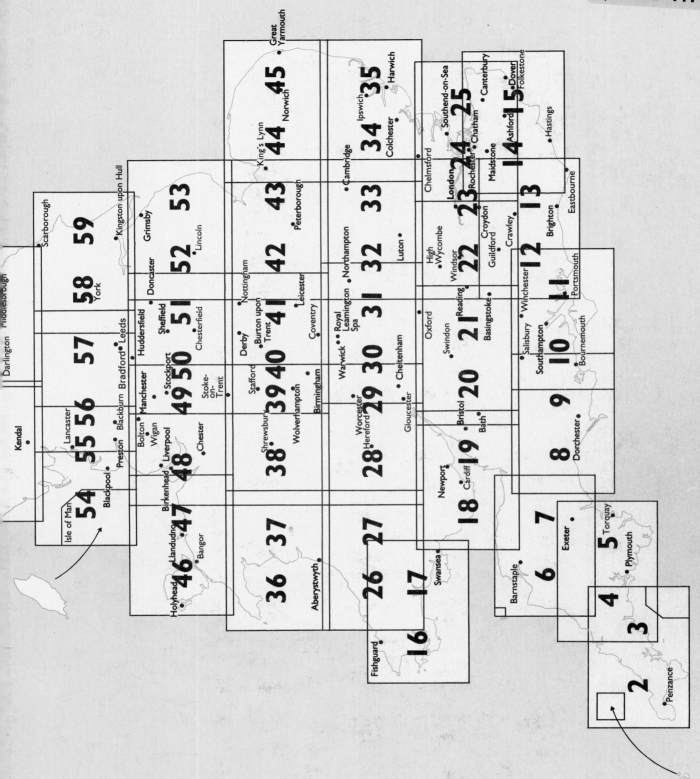

COMPREHENSIVE
ROAD ATLAS
BRITAIN

COMPREHENSIVE
ROAD ATLAS
BRITAIN

Bartholomew

A Division of HarperCollins*Publishers*

Published by Bartholomew
a Division of HarperCollins *Publishers*
Duncan Street, Edinburgh EH9 1TA
© Bartholomew November 1993
New 1994 edition
ISBN 0 7028 2516 6
Printed and bound in the UK
by Bartholomew, The Edinburgh Press Limited

Details included in this atlas are subject to change without notice.
Whilst every effort is made to keep information up to date
Bartholomew will not be held responsible for any loss, damage or
inconvenience caused by any inaccuracies in this atlas.
The publishers are always pleased to acknowledge any corrections
brought to their notice, and record their appreciation of the
valuable services rendered in the past by map users in assisting
to maintain the accuracy of their publications.

GB 7163

CONTENTS

VI-VII   ROUTE PLANNING MAP

VIII   WEATHER HAZARDS

1   KEY TO SYMBOLS

2-107   MAIN MAP SECTION

108-111   DISTANCE FINDER DIAGRAMS

112   CHANNEL FERRIES

113-121   LONDON MAPS

122-128   LONDON INDEX

129-146   TOWN PLANS

147-198   INDEX

199   MILEAGE CHART

200   CONVERSION TABLES

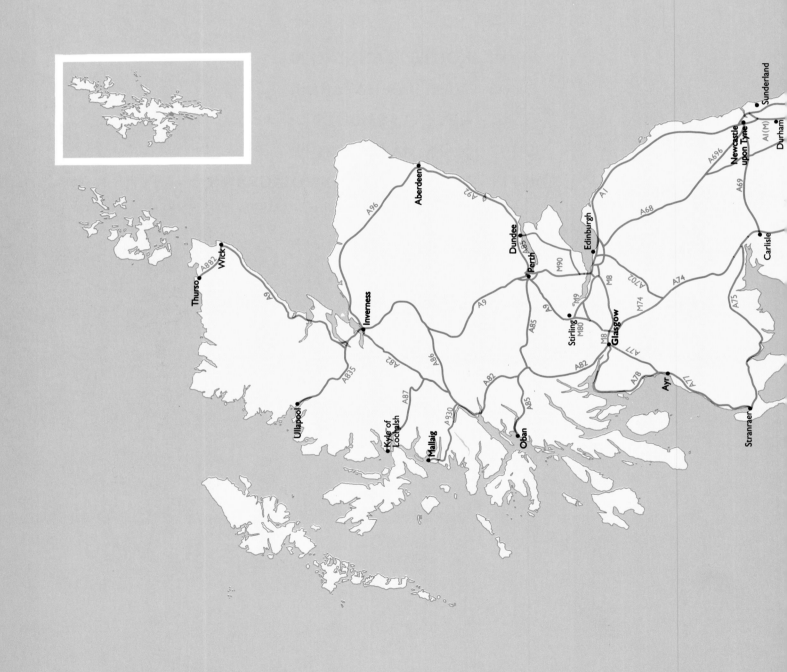

Sunderland

Newcastle
upon Tyne

A1(M)

Durham

A696

A69

A68

A1

Carlisle

Aberdeen

A96

A92

Edinburgh

Dundee

A85

Perth

A702

A74

A75

M90

M8

M9

A90

Inverness

A835

A82

A9

A85

Stirling

M80

A74

M74

M8

Glasgow

Thurso

Wick

A882

A9

Ullapool

A87

A96

A82

A82

A77

Ayr

A78

A77

Kyle of
Lochalsh

Mallaig

A830

Oban

A85

Stranraer

Route Planning Map

approx 40 miles to 1 inch

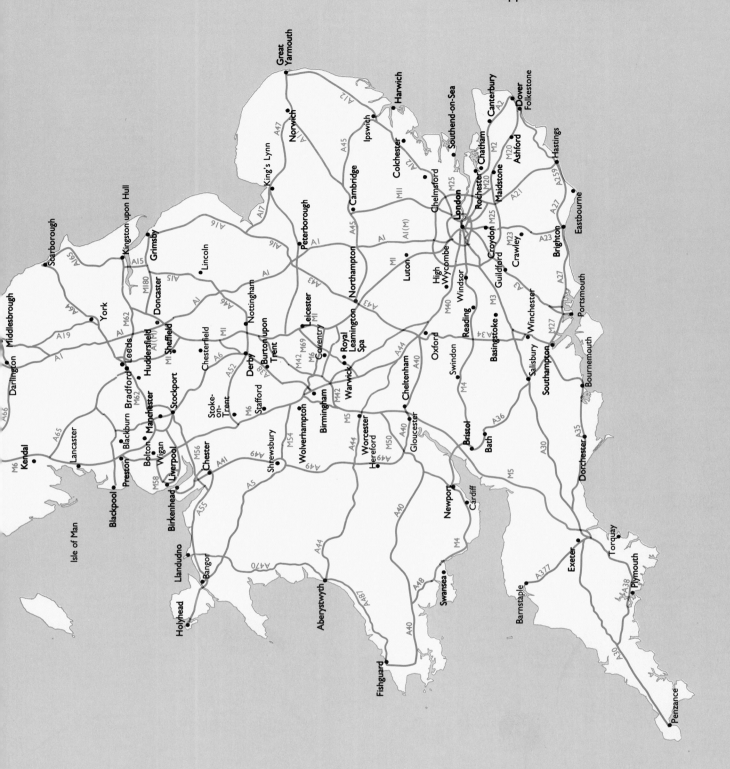

Weather Hazards

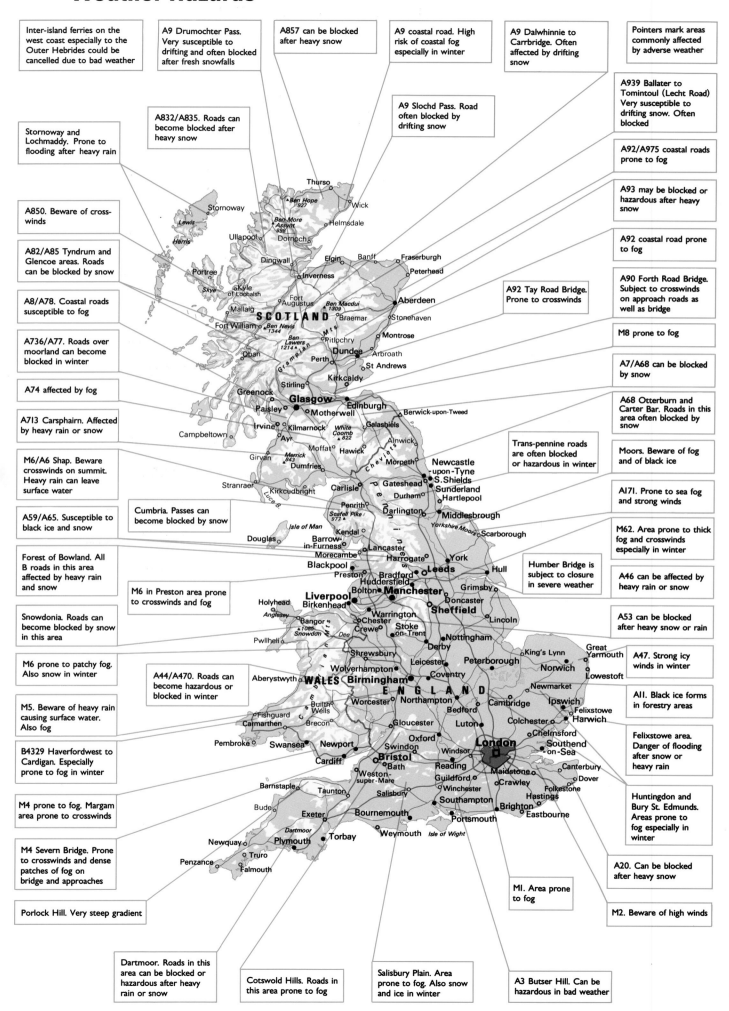

Inter-island ferries on the west coast especially to the Outer Hebrides could be cancelled due to bad weather

A9 Drumochter Pass. Very susceptible to drifting and often blocked after fresh snowfalls

A857 can be blocked after heavy snow

A9 coastal road. High risk of coastal fog especially in winter

A9 Dalwhinnie to Carrbridge. Often affected by drifting snow

Pointers mark areas commonly affected by adverse weather

A832/A835. Roads can become blocked after heavy snow

A9 Slochd Pass. Road often blocked by drifting snow

A939 Ballater to Tomintoul (Lecht Road) Very susceptible to drifting snow. Often blocked

Stornoway and Lochmaddy. Prone to flooding after heavy rain

A92/A975 coastal roads prone to fog

A850. Beware of cross-winds

A93 may be blocked or hazardous after heavy snow

A92 coastal road prone to fog

A82/A85 Tyndrum and Glencoe areas. Roads can be blocked by snow

A90 Forth Road Bridge. Subject to crosswinds on approach roads as well as bridge

A8/A78. Coastal roads susceptible to fog

A92 Tay Road Bridge. Prone to crosswinds

M8 prone to fog

A736/A77. Roads over moorland can become blocked in winter

A7/A68 can be blocked by snow

A74 affected by fog

A68 Otterburn and Carter Bar. Roads in this area often blocked by snow

A713 Carsphairn. Affected by heavy rain or snow

Trans-pennine roads are often blocked or hazardous in winter

Moors. Beware of fog and of black ice

M6/A6 Shap. Beware crosswinds on summit. Heavy rain can leave surface water

A171. Prone to sea fog and strong winds

A59/A65. Susceptible to black ice and snow

Cumbria. Passes can become blocked by snow

M62. Area prone to thick fog and crosswinds especially in winter

Forest of Bowland. All B roads in this area affected by heavy rain and snow

Humber Bridge is subject to closure in severe weather

A46 can be affected by heavy rain or snow

M6 in Preston area prone to crosswinds and fog

A53 can be blocked after heavy snow or rain

Snowdonia. Roads can become blocked by snow in this area

M6 prone to patchy fog. Also snow in winter

A47. Strong icy winds in winter

A44/A470. Roads can become hazardous or blocked in winter

A11. Black ice forms in forestry areas

M5. Beware of heavy rain causing surface water. Also fog

Felixstowe area. Danger of flooding after snow or heavy rain

B4329 Haverfordwest to Cardigan. Especially prone to fog in winter

M4 prone to fog. Margam area prone to crosswinds

Huntingdon and Bury St. Edmunds. Areas prone to fog especially in winter

M4 Severn Bridge. Prone to crosswinds and dense patches of fog on bridge and approaches

A20. Can be blocked after heavy snow

Porlock Hill. Very steep gradient

M1. Area prone to fog

M2. Beware of high winds

Dartmoor. Roads in this area can be blocked or hazardous after heavy rain or snow

Cotswold Hills. Roads in this area prone to fog

Salisbury Plain. Area prone to fog. Also snow and ice in winter

A3 Butser Hill. Can be hazardous in bad weather

viii

KEY

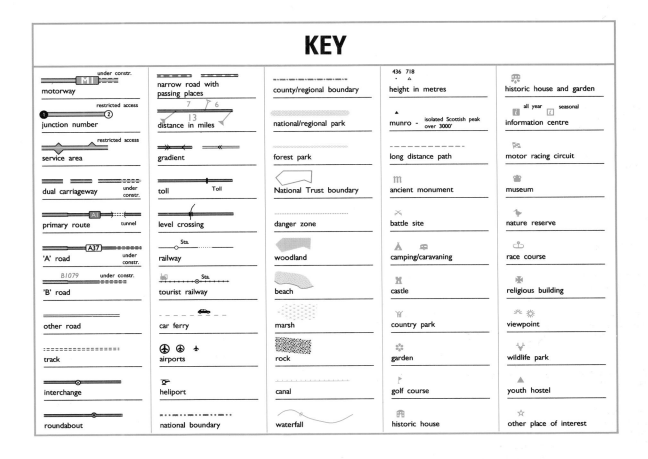

motorway	narrow road with passing places	county/regional boundary	height in metres	historic house and garden
junction number	distance in miles	national/regional park	munro - *isolated Scottish peak over 3000'*	information centre
service area	gradient	forest park	long distance path	motor racing circuit
dual carriageway	toll	National Trust boundary	ancient monument	museum
primary route	level crossing	danger zone	battle site	nature reserve
'A' road	railway	woodland	camping/caravaning	race course
'B' road	tourist railway	beach	castle	religious building
other road	car ferry	marsh	country park	viewpoint
track	airports	rock	garden	wildlife park
interchange	heliport	canal	golf course	youth hostel
roundabout	national boundary	waterfall	historic house	other place of interest

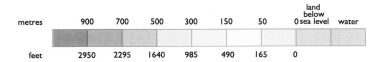

metres	900	700	500	300	150	50	land below 0 sea level	water
feet	2950	2295	1640	985	490	165	0	

Scale

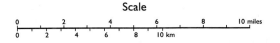

0   2   4   6   8   10 miles

0   2   4   6   8   10 km

18 19 20 21 22

A

LUNDY (NT)

North West Point

Shutter Rock
Rat Island

same scale as main map

Map labels (North Devon & Cornwall)

BARNSTAPLE
OR
BIDEFORD BAY

BUDE BAY

CORNWALL

DARTMOOR

DARTMOOR NATIONAL PARK

Ilfracombe · Hele · Berrynarbor · Combe Martin · Heale · Martinhoe · Trentishoe
Heddon's Mouth · Widmouth Head · Bull Point · Lee · Slade · Mortehoe · Morte Point
Mollacott Cross · Sterridge · Parracombe · Beccott · Arlington · Knightacott · Loxhore
Woolacombe · Morte Bay · Trinstone · West Down · East Down · Patchole · Kentisbury
Berry Down Cross · Bittadon · Blackmoor Gate · Challacombe Common
Baggy Point · Pickwell · North Buckland · Georgeham · Halsinger · Milltown · Muddiford · Shirwell · Bratton Fleming · Leworthy
Croyde · Croyde Bay · Knowle · Marwood · Marwood Hill · Prixford · Kingsheanton · Shirwell Cross · Benton
Saunton · Braunton · Pippacott · Heanton Punchardon · Wrafton · Ashford · Goodleigh · Northleigh · Gunn
Saunton Sands · Braunton Burrows · Toll · Pilton · Barnstaple · Newport · Landkey · Bishop's Tawton · Swimbridge · West Buckland · East Buckland · Yarnacott
Northam Burrows · The Neck · Bickington · Fremington · Yelland · Tawstock · St John Chapel
Appledore · Instow · Bickleton · Newton Tracey · Cobbaton · Filleigh
Westward Ho! · Tapeley · Westleigh · Horwood · Loveacott · Hiscott · Herner · Chittlehampton
Northam · Bideford · East-the-Water · Eastleigh · Woodtown · Alverdiscott · Ensis · Langridge
Abbotsham · Gammaton Moor · Yarnscombe · Fishley Barton · Hudscott · Clapworthy
Fairy Cross · Ford · Yeo Vale · Littleham · Landcross · Weare Giffard · Huntshaw Cross · Umberleigh · Warkleigh · Satterleigh
Clovelly · Buck's Mills · Horns Cross · Goldworthy · Monkleigh · High Bullen · Sherwood Green · High Bickington · Chittlehamholt
Titchberry · Windbury Point · Gallantry Bower · Clovelly Cross · Buck's Cross · Parkham Ash · Parkham · Great Torrington · St Giles in the Wood · Kingscott · Portsmouth Arms
Hartland Point · Stoke · Hartland · Philham · Dyke · Cranford · Almiston Cross · Buckland Brewer · Frithelstock · Frithelstock Stone · Taddiport · Roborough · Northcote Manor
Milford · Edistone · Tosberry · Woolfardisworthy · Ash · Melbury · Powler's Piece · Little Torrington · Villavin · Burrington · Elstone
Elmscott · South Hole · Welcombe · Ashmansworthy · Kismeblon Bridge · East Putford · Langtree · Beaford · Riddlecombe · Copy Lake · Colleton
Knaps Longpeak · Meddon · Youlstone · Dinworthy · West Putford · Bulkworthy · Stibb Cross · Winswell · Merton · Dolton · Ashreigney
Gooseham · Eastcott · Bradworthy · Brendon · Abbots Bickington · Sutcombe · Newton St Petrock · Peters Marland · Woollaton · Heanton Satchville · Huish · Dowland · Eggesford Barton
Morwenstow · Shop · Woodford · Alfardisworthy · Soldon Cross · Milton Damerel · Shebbear · North Town · Petrockstow · Meeth · Iddesleigh · Hollocombe · Ashley · Wembworthy · Nymet
Lower Sharpnose Point · Taylors Cross · Kilkhampton · Youldonmoor Cross · Youldon · Thornbury · Buckland Filleigh · Ash · Winkleigh · Brushford Barton
Coombe · Stibb · Youldon · Holsworthy Beacon · Bradford · Sheepwash · Black Torrington · Hele Bridge · Monkokehampton · Broadwood · Taw Bridge · Kelly
Poughill · Hersham · Grimscott · Chilsworthy · Cookbury · Brandis Corner · Dunsland Cross · Highampton · Hatherleigh · Bassett's Cross · Exbourne · Bondleigh
Flexbury · Bude · Stratton · Launcells Cross · Pancrasweek · Holsworthy · Anvil Corner · Graddon Moor · Lydacott · Jacobstowe · Sampford Courtenay · North Tawton
Helebridge · Launcells · Red Post · Marhamchurch · Rydon · Pyworthy · Chasty · Hollacombe · Halwill Forest · Northlew · Inwardleigh · Shilstone
Widemouth Bay · Titson · Bridgerule · Yeomadon · Halwill Junction · Halwill · Beaworthy · Ashbury · Oak Cross · Folly Gate · Belstone Corner · Itton
Coppathorne · Week Orchard · Herdicott · Clawton · Upcott · Broadbury · Northlew · Okehampton · Sticklepath · South Tawton · Taw Green
Poundstock · Treskinnick Cross · Tinney · Cofcott Green · Quoditch · Belstone · Okehampton Camp · Finch Foundry · South Zeal
Tregole · Trewint · Whitstone · North Tamerton · Tetcott · Lana · Ashwater · Germansweek · Boasley Cross · Thornton Cross · Yelland · Hewton · Meldon
Wainhouse Corner · Week St Mary · Trebarrow · Luffincott · Henford · Chapman's Well · Virginstow · Bratton Clovelly · Bridestowe · Sourton · Yes Tor · High Willhays
Jacobstow · South Wheatley · Maxworthy · West Curry · Clubworthy · Northcott · Boyton · East Panson · Gridley Corner · Broadwoodwidger · Bridestowe and Sourton Common · Amicombe Hill · Great Kneeset · Cranmere Pool
Collamoor Head · Langdon · Caudworthy Water · Troswell · Bennacott · St Giles on the Heath · Bridgetown · Broadwoodwidger · Shortacombe · Hangingstone Hill · Whitehorse Hill
Marshgate · Otterham · Warbstow · Brazacott · North Petherwin · Polapit Tamar · Cross Green · Thrushelton · Lewdown · Lydford · Beardon · White Ridge
Trelash · Tremaine · Treneglos · Yeolmbridge · Langore · Ladycross · Werrington · Stowford · Coryton · Lydford Gorge · Sittaford Tor · Fernworthy Reservoir
Hallworthy · Tresmeer · St Stephens · Liftondown · Lifton · Portgate · Lewtrenchard · Downton · North Brentor · Willsworthy · Frenchbeer
Tremail · Tregeare · Egloskerry · Newport · Launceston · Lawrence · Lifton · Tinhay · Brentor · Chillaton · Black Down · Cut Hill
St Clether · Downhead · Laneast · Trewen · Tregadillett · Kennards House · Lawhitton · Kelly · Marystow · Horndon · Lynch Tor · Rough Tor
Altarnun · Fivelanes · Polyphant · Trebullett · South Petherwin · Bradstone · Felldownhead · Mary Tavy · Peter Tavy · Cowsic Head
Brown Willy · Codda · Congdon's Shop · Lezant · Dunterton · Abbot · Higher Postbridge · Bellever

Roads: A39 · A361 · A399 · A3123 · A377 · A388 · A386 · A3072 · A3079 · A30 · A395 · A388 · B3230 · B3231 · B3227 · B3237 · B3248 · B3254 · B3262 · B3314 · B3220 · B3226 · B3217 · B3219 · B3211

NATIONAL PARK · settlements

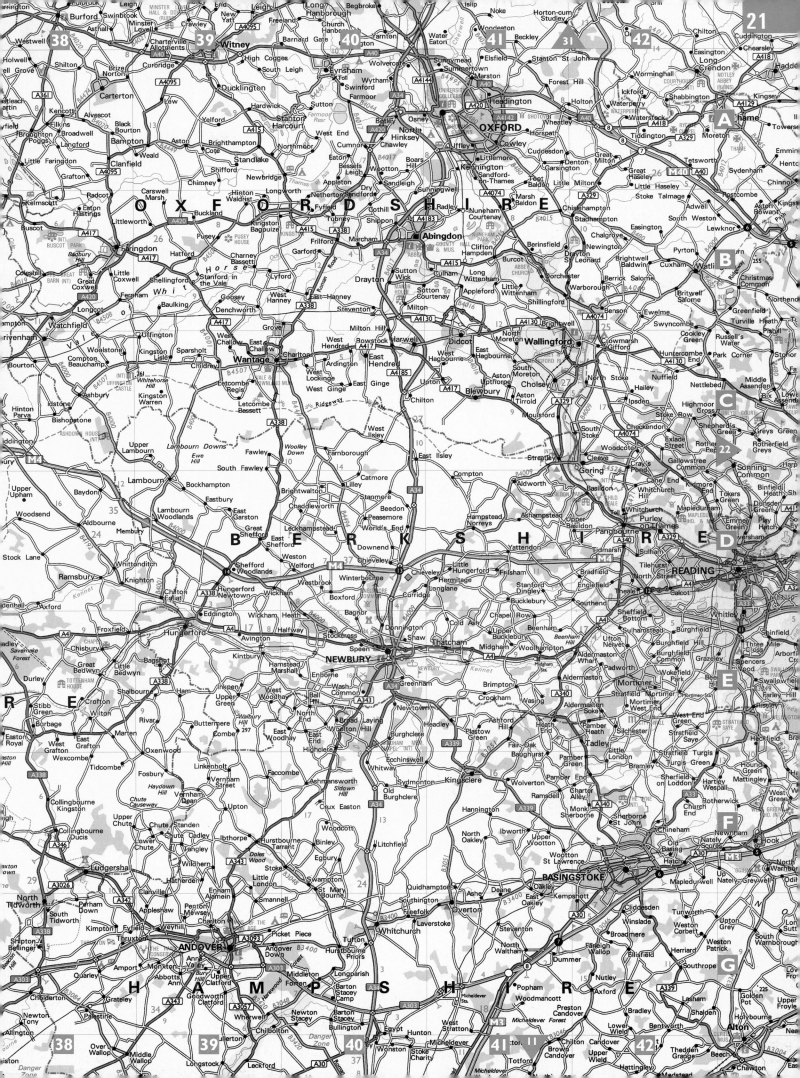

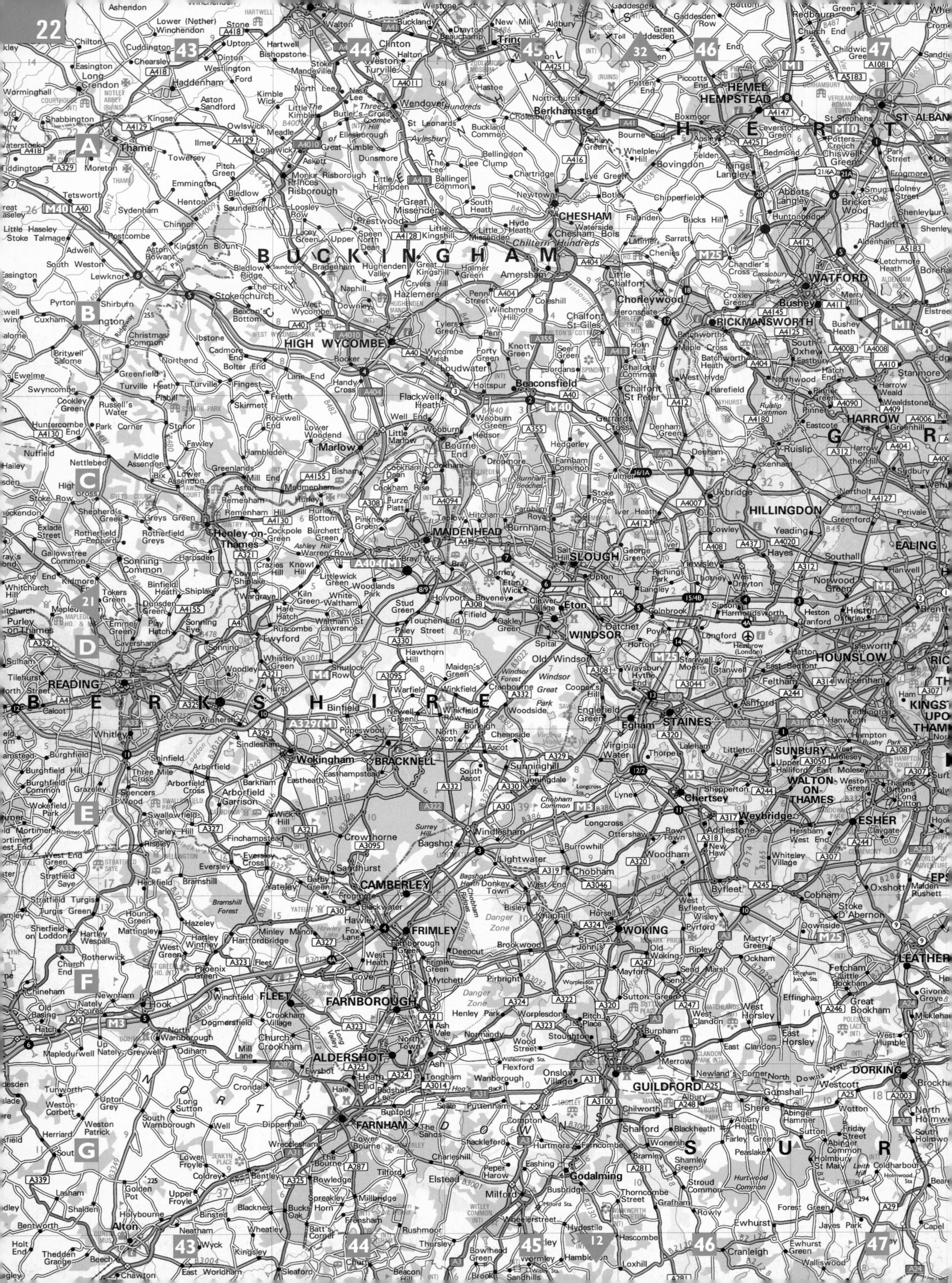

BUCKINGHAM

BERKSHIRE

HERT

SURREY

DORSET

Major towns: Thame, Aylesbury, Tring, Berkhamsted, Hemel Hempstead, St Albans, Chesham, Amersham, Watford, Rickmansworth, Harrow, High Wycombe, Beaconsfield, Marlow, Maidenhead, Slough, Windsor, Eton, Uxbridge, Hillingdon, Ealing, Hounslow, Reading, Henley-on-Thames, Wokingham, Bracknell, Staines, Sunbury, Walton-on-Thames, Chertsey, Weybridge, Esher, Camberley, Frimley, Woking, Leatherhead, Dorking, Guildford, Farnham, Aldershot, Farnborough, Fleet, Godalming

Grid references (top): 43, 44, 45, 32, 46, 47

Grid references (bottom): 43, 44, 45, 12, 46, 47

Grid rows: A, B, C, D, E, F, G

Roads: M40, M4, M25, M3, M10, M1, A40, A41, A404, A355, A413, A4010, A418, A329, A30, A31, A3, A322, A331, A325, A320, A309, A217

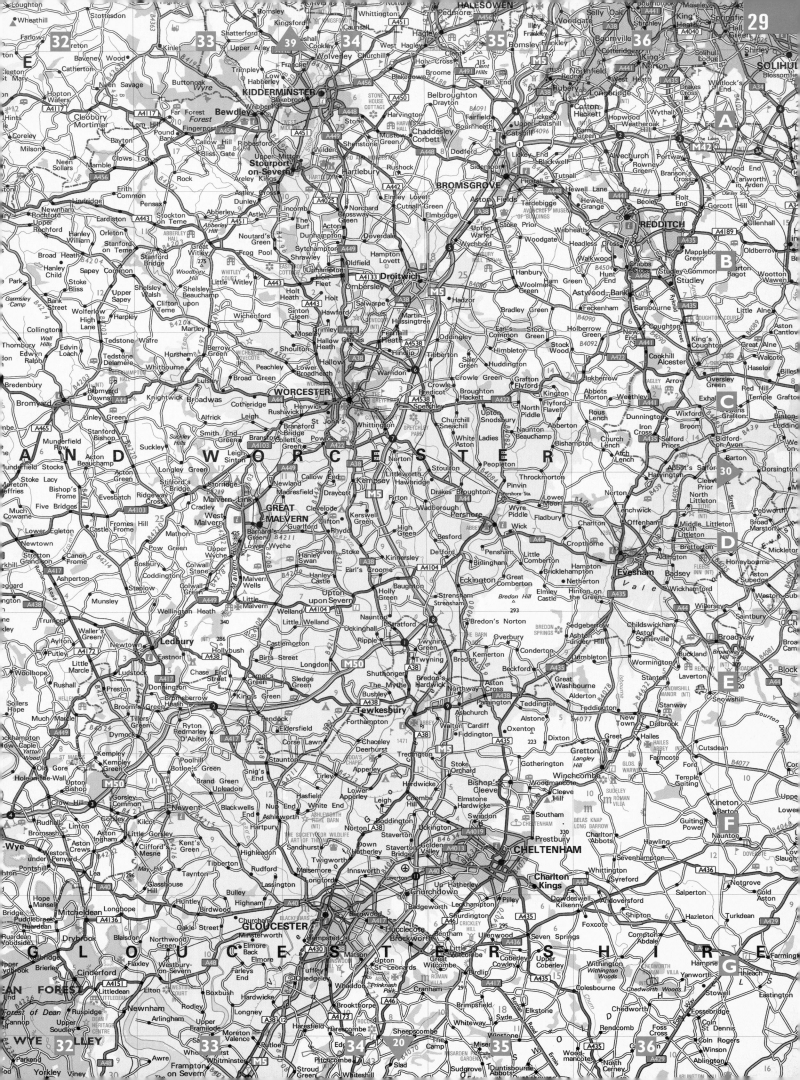

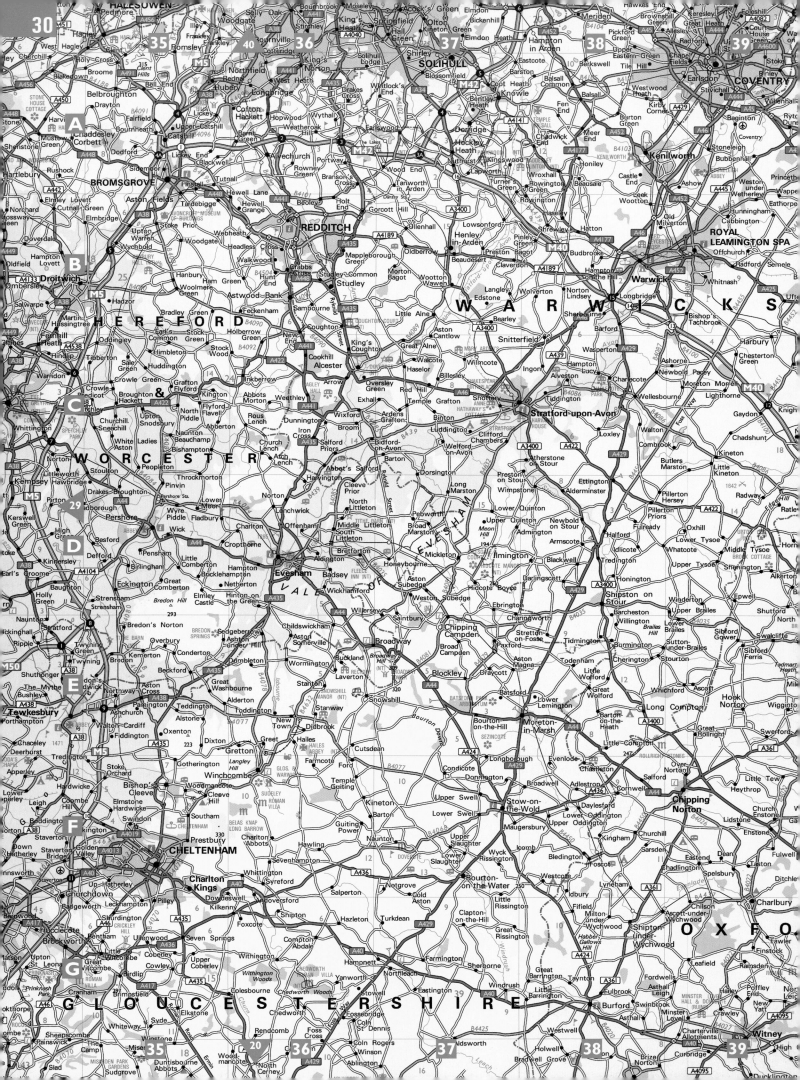

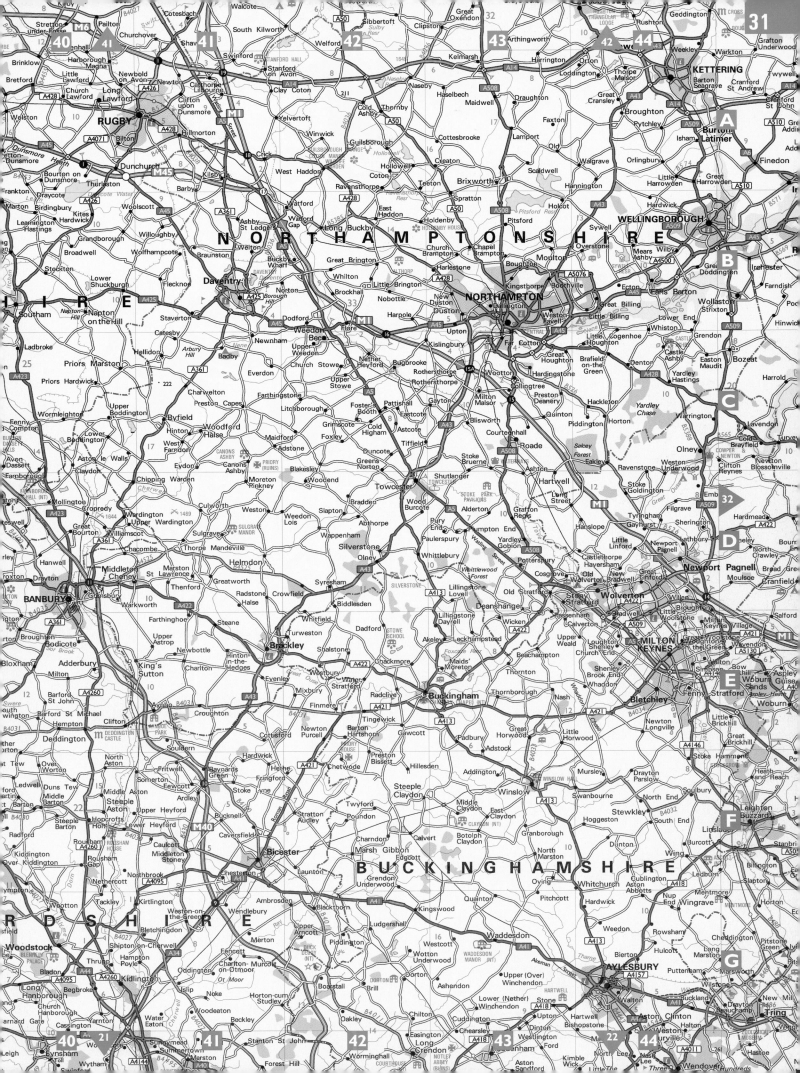

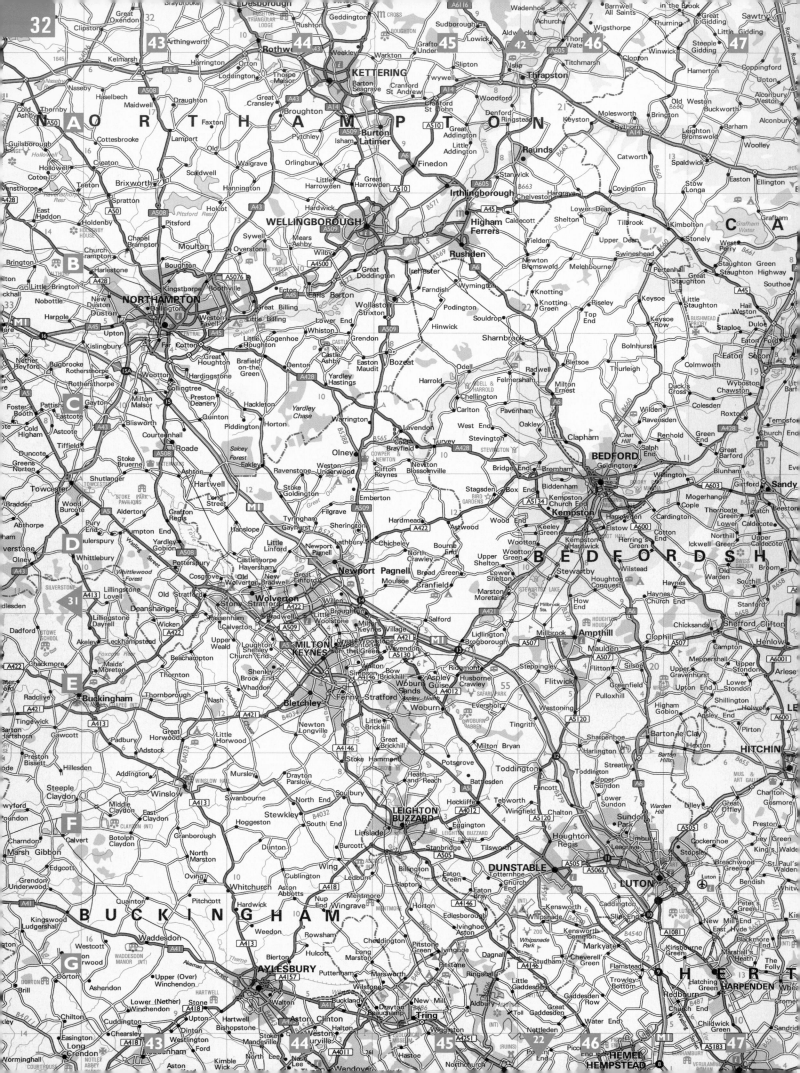

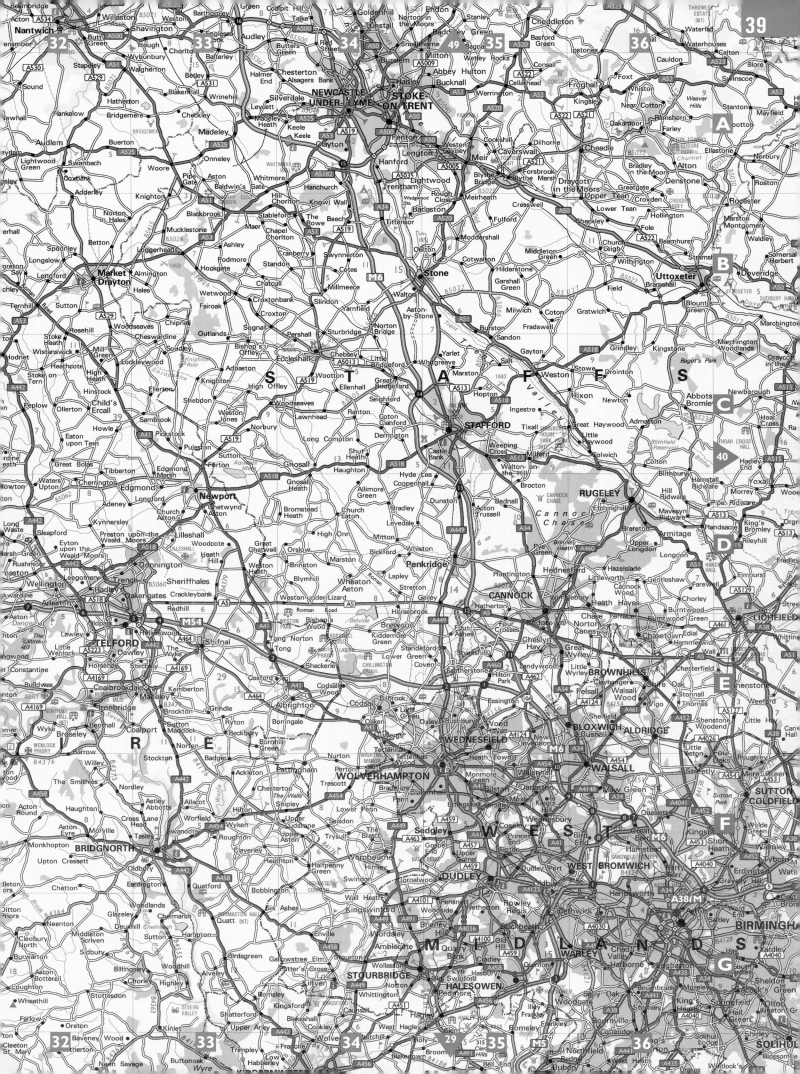

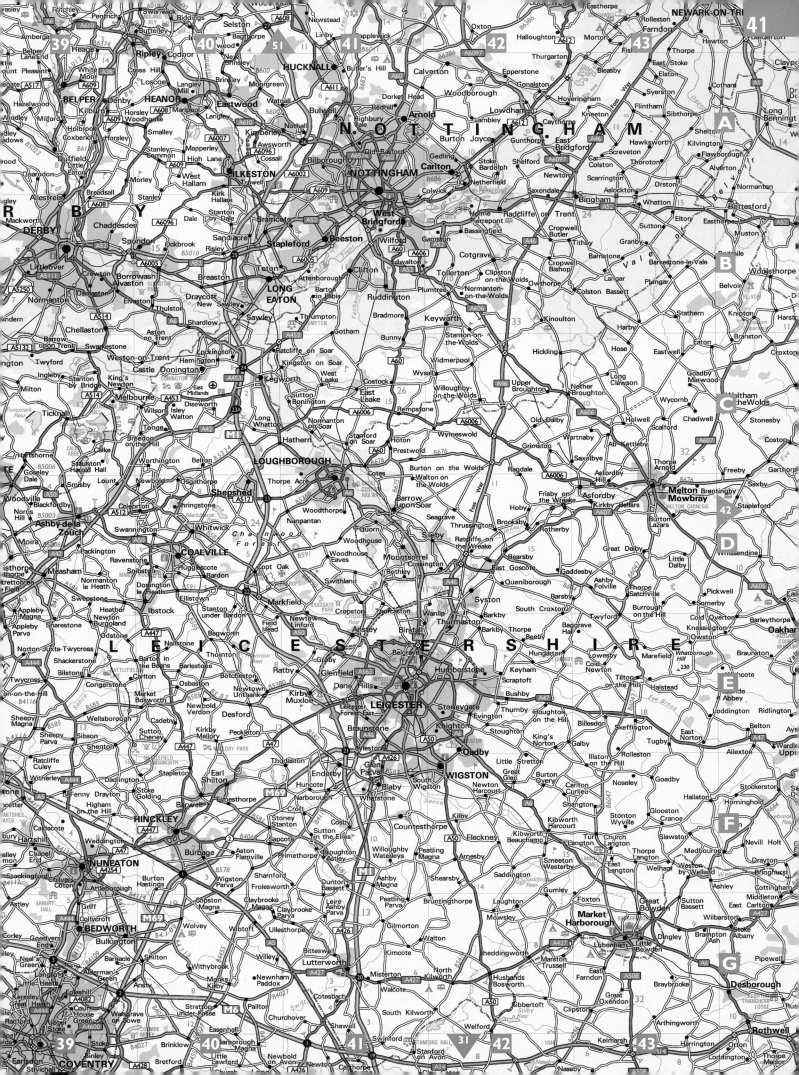

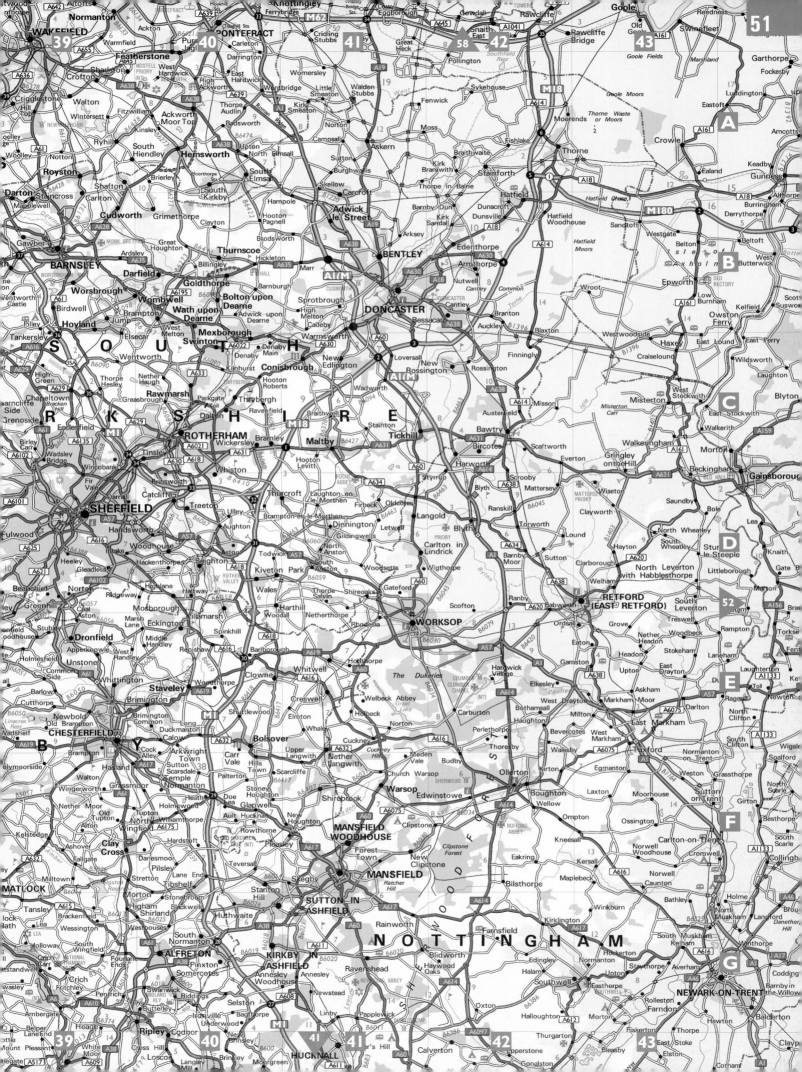

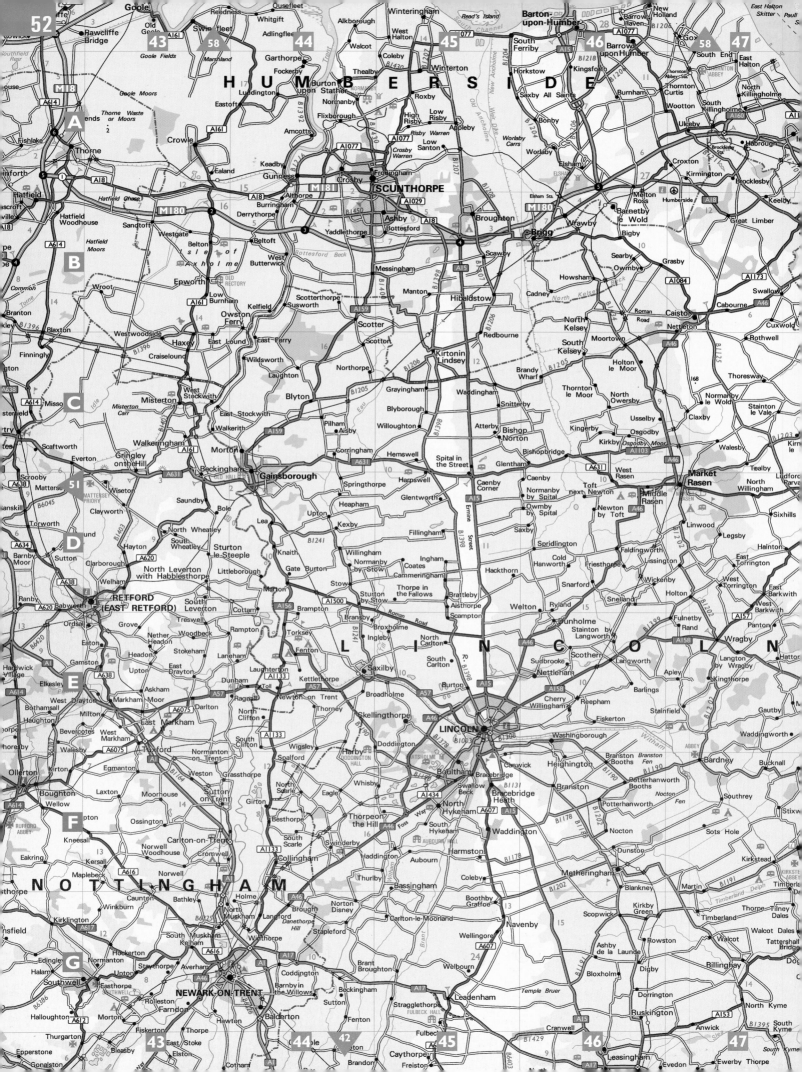

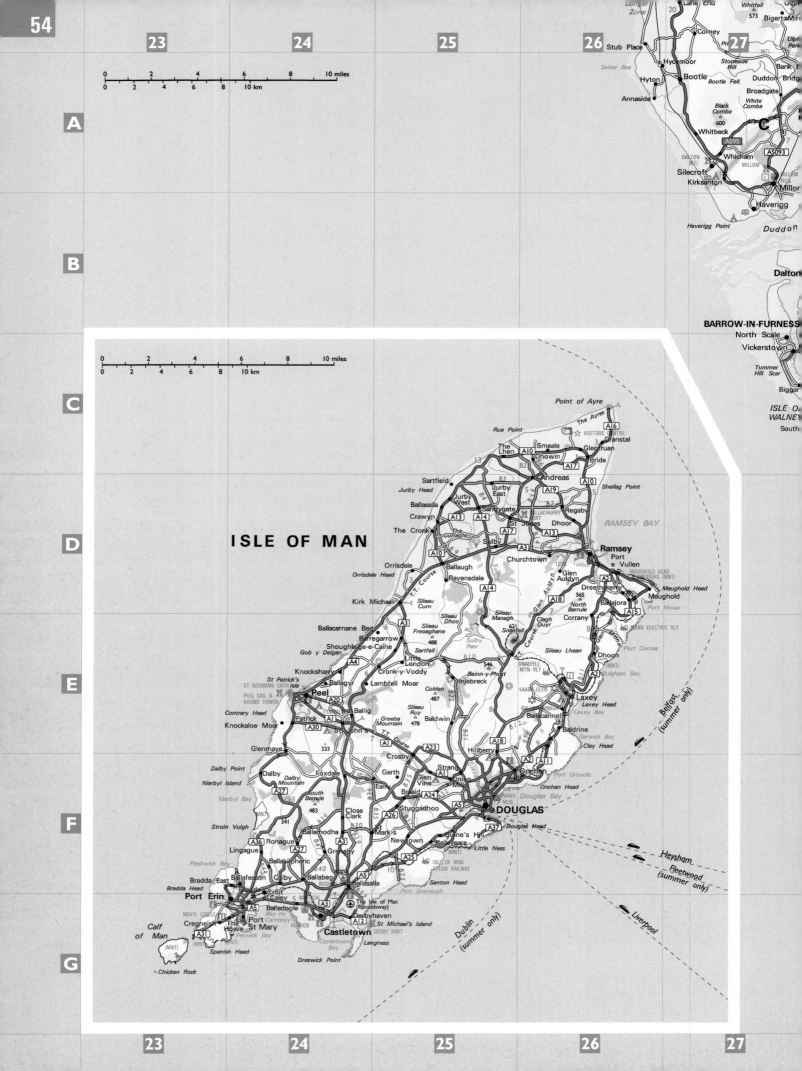

ISLE OF MAN

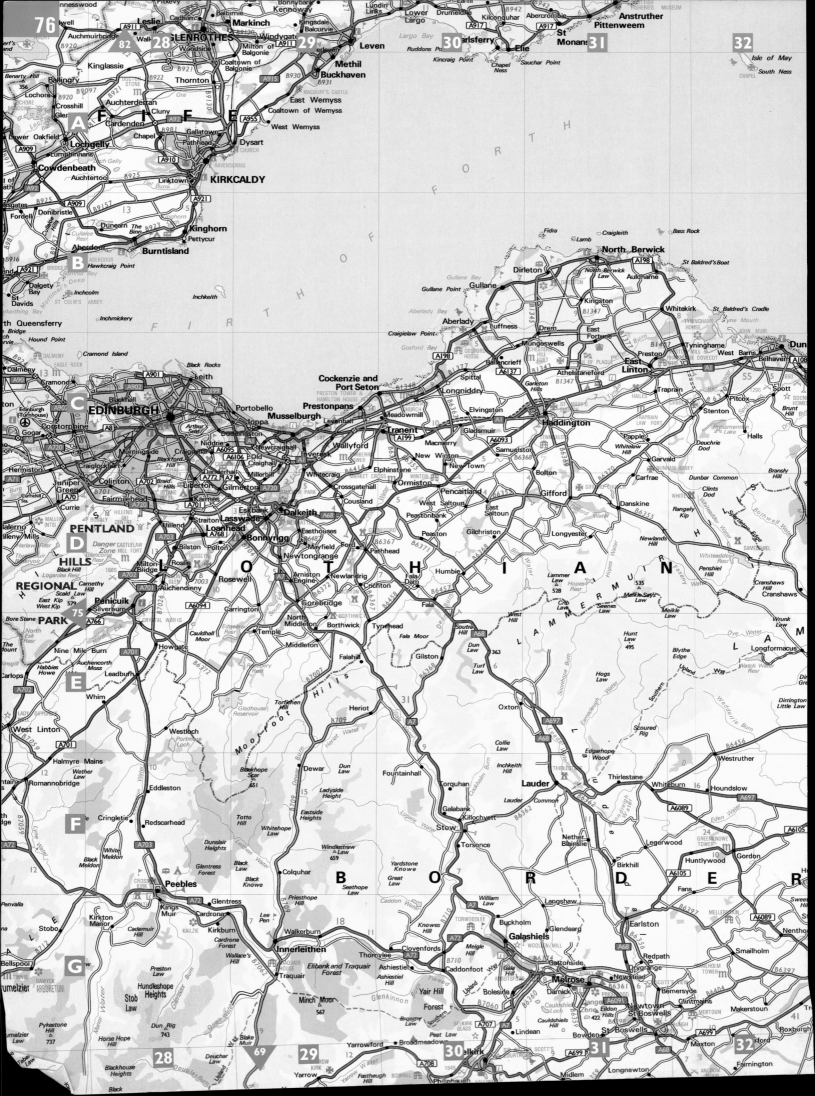

Lochboisdale

Castlebay

Point of Ardna

A

Eag na Maoile

Eilean Mor

Rubha Mor

Rubh' a'Bhinnein

Bousd

Rubha Sgor-Innis

Sorisdale

Torastan

Loch
Fada

Bagh na Coille

Cliad

Grishipoll Bay

Arnabost

Grishipoll

B8072

Clabhach

Ben Hogh

B8071

73

Ballyhaugh

Loch
Cliad

Hogh Bay

104

Totamore

Arinagour

B

Totronald

Uig

Acha

C O L L

Loch Eatharna

Arileod

Eilean Ornsay

Port Mine

Feall Bay

Quini

Calgary Point

Crossapol

Gorton

Port na Earba

Caliach Point

Sunipol

Gunna

Crossapol
Bay

Friesland
Bay

Langamull

Loch Breac-fhacha

Rubha Fasadh

Mornish

Port a'Mhurain

Soa

Cruach Sleibhe

166

Urvaig

Miodar

Rubha nan Oirean

Calgary

Sgeir Bharrach

Vaul

Caolas Ban

Ruaig

Rubha Dubh

Treshnish Point

Treshnish

Ensay

Balephetrish
Hill

Caolas

B8073

Balephetrish Bay

B8069

Brock

Beinn Duill

Cruach

The Green

191

Odha

256

Rubha Liath

Port Ban

Rubh' a'Chaoil

Tostarie

Hough Bay

Gott Bay

Rubh' an t-Suibhein

Port

Soa

C

Kilkenneth

T I R E E

Scarinish

Cairn na Burgh More

Cairn na Burgh Beg

Loch Tuat

Moss

B8068

Tiree

Fladda

Saundaig

Heylipoll

Crossapol

Heanish

Sgeir a Chaistell

Eilean Dioghlum

Barrapoll

B8067

Baugh

Hynish
Bay

Lunga

Rubha Maol
na Mine

Gometra
Ho.

Be

Balemartine

B8066

Gometra

Balephuil

Mannel

Maisgeir

Eolasar

Rinn Thorbhais

Hynish

Treshnish Isles

SKERRYVORE
MUSEUM

Bac Mor or
Dutchman's Cap

Little
Colonsay

Bac Beag

Staffa

Eilean Dubh

STAFFA (NTS)

D

Fingal's
Cave

Erisgeir

Aird na h-Iol

Reidh Eilean

Eilean
Chalbha

MACLEAN'S CROSS

Car
Mhic T

IONA ABBEY

Kintra

Rubha nan Cearc

Port an Duine Mhairbh

Dun

Beinn Chladan

E

IONA (NTS)

Fionnphort

Eorabus

Ruanaich

Aridhglas

Loch na
Lathaich

Ard

I o n a

Stac an Aoineidh

A849

Bunessan

Fidden

Rubha na
Carraig-geire

R O S S

O F

Soa Island

Knockvologan

Ardalanish

Uis

Erraid

Torr Fada

Ardchiavaig

Eilean Dubh

Eilean a'Chalmain

Aird Mor

Port
Mor

Eilean Mor

Rubh' Ardalanish

F

Torran Rocks

Dearg Sgeir

Na Torrain

Ruadh Sgeir

West Reef

Torran Sgoilte

McPhail's Anvil

Sgeir Ghobhlach

Otter Rock

G

0 2 4 6 8 10 miles

0 2 4 6 8 10 km

Dubh Artach

Kilorar Ba

Loch an Spoor

Neui

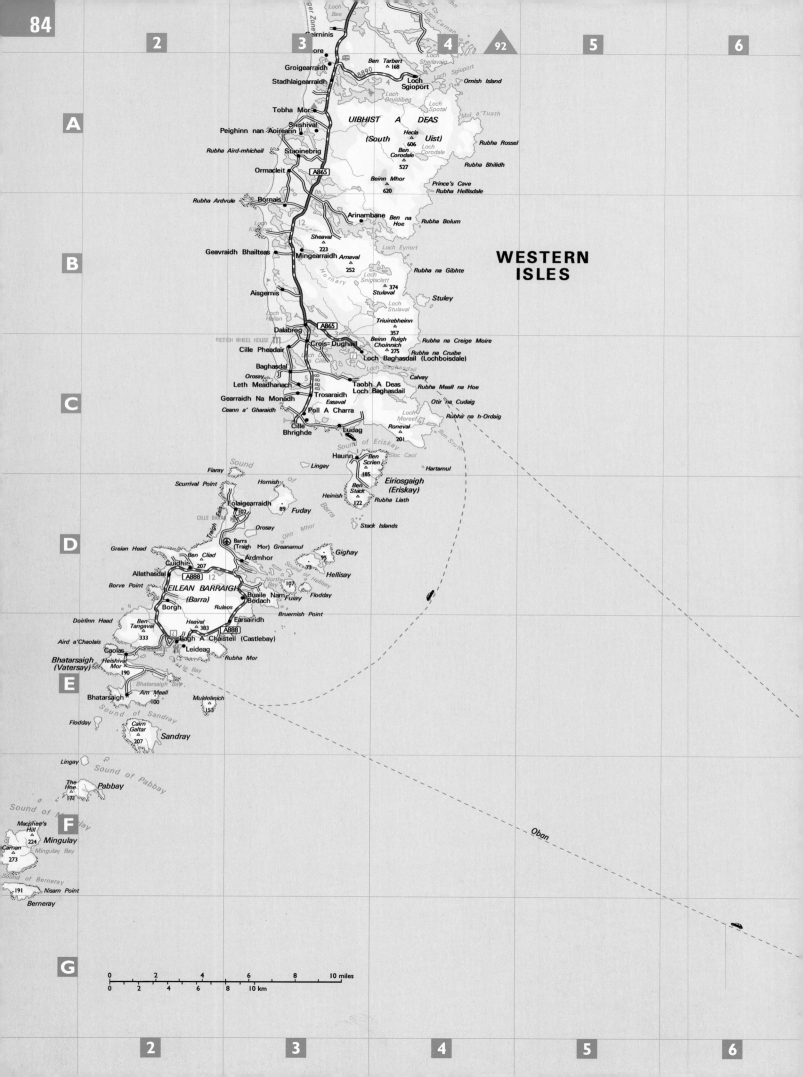

WESTERN ISLES

UIBHIST A DEAS
(South Uist)

Loch Sgioport

Ben Tarbert △ 168

Ornish Island

Rubha Rossel

Hecla △ 606
Ben Corodale △ 527

Rubha Bhilidh

Beinn Mhor △ 620

Prince's Cave
Rubha Hellisdale

Groigearraidh
Stadhlaigearraidh
Tobha Mor
Snishival
Peighinn nan Aoireann
Rubha Aird-mhicheil
Staoinebrig
Ormacleit
Bornais
Rubha Ardvule

A865

Arinambane
Ben na Hoe
Rubha Bolum

Geavraidh Bhailteas
Mingearraidh
Sheaval △ 223
Arnaval △ 252

Rubha na Gibhte

Aisgernis
Stulaval △ 374

Stuley

Dalabreg
A865
Creis-Dughaill
Cille Pheadair
Baghasdal

Triuirebheinn △ 357
Beinn Ruigh Choinnich △ 275

Rubha na Creige Moire
Rubha na Cruibe

Loch Baghasdail (Lochboisdale)

Calvay
Rubha Meall na Hoe

Orosay
Leth Meadhanach
Gearraidh Na Monadh
Ceann a' Gharaidh
Poll A Charra
Cille Bhrighde

Trosaraidh
Easaval
Taobh A Deas
Loch Baghasdail

Otir na Cudaig
Rubha na h-Ordaig

Ludag

Roneval △ 201

Haunn
Ben Scrien △ 185

Hartamul

Sound of Eriskay

Eiriosgaigh
(Eriskay)

Fiaray
Lingay

Scurrival Point
Hornish
Heinish
Rubha Liath

Eolaigearraidh
CILLE BARRA
Fuday
Stack Islands

Orosay

Barra (Traigh Mor)
Ardmhor
Greanamul
Gighay

Greian Head
Ben Cliad △ 207
Cuidhir
A888
Hellisay

Allathasdal
Borve Point

EILEAN BARRAIGH
(Barra)
Buaile Nam Bodach
Fuiay
Floddday

Borgh
Ruleos
Bruernish Point

Doirlinn Head
Ben Tangaval △ 333
Heaval △ 383
Earsairidh
A888

Aird a'Chaolais
Bagh A Chaisteil (Castlebay)
Leideag

Caolas
Heishival Mor △ 190
Rubha Mor

Bhatarsaigh (Vatersay)

Bhatarsaigh
Am Meall △ 100

Muldoanich △ 153

Sound of Sandray

Floddday
Cairn Galtar △ 207
Sandray

Lingay
Sound of Pabbay

The Hoe
Pabbay △ 174

Sound of Mingulay

Macphee's Hill △ 224
Carnan △ 273
Mingulay
Mingulay Bay

Sound of Berneray

△ 191
Nisam Point
Berneray

Oban

PICTISH WHEEL HOUSE

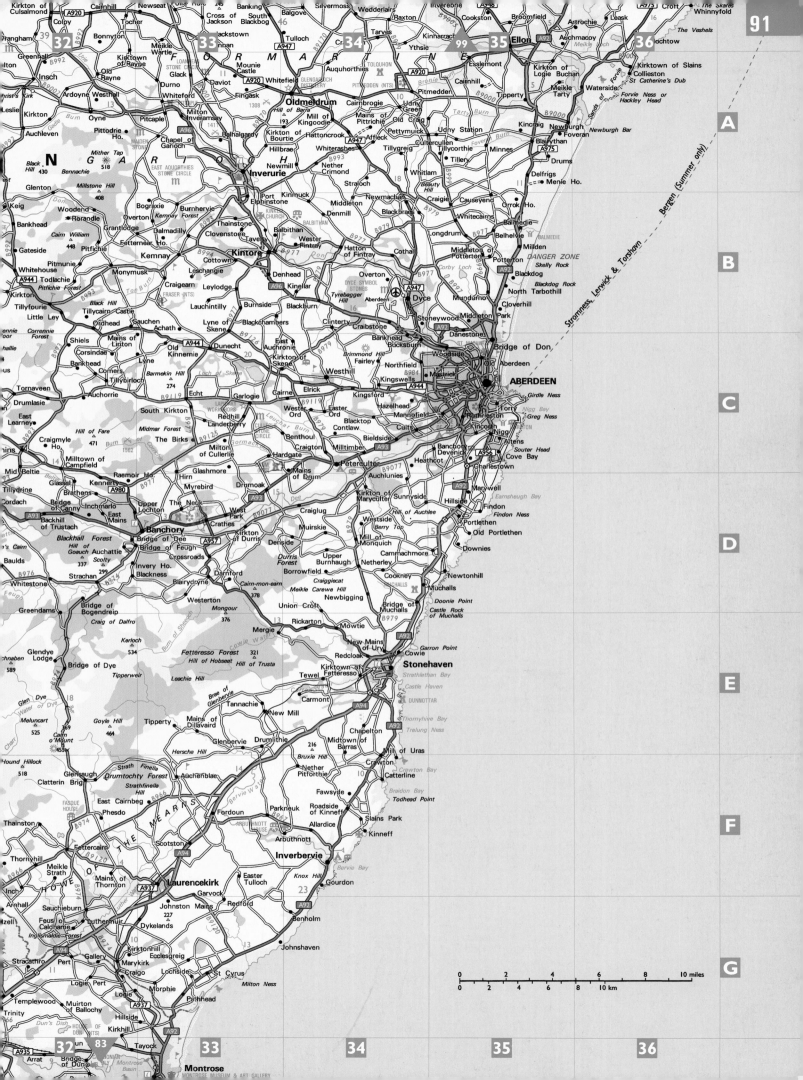

THE MINCH

Stornoway

Summer Isles

Tanera Beg

Glas-leac Mor

Priest Island

Bottle Island

Eilean Mullagrach

Glas-leac Beag

Eilean Dubh

Cailleach Head

Greenstone Point

Obinan
Rubha Mor
Mellon Udrigle
Rubha Beag
Leac Mhor

Gruinard Island

Stattic Point

Badluarchrach

Mungasdale

Achgarve

Gruinard Bay

Eilean Furadh Mor

Slaggan Bay

Cove

Mellon Charles
Ormiscaig
Laide
First Coast
Second Coast
Little Gruinard

Rubha Reidh

Carnas Mor

Loch an Draing

An Cuaidh 296

Aultbea
Bualnaluib
Drumchork

Isle of Ewe

Loch Sguod

A832

Creag-mheall Beag

Creag-mheall Mor 347

Melvaig
Aultgrishan

Inverasdale
Midtown

Loch Ewe

Loch Thurnaig

Tuirnaig

Beinn a'Chaisgein Beag 680

Fisherfield

Cnoc Breac 293

Peterburn

B8021

Naast
Boor
Poolewe
Londubh

INVEREWE (NTS)

Meall na Meine 251

Beinn a'Chaisgein 857

North Erradale

B8057

Loch na Moine

Lochan Beannoch
Beinn Airigh Charr 791

Big Sand
Carn Dearg

Mial
Gairloch
Auchtercairn 349

Loch na Curra

Loch Tollaidh

Meall A'irigh Mhic Craidh

Loch Airigh a' Phuill

Meall Mheannaidh

Longa Island

Gair Loch
Strath Bay

GAIRLOCH HERITAGE MUSEUM

Beinn Lair 860

Eilean Troddday

Rubha na h-Aiseig

Eilean Horrisdale

Charlestown

Kerrysdale

Eilean Ruairidh Mor

Eilean Suthainn

Port Henderson
Opinan

Badachro

Meall Aundary 329

B8056

Kerry

Shieldaig

Loch Bad an Sgalaig

A832

Slattadale

Letterewe

Furnace

Almaluag Bay

Galta Mor

Sgeir Eirinn

Eilean Flodigarry

South Erradale

Loch Clair

Loch Braigh Horrisdale

Loch Kerry

VICTORIA FALLS

Talladale

18

na Quiraing

Digg
The Needle

Staffin Bay

Staffin Island
Rubha Garbhaig

Redpoint
Maol Ruadh

Dubh Loch

Loch Ghabhaig

Loch Gaineamhach

Strath Lungard

Meall a' Ghiubhais

Stenscholl
Staffin
Loch Cleap

Red Point

Meall na h-Uamha 288

Craig

Shieldaig Forest

Baosbheinn 875

Beinn an Eoin 855

Beinn a'Chearcaill

Maligar

L. Mealt

Elishader

Craig

Beinn Bhreac 624

Loch a'Bhealaich

Loch na Oidhche

Marishader
Garros
Culnaknock

Rubha nam Brathairean

Loch a'Ghobhainn

An Ruadh-mheallan

Sgurr Mhor 985

Beinn Dearg 914

Ruadh-stac Mor
Sail Mhor 1010

Beinn Edra 611

Lealt

Loch Torridon

Rubha na Fearn

Lower Diabaig

Upper Diabaig 672

Beinn Alligin 922

981

Beinn Eighe

Creag a'Lain

Baca Ruadh 608

637

Rigg

Fearnmore

Fearnbeg

L. Diabaig

Loch Diabaigas Airde

Spidean a'Choire Leith 1054

Hartaval

719

Arinacrinachd

Alligin Shuas
Inverpilligan

Mullach an Rathain 1023

Liathach

Sgurr Dubh 782

Dry Harbour

Rona

125

Cuaig
Kenmore

Loch a'Creagach

UPPER LOCH TORRIDON

Fasag
Torridon
Annat

Torridon 16

436

Loch Bharanachd

Coulin Forest

Ardheslaig

Rubha na Feola

Balgy

Seana Mheallan

Lochan Uaine 925 876

Eilean Tigh

Beinnna h-Iolaire 254

Inverbain

Shieldaig Island

A896

Ben-damph Forest

737

960

Torran

Eilean Fladday

Shieldaig

Ben Shieldaig 516

Beinn na h-Eaglaise 792

Maol Chean-dearg 933

Sgorr Ruadh 960

A855

Ben Dearg 552

Arnish

An Garbh-mheall 493

Croic-bheinn 493

An Fur 387

Beinn Damh 902

Fuar Tholl 907

Brochel

Lonbain

Meall na Fhuaid 518

Glenshieldaig Forest

Loch Lundie

An Staonach 513

Meall na Saobhaidhe 368

An Ruadh-stac 892

Annain Bhuidheach

Balnacra

SKYE

A850

Sithean Bhealaich Chumhaing 392

Prince Charles's Cave

Loch Arnish

Manish Point

Loch nan Eun

Applecross

Applecross Forest

Beinn Bhan 896

Sgurr a Gharaidh 730

Coulags

A890

Glengrasco

Aoryaig

Hartfield

646

A890

Borve

Portree

RAASAY

Applecross
Milton
Camusteel
Camasterach

Sgurr a' Chaorachain 776

Bealach na Ba 710

Meall Gorm 792

626

Loch Coultrie

Loch Kishorn

Sgurr 392

Strathcarron Sta.

Achintee

Penifiler

Glame 385

Culduie

Sron na h-Airde Baine

Russel

Lochcarron

A896

Carn Geuradainn 594

Glenmore

Ben Tianavaig 413

Balachuirn

Dun Caan 443

Toscaig

Achintraid

Sgeir Fhada

Attadale

Camastianavaig

Stroc-bheinn 400

Oskaig Point

Oskaig

Rubha na' Leac

85

86

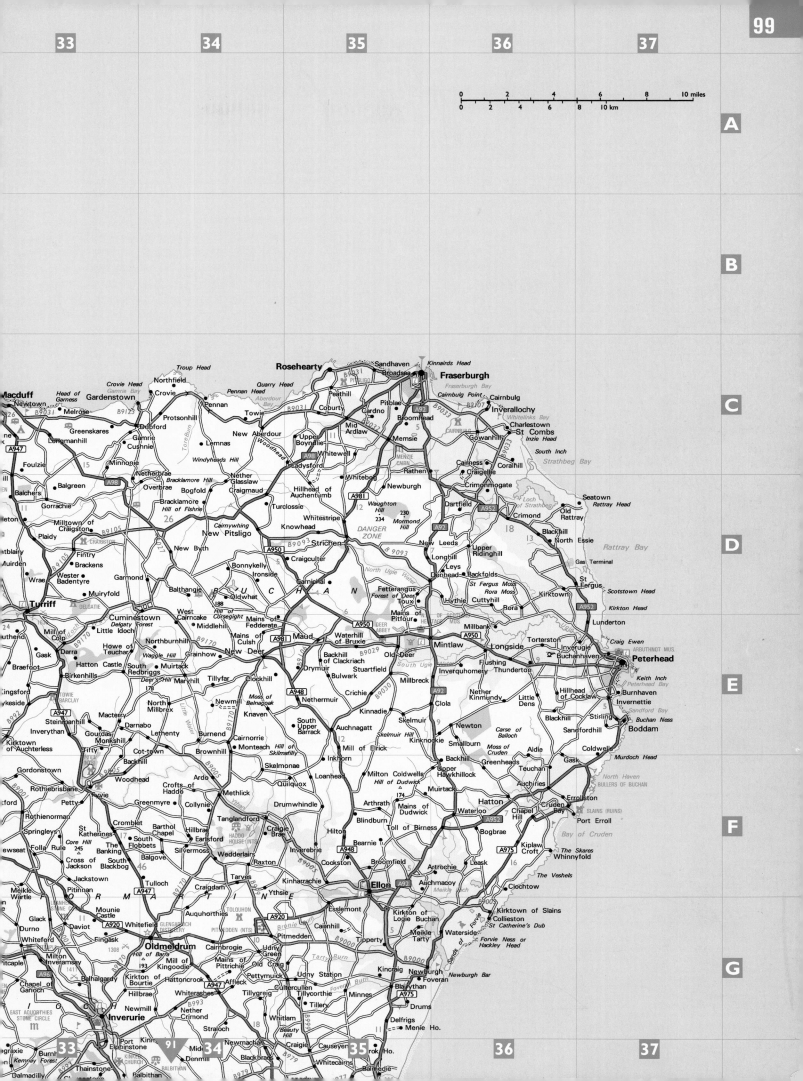

33   34   35   36   37

A

B

10 miles
0 2 4 6 8
0 2 4 6 8 10 km

C

Troup Head   Rosehearty   Sandhaven   Kinnairds Head
Crovie Head   Northfield   Broadsea   Fraserburgh
Macduff   Head of   Gardenstown   Crovie   Pennan   Quarry Head   Peathill   Pitligo   Fraserburgh Bay
Newtown   Garness   Gamrie Bay   Pennan Head   Towie   Coburty   Pitblae   Cairnbulg Point   Cairnbulg
B9031   Melrose   B9123   Dubford   Aberdour   Pitlae   Cardno   Broomhead   Inverallochy
A947   Greenskares   Gamrie   Protsonhill   Bay   New Aberdour   Upper   Mid   Memsie   Charlestown   St Combs
Longmanhill   Cushnie   Woodhead   Boyndlie   Ardlaw   Rathen   Inzie Head
Foulzie   Minnonie   Netherbrae   Whitewell   Whitebog   Newburgh   Cairness   Gowanhill   South Inch   Strathbeg Bay
Balgreen   A98   Overbrae   Bogfold   Craigmaud   Hillhead of   Craigellie
Gorrachie   Bracklamore   Nether   Turclossie   Auchentumb   Dartfield   Crimonmogate   Seatown   Rattray Head
Milltown of   Hill of Fishrie   Glasslaw   Whitestripe   Waughton   230   Crimond   Old Rattray
Craigston   Bracklamore   Knowhead   Hill   Mormond   Blackhill   North Essie   Rattray Bay
Plaidy   B9105   New Byth   DANGER   Hill   New Leeds   Gas Terminal
Fintry   CRAIGSTON   New Pitsligo   A950   Strichen   ZONE   Longhill   Upper   St Fergus   Scotstown Head
Brackens   Garmond   Craigculter   North Ugie Water   Leys   Ridinghill   Kirktown   Kirkton Head
Wester   Balthangie   Bonnykelly   Carnichal   Fetterangus   Denhend   Backfolds   A952   Lunderton
Badentyre   Oldwhat   Ironside   Forest of Deer   Hythie   Cuttyhill
Turriff   Muiryfold   BUCHAN   Troux   Mains of   Rora
West   Hill of   Mains of   B9093   Pitfour   Millbank   Torterston   Craig Ewen
Cuminestown   Cairncake   Corseght   Waterhill   Old Deer   Mintlaw   Longside   Inverugie   Peterhead
Mill of   Delgaty Forest   Middlehill   Culsh   of Bruxie   Flushing   Buchanhaven   Peterhead Bay
Colp   Howe of   A981   Maud   B9029   Thunderton   Inverquhomery   Burnhaven
Gask   Teuchar   Grainhow   New Deer   Backhill   Nether   Invernettie
Darra   Waggle Hill   of Clackriach   Millbreck   Kinmundy   Little   Blackhill   Sandford Bay
Hatton Castle   South   Muirtack   Drymuir   Stuartfield   A92   Dens   Stirling   Buchan Ness
Birkenhills   Redbriggs   Maryhill   Tillyfar   Clockhill   Bulwark   Crichie   Newton   Sandfordhill   Boddam
Kingsford   Deer's Hill   A948   Nethermuir   Kinnadie   Clola   Carse of   Aldie   Coldwells
Braefoot   TOWIE   Macterry   North   Newmill   Moss of   Skelmuir   Kinknockie   Balloch   Gask   Murdoch Head
BARCLAY   Steinmanhill   Millbrex   Belnagoak   Auchnagatt   Smallburn   Backhill   Teuchan   North Haven
Kirktown of   A947   Inverythan   Darnabo   Knaven   South   Skelmuir   Mill of Elrick   Moss of   Greenheads   Auchiries   BULLERS OF BUCHAN
Auchterless   Tifty   Gourdas   Monkshill   Lethenty   Burnend   Upper   Inkhorn   Cruden   Errolston
Gordonstown   Backhill   Cairnorrie   Barrack   Milton Coldwells   Hatton   Cruden   SLAINS (RUINS)
Rothiebrisbane   Woodhead   Ardo   Monteach   Hill of   Loanhead   Upper   Bay   Port Erroll
Fyvie   Crofts of   Brownhill   Skilmafilly   Hawhillock   Waterloo   Chapel   Bay of Cruden
Petty   Haddo   Methlick   Skelmonae   Hill of Dudwick   Muirtack   Hill   Bogbrae   The Skares
Rothienorman   Greenmyre   Collynie   Drumwhindle   Arthrath   Mains of   A952   Kiplaw   Whinnyfold
Springleys   Cromblet   Barthol   Tanglandford   Craigie   Blindburn   Dudwick   A975   Croft   The Veshels
St Katherines   Chapel   Earlsford   Brae   Hilton   Bearnie   Toll of Birness   Leask   Forvie Ness or
Folla Rule   The Banking   Silvermoss   Wedderlairs   Inverebrie   A948   Cookston   Broomfield   Artrochie   Clochtow   Hackley Head
Cross of   South Blackbog   Balgove   Raxton   Kinharrachie   Ellon   Auchmacoy   Kirktown of Slains
Jackstown   Tulloch   Craigdam   Tarves   Ythsie   A92   Colliston   St Catherine's Dub
Meikle   Pitinnan   A947   Ythsie   Esslemont   Kirkton of   Waterside   Forvie Ness or
Wartle   Mounie   Auquhorthies   Cairnhill   Logie Buchan   Meikle   Hackley Head
Glack   Castle   Daviot   A920   Whitefield   TOLOUHON   A920   Pitmedden   Tipperty   Tarty   Sands of
Whiteford   Fingask   Cairnbrogie   Udny   B9000   Newburgh
Chapel of   Milton   Mains of   Green   Kincraig   Newburgh
Garioch   Inveramsay   Balhalgardy   Mill of   Kingoodie   Old Craig   Udny Station   Foveran   Newburgh Bar
Kirkton of   Pettymuick   Minnes   Blairython
Bourtie   Hattoncrook   Affleck   Cultercullen   A975
Oldmeldrum   Hillbrae   Whiterashes   Tillygreig   Tillycorthie   Drums
Newmill   Nether   Tillery   Delfrigs
Inverurie   Crimond   Whitlam   Menie Ho.
EAST AQUHORTHIES   Stralloch   Beauty   Craigie
STONE CIRCLE   Hill   Causeyen   Menie Ho.
Port Kinn   Newmachar   Whitecairns
Elphinstone   KINKEL   Blackbraes   Balmedie
CHURCH   Denmill

33   91   34   35   36   37

D

E

F

G

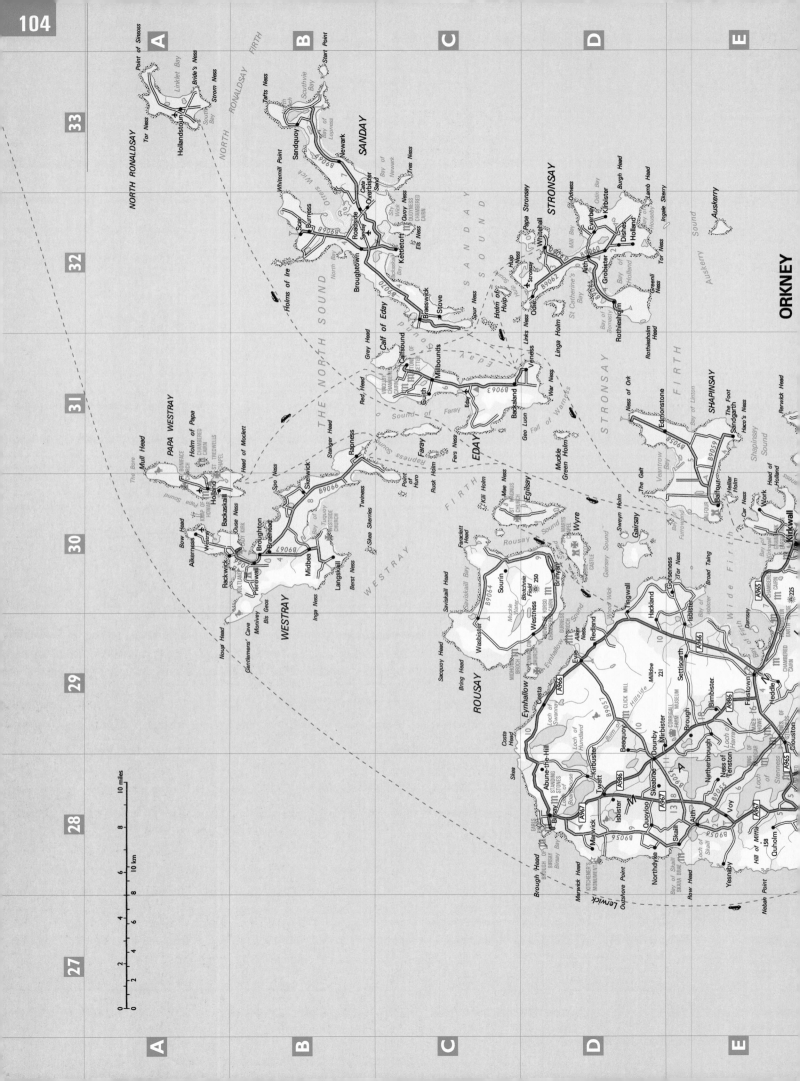

ORKNEY

NORTH RONALDSAY

SANDAY

STRONSAY

WESTRAY

PAPA WESTRAY

EDAY

ROUSAY

SHAPINSAY

Kirkwall

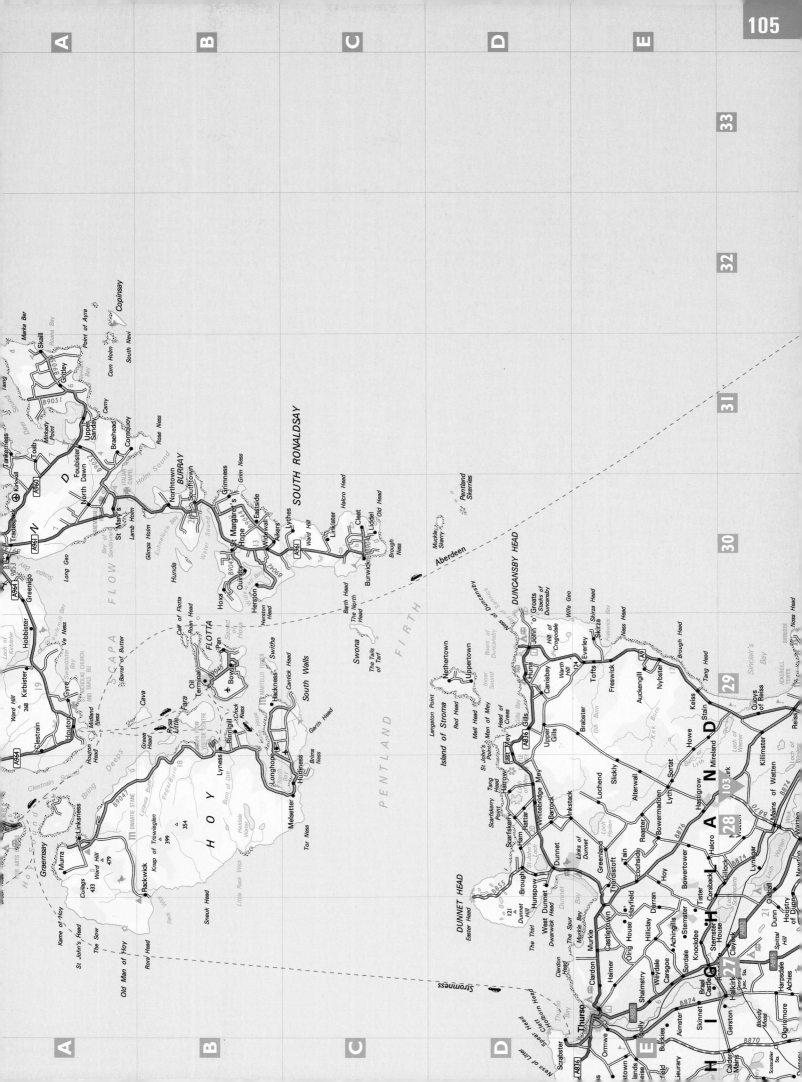

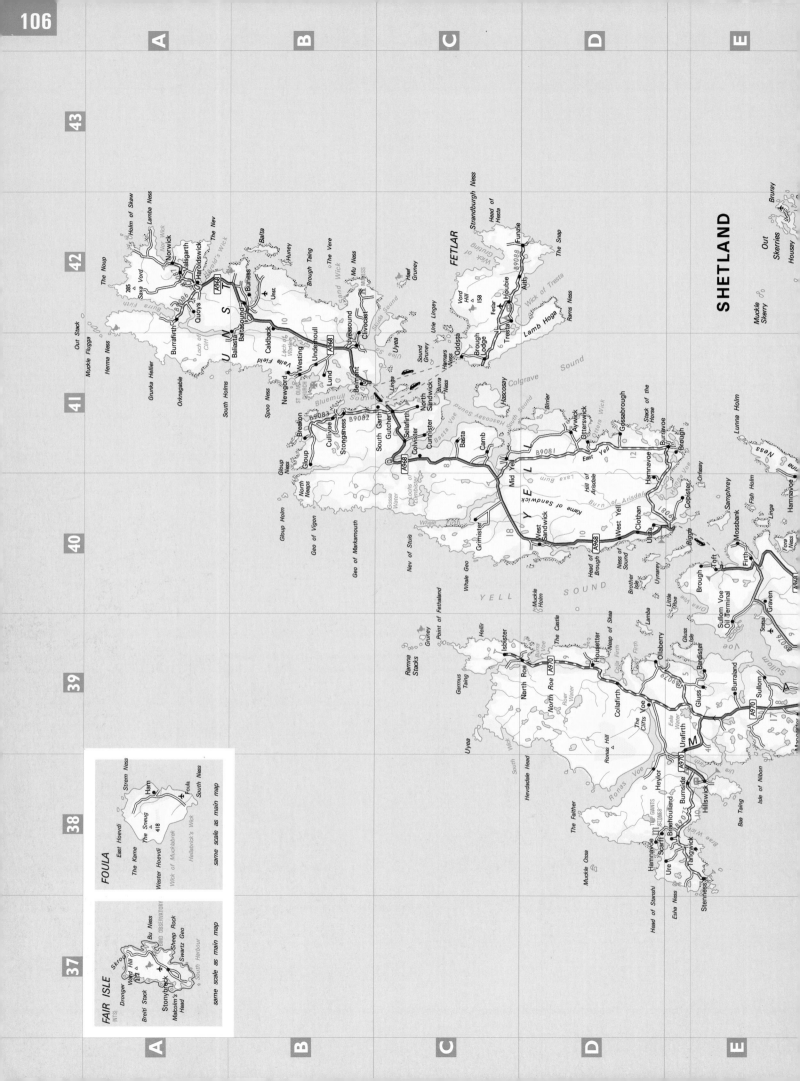

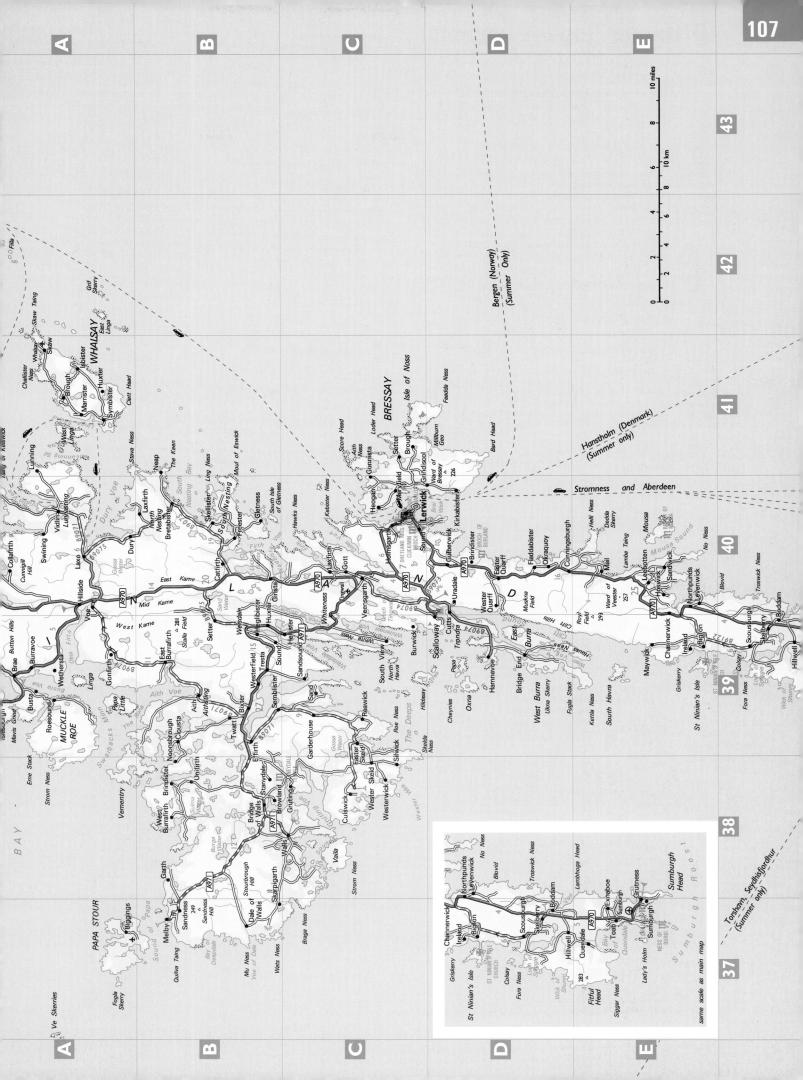

Fifteen Route Centres - key points in the nation's network of motorways and main roads - have been selected to represent different areas throughout Britain. They are as follows:

London
Aberdeen
Birmingham
Bristol
Cardiff
Edinburgh
Exeter
Glasgow
Inverness
Leeds
Liverpool
Manchester
Newcastle
Norwich
Southampton

For each Route Centre a set of useful destinations has been selected e.g. major cities, holiday resorts, cross-channel ferry ports - and the shortest road distances to these destinations using motorways and A roads are indicated. The distances are shown in miles, with the kilometric equivalent in italics.

LONDON

Inverness **540** *869*
Aberdeen **507** *816*
Dundee **445** *716*
Glasgow **387** *623*
Edinburgh **378** *608*
Newcastle **274** *441*
Carlisle **292** *470*
Hull **173** *278*
188 *303* Manchester
Holyhead **250** *402*
Liverpool **202** *325*
Norwich **106** *171*
Birmingham **106** *171*
Cambridge **53** *85*
Fishguard **267** *430*
Harwich **73** *117*
Swansea **187** *301*
Cardiff **147** *237*
Bristol **122** *196*
LONDON
Dover **71** *114*
Southampton **81** *130*
Brighton **54** *87*
Penzance **273** *439*
Plymouth **218** *351*

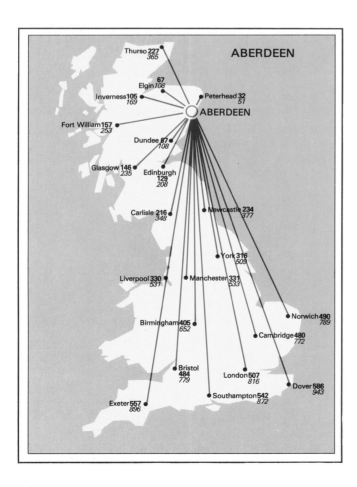

ABERDEEN

Thurso **227** *365*
Elgin **67** *108*
Inverness **105** *169*
Peterhead **32** *51*
ABERDEEN
Fort William **157** *253*
Dundee **87** *108*
Glasgow **146** *235*
Edinburgh **129** *208*
Carlisle **216** *348*
Newcastle **234** *377*
York **316** *509*
Liverpool **330** *531*
Manchester **331** *533*
Norwich **490** *789*
Birmingham **405** *652*
Cambridge **480** *772*
Bristol **484** *779*
London **507** *816*
Dover **586** *943*
Southampton **542** *872*
Exeter **557** *896*

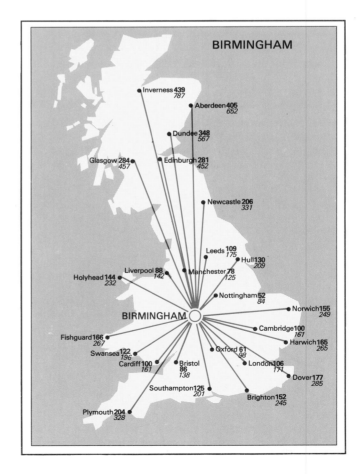

BIRMINGHAM

Inverness **439** *787*
Aberdeen **405** *652*
Dundee **348** *567*
Glasgow **284** *457*
Edinburgh **281** *452*
Newcastle **206** *331*
Leeds **109** *175*
Hull **130** *209*
Holyhead **144** *232*
Liverpool **88** *142*
Manchester **78** *125*
Nottingham **52** *84*
Norwich **155** *249*
BIRMINGHAM
Fishguard **166** *267*
Cambridge **100** *161*
Swansea **122** *196*
Harwich **165** *265*
Cardiff **100** *161*
Oxford **61** *98*
Bristol **86** *138*
London **106** *171*
Dover **177** *285*
Southampton **125** *201*
Brighton **152** *245*
Plymouth **204** *328*

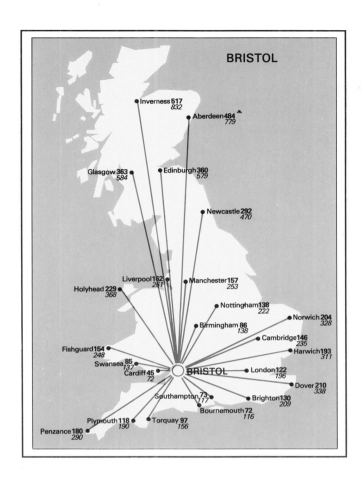

BRISTOL

Inverness 517 / 832
Aberdeen 484 / 779
Glasgow 363 / 584
Edinburgh 360 / 579
Newcastle 292 / 470
Liverpool 162 / 261
Manchester 157 / 253
Holyhead 229 / 368
Nottingham 138 / 222
Norwich 204 / 328
Birmingham 86 / 138
Cambridge 146 / 235
Harwich 193 / 311
Fishguard 154 / 248
Swansea 85 / 137
Cardiff 45 / 72
London 122 / 196
Dover 210 / 338
Southampton 73 / 117
Brighton 130 / 209
Bournemouth 72 / 116
Plymouth 118 / 190
Torquay 97 / 156
Penzance 180 / 290

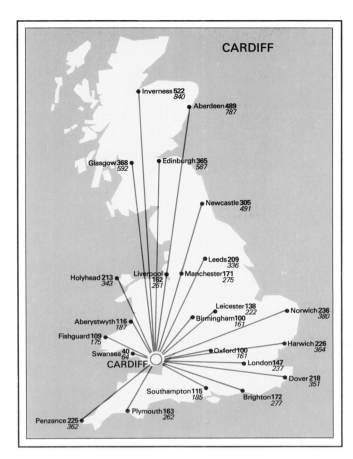

CARDIFF

Inverness 522 / 840
Aberdeen 489 / 787
Glasgow 368 / 592
Edinburgh 365 / 587
Newcastle 305 / 491
Leeds 209 / 336
Holyhead 213 / 343
Liverpool 162 / 261
Manchester 171 / 275
Leicester 138 / 222
Norwich 236 / 380
Aberystwyth 116 / 187
Birmingham 100 / 161
Fishguard 109 / 175
Oxford 100 / 161
Harwich 226 / 364
Swansea 40 / 64
London 147 / 237
Dover 218 / 351
Southampton 115 / 185
Brighton 172 / 277
Plymouth 163 / 262
Penzance 225 / 362

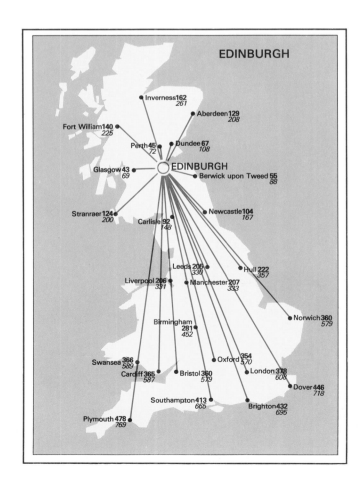

EDINBURGH

Inverness 162 / 261
Aberdeen 129 / 208
Fort William 140 / 225
Perth 45 / 72
Dundee 67 / 108
Glasgow 43 / 69
Berwick upon Tweed 55 / 88
Stranraer 124 / 200
Newcastle 104 / 167
Carlisle 92 / 148
Leeds 205 / 330
Hull 222 / 357
Liverpool 206 / 331
Manchester 207 / 333
Norwich 360 / 579
Birmingham 281 / 452
Swansea 366 / 589
Oxford 354 / 570
Cardiff 365 / 587
Bristol 360 / 579
London 378 / 608
Dover 446 / 718
Southampton 413 / 665
Brighton 432 / 695
Plymouth 478 / 769

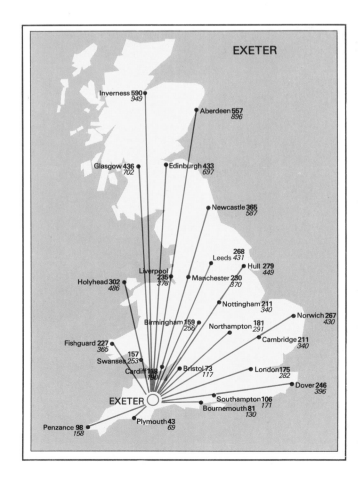

EXETER

Inverness 590 / 949
Aberdeen 557 / 896
Glasgow 436 / 702
Edinburgh 433 / 697
Newcastle 365 / 587
Leeds 268 / 431
Hull 279 / 449
Liverpool 235 / 378
Manchester 230 / 370
Holyhead 302 / 486
Nottingham 211 / 340
Birmingham 159 / 256
Northampton 181 / 291
Norwich 267 / 430
Cambridge 211 / 340
Fishguard 227 / 365
Swansea 157 / 253
Cardiff 108 / 160
Bristol 73 / 117
London 175 / 282
Dover 246 / 396
Southampton 106 / 171
Bournemouth 81 / 130
Penzance 98 / 158
Plymouth 43 / 69

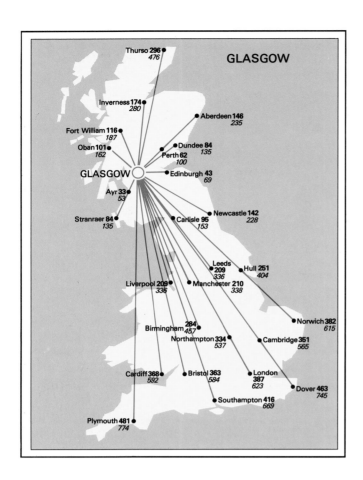

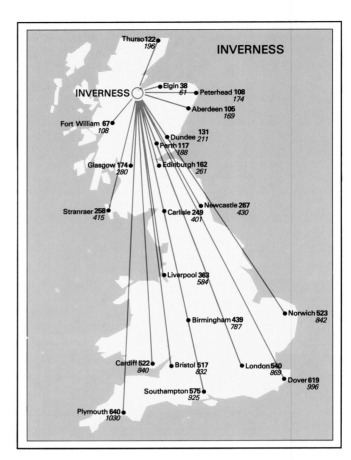

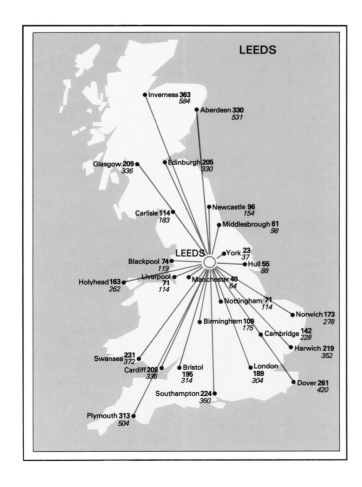

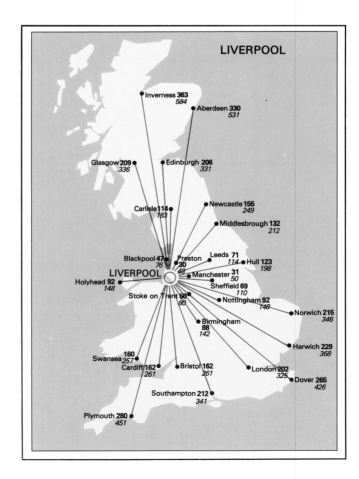

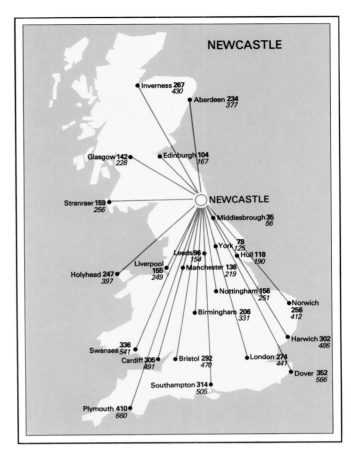

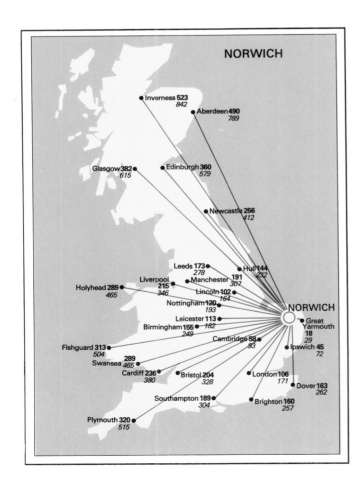

Channel Ferries

NETHERLANDS

To Hoek van Holland 6–8hrs
To Esbjerg 22½hrs
To Hamburg 19hrs
To Rotterdam 20½hrs
To Kingston upon Hull 15hrs
To Göteborg 22½hrs

BELGIUM

Vlissingen
Breskens
Zeebrugge
Brugge
Oostende

Kortijk
Tournai
Tourcoing
Roubaix
Armentières
Lille
Béthune
Valenciennes
Cambrai
St Quentin
Soissons
Compiègne
Beauvais
Arras
Douai
Amiens
Abbeville

Dunkerque
Dunkerque Ouest
Calais
Boulogne
C. Gris Nez
Le Touquet-Paris-Plage
Dieppe
Rouen

FRANCE

Felixstowe
Harwich
The Naze
Clacton-on-Sea
Colchester
Chelmsford
Hertford
Luton
St Albans
Watford

Southend-on-Sea
Sheerness
Margate
N. Foreland
Ramsgate
Canterbury
Dover
Folkestone
Dungeness
Hastings
Eastbourne
Beachy Head

Romford
LONDON
Croydon
Crawley
Guildford
Reading
Windsor
Oxford
Newbury

ENGLAND

Maidstone
Gillingham
Royal Tunbridge Wells
Brighton
Worthing
Newhaven
Chichester
Portsmouth
Selsey Bill

Winchester
Southampton
Cowes
Newport
Isle of Wight
St. Catherine's Pt

Salisbury
Bournemouth
Poole
Weymouth
Dorchester
Bill of Portland
Yeovil

Swindon
Cheltenham
Gloucester
Monmouth
Bath
Bristol

ENGLISH CHANNEL

Le Havre
Deauville
Bayeux
Ouistreham
Caen
Cherbourg
Cap de la Hague

CHANNEL ISLANDS
Alderney
Sark
Guernsey
St Peter Port
Jersey
St Helier

7hrs
5–8hrs
4hrs
3½hrs
2½hrs
½–1¼hrs
1hr
4hrs
5½hrs
5½hrs
2hrs
5–8hrs
4½–7½hrs
4½hrs
5½hrs
7hrs
6hrs
2½hrs
7–8½hrs
8½hrs–10hrs to St Malo
4hrs
1¾hrs

Santander (Winter only) & Bilbao 29–33hrs
To Rosslare

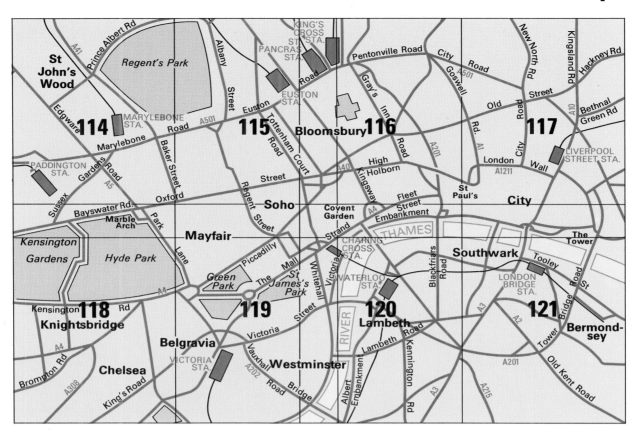

KEY TO MAP SYMBOLS

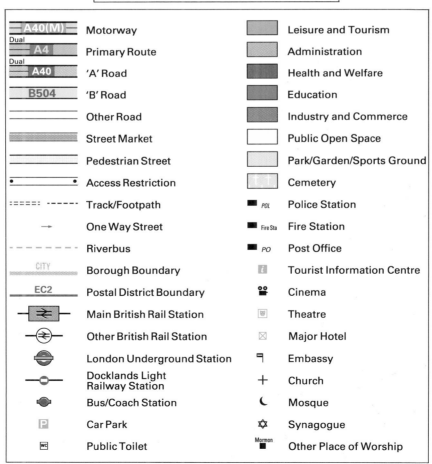

A40(M) Dual	Motorway
A4 Dual	Primary Route
A40	'A' Road
B504	'B' Road
—	Other Road
—	Street Market
—	Pedestrian Street
• — •	Access Restriction
====== ------	Track/Footpath
→	One Way Street
– – –	Riverbus
CITY	Borough Boundary
EC2	Postal District Boundary
⊠	Main British Rail Station
⊕	Other British Rail Station
⊖	London Underground Station
⊖	Docklands Light Railway Station
⊖	Bus/Coach Station
P	Car Park
WC	Public Toilet

■	Leisure and Tourism
■	Administration
■	Health and Welfare
■	Education
■	Industry and Commerce
□	Public Open Space
□	Park/Garden/Sports Ground
▦	Cemetery
■ POL	Police Station
■ Fire Sta	Fire Station
■ PO	Post Office
i	Tourist Information Centre
🎥	Cinema
▣	Theatre
⊠	Major Hotel
⊐	Embassy
+	Church
☾	Mosque
✡	Synagogue
Mormon ■	Other Place of Worship

Scale 1:10,000 (6.3 inches to 1 mile)

0	0.25	0.50	0.75	1 kilometre

0		¼		½ mile

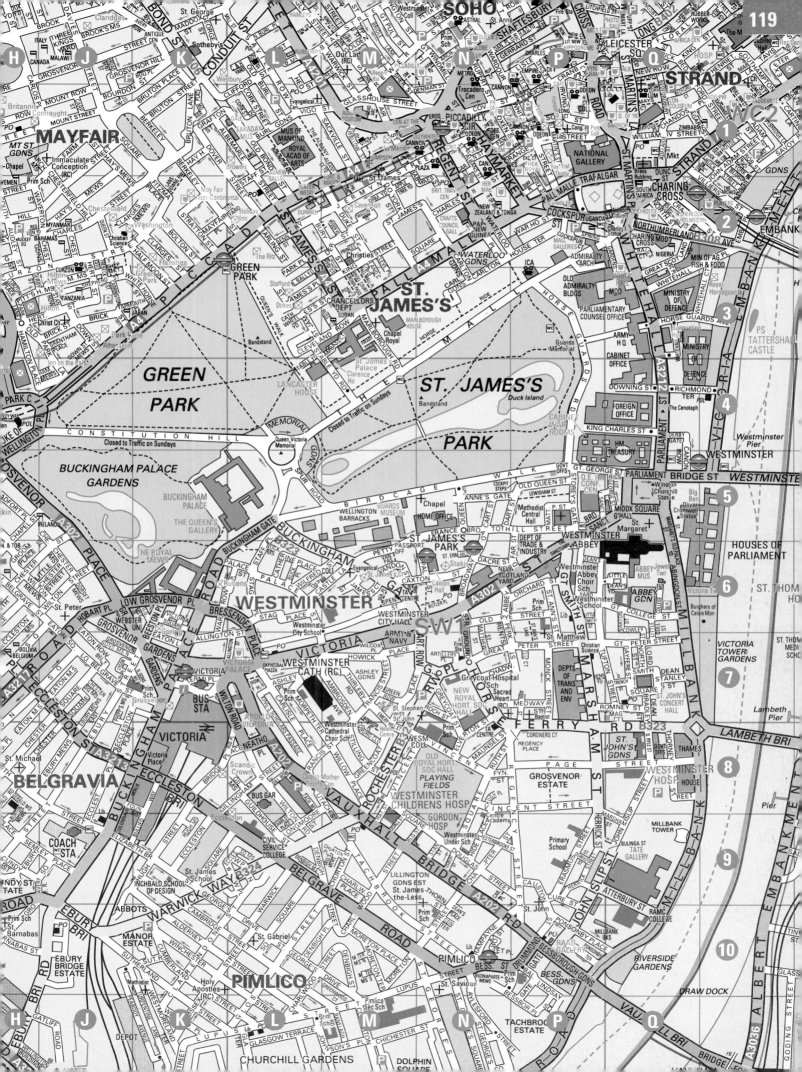

Abbey Orchard St. SW1 **119 P6**
Abbey St. SE1 **121 N6**
Abbots La. SE1 **121 N3**
Abbots Manor Est. SW1 **119 J10**
Abchurch La. EC4 **117 L10**
Abchurch Yd. EC4 **117 K10**
Aberdeen Pl. NW8 **114 A4**
Aberdour St. SE1 **121 M8**
Abingdon Clo. SE1 **121 Q9**
Abingdon St. SW1 **119 Q6**
Achilles Way W1 **118 H3**
Acton St. WC1 **116 B3**
Adam & Eve Ct. W1 **115 M8**
Adam St. WC2 **120 A1**
Adams Ct. EC2 **117 L8**
Adams Row W1 **118 H1**
Addington St. SE1 **120 C5**
Addle Hill EC4 **116 G9**
Addle St. EC2 **117 J7**
Adelaide St. WC2 **119 Q1**
Adeline Pl. WC1 **115 P7**
Adelphi Ter. WC2 **120 A1**
Adpar St. W2 **114 A6**
Affleck St. N1 **116 C1**
Agar St. WC2 **119 Q1**
Agdon St. EC1 **116 F4**
Air St. W1 **119 M1**
Alaska St. SE1 **120 D3**
Albany, The W1 **119 L1**
Albany Ctyd. SW1 **119 M1**
Albemarle St. W1 **119 L1**
Albemarle Way EC1 **116 F5**
Albert Ct. SW7 **118 A5**
Albert Hall Mans. SW7 **118 A5**
Alberta Est. SE17 **120 G10**
Alberta St. SE17 **120 F10**
Albion Clo. W2 **114 D10**
Albion Ms. W2 **114 D10**
Albion Pl. EC1 **116 F6**
Albion Pl. EC2 **117 L7**
Albion St. W2 **114 D9**
Albion Way EC1 **116 H7**
Aldbridge St. SE17 **121 N10**
Aldenham St. NW1 **115 M1**
Aldermanbury EC2 **117 J8**
Aldermanbury Sq. EC2 **117 J7**
Alderman's Wk. EC2 **117 M7**
Alderney St. SW1 **119 K10**
Aldersgate St. EC1 **116 H6**
Aldford St. W1 **118 G2**
Aldgate EC3 **117 P9**
Aldgate Ave. E1 **117 P8**
Aldgate High St. EC3 **117 P9**
Aldwych WC2 **116 B10**
Alexander Pl. SW7 **118 C8**
Alexander Sq. SW3 **118 C8**
Alford Pl. N1 **117 J1**
Alfred Ms. W1 **115 N6**
Alfred Pl. WC1 **115 N6**
Alice St. SE1 **121 M7**
Alie St. E1 **117 Q9**
All Souls Pl. W1 **115 K7**
Allgood St. E2 **117 Q1**
Allhallows La. EC4 **121 K1**
Allington St. SW1 **119 K7**
Allitsen Rd. NW8 **114 C1**
Allsop Pl. NW1 **114 F5**
Alma Gro. SE1 **121 Q9**
Alpha Clo. NW1 **114 D3**
Alsace Rd. SE17 **121 M10**
Alscot Rd. SE1 **121 Q8**
Alscot Way SE1 **121 P8**
Alvey Est. SE17 **121 M9**
Alvey St. SE17 **121 M10**
Ambassador's Ct. SW1 **119 M3**
Ambergate St. SE17 **120 G10**
Ambrosden Ave. SW1 **119 M7**
Amelia St. SE17 **120 H10**
Amen Cor. EC4 **116 G9**
Amen Ct. EC4 **116 G8**
America Sq. EC3 **117 P10**
America St. SE1 **121 H3**
Ampthill Sq. Est. NW1 **115 M1**
Ampton Pl. WC1 **116 B3**
Ampton St. WC1 **116 B3**
Amwell St. EC1 **116 D2**
Anchor Yd. EC1 **117 J4**
Anderson St. SW3 **118 E10**
Andrew Borde St. WC2 **115 P8**
Andrews Crosse WC2 **116 D9**
Angel All. E1 **117 Q8**
Angel Ct. EC2 **117 L8**
Angel Ct. SW1 **119 M3**
Angel Ms. N1 **116 E1**
Angel Pas. EC4 **121 K1**
Angel Pl. SE1 **121 K4**
Angel St. EC1 **116 H8**
Anning St. EC2 **117 N4**
Ann's Clo. SW1 **118 F5**
Ann's Pl. E1 **117 P7**
Apothecary St. EC4 **116 F9**
Apple Tree Yd. SW1 **119 M2**
Appleby St. E2 **117 P1**
Appold St. EC2 **117 M6**
Aquinas St. SE1 **120 E3**
Arcade, The EC2 **117 M7**
Arch St. SE1 **121 H7**
Archer St. W1 **115 N10**
Archery Clo. W2 **114 D9**
Arches, The WC2 **120 A2**
Archibald Ms. W1 **119 J1**
Arden Est. N1 **117 M1**

Argent St. SE1 **120 G4**
Argyle Sq. WC1 **116 A2**
Argyle St. WC1 **115 Q2**
Argyle Wk. WC1 **115 Q3**
Argyll St. W1 **115 L9**
Arlington St. SW1 **119 L2**
Arlington Way EC1 **116 E2**
Armstrong Rd. SW7 **118 A7**
Arne St. WC2 **116 A9**
Arneway St. SW1 **119 P7**
Arnold Circ. E2 **117 P3**
Arnold Est. SE1 **121 Q5**
Arthur St. EC4 **117 L10**
Artillery La. E1 **117 N7**
Artillery Pas. E1 **117 N7**
Artillery Pl. SW1 **119 N7**
Artillery Row SW1 **119 N7**
Artizan St. E1 **117 N8**
Arundel Great Ct. WC2 **116 C10**
Arundel St. WC2 **116 C10**
Ashbridge St. NW8 **114 C5**
Ashby St. EC1 **116 G3**
Ashford St. N1 **117 M2**
Ashland Pl. W1 **114 G6**
Ashley Gdns. SW1 **119 M7**
Ashley Pl. SW1 **119 L7**
Ashmill St. NW1 **114 C6**
Aske St. N1 **117 M2**
Astell St. SW3 **118 D10**
Atterbury St. SW1 **119 Q9**
Attneave St. WC1 **116 D3**
Audley Sq. W1 **119 H2**
Augustus St. NW1 **115 K1**
Austin Friars EC2 **117 L8**
Austin Friars Pas. EC2 **117 L8**
Austin Friars Sq. EC2 **117 L8**
Austin St. E2 **117 P3**
Austral St. SE11 **120 F8**
Ave Maria La. EC4 **116 G9**
Avery Fm. Row SW1 **119 J9**
Avery Row W1 **115 K10**
Avon Pl. SE1 **121 J5**
Avonmouth St. SE1 **121 H6**
Aybrook St. W1 **114 G7**
Aylesbury St. EC1 **116 F5**
Aylwin Est. SE1 **121 N6**
Ayres St. SE1 **121 J4**
Ayrton Rd. SW7 **118 A6**

B

Babmaes St. SW1 **119 N2**
Bacchus Wk. N1 **117 M1**
Baches St. N1 **117 L3**
Back Hill EC1 **116 D5**
Backhouse Pl. SE1 **121 N9**
Bacon Gro. SE1 **121 P7**
Bacon St. E1 **117 Q4**
Bacon St. E2 **117 Q4**
Baden Pl. SE1 **121 K4**
Bainbridge St. WC1 **115 P8**
Baird St. EC1 **117 J4**
Baker St. NW1 **114 F5**
Baker St. W1 **114 F6**
Baker's Ms. W1 **114 G8**
Baker's Rents E2 **117 P3**
Baker's Row EC1 **116 D5**
Balaclava Rd. SE1 **121 Q9**
Balcombe St. NW1 **114 E4**
Balderton St. W1 **114 H9**
Baldwin St. EC1 **117 K3**
Baldwin's Gdns. EC1 **116 D6**
Balfe St. N1 **116 A1**
Balfour Ms. W1 **118 H2**
Balfour Pl. W1 **118 H1**
Balfour St. SE17 **121 K8**
Balniel Gate SW1 **119 P10**
Baltic St. EC1 **116 H5**
Banbury Ct. WC2 **115 Q10**
Bank End SE1 **121 J2**
Bankside SE1 **121 H1**
Barbara Brosnan Ct. NW8 **114 A1**
Barbican, The EC2 **117 H6**
Barbon Clo. WC1 **116 A6**
Barge Ho. St. SE1 **120 E2**
Barley Mow Pas. EC1 **116 G7**
Barlow Pl. W1 **119 K1**
Barlow St. SE17 **121 L9**
Barnard's Inn EC1 **116 D8**
Barnby St. NW1 **115 M2**
Barnham St. SE1 **121 N4**
Baron St. N1 **116 D1**
Baroness Rd. E2 **117 Q2**
Barons Pl. SE1 **120 E5**
Barrett St. W1 **114 H9**
Barrie St. W2 **114 A10**
Barrow Hill Est. NW8 **114 C1**
Barrow Hill Rd. NW8 **114 C1**
Barter St. WC1 **116 A7**
Bartholomew Clo. EC1 **116 H7**
Bartholomew La. EC2 **117 L9**
Bartholomew Pl. EC1 **116 H7**
Bartholomew Sq. EC1 **117 J4**
Bartholomew St. SE1 **121 L7**
Bartlett Ct. EC4 **116 E8**
Barton St. SW1 **119 Q6**
Basil St. SW3 **118 E6**
Basing Ho. Yd. E2 **117 N2**
Basing Pl. E2 **117 N2**
Basinghall Ave. EC2 **117 K7**
Basinghall St. EC2 **117 K8**
Bastwick St. EC1 **116 H4**

Bateman St. W1 **115 N9**
Bateman's Bldgs. W1 **115 N9**
Bateman's Row EC2 **117 N4**
Bath Ct. EC1 **116 D5**
Bath St. EC1 **117 J3**
Bath Ter. SE1 **121 H7**
Bathurst Ms. W2 **114 B10**
Bathurst St. W2 **114 B10**
Battle Bri. La. SE1 **121 M3**
Battle Bri. Rd. NW1 **115 Q1**
Bayley St. WC1 **115 N7**
Baylis Rd. SE1 **120 D5**
Beak St. W1 **115 M10**
Bear All. EC4 **116 F8**
Bear Gdns. SE1 **121 H2**
Bear La. SE1 **120 G3**
Bear St. WC2 **115 P10**
Beauchamp Pl. SW3 **118 D6**
Beaufort Gdns. SW3 **118 D6**
Beaufoy Wk. SE11 **120 C9**
Beaumont Ms. W1 **114 H6**
Beaumont Pl. W1 **115 M4**
Beaumont St. W1 **115 H6**
Becket St. SE1 **121 K6**
Beckway St. SE17 **121 M9**
Bedale St. SE1 **121 K3**
Bedford Ave. WC1 **115 P7**
Bedford Ct. WC2 **119 Q1**
Bedford Pl. WC1 **115 Q6**
Bedford Row WC1 **116 C6**
Bedford Sq. WC1 **115 P7**
Bedford St. WC2 **115 Q10**
Bedford Way WC1 **115 P5**
Bedfordbury WC2 **119 Q1**
Beech St. EC2 **117 H6**
Beehive Pas. EC3 **117 M9**
Beeston Pl. SW1 **119 K7**
Belgrave Ms. N. SW1 **118 G5**
Belgrave Ms. S. SW1 **118 H6**
Belgrave Ms. W. SW1 **118 G6**
Belgrave Pl. SW1 **118 H6**
Belgrave Rd. SW1 **119 L9**
Belgrave Sq. SW1 **118 G6**
Belgrave Yd. SW1 **119 J7**
Belgrove St. WC1 **116 A2**
Bell Inn Yd. EC3 **117 L9**
Bell La. E1 **117 P7**
Bell St. NW1 **114 C6**
Bell Yd. WC2 **116 D9**
Belvedere Bldgs. SE1 **120 G5**
Belvedere Pl. SE1 **120 G5**
Belvedere Rd. SE1 **120 C4**
Bendall Ms. NW1 **114 D6**
Benjamin St. EC1 **116 F6**
Bennet's Hill EC4 **116 G10**
Bennett St. SW1 **119 L2**
Bennetts Yd. SW1 **119 P7**
Bentinck Ms. W1 **115 H8**
Bentinck St. W1 **115 H8**
Berkeley Ms. W1 **114 F9**
Berkeley Sq. W1 **119 K1**
Berkeley St. W1 **119 K2**
Bermondsey Sq. SE1 **121 N6**
Bermondsey St. SE1 **121 M3**
Bernard St. WC1 **115 Q5**
Berners Ms. W1 **115 M7**
Berners Pl. W1 **115 M8**
Berners St. W1 **115 M7**
Berry Pl. EC1 **116 G3**
Berry St. EC1 **116 G4**
Berryfield Rd. SE17 **120 G10**
Berwick St. W1 **115 M8**
Bessborough Gdns. SW1 **119 P10**
Bessborough Pl. SW1 **119 N10**
Bessborough St. SW1 **119 N10**
Bethnal Grn. Rd. E1 **117 P4**
Betterton St. WC2 **115 Q9**
Bevenden St. N1 **117 L2**
Beverley NW8 **114 C3**
Bevin Way WC1 **116 D2**
Bevis Marks EC3 **117 N8**
Bickenhall St. W1 **114 F6**
Bidborough St. WC1 **115 Q3**
Bidford Ms. W1 **115 K6**
Billiter Sq. EC3 **117 N9**
Billiter St. EC3 **117 N9**
Bingham Pl. W1 **114 G6**
Binney St. W1 **115 H9**
Birchin La. EC3 **117 L9**
Bird St. W1 **115 H9**
Birdcage Wk. SW1 **119 M5**
Birkenhead St. WC1 **116 A2**
Bishop's Ct. EC4 **116 F8**
Bishop's Ct. WC2 **116 D8**
Bishops Ter. SE11 **120 E8**
Bishopsgate EC2 **117 N7**
Bishopsgate Chyd. EC2 **117 M8**
Bittern St. SE1 **121 H5**
Black Friars Ct. EC4 **116 F10**
Black Friars La. EC4 **116 F10**
Black Horse Ct. SE1 **121 L6**
Black Prince Rd. SE1 **120 A9**
Black Prince Rd. SE11 **120 C9**
Black Swan Yd. SE1 **121 M4**
Blackall St. EC2 **117 M4**
Blackbird Yd. E2 **117 Q2**
Blackburnes Ms. W1 **118 G1**
Blackfriars Pas. EC4 **116 F10**
Blackfriars Rd. SE1 **120 F2**
Blackland Ter. SW3 **118 E9**
Blackwood St. SE17 **121 K10**
Blandford Sq. NW1 **114 D5**
Blandford St. W1 **114 F8**

Bleeding Heart Yd. EC1 **116 E7**
Blenheim St. W1 **115 J9**
Bletchley Ct. N1 **117 K1**
Bletchley St. N1 **117 J1**
Blomfield St. EC2 **117 L7**
Bloomburg St. SW1 **119 M9**
Bloomfield Pl. W1 **115 K10**
Bloomfield Ter. SW1 **118 H10**
Bloomsbury Ct. WC1 **116 A7**
Bloomsbury Pl. WC1 **116 A6**
Bloomsbury Sq. WC1 **116 A7**
Bloomsbury St. WC1 **115 P7**
Bloomsbury Way WC1 **115 Q8**
Blore Ct. W1 **115 N10**
Blossom St. E1 **117 N5**
Blue Ball Yd. SW1 **119 L3**
Bolsover St. W1 **115 K5**
Bolt Ct. EC4 **116 E9**
Bolton St. W1 **119 K2**
Bond Ct. EC4 **117 K9**
Bonhill St. EC2 **117 L5**
Book Ms. WC2 **115 P9**
Boot St. N1 **117 M3**
Booth's Pl. W1 **115 M7**
Boreas Wk. E1 **117 P7**
Borer's Pas. E1 **117 N8**
Borough High St. SE1 **121 J5**
Borough Rd. SE1 **120 G6**
Borough Sq. SE1 **121 H5**
Boscobel Pl. SW1 **118 H8**
Boscobel St. NW8 **114 B5**
Boss St. SE1 **121 P4**
Boston Pl. NW1 **114 E5**
Boswell Ct. WC1 **116 A6**
Boswell St. WC1 **116 A6**
Botolph All. EC3 **121 M1**
Botolph La. EC3 **121 M1**
Boundary Pas. E2 **117 P4**
Boundary Row SE1 **120 F4**
Boundary St. E2 **117 P3**
Bourchier St. W1 **115 N10**
Bourdon Pl. W1 **115 K10**
Bourdon St. W1 **119 J1**
Bourlet Clo. W1 **115 L7**
Bourne Est. EC1 **116 D6**
Bourne St. SW1 **118 G9**
Bouverie Pl. W2 **114 B8**
Bouverie St. EC4 **116 E9**
Bow Chyd. EC4 **117 J9**
Bow La. EC4 **117 J9**
Bow St. WC2 **116 A9**
Bowden St. SE11 **120 E10**
Bowland Yd. SW1 **118 F5**
Bowling Grn. Ct. EC2 **117 N5**
Bowling Grn. La. EC1 **116 E4**
Bowling Grn. Pl. SE1 **121 K4**
Bowling Grn. Wk. N1 **117 M2**
Boyce St. SE1 **120 D3**
Boyfield St. SE1 **120 G5**
Boyle St. W1 **115 L10**
Brabant Ct. EC3 **117 M10**
Brackley St. EC1 **117 J6**
Brad St. SE1 **120 E3**
Braham St. E1 **117 Q9**
Braidwood St. SE1 **121 M3**
Brandon St. SE17 **121 J9**
Bray Pl. SW3 **118 E9**
Bread St. EC4 **117 J10**
Bream's Bldgs. EC4 **116 D8**
Brendon St. W1 **114 D8**
Bressenden Pl. SW1 **119 K6**
Brewer St. W1 **115 M10**
Brewer's Grn. SW1 **119 M6**
Brewhouse Yd. EC1 **116 F4**
Brick Ct. EC4 **116 D9**
Brick La. E1 **117 Q3**
Brick La. E2 **117 Q5**
Brick St. W1 **119 J3**
Bricklayer's Arms SE1 **121 N8**
Bride Ct. EC4 **116 F9**
Bride La. EC4 **116 F9**
Bridewell Pl. EC4 **116 F9**
Bridford Ms. W1 **115 K6**
Bridge Pl. SW1 **119 K8**
Bridge St. SW1 **119 Q5**
Bridge Yd. SE1 **121 L2**
Bridgeman St. NW8 **114 C1**
Bridgewater Sq. EC2 **117 H6**
Bridgewater St. EC2 **117 H6**
Bridgeway St. NW1 **115 M1**
Bridle La. W1 **115 M10**
Brill Pl. NW1 **115 P1**
Brinton Wk. SE1 **120 F3**
Briset St. EC1 **116 F6**
Britannia St. WC1 **116 B2**
Britannia Wk. N1 **117 K2**
Britton St. EC1 **116 F5**
Broad Ct. WC2 **116 A9**
Broad Sanctuary SW1 **119 P5**
Broad St. Ave. EC2 **117 M7**
Broad St. Pl. EC2 **117 L7**
Broad Wk. W1 **118 G2**
Broad Yd. EC1 **116 F5**
Broadbent St. W1 **115 J10**
Broadgate Circle EC2 **117 M6**
Broadley St. NW8 **114 B6**
Broadley Ter. NW1 **114 D5**
Broadmayne SE17 **121 K10**
Broadstone Pl. W1 **114 G7**
Broadwall SE1 **120 E2**
Broadway SW1 **119 N6**
Broadwick St. W1 **115 M10**

Brockham St. SE1 **121 J6**
Brodie St. SE1 **121 Q10**
Bromley Pl. W1 **115 L6**
Brompton Arc. SW3 **118 E5**
Brompton Pl. SW3 **118 D6**
Brompton Rd. SW1 **118 E5**
Brompton Rd. SW3 **118 C8**
Brompton Rd. SW7 **118 C7**
Brompton Sq. SW3 **118 C6**
Brook Dr. SE11 **120 E7**
Brook Gate W1 **118 F1**
Brook St. W1 **115 J10**
Brook St. W2 **114 B10**
Brooke St. EC1 **116 D7**
Brooke's Ct. EC1 **116 D6**
Brook's Ms. W1 **115 J10**
Brown Hart Gdns. W1 **114 H10**
Brown St. W1 **114 E8**
Browning Est. SE17 **121 J10**
Browning Ms. W1 **115 H7**
Browning St. SE17 **121 J10**
Brownlow Ms. WC1 **116 C5**
Brownlow St. WC1 **116 C7**
Brune St. E1 **117 P7**
Brunswick Cen. WC1 **115 Q4**
Brunswick Ct. SE1 **121 N4**
Brunswick Ms. W1 **114 F8**
Brunswick Pl. N1 **117 L3**
Brunswick Sq. WC1 **116 A4**
Brushfield St. E1 **117 N6**
Bruton La. W1 **119 K1**
Bruton Pl. W1 **119 K1**
Bruton St. W1 **119 K1**
Bryanston Ms. E. W1 **114 E7**
Bryanston Ms. W. W1 **114 E7**
Bryanston Pl. W1 **114 E7**
Bryanston Sq. W1 **114 E7**
Bryanston St. W1 **114 E9**
Brydges Pl. WC2 **119 Q1**
Buck Hill Wk. W2 **118 B1**
Buckingham Arc. WC2 **120 A1**
Buckingham Gate SW1 **119 L5**
Buckingham Ms. SW1 **119 L6**
Buckingham Palace Rd. SW1 **119 J9**
Buckingham Pl. SW1 **119 L6**
Buckingham St. WC2 **120 A1**
Buckland St. N1 **117 L1**
Buckle St. E1 **117 Q8**
Bucklersbury EC4 **117 K9**
Budge Row EC4 **117 K10**
Bulinga St. SW1 **119 Q9**
Bull Inn Ct. WC2 **120 A1**
Bull Wf. La. EC4 **117 J10**
Bullied Way SW1 **119 K9**
Bulls Gdns. SW3 **118 D8**
Bull's Head Pas. EC3 **117 M9**
Bulstrode Pl. W1 **115 H7**
Bulstrode St. W1 **115 H8**
Bunhill Row EC1 **117 K4**
Bunhouse Pl. SW1 **118 G10**
Buonaparte Ms. SW1 **119 N10**
Burbage Clo. SE1 **121 K7**
Burdett St. SE1 **120 D6**
Burge St. SE1 **121 L7**
Burgon St. EC4 **116 G9**
Burleigh St. WC2 **116 A10**
Burlington Arc. W1 **119 L1**
Burlington Gdns. W1 **119 L1**
Burne St. NW1 **114 C6**
Burnell Wk. SE1 **121 Q10**
Burnham Clo. SE1 **121 Q9**
Burnsall St. SW3 **118 D10**
Burrell St. SE1 **120 F2**
Burrows Ms. SE1 **120 F4**
Burton Ms. SW1 **119 H9**
Burton Pl. WC1 **115 P3**
Burton St. WC1 **115 P3**
Burwash Ho. SE1 **121 L5**
Burwood Pl. W2 **114 D8**
Bury Ct. EC3 **117 N8**
Bury Pl. WC1 **115 Q7**
Bury St. EC3 **117 N9**
Bury St. SW1 **119 M2**
Bury Wk. SW3 **118 C9**
Busby St. E2 **117 Q4**
Bush La. EC4 **117 K10**
Bushbaby Clo. SE1 **121 M7**
Bushwood Dr. SE1 **121 Q9**
Bute St. SW7 **118 A8**
Butler Pl. SW1 **119 N6**
Buttesland St. N1 **117 L2**
Buxton Ct. N1 **117 J2**
Buxton St. E1 **117 Q5**
Byng Pl. WC1 **115 N5**
Byward St. EC3 **121 N1**
Bywater St. SW3 **118 E10**
Bywell Pl. W1 **115 L7**

C

Cabbell St. NW1 **114 C7**
Cadbury Way SE16 **121 Q7**
Cadell Clo. E2 **117 Q1**
Cadet Dr. SE1 **121 Q10**
Cadogan Gdns. SW3 **118 F8**
Cadogan Gate SW1 **118 F8**
Cadogan La. SW1 **118 G7**
Cadogan Pl. SW1 **118 F6**

Cadogan Sq. SW1 **118 F7**
Cadogan St. SW3 **118 E9**
Cahill St. EC1 **117 J5**
Cale St. SW3 **118 C10**
Caleb St. SE1 **120 H4**
Caledonia St. N1 **116 A1**
Caledonian Rd. N1 **116 A1**
Callendar Rd. SW7 **118 A6**
Calthorpe St. WC1 **116 C4**
Calvert Ave. E2 **117 N3**
Calvert's Bldgs. SE1 **121 K3**
Calvin St. E1 **117 P5**
Cambridge Gate NW1 **115 K4**
Cambridge Gate Ms. NW1 **115 K4**
Cambridge Sq. W2 **114 C8**
Cambridge St. SW1 **119 K10**
Cambridge Ter. NW1 **115 J3**
Cambridge Ter. Ms. NW1 **115 K3**
Camlet St. E2 **117 P4**
Camomile St. EC3 **117 M8**
Camperdown St. E1 **117 Q9**
Candover St. W1 **115 L7**
Cannon St. EC4 **117 H9**
Canon Row SW1 **119 Q5**
Canterbury Pl. SE17 **120 G9**
Canvey St. SE1 **120 G2**
Capel Ct. EC2 **117 L9**
Capener's Clo. SW1 **118 G5**
Capland St. NW8 **114 B4**
Capper St. WC1 **115 M5**
Carburton St. W1 **115 K6**
Cardigan St. SE11 **120 D10**
Cardinal Bourne St. SE1 **121 L7**
Cardington St. NW1 **115 M2**
Carey La. EC2 **117 H8**
Carey Pl. SW1 **119 N9**
Carey St. WC2 **116 C9**
Carlisle Ave. EC3 **117 P9**
Carlisle La. SE1 **120 C7**
Carlisle Ms. NW8 **114 B6**
Carlisle Pl. SW1 **119 L7**
Carlisle St. W1 **115 N9**
Carlos Pl. W1 **115 H10**
Carlton Gdns. SW1 **119 N3**
Carlton Ho. Ter. SW1 **119 N3**
Carlton St. SW1 **119 N1**
Carlton Twr. Pl. SW1 **118 F6**
Carmelite St. EC4 **116 E10**
Carnaby St. W1 **115 L9**
Caroline Gdns. E2 **117 N2**
Caroline Ter. SW1 **118 G9**
Carpenter St. W1 **119 J1**
Carrington St. W1 **119 J3**
Carter La. EC4 **116 G9**
Carteret St. SW1 **119 N5**
Carthusian St. EC1 **116 H6**
Carting La. WC2 **120 A1**
Carton St. W1 **114 F8**
Cartwright Gdns. WC1 **115 Q3**
Cartwright St. E1 **121 Q1**
Castle Baynard St. EC4 **116 G10**
Castle Ct. EC3 **117 L9**
Castle La. SW1 **119 L6**
Castle Yd. SE1 **120 G2**
Castlereagh St. W1 **114 D8**
Catesby St. SE17 **121 L9**
Cathedral Pl. EC4 **116 H9**
Cathedral St. SE1 **121 K2**
Catherine Griffiths Ct. EC1 **116 E4**
Catherine Pl. SW1 **119 L6**
Catherine St. WC2 **116 B10**
Catherine Wheel All. E1 **117 N7**
Catherine Wheel Yd. SW1 **119 L3**
Cato St. W1 **114 D7**
Catton St. WC1 **116 B7**
Causton St. SW1 **119 P9**
Cavendish Ave. NW8 **114 A1**
Cavendish Clo. NW8 **114 B2**
Cavendish Ct. EC3 **117 N8**
Cavendish Ms. N. W1 **115 K6**
Cavendish Ms. S. W1 **115 K7**
Cavendish Pl. W1 **115 K8**
Cavendish Sq. W1 **115 K8**
Cavendish St. N1 **117 K1**
Caxton St. SW1 **119 M6**
Cayton Pl. EC1 **117 K3**
Cayton St. EC1 **117 K3**
Cecil Ct. WC2 **119 Q1**
Centaur St. SE1 **120 C6**
Central Mkts. EC1 **116 G7**
Central St. EC1 **116 H2**
Cerney Ms. W2 **114 A10**
Chadwell St. EC1 **116 E2**
Chadwick St. SW1 **119 N7**
Chagford St. NW1 **114 E5**
Chamber St. E1 **117 Q10**
Chambord St. E2 **117 Q3**
Chance St. E1 **117 P4**
Chancel St. SE1 **120 F3**
Chancery La. WC2 **116 D8**
Chandos Pl. WC2 **119 Q1**
Chandos St. W1 **115 K7**
Change All. EC3 **117 L9**
Chapel Ct. SE1 **121 K4**
Chapel Pl. EC2 **117 M3**
Chapel Pl. W1 **115 J9**
Chapel St. NW1 **114 C7**
Chapel St. SW1 **119 H5**
Chaplin Clo. SE1 **120 E4**
Chapone Pl. W1 **115 N9**
Chapter Ho. Ct. EC4 **116 G9**
Chapter St. SW1 **119 N9**
Charing Cross WC2 **119 Q2**
Charing Cross Rd. WC2 **115 P9**
Charles Pl. NW1 **115 M3**
Charles II St. SW1 **119 N2**
Charles Sq. N1 **117 L3**
Charles St. W1 **119 J2**
Charleston St. SE17 **121 J9**
Charlotte Ms. W1 **115 M6**
Charlotte Pl. SW1 **119 L9**
Charlotte Pl. W1 **115 M7**
Charlotte Rd. EC2 **117 M3**
Charlotte St. W1 **115 M6**
Charlwood Pl. SW1 **119 M9**
Charlwood St. SW1 **119 M10**
Chart St. N1 **117 L2**
Charterhouse Bldgs. EC1 **116 G5**
Charterhouse Sq. EC1 **116 G6**
Charterhouse St. EC1 **116 F6**
Chatham St. SE17 **121 K8**
Chaucer Dr. SE1 **121 Q9**
Cheapside EC2 **117 H9**
Chelsea Bri. Rd. SW1 **118 G10**
Chelsea Cloisters SW3 **118 D9**
Chelsea Sq. SW3 **118 B10**
Cheltenham Ter. SW3 **118 F10**
Cheney Rd. NW1 **115 Q1**
Chenies Ms. WC1 **115 N5**
Chenies St. WC1 **115 N6**
Chequer St. EC1 **117 J5**
Cherbury St. N1 **117 L1**
Chesham Clo. SW1 **118 G7**
Chesham Ms. SW1 **118 G6**
Chesham Pl. SW1 **118 G7**
Chesham St. SW1 **118 G7**
Cheshire St. E2 **117 Q4**
Chester Clo. SW1 **119 J5**
Chester Clo. N. NW1 **115 K2**
Chester Clo. S. NW1 **115 K3**
Chester Cotts. SW1 **118 G9**
Chester Ct. NW1 **115 K2**
Chester Gate NW1 **115 J3**
Chester Ms. SW1 **119 J6**
Chester Pl. NW1 **115 J2**
Chester Rd. NW1 **115 H3**
Chester Row SW1 **118 G9**
Chester Sq. SW1 **119 H8**
Chester Sq. Ms. SW1 **119 J7**
Chester St. SW1 **119 H6**
Chester Ter. NW1 **115 J2**
Chester Way SE11 **120 E9**
Chesterfield Gdns. W1 **119 J2**
Chesterfield Hill W1 **119 J2**
Chesterfield St. W1 **119 J2**
Chettle Clo. SE1 **121 K6**
Cheval Pl. SW7 **118 D6**
Chicheley St. SE1 **120 C4**
Chichester Rents WC2 **116 D8**
Chicksand St. E1 **117 Q7**
Chiltern St. W1 **114 G6**
Chilton St. E2 **117 Q4**
Chilworth Ms. W2 **114 A9**
Ching Ct. WC2 **115 Q9**
Chiswell St. EC1 **117 K6**
Chitty St. W1 **115 M6**
Christina St. EC2 **117 M4**
Christopher Pl. NW1 **115 P3**
Christopher St. EC2 **117 L5**
Church Pl. SW1 **119 M1**
Church St. NW8 **114 B6**
Church St. W2 **114 B6**
Church St. Est. NW8 **114 B5**
Church Yd. Row SE11 **120 G8**
Churchway NW1 **115 P2**
Churton Pl. SW1 **119 M9**
Churton St. SW1 **119 M9**
Circus Ms. W1 **114 E6**
Circus Pl. EC2 **117 L7**
Circus Rd. NW8 **114 A2**
Citadel Pl. SE11 **120 B10**
City Gdn. Row N1 **116 G1**
City Rd. EC1 **116 F1**
Clabon Ms. SW1 **118 E7**
Clare Mkt. WC2 **116 B9**
Claremont Clo. N1 **116 D1**
Claremont Sq. N1 **116 D1**
Clarence Gdns. NW1 **115 K3**
Clarence Pas. NW1 **115 Q1**
Clarence Ter. NW1 **114 F4**
Clarendon Clo. W2 **114 C10**
Clarendon Gro. NW1 **115 N2**
Clarendon Ms. W2 **114 C10**
Clarendon Pl. W2 **114 C10**
Clarendon St. SW1 **119 K10**
Clarges Ms. W1 **119 J2**
Clarges St. W1 **119 K2**
Clarke's Ms. W1 **115 H6**
Clarks Pl. EC2 **117 M8**
Clay St. W1 **114 F7**
Cleaver Sq. SE11 **120 E10**
Cleaver St. SE11 **120 E10**
Clement's Inn WC2 **116 C9**
Clement's Inn Pas. WC2 **116 C9**
Clements La. EC4 **117 L10**
Clenham St. SE1 **121 J4**
Clenston Ms. W1 **114 E8**
Clere St. EC2 **117 L4**
Clerkenwell Clo. EC1 **116 E4**
Clerkenwell Grn. EC1 **116 E5**
Clerkenwell Rd. EC1 **116 D5**
Cleveland Ms. W1 **115 L6**
Cleveland Pl. SW1 **119 M2**
Cleveland Row SW1 **119 L3**
Cleveland St. W1 **115 K5**
Clifford St. W1 **119 L1**
Clifton Ct. NW8 **114 A4**
Clifton Pl. W2 **114 B9**
Clifton St. EC2 **117 M6**
Clink St. SE1 **121 K2**
Clipstone Ms. W1 **115 L5**
Clipstone St. W1 **115 K6**
Cliveden Pl. SW1 **118 G8**
Cloak La. EC4 **117 K10**
Cloth Ct. EC1 **116 G7**
Cloth Fair EC1 **116 G7**
Cloth St. EC1 **116 H6**
Club Row E1 **117 P4**
Club Row E2 **117 P4**
Clunbury St. N1 **117 L1**
Cluny Est. SE1 **121 M6**
Cluny Pl. SE1 **121 M6**
Coach & Horses Yd. W1 **115 L10**
Cobb St. E1 **117 P7**
Cobourg St. NW1 **115 M3**
Coburg Clo. SW1 **119 M8**
Cochrane Ms. NW8 **114 B1**
Cochrane St. NW8 **114 B1**
Cock Hill E1 **117 N7**
Cock La. EC1 **116 F7**
Cockpit Steps SW1 **119 P5**
Cockpit Yd. WC1 **116 C6**
Cockspur Ct. SW1 **119 P2**
Cockspur St. SW1 **119 P2**
Code St. E1 **117 Q5**
Coin St. SE1 **120 D2**
Colchester St. E1 **117 Q8**
Coldbath Sq. EC1 **116 D4**
Cole St. SE1 **121 J5**
Colebrooke Row N1 **116 F1**
Coleman St. EC2 **117 K8**
Coley St. WC1 **116 C5**
College Hill EC4 **117 J10**
College Ms. SW1 **119 Q6**
College St. EC4 **117 K10**
Collier St. N1 **116 B1**
Collinson St. SE1 **120 H5**
Collinson Wk. SE1 **121 H5**
Colnbrook St. SE1 **120 F7**
Colombo St. SE1 **120 F3**
Colonade Wk. SW1 **119 J9**
Colonnade WC1 **116 A5**
Columbia Rd. E2 **117 P2**
Colville Pl. W1 **115 M7**
Colworth Gro. SE17 **121 J9**
Commercial St. E1 **117 P5**
Commodity Quay E1 **121 Q1**
Compton Clo. NW1 **115 K3**
Compton Pas. EC1 **116 G4**
Compton Pl. WC1 **115 Q4**
Compton St. EC1 **116 F4**
Comus Pl. SE17 **121 M9**
Concert Hall App. SE1 **120 C3**
Conduit Ct. WC2 **115 Q10**
Conduit Ms. W2 **114 A9**
Conduit Pas. W2 **114 A9**
Conduit Pl. W2 **114 A9**
Conduit St. W1 **115 K10**
Congreve St. SE17 **121 M9**
Connaught Clo. W2 **114 C9**
Connaught Ms. W2 **114 E9**
Connaught Pl. W2 **114 E9**
Connaught Sq. W2 **114 E9**
Connaught St. W2 **114 D9**
Cons St. SE1 **120 E4**
Constitution Hill SW1 **119 J4**
Content St. SE17 **121 J9**
Conway Ms. W1 **115 L5**
Conway St. W1 **115 L5**
Coombs St. N1 **116 G1**
Cooper Clo. SE1 **120 E5**
Coopers La. NW1 **115 P1**
Cooper's Row EC3 **117 P10**
Copperfield St. SE1 **120 G4**
Copthall Ave. EC2 **117 L8**
Copthall Bldgs. EC2 **117 L8**
Copthall Clo. EC2 **117 K8**
Copthall Ct. EC2 **117 L8**
Coptic St. WC1 **115 Q7**
Coral St. SE1 **120 E5**
Coram St. WC1 **115 Q5**
Corbet Ct. EC3 **117 L9**
Corbet Pl. E1 **117 P6**
Cork St. W1 **119 L1**
Cork St. Ms. W1 **119 L1**
Corlett St. NW1 **114 C6**
Corner Ho. St. WC2 **119 Q2**
Cornhill EC3 **117 L9**
Cornwall Rd. SE1 **120 D2**
Cornwall Ter. NW1 **114 F5**
Cornwall Ter. Ms. NW1 **114 F5**
Coronet St. N1 **117 M3**
Corporation Row EC1 **116 E4**
Corsham St. N1 **117 L3**
Cosmo Pl. WC1 **116 A6**
Cosser St. SE1 **120 D6**
Cosway St. NW1 **114 D6**
Cotham St. SE17 **121 J9**
Cottage Pl. SW3 **118 C7**
Cottington Clo. SE11 **120 F9**
Cottington St. SE11 **120 E10**
Cottons Gdns. E2 **117 N2**
Cottons La. SE1 **121 L2**
Coulson St. SW3 **118 E10**
Counter Ct. SE1 **121 K3**
Counter St. SE1 **121 M3**
County St. SE1 **121 J7**
Courtenay St. SE11 **120 D10**
Cousin La. EC4 **121 K1**
Covent Gdn. WC2 **116 A10**
Coventry St. W1 **119 N1**
Cowcross St. EC1 **116 F6**
Cowley St. SW1 **119 Q6**
Cowper St. EC2 **117 L4**
Coxson Pl. SE1 **121 P5**
Crace St. NW1 **115 N2**
Craigs Ct. SW1 **119 Q2**
Crail Row SE17 **121 L9**
Cramer St. W1 **114 H7**
Crampton St. SE17 **120 H10**
Cranbourn All. WC2 **115 P10**
Cranbourn St. WC2 **115 P10**
Crane Ct. EC4 **116 E9**
Cranfield Row SE1 **120 E6**
Cranleigh St. NW1 **115 M1**
Cranley Pl. SW7 **118 A9**
Cranmer Ct. SW3 **118 D9**
Cranston Est. N1 **117 L1**
Cranwood St. EC1 **117 L3**
Craven Pas. WC2 **119 Q2**
Craven St. WC2 **119 Q2**
Crawford Ms. W1 **114 E7**
Crawford Pas. EC1 **116 D5**
Crawford Pl. W1 **114 D8**
Crawford St. W1 **114 D7**
Creasy Est. SE1 **121 M7**
Creechurch La. EC3 **117 N9**
Creechurch Pl. EC3 **117 N9**
Creed La. EC4 **116 G9**
Cremer St. E2 **117 P1**
Crescent, The EC3 **117 P10**
Crescent Pl. SW3 **118 C8**
Crescent Row EC1 **116 H5**
Crestfield St. WC1 **116 A2**
Cricketers Ct. SE11 **120 F9**
Crimscott St. SE1 **121 N7**
Cripplegate St. EC2 **117 H6**
Crispin St. E1 **117 P7**
Cromer St. WC1 **116 A3**
Crompton St. W2 **114 A5**
Cromwell Gdns. SW7 **118 B7**
Cromwell Ms. SW7 **118 B8**
Cromwell Pl. SW7 **118 B8**
Cromwell Rd. SW7 **118 A8**
Crondall St. N1 **117 M1**
Crosby Ct. SE1 **121 K4**
Crosby Row SE1 **121 K4**
Crosby Sq. EC3 **117 M9**
Cross Keys Clo. W1 **115 H7**
Cross La. EC3 **121 M1**
Crosslet St. SE17 **121 L8**
Crosswall EC3 **117 P10**
Crown Ct. EC2 **117 J9**
Crown Ct. WC2 **116 A9**
Crown Office Row EC4 **116 D10**
Crown Pas. SW1 **119 M3**
Crucifix La. SE1 **121 M4**
Cruikshank St. WC1 **116 D2**
Crutched Friars EC3 **117 N10**
Cubitt St. WC1 **116 C3**
Cubitts Yd. WC2 **116 A10**
Cuff Pt. E2 **117 P2**
Culford Gdns. SW3 **118 F9**
Cullum St. EC3 **117 M10**
Culross St. W1 **118 G1**
Culworth St. NW8 **114 C1**
Cumberland Gdns. WC1 **116 C2**
Cumberland Gate W1 **114 E10**
Cumberland Mkt. NW1 **115 K2**
Cumberland Mkt. Est. NW1 **115 K2**
Cumberland Pl. NW1 **115 J2**
Cumberland St. SW1 **119 K10**
Cumberland Ter. NW1 **115 J1**
Cumberland Ter. Ms. NW1 **115 J1**
Cumming St. N1 **116 C1**
Cunard Pl. EC3 **117 N9**
Cundy St. SW1 **119 H9**
Cundy St. Est. SW1 **119 H9**
Cunningham Pl. NW8 **114 A4**
Cureton St. SW1 **119 P9**
Curlew St. SE1 **121 P4**
Cursitor St. EC4 **116 D8**
Curtain Rd. EC2 **117 N3**
Curtis St. SE1 **121 P8**
Curtis Way SE1 **121 P8**
Curzon Gate W1 **118 H3**
Curzon Pl. W1 **119 H3**
Curzon St. W1 **119 H3**
Cut, The SE1 **120 E4**
Cuthbert St. W2 **114 A6**
Cutler St. E1 **117 N8**
Cutlers Gdns. E1 **117 N8**
Cygnet St. E1 **117 Q4**
Cynthia St. N1 **116 C1**
Cypress Pl. W1 **115 M5**
Cyrus St. EC1 **116 G4**

D

Dacre St. SW1 **119 N6**
Dalehead NW1 **115 L1**
Dallington St. EC1 **116 G4**
Dane St. WC1 **116 B7**
Dansey Pl. W1 **115 N10**
Dante Pl. SE11 **120 G9**
Dante Rd. SE11 **120 F8**
Danube St. SW3 **118 D10**
D'Arblay St. W1 **115 M9**
Dartmouth St. SW1 **119 P5**
Darwin St. SE17 **121 L8**
Daventry St. NW1 **114 C6**
David Ms. W1 **114 G6**
Davidge St. SE1 **120 G5**
Davies Ms. W1 **115 J10**
Davies St. W1 **115 J10**
Dawes Ho. SE17 **121 K9**
Dawes St. SE17 **121 L10**
Dawson St. E2 **117 Q1**
De Walden St. W1 **115 H7**
Deacon Way SE17 **121 H8**
Dean Bradley St. SW1 **119 Q7**
Dean Farrar St. SW1 **119 P6**
Dean Ryle St. SW1 **119 Q8**
Dean Stanley St. SW1 **119 Q7**
Dean St. W1 **115 N8**
Dean Trench St. SW1 **119 Q7**
Deanery Ms. W1 **119 H2**
Deanery St. W1 **118 H2**
Deans Bldgs. SE17 **121 L9**
Dean's Ct. EC4 **116 G9**
Deans Ms. W1 **115 K8**
Dean's Pl. SW1 **119 N10**
Dean's Yd. SW1 **119 P6**
Decima St. SE1 **121 M6**
Dell's Ms. SW1 **119 M9**
Denbigh Ms. SW1 **119 L9**
Denbigh Pl. SW1 **119 L10**
Denbigh St. SW1 **119 L9**
Denman St. W1 **119 N1**
Denmark Pl. WC2 **115 P8**
Denmark St. WC2 **115 P9**
Denny Cres. SE11 **120 E10**
Denny St. SE11 **120 E10**
Denyer St. SW3 **118 D9**
Derby Gate SW1 **119 Q4**
Derby St. W1 **119 H3**
Dereham Pl. EC2 **117 N3**
Dering St. W1 **115 J9**
Deverell St. SE1 **121 K7**
Devereux Ct. WC2 **116 D9**
Devonshire Clo. W1 **115 J6**
Devonshire Ms. N. W1 **115 J6**
Devonshire Ms. S. W1 **115 J6**
Devonshire Ms. W. W1 **115 J5**
Devonshire Pl. W1 **115 H5**
Devonshire Pl. Ms. W1 **115 H5**
Devonshire Row EC2 **117 N7**
Devonshire Row Ms. W1 **115 K5**
Devonshire Sq. EC2 **117 N7**
Devonshire St. W1 **114 H6**
Diadem Ct. W1 **115 N9**
Diana Pl. NW1 **115 K4**
Dickens Sq. SE1 **121 J6**
Dingley Pl. EC1 **117 J3**
Dingley Rd. EC1 **117 H3**
Disney Pl. SE1 **121 J4**
Disney St. SE1 **121 J4**
Diss St. E2 **117 P2**
Distaff La. EC4 **116 H10**
Distin St. SE11 **120 D9**
Dockhead SE1 **121 Q5**
Dodson St. SE1 **120 E5**
Dolben St. SE1 **120 G3**
Dombey St. WC1 **116 B6**
Domingo St. EC1 **117 H4**
Dominion St. EC2 **117 L6**
Donegal St. N1 **116 C1**
Donne Pl. SW3 **118 D8**
Doon St. SE1 **120 D2**
Doric Way NW1 **115 N2**
Dorrington St. EC1 **116 D6**
Dorset Bldgs. EC4 **116 F9**
Dorset Clo. NW1 **114 E6**
Dorset Est. E2 **117 Q2**
Dorset Ms. SW1 **119 J6**
Dorset Pl. SW1 **119 N10**
Dorset Ri. EC4 **116 F9**
Dorset Sq. NW1 **114 E5**
Dorset St. W1 **114 F7**
Doughty Ms. WC1 **116 B5**
Doughty St. WC1 **116 B4**
Douglas St. SW1 **119 N9**
Dove Ct. EC2 **117 K9**
Dove Wk. SW1 **118 G10**
Dovehouse St. SW3 **118 C10**
Dover St. W1 **119 K1**
Dover Yd. W1 **119 K2**
Dowgate Hill EC4 **117 K10**
Down St. W1 **119 J3**
Down St. Ms. W1 **119 J3**
Downing St. SW1 **119 Q4**
Doyce St. SE1 **121 H4**
D'Oyley St. SW1 **118 G8**
Drake St. WC1 **116 B7**
Draycott Ave. SW3 **118 D8**
Draycott Pl. SW3 **118 E9**
Draycott Ter. SW3 **118 F9**
Druid St. SE1 **121 N4**
Drum St. E1 **117 Q8**
Drummond Cres. NW1 **115 N2**
Drummond Gate SW1 **119 P10**
Drummond St. NW1 **115 L4**
Drury La. WC2 **116 A8**
Dryden Ct. SE11 **120 E9**
Dryden St. WC2 **116 A9**
Drysdale Pl. N1 **117 N2**
Drysdale St. N1 **117 N2**
Ducal St. E2 **117 Q3**

Duchess Ms. W1 **115 K7**
Duchess St. W1 **115 K7**
Duchy St. SE1 **120 E2**
Duck La. W1 **115 N9**
Dudley St. W2 **114 A7**
Dudmaston Ms. SW3 **118 B10**
Dufferin Ave. EC1 **117 K5**
Dufferin St. EC1 **117 J5**
Dufour's Pl. W1 **115 M9**
Duke of Wellington Pl. SW1 **119 H4**
Duke of York St. SW1 **119 M2**
Duke St. SW1 **119 M2**
Duke St. W1 **114 H8**
Duke St. Hill SE1 **121 L2**
Duke's Ms. W1 **114 H8**
Dukes Pl. EC3 **117 N9**
Duke's Rd. WC1 **115 P3**
Duke's Yd. W1 **115 H10**
Duncan Ter. N1 **116 F1**
Duncannon St. WC2 **119 Q1**
Dunloe St. E2 **117 Q1**
Dunlop Pl. SE16 **121 Q7**
Dunmore Pt. E2 **117 P3**
Dunns Pas. WC1 **116 A8**
Dunraven St. W1 **114 F10**
Dunstable Ms. W1 **115 H6**
Dunster Ct. EC3 **117 M10**
Dunsterville Way SE1 **121 L5**
Dunton Rd. SE1 **121 P9**
Duplex Ride SW1 **118 F5**
Durham Ho. St. WC2 **120 A1**
Durweston Ms. W1 **114 F6**
Durweston St. W1 **114 F7**
Dyer's Bldgs. EC1 **116 D7**
Dyott St. WC1 **115 P8**
Dysart St. EC2 **117 M5**

E

Eagle Ct. EC1 **116 F6**
Eagle Pl. SW1 **119 M1**
Eagle St. WC1 **116 B7**
Earl Rd. SE1 **121 P10**
Earl St. EC2 **117 L6**
Earlham St. WC2 **115 P9**
Earlstoke St. EC1 **116 F2**
Earnshaw St. WC2 **115 P8**
Easley's Ms. W1 **115 H8**
East Harding St. EC4 **116 E8**
East Pas. EC1 **116 H6**
East Poultry Ave. EC1 **116 F7**
East Rd. N1 **117 L2**
East Smithfield E1 **121 Q1**
East St. SE17 **121 J10**
East Tenter St. E1 **117 Q9**
Eastcastle St. W1 **115 L8**
Eastcheap EC3 **117 L10**
Easton St. WC1 **116 D3**
Eaton Clo. SW1 **118 G9**
Eaton Gate SW1 **118 G8**
Eaton La. SW1 **119 K7**
Eaton Ms. N. SW1 **118 G7**
Eaton Ms. S. SW1 **119 J7**
Eaton Ms. W. SW1 **118 H8**
Eaton Pl. SW1 **118 G7**
Eaton Row SW1 **119 J7**
Eaton Sq. SW1 **118 H8**
Eaton Ter. SW1 **118 G8**
Eaton Ter. Ms. SW1 **118 G8**
Ebenezer St. N1 **117 K2**
Ebor St. E1 **117 P4**
Ebury Bri. SW1 **119 J10**
Ebury Bri. Est. SW1 **119 J10**
Ebury Ms. SW1 **119 J8**
Ebury Ms. E. SW1 **119 J7**
Ebury Sq. SW1 **119 H9**
Ebury St. SW1 **118 H9**
Eccleston Bri. SW1 **119 K8**
Eccleston Ms. SW1 **119 H7**
Eccleston Pl. SW1 **119 J8**
Eccleston Sq. SW1 **119 K9**
Eccleston Sq. Ms. SW1 **119 K9**
Eccleston St. SW1 **119 H7**
Edgware Rd. W2 **114 A5**
Edinburgh Gate SW1 **118 E5**
Edward Ms. NW1 **115 K1**
Edwards Ms. W1 **114 G9**
Egerton Cres. SW3 **118 D8**
Egerton Gdns. SW3 **118 C7**
Egerton Gdns. Ms. SW3 **118 D7**
Egerton Pl. SW3 **118 D7**
Egerton Ter. SW3 **118 D7**
Elba Pl. SE17 **121 J8**
Elder St. E1 **117 P5**
Eldon St. EC2 **117 L7**
Elephant & Castle SE1 **120 G8**
Elephant Rd. SE17 **120 H8**
Elia Ms. N1 **116 F1**
Elia St. N1 **116 F1**
Elim Est. SE1 **121 M6**
Elizabeth Bri. SW1 **119 J9**
Elizabeth Ct. SW1 **119 P7**
Elizabeth St. SW1 **118 H8**
Elliotts Row SE11 **120 F8**
Ellis St. SW1 **118 F8**
Elm Ct. EC4 **116 D10**
Elm Pl. SW7 **118 A10**
Elm St. WC1 **116 C5**
Elm Tree Clo. NW8 **114 A2**
Elm Tree Rd. NW8 **114 A2**
Elms Ms. W2 **114 A10**
Elsted St. SE17 **121 L9**
Elverton St. SW1 **119 N8**
Ely Ct. EC1 **116 E7**
Ely Pl. EC1 **116 E7**
Elystan Pl. SW3 **118 D10**
Elystan St. SW3 **118 C9**
Embankment Pl. WC2 **120 A2**
Emerald St. WC1 **116 B6**
Emerson St. SE1 **121 H2**
Emery Hill St. SW1 **119 M7**
Emery St. SE1 **120 E6**
Endell St. WC2 **115 Q8**
Endsleigh Gdns. WC1 **115 N4**
Endsleigh Pl. WC1 **115 P4**
Endsleigh St. WC1 **115 P4**
Enford St. W1 **114 E6**
English Grds. SE1 **121 M3**
Enid St. SE16 **121 Q6**
Ennismore Gdns. SW7 **118 C6**
Ennismore Gdns. Ms. SW7 **118 C6**
Ennismore Ms. SW7 **118 C6**
Ennismore St. SW7 **118 C6**
Ensor Ms. SW7 **118 A10**
Epworth St. EC2 **117 L5**
Erasmus St. SW1 **119 P9**
Errol St. EC1 **117 J5**
Essex Ct. EC4 **116 D9**
Essex St. WC2 **116 D10**
Esterbrooke St. SW1 **119 N9**
Ethel St. SE17 **121 J9**
Europa Pl. EC1 **117 H3**
Euston Gro. NW1 **115 N3**
Euston Rd. NW1 **115 K5**
Euston Sq. NW1 **115 N3**
Euston Sta. Colonnade NW1 **115 N3**
Euston St. NW1 **115 M3**
Evelyn Ct. N1 **117 K1**
Evelyn Wk. N1 **117 K1**
Evelyn Yd. W1 **115 N8**
Everton Bldgs. NW1 **115 L3**
Ewer St. SE1 **120 H3**
Excel Ct. WC2 **119 P1**
Exchange Arc. EC2 **117 N6**
Exchange Ct. WC2 **120 A1**
Exchange Pl. EC2 **117 M6**
Exeter St. WC2 **116 A10**
Exhibition Rd. SW7 **118 B6**
Exmouth Mkt. EC1 **116 D4**
Exmouth Ms. NW1 **115 M3**
Exon St. SE17 **121 M9**
Exton St. SE1 **120 D3**
Eyre St. Hill EC1 **116 D5**
Ezra St. E2 **117 Q2**

F

Fair St. SE1 **121 N4**
Fairchild Pl. EC2 **117 N5**
Fairchild St. EC2 **117 N5**
Fairholt St. SW7 **118 D6**
Falcon Clo. SE1 **120 G2**
Falconberg Ct. W1 **115 P8**
Falconberg Ms. W1 **115 N8**
Falkirk St. N1 **117 N1**
Falmouth Rd. SE1 **121 J7**
Fann St. EC1 **117 H5**
Fanshaw St. N1 **117 M2**
Fareham St. W1 **115 N8**
Farm St. W1 **119 J1**
Farnham Pl. SE1 **120 G3**
Farringdon La. EC1 **116 E5**
Farringdon St. EC4 **116 F8**
Fashion St. E1 **117 Q7**
Faulkner's All. EC1 **116 F6**
Featherstone St. EC1 **117 K4**
Fellows Ct. E2 **117 P1**
Fen Ct. EC3 **117 M10**
Fenchurch Ave. EC3 **117 M9**
Fenchurch Bldgs. EC3 **117 N9**
Fenchurch Pl. EC3 **117 N10**
Fenchurch St. EC3 **117 M10**
Fendall St. SE1 **121 N7**
Fenning St. SE1 **121 M4**
Fernsbury St. WC1 **116 D3**
Fetter La. EC4 **116 E9**
Field Ct. WC1 **116 C7**
Field St. WC1 **116 B2**
Finch La. EC3 **117 L9**
Finsbury Ave. EC2 **117 L7**
Finsbury Circ. EC2 **117 L7**
Finsbury Est. EC1 **116 E3**
Finsbury Mkt. EC2 **117 M5**
Finsbury Pavement EC2 **117 L6**
Finsbury Sq. EC2 **117 L5**
Finsbury St. EC2 **117 K6**
First St. SW3 **118 D8**
Fish St. Hill EC3 **121 L1**
Fisher St. WC1 **116 B7**
Fisherton St. NW8 **114 A4**
Fitzalan St. SE11 **120 D8**
Fitzhardinge St. W1 **114 G8**
Fitzmaurice Pl. W1 **119 K2**
Fitzroy Ct. W1 **115 M5**
Fitzroy Ms. W1 **115 L5**
Fitzroy Sq. W1 **115 L5**
Fitzroy St. W1 **115 L5**
Flaxman Ct. W1 **115 N9**
Flaxman Ter. WC1 **115 P3**
Fleet La. EC4 **116 F8**
Fleet Sq. WC1 **116 C3**
Fleet St. EC4 **116 E9**
Fleming Ct. W2 **114 A6**
Fleur de Lis St. E1 **117 N5**
Flint St. SE17 **121 L9**
Flinton St. SE17 **121 N10**
Flitcroft St. WC2 **115 P9**
Floral St. WC2 **115 Q10**
Flower & Dean Wk. E1 **117 Q7**
Foley St. W1 **115 L7**
Folgate St. E1 **117 N6**
Fore St. EC2 **117 J7**
Fore St. Ave. EC2 **117 K7**
Forset St. W1 **114 D8**
Fort Rd. SE1 **121 Q9**
Fort St. E1 **117 N7**
Fortune St. EC1 **117 J5**
Foster La. EC2 **117 H8**
Foubert's Pl. W1 **115 L9**
Foulis Ter. SW7 **118 B10**
Founders Ct. EC2 **117 K8**
Foundry Ms. NW1 **115 M4**
Fountain Ct. EC4 **116 D10**
Fountain Sq. SW1 **119 J8**
Fournier St. E1 **117 Q6**
Fox and Knot St. EC1 **116 G6**
Frampton St. NW8 **114 B5**
Francis St. SW1 **119 L8**
Frankland Rd. SW7 **118 A7**
Franklin's Row SW3 **118 F10**
Frazier St. SE1 **120 D5**
Frederic Ms. SW1 **118 F5**
Frederick Clo. W2 **114 D10**
Frederick St. WC1 **116 B3**
Frederick's Pl. EC2 **117 K9**
Frederick's Row EC1 **116 F2**
Fremantle St. SE17 **121 M10**
French Pl. E1 **117 N4**
Friar St. EC4 **116 G9**
Friary Ct. SW1 **119 M3**
Friday St. EC4 **117 H10**
Friend St. EC1 **116 F2**
Frith St. W1 **115 N9**
Frying Pan All. E1 **117 P7**
Fullwoods Ms. N1 **117 L2**
Fulwood Pl. WC1 **116 C7**
Furnival St. EC4 **116 D8**
Fynes St. SW1 **119 N8**

G

Gage St. WC1 **116 A6**
Gainsford St. SE1 **121 P4**
Galen Pl. WC1 **116 A7**
Galway St. EC1 **117 J3**
Gambia St. SE1 **120 G3**
Ganton St. W1 **115 L10**
Garbutt Pl. W1 **114 H6**
Gard St. EC1 **116 G2**
Garden Ct. EC4 **116 D10**
Garden Row SE1 **120 F7**
Garden Ter. SW1 **119 N10**
Garden Wk. EC2 **117 M3**
Garlick Hill EC4 **117 J10**
Garnault Ms. EC1 **116 E3**
Garnault Pl. EC1 **116 E3**
Garrett St. EC1 **117 J4**
Garrick St. WC2 **115 Q10**
Gascoigne Pl. E2 **117 P2**
Gate Ms. SW7 **118 D5**
Gate St. WC2 **116 B8**
Gateforth St. NW8 **114 C5**
Gatesborough St. EC2 **117 M4**
Gateways, The SW3 **118 D9**
Gaunt St. SE1 **120 G6**
Gavel St. SE17 **121 L8**
Gayfere St. SW1 **119 Q7**
Gaywood Est. SE1 **120 G7**
Gaywood St. SE1 **120 G7**
Gedling Pl. SE1 **121 Q6**
Gee St. EC1 **116 H4**
Gees Ct. W1 **115 H9**
Geffrye Ct. N1 **117 N1**
Geffrye St. E2 **117 P1**
George Ct. WC2 **120 A1**
George Inn Yd. SE1 **121 K3**
George Loveless Ho. E2 **117 Q2**
George Ms. NW1 **115 L3**
George St. EC4 **117 K9**
George St. W1 **114 E8**
George Yd. EC3 **117 L9**
George Yd. W1 **114 H10**
Georgina Gdns. E2 **117 Q2**
Gerald Ms. SW1 **119 H8**
Gerald Rd. SW1 **119 H8**
Geraldine St. SE11 **120 F7**
Gerrard Pl. W1 **115 P10**
Gerrard St. W1 **115 P10**
Gerridge St. SE1 **120 E6**
Gibraltar Wk. E2 **117 Q3**
Gibson Rd. SE11 **120 C9**
Gilbert Pl. WC1 **115 Q7**
Gilbert Rd. SE11 **120 E9**
Gilbert St. W1 **115 H9**
Gildea St. W1 **115 K7**
Gillfoot NW1 **115 L1**
Gillingham Ms. SW1 **119 L8**
Gillingham Row SW1 **119 L8**
Gillingham St. SW1 **119 K8**
Giltspur St. EC1 **116 G8**
Gladstone St. SE1 **120 F6**
Glasshill St. SE1 **120 G4**
Glasshouse All. EC4 **116 E9**
Glasshouse St. W1 **119 M1**
Glasshouse Wk. SE11 **120 A10**
Glasshouse Yd. EC1 **116 H5**
Glendower Pl. SW7 **118 A8**
Glentworth St. NW1 **114 F5**
Globe St. SE1 **121 K5**
Globe Yd. W1 **115 J9**
Gloucester Ct. EC3 **121 N1**
Gloucester Pl. NW1 **114 E4**
Gloucester Pl. W1 **114 F6**
Gloucester Pl. Ms. W1 **114 F7**
Gloucester Sq. W2 **114 B9**
Gloucester Way EC1 **116 E3**
Glynde Ms. SW3 **118 D7**
Godfrey St. SW3 **118 D10**
Godliman St. EC4 **116 H9**
Golden La. EC1 **117 H5**
Golden La. Est. EC1 **116 H5**
Golden Sq. W1 **115 M10**
Goldsmith St. EC2 **117 J8**
Goodge Pl. W1 **115 M7**
Goodge St. W1 **115 M7**
Goodmans Yd. E1 **117 P10**
Goodwins Ct. WC2 **115 Q10**
Gophir La. EC4 **117 K10**
Gordon Sq. WC1 **115 N4**
Gordon St. WC1 **115 N4**
Goring St. EC3 **117 N8**
Gorsuch Pl. E2 **117 P2**
Gorsuch St. E2 **117 P2**
Gosfield St. W1 **115 L6**
Goslett Yd. WC2 **115 P9**
Gosset St. E2 **117 Q3**
Goswell Rd. EC1 **116 F1**
Gough Sq. EC4 **116 E8**
Gough St. WC1 **116 C4**
Goulston St. E1 **117 P8**
Gower Ct. WC1 **115 N4**
Gower Ms. WC1 **115 P7**
Gower Pl. WC1 **115 M4**
Gower St. WC1 **115 N5**
Gracechurch St. EC3 **117 L10**
Grafton Ms. W1 **115 L5**
Grafton Pl. NW1 **115 N3**
Grafton St. W1 **119 K1**
Grafton Way W1 **115 L5**
Grafton Way WC1 **115 M5**
Graham St. N1 **116 G1**
Graham Ter. SW1 **118 G9**
Granby Bldgs. SE11 **120 B9**
Granby Ter. NW1 **115 L1**
Grand Ave. EC1 **116 G6**
Grange, The SE1 **121 P6**
Grange Ct. WC2 **116 C9**
Grange Rd. SE1 **121 N7**
Grange Wk. SE1 **121 N6**
Grange Yd. SE1 **121 P7**
Grantham Pl. W1 **119 J3**
Granville Pl. W1 **114 G9**
Granville Sq. WC1 **116 C3**
Granville St. WC1 **116 C3**
Grape St. WC2 **115 Q8**
Graphite Sq. SE11 **120 B10**
Gravel La. E1 **117 P8**
Gray St. SE1 **120 E5**
Gray's Inn Pl. WC1 **116 C7**
Gray's Inn Rd. WC1 **116 A2**
Gray's Inn Sq. WC1 **116 D6**
Gray's Yd. W1 **114 H8**
Great Bell All. EC2 **117 K8**
Great Castle St. W1 **115 K8**
Great Cen. St. NW1 **114 E6**
Great Chapel St. W1 **115 N8**
Great College St. SW1 **119 Q6**
Great Cumberland Ms. W1 **114 E9**
Great Cumberland Pl. W1 **114 F8**
Great Dover St. SE1 **121 K5**
Great Eastern St. EC2 **117 M3**
Great Eastern Wk. EC2 **117 M7**
Great George St. SW1 **119 P5**
Great Guildford St. SE1 **120 H3**
Great James St. WC1 **116 B6**
Great Marlborough St. W1 **115 L9**
Great Maze Pond SE1 **121 L4**
Great New St. EC4 **116 E8**
Great Newport St. WC2 **115 P10**
Great Ormond St. WC1 **116 A6**
Great Percy St. WC1 **116 C2**
Great Peter St. SW1 **119 N7**
Great Portland St. W1 **115 K6**
Great Pulteney St. W1 **115 M10**
Great Queen St. WC2 **116 A9**
Great Russell St. WC1 **115 P8**
Great St. Helens EC3 **117 M8**
Great St. Thomas Apostle EC4 **117 J10**
Great Scotland Yd. SW1 **119 Q2**
Great Smith St. SW1 **119 P6**
Great Suffolk St. SE1 **120 G3**
Great Sutton St. EC1 **116 G5**
Great Swan All. EC2 **117 K8**
Great Titchfield St. W1 **115 L6**
Great Twr. St. EC3 **117 M10**
Great Trinity La. EC4 **117 J10**
Great Turnstile WC1 **116 C7**
Great Winchester St. EC2 **117 L8**
Great Windmill St. W1 **115 N10**
Great Yd. SE1 **121 N4**
Greek Ct. W1 **115 P9**
Greek St. W1 **115 P9**
Greek Yd. WC2 **115 Q10**
Green Arbour Ct. EC1 **116 F8**
Green Dragon Ct. SE1 **121 K2**
Green St. W1 **114 F10**
Green Wk. SE1 **121 M7**
Greenberry St. NW8 **114 C1**
Greencoat Pl. SW1 **119 M8**
Greencoat Row SW1 **119 M7**
Greenham Clo. SE1 **120 D5**
Greenhill's Rents EC1 **116 F6**
Green's Ct. W1 **115 N10**
Greenwell St. W1 **115 K5**
Greet St. SE1 **120 E3**
Grendon St. NW8 **114 C4**
Grenville St. WC1 **116 A5**
Gresham St. EC2 **117 J8**
Gresse St. W1 **115 N8**
Greville St. EC1 **116 E7**
Grey Eagle St. E1 **117 Q5**
Greycoat Pl. SW1 **119 N7**
Greycoat St. SW1 **119 N7**
Greyfriars Pas. EC1 **116 G8**
Greystoke Pl. EC4 **116 D8**
Griggs Pl. SE1 **121 N6**
Grimsby St. E2 **117 Q5**
Grindal St. SE1 **120 D5**
Grocer's Hall Ct. EC2 **117 K9**
Groom Pl. SW1 **119 H6**
Grosvenor Cotts. SW1 **118 G8**
Grosvenor Cres. SW1 **118 H5**
Grosvenor Cres. Ms. SW1 **118 G5**
Grosvenor Est. SW1 **119 P8**
Grosvenor Gdns. SW1 **119 K7**
Grosvenor Gdns. Ms. E. SW1 **119 K6**
Grosvenor Gdns. Ms. N. SW1 **119 J7**
Grosvenor Gdns. Ms. S. SW1 **119 K7**
Grosvenor Gate W1 **118 F1**
Grosvenor Hill W1 **115 J10**
Grosvenor Pl. SW1 **119 H5**
Grosvenor Sq. W1 **114 H10**
Grosvenor St. W1 **115 J10**
Grotto Pas. W1 **114 H6**
Grove End Rd. NW8 **114 A2**
Grove Gdns. NW8 **114 D3**
Groveland Ct. EC4 **117 J9**
Guildhall Bldgs. EC2 **117 K8**
Guildhouse St. SW1 **119 L8**
Guilford Pl. WC1 **116 B5**
Guilford St. WC1 **116 A5**
Guinness Bldgs. SE1 **121 M7**
Guinness Sq. SE1 **121 M8**
Guinness Trust Bldgs. SE11 **120 F10**
Guinness Trust Bldgs. SW3 **118 E9**
Gun St. E1 **117 P7**
Gunpowder Sq. EC4 **116 E8**
Gunthorpe St. E1 **117 Q7**
Guthrie St. SW3 **118 C10**
Gutter La. EC2 **117 J8**
Guy St. SE1 **121 L4**
Gwynne Pl. WC1 **116 C3**

H

Haberdasher Pl. N1 **117 L2**
Haberdasher St. N1 **117 L2**
Hackney Rd. E2 **117 P2**
Half Moon Ct. EC1 **116 H7**
Half Moon Pas. E1 **117 Q9**
Half Moon St. W1 **119 K2**
Halkin Arc. SW1 **118 G6**
Halkin Ms. SW1 **118 G6**
Halkin Pl. SW1 **118 G6**
Halkin St. SW1 **118 H5**
Hall Pl. W2 **114 A5**
Hall St. EC1 **116 G2**
Hallam Ms. W1 **115 K6**
Hallam St. W1 **115 K5**
Halpin Pl. SE17 **121 L9**
Halsey Ms. SW3 **118 E8**
Halsey St. SW3 **118 E8**
Halstead Ct. N1 **117 L1**
Ham Yd. W1 **115 N10**
Hamilton Clo. NW8 **114 A3**
Hamilton Ms. W1 **119 J4**
Hamilton Pl. W1 **119 H3**
Hamilton Sq. SE1 **121 L4**
Hammett St. EC3 **117 P10**
Hampden Clo. NW1 **115 P1**
Hampden Gurney St. W1 **114 E9**
Hampstead Rd. NW1 **115 L1**
Hampton St. SE1 **120 G9**
Hampton St. SE17 **120 G9**
Hanbury St. E1 **117 Q6**
Hand Ct. WC1 **116 C7**
Handel St. WC1 **115 Q4**
Hankey Pl. SE1 **121 L5**
Hanover Gate NW1 **114 D3**
Hanover Pl. WC2 **116 A9**
Hanover Sq. W1 **115 K9**
Hanover St. W1 **115 K9**
Hanover Ter. NW1 **114 D3**
Hanover Ter. Ms. NW1 **114 D3**
Hans Cres. SW1 **118 E6**
Hans Pl. SW1 **118 F6**
Hans Rd. SW3 **118 E6**
Hans St. SW1 **118 F7**
Hanson St. W1 **115 L6**
Hanway Pl. W1 **115 N8**
Hanway St. W1 **115 N8**

Harbet Rd. W2 114 B7
Harcourt St. W1 114 D7
Hardwick St. EC1 116 E3
Hardwidge St. SE1 121 M4
Hare Ct. EC4 116 D9
Hare Pl. EC4 116 E9
Hare Wk. N1 117 N1
Harewood Ave. NW1 114 D5
Harewood Pl. W1 115 K9
Harewood Row NW1 114 D6
Harley Pl. W1 115 J7
Harley St. W1 115 J5
Harold Est. SE1 121 N7
Harp All. EC4 116 F8
Harp La. EC3 121 M1
Harper Rd. SE1 121 J6
Harpur Ms. WC1 116 B6
Harpur St. WC1 116 B6
Harriet St. SW1 118 F5
Harriet Wk. SW1 118 F5
Harrington Rd. SW7 118 B8
Harrington Sq. NW1 115 L1
Harrington St. NW1 115 L1
Harrison St. WC1 116 A3
Harrow Pl. E1 117 P8
Harrowby St. W1 114 D8
Hart St. EC3 117 N10
Hartshorn All. EC3 117 N9
Harwich La. EC2 117 N6
Hasker St. SW3 118 D8
Hassard St. E2 117 Q1
Hastings St. WC1 115 Q3
Hat and Mitre Ct. EC1 116 G5
Hatfields SE1 120 E2
Hatherley St. SW1 119 M9
Hatton Gdn. EC1 116 E6
Hatton Row NW8 114 B5
Hatton St. NW8 114 B5
Hatton Wall EC1 116 D6
Haunch of Venison Yd. W1 115 J9
Haverstock St. N1 116 G1
Hay Hill W1 119 K1
Haydon St. EC3 117 P10
Haydon Wk. E1 117 Q10
Hayes Pl. NW1 114 D5
Hayles St. SE11 120 F8
Haymarket SW1 119 N1
Haymarket Arc. SW1 119 N1
Hayne St. EC1 116 G6
Hay's La. SE1 121 M3
Hay's Ms. W1 119 J2
Hayward's Pl. EC1 116 F5
Hazel Way SE1 121 P8
Headfort Pl. SW1 119 H5
Hearn St. EC2 117 N5
Hearn's Bldgs. SE17 121 L9
Heathcote St. WC1 116 B4
Heddon St. W1 115 L10
Helmet Row EC1 117 J4
Hemp Wk. SE17 121 L8
Henderson Dr. NW8 114 A4
Hendre Rd. SE1 121 N9
Heneage La. EC3 117 N9
Heneage St. E1 117 Q6
Henley Dr. SE1 121 Q8
Henrietta Ms. WC1 116 A4
Henrietta Pl. W1 115 J8
Henrietta St. WC2 116 A10
Henshaw St. SE17 121 K8
Herald's Ct. SE11 120 F9
Herald's Pl. SE11 120 E8
Herbal Hill EC1 116 E5
Herbert Cres. SW1 118 F6
Herbrand St. WC1 115 Q4
Hercules Rd. SE1 120 C7
Hermes St. N1 116 D1
Hermit St. EC1 116 F2
Hermitage St. W2 114 A7
Herrick St. SW1 119 P9
Hertford Pl. W1 115 L5
Hertford St. W1 119 H3
Hewett St. EC2 117 N5
Heygate St. SE17 121 H9
Hide Pl. SW1 119 N9
High Holborn WC1 115 Q8
Hill St. W1 119 H2
Hillery Clo. SE17 121 L9
Hills Pl. W1 115 L9
Hind Ct. EC4 116 E9
Hinde St. W1 114 H8
Hobart Pl. SW1 119 J6
Hocker St. E2 117 P3
Hogans Ms. W2 114 A6
Hogarth Ct. EC3 117 N10
Holbein Ms. SW1 118 G10
Holbein Pl. SW1 118 G9
Holborn EC1 116 D7
Holborn Circ. EC1 116 E7
Holborn Pl. WC1 116 B7
Holborn Viaduct EC1 116 E7
Holford Pl. WC1 116 C2
Holford St. WC1 116 D2
Holland St. SE1 120 G2
Hollen St. W1 115 M8
Holles St. W1 115 K8
Holmes Ter. SE1 120 D4
Holsworthy Sq. WC1 116 C5
Holyoak Rd. SE11 120 F8
Holyrood St. SE1 121 M3
Holywell La. EC2 117 N4
Holywell Row EC2 117 M5
Homefield St. N1 117 M1
Homer Row W1 114 D7
Homer St. W1 114 D7
Honduras St. EC1 117 H4
Honey La. EC2 117 J9
Hood Ct. EC4 116 E9
Hooper's Ct. SW3 118 E5
Hop Gdns. WC2 119 Q1
Hopetown St. E1 117 Q7
Hopkins St. W1 115 M9
Hopton Gdns. SE1 120 G2
Hopton St. SE1 120 G2
Horatio St. E2 117 Q1
Hornbeam Clo. SE11 120 D8
Horse and Dolphin Yd. W1 115 P10
Horse Guards Ave. SW1 119 Q3
Horse Guards Rd. SW1 119 P3
Horse Ride SW1 119 N3
Horse Shoe Yd. W1 115 K10
Horseferry Rd. SW1 119 N7
Horselydown La. SE1 121 P4
Hosier La. EC1 116 F7
Hotspur St. SE11 120 D10
Houghton St. WC2 116 C9
Houndsditch EC3 117 N8
Howard Pl. SW1 119 L7
Howell Wk. SE1 120 G9
Howick Pl. SW1 119 M7
Howland Ms. E. W1 115 M6
Howland St. W1 115 L6
Hoxton Mkt. N1 117 M3
Hoxton Sq. N1 117 M3
Hudson's Pl. SW1 119 L8
Huggin Ct. EC4 117 J10
Huggin Hill EC4 117 J10
Hugh Ms. SW1 119 K9
Hugh Pl. SW1 119 N8
Hugh St. SW1 119 K9
Hull St. EC1 117 H3
Humphrey St. SE1 121 P10
Hungerford Bri. SE1 120 B3
Hungerford Bri. WC2 120 B3
Hungerford La. WC2 120 A2
Hunter Clo. SE1 121 L7
Hunter St. WC1 116 A4
Huntley St. WC1 115 M5
Hunt's Ct. WC2 119 P1
Huntsman St. SE17 121 L9
Huntsworth Ms. NW1 114 E5
Hutton St. EC4 116 E9
Hyde Pk. W2 118 C2
Hyde Pk. Cor. W1 118 H4
Hyde Pk. Cres. W2 114 C9
Hyde Pk. Gdns. W2 114 B10
Hyde Pk. Gdns. Ms. W2 114 B10
Hyde Pk. Pl. W2 114 D10
Hyde Pk. Sq. W2 114 C9
Hyde Pk. Sq. Ms. W2 114 C9
Hyde Pk. St. W2 114 C9

I

Idol La. EC3 121 M1
Iliffe St. SE17 120 G10
Iliffe Yd. SE17 120 G10
Imperial College Rd. SW7 118 A6
India St. EC3 117 P9
Ingestre Pl. W1 115 M9
Inglebert St. EC1 116 D2
Ingram Clo. SE11 120 C8
Inigo Pl. WC2 115 Q10
Inner Circle NW1 114 G3
Inner Temple La. EC4 116 D9
Insurance St. WC1 116 D3
Ireland Yd. EC4 116 G9
Ironmonger La. EC2 117 K9
Ironmonger Pas. EC1 117 J3
Ironmonger Row EC1 117 J3
Irving St. WC2 119 P1
Isabella St. SE1 120 F3
Ives St. SW3 118 D8
Ivor Pl. NW1 114 E5
Ivybridge La. WC2 120 A1
Ivychurch La. SE17 121 N10
Ixworth Pl. SW3 118 C10

J

Jacob's Well Ms. W1 114 H8
Jamaica Rd. SE1 121 Q5
James Hammett Ho. E2 117 Q2
James St. W1 115 H8
James St. WC2 116 A10
Jasper Wk. N1 117 K1
Jermyn St. SW1 119 M2
Jerome Cres. NW8 114 C4
Jerome St. E1 117 P5
Jerrard St. N1 117 N1
Jerusalem Pas. EC1 116 F5
Jervis Ct. W1 115 K9
Jewry St. EC3 117 P9
Joan St. SE1 120 F3
Jockey's Flds. WC1 116 C6
Johanna St. SE1 120 D5
John Adam St. WC2 120 A1
John Carpenter St. EC4 116 E10
John Islip St. SW1 119 P10
John Princes St. W1 115 K8
John St. WC1 116 C5
John's Ms. WC1 116 C5
Joiner St. SE1 121 L3
Jonathan St. SE11 120 B10
Jones St. W1 119 J1
Jubilee Pl. SW3 118 D10
Judd St. WC1 115 Q3
Junction Ms. W2 114 C8
Junction Pl. W2 114 B8
Junction Wf. N1 116 H1
Juxon St. SE11 120 C8

K

Kean St. WC2 116 B9
Keats Clo. SE1 121 P9
Keats Pl. EC2 117 K7
Keeley St. WC2 116 B9
Kell St. SE1 120 G6
Kemble St. WC2 116 B9
Kemp's Ct. W1 115 M9
Kempsford Rd. SE11 120 F9
Kendal St. W2 114 D9
Kendall Pl. W1 114 G7
Kendrick Ms. SW7 118 A8
Kendrick Pl. SW7 118 A9
Kennet Wf. La. EC4 117 J10
Kennings Way SE11 120 F10
Kennington Rd. SE1 120 D6
Kennington Rd. SE11 120 D8
Kenrick Pl. W1 114 G7
Kensington Gore SW7 118 A5
Kent Pas. NW1 114 E4
Kent Ter. NW1 117 Q3
Kent Yd. SW7 118 D5
Kentish Bldgs. SE1 121 K4
Kenton St. WC1 115 Q4
Keppel Row SE1 121 H3
Keppel St. WC1 115 P6
Kestrel Ho. EC1 116 H2
Keyse Rd. SE1 121 P7
Keystone Cres. N1 116 A1
Keyworth Pl. SE1 120 G6
Keyworth St. SE1 120 G6
Kiffen St. EC2 117 L4
Kimbolton Row SW3 118 C9
King & Queen St. SE17 121 J10
King Charles St. SW1 119 Q4
King Edward St. EC1 116 H8
King Edward Wk. SE1 120 E6
King James St. SE1 120 G5
King John Ct. EC2 117 N4
King Sq. EC1 116 H3
King St. EC2 117 J9
King St. SW1 119 M3
King St. WC2 115 Q10
King William St. EC4 121 L1
Kinghorn St. EC1 116 H7
Kinglake Est. SE17 121 N10
Kingly Ct. W1 115 M10
Kingly St. W1 115 L10
Kings Arms Yd. EC2 117 K8
Kings Bench St. SE1 120 G4
Kings Bench Wk. EC4 116 E9
King's Cross Rd. WC1 116 B2
Kings Head Yd. SE1 121 K3
King's Ms. WC1 116 C5
Kings Pl. SE1 121 H5
King's Reach Twr. SE1 120 E2
King's Rd. SW1 118 H8
King's Scholars' Pas. SW1 119 L7
Kingscote St. EC4 116 F10
Kingsland Rd. E2 117 N2
Kingsway WC2 116 B8
Kinnerton Pl. N. SW1 118 F5
Kinnerton Pl. S. SW1 118 F5
Kinnerton St. SW1 118 G5
Kinnerton Yd. SW1 118 F5
Kintore Way SE1 121 P8
Kipling Est. SE1 121 L5
Kipling St. SE1 121 L5
Kirby Gro. SE1 121 M4
Kirby St. EC1 116 E6
Kirkman Pl. W1 115 N7
Kirton Gdns. E2 117 Q3
Knightrider St. EC4 116 G10
Knights Arc. SW1 118 E5
Knights Wk. SE11 120 F9
Knightsbridge SW1 118 F4
Knightsbridge SW7 118 D5
Knightsbridge Grn. SW1 118 E5
Knox St. W1 114 E6

L

Lackington St. EC2 117 L6
Lafone St. SE1 121 P4
Lamb St. E1 117 P6
Lamb Wk. SE1 121 M5
Lambeth Bri. SE1 120 A8
Lambeth Bri. SW1 120 A8
Lambeth High St. SE1 120 B8
Lambeth Hill EC4 117 H10
Lambeth Palace Rd. SE1 120 B7
Lambeth Rd. SE1 120 D7
Lambeth Wk. SE11 120 C8
Lamb's Bldgs. EC1 117 K5
Lambs Conduit Pas. WC1 116 B6
Lamb's Conduit St. WC1 116 B5
Lamb's Pas. EC1 117 K6
Lamlash St. SE11 120 F8
Lancashire Ct. W1 115 K10
Lancaster Pl. WC2 116 B10
Lancaster St. SE1 120 G5
Lancaster Ter. W2 114 A10
Lancelot Pl. SW7 118 E5
Lancing St. NW1 115 N3
Landon Pl. SW1 118 E6
Langham Pl. W1 115 K7
Langham St. W1 115 K7
Langley Ct. WC2 115 Q10
Langley St. WC2 115 Q9
Langthorn Ct. EC2 117 L8
Langton Clo. WC1 116 C4
Lansdowne Pl. SE1 121 L6
Lansdowne Row W1 119 K2
Lansdowne Ter. WC1 116 A5
Lant St. SE1 121 H4
Larcom St. SE17 121 J9
Larissa St. SE17 121 L10
Laud St. SE11 120 B10
Launcelot St. SE1 120 D5
Laurence Pountney Hill EC4 117 K10
Laurence Pountney La. EC4 117 K10
Lavington St. SE1 120 G3
Law St. SE1 121 L6
Lawrence La. EC2 117 J9
Lawson Est. SE1 121 K7
Laxton Pl. NW1 115 K4
Laystall St. EC1 116 D5
Laytons Bldgs. SE1 121 K4
Leadenhall Mkt. EC3 117 M9
Leadenhall Pl. EC3 117 M9
Leadenhall St. EC3 117 M9
Leake Ct. SE1 120 C4
Leake St. SE1 120 C4
Leather La. EC1 116 D6
Leathermarket St. SE1 121 M5
Lecky St. SW7 118 A10
Leeke St. WC1 116 B2
Lees Pl. W1 114 G10
Leicester Ct. WC2 115 P10
Leicester Pl. WC2 115 P10
Leicester Sq. WC2 119 P1
Leicester St. WC2 115 P10
Leigh Hunt St. SE1 121 H4
Leigh St. WC1 115 Q4
Leman St. E1 117 Q9
Lennox Gdns. SW1 118 E7
Lennox Gdns. Ms. SW1 118 E7
Leo Yd. EC1 116 G5
Leonard St. EC2 117 L4
Leopards Ct. EC1 116 D6
Leroy St. SE1 121 M7
Lever St. EC1 116 G3
Leverett St. SW3 118 D8
Lewisham St. SW1 119 P5
Lexington St. W1 115 M10
Leyden St. E1 117 P7
Library St. SE1 120 F5
Lidlington Pl. NW1 115 M1
Ligonier St. E2 117 P4
Lilac Pl. SE11 120 B9
Lilestone St. NW8 114 C4
Lillington Gdns. Est. SW1 119 M9
Lily Pl. EC1 116 E6
Lime St. EC3 117 M10
Lime St. Pas. EC3 117 M10
Lincoln St. SW3 118 E9
Lincoln's Inn Flds. WC2 116 B8
Lindsey St. EC1 116 G6
Linhope St. NW1 114 E4
Lisle St. WC2 115 P10
Lisson Grn. Est. NW8 114 C3
Lisson Gro. NW1 114 D5
Lisson Gro. NW8 114 B4
Lisson St. NW1 114 C6
Litchfield St. WC2 115 P10
Little Albany St. NW1 115 K3
Little Argyll St. W1 115 L9
Little Britain EC1 116 G7
Little Chester St. SW1 119 J6
Little College St. SW1 119 Q6
Little Dean's Yd. SW1 119 Q6
Little Dorrit Ct. SE1 121 J4
Little Edward St. NW1 115 K2
Little Essex St. WC2 116 D10
Little George St. SW1 119 Q5
Little Marlborough St. W1 115 L9
Little New St. EC4 116 E8
Little Newport St. WC2 115 P10
Little Portland St. W1 115 K8
Little Russell St. WC1 115 Q7
Little St. James's St. SW1 119 L3
Little Sanctuary SW1 119 P5
Little Smith St. SW1 119 P6
Little Somerset St. E1 117 P9
Little Titchfield St. W1 115 L7
Little Trinity La. EC4 117 J10
Little Turnstile WC1 116 B7
Liverpool St. EC2 117 M7
Livonia St. W1 115 M9
Lizard St. EC1 117 J3
Lloyd Baker St. WC1 116 C3
Lloyd Sq. WC1 116 D2
Lloyd St. WC1 116 D2
Lloyd's Ave. EC3 117 N9
Lloyd's Row EC1 116 F3
Lockyer Est. SE1 121 L4
Lockyer St. SE1 121 L5
Lodge Rd. NW8 114 B3
Lolesworth Clo. E1 117 Q7
Lollard St. SE11 120 C8
Loman St. SE1 120 G4
Lombard Ct. EC3 117 L10
Lombard La. EC4 116 E9
Lombard St. EC3 117 L9
London Bri. EC4 121 L2
London Bri. SE1 121 L2
London Bri. St. SE1 121 L3
London Ms. W2 114 B9
London Rd. SE1 120 F6
London St. EC3 117 N10
London St. W2 114 A8
London Wall EC2 117 J7
Long Acre WC2 115 Q10
Long Ct. WC2 119 P1
Long La. EC1 116 G6
Long La. SE1 121 K5
Long St. E2 117 P2
Long Wk. SE1 121 N6
Long Yd. WC1 116 B5
Longfellow Way SE1 121 Q9
Longfield Est. SE1 121 Q9
Longford St. NW1 115 K4
Longmoore St. SW1 119 L9
Longville Rd. SE11 120 G8
Lord N. St. SW1 119 Q7
Lords Vw. NW8 114 C3
Lorenzo St. WC1 116 B1
Lorne Clo. NW8 114 D3
Lothbury EC2 117 K8
Lovat La. EC3 121 M1
Love La. EC2 117 J8
Lover's Wk. W1 118 G2
Lower Belgrave St. SW1 119 J7
Lower Grosvenor Pl. SW1 119 J6
Lower James St. W1 115 M10
Lower John St. W1 115 M10
Lower Marsh SE1 120 D5
Lower Robert St. WC2 120 A1
Lower Sloane St. SW1 118 G9
Lower Thames St. EC3 121 L1
Lowndes Clo. SW1 118 H7
Lowndes Pl. SW1 118 G7
Lowndes Sq. SW1 118 F5
Lowndes St. SW1 118 F6
Lowther Gdns. SW7 118 A5
Loxham St. WC1 116 A3
Lucan Pl. SW3 118 C9
Ludgate Bdy. EC4 116 F9
Ludgate Circ. EC4 116 F9
Ludgate Ct. EC4 116 F9
Ludgate Hill EC4 116 F9
Ludgate Sq. EC4 116 G9
Ludlow St. EC1 116 H4
Luke St. EC2 117 M4
Lulworth SE17 121 K10
Lumley Ct. WC2 120 A1
Lumley St. W1 114 H9
Luton St. NW8 114 B5
Luxborough St. W1 114 G5
Lyall Ms. SW1 118 G7
Lyall Ms. W. SW1 118 G7
Lyall St. SW1 118 G7
Lygon Pl. SW1 119 J7
Lynton Rd. SE1 121 Q9
Lyons Pl. NW8 114 A5

M

Mabledon Pl. WC1 115 P3
Macclesfield Rd. EC1 116 H2
Macclesfield St. W1 115 P10
Macfarren Pl. NW1 114 H5
Macklin St. WC2 116 A8
Mackworth St. NW1 115 L2
Maddox St. W1 115 K10
Madron St. SE17 121 N10
Magdalen Pas. E1 117 Q10
Magdalen St. SE1 121 M3
Maggie Blake's Cause SE1 121 P3
Magpie All. EC4 116 E9
Maguire St. SE1 121 Q4
Maiden La. SE1 121 J2
Maiden La. WC2 116 A10
Maidstone Bldgs. SE1 121 K3
Mail Coach Yd. N1 117 N2
Makins St. SW3 118 D9
Malet Pl. WC1 115 N5
Malet St. WC1 115 N5
Mall, The SW1 119 M4
Mallory St. NW8 114 C5
Mallow St. EC1 117 K4
Malta St. EC1 116 G4
Maltby St. SE1 121 P5
Maltravers St. WC2 116 C10
Malvern Ct. SW7 118 B8
Manchester Ms. W1 114 G7
Manchester Sq. W1 114 G8
Manchester St. W1 114 G7
Manciple St. SE1 121 L5
Mandela Way SE1 121 N8
Mandeville Pl. W1 115 H8
Manette St. W1 115 P9
Manningford Clo. EC1 116 F2
Manor Pl. SE17 120 H10
Mansell St. E1 117 Q9
Mansfield Ms. W1 115 J7
Mansfield St. W1 115 J7
Mansion Ho. Pl. EC4 117 K9
Manson Ms. SW7 118 A9
Manson Pl. SW7 118 A9
Maple Pl. W1 115 M5
Maple St. W1 115 L6
Marble Arch W1 114 E10
Marchmont St. WC1 115 Q4
Marcia Rd. SE1 121 N9

Margaret Ct. W1 **115 L8**
Margaret St. W1 **115 K8**
Margery St. WC1 **116 D3**
Marigold All. SE1 **120 F1**
Mark La. EC3 **117 N10**
Mark St. EC2 **117 M4**
Market Ct. W1 **115 L8**
Market Ms. W1 **119 J3**
Market Pl. W1 **115 L8**
Markham Pl. SW3 **118 E10**
Markham Sq. SW3 **118 E10**
Markham St. SW3 **118 D10**
Marlborough Bldgs. SW3 **118 D8**
Marlborough Clo. SE17 **120 H9**
Marlborough Gate Ho. W2 **114 A10**
Marlborough Rd. SW1 **119 M3**
Marlborough St. SW3 **118 C9**
Marshall St. W1 **115 M9**
Marshalls Pl. SE16 **121 Q7**
Marshalsea Rd. SE1 **121 J4**
Marsham St. SW1 **119 P7**
Mart St. WC2 **116 A10**
Martin La. EC4 **117 L10**
Martlett Ct. WC2 **116 A9**
Marylebone Flyover NW1 **114 C7**
Marylebone Flyover W2 **114 B7**
Marylebone High St. W1 **114 H6**
Marylebone La. W1 **115 H8**
Marylebone Ms. W1 **115 J7**
Marylebone Pas. W1 **115 M8**
Marylebone Rd. NW1 **114 F6**
Marylebone St. W1 **115 H7**
Marylee Way SE11 **120 C10**
Mason St. SE17 **121 L8**
Masons Arms Ms. W1 **115 K10**
Masons Ave. EC2 **117 K8**
Mason's Pl. EC1 **116 H2**
Mason's Yd. SW1 **119 M2**
Massinger St. SE17 **121 M9**
Matthew Parker St. SW1 **119 P5**
Matthews Yd. WC2 **115 Q9**
Maunsel St. SW1 **119 N8**
Mayfair Pl. W1 **119 K2**
Mays Ct. WC2 **119 Q1**
McAuley Clo. SE1 **120 D6**
McCoid Way SE1 **120 H5**
Mead Row SE1 **120 D6**
Meadow Row SE1 **121 H7**
Meakin Est. SE1 **121 M6**
Meard St. W1 **115 N9**
Mecklenburgh Pl. WC1 **116 B4**
Mecklenburgh Sq. WC1 **116 B4**
Mecklenburgh St. WC1 **116 B4**
Medway St. SW1 **119 P7**
Melbourne Pl. WC2 **116 C9**
Melbury Ter. NW1 **114 D5**
Melcombe Pl. NW1 **114 E6**
Melcombe St. NW1 **114 F5**
Melina Pl. NW8 **114 A3**
Melior Pl. SE1 **121 M4**
Melior St. SE1 **121 M4**
Melton Ct. SW7 **118 B9**
Melton St. NW1 **115 M3**
Memel Ct. EC1 **117 H5**
Memel St. EC1 **116 H5**
Mepham St. SE1 **120 D3**
Mercer St. WC2 **115 Q9**
Meredith St. EC1 **116 F3**
Merlin St. WC1 **116 D3**
Mermaid Ct. SE1 **121 K4**
Merrick Sq. SE1 **121 K6**
Merrow Wk. SE17 **121 L10**
Meymott St. SE1 **120 F3**
Micawber St. N1 **117 J2**
Middle St. EC1 **116 H6**
Middle Temple La. EC4 **116 D9**
Middle Yd. SE1 **121 M2**
Middlesex Pas. EC1 **116 G7**
Middlesex St. E1 **117 N7**
Middleton Bldgs. W1 **115 L7**
Midford Pl. W1 **115 M5**
Midhope St. WC1 **116 A3**
Midland Rd. NW1 **115 P1**
Milcote St. SE1 **120 F5**
Miles Pl. NW1 **114 C6**
Milford La. WC2 **116 D10**
Milk St. EC2 **117 J8**
Mill St. SE1 **121 Q5**
Mill St. W1 **115 L10**
Millbank SW1 **119 Q6**
Millbank Twr. SW1 **119 Q9**
Millman Ms. WC1 **116 B5**
Millman St. WC1 **116 B5**
Mills Ct. EC2 **117 M4**
Millstream Rd. SE1 **121 P5**
Milner St. SW3 **118 E8**
Milroy Wk. SE1 **120 F2**
Milton Clo. SE1 **121 P9**
Milton Ct. EC2 **117 K6**
Milton St. EC2 **117 K6**
Mincing La. EC3 **117 M10**
Minera Ms. SW1 **118 H8**
Minnow Wk. SE17 **121 N9**
Minories EC3 **117 P9**
Mint St. SE1 **121 H4**
Mitchell St. EC1 **117 H4**
Mitre Ct. EC2 **117 J8**
Mitre Ct. EC4 **116 E9**
Mitre Rd. SE1 **120 E4**
Mitre Sq. EC3 **117 N9**
Mitre St. EC3 **117 N9**
Molyneux St. W1 **114 D7**
Monck St. SW1 **119 P7**
Moncorvo Clo. SW7 **118 C5**
Monkton St. SE11 **120 E8**
Monkwell Sq. EC2 **117 J7**
Monmouth St. WC2 **115 Q10**
Montagu Mans. W1 **114 F6**
Montagu Ms. N. W1 **114 F7**
Montagu Ms. S. W1 **114 F8**
Montagu Ms. W. W1 **114 F8**
Montagu Pl. W1 **114 E7**
Montagu Row W1 **114 F7**
Montagu Sq. W1 **114 F7**
Montagu St. W1 **114 F8**
Montague Clo. SE1 **121 K2**
Montague Pl. WC1 **115 P6**
Montague St. EC1 **116 H7**
Montague St. WC1 **115 Q6**
Montclare St. E2 **117 P4**
Montpelier Ms. SW7 **118 D6**
Montpelier Pl. SW7 **118 D6**
Montpelier Sq. SW7 **118 D6**
Montpelier St. SW7 **118 D5**
Montpelier Ter. SW7 **118 D5**
Montpelier Wk. SW7 **118 C6**
Montreal Pl. WC2 **116 B10**
Montrose Ct. SW7 **118 B5**
Montrose Pl. SW1 **118 H5**
Monument St. EC3 **117 L10**
Moor La. EC2 **117 K7**
Moor Pl. EC2 **117 K7**
Moor St. W1 **115 P9**
Moore St. SW3 **118 E8**
Moorfields EC2 **117 K7**
Moorgate EC2 **117 K7**
Moorgate Pl. EC2 **117 K8**
Mora St. EC1 **117 J3**
Morecambe St. SE17 **121 J9**
Moreland St. EC1 **116 G2**
Moreton Pl. SW1 **119 M10**
Moreton St. SW1 **119 M10**
Moreton Ter. SW1 **119 M10**
Moreton Ter. Ms. N. SW1 **119 M10**
Moreton Ter. Ms. S. SW1 **119 M10**
Morgans La. SE1 **121 M3**
Morley St. SE1 **120 E6**
Morocco St. SE1 **121 M5**
Morpeth Ter. SW1 **119 L7**
Mortimer Mkt. WC1 **115 M5**
Mortimer St. W1 **115 L8**
Morton Pl. SE1 **120 D7**
Morwell St. WC1 **115 P7**
Mossop St. SW3 **118 D8**
Motcomb St. SW1 **118 F6**
Mount Mills EC1 **116 G3**
Mount Pleasant WC1 **116 D5**
Mount Row W1 **119 J1**
Mount St. W1 **118 G1**
Moxon St. W1 **114 G7**
Mozart Ter. SW1 **118 H9**
Mulready St. NW8 **114 C5**
Mulvaney Way SE1 **121 L5**
Mumford Ct. EC2 **117 J8**
Mundy St. N1 **117 N2**
Munster Sq. NW1 **115 K3**
Munton Rd. SE17 **121 J8**
Murphy St. SE1 **120 D5**
Murray Gro. N1 **117 J1**
Muscovy St. EC3 **121 N1**
Museum St. WC1 **115 Q7**
Myddelton Pas. EC1 **116 E2**
Myddelton Sq. EC1 **116 E2**
Myddelton St. EC1 **116 E3**
Mylne St. EC1 **116 D2**
Myrtle Wk. N1 **117 M1**

N

Nag's Head Ct. EC1 **117 J5**
Nantes Pas. E1 **117 P6**
Nash St. NW1 **115 K2**
Nassau St. W1 **115 L7**
Nathaniel Clo. E1 **117 Q7**
Navarre St. E2 **117 P4**
Nazrul St. E2 **117 P2**
Neal St. WC2 **115 Q9**
Neal's Yd. WC2 **115 Q9**
Neathouse Pl. SW1 **119 L8**
Nebraska St. SE1 **121 K5**
Neckinger SE16 **121 Q6**
Neckinger Est. SE16 **121 Q6**
Neckinger St. SE1 **121 Q6**
Nelson Pas. EC1 **117 J3**
Nelson Pl. N1 **116 G1**
Nelson Sq. SE1 **120 F4**
Nelson Ter. N1 **116 G1**
Netley St. NW1 **115 L3**
Neville Clo. NW1 **115 P1**
Neville St. SW7 **118 A10**
Neville Ter. SW7 **118 A10**
New Bond St. W1 **115 J9**
New Bri. St. EC4 **116 F9**
New Broad St. EC2 **117 M7**
New Burlington Ms. W1 **115 L10**
New Burlington Pl. W1 **115 L10**
New Burlington St. W1 **115 L10**
New Cavendish St. W1 **115 H7**
New Change EC4 **117 H9**
New Charles St. EC1 **116 G2**
New Compton St. WC2 **115 P9**
New Ct. EC4 **116 D10**
New Coventry St. W1 **119 P1**
New Fetter La. EC4 **116 E8**
New Goulston St. E1 **117 P8**
New Inn Bdy. EC2 **117 N4**
New Inn Pas. WC2 **116 C9**
New Inn St. EC2 **117 N4**
New Inn Yd. EC2 **117 N4**
New Kent Rd. SE1 **121 H7**
New London St. EC3 **117 N10**
New N. Pl. EC2 **117 M5**
New N. St. WC1 **116 B6**
New Oxford St. WC1 **115 P8**
New Quebec St. W1 **114 F9**
New Ride SW7 **118 C4**
New Row WC2 **115 Q10**
New Sq. WC2 **116 C8**
New St. EC2 **117 N7**
New St. Sq. EC4 **116 E8**
New Turnstile WC1 **116 B7**
New Union St. EC2 **117 K7**
Newburgh St. W1 **115 L9**
Newbury St. EC1 **116 H6**
Newcastle Clo. EC4 **116 F8**
Newcastle Pl. W2 **114 B7**
Newcastle Row EC1 **116 E5**
Newcomen St. SE1 **121 K4**
Newcourt St. NW8 **114 C1**
Newgate St. EC1 **116 G8**
Newhams Row SE1 **121 N5**
Newington Butts SE1 **120 G9**
Newington Butts SE11 **120 G9**
Newington Causeway SE1 **120 G7**
Newman Pas. W1 **115 M7**
Newman St. W1 **115 M7**
Newman Yd. W1 **115 M8**
Newman's Ct. EC3 **117 L9**
Newman's Row WC2 **116 C7**
Newnham Ter. SE1 **120 D6**
Newport Ct. WC2 **115 P10**
Newport Pl. WC2 **115 P10**
Newport St. SE11 **120 B9**
Newton St. WC2 **116 A8**
Nicholas La. EC4 **117 L10**
Nicholson St. SE1 **120 F3**
Nile St. N1 **117 J2**
Noble St. EC2 **117 H8**
Noel St. W1 **115 M9**
Norfolk Cres. W2 **114 C8**
Norfolk Pl. W2 **114 B8**
Norfolk Row SE1 **120 B8**
Norfolk Sq. W2 **114 B9**
Norfolk Sq. Ms. W2 **114 B9**
Norman St. EC1 **117 H3**
Norris St. SW1 **119 N1**
North Audley St. W1 **114 G9**
North Bank NW8 **114 C3**
North Carriage Dr. W2 **114 C10**
North Ct. W1 **115 M6**
North Cres. WC1 **115 N6**
North Gower St. NW1 **115 M3**
North Ms. WC1 **116 C5**
North Ride W2 **118 C1**
North Row W1 **114 F10**
North Tenter St. E1 **117 Q9**
North Ter. SW3 **118 C7**
North Wf. Rd. W2 **114 A7**
Northampton Rd. EC1 **116 E4**
Northampton Sq. EC1 **116 F3**
Northburgh St. EC1 **116 G5**
Northchurch SE17 **121 L10**
Northington St. WC1 **116 C5**
Northumberland All. EC3 **117 N9**
Northumberland Ave. WC2 **119 Q2**
Northumberland St. WC2 **119 Q2**
Northwick Clo. NW8 **114 A4**
Northwick Ter. NW8 **114 A4**
Norton Folgate E1 **117 N6**
Norwich St. EC4 **116 D8**
Nottingham Ct. WC2 **115 Q9**
Nottingham Pl. W1 **114 G5**
Nottingham St. W1 **114 G6**
Nottingham Ter. NW1 **114 G5**
Nun Ct. EC2 **117 K8**
Nutford Pl. W1 **114 D8**

O

Oak Tree Rd. NW8 **114 B3**
Oakden St. SE11 **120 E8**
Oakey La. SE1 **120 D6**
Oakley Cres. EC1 **116 G1**
Oat La. EC2 **117 J8**
Occupation Rd. SE17 **121 H10**
Octagon Arc. EC2 **117 M7**
Odhams Wk. WC2 **115 Q9**
Ogle St. W1 **115 L6**
Old Bailey EC4 **116 G9**
Old Barge Ho. All. SE1 **120 E2**
Old Barrack Yd. SW1 **118 G5**
Old Bond St. W1 **119 L1**
Old Brewers Yd. WC2 **115 Q9**
Old Broad St. EC2 **117 L9**
Old Bldgs. WC2 **116 D8**
Old Burlington St. W1 **115 L10**
Old Castle St. E1 **117 P8**
Old Cavendish St. W1 **115 J8**
Old Compton St. W1 **115 N10**
Old Fish St. Hill EC4 **117 H10**
Old Gloucester St. WC1 **116 A6**
Old Jewry EC2 **117 K9**
Old Kent Rd. SE1 **121 M8**
Old Marylebone Rd. NW1 **114 D7**
Old Nichol St. E2 **117 P4**
Old N. St. WC1 **116 B6**
Old Palace Yd. SW1 **119 Q6**
Old Paradise St. SE11 **120 B8**
Old Pk. La. W1 **119 H3**
Old Pye St. SW1 **119 N6**
Old Quebec St. W1 **114 F9**
Old Queen St. SW1 **119 P5**
Old Seacoal La. EC4 **116 F9**
Old Sq. WC2 **116 C8**
Old St. EC1 **116 H5**
Oldbury Pl. W1 **114 H6**
Olivers Yd. EC1 **117 L4**
O'Meara St. SE1 **121 J3**
Omega Pl. N1 **116 A1**
Onslow Gdns. SW7 **118 A10**
Onslow Ms. E. SW7 **118 A9**
Onslow Ms. W. SW7 **118 A9**
Onslow Sq. SW7 **118 B9**
Onslow St. EC1 **116 E5**
Ontario St. SE1 **120 G7**
Opal St. SE11 **120 F10**
Orange St. WC2 **119 P1**
Orange Yd. W1 **115 P9**
Oratory La. SW3 **118 B10**
Orb St. SE17 **121 K9**
Orchard St. W1 **114 G9**
Orchardson St. NW8 **114 A5**
Orde Hall St. WC1 **116 B6**
Orient St. SE11 **120 F8**
Ormond Clo. WC1 **116 A6**
Ormond Ms. WC1 **116 A5**
Ormond Yd. SW1 **119 M2**
Ormonde Pl. SW1 **118 G9**
Ormsby St. E2 **117 P1**
Orsett St. SE11 **120 C10**
Osbert St. SW1 **119 N9**
Osborn St. E1 **117 Q7**
Oslo Ct. NW8 **114 C1**
Osnaburgh St. NW1 **115 K4**
Osnaburgh Ter. NW1 **115 K4**
Osric Path N1 **117 M1**
Ossington Bldgs. W1 **114 G6**
Ossulston St. NW1 **115 N1**
Oswin St. SE11 **120 G8**
Othello Clo. SE11 **120 F10**
Outwich St. EC3 **117 N8**
Ovington Gdns. SW3 **118 D7**
Ovington Ms. SW3 **118 D7**
Ovington Sq. SW3 **118 D7**
Ovington St. SW3 **118 D7**
Owen St. EC1 **116 E1**
Owen's Ct. EC1 **116 F2**
Owen's Row EC1 **116 F2**
Oxendon St. SW1 **119 N1**
Oxenholme NW1 **115 M1**
Oxford Circ. Ave. W1 **115 L9**
Oxford Ct. EC4 **117 K10**
Oxford Sq. W2 **114 D9**
Oxford St. W1 **114 G9**
Oxley Clo. SE1 **121 Q10**

P

Padbury Ct. E2 **117 Q3**
Paddington Grn. W2 **114 B6**
Paddington St. W1 **114 G6**
Page St. SW1 **119 P8**
Pages Wk. SE1 **121 M8**
Paget St. EC1 **116 F2**
Pakenham St. WC1 **116 C3**
Palace Ms. SW1 **118 H9**
Palace Pl. SW1 **119 L6**
Palace St. SW1 **119 L6**
Palissy St. E2 **117 P3**
Pall Mall SW1 **119 M3**
Pall Mall E. SW1 **119 P2**
Pall Mall Pl. SW1 **119 M3**
Palmer St. SW1 **119 N6**
Pancras La. EC4 **117 J9**
Panton St. SW1 **119 N1**
Panyer All. EC4 **116 H8**
Paragon Ms. SE1 **121 L8**
Pardon St. EC1 **116 G4**
Pardoner St. SE1 **121 L6**
Paris Gdn. SE1 **120 F2**
Park Clo. SW1 **118 E5**
Park Cres. W1 **115 J5**
Park Cres. Ms. E. W1 **115 K5**
Park Cres. Ms. W. W1 **115 J5**
Park Gdn. Pl. W2 **114 B9**
Park La. W1 **114 F10**
Park Pl. SW1 **119 L3**
Park Rd. NW1 **114 E4**
Park Rd. NW8 **114 C2**
Park Sq. E. NW1 **115 J4**
Park Sq. Ms. NW1 **115 J5**
Park Sq. W. NW1 **115 J4**
Park St. SE1 **120 H2**
Park St. W1 **114 G10**
Park W. W2 **114 B9**
Park W. Pl. W2 **114 D8**
Parker Ms. WC2 **116 A8**
Parker St. WC2 **116 A8**
Parkers Row SE1 **121 Q5**
Parliament Sq. SW1 **119 Q5**
Parliament St. SW1 **119 Q5**
Passing All. EC1 **116 F5**
Passmore St. SW1 **118 G9**
Pastor St. SE11 **120 G8**
Paternoster Row EC4 **116 H9**
Paternoster Sq. EC4 **116 G8**
Paton St. EC1 **117 H3**
Paul St. EC2 **117 L5**
Paveley St. NW8 **114 D3**
Pavilion Rd. SW1 **118 F5**
Pavilion St. SW1 **118 F7**
Peabody Dws. WC1 **115 Q4**
Peabody Est. EC1 **117 J5**
Peabody Sq. SE1 **120 F5**
Peacock St. SE17 **120 G9**
Peacock Yd. SE17 **120 G9**
Pear Pl. SE1 **120 D4**
Pear Tree Ct. EC1 **116 E5**
Pear Tree St. EC1 **116 G4**
Pearman St. SE1 **120 E6**
Pedley St. E1 **117 Q5**
Peerless St. EC1 **117 K3**
Pelham Cres. SW7 **118 C9**
Pelham Pl. SW7 **118 C8**
Pelham St. SW7 **118 B8**
Pelter St. E2 **117 P2**
Pemberton Row EC4 **116 E8**
Pembroke Clo. SW1 **118 H5**
Penfold Pl. NW1 **114 C6**
Penfold St. NW1 **114 C6**
Penfold St. NW8 **114 B5**
Penry St. SE1 **121 N9**
Penton Gro. N1 **116 D1**
Penton Pl. SE17 **120 G10**
Penton Ri. WC1 **116 C2**
Penton St. N1 **116 D1**
Pentonville Rd. N1 **116 B1**
Pepper St. SE1 **120 H4**
Pepys St. EC3 **117 N10**
Percival St. EC1 **116 F4**
Percy Circ. WC1 **116 C2**
Percy Ms. W1 **115 N7**
Percy Pas. W1 **115 M7**
Percy St. W1 **115 N7**
Percy Yd. WC1 **116 C2**
Peregrine Ho. EC1 **116 G2**
Perkin's Rents SW1 **119 N6**
Perrys Pl. W1 **115 N8**
Peter St. W1 **115 N10**
Peters Hill EC4 **116 H10**
Peters La. EC1 **116 F6**
Peto Pl. NW1 **115 K4**
Petticoat Sq. E1 **117 P8**
Petty France SW1 **119 M6**
Petyward SW3 **118 D9**
Philpot La. EC3 **117 M10**
Phipp St. EC2 **117 M4**
Phipp's Ms. SW1 **119 J7**
Phoenix Pl. WC1 **116 C4**
Phoenix Rd. NW1 **115 N2**
Phoenix St. WC2 **115 P9**
Piccadilly W1 **119 K3**
Piccadilly Arc. SW1 **119 L2**
Piccadilly Circ. W1 **119 N1**
Piccadilly Pl. W1 **119 M1**
Pickard St. EC1 **116 G2**
Pickering Pl. SW1 **119 M3**
Pickford Wf. N1 **116 H1**
Pickwick St. SE1 **121 H5**
Picton Pl. W1 **114 H9**
Pilgrim St. EC4 **116 F9**
Pilgrimage St. SE1 **121 K5**
Pimlico Rd. SW1 **118 G10**
Pimlico Wk. N1 **117 M2**
Pindar St. EC2 **117 M6**
Pine St. EC1 **116 D4**
Pineapple Ct. SW1 **119 L6**
Pitfield Est. N1 **117 M2**
Pitfield St. N1 **117 M3**
Pitt's Head Ms. W1 **119 H3**
Plantain Pl. SE1 **121 K4**
Platina St. EC2 **117 L4**
Playhouse Yd. EC4 **116 F9**
Pleydell St. EC4 **116 E9**
Plough Ct. EC3 **117 L10**
Plough Pl. EC4 **116 E8**
Plough Yd. EC2 **117 N5**
Plumtree Ct. EC4 **116 F8**
Plympton Pl. NW8 **114 C5**
Plympton St. NW8 **114 C5**
Pocock St. SE1 **120 F4**
Poland St. W1 **115 M8**
Pollen St. W1 **115 L9**
Pollitt Dr. NW8 **114 B4**
Polygon Rd. NW1 **115 N1**
Pomell Way E1 **117 Q8**
Pond Pl. SW3 **118 C9**
Ponsonby Pl. SW1 **119 P10**
Ponsonby Ter. SW1 **119 P10**
Pont St. SW1 **118 E7**
Pont St. Ms. SW1 **118 E7**
Pontypool Pl. SE1 **120 F4**
Pooles Bldgs. EC1 **116 D5**
Pope St. SE1 **121 N5**
Poppins Ct. EC4 **116 F9**
Porchester Pl. W2 **114 D9**
Porlock St. SE1 **121 L4**
Porter St. SE1 **121 J2**
Porter St. W1 **114 F6**
Portland Ms. W1 **115 M9**
Portland Pl. W1 **115 J5**
Portland St. SE17 **121 K10**
Portman Clo. W1 **114 F8**
Portman Ms. S. W1 **114 G9**
Portman Sq. W1 **114 G8**
Portman St. W1 **114 G9**

Portpool La. EC1 **116 D6**
Portsea Ms. W2 **114 D9**
Portsea Pl. W2 **114 D9**
Portsmouth St. WC2 **116 B9**
Portsoken St. E1 **117 P10**
Portugal St. WC2 **116 B9**
Post Office Ct. EC3 **117 L9**
Potier St. SE1 **121 L7**
Poultry EC2 **117 K9**
Powis Pl. WC1 **116 A5**
Praed Ms. W2 **114 B8**
Praed St. W2 **114 B8**
Pratt Wk. SE11 **120 C8**
Prescot St. E1 **117 Q10**
President St. EC1 **116 H2**
Preston Clo. SE1 **121 M8**
Prestwood St. N1 **117 J1**
Price's St. SE1 **120 G3**
Prideaux Pl. WC1 **116 C2**
Priest St. EC2 **117 H8**
Primrose Hill EC4 **116 E9**
Primrose St. EC2 **117 M6**
Prince Albert Rd. NW1 **114 D1**
Prince Albert Rd. NW8 **114 D1**
Prince Consort Rd. SW7 **118 A6**
Prince of Wales Gate SW7 **118 C5**
Prince of Wales Pas. NW1 **115 L3**
Princelet St. E1 **117 Q6**
Prince's Arc. SW1 **119 M2**
Princes Gdns. SW7 **118 B6**
Princes Gate SW7 **118 B5**
Princes Gate Ct. SW7 **118 B5**
Princes Gate Ms. SW7 **118 B6**
Princes Pl. SW1 **119 M2**
Princes St. EC2 **117 K9**
Princes St. W1 **115 K9**
Princess St. SE1 **120 G7**
Princeton St. WC1 **116 B7**
Printer St. EC4 **116 E8**
Printing Ho. Yd. E2 **117 N3**
Prioress St. SE1 **121 L7**
Procter St. WC1 **116 B7**
Providence Ct. W1 **114 H10**
Providence Row N1 **116 B1**
Provost Est. N1 **117 K2**
Provost St. N1 **117 K1**
Prudent Pas. EC2 **117 K8**
Pudding La. EC3 **121 L1**
Puddle Dock EC4 **116 G10**
Puma Ct. E1 **117 P6**
Pump Ct. EC4 **116 D9**
Purbrook Est. SE1 **121 N5**
Purbrook St. SE1 **121 N6**

Q

Quadrant Arc. W1 **119 M1**
Quaker St. E1 **117 P5**
Quality Ct. WC2 **116 D8**
Quebec Ms. W1 **114 F9**
Queen Anne Ms. W1 **115 K7**
Queen Anne St. W1 **115 J8**
Queen Anne's Gate SW1 **119 N5**
Queen Anne's Wk. WC1 **116 A5**
Queen Elizabeth St. SE1 **121 P4**
Queen Sq. WC1 **116 A6**
Queen Sq. Pl. WC1 **116 A5**
Queen St. EC4 **117 J10**
Queen St. W1 **119 J2**
Queen St. Pl. EC4 **121 J1**
Queen Victoria St. EC4 **116 G10**
Queenhithe EC4 **117 J10**
Queens Head Yd. SE1 **121 K3**
Queen's Wk. SW1 **119 L3**
Queens Yd. WC1 **115 M5**
Queensberry Ms. W. SW7 **118 A8**
Queensberry Pl. SW7 **118 A8**
Queensberry Way SW7 **118 A8**
Queensbridge Rd. E2 **117 Q1**
Quick St. N1 **116 G1**
Quilp St. SE1 **121 H4**

R

Radnor Ms. W2 **114 B9**
Radnor Pl. W2 **114 C9**
Radnor St. EC1 **117 J3**
Railway App. SE1 **121 L3**
Railway St. N1 **116 A1**
Rainsford St. W2 **114 C8**
Ramillies Pl. W1 **115 L9**
Ramillies St. W1 **115 L9**
Rampayne St. SW1 **119 N10**
Randall Rd. SE11 **120 B9**
Randall Row SE11 **120 B9**
Ranelagh Gro. SW1 **119 H10**
Ranston St. NW1 **114 C6**
Raphael St. SW7 **118 E5**
Rathbone Pl. W1 **115 N7**
Rathbone St. W1 **115 M7**
Ravenscroft St. E2 **117 Q1**
Ravent Rd. SE11 **120 C8**
Ravey St. EC2 **117 M4**
Rawlings St. SW3 **118 E8**
Rawstorne Pl. EC1 **116 F2**
Rawstorne St. EC1 **116 F2**
Ray St. EC1 **116 E5**
Ray St. Bri. EC1 **116 E5**
Raymond Bldgs. WC1 **116 C6**
Red Lion Ct. EC4 **116 E9**
Red Lion Sq. WC1 **116 B7**
Red Lion St. WC1 **116 B6**

Red Lion Yd. W1 **119 H2**
Red Pl. W1 **114 G10**
Redchurch St. E2 **117 P4**
Redcross Way SE1 **121 J4**
Redhill St. NW1 **115 K2**
Redvers St. N1 **117 N2**
Reece Ms. SW7 **118 A8**
Reedworth St. SE11 **120 E9**
Reeves Ms. W1 **118 G1**
Regan Way N1 **117 M1**
Regency Pl. SW1 **119 P8**
Regency St. SW1 **119 P8**
Regent Pl. W1 **115 M10**
Regent Sq. WC1 **116 A3**
Regent St. SW1 **119 N1**
Regent St. W1 **115 K8**
Regents Pk. NW1 **114 E1**
Regents Pk. Est. NW1 **115 L3**
Regnart Bldgs. NW1 **115 M4**
Relton Ms. SW1 **118 D6**
Rembrandt Clo. SW1 **118 G9**
Remington St. N1 **116 G1**
Remnant St. WC2 **116 B8**
Renfrew Rd. SE11 **120 F8**
Rennie St. SE1 **120 F2**
Rephidim St. SE1 **121 L7**
Retford St. N1 **117 N1**
Rex Pl. W1 **118 H1**
Rhoda St. E2 **117 Q4**
Richards St. SW3 **118 D8**
Richardson's Ms. W1 **115 L5**
Richbell Pl. WC1 **116 B6**
Richmond Bldgs. W1 **115 N9**
Richmond Ms. W1 **115 N9**
Richmond Ter. SW1 **119 Q4**
Ridgmount Gdns. WC1 **115 N6**
Ridgmount Pl. WC1 **115 N6**
Ridgmount St. WC1 **115 N6**
Riding Ho. St. W1 **115 K7**
Riley Rd. SE1 **121 P6**
Ring, The W2 **114 C10**
Risborough St. SE1 **120 G4**
Rising Sun Ct. EC1 **116 G7**
River St. EC1 **116 D2**
Riverside Wk. SE1 **120 C2**
Rivington Pl. EC2 **117 N3**
Rivington St. EC2 **117 M3**
Robert Adam St. W1 **114 G8**
Robert Dashwood Way SE17
  120 H9
Robert St. NW1 **115 K3**
Robert St. WC2 **120 A1**
Roberts Ms. SW1 **118 G7**
Robert's Pl. EC1 **116 E4**
Rochelle St. E2 **117 P3**
Rochester Row SW1 **119 M8**
Rochester St. SW1 **119 N7**
Rochester Wk. SE1 **121 K2**
Rockingham Est. SE1 **121 H7**
Rockingham St. SE1 **120 H7**
Rocliffe St. N1 **116 G1**
Rodmarton St. W1 **114 F7**
Rodney Pl. SE17 **121 J8**
Rodney Rd. SE17 **121 J8**
Roger St. WC1 **116 C5**
Rolls Bldgs. EC4 **116 D8**
Rolls Pas. EC4 **116 D8**
Rolls Rd. SE1 **121 Q10**
Romilly St. W1 **115 N10**
Romney St. SW1 **119 Q7**
Rood La. EC3 **117 M10**
Ropemaker St. EC2 **117 K6**
Roper La. SE1 **121 N5**
Roscoe St. EC1 **117 J5**
Rose All. SE1 **121 J2**
Rose & Crown Ct. EC2 **117 H8**
Rose & Crown Yd. SW1 **119 M2**
Rose St. WC2 **115 Q10**
Rosebery Ave. EC1 **116 D4**
Rosebery Sq. EC1 **116 D5**
Rosemoor St. SW3 **118 E9**
Rosoman Pl. EC1 **116 E4**
Rosoman St. EC1 **116 E3**
Rossmore Rd. NW1 **114 D5**
Rotary St. SE1 **120 F6**
Rotherham Wk. SE1 **120 F3**
Rothsay St. SE1 **121 M6**
Rotten Row SW1 **118 E4**
Rotten Row SW7 **118 D4**
Roupell St. SE1 **120 E3**
Rowcross St. SE1 **121 Q10**
Royal Arc. W1 **119 L1**
Royal Ave. SW3 **118 E10**
Royal Ex. EC3 **117 L9**
Royal Ex. Ave. EC3 **117 L9**
Royal Ex. Bldgs. EC3 **117 L9**
Royal Mint Pl. E1 **117 Q10**
Royal Mint St. E1 **117 Q10**
Royal Opera Arc. SW1 **119 N2**
Royal St. SE1 **120 C6**
Royalty Ms. W1 **115 N9**
Rufus St. N1 **117 M3**
Rugby St. WC1 **116 B5**
Rupert St. W1 **115 N10**
Rupert St. W1 **115 N10**
Rushworth St. SE1 **120 G4**
Russell St. SW1 **119 M3**
Russell Sq. WC1 **115 Q5**
Russell St. WC2 **116 A10**
Russia Ct. EC2 **117 J9**
Russia Row EC2 **117 J9**
Rutherford St. SW1 **119 N8**

Rutland Gdns. SW7 **118 D5**
Rutland Gdns. Ms. SW7 **118 D5**
Rutland Gate SW7 **118 D5**
Rutland Gate Ms. SW7 **118 C5**
Rutland Ms. E. SW7 **118 C6**
Rutland Ms. S. SW7 **118 C6**
Rutland Pl. EC1 **116 G6**
Rutland St. SW7 **118 D6**
Ryder Ct. SW1 **119 M2**
Ryder St. SW1 **119 M2**
Ryder Yd. SW1 **119 M2**
Rysbrack St. SW3 **118 E6**

S

Sackville St. W1 **119 M1**
Saffron Hill EC1 **116 E6**
Saffron St. EC1 **116 E6**
Sage Way WC1 **116 B3**
Sail St. SE11 **120 C8**
St. Albans Ms. W2 **114 B6**
St. Albans St. SW1 **119 N1**
St. Alphage Gdns. EC2 **117 J7**
St. Andrew St. EC4 **116 E7**
St. Andrew's Hill EC4 **116 G10**
St. Andrews Pl. NW1 **115 K4**
St. Anne's Ct. W1 **115 N9**
St. Ann's La. SW1 **119 P6**
St. Ann's St. SW1 **119 P6**
St. Anselms Pl. W1 **114 A1**
St. Barnabas St. SW1 **119 H10**
St. Benet's Pl. EC3 **117 L10**
St. Botolph Row EC3 **117 P9**
St. Botolph St. EC3 **117 P8**
St. Bride St. EC4 **116 F8**
St. Bride's Pas. EC4 **116 F9**
St. Catherine's Ms. SW3 **118 E8**
St. Chad's Pl. WC1 **116 A2**
St. Chad's St. WC1 **116 A2**
St. Christopher's Pl. W1 **115 H8**
St. Clare St. EC3 **117 P9**
St. Clement's La. WC2 **116 C9**
St. Cross St. EC1 **116 E6**
St. Dunstan's All. EC3 **121 M1**
St. Dunstan's Hill EC3 **121 M1**
St. Dunstan's La. EC3 **121 M1**
St. Ermin's Hill SW1 **119 N6**
St. George St. W1 **115 K10**
St. Georges Circ. SE1 **120 F6**
St. George's Dr. SW1 **119 K9**
St. Georges Flds. W2 **114 D9**
St. Georges La. EC3 **117 L10**
St. Georges Rd. SE1 **120 E6**
St. Giles High St. WC2 **115 P9**
St. Giles Pas. WC2 **115 P9**
St. Helena St. WC1 **116 D3**
St. Helens Pl. EC3 **117 M8**
St. James's Ct. SW1 **119 M6**
St. James's Mkt. SW1 **119 N1**
St. James's Pk. SW1 **119 N6**
St. James's Pas. EC3 **117 N9**
St. James's Pl. SW1 **119 L3**
St. James's Sq. SW1 **119 M2**
St. James's Row EC1 **116 F4**
St. James's Wk. EC1 **116 F4**
St. John St. EC1 **116 F2**
St. Johns Est. N1 **117 L1**
St. John's Est. SE1 **121 P5**
St. John's La. EC1 **116 F5**
St. John's Path EC1 **116 F5**
St. John's Pl. EC1 **116 F5**
St. John's Sq. EC1 **116 F5**
St. John's Wd. Ct. NW8 **114 B3**
St. John's Wd. High St. NW8
  114 B1
St. John's Wd. Rd. NW8 **114 A4**
St. John's Wd. Ter. NW8 **114 B1**
St. Katharine's Way E1 **121 Q2**
St. Katherine's Row EC3 **117 N10**
St. Leonards Ct. N1 **117 L2**
St. Luke's Est. EC1 **117 K3**
St. Luke's St. SW3 **118 D10**
St. Margaret's Ct. SE1 **121 K3**
St. Margaret's St. SW1 **119 Q5**
St. Mark St. E1 **117 Q9**
St. Martin's Ct. WC2 **115 Q10**
St. Martin's La. WC2 **115 Q10**
St. Martin's le Grand EC1 **117 H8**
St. Martin's Pl. WC2 **119 P1**
St. Martin's St. WC2 **119 P1**
St. Mary at Hill EC3 **121 M1**
St. Mary Axe EC3 **117 M9**
St. Mary's Gdns. SE11 **120 E8**
St. Marys Mans. W2 **114 A6**
St. Marys Sq. W2 **114 A6**
St. Marys Ter. W2 **114 A6**
St. Mary's Wk. SE11 **120 E8**
St. Matthew St. SW1 **119 N7**
St. Michael's All. EC3 **117 L9**
St. Michaels St. W2 **114 B8**
St. Mildred's Ct. EC2 **117 K9**
St. Olaves Ct. EC2 **117 Q2**
St. Olave's Est. SE1 **121 N4**
St. Olaves Gdns. SE11 **120 D8**
St. Oswulf St. SW1 **119 P9**
St. Paul's Chyd. EC4 **116 G9**
St. Peter's All. EC3 **117 L9**
St. Saviour's Est. SE1 **121 P6**
St. Stephens Row EC4 **117 K10**
St. Swithin's La. EC4 **117 K10**
St. Thomas St. SE1 **121 L3**

St. Vincent St. W1 **114 H7**
Salamanca Pl. SE11 **120 B9**
Salamanca St. SE11 **120 B9**
Sale Pl. W2 **114 C7**
Salisbury Clo. SE17 **121 K8**
Salisbury Ct. EC4 **116 E9**
Salisbury Pl. W1 **114 E6**
Salisbury Sq. EC4 **116 E9**
Salisbury St. NW8 **114 C5**
Salters Hall Ct. EC4 **117 K10**
Samford St. NW8 **114 C5**
Samuel Lewis Trust Dws. SW3
  118 C9
Sancroft St. SE11 **120 C10**
Sanctuary, The SW1 **119 P6**
Sanctuary St. SE1 **121 J5**
Sandell St. SE1 **120 D4**
Sandland St. WC1 **116 C7**
Sandwich St. WC1 **115 Q3**
Sandys Row E1 **117 N7**
Sans Wk. EC1 **116 E4**
Saracen's Head Yd. EC3 **117 P9**
Sarah St. N1 **117 N2**
Sardinia St. WC2 **116 B9**
Satchwell Rd. E2 **117 Q3**
Satchwell St. E2 **117 Q3**
Savage Gdns. EC3 **117 N10**
Savile Row W1 **115 L10**
Savoy Bldgs. WC2 **120 B1**
Savoy Ct. WC2 **120 A1**
Savoy Hill WC2 **120 B1**
Savoy Pl. WC2 **120 A1**
Savoy Row WC2 **120 B1**
Savoy St. WC2 **120 B1**
Savoy Steps WC2 **120 B1**
Savoy Way WC2 **120 B1**
Sawyer St. SE1 **120 H4**
Scala St. W1 **115 M6**
Scarborough St. E1 **117 Q9**
Scawfell St. E2 **117 Q1**
Sclater St. E1 **117 P4**
Scoresby St. SE1 **120 F3**
Scotland Pl. SW1 **119 Q3**
Scotswood St. EC1 **116 E4**
Scott Ellis Gdns. NW8 **114 A3**
Scott's Yd EC4 **117 K10**
Scovell Cres. SE1 **121 H5**
Scovell Rd. SE1 **120 H5**
Scrutton St. EC2 **117 M5**
Seacoal La. EC4 **116 F9**
Seaford St. WC1 **116 A3**
Seaforth Pl. SW1 **119 M6**
Searles Rd. SE1 **121 L8**
Seaton Clo. SE11 **120 E10**
Seaton Pl. NW1 **115 L4**
Sebastian St. EC1 **116 G3**
Secker St. SE1 **120 D3**
Sedan Way SE17 **121 M10**
Sedding St. SW1 **118 G8**
Seddon St. WC1 **116 C3**
Sedley Pl. W1 **115 J9**
Seething La. EC3 **117 N10**
Sekforde St. EC1 **116 F5**
Sellon Ms. SE11 **120 C9**
Selwood Pl. SW7 **118 A10**
Selwood Ter. SW7 **118 A10**
Semley Pl. SW1 **119 H9**
Serjeants Inn EC4 **116 E9**
Serle St. WC2 **116 C8**
Serpentine Rd. W2 **118 E3**
Setchell Rd. SE1 **121 P8**
Setchell Way SE1 **121 P8**
Seville St. SW1 **118 F5**
Seward St. EC1 **116 G3**
Seymour Ms. W1 **114 G8**
Seymour Pl. W1 **114 D6**
Seymour St. W1 **114 E9**
Seymour St. W2 **114 E9**
Shacklewell St. E2 **117 Q4**
Shad Thames SE1 **121 P3**
Shaftesbury Ave. W1 **115 N10**
Shaftesbury Ave. WC2 **119 N1**
Shaftesbury St. N1 **117 J1**
Shafto Ms. SW1 **118 E7**
Shand St. SE1 **121 N3**
Shavers Pl. SW1 **119 N1**
Sheffield St. WC2 **116 B9**
Shelton St. WC2 **115 Q9**
Shenfield St. N1 **117 N1**
Shepherd Mkt. W1 **119 J3**
Shepherd St. W1 **119 J3**
Shepherdess Pl. N1 **117 J2**
Shepherdess Wk. N1 **117 J1**
Shepherds Pl. W1 **114 G10**
Sheraton St. W1 **115 N9**
Sherborne La. EC4 **117 K10**
Sherlock Ms. W1 **114 G6**
Sherwood St. W1 **115 M10**
Shillibeer Pl. W1 **114 D7**
Ship and Mermaid Row SE1
  121 L4
Ship Tavern Pas. EC3 **117 M10**
Shipton St. E2 **117 Q3**
Shoe La. EC4 **116 E8**
Shoreditch High St. E1 **117 N5**
Shorncliffe Rd. SE1 **121 P10**
Short St. SE1 **120 E4**
Shorter St. E1 **117 Q10**
Shorts Gdns. WC2 **115 Q9**
Shouldham St. W1 **114 D7**
Shropshire Pl. WC1 **115 M5**
Shroton St. NW1 **114 C6**

Sicilian Ave. WC1 **116 A7**
Siddons La. NW1 **114 F5**
Sidford Pl. SE1 **120 C7**
Sidmouth St. WC1 **116 A3**
Sidney Gro. EC1 **116 F1**
Silbury St. N1 **117 K2**
Silex St. SE1 **120 G5**
Silk St. EC2 **117 J6**
Silver Pl. W1 **115 M10**
Silvester St. SE1 **121 K5**
Simla Ho. SE1 **121 L5**
Singer St. EC2 **117 L3**
Sise La. EC4 **117 K9**
Sivill Ho. E2 **117 Q2**
Skinner Pl. SW1 **118 G9**
Skinner St. EC1 **116 E3**
Skinners La. EC4 **117 J10**
Skipton St. SE1 **120 G7**
Slingsby Pl. WC2 **115 Q10**
Sloane Ave. SW3 **118 D9**
Sloane Ct. E. SW3 **118 G10**
Sloane Ct. W. SW3 **118 G10**
Sloane Gdns. SW1 **118 G9**
Sloane Sq. SW1 **118 F9**
Sloane St. SW1 **118 F6**
Sloane Ter. SW1 **118 F8**
Smallbrook Ms. W2 **114 A9**
Smart's Pl. WC2 **116 A8**
Smith Sq. SW1 **119 Q7**
Smith St. SW3 **118 E10**
Smithfield St. EC1 **116 F7**
Smith's Ct. W1 **115 M10**
Snow Hill EC1 **116 F7**
Snow Hill Ct. EC1 **116 G8**
Snowden St. EC2 **117 M5**
Snowsfields SE1 **121 L4**
Soho Sq. W1 **115 N8**
Soho St. W1 **115 N8**
Soley Ms. WC1 **116 D2**
Somers Cres. W2 **114 C9**
Somers Ms. W2 **114 C9**
South Audley St. W1 **118 H1**
South Carriage Dr. SW7 **118 C4**
South Cres. WC1 **115 N7**
South Eaton Pl. SW1 **118 H8**
South Molton La. W1 **115 J9**
South Molton St. W1 **115 J9**
South Par. SW3 **118 B10**
South Pl. EC2 **117 L7**
South Pl. Ms. EC2 **117 L7**
South Sq. WC1 **116 D7**
South St. W1 **118 H2**
South Tenter St. E1 **117 Q9**
South Ter. SW7 **118 C8**
South Wf. Rd. W2 **114 A8**
Southall Pl. SE1 **121 K5**
Southampton Bldgs. WC1 **116 D7**
Southampton Pl. WC1 **116 A7**
Southampton Row WC1 **116 A6**
Southampton St. WC2 **116 A10**
Southwark Bri. EC4 **121 J1**
Southwark Bri. SE1 **121 J1**
Southwark Bri. Rd. SE1 **120 H5**
Southwark Gro. SE1 **120 H3**
Southwark Pk. Rd. SE16 **121 Q8**
Southwark St. SE1 **120 G2**
Southwick Ms. W2 **114 B8**
Southwick Pl. W2 **114 C9**
Southwick St. W2 **114 C8**
Spa Grn. Est. EC1 **116 E2**
Spa Rd. SE16 **121 P7**
Spafield St. EC1 **116 D4**
Spanish Pl. W1 **114 H8**
Speedy Pl. WC1 **115 Q3**
Spencer St. EC1 **116 F3**
Spenser St. SW1 **119 M6**
Spital Sq. E1 **117 N6**
Spital Yd. E1 **117 N6**
Spitalfields Mkt. E1 **117 P6**
Sprimont Pl. SW3 **118 E10**
Spring Gdns. SW1 **119 P2**
Spring Ms. W1 **114 F6**
Spring St. W2 **114 A9**
Spur Rd. SW1 **119 L5**
Spurgeon St. SE1 **121 K7**
Stable Yd. SW1 **119 L4**
Stable Yd. Rd. SW1 **119 M4**
Stables Way SE11 **120 D10**
Stacey St. WC2 **115 P9**
Stackhouse St. SW3 **118 E6**
Staff St. EC1 **117 L3**
Stafford Pl. SW1 **119 L6**
Stafford St. W1 **119 L2**
Stag Pl. SW1 **119 L6**
Stainer St. SE1 **121 L3**
Staining La. EC2 **117 J8**
Stalbridge St. NW1 **114 D6**
Stamford St. SE1 **120 D3**
Stamp Pl. E2 **117 P2**
Standard Pl. EC2 **117 N3**
Stanford Pl. SE17 **121 M9**
Stanford St. SW1 **119 N9**
Stanhope Gate W1 **118 H2**
Stanhope Par. NW1 **115 L2**
Stanhope Pl. W2 **114 E9**
Stanhope Row W1 **119 J3**
Stanhope St. NW1 **115 L2**
Stanhope Ter. W2 **114 B10**
Stanley Ms. SW1 **115 Q1**
Stanworth St. SE1 **121 P5**
Staple Inn Bldgs. WC1 **116 D7**
Staple St. SE1 **121 L5**

Star St. W2 **114 B8**
Star Yd. WC2 **116 D8**
Starcross St. NW1 **115 M3**
Stead St. SE17 **121 K9**
Stedham Pl. WC1 **115 Q8**
Steedman St. SE17 **120 H9**
Stephen Ms. W1 **115 N7**
Stephen St. W1 **115 N7**
Stephenson Way NW1 **115 M4**
Sterling St. SW7 **118 D5**
Sterry St. SE1 **121 K5**
Stevens St. SE1 **121 N6**
Steward St. E1 **117 N6**
Stewart's Gro. SW3 **118 C10**
Stillington St. SW1 **119 M8**
Stone Bldgs. WC2 **116 C7**
Stone Ho. Ct. SE1 **117 N8**
Stonecutter St. EC4 **116 F8**
Stones End St. SE1 **121 H5**
Stoney La. E1 **117 P8**
Stoney St. SE1 **121 K2**
Store St. W1 **115 N7**
Storey's Gate SW1 **119 P5**
Stothard Pl. EC2 **117 N6**
Stoughton Clo. SE11 **120 C9**
Stourcliffe St. W1 **114 E9**
Strand WC2 **119 Q1**
Strand La. WC2 **116 C10**
Stratford Pl. W1 **115 J9**
Strathearn Pl. W2 **114 C10**
Stratton St. W1 **119 K2**
Streatham St. WC1 **115 Q8**
Strouts Pl. E2 **117 P2**
Strutton Grd. SW1 **119 N6**
Strype St. E1 **117 P7**
Studio Pl. SW1 **118 F5**
Studland SE17 **121 K10**
Stukeley St. WC2 **116 A8**
Sturge St. SE1 **120 H4**
Sturt St. N1 **117 J1**
Sudeley St. N1 **116 G1**
Sudrey St. SE1 **120 H5**
Suffolk La. EC4 **117 K10**
Suffolk Pl. SW1 **119 P2**
Suffolk St. SW1 **119 P1**
Sugar Bakers Ct. EC3 **117 N9**
Sullivan Rd. SE11 **120 E8**
Summers St. EC1 **116 D5**
Sumner Pl. SW7 **118 B9**
Sumner Pl. Ms. SW7 **118 B9**
Sumner St. SE1 **120 G2**
Sun Ct. EC3 **117 L9**
Sun St. EC2 **117 L6**
Sun St. Pas. EC2 **117 M7**
Surrey Lo. SE1 **120 D7**
Surrey Row SE1 **120 F4**
Surrey Sq. SE17 **121 M10**
Surrey St. WC2 **116 C10**
Surrey Ter. SE17 **121 N10**
Sussex Gdns. W2 **114 A10**
Sussex Ms. E. W2 **114 B9**
Sussex Ms. W. W2 **114 B10**
Sussex Pl. NW1 **114 E3**
Sussex Pl. W2 **114 B9**
Sussex Sq. W2 **114 B10**
Sutherland Row SW1 **119 K10**
Sutherland St. SW1 **119 J10**
Sutton Est. SW3 **118 D10**
Sutton Row W1 **115 P8**
Sutton's Way EC1 **117 J5**
Swallow Pas. W1 **115 K9**
Swallow Pl. W1 **115 K9**
Swallow St. W1 **119 M1**
Swan La. EC4 **121 K1**
Swan Mead SE1 **121 M7**
Swan St. SE1 **121 J6**
Swanfield St. E2 **117 P3**
Sweeney Cres. SE1 **121 Q5**
Swinton Pl. WC1 **116 B2**
Swinton St. WC1 **116 B2**
Sycamore St. EC1 **116 H5**
Sydney Clo. SW3 **118 B9**
Sydney Ms. SW3 **118 B9**
Sydney Pl. SW7 **118 B9**
Sydney St. SW3 **118 C10**
Symons St. SW3 **118 F9**

T
Tabard Gdn. Est. SE1 **121 L5**
Tabard St. SE1 **121 K5**
Tabernacle St. EC2 **117 L5**
Tachbrook Ms. SW1 **119 L8**
Tachbrook St. SW1 **119 M9**
Talbot Ct. EC3 **117 L10**
Talbot Sq. W2 **114 B9**
Talbot Yd. SE1 **121 K3**
Tallis St. EC4 **116 E10**
Tankerton St. WC1 **116 A3**
Tanner St. SE1 **121 N5**
Tanswell Est. SE1 **120 E5**
Tanswell St. SE1 **120 D5**
Taplow SE17 **121 L10**
Taplow St. N1 **117 J1**
Tarn St. SE1 **120 H7**
Tarrant Pl. W1 **114 E7**
Tatum St. SE17 **121 L9**
Taunton Ms. NW1 **114 E5**
Taunton Pl. NW1 **114 E4**
Tavistock Ms. W2 **114 A8**
Tavistock Pl. WC1 **115 Q4**
Tavistock Sq. WC1 **115 P4**
Tavistock St. WC2 **116 A10**
Taviton St. WC1 **115 N4**

Tavy Clo. SE11 **120 E10**
Telegraph St. EC2 **117 K8**
Temple EC4 **116 D10**
Temple Ave. EC4 **116 E10**
Temple La. EC4 **116 E9**
Temple Pl. WC2 **116 C10**
Temple W. Ms. SE11 **120 F7**
Tenison Ct. W1 **115 L10**
Tenison Way SE1 **120 C3**
Tennis St. SE1 **121 K4**
Tenter Grd. E1 **117 P7**
Tenterden St. W1 **115 K9**
Thanet St. WC1 **115 Q3**
Thavies Inn EC1 **116 E8**
Thayer St. W1 **114 H7**
Theed St. SE1 **120 E3**
Theobald St. SE1 **121 K7**
Theobald's Rd. WC1 **116 A7**
Theseus Wk. N1 **116 G1**
Thirleby Rd. SW1 **119 M7**
Thomas Doyle St. SE1 **120 G6**
Thoresby St. N1 **117 J2**
Thorndike St. SW1 **119 N9**
Thorney St. SW1 **119 Q8**
Thornhaugh Ms. WC1 **115 P5**
Thornhaugh St. WC1 **115 P6**
Thornton Pl. W1 **114 E6**
Thrale St. SE1 **121 J3**
Thrawl St. E1 **117 Q7**
Threadneedle St. EC2 **117 L9**
Three Cups Yd. WC1 **116 C7**
Three Kings Yd. W1 **115 J10**
Three Oak La. SE1 **121 P4**
Throgmorton Ave. EC2 **117 L8**
Throgmorton St. EC2 **117 L8**
Thrush St. SE17 **120 H10**
Thurloe Clo. SW7 **118 C8**
Thurloe Pl. SW7 **118 B8**
Thurloe Pl. Ms. SW7 **118 B8**
Thurloe Sq. SW7 **118 C8**
Thurloe St. SW7 **118 B8**
Thurlow St. SE17 **121 L10**
Tilney Ct. EC1 **117 J4**
Tilney St. W1 **119 H2**
Timber St. EC1 **117 H4**
Tinworth St. SE11 **120 A10**
Tisbury Ct. W1 **115 N10**
Tisdall Pl. SE17 **121 L9**
Titchborne Row W2 **114 D9**
Tiverton St. SE1 **120 H6**
Tokenhouse Yd. EC2 **117 K8**
Tolmers Sq. NW1 **115 M4**
Tomlinson Clo. E2 **117 Q3**
Tompion St. EC1 **116 F3**
Tonbridge St. WC1 **115 Q2**
Tonbridge Wk. WC1 **115 Q2**
Took's Ct. EC4 **116 D8**
Tooley St. SE1 **121 L2**
Topham St. EC1 **116 D4**
Torrens St. N1 **116 E1**
Torrington Pl. WC1 **115 M6**
Torrington Sq. WC1 **115 P5**
Tothill St. SW1 **119 N5**
Tottenham Ct. Rd. W1 **115 M5**
Tottenham Ms. W1 **115 M6**
Tottenham St. W1 **115 M7**
Toulmin St. SE1 **121 H5**
Tower Bri. E1 **121 P3**
Tower Bri. SE1 **121 P3**
Tower Bri. App. E1 **121 P2**
Tower Bri. Rd. SE1 **121 M7**
Tower Ct. WC2 **115 Q9**
Tower Hill EC3 **121 P1**
Tower Pl. EC3 **121 N1**
Tower Royal EC4 **117 J10**
Tower St. WC2 **115 P9**
Townley St. SE17 **121 K10**
Townsend St. SE17 **121 M8**
Toynbee St. E1 **117 P7**
Trafalgar Sq. WC2 **119 P2**
Trafalgar St. SE17 **121 K10**
Transept St. NW1 **114 D7**
Trebeck St. W1 **119 J2**
Tresham Cres. NW8 **114 C4**
Treveris St. SE1 **120 G3**
Trevor Pl. SW7 **118 D5**
Trevor Sq. SW7 **118 E5**
Trevor St. SW7 **118 D5**
Trinity Ch. Sq. SE1 **121 J6**
Trinity Sq. EC3 **121 N1**
Trinity St. SE1 **121 J5**
Trio Pl. SE1 **121 J5**
Triton Sq. NW1 **115 L4**
Trump St. EC2 **117 J9**
Trundle St. SE1 **121 H4**
Tryon St. SW3 **118 E10**
Tudor Pl. W1 **115 N8**
Tudor St. EC4 **116 E10**
Tufton St. SW1 **120 A7**
Turk's Head Yd. EC1 **116 F6**
Turks Row SW3 **118 F10**
Turnagain La. EC4 **116 F8**
Turnmill St. EC1 **116 E5**
Turnpike Ho. EC1 **116 G3**
Turquand St. SE17 **121 J9**
Turville St. E2 **117 Q4**
Tweezer's All. WC2 **116 D10**
Twyford Pl. WC2 **116 B8**
Tyburn Way W1 **114 F10**
Tyers Est. SE1 **121 M4**
Tyers Gate SE1 **121 M5**

Tyler's Ct. W1 **115 N9**
Tyne St. E1 **117 Q8**
Tysoe St. EC1 **116 D3**
Tyssen St. N1 **117 N1**

U
Udall St. SW1 **119 M9**
Ufford St. SE1 **120 E4**
Ulster Pl. NW1 **115 J5**
Ulster Ter. NW1 **115 J4**
Undershaft EC3 **117 M9**
Underwood Row N1 **117 J2**
Underwood St. N1 **117 J2**
Union Ct. SE1 **117 M8**
Union St. SE1 **120 G3**
Union Wk. E2 **117 N2**
University St. WC1 **115 M5**
Unwin Rd. SW7 **118 A6**
Upnor Way SE17 **121 N10**
Upper Belgrave St. SW1 **119 H6**
Upper Berkeley St. W1 **114 E9**
Upper Brook St. W1 **118 G1**
Upper Grosvenor St. W1 **118 G1**
Upper Grd. SE1 **120 D2**
Upper Harley St. NW1 **115 H5**
Upper James St. W1 **115 M10**
Upper John St. W1 **115 M10**
Upper Marsh SE1 **120 C6**
Upper Montagu St. W1 **114 E6**
Upper St. Martin's La. WC2 **115 Q10**
Upper Tachbrook St. SW1 **119 M8**
Upper Thames St. EC4 **116 G10**
Upper Wimpole St. W1 **115 H6**
Upper Woburn Pl. WC1 **115 P3**

V
Valentine Pl. SE1 **120 F4**
Valentine Row SE1 **120 F5**
Vandon Pas. SW1 **119 M6**
Vandon St. SW1 **119 M6**
Vandy St. EC2 **117 M5**
Vane St. SW1 **119 M8**
Varndell St. NW1 **115 L2**
Vauban Est. SE16 **121 Q7**
Vauban St. SE16 **121 Q7**
Vauxhall Bri. Rd. SW1 **119 M8**
Vauxhall Wk. SE11 **120 B10**
Venables St. NW8 **114 B5**
Vere St. W1 **115 J9**
Vernon Pl. WC1 **116 A7**
Vernon Ri. WC1 **116 C2**
Vernon Sq. WC1 **116 C2**
Verulam Bldgs. WC1 **116 C6**
Verulam St. WC1 **116 D6**
Vestry St. N1 **117 K2**
Victoria Ave. EC2 **117 N7**
Victoria Embk. EC4 **116 D10**
Victoria Embk. SW1 **120 A4**
Victoria Embk. WC2 **120 C1**
Victoria Sq. SW1 **119 K6**
Victoria Sta. SW1 **119 K8**
Victoria St. SW1 **119 L7**
Victory Pl. SE17 **121 J8**
Vigo St. W1 **119 L1**
Villiers St. WC2 **120 A2**
Vince St. EC1 **117 L3**
Vincent Sq. SW1 **119 N8**
Vincent St. SW1 **119 N8**
Vine Hill EC1 **116 D5**
Vine La. SE1 **121 N3**
Vine St. EC3 **117 P9**
Vine St. W1 **119 M1**
Vine St. Bri. EC1 **116 E5**
Vine Yd. SE1 **121 J5**
Vinegar Yd. SE1 **121 M4**
Vineyard Wk. EC1 **116 D4**
Vintners Pl. EC4 **117 J10**
Virgil Pl. W1 **114 E7**
Virgil St. SE1 **120 C6**
Virginia Rd. E2 **117 P3**
Viscount St. EC1 **117 H6**

W
Wadding St. SE17 **121 K9**
Waithman St. EC4 **116 F9**
Wakefield Ms. WC1 **116 A3**
Wakefield St. WC1 **116 A3**
Wakley St. EC1 **116 F2**
Walbrook EC4 **117 K10**
Walcorde Ave. SE17 **121 J9**
Walcot Sq. SE11 **120 E8**
Walcott St. SW1 **119 M8**
Walkers Ct. W1 **115 N10**
Wallis All. SE1 **121 J5**
Walmer Pl. W1 **114 E6**
Walmer St. W1 **114 E6**
Walnut Tree Wk. SE11 **120 D8**
Walpole St. SW3 **118 E10**
Walton Pl. SW3 **118 E6**
Walton St. SW3 **118 D8**
Walworth Rd. SE1 **121 H9**
Walworth Rd. SE17 **120 H9**
Wansey St. SE17 **121 J9**
Wardens Gro. SE1 **120 H3**
Wardour Ms. W1 **115 M9**
Wardour St. W1 **115 M8**
Wardrobe Pl. EC4 **116 G9**
Wardrobe Ter. EC4 **116 G10**
Warner St. EC1 **116 D5**
Warner Yd. EC1 **116 D5**
Warren Ms. W1 **115 L5**

Warren St. W1 **115 K5**
Warwick Ct. WC1 **116 C7**
Warwick Ho. St. SW1 **119 P2**
Warwick La. EC4 **116 G9**
Warwick Pl. N. SW1 **119 L9**
Warwick Row SW1 **119 K6**
Warwick Sq. EC4 **116 G8**
Warwick Sq. SW1 **119 L10**
Warwick Sq. Ms. SW1 **119 N9**
Warwick St. W1 **115 M10**
Warwick Way SW1 **119 K10**
Warwick Yd. EC2 **117 J5**
Water St. WC2 **116 C10**
Watergate EC4 **116 F10**
Watergate Wk. WC2 **120 A1**
Waterloo Bri. SE1 **120 B1**
Waterloo Bri. WC2 **120 B1**
Waterloo Pl. SW1 **119 N2**
Waterloo Rd. SE1 **120 D4**
Waterson St. E2 **117 N2**
Watling Ct. EC4 **117 J9**
Watling St. EC4 **117 H9**
Watson Ms. W1 **114 D7**
Watts Way SW7 **118 B6**
Waverton St. W1 **119 H1**
Webb St. SE1 **121 M7**
Webber Row SE1 **120 E5**
Webber St. SE1 **120 F5**
Wedgwood Ms. W1 **115 P9**
Weighouse St. W1 **115 H9**
Weir's Pas. NW1 **115 P2**
Welbeck St. W1 **115 H7**
Welbeck Way W1 **115 J8**
Well Ct. EC4 **117 J9**
Weller St. SE1 **121 H4**
Wellers Ct. NW1 **115 Q1**
Wellesley Pl. NW1 **115 N3**
Wellesley Ter. N1 **117 J2**
Wellington Ct. NW8 **114 A1**
Wellington Pl. NW8 **114 B2**
Wellington Row E2 **117 Q2**
Wellington Sq. SW3 **118 E10**
Wellington St. WC2 **116 A10**
Wells Ms. W1 **115 M7**
Wells Sq. WC1 **116 B3**
Wells St. W1 **115 L7**
Wells Way SW7 **118 A6**
Wendover SE17 **121 M10**
Wenlock Ct. N1 **117 L1**
Wenlock Rd. N1 **117 H1**
Wenlock St. N1 **117 J1**
Wentworth St. E1 **117 P8**
Werrington St. NW1 **115 M1**
Wesley Clo. SE17 **120 G9**
Wesley St. W1 **115 H7**
West Carriage Dr. W2 **118 C1**
West Cen. St. WC1 **115 Q8**
West Eaton Pl. SW1 **118 G8**
West Eaton Pl. Ms. SW1 **118 G7**
West Halkin St. SW1 **118 G6**
West Harding St. EC4 **116 E8**
West Ms. SW1 **119 L9**
West Poultry Ave. EC1 **116 F7**
West Smithfield EC1 **116 F7**
West Sq. SE11 **120 F7**
West St. WC2 **115 P10**
West Tenter St. E1 **117 Q9**
West Warwick Pl. SW1 **119 L9**
Westbourne Cres. W2 **114 A10**
Westbourne Cres. Ms. W2 **114 A10**
Westbourne St. W2 **114 A10**
Westland Pl. N1 **117 K2**
Westminster Bri. SE1 **120 A5**
Westminster Bri. SW1 **120 A5**
Westminster Bri. Rd. SE1 **120 C5**
Westminster Cathedral Piazza SW1 **119 L7**
Westmoreland St. W1 **115 H7**
Weston Ri. WC1 **116 C1**
Weston St. SE1 **121 L4**
Weymouth Ms. W1 **115 J6**
Weymouth St. W1 **115 H7**
Whalebone Ct. EC2 **117 L8**
Wharf Rd. N1 **117 H1**
Wharton St. WC1 **116 C3**
Wheatley St. W1 **115 H7**
Wheler St. E1 **117 P5**
Whetstone Pk. WC2 **116 B8**
Whichcote St. SE1 **120 B3**
Whidborne St. WC1 **116 A3**
Whiskin St. EC1 **116 F3**
Whitby St. E1 **117 P4**
Whitcomb St. WC2 **119 P1**
White Hart St. SE11 **120 E8**
White Hart Yd. SE1 **121 K3**
White Horse St. W1 **119 K3**
White Kennet St. E1 **117 N8**
White Lion Hill EC4 **116 G10**
White Lion St. N1 **116 D1**
White Lion Yd. W1 **115 J10**
Whitechapel High St. E1 **117 Q8**
Whitecross Pl. EC2 **117 L6**
Whitecross St. EC1 **117 J4**
Whitecross St. EC2 **117 J6**
Whitefriars St. EC4 **116 E9**
Whitehall SW1 **119 Q2**
Whitehall Ct. SW1 **120 A3**
Whitehall Gdns. SW1 **119 Q3**
Whitehall Pl. E7 **119 Q3**
Whitehaven St. NW8 **114 C5**

Whitehead's Gro. SW3 **118 D10**
Whitehorse Rd. SE1 **120 E6**
Whites Grds. SE1 **121 N5**
Whites Grds. Est. SE1 **121 N4**
White's Row E1 **117 P7**
Whitfield Pl. W1 **115 L5**
Whitfield St. W1 **115 L5**
Whitgift St. SE11 **120 B8**
Whittaker St. SW1 **118 G9**
Whittington Ave. EC3 **117 M9**
Whittlesey St. SE1 **120 E3**
Wickham St. SE11 **120 B10**
Wicklow St. WC1 **116 B2**
Widegate St. E1 **117 N7**
Wigmore Pl. W1 **115 J8**
Wigmore St. W1 **114 G9**
Wilbraham Pl. SW1 **118 F8**
Wilcox Pl. SW1 **119 M7**
Wild Ct. WC2 **116 B8**
Wild St. WC2 **116 A9**
Wild's Rents SE1 **121 M6**
Wilfred St. SW1 **119 L6**
Wilkes St. E1 **117 Q6**
Wilks Pl. N1 **117 N1**
William IV St. WC2 **119 Q1**
William Ms. SW1 **118 F5**
William Rd. NW1 **115 L3**
William St. SW1 **118 F5**
Willoughby St. WC1 **115 Q7**
Willow Pl. SW1 **119 M8**
Willow St. EC2 **117 M4**
Willow Wk. SE1 **121 N8**
Wilmington Sq. WC1 **116 D3**
Wilmington St. WC1 **116 D3**
Wilson St. EC2 **117 L6**
Wilton Cres. SW1 **118 G5**
Wilton Ms. SW1 **119 H6**
Wilton Pl. SW1 **118 G5**
Wilton Rd. SW1 **119 K7**
Wilton Row SW1 **118 G5**
Wilton St. SW1 **119 J6**
Wilton Ter. SW1 **118 G6**
Wiltshire Clo. SW3 **118 E9**
Wimpole Ms. W1 **115 J6**
Wimpole St. W1 **115 J7**
Winchester Clo. SE17 **120 G9**
Winchester Sq. SE1 **121 K2**
Winchester St. SW1 **119 K10**
Winchester Wk. SE1 **121 K2**
Wincott St. SE11 **120 E9**
Windmill St. W1 **115 N7**
Windmill Wk. SE1 **120 E3**
Windsor Pl. SW1 **119 M7**
Windsor Ter. N1 **117 J2**
Wine Office Ct. EC4 **116 E9**
Winnett St. W1 **115 N10**
Winsland Ms. W2 **114 A8**
Winsland St. W2 **114 A8**
Winsley St. W1 **115 L8**
Woburn Pl. WC1 **115 P4**
Woburn Sq. WC1 **115 P5**
Woburn Wk. WC1 **115 P3**
Wollaston Clo. SE1 **120 H8**
Wolseley St. SE1 **121 Q5**
Wolverton SE17 **121 M10**
Wood St. EC2 **117 J9**
Woodbridge St. EC1 **116 F4**
Woods Ms. W1 **114 G10**
Woods Pl. SE1 **121 N7**
Woodseer St. E1 **117 Q6**
Woodstock Ms. W1 **115 H7**
Woodstock St. W1 **115 J9**
Wootton St. SE1 **120 E3**
Worcester Pl. EC4 **117 J10**
Wordsworth Rd. SE1 **121 P9**
Worgan St. SE11 **120 B10**
World Trade Cen. E1 **121 Q1**
Wormwood St. EC2 **117 M8**
Worship St. EC2 **117 L5**
Wren St. WC1 **116 C4**
Wybert St. NW1 **115 L4**
Wyclif St. EC1 **116 F3**
Wyndham Ms. W1 **114 E7**
Wyndham Pl. W1 **114 E7**
Wyndham St. W1 **114 E6**
Wyndham Yd. W1 **114 E7**
Wynyard Ter. SE11 **120 C10**
Wynyatt St. EC1 **116 F3**
Wythburn Pl. W1 **114 E9**

Y
Yardley St. WC1 **116 D3**
Yarmouth Pl. W1 **119 J3**
Yeoman's Row SW3 **118 D7**
Yeomans Yd. E1 **117 Q10**
York Bri. NW1 **114 G4**
York Bldgs. WC2 **120 A1**
York Gate NW1 **114 G5**
York Pl. WC2 **120 A1**
York Rd. SE1 **120 C4**
York St. W1 **114 E7**
York Ter. E. NW1 **114 H5**
York Ter. W. NW1 **114 G5**
Yorkshire Grey Yd. WC1 **116 B7**
Young's Bldgs. EC1 **117 J4**

Z
Zoar St. SE1 **120 H2**

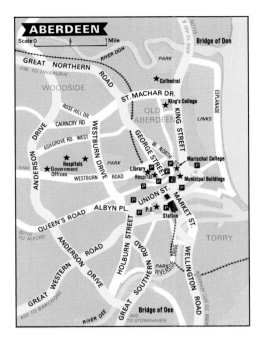

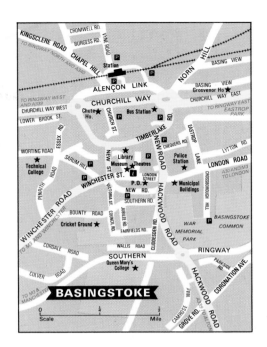

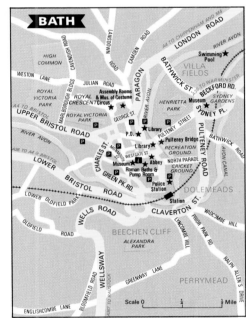

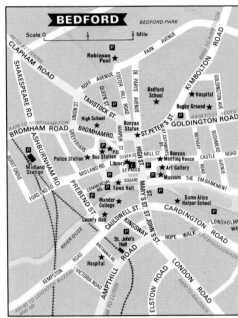

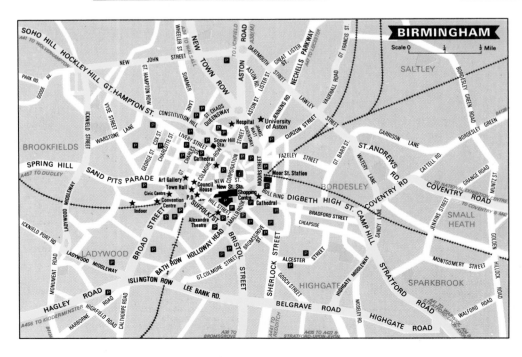

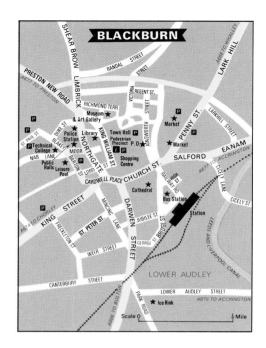

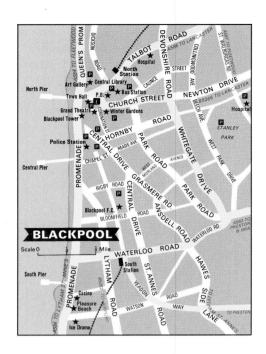

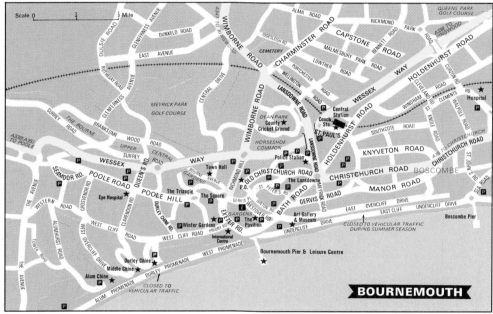

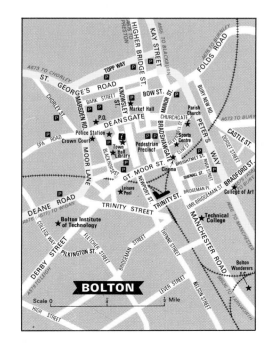

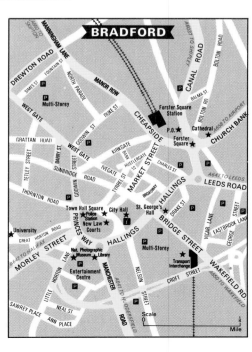

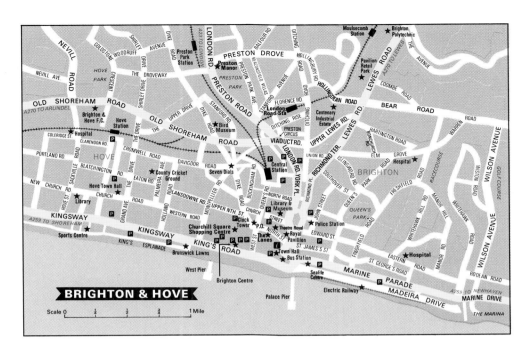

BRIGHTON & HOVE

Scale 0 ¼ ½ ¾ 1 Mile

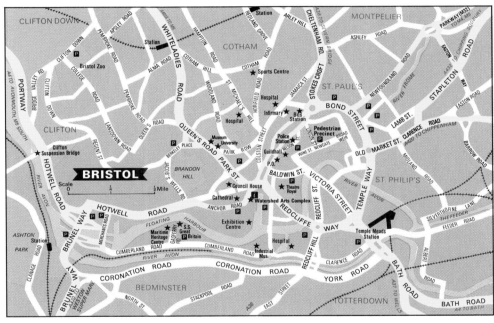

BRISTOL

Scale 0 ¼ ½ Mile

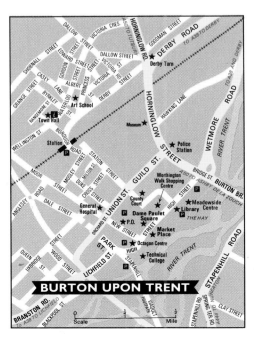

BURTON UPON TRENT

Scale 0 ½ Mile

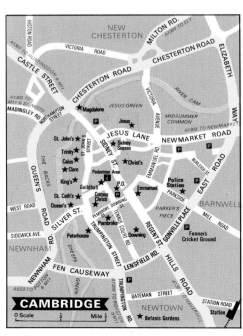

CAMBRIDGE

0 Scale ¼ ½ Mile

Town Plans

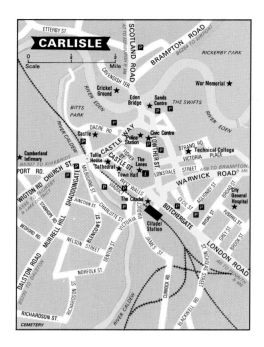

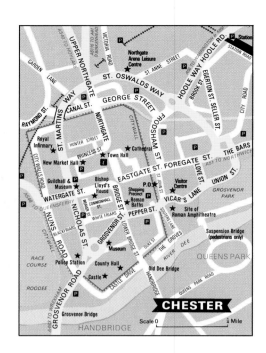

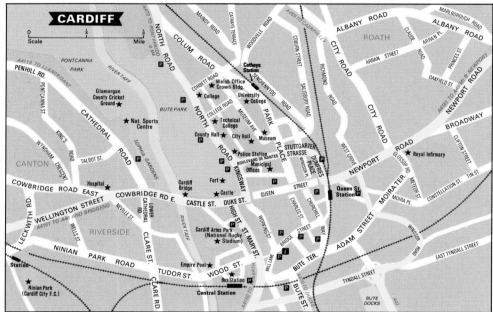

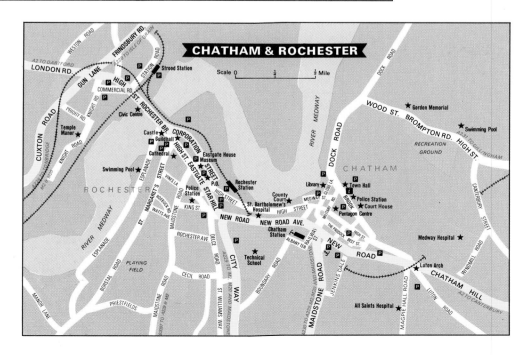

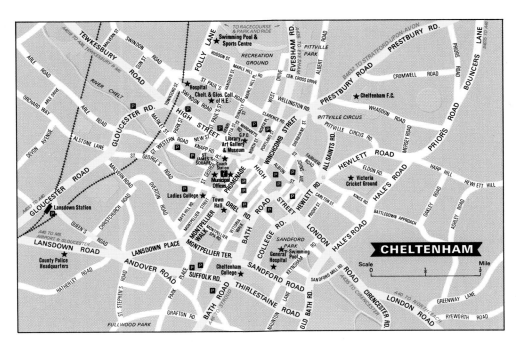

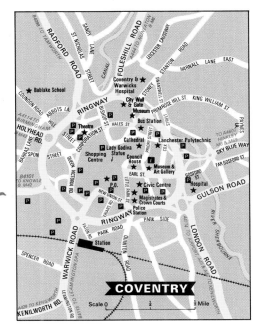

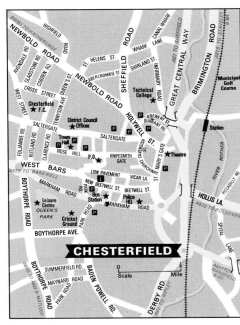

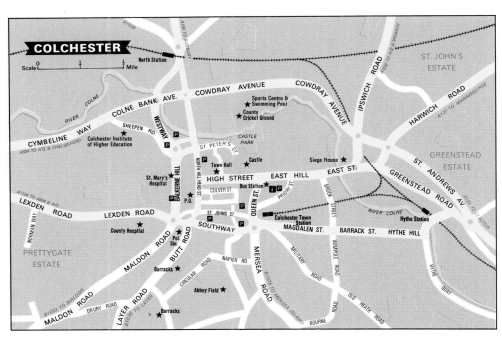

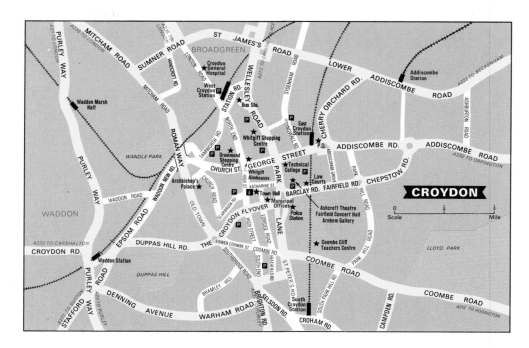

CROYDON

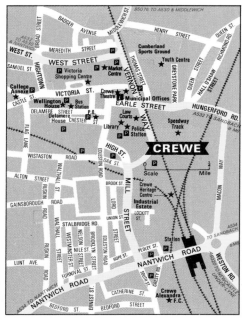

CREWE

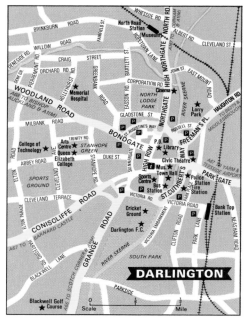

DARLINGTON

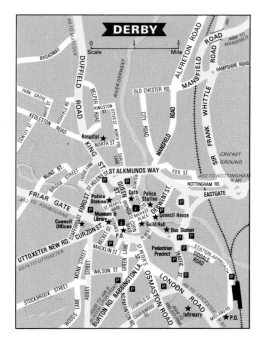

DERBY

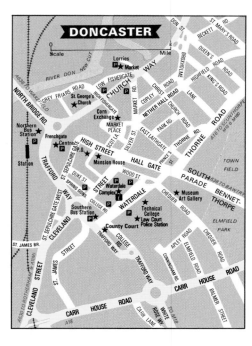

DONCASTER

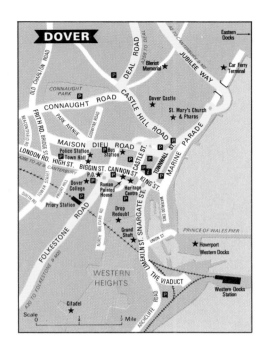

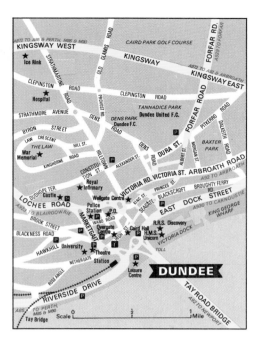

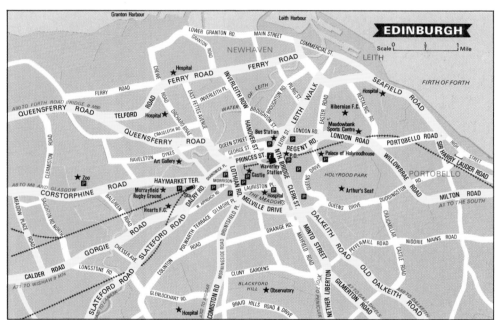

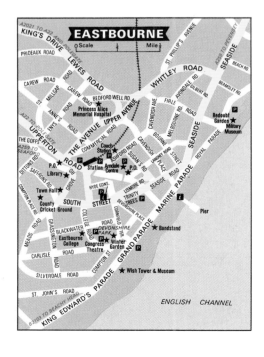

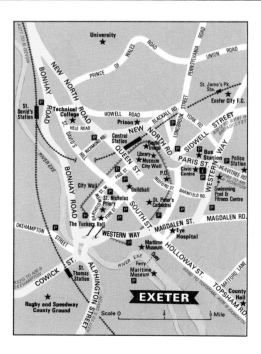

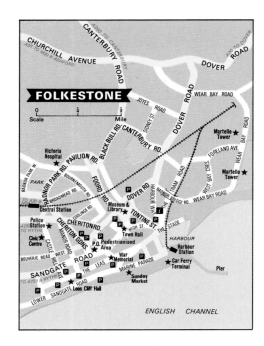

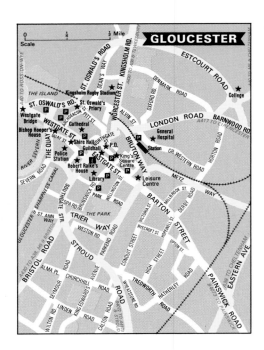

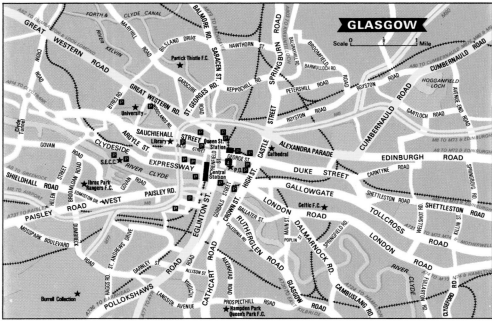

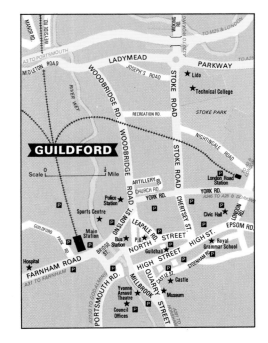

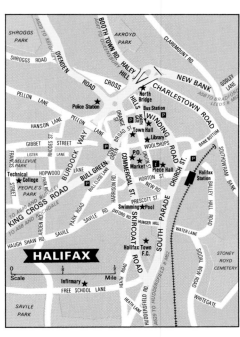

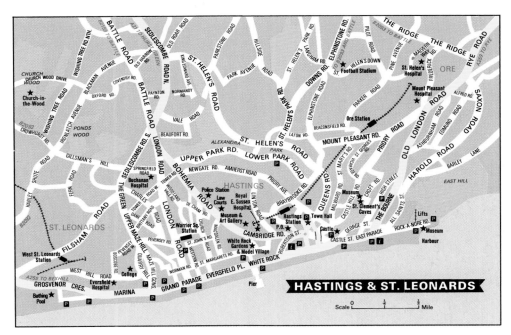

HASTINGS & ST. LEONARDS

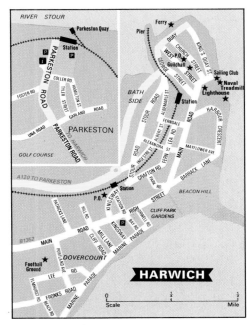

HARWICH

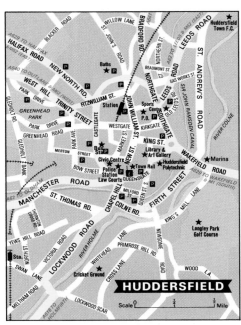

HUDDERSFIELD

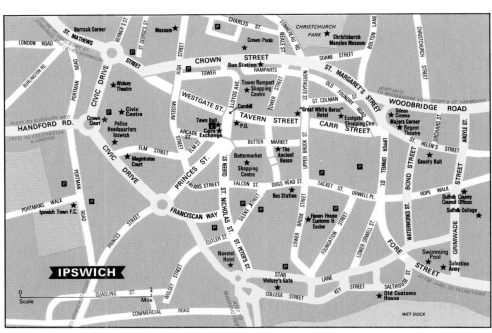

IPSWICH

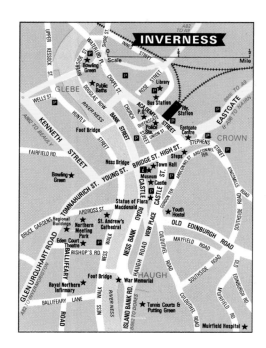

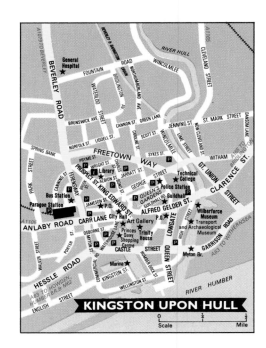

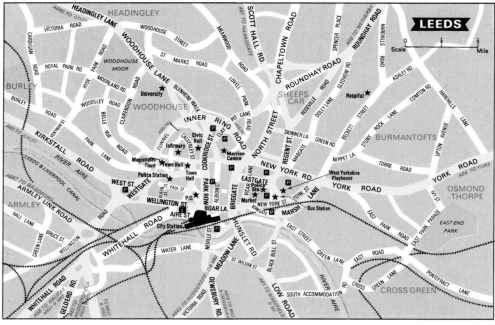

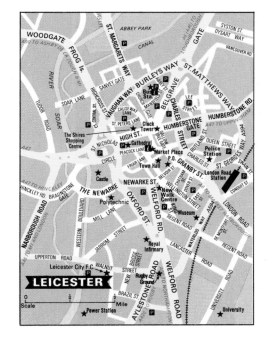

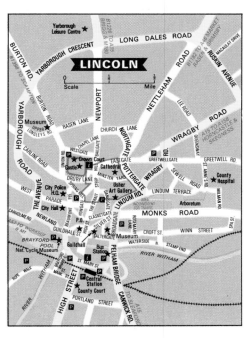

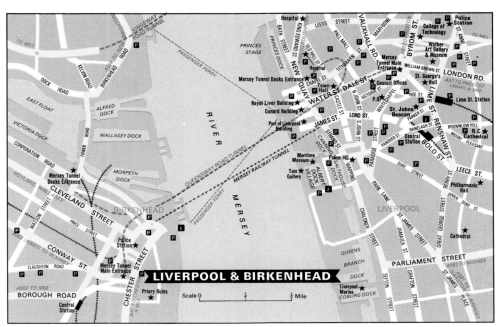

LIVERPOOL & BIRKENHEAD

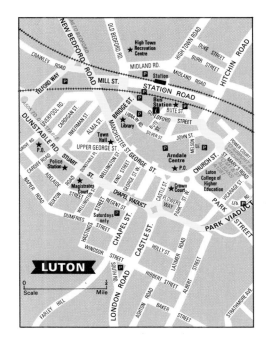

LUTON

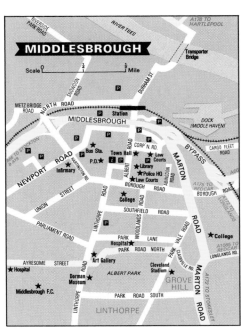

MIDDLESBROUGH

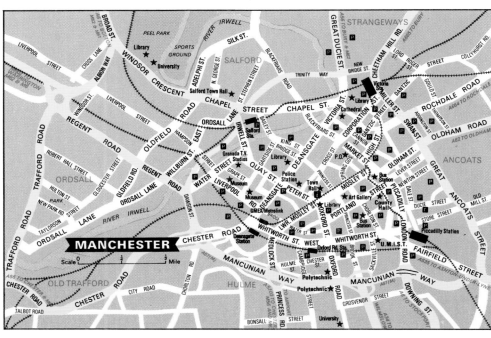

MANCHESTER

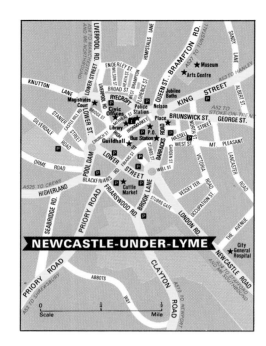

NEWCASTLE-UNDER-LYME

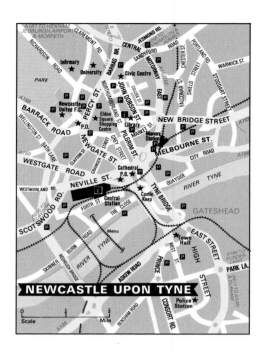

NEWCASTLE UPON TYNE

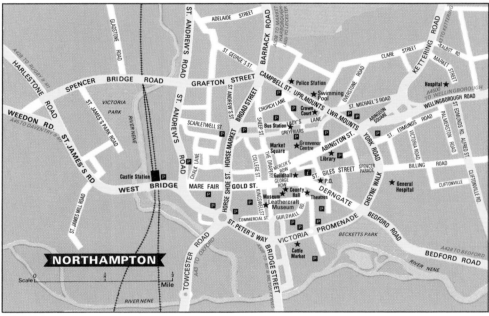

NORTHAMPTON

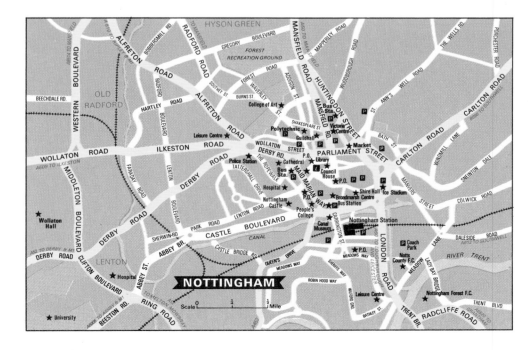

NOTTINGHAM

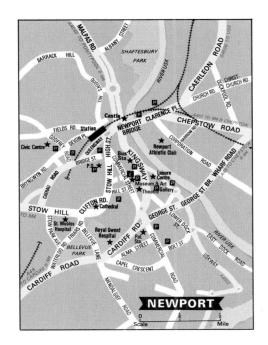

NEWPORT

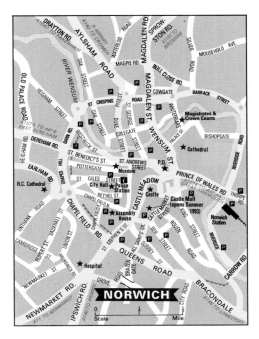

NORWICH

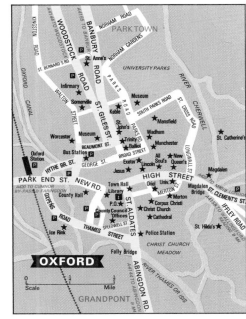

OXFORD

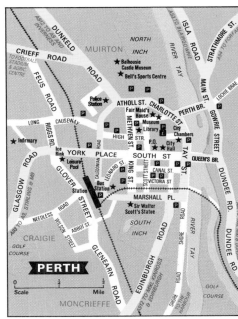

PERTH

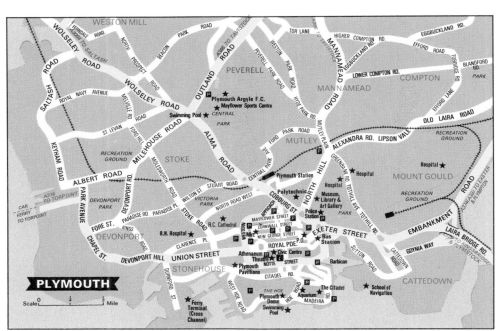

PLYMOUTH

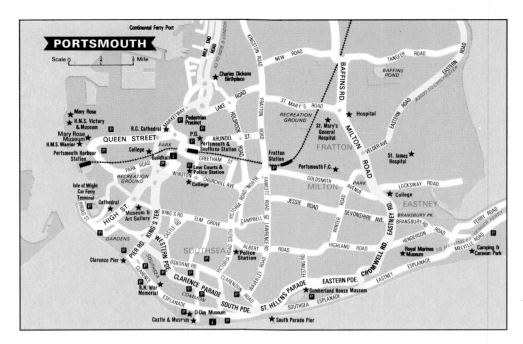

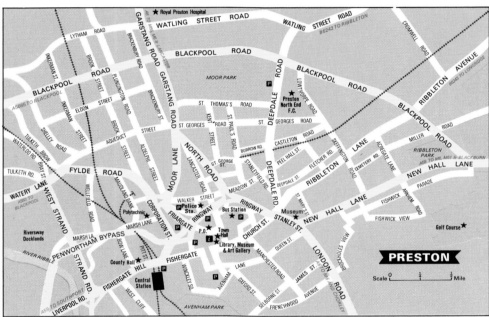

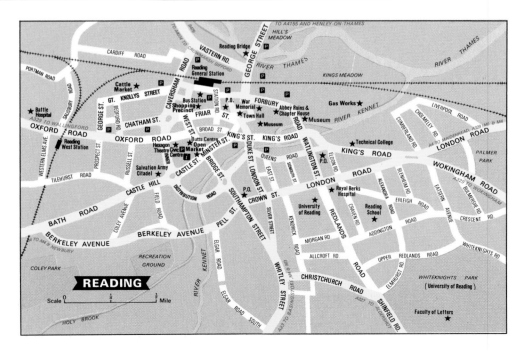

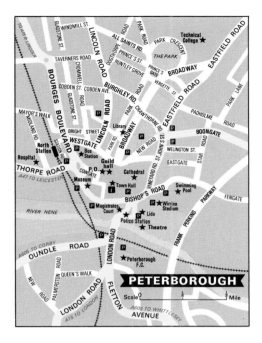

PETERBOROUGH

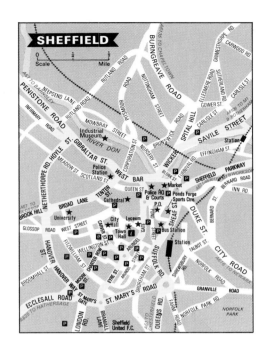

SHEFFIELD

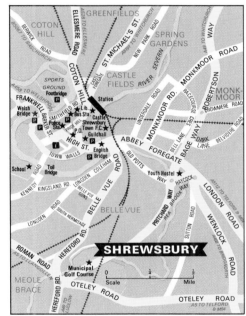

SHREWSBURY

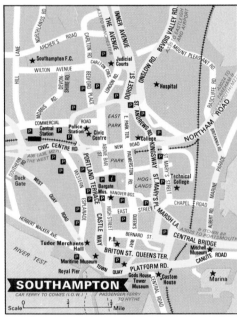

SOUTHAMPTON

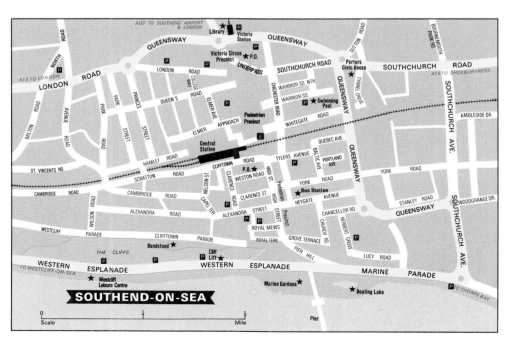

SOUTHEND-ON-SEA

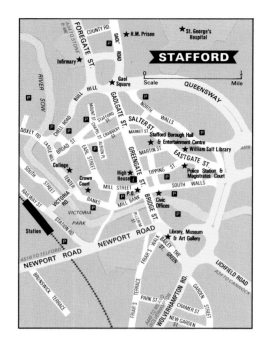

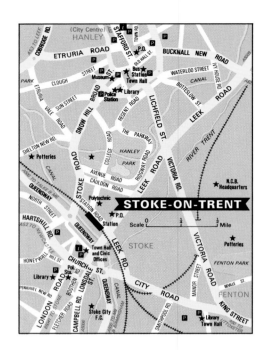

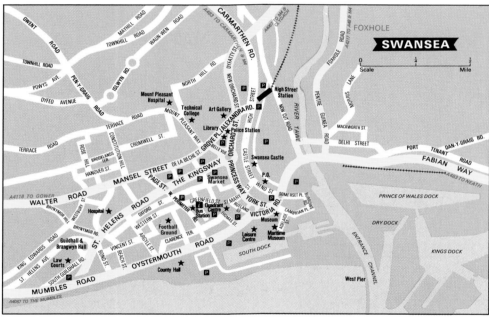

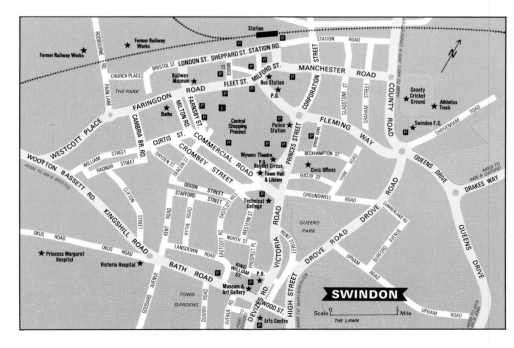

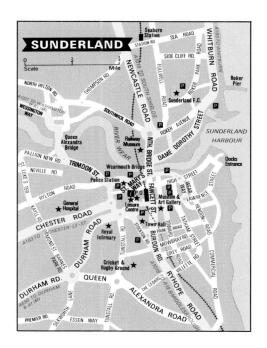

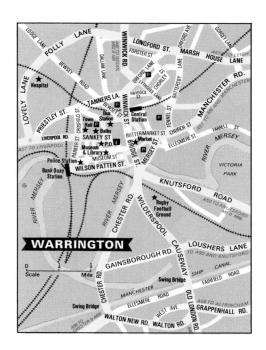

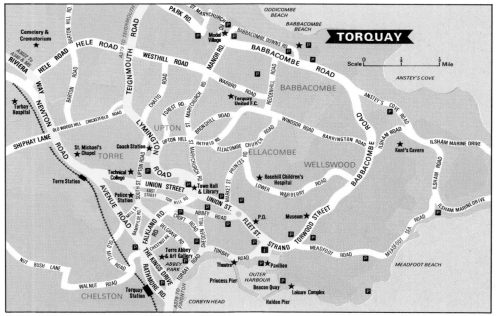

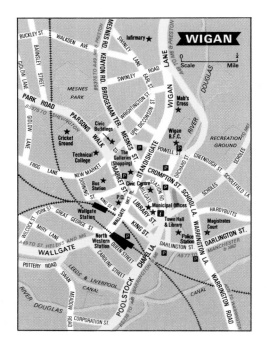

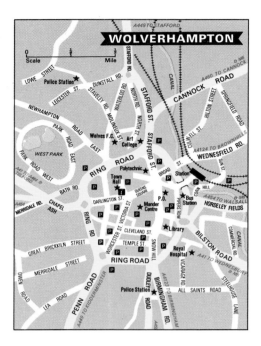

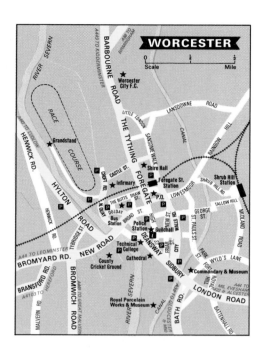

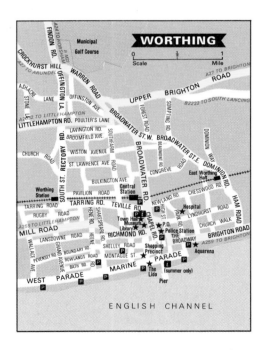

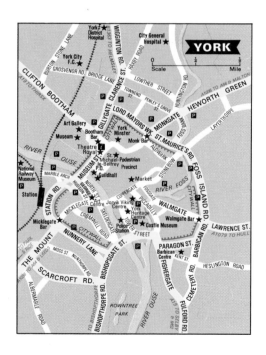

INDEX

Abbreviations

Bfd.	Bedfordshire	*D.&G.*	Dumfries & Galloway	*Hfs.*	Hertfordshire	*Nfk*	Norfolk	*Sry*	Surrey
Bkh.	Buckinghamshire	*Dor.*	Dorset	*Hgh.*	Highland	*Nmp.*	Northamptonshire	*Stf.*	Staffordshire
Bor.	Borders	*Drm*	Durham	*Hum.*	Humberside	*Nor.*	Northumberland	*Str.*	Strathclyde
Brk.	Berkshire	*Dyf.*	Dyfed	*H.&W.*	Hereford & Worcester	*Not.*	Nottinghamshire	*S.Y.*	South Yorkshire
Cbs.	Cambridge	*E.S.*	East Sussex	*I.o.M.*	Isle of Man	*N.Y.*	North Yorkshire	*Tay.*	Tayside
Cen.	Central	*Esx*	Essex	*I.o.S.*	Isles of Scilly	*Ork.*	Orkney	*T.&W.*	Tyne & Wear
Che.	Cheshire	*G.L.*	Greater London	*I.o.W.*	Isle of Wight	*Oxf.*	Oxfordshire	*War.*	Warwickshire
C.I.	Channel Islands	*Glo.*	Gloucestershire	*Lan.*	Lancashire	*Pow.*	Powys	*W.G.*	West Glamorgan
Cle.	Cleveland	*G.M.*	Greater Manchester	*Lcn.*	Lincolnshire	*Sfk*	Suffolk	*W.I.*	Western Isles
Clw.	Clwyd	*Grm.*	Grampian	*Lei.*	Leicestershire	*S.G.*	South Glamorgan	*W.M.*	West Midlands
Cnw.	Cornwall	*Gwe.*	Gwent	*Ltn*	Lothian	*She.*	Shetland	*W.S.*	West Sussex
Cum.	Cumbria	*Gwy.*	Gwynedd	*Mer.*	Merseyside	*Shr.*	Shropshire	*Wts.*	Wiltshire
Dby.	Derbyshire	*Ham.*	Hampshire	*M.G.*	Mid Glamorgan	*Som.*	Somerset	*W.Y.*	West Yorkshire
Dev.	Devon								

A

Abbas Combe 9 B32
Abberley 29 B33
Abberton *H.&W.* 29 C35
Abberton *Esx* 34 G56
Abberwick 71 B37
Abbess Roding 33 G51
Abbeycwmhir 27 A26
Abbey Dore 28 E29
Abbey Hulton 40 A35
Abbey St Bathans 77 D33
Abbeystead 55 D31
Abbeytown 60 A27
Abbey Wood 23 D50
Abbotrule 70 B31
Abbots Bickington 6 D19
Abbots Bromley 40 C36
Abbotsbury 8 F31
Abbotsham 6 C19
Abbotskerswell 5 D24
Abbots Langley 22 A46
Abbots Leigh 19 D31
Abbotsley 33 C48
Abbots Morton 30 C36
Abbots Ripton 32 A47
Abbot's Salford 30 C36
Abbotts Ann 21 G39
Abbottswood 10 B39
Abdon 38 G31
Aber *Gwy.* 36 B18
Aber *Dyf.* 26 D20
Aber *Gwy.* 46 E22
Aber *M.G.* 18 B25
Aberaeron 26 B20
Aberaman 18 A25
Aberangell 37 E24
Aberarad 17 A18
Aberarder 88 F20
Aberarder Ho. 88 B22
Aberargie 82 F27
Aberarth 26 B20
Aberavon 18 B23
Aber-banc 26 D19
Aber Bargoed 18 A27
Aberbeeg 18 A27
Aber Bowlan 17 A22
Abercanaid 18 A26
Abercarn 18 B27
Abercastle 16 A14
Abercegir 37 E23
Aberchalder 88 D19
Aberchirder 98 D31
Abercorn 75 C26
Abercraf 27 G24
Abercrombie 83 G30
Abercrychan 27 E23
Abercwmboi 18 A25
Abercych 26 C18
Abercynafon 27 G26
Abercynon 18 B26
Aber-cywarch 37 D24
Aberdalgie 82 E26
Aberdare 18 A25
Aberdaron 36 C17
Aberdeen 91 C35
Aberdesach 46 G20
Aberdour 75 B27
Aberduhonw 27 C26
Aberdulais 18 B23
Aberdyfi 36 F21
Aberedw 27 D26
Abereiddy 16 A13
Abererch 36 B19
Aberfan 18 A26
Aberfeldy 81 C24
Aberffraw 46 F19
Aberffrwd 27 A22

Aberford 57 F40
Aberfoyle 81 G21
Abergarw 18 C25
Abergavenny 28 G28
Abergele 47 E25
Abergiar 26 D20
Abergorlech 17 A21
Abergwesyn 27 C24
Abergwili 17 B20
Abergwydol 37 E23
Abergwynant 37 D22
Abergwynfi 18 B24
Abergynolwyn 37 E22
Aberhafesp 37 F26
Aberhosan 37 F23
Aberkenfig 18 C24
Aberlady 76 B30
Aberlemno 83 B30
Aberllefenni 37 E23
Aber-Ilia 27 G25
Abermad 26 A21
Abermeurig 26 C21
Abermule 38 F27
Aber-Naint 38 C27
Aber-nant 18 A25
Abernant 17 B19
Abernethy 82 F27
Abernyte 82 D28
Aber-pergwm 18 A24
Aberporth 26 C18
Aberriw (Berriew) 38 E27
Aberscross 96 A23
Abersky 88 B21
Abersoch 36 C18
Abersychan 19 A28
Aberthin 18 D26
Abertillery 18 A27
Abertridwr *M.G.* 18 C26
Abertridwr *Pow.* 37 D26
Abertysswg 18 A27
Aberuthven 82 F25
Aberyscir 27 F25
Aberystwyth 36 G21
Abhainnsuidhe 100 G6
Abingdon 21 B40
Abinger Common 22 G47
Abinger Hammer 22 G46
Abington 68 A25
Abington Pigotts 33 D48
Abingworth 12 E47
Ab Kettleby 41 C42
Ablington 20 A36
Abney 50 E37
Aboyne 90 D31
Abram 49 B32
Abriachan 88 A21
Abridge 23 B50
Abson 19 D32
Abthorpe 31 D42
Abune-the-Hill 104 D28
Aby 53 E50
Acaster Malbis 58 E41
Acaster Selby 58 E41
Accrington 56 G33
Accurrach 80 E16
Acha 78 B7
Achacha 80 C15
Achadacaie 73 D14
Achadunan 80 F17
Achagavel 79 B13
Achaglass 72 F12
Achahoish 73 C13
Achalader 82 C27
Achallader 80 C19
Acha Mor 100 E9
Achamore 72 C11
Achanamara 73 B13

Achandunie 96 D22
Achany 96 A21
Achaphubuil 87 G16
Acharacle 79 A12
Achargary 102 C22
Acharn *Tay.* 81 C23
Acharn *Str.* 80 D17
Acharosson 73 C15
Achateny 79 A11
Achath 91 B33
Achavanich 103 D27
Achavraie 95 A16
Achduart 95 A16
Achentoul 102 E24
Achfary 101 D18
Achgarve 94 B14
Achiemore *Hgh.* 101 B19
Achiemore *Hgh.* 102 C24
Achies 103 C27
A'Chill 85 D8
Achiltibuie 94 A15
Achina 102 B22
Achindown 97 G24
Achinduich 96 A21
Achingills 103 B27
Achintee 94 G15
Achintee Ho 87 G17
Achintraid 86 A14
Achlean 89 E24
Achleek 79 B13
Achlian 80 E17
Achlyness 101 C18
Achmelvich 101 F16
Achmony 88 A20
Achmore *Hgh.* 86 A14
Achmore *Hgh.* 95 B16
Achmore *Cen.* 81 D21
Achnaba 73 B14
Achnabat 88 A21
Achnabourin 102 C22
Achnacairn 80 D15
Achnacarnin 101 E16
Achnaclerach 96 E19
Achnacloich 80 D15
Achnacloich 86 D11
Achnaclyth 103 E26
Achnacraig 79 C10
Achnacroish 79 C14
Achnadrish 79 B10
Achnafalnich 80 E17
Achnafauld 81 D24
Achnagairn 96 G21
Achnagarron 96 D22
Achnaha *Hgh.* 79 C12
Achnaha *Hgh.* 79 A10
Achnahanat 96 B20
Achnahannet 89 B25
Achnairn 102 G21
Achnalea 79 A14
Achnanellan 79 A13
Achnasaul 87 F17
Achnasheen 95 F17
Achnashelloch 73 A14
Achnastank 98 F28
Achorn 103 E27
Achosnich *Hgh.* 79 A10
Achosnich *Hgh.* 96 B22
Achreamie 103 B25
Achriabhach 80 A17
Achriesgill 101 C18
Achrimsdale 97 A24
Achronich 79 D10
Achtoty 102 B22
Achurch 42 G46
Achuvoldrach 102 C21
Achvaich 96 B22
Achvarasdal 103 B25
Achvlair 80 B15

Achvraie 95 A16
Ackergill 103 C29
Acklam *Cle.* 62 E40
Acklam *N.Y.* 58 C43
Ackleton 39 F33
Acklington 71 C38
Ackton 57 G40
Ackworth Moor Top 51 A40
Acle 45 D59
Acock's Green 40 G36
Acol 25 E58
Acomb *N.Y.* 58 D41
Acomb *Nor.* 70 G35
Aconbury 28 E30
Acre 56 G33
Acrefair 38 A28
Acrise Place 15 C57
Acton *Shr.* 38 G28
Acton *H.&W.* 29 B34
Acton *G.L.* 22 C47
Acton *Sfk* 34 D54
Acton *Che.* 49 G32
Acton Beauchamp 29 C32
Acton Bridge 48 E31
Acton Burnell 38 E31
Acton Green 29 D32
Acton Pigott 38 E31
Acton Round 39 F32
Acton Scott 38 G30
Acton Trussell 40 D35
Acton Turville 20 C34
Adamhill 74 G20
Adbaston 39 C33
Adber 8 B31
Adderbury 31 E40
Adderley 39 B32
Adderstone 77 G37
Addiewell 75 D25
Addingham 57 E36
Addington *Bkh.* 31 F43
Addington *Kent* 23 F52
Addington *G.L.* 23 E49
Addlestone 22 E46
Addlethorpe 53 F51
Adel 57 F38
Adeney 39 D32
Adfa 37 E26
Adforton 28 A29
Adisham 15 B57
Adlestrop 30 F38
Adlingfleet 58 G44
Adlington *Che.* 49 D35
Adlington *Lan.* 48 A31
Admaston *Shr.* 39 D32
Admaston *Stf.* 40 C36
Admington 30 D37
Adsborough 8 B28
Adsdean 11 D43
Adstock 31 E43
Adstone 31 C41
Adversane 12 D46
Adwalton 57 G38
Adwell 21 B42
Adwick le Street 51 B41
Adwick upon Dearne 51 B40
Ae Village 68 E25
Affeck *Tay.* 83 D30
Affleck *Grm.* 91 A34
Affpuddle 9 E33
Afon-wen 47 E27
Afton Bridgend 68 B22
Agglethorpe 57 A36
Aigburth 48 D29
Aignis 100 D10
Aike 59 E46
Aikerness 104 A30
Aikers 105 B30
Aiketgate 61 B30
Aikshaw 60 B27

Aikton 60 A28
Aikwood Tower 69 A30
Ailey 28 D29
Ailsworth 42 F47
Aimster 103 B27
Ainderby Quernhow 57 A39
Ainderby Steeple 62 G39
Aingers Green 35 G57
Ainsdale 48 A29
Ainstable 61 B31
Ainsworth 49 A33
Ainthorpe 63 F42
Aintree 48 C29
Aird 92 F3
Aird a'Chaolais 84 E2
Aird A Mhachair 92 G3
Aird A Mhulaidh 100 F7
Aird Asaig 100 G7
Aird Dhail 100 A10
Aird Leimhe 92 C6
Aird Mhige 92 B6
Aird Mhighe 92 C6
Aird of Sleat 86 D11
Airdrie *Fife* 83 G31
Airdrie *Str.* 75 D23
Aird Thunga 100 D10
Aird Uige 100 D6
Airidh A Bhruaich 100 F8
Airieland 65 E23
Airigh-drishaig 86 A13
Airmyn 58 G43
Airntully 82 D26
Airor 86 D13
Airth 75 B24
Airton 56 D35
Airyhassen 64 F19
Aisby *Lcn.* 42 B46
Aisby *Lcn.* 52 C44
Aisgernis 84 B3
Aiskew 57 A38
Aislaby *N.Y.* 58 A43
Aislaby *N.Y.* 63 F44
Aislaby *Cle.* 62 E39
Aisthorpe 52 D43
Aith *Ork.* 104 E28
Aith *She.* 106 D42
Aith *She.* 107 B39
Aith *Ork.* 104 D32
Aitnoch 89 A25
Akeld 70 A35
Akeley 31 E42
Akenham 35 D57
Albaston 4 C20
Alberbury 38 D29
Albourne 13 E48
Albrighton *Shr.* 39 E33
Albrighton *Shr.* 38 D30
Alburgh 45 G58
Albury *Sry* 22 G46
Albury *Hfs.* 33 F50
Albury Heath 22 G46
Alby Hill 45 B57
Alcaig 96 F21
Alcaston 38 G30
Alcester 30 C36
Alciston 13 F50
Alcombe 7 A25
Alconbury 32 A47
Alconbury Hill 32 A47
Alconbury Weston 32 A47
Aldborough *Nfk* 45 B57
Aldborough *N.Y.* 57 C40
Aldbourne 21 D38
Aldbrough 59 F48
Aldbrough St John 62 E37
Aldbrough 57 B38
Aldbury 32 G45
Aldclune 81 A24

Aldeburgh 35 C60
Aldeby 45 F60
Aldenham 22 B47
Alderbury 10 B37
Alderford 45 D57
Alderholt 10 C37
Alderley 20 B33
Alderley Edge 49 E34
Alderman's Green 41 G39
Aldermaston 21 E41
Aldermaston Soke 21 E41
Aldermaston Wharf 21 E42
Alderminster 30 D38
Aldersey Green 48 G30
Aldershot 22 F43
Alderton *Wts.* 20 C34
Alderton *Shr.* 38 C30
Alderton *Sfk.* 35 D59
Alderton *Nmp.* 31 D43
Alderton *Glo.* 29 E35
Alderwasley 50 G38
Aldfield 57 C38
Aldford 48 G29
Aldham *Esx* 34 F55
Aldham *Sfk* 34 F56
Aldie *Grm.* 99 E36
Aldie *Hgh.* 96 C23
Aldingbourne 12 F44
Aldingham 55 B28
Aldington *H.&W.* 30 D36
Aldington *Kent* 15 D56
Aldivalloch 90 A29
Aldochlay 74 A19
Aldons 67 E17
Aldreth 33 A50
Aldridge 40 E36
Aldringham 35 B60
Aldro 58 C44
Aldsworth 20 A37
Aldunie 90 A29
Aldville 82 D25
Aldwark *N.Y.* 57 C40
Aldwark *Dby.* 50 G38
Aldwick 12 G45
Aldwincle 42 G45
Aldworth 21 D41
Alexandria 74 C19
Alfardisworthy 6 D18
Alfington 7 F27
Alfold 12 C46
Alfold Crossways 12 C46
Alford *Grm.* 90 B31
Alford *Som.* 9 A32
Alford *Lcn.* 53 E50
Alfreton 51 G39
Alfrick 29 C33
Alfriston 13 F50
Algarkirk 43 B48
Alhampton 9 A32
Alkborough 58 G44
Alkerton 30 D39
Alkham 15 C58
Alkington 38 B31
Alkmonton 40 B37
Allaleigh 5 E24
Allanaquoich 89 E26
Allancreich 90 D31
Allangillfoot 69 D28
Allanton *D.&G.* 68 E24
Allanton *Bor.* 77 E34
Allanton *Str.* 75 E24
Allanton *Str.* 75 E23
Allardice 91 F33
Allathasdal 84 D2
All Cannings 20 E36
Allendale Town 61 A34
Allenheads 61 B34
Allensford 62 A36
Allen's Green 33 G50
Allensmore 28 E30
Aller 8 B29
Allerby 60 C26
Allerford *Dev.* 6 G20
Allerford *Som.* 7 A25
Allerston 58 A44
Allerthorpe 58 E43
Allerton *W.Y.* 57 F37
Allerton *Mer.* 48 D30
Allerton Bywater 57 F39
Allesley 40 G38
Allestree 41 B39
Allexton 42 E44
Allgreave 49 F35
Allhallows 24 C54
Alligin Shuas 94 F13
Allimore Green 40 D34
Allington *Wts.* 10 A38
Allington *Wts.* 20 E36
Allington *Lcn.* 42 A44
Allithwaite 55 B29
Allnabad 102 D20
Alloa 75 A24
Allonby 60 B26
Alloway 67 B19
All Saints South Elmham
  45 G59

Allscot 39 F33
All Stretton 38 F30
Alltachonaich 79 B13
Alltan Dubh 101 G15
Alltbeithe 87 B16
Alltforgan 37 C25
Alltmawr 27 D26
Alltnacaillich 102 D20
Allt na h-Airbhe 95 B16
Allt-na-subh 86 B14
Alltsigh 88 C20
Alltwalis 17 A20
Alltwen 18 A23
Alltyblaca 26 D21
Allweston 9 C32
Almeley 28 C29
Almer 9 E34
Almington 39 B33
Almiston Cross 6 C19
Almondbank 82 E26
Almondbury 50 A37
Almondsbury 19 C31
Alne 57 C40
Alness 96 E22
Alnham 70 B35
Alnmouth 71 B38
Alnwick 71 B37
Alphamstone 34 E54
Alpheton 34 C54
Alphington 7 G25
Alpington 45 E58
Alport 50 F38
Alpraham 48 G31
Alresford 34 F56
Alrewas 40 D37
Alrick 82 A27
Alsager 49 G33
Alsagers Bank 40 A34
Alsop en le Dale 50 G37
Alston *Dev.* 8 D29
Alston *Cum.* 61 B33
Alstone 29 E35
Alstonefield 50 G36
Alswear 6 C22
Altanduin 102 F23
Altarnun 4 B18
Altass 96 A20
Altens 91 C35
Alterwall 103 B28
Altham 56 F33
Althorne 25 B55
Althorpe 52 B44
Alticry 64 E18
Altnafeadh 80 B17
Altnaharra 102 E21
Altofts 57 G39
Alton *Ham.* 22 G43
Alton *Dby.* 51 F39
Alton *Stf.* 40 A36
Alton Barnes 20 E37
Alton Pancras 9 D32
Alton Priors 20 E37
Altonside 98 D28
Altrincham 49 D33
Altura 87 E18
Alva 75 A24
Alvanley 48 E30
Alvaston 41 B39
Alvechurch 30 A36
Alvecote 40 E38
Alvediston 9 B35
Alveley 39 G33
Alverdiscott 6 C21
Alverstoke 11 E42
Alverstone 11 F41
Alverton 42 A43
Alves 97 E27
Alvescot 21 A38
Alveston *War.* 30 C38
Alveston *Avon* 19 C32
Alvie 89 D24
Alvingham 53 C49
Alvington 19 A31
Alwalton 42 F47
Alwinton 70 C34
Alwoodley Gates 57 E39
Alyth 82 C28
Amalebra 2 E10
Ambergate 51 G39
Amber Hill 43 A48
Amberley *Glo.* 20 A34
Amberley *W.S.* 12 E46
Amble 71 C38
Amblecote 40 G34
Ambleside 60 F29
Ambleston 16 B15
Ambrismore 73 E16
Ambrosden 31 G41
Amcotts 52 A44
Amersham 22 B45
Amesbury 20 G37
Amington 40 E38
Amisfield Town 68 E25
Amlwch 46 C20
Amlwch Port 46 C20
Ammanford 17 C21

Amotherby 58 B43
Ampfield 10 B39
Ampleforth 58 B41
Ampleforth College 58 B41
Ampney Crucis 20 A36
Ampney St Mary 20 A36
Ampney St Peter 20 A36
Amport 21 G38
Ampthill 32 E46
Ampton 34 A54
Amroth 16 D17
Amulree 81 D24
Anaboard 89 A25
Anaheilt 79 A14
Ancaster 42 A45
Anchor 38 G27
Ancroft 77 F35
Ancrum 70 A32
Ancton 12 F45
Anderby 53 E51
Anderson 9 E34
Anderton 49 E32
Andover 21 G38
Andover Down 21 G39
Andoversford 29 G35
Andreas 54 D25
Anelog 36 C17
Angarrack 2 E11
Angersleigh 7 D27
Angerton 60 A28
Angle 16 D14
Angler's Retreat 37 F23
Angmering 12 F46
Angram 57 E40
Anie 81 F21
Ankerville 96 D23
Anlaby 59 G46
Anmer 44 C53
Anmore 11 C42
Annan 69 G27
Annaside 54 A26
Annat *Str.* 80 E16
Annat *Hgh.* 94 F14
Anna Valley 21 G39
Annbank 67 A20
Annesley 51 G40
Annesley Woodhouse 51 G40
Annfield Plain 62 A37
Annscroft 38 E30
Ansdell 55 G29
Ansford 9 A32
Ansley 40 F38
Anslow 40 C37
Anslow Gate 40 C37
Anstey *Lei.* 41 E41
Anstey *Hfs.* 33 E50
Anstruther 83 G31
Ansty *W.S.* 13 D48
Ansty *Wts.* 9 B35
Ansty *War.* 41 G39
Anthill Common 11 C42
Anthorn 60 A27
Antingham 45 B58
An T-ob 92 C5
Antony 4 E20
Antrobus 49 E32
Anvil Corner 6 E19
Anwick 52 G47
Anwoth 65 E21
Aoradh 72 D8
Apes Hall 43 G51
Apethorpe 42 F46
Apley 52 E46
Apperknowle 51 E39
Apperley 29 F34
Appin Ho. 80 C15
Appleby 52 A45
Appleby Magna 41 D39
Appleby Parva 41 E39
Applecross 94 G12
Appledore *Kent* 14 E55
Appledore *Dev.* 7 D26
Appledore *Dev.* 6 B20
Appledore Heath 14 D55
Appleford 21 B41
Appleshaw 21 G39
Applethwaite 60 D28
Appleton 21 A40
Appleton-le-Moors 58 A43
Appleton-le-Street 58 B43
Appleton Roebuck 58 E41
Appleton Thorn 49 D32
Appleton Wiske 62 F39
Appletreehall 69 B30
Appletreewick 57 C36
Appley 7 C26
Appley Bridge 48 A31
Apse Heath 11 F41
Apsley 22 A46
Apsley End 32 E47
Apuldram 12 F44
Arbirlot 83 C31
Arborfield 22 E43
Arborfield Cross 22 E43
Arborfield Garrison 22 E43
Arbroath 83 D32
Arbuthnott 91 F33

Archdeacon Newton 62 E38
Archiestown 97 G27
Arclid 49 F33
Ard a'Chapuill 73 C16
Ardacheranbeg 73 B16
Ardacheranmor 73 B16
Ardachoil 79 D12
Ardachvie 87 E17
Ardailly 72 F12
Ardalanish 78 F9
Ardanaiseig 80 E16
Ardaneaskan 86 A14
Ardanstur 79 F14
Ardantiobairt 79 B12
Ardantrive 79 E14
Ardarroch 86 A14
Ardbeg *Str.* 73 D16
Ardbeg *Str.* 73 B17
Ardbeg *Str.* 72 F10
Ardblair 88 A20
Ardbrecknish 80 E16
Ardcharnich 95 C17
Ardchiavaig 78 F9
Ardchonnel 79 D14
Ardchonnell 80 F15
Ardchrishnish 78 E9
Ardchronie 96 C21
Ardchuilk 87 A18
Ardchullarie More 81 F21
Ardchyle 81 E21
Arddleen 38 D28
Ardeley 33 F48
Ardelve 86 B14
Arden 74 B19
Ardencaple 79 F13
Ardens Grafton 30 C37
Ardentallan 79 E14
Ardentinny 73 B17
Ardeonaig 81 D22
Ardersier 96 F23
Ardery 79 A13
Ardessie 95 C16
Ardfad 79 F13
Ardfern 79 G13
Ardfin 72 D10
Ardgartan 80 G18
Ardgay 96 B21
Ardgenavan 80 F17
Ardgowan 73 C17
Ardgowse 90 B31
Ardgye 97 E27
Ardhallow 73 C17
Ardheslaig 94 F13
Ardiecow 98 C31
Ardinamar 79 F13
Ardindrean 95 C17
Ardingly 13 D49
Ardington 21 C40
Ardintoul 86 B14
Ardkinglas Ho 80 G17
Ardlair 90 A31
Ardlamont 73 D15
Ardleigh 34 F56
Ardleish 80 F19
Ardler 82 C28
Ardley 31 F41
Ardlui 80 F19
Ardlussa 72 B12
Ardmaddy 80 D16
Ardmair 95 B16
Ardmaleish 73 D16
Ardmay 80 G18
Ardmenish 72 C11
Ardmhor 84 D3
Ardminish 72 F12
Ardmolich 86 B13
Ardmore *Str.* 79 E13
Ardmore *Str.* 74 C19
Ardmore *Str.* 72 C10
Ardmore *Hgh.* 96 C23
Ardnackaig 73 A13
Ardnacross 72 C11
Ardnadam 73 C17
Ardnadrochet 79 D12
Ardnagoine 94 A15
Ardnagowan 80 G16
Ardnagrask 96 G20
Ardnahein 73 A17
Ardnahoe 72 C10
Ardnarff 86 A14
Ardnastang 79 A13
Ardnave 72 C8
Ardno 80 G17
Ardo 99 F36
Ardoch *Grm.* 97 F27
Ardoch *D.&G.* 68 C24
Ardoch *Tay.* 82 D26
Ardochrig 74 F22
Ardochu 96 A22
Ardoyne 91 A32
Ardpatrick 73 D13
Ardpeaton 73 B17
Ardradnaig 81 C22
Ardrishaig 73 B14
Ardroe 101 F16
Ardross 96 A22
Ardrossan 73 F17

Ardscalpsie 73 E16
Ardshave 96 B23
Ardshealach 79 A12
Ardshellach 79 F13
Ardsley 51 B39
Ardslignish 79 A11
Ardtalla 72 E10
Ardtalnaig 81 D22
Ardtarig 73 B16
Ardteatle 80 E17
Ardtoe 86 G12
Ardtornish 79 C12
Ardtrostan 81 E22
Ardtur 80 C15
Arduaine 79 F13
Ardullie 96 E21
Ardura 79 D12
Ardvar 101 E17
Ardvasar 86 F13
Ardveich 81 E22
Ardverikie 88 F20
Ardvorlich *Tay.* 81 E22
Ardvorlich *Str.* 80 F19
Ardwall 65 E21
Ardwell *Str.* 67 D17
Ardwell *D.&G.* 64 F17
Ardwell *Grm.* 98 F29
Areley Kings 29 A33
Arford 12 C44
Argaty 81 G23
Argoed 18 B27
Argoed Mill 27 B25
Argrennan 65 E22
Arichamish 79 G14
Arichastlich 80 D18
Arichonan 73 A13
Aridhglas 78 E9
Arienskill 86 F13
Arileod 78 B7
Arinacrinachd 94 F13
Arinafad Beg 73 B13
Arinagour 78 B8
Arinambane 84 B3
Arisaig 86 F12
Arivegaig 79 A12
Arkendale 57 C39
Arkesden 33 E50
Arkholme 55 B31
Arkleby 60 B27
Arkleside 57 A36
Arkleton 69 D29
Arkley 23 B48
Arksey 51 A40
Arkwright Town 51 F40
Arlary 82 G27
Arlecdon 60 E26
Arlesey 32 E47
Arleston 39 D32
Arley 49 D32
Arlingham 29 G32
Arlington *Dev.* 6 A22
Arlington *Glo.* 20 A36
Arlington *E.S.* 13 F51
Arlington Beccott 6 A22
Armadale *Ltn* 75 D25
Armadale *Hgh.* 102 B23
Armadale *Hgh.* 86 D12
Armathwaite 61 B30
Arminghall 45 E58
Armitage 40 D36
Armscote 30 D38
Armston 42 G46
Armthorpe 51 B42
Arnabost 78 B7
Arncliffe 56 B35
Arncliffe Cote 56 B35
Arncroach 83 G30
Arne 9 F35
Arnesby 41 F42
Arngask 82 F27
Arngibbon 74 A22
Arngomery 74 A22
Arnhall 83 A31
Arnicle 73 G13
Arnipol 86 F13
Arnisdale 86 C14
Arnish 94 G12
Arniston Engine 76 D29
Arnol 100 C8
Arnold 41 A41
Arnprior 74 A21
Arnside 55 B30
Arowry 38 B30
Arrad Foot 55 A29
Arradoul 98 C30
Arram 59 E46
Arrat 83 B32
Arrathorne 62 G37
Arreton 11 F41
Arrington 33 C49
Arrivain 80 D18
Arrochar 80 F18
Arrow 30 C36
Arscaig 102 G20
Arthington 57 E38
Arthingworth 42 G43

Arthog 37 D22
Arthrath 99 F35
Arthurstone 82 C28
Aruadh 72 D8
Arundel 12 F46
Aryhoulan 80 A15
Asby 60 D26
Ascog 73 D17
Ascot 22 E45
Ascott 38 E39
Ascott-under-Wychwood 30 G39
Ascreavie 82 B29
Asenby 57 B39
Asfordby 41 D42
Asfordby Hill 42 D43
Asgarby Lcn. 42 A47
Asgarby Lcn. 53 F49
Ash Som. 8 B30
Ash Dev. 6 E21
Ash Kent 15 B58
Ash Kent 23 E51
Ash Sry 22 F44
Ashampstead 21 D41
Ashbocking 35 C57
Ashbourne 40 A37
Ashbrittle 7 C26
Ash Bullayne 7 E23
Ashburnham Place 13 E52
Ashburton 5 C23
Ashbury Dev. 6 F21
Ashbury Oxf. 21 C38
Ashby 52 B45
Ashby by Partney 53 F50
Ashby cum Fenby 53 B48
Ashby de la Launde 52 G46
Ashby de la Zouch 41 D39
Ashby Folville 42 D43
Ashby Magna 41 F41
Ashby Parva 41 G41
Ashby Puerorum 53 E49
Ashby St Ledgers 31 B41
Ashby St Mary 45 E59
Ashchurch 29 E35
Ashcombe 5 C25
Ashdon 33 D51
Ashe 21 G41
Asheldham 25 A55
Ashen 34 D53
Ashenden 14 D54
Ashendon 31 G42
Ashens 73 C14
Ashfield Str. 73 B13
Ashfield Cen. 81 G23
Ashfield Sfk 35 B57
Ashfield Green 35 A58
Ashford Crossways 13 D48
Ashford Kent 14 C55
Ashford Sry 22 D46
Ashford Dev. 6 B21
Ashford Dev. 5 F22
Ashford Ham. 10 C37
Ashford Bowdler 28 A30
Ashford Carbonel 28 A31
Ashford Hill 21 E41
Ashford in the Water 50 E37
Ashgill 75 E23
Ashiestiel 76 G30
Ashill Dev. 7 D26
Ashill Som. 8 C29
Ashill Nfk 44 E54
Ashingdon 24 B54
Ashington W.S. 12 E47
Ashington Som. 8 B31
Ashington Nor. 71 E38
Ashkirk 69 A30
Ashleworth 29 F33
Ashley Cbs. 33 B52
Ashley Stf. 39 B33
Ashley Nmp. 42 F43
Ashley Ham. 10 A39
Ashley Wts. 20 E33
Ashley Glo. 20 B35
Ashley Che. 49 D33
Ashley Dev. 6 D22
Ashley Ham. 10 E38
Ashley Kent 15 C58
Ashley Green 22 A45
Ashley Heath 10 D37
Ash Magna 38 B31
Ashmanhaugh 45 C59
Ashmansworth 21 F40
Ashmansworthy 6 D18
Ash Mill 7 C23
Ashmore Dor. 9 C35
Ashmore Tay. 82 B27
Ashorne 30 C38
Ashover 51 F39
Ashow 30 A38
Ashperton 29 D32
Ashprington 5 E23
Ash Priors 7 C27
Ashreigney 6 D21
Ashtead 22 F47

Ash Thomas 7 D26
Ashton Che. 48 F30
Ashton Nmp. 31 C43
Ashton Nmp. 42 G46
Ashton H.&W. 28 B31
Ashton Cnw. 2 F11
Ashton Cnw. 4 D19
Ashton Common 20 F34
Ashton-in-Makerfield 48 C31
Ashton Keynes 20 B36
Ashton under Hill 29 E35
Ashton-under-Lyne 49 C35
Ashton upon Mersey 49 C33
Ashurst Ham. 10 C39
Ashurst E.S. 13 C50
Ashurst W.S. 12 E47
Ashurstwood 13 C50
Ash Vale 22 F44
Ashwater 6 F19
Ashwell Lei. 42 D44
Ashwell Hfs. 33 E48
Ashwellthorpe 45 F57
Ashwick 19 G32
Ashwicken 44 D53
Ashybank 70 B31
Askam in Furness 55 B28
Askern 51 A41
Askerswell 8 E31
Askett 22 A44
Askham Not. 51 E43
Askham Cum. 61 D30
Askham Bryan 58 E41
Askham Richard 58 E41
Asknish 73 A15
Askrigg 61 G35
Askwith 57 E37
Aslackby 42 B46
Aslacton 45 F57
Aslockton 42 A43
Asloun 90 B31
Aspall 35 B57
Aspatria 60 B27
Aspenden 33 F49
Aspley Guise 32 E45
Aspull 49 B32
Asselby 58 G42
Assington 34 E55
Astbury 49 F34
Astcote 31 C42
Asterby 53 E48
Asterley 38 E29
Asterton 38 F29
Asthall 30 G38
Asthall Leigh 30 G38
Astley H.&W. 29 B33
Astley Shr. 38 D31
Astley War. 41 G39
Astley Abbotts 39 F33
Astley Bridge 49 A33
Astley Cross 29 A33
Astley Green 49 C32
Aston Dby. 50 D37
Aston Che. 48 E31
Aston Clw. 48 F29
Aston Oxf. 21 A39
Aston W.M. 40 G36
Aston Shr. 39 E32
Aston S.Y. 51 D40
Aston Stf. 39 A33
Aston Che. 38 A31
Aston Hfs. 33 F48
Aston Bkh. 22 C43
Aston Abbotts 32 F44
Aston Botterell 39 G32
Aston-by-Stone 40 B34
Aston Cantlow 30 B37
Aston Clinton 32 G44
Aston Crews 29 F31
Aston Cross 29 E35
Aston End 33 F48
Aston Eyre 39 F32
Aston Fields 29 B35
Aston Flamville 41 F40
Aston Ingham 29 F32
Aston juxta Mondrum 49 G32
Aston le Walls 31 C40
Aston Magna 30 E37
Aston Munslow 38 G31
Aston on Clun 38 G29
Aston on Trent 41 B40
Aston Rogers 38 E29
Aston Rowant 22 B43
Aston Sandford 22 A43
Aston Somerville 30 E36
Aston Subedge 30 D37
Aston Tirrold 21 C41
Astwick 33 E48
Astwood 32 D45
Astwood Bank 30 B36
Aswarby 42 A46
Aswardby 53 E49
Aswick Grange 43 D48
Atcham 38 E31

Atch Lench 30 C36
Athelington 35 A58
Athelney 8 B29
Athelstaneford 76 C30
Atherington 6 C21
Atherstone 40 F38
Atherstone on Stour 30 C38
Atherton 49 B32
Athlinne 100 F7
Atlow 40 A38
Attadale 86 A15
Attenborough 41 B40
Atterby 52 C45
Attleborough War. 41 F39
Attleborough Nfk 44 F56
Attlebridge 45 D57
Atwick 59 D47
Atworth 20 E34
Aubourn 52 F45
Auch 80 D19
Auchachenna 80 E15
Auchairne 66 E16
Auchallater 90 E27
Auchameanach 73 E14
Aucharnie 98 E32
Aucharrigill 96 A20
Auchattie 91 D32
Auchavan 82 A27
Auchbraad 73 B14
Auchbreck 90 A27
Auchenblae 91 F33
Auchenbothie 74 C19
Auchenbrack 68 D23
Auchenbreck 73 B16
Auchencairn 65 E23
Auchencrow 77 D34
Auchendinny 76 D28
Auchendolly 65 D23
Auchenfoyle 74 C19
Auchengray 75 E25
Auchenhalrig 98 C29
Auchenheath 75 F24
Auchenhessnane 68 D23
Auchenlochan 73 C15
Auchenmalg 64 E18
Auchenrivock 69 E23
Auchentiber 74 F19
Auchessan 81 E20
Auchgourish 89 C25
Auchinafaud 72 E12
Auchincruive 67 A19
Auchindarrach 73 B14
Auchindarroch 80 B15
Auchindrain 80 G16
Auchindrean 95 C17
Auchininna 98 E32
Auchinleck 67 A21
Auchinloch 74 C22
Auchinner 81 F22
Auchinroath 98 D28
Auchintoul Grm. 98 D31
Auchintoul Grm. 90 B31
Auchintoul Hgh. 96 A21
Auchinvennal 74 B18
Auchiries 91 A32
Auchleven 91 A32
Auchlochan 75 G23
Auchlunachan 95 C17
Auchlunies 91 D34
Auchlunkart 98 E29
Auchlyne 81 E20
Auchmacoy 99 F35
Auchmair 90 A29
Auchmantle 64 D17
Auchmithie 83 C32
Auchmuirbridge 82 G27
Auchmull 90 F31
Auchnabony 65 F23
Auchnabreac 80 G16
Auchnacloich 81 D24
Auchnacraig 79 E13
Auchnacree 83 A30
Auchnafree 81 D23
Auchnagallin 89 A26
Auchnagatt 99 E35
Auchnaha 73 B15
Auchnangoul 80 G16
Aucholzie 90 D29
Auchorrie 91 C32
Auchraw 81 E21
Auchreoch 80 E19
Auchronie 90 E30
Auchterarder 82 F25
Auchtercairn 94 D14
Auchterderran 75 A27
Auchterhouse 82 D28
Auchtermuchty 82 F28
Auchterneed 96 E20
Auchtertool 75 A27
Auchtertyre Tay. 82 C28
Auchtertyre Cen. 80 E19
Auchtertyre Grm. 97 F27
Auchtoo 81 E21
Auckengill 103 B29
Auckley 51 B42
Audenshaw 49 C35

Audlem 39 A32
Audley 49 G33
Audley End 33 E50
Auds 98 C32
Aughton Lan. 48 B29
Aughton Lan. 55 C31
Aughton S.Y. 51 D40
Aughton Hum. 58 F42
Aughton Park 48 B29
Auldearn 97 F25
Aulden 28 C30
Auldhame 76 B31
Auldhouse 74 E21
Aulich 81 B21
Ault a'chruinn 86 C15
Aultanrynie 101 E19
Aultbea 94 C14
Aultgrishan 94 C13
Aultguish Inn 96 D19
Ault Hucknall 51 F40
Aultibea 103 F26
Aultiphurst 102 B23
Aultmore 98 D29
Aultnagoire 88 B21
Aultnamain Inn 96 C22
Aultnapaddock 98 E29
Aulton 90 A31
Aultvoulin 86 D13
Aundorach 89 C25
Aunk 7 E26
Aunsby 42 B46
Auquhorthies 91 A34
Aust 19 C31
Austerfield 51 C42
Austonley 50 B37
Austrey 40 E38
Austwick 56 C33
Authorpe 53 D49
Authorpe Row 53 E51
Avebury 20 D36
Aveley 23 D51
Avening 20 B34
Averham 51 G43
Aveton Gifford 5 F22
Avielochan 89 C24
Aviemore 89 C24
Avington Ham. 11 A41
Avington Brk. 21 E39
Avoch 96 F22
Avon 10 E37
Avonbridge 75 C25
Avon Dassett 31 C40
Avonmouth 19 D30
Avonwick 5 E23
Awbridge 10 B39
Awhirk 64 E16
Awkley 19 C31
Awliscombe 7 E27
Awre 19 A32
Awsworth 41 A40
Axbridge 19 F29
Axford Ham. 21 G42
Axford Wts. 21 D38
Axminster 8 E29
Axmouth 8 E28
Aycliffe 62 D38
Aydon 71 G36
Aylburton 19 A31
Ayle 61 B33
Aylesbeare 7 F26
Aylesbury 31 G43
Aylesby 53 B48
Aylesford 14 B53
Aylesham 15 B58
Aylestone 41 E41
Aylmerton 45 B57
Aylsham 45 C57
Aylton 29 E32
Aymestrey 28 B29
Aynho 31 E40
Ayot St Lawrence 32 G47
Ayot St Peter 32 G47
Ayr 67 A19
Aysgarth 56 A35
Ayshford 7 D26
Ayside 55 A29
Ayston 42 E44
Aythorpe Roding 33 G51
Ayton Tay. 82 F27
Ayton Bor. 77 D35
Aywick 106 D41
Azerley 57 B38

B

Babbacombe 5 D25
Babbinswood 38 B29
Babcary 8 B31
Babel 27 E24
Babell 47 E27
Babeny 5 C22
Babraham 33 C50
Babworth 51 D42
Bac 100 C10
Backaland 104 C31
Backaskaill 104 A30

Backbarrow 55 A29
Backburn 98 F32
Backfolds 99 D36
Backford 48 E29
Backhill Grm. 99 F33
Backhill Grm. 99 F36
Backhill of Clackriach 99 E35
Backhill of Trustach 91 D32
Backies Grm. 98 D30
Backies Hgh. 97 A24
Backlass 103 C27
Backmuir of New Gilston 83 G30
Back of Keppoch 86 F12
Backside 98 F29
Backwell 19 E30
Backworth 71 F38
Bacon End 33 G51
Baconsthorpe 45 B57
Bacton Nfk 45 B59
Bacton H.&W. 28 E29
Bacton Sfk 34 B56
Bacup 56 G34
Badachro 94 D13
Badanloch Lodge 102 E23
Badavanich 95 F16
Badbea 103 G26
Badbury 20 C37
Badby 31 C41
Badcall Hgh. 101 C18
Badcall Hgh. 101 D17
Badcaul 94 B15
Baddeley Green 49 G35
Badden 73 B14
Baddesley Ensor 40 F38
Baddidarach 101 F16
Badenscoth 98 F32
Badenyon 90 B29
Badger 39 F33
Badgerbank 49 E34
Badgers Mount 23 E50
Badgeworth 29 G34
Badgworth 19 F29
Badicaul 86 B13
Badingham 35 B59
Badintagairt 102 G20
Badlesmere 14 B55
Badley 34 C56
Badlipster 103 D28
Badluarchrach 94 B15
Badminton 20 C34
Badnaban 101 F16
Badnabay 101 D17
Badnafrave 90 B27
Badnagie 103 E27
Badnambiast 88 G22
Badninish 96 B23
Badrallach 95 B16
Badsey 30 D36
Badshot Lea 22 G44
Badsworth 51 A40
Badwell Ash 34 B55
Badyo 82 A25
Bagby 57 A40
Bag Enderby 53 E49
Bagendon 20 A35
Baggrave Hall 41 E42
Baggrow 60 B27
Bagh A Chaisteil (Castlebay) 84 E2
Baghasdal 84 C3
Bagillt 48 E28
Baginton 30 A39
Baglan 18 B23
Bagley 38 C30
Bagnall 49 G35
Bagnor 21 E40
Bagshot Sry 22 E44
Bagshot Wts. 21 E39
Bagstone 19 C32
Bagthorpe 51 G40
Baguley 49 D33
Bagworth 41 E40
Bagwyllydiart 28 F30
Baildon 57 F37
Baile Ailein 100 E8
Baile A Mhanaich (Balivanich) 92 F3
Baile an Truiseil 100 B9
Bailebeag 88 C20
Baile Boidheach 73 C13
Baile Gharbhaidh 92 G3
Baile Glas 92 F4
Baileguish 89 E24
Bailemeonach 79 C12
Baile Mhartainn 92 D3
Baile Mor 92 E3
Bailenacille 92 C4
Baile nan Cailleach 92 F3
Baile Raghaill 92 E2
Bailetonach 86 G12
Bailliesward 98 F30
Bainbridge 61 G35
Bainsford 75 B24
Bainshole 98 F31
Bainton Cbs. 42 E47

Bainton *Hum.* 59 D45
Bairnkine 70 B32
Bakebare 98 F29
Baker's End 33 G49
Baker Street 24 C52
Bakewell 50 F37
Bala 37 B25
Balachuirn 94 G11
Balafark 74 A22
Balaldie 97 D24
Balameanach 73 A14
Balavil 88 D23
Balbeg *Hgh.* 88 A20
Balbeg *Hgh.* 88 B20
Balbeggie 82 E27
Balbirnie 82 G28
Balbithan 91 B33
Balblair *Hgh.* 96 B21
Balblair *Hgh.* 96 E22
Balcharn 96 A21
Balcherry 96 C23
Balchers 98 D32
Balchladich 101 E16
Balchraggan *Hgh.* 96 G21
Balchraggan *Hgh.* 88 A21
Balchrick 101 B17
Balcombe 13 C49
Balcurvie 82 G29
Baldernock 74 C21
Baldersby 57 B39
Balderstone 56 F32
Balderton 52 G44
Baldhu 2 D13
Baldinnie 83 F30
Baldock 33 E48
Baldovie *Tay.* 82 B29
Baldovie *Tay.* 83 D30
Baldrine 54 E26
Baldslow 14 F54
Baldwin 54 E25
Baldwinholme 60 A29
Baldwin's Gate 39 A33
Bale 44 B56
Balelone 92 D3
Balemartine 78 C5
Balendoch 82 C28
Balephuil 78 C5
Balerno 75 D27
Balernock 74 B18
Baleromindubh 72 A9
Balerominmore 72 A9
Balevulin 79 E10
Balfield 83 A31
Balfour *Grm.* 90 D31
Balfour *Ork.* 104 E30
Balfron 74 B21
Balfron Station 74 B21
Balgavies 83 B31
Balgedie 82 G27
Balgonar 75 A25
Balgove 99 F34
Balgowan *D.&G.* 64 F17
Balgowan *Hgh.* 88 E22
Balgown 93 E9
Balgray 82 D29
Balgreen 99 D33
Balgreggan 64 E16
Balgy 94 F14
Balhaldie 81 G23
Balhary 82 C28
Balhelvie 82 E28
Balhousie 83 G30
Baliasta 106 B41
Baligill 102 B24
Baligrundle 79 D14
Balindore 80 D15
Balintore 97 D24
Balintraid 96 D23
Balintyre 81 C22
Balivanich (Baile A Mhanaich) 92 F3
Balkeerie 82 C29
Balkholme 58 G43
Balkissock 67 E17
Ball 38 C29
Ballabeg 54 F24
Ballacannell 54 E26
Ballacarnane Beg 54 E24
Ballachulish 80 B16
Balladoole 54 G24
Ballafesson 54 F23
Ballagyr 54 E24
Ballajora 54 D26
Ballakilpheric 54 F24
Ballamodha 54 F24
Ballantrae 66 E16
Ballards Gore 25 B55
Ballasalla *I.o.M.* 54 D25
Ballasalla *I.o.M.* 54 F24
Ballater 90 D29
Ballaterach 90 D29
Ballaugh 54 D25
Ballaveare 54 F25
Ballechin 82 B25
Balleich 81 G20

Ballencrieff 76 C30
Ball Haye Green 49 G35
Ball Hill 21 E40
Ballidon 50 G37
Balliekine 73 G14
Balliemeanoch 80 G16
Balliemore *Tay.* 81 B23
Balliemore *Str.* 73 A16
Balliemore *Str.* 79 E14
Ballig 54 E24
Ballimeanoch 80 F15
Ballimore *Cen.* 81 F21
Ballimore *Str.* 73 B15
Ballinaby 72 D8
Ballindean 82 E28
Ballingdon 34 D54
Ballinger Common 22 A44
Ballingham 28 E31
Ballingry 75 A27
Ballinlick 82 C25
Ballinluig *Tay.* 82 B25
Ballinluig *Tay.* 82 B26
Ballintuim 82 B26
Balloch *Tay.* 82 B29
Balloch *Tay.* 81 F24
Balloch *Hgh.* 96 G23
Balloch *Str.* 74 B19
Ballochan 90 D31
Ballochandrain 73 B15
Ballochford 98 F29
Ballochgair 66 A13
Ballochmartin 73 E17
Ballochmorrie 67 E17
Ballochmyle 67 A21
Ballochroy 73 E13
Ballogie 90 D31
Balls Cross 12 D45
Ballyaurgan 73 C13
Ballygown 79 C10
Ballygrant 72 D9
Ballyhaugh 78 B7
Ballymichael 73 G14
Balmacara 86 B13
Balmaclellan 65 C22
Balmacneil 82 B25
Balmadies 83 C31
Balmae 65 F22
Balmaha 74 A20
Balmalcolm 82 G28
Balmeanach 79 D10
Balmedie 91 B35
Balmerino 82 E29
Balmerlawn 10 D39
Balminnoch 64 D18
Balmore *Hgh.* 97 G24
Balmore *Str.* 74 C22
Balmore *Hgh.* 88 A19
Balmore *Hgh.* 93 G8
Balmullo 83 E30
Balmungie 96 F23
Balmyle 82 B26
Balnaboth 82 A28
Balnabruaich 96 D23
Balnacra 94 G15
Balnafoich 88 A22
Balnagall 97 C24
Balnagown Castle 96 D23
Balnaguard 82 B25
Balnaguisich 96 D22
Balnahard *Str.* 79 D10
Balnahard *Str.* 72 A10
Balnain 88 A20
Balnakeil 101 B19
Balnaknock 93 E10
Balnamoon 83 A31
Balnapaling 96 E23
Balnespick 89 D24
Balquhidder 81 E21
Balsall 30 A38
Balsall Common 30 A38
Balscote 30 D39
Balsham 33 C51
Baltasound 106 B41
Balterley 39 A33
Baltersan 64 D20
Balthangie 99 D34
Balthayock 82 E27
Baltonsborough 8 A31
Baluachraig 73 A14
Balulive 72 D9
Balure *Str.* 80 D16
Balure *Str.* 79 D14
Balvaird 96 F21
Balvarran 82 A26
Balvicar 79 F13
Balvraid *Hgh.* 86 C14
Balvraid *Hgh.* 89 A24
Bamber Bridge 55 G31
Bamber's Green 33 F51
Bamburgh 77 G37
Bamff 82 B28
Bamford 50 D37
Bampton *Oxf.* 21 A38
Bampton *Cum.* 61 E30
Bampton *Dev.* 7 C25
Banavie 87 G16

Banbury 31 D40
Bancffosfelen 17 C20
Banchor 97 G24
Banchory 91 D32
Banchory-Devenick 91 C35
Bancycapel 17 C18
Banc-y-ffordd 17 A19
Bandon 82 G28
Banff 98 C32
Bangor 46 E21
Bangor-is-y-coed 38 A29
Bangor Teifi 26 D19
Banham 44 G56
Bank 10 D38
Bankend *Str.* 75 G24
Bank End 54 A27
Bankend *D.&G.* 69 G26
Bankfoot 82 D26
Bankhead *Grm.* 91 C32
Bankhead *Grm.* 91 C34
Bankhead *Grm.* 91 B32
Bankhead *D.&G.* 65 F23
Bank Newton 56 D35
Banknock 75 C23
Banks *Cum.* 70 G31
Banks *Lan.* 55 G29
Bankshill 69 E27
Bank Street 29 B32
Banningham 45 C58
Bannister Green 33 F52
Bannockburn 75 A24
Banstead 23 F48
Bantham 5 F22
Banton 75 C23
Banwell 19 F29
Bapchild 25 E55
Baptiston 74 B21
Barabhas 100 B9
Barachander 80 E16
Barassie 74 G18
Barbaraville 96 D23
Barber Booth 50 D37
Barbon 56 A32
Barbrook 7 A23
Barby 31 A41
Barcaldine 80 C15
Barcaple 65 E22
Barcheston 30 D38
Barcombe 13 E50
Barcombe Cross 13 E50
Barden 62 G37
Bardennoch 67 D21
Bardfield End Green 33 E52
Bardfield Saling 33 F52
Bardister 106 E39
Bardney 52 F47
Bardon *Lei.* 41 D40
Bardon *Grm.* 97 F28
Bardon Mill 70 G33
Bardsea 55 B29
Bardsey 57 E39
Bardsley 49 B35
Bardwell 34 A55
Barewood 28 C29
Barfad 73 D14
Barford *War.* 30 B38
Barford *Nfk* 45 E57
Barford St John 31 E40
Barford St Martin 10 A36
Barford St Michael 30 E39
Barfreston 15 B58
Bargaly 64 D20
Bargany 67 C18
Bargoed 18 B27
Bargrennan 64 C19
Barham *Cbs.* 32 A47
Barham *Sfk* 35 C57
Barham *Kent* 15 B57
Barharrow 65 E21
Bar Hill 33 B49
Barholm *Lcn.* 42 D46
Barholm *D.&G.* 64 E20
Barkby 41 E42
Barkby Thorpe 41 E42
Barkestone-le-Vale 42 B43
Barkham 22 E43
Barking *G.L.* 23 C50
Barking *Sfk* 34 C56
Barking & Dagenham 23 C50
Barkingside 23 C50
Barkisland 50 A36
Barkston *Lcn.* 42 A45
Barkston *N.Y.* 57 F40
Barkway 33 E49
Barlae 64 D18
Barlaston 40 B34
Barlavington 12 E45
Barlay 65 E21
Barlborough 51 E40
Barlby 58 F42
Barlestone 41 E40
Barley *Hfs.* 33 E49
Barley *Lan.* 56 E34
Barleycroft End 33 F49
Barleyhill 62 A36
Barleythorpe 42 E44

Barling 25 C55
Barlings 52 E46
Barlow *Dby.* 51 E39
Barlow *T.&W.* 71 G37
Barlow *N.Y.* 58 G42
Barmby Moor 58 E43
Barmby on the Marsh 58 G42
Barmolloch 73 A14
Barmoor Lane End 77 F35
Barmouth 36 D21
Barmpton 62 E38
Barmston 59 D47
Barnacabber 73 B17
Barnacarry 73 A16
Barnack 42 E46
Barnacle 41 G40
Barnamuc 80 C16
Barnard Castle 62 E36
Barnard Gate 31 G40
Barnardiston 33 D52
Barnard's Green 29 D33
Barnbarroch *D.&G.* 65 E24
Barnbarroch *D.&G.* 64 E19
Barnburgh 51 B40
Barnby 45 F60
Barnby Dun 51 B41
Barnby in the Willows 52 G44
Barnby Moor 51 D42
Barndennoch 68 E24
Barnes 23 D48
Barnet 23 B48
Barnetby le Wold 52 B46
Barney 44 B55
Barnham *W.S.* 12 F45
Barnham *Sfk* 34 A54
Barnham Broom 44 E56
Barnhead 83 B32
Barnhill 97 F27
Barningham *Sfk* 34 A55
Barningham *Drm* 62 E36
Barnoldby le Beck 53 B48
Barnoldswick 56 E34
Barns Green 12 D47
Barnsley *S.Y.* 51 B39
Barnsley *Glo.* 20 A36
Barnstaple 6 B21
Barnston *Mer.* 48 D28
Barnston *Esx* 33 G52
Barnstone 42 B43
Barnt Green 30 A36
Barnton 49 E32
Barnwell All Saints 42 G46
Barnwell St Andrew 42 G46
Barnwood 29 G34
Barr *Str.* 72 D9
Barr *Hgh.* 79 B12
Barr *Str.* 67 D18
Barrackan 79 G13
Barraer 64 D19
Barraglom 100 D7
Barrahormid 72 B12
Barran 78 C5
Barrapoll 78 C5
Barrasford 70 F34
Barra (Traigh Mor) Airport 84 D3
Barravullin 79 G13
Barregarrow 54 E24
Barr Hall 34 E53
Barrhead 74 E21
Barrhill 67 E18
Barrington *Som.* 8 C29
Barrington *Cbs.* 33 D49
Barripper 74 D19
Barrisdale 86 D14
Barrmill 74 E19
Barrnacarry 79 E13
Barrock 103 A28
Barrow *Sfk* 34 B53
Barrow *Shr.* 39 E32
Barrow *Lei.* 42 D44
Barrow *Lan.* 56 F34
Barrow *Som.* 9 A33
Barrowby 42 B44
Barrowden 42 E45
Barrowford 56 F34
Barrow Gurney 19 E31
Barrow Haven 59 G46
Barrow-in-Furness 54 B27
Barrow Nook 48 B30
Barrow Street 9 A34
Barrow upon Humber 59 G46
Barrow upon Soar 41 D41
Barrow upon Trent 41 C39
Barry *S.G.* 18 E27
Barry *Tay.* 83 D31
Barsby 41 D42
Barsham 45 F59
Barskimming 67 A20
Barsloisnoch 73 A13
Barston 30 A37
Bartestree 28 D31
Barthol Chapel 99 F34
Barthomley 49 G33
Bartley 10 C39
Bartlow 33 D51

Barton *Glo.* 30 F36
Barton *War.* 30 C37
Barton *Lan.* 48 B29
Barton *Che.* 48 G30
Barton *Dev.* 5 D25
Barton *N.Y.* 62 F38
Barton *Cbs.* 33 C49
Barton *Lan.* 55 F30
Barton Bendish 44 E53
Barton Common 45 C59
Barton End 20 B34
Barton Hartshorn 31 E42
Barton in Fabis 41 B41
Barton in the Beans 41 E40
Barton-le-Clay 32 E46
Barton-le-Street 58 B43
Barton-le-Willows 58 C43
Barton Mills 34 A53
Barton on Sea 10 E38
Barton-on-the-Heath 30 E38
Barton Seagrave 32 A44
Barton Stacey 21 G40
Barton Stacey Camp 21 G40
Barton St David 8 A31
Barton Turf 45 C59
Barton-under-Needwood 40 D37
Barton-upon-Humber 59 G45
Barway 33 A51
Barwell 41 F40
Barwhinnock 65 E22
Barwick 8 C31
Barwick in Elmet 57 F39
Barwinnock 64 F19
Baschurch 38 C29
Bascote 30 B39
Basford Green 49 G35
Bashall Eaves 56 E32
Bashall Town 56 E32
Bashley 10 E38
Basildon *Esx* 24 C53
Basildon *Brk.* 21 D42
Basingstoke 21 F41
Baslow 50 E38
Bason Bridge 19 G29
Bassaleg 19 C28
Bassenthwaite 60 C27
Bassett 11 C40
Bassett's Cross 6 E21
Bassingbourn 33 D48
Bassingfield 41 B42
Bassingham 52 F44
Bassingthorpe 42 C45
Basta 106 C41
Baston 42 D47
Bastwick 45 D60
Batavaime 81 D20
Batchworth 22 B46
Batchworth Heath 22 B46
Batcombe *Som.* 9 A32
Batcombe *Dor.* 9 D32
Bate Heath 49 E32
Bath 20 E33
Bathampton 20 E33
Bathealton 7 C26
Batheaston 20 E33
Bathford 20 E33
Bathgate 75 D25
Bathley 51 G43
Bathpool *Cnw.* 4 C18
Bathpool *Som.* 8 B28
Batley 57 G38
Batsford 30 E37
Battersby 63 F41
Battersea 23 D48
Battisborough Cross 5 F22
Battisford 34 C56
Battisford Tye 34 C56
Battle *Pow.* 27 E25
Battle *E.S.* 14 F53
Battlefield 38 D31
Battlesbridge 24 B53
Battlesden 32 F45
Battleton 7 C24
Battramsley 10 E38
Batt's Corner 22 G44
Bauds of Cullen 98 C30
Baugh 78 C6
Baughton 29 D34
Baughurst 21 F41
Baulds 90 D31
Baulking 21 B39
Baumber 53 E48
Baunton 20 A36
Baveney Wood 29 A32
Baverstock 10 A36
Bawburgh 45 E57
Bawdeswell 44 C56
Bawdrip 8 A29
Bawdsey 35 D59
Bawtry 51 C42
Baxenden 56 G33
Baxterley 40 F38
Baycliff 55 B28
Baydon 21 D38
Bayford *Bfd.* 23 A48

Bayford *Som.* 9 B33
Bayfordbury 33 G48
Bayham Abbey 13 C52
Bayles 61 B32
Baylham 34 C56
Baynards Green 31 F41
Baysham 28 F31
Bayston Hill 38 E30
Baythorn End 34 D53
Bayton 29 A32
Beach 79 B13
Beachampton 31 E43
Beacharr 72 F12
Beachborough 15 D57
Beachley 19 B31
Beacon 7 E27
Beacon End 34 F55
Beacon Hill 12 C44
Beacon's Bottom 22 B43
Beaconsfield 22 B45
Beadlam 58 A42
Beadnell 71 A38
Beaford 6 D21
Beal *Nor.* 77 F36
Beal *N.Y.* 58 G41
Bealach 80 B15
Beambridge 49 G32
Beamhurst 40 B36
Beaminster 8 D30
Beamish 62 A38
Beamsley 57 D36
Bean 23 D51
Beanacre 20 E34
Beanley 71 B36
Beaquoy 104 D28
Beardon 6 G21
Beare Green 22 G47
Bearley 30 B37
Bearnie 99 F35
Bearnock 88 A19
Bearnus 78 C9
Bearpark 62 B38
Bearsbridge 61 A33
Bearsden 74 C21
Bearsted 14 B53
Bearwood 10 E36
Beattock 69 C26
Beauchamp Roding 33 G51
Beauchief 51 D39
Beaudesert 30 B37
Beaufort 28 G27
Beaulieu 10 D39
Beauly 96 G21
Beaumaris 46 E21
Beaumont *Esx* 35 F57
Beaumont *Cum.* 60 A29
Beausale 30 A38
Beauworth 11 B41
Beaworthy 6 F20
Beazley End 34 F53
Bebington 48 D29
Bebside 71 E38
Beccles 45 F60
Becconsall 55 G30
Beckbury 39 E33
Beckenham 23 E49
Beckermet 60 F25
Beck Foot 61 G32
Beckfoot *Cum.* 60 B26
Beckfoot *Cum.* 60 F27
Beckford 29 E35
Beckhampton 20 E36
Beck Hole 63 F44
Beckingham *Lcn.* 52 G44
Beckingham *Not.* 51 C43
Beckington 20 F33
Beckley *E.S.* 14 E54
Beckley *Oxf.* 31 G41
Beck Row 33 A52
Beck Side 55 A28
Beckton 23 C50
Beckwithshaw 57 D38
Becontree 23 C50
Bedale 57 A38
Bedburn 62 C36
Bedchester 9 C34
Beddau 18 C26
Beddgelert 36 A21
Beddingham 13 F50
Beddington 23 E48
Beddington Corner 23 E48
Bedfield 35 B57
Bedford 32 C46
Bedgebury Cross 13 C52
Bedhampton 11 D43
Bedingfield 35 B57
Bedlington 71 E38
Bedlinog 18 A26
Bedmond 22 A46
Bednall 40 D35
Bedol 48 E28
Bedrule 70 B31
Bedstone 28 A29
Bedwas 18 C27
Bedwellty 18 A27
Bedworth 41 G39

Beeby 41 E42
Beech *Stf.* 40 B34
Beech *Ham.* 11 A42
Beechamwell 44 E53
Beech Hill 21 E42
Beechingstoke 20 F36
Beedon 21 D40
Beeford 59 D47
Beeley 50 F38
Beelsby 53 B48
Beenham 21 E41
Beer 8 F28
Beercrocombe 8 B29
Beer Hackett 9 C32
Beesands 5 F24
Beesby 53 D50
Beeson 5 F23
Beeston *Che.* 48 G31
Beeston *Not.* 41 B41
Beeston *Bfd.* 32 D47
Beeston *W.Y.* 57 F38
Beeston *Nfk* 44 D55
Beeston Regis 45 A57
Beeston St Lawrence 45 C59
Beeswing 65 D24
Beetham 55 B30
Beetley 44 D55
Began 19 C28
Begbroke 31 G40
Begelly 16 D17
Beggshill 98 F31
Beguildy 28 A27
Beighton *Dby.* 51 D40
Beighton *Nfk* 45 E59
Beith 74 E19
Bekesbourne 15 B57
Belaugh 45 D58
Belbroughton 29 A34
Belchamp Otten 34 D54
Belchamp St Paul 34 D53
Belchamp Walter 34 D54
Belchford 53 E48
Belford 77 G36
Belgrave 41 E41
Belhaven 76 C32
Belhelvie 91 B35
Belhinnie 90 A30
Bellabeg 90 B29
Belladrum 96 G21
Bellanoch 73 A13
Bellasize 58 G44
Bellaty 82 B28
Bell Bar 23 A48
Bell Busk 56 D35
Belleau 53 E49
Bell End 29 A35
Bellerby 62 G37
Bellever 5 C22
Belliehill 83 A31
Bellingdon 22 A45
Bellingham 70 E34
Belloch 72 G12
Bellochantuy 72 G12
Bellsdyke 75 B25
Bellshill *Nor.* 77 G37
Bellshill *Str.* 75 E23
Bellside 75 E24
Bellspool 75 G27
Bellsquarry 75 D26
Bells Yew Green 13 C52
Belluton 19 E31
Belmaduthy 96 F22
Belmesthorpe 42 D46
Belmont *She.* 106 B41
Belmont *Lan.* 49 A32
Belmont *G.L.* 23 E48
Belowda 3 B15
Belper 41 A39
Belper Lane End 51 G39
Belsay 71 F36
Belsford 5 E23
Belstead 35 D57
Belston 67 A19
Belstone 6 F21
Belstone Corner 6 F22
Belsyde 75 C25
Belthorn 56 G33
Beltinge 25 E57
Beltoft 52 B44
Belton *Hum.* 51 B43
Belton *Lei.* 42 E44
Belton *Lei.* 41 C40
Belton *Lcn.* 42 B45
Belton *Nfk* 45 E60
Beltring 23 G52
Belvedere 23 D50
Belvoir 42 B44
Bembridge 11 F42
Bemersyde 76 G31
Bempton 59 B47
Benacre 45 G61
Ben Alder Cottage 81 A20
Ben Alder Lodge 88 G21
Benbecula (Bhaile A Mhanaich)
  Airport 92 F3
Benbuie 68 D22

Benderloch 79 D14
Bendish 32 F47
Benenden 14 D54
Benfield 64 D19
Bengate 45 C58
Bengeo 33 G49
Benholm 91 G34
Beningbrough 58 D41
Benington *Hfs.* 33 F48
Benington *Lcn.* 43 A49
Benington Sea End 43 A50
Benllech 46 D20
Benmore *Str.* 73 B17
Benmore *Cen.* 81 E20
Bennacott 4 A18
Bennan 65 C22
Benniworth 53 D48
Benover 14 C53
Benson 21 B42
Benthall *Nor.* 71 A38
Benthall *Shr.* 39 E32
Bentham 29 G35
Benthoul 91 C33
Bentley *Ham.* 22 G43
Bentley *Hum.* 59 F46
Bentley *War.* 40 F38
Bentley *S.Y.* 51 B41
Bentley Heath 30 A37
Benton 6 B22
Benton Square 71 G39
Bentpath 69 D28
Bentworth 21 G42
Benvie 82 D29
Benville Lane 8 D31
Benwick 43 G49
Beoley 30 B36
Bepton 12 E44
Berden 33 F50
Berea 16 B13
Bere Alston 4 D20
Bere Ferrers 4 D20
Berepper 2 F12
Bere Regis 9 E34
Bergh Apton 45 E59
Berinsfield 21 B41
Berkeley 19 B32
Berkhamsted 22 A45
Berkley 20 G33
Berkswell 30 A38
Bermondsey 23 D49
Bernera 86 B14
Berners Roding 24 A52
Bernice 73 A17
Bernisdale 93 F9
Berrick Salome 21 B42
Berriedale 103 F26
Berriew (Aberriw) 38 E27
Berrington *Shr.* 38 E31
Berrington *Nor.* 77 F35
Berrow 19 F28
Berrow Green 29 C33
Berry Down Cross 6 A21
Berry Hill *Dyf.* 16 A16
Berry Hill *Glo.* 28 G31
Berryhillock 98 C30
Berrynarbor 6 A21
Berry Pomeroy 5 D24
Bersham 38 A28
Berstane 104 E30
Berwick 13 F50
Berwick Bassett 20 D36
Berwick Hill 71 F37
Berwick St James 10 A36
Berwick St John 9 B35
Berwick St Leonard 9 A35
Berwick-upon-Tweed 77 E35
Bescar 48 A29
Besford *Shr.* 38 C31
Besford *H.&W.* 29 D35
Bessacarr 51 B41
Bessels Leigh 21 A40
Bessingby 59 C47
Bessingham 45 B57
Best Beech Hill 13 C52
Besthorpe *Nfk* 44 F56
Besthorpe *Not.* 52 F44
Beswick 59 E46
Betchworth 23 F48
Bethania *Dyf.* 26 B21
Bethania *Gwy.* 37 A22
Bethel *Gwy.* 37 A25
Bethel *Gwy.* 46 F21
Bethel *Gwy.* 46 E19
Bethersden 14 D55
Bethesda *Gwy.* 46 F21
Bethesda *Dyf.* 16 C16
Bethlehem 17 B22
Bethnal Green 23 C49
Betley 39 A33
Betsham 24 D52
Betteshanger 15 B58
Bettisfield 38 B30
Betton *Shr.* 38 E29
Betton *Shr.* 39 B32
Bettws 19 B28

Bettws Bledrws 26 C21
Bettws Cedewain 38 F27
Bettws Evan 26 D18
Bettws Gwerfil Goch 37 A26
Bettws-Newydd 19 A29
Bettws-y-crwyn 38 G27
Bettyhill 102 B22
Betws *M.G.* 18 C24
Betws *Dyf.* 17 C22
Betws Disserth 27 C26
Betws Garmon 46 G21
Betws-y-coed 47 G23
Betws-yn-Rhos 47 E24
Beulah *Pow.* 27 C25
Beulah *Dyf.* 26 D18
Bevendean 13 F49
Bevercotes 51 E42
Beverley 59 F46
Beverstone 20 B34
Bevington 19 B32
Bewaldeth 60 C27
Bewcastle 70 F31
Bewdley 29 A33
Bewerley 57 C37
Bewholme 59 E47
Bewley Common 20 E35
Bexhill 14 G53
Bexley 23 D50
Bexleyheath 23 D50
Bexwell 44 E52
Beyton 34 B55
Beyton Green 34 B55
Bhalamus 100 G8
Bhaltos 100 D6
Bhatarsaigh 84 E2
Biallaid 88 E22
Bibury 20 A37
Bicester 31 F41
Bickenhall 8 C28
Bickenhill 40 G37
Bicker 43 B48
Bickerstaffe 48 B30
Bickerton *Che.* 48 G30
Bickerton *N.Y.* 57 D40
Bickford 40 D34
Bickham Bridge 5 E23
Bickham House 7 G25
Bickington *Dev.* 6 B21
Bickington *Dev.* 5 C23
Bickleigh *Dev.* 7 E25
Bickleigh *Dev.* 5 D21
Bickleton 6 B21
Bickley 23 E50
Bickley Moss 38 A31
Bickley Town 38 A31
Bicknacre 24 A53
Bicknoller 7 B26
Bicknor 14 B54
Bickton 10 C37
Bicton *Shr.* 38 G28
Bicton *Shr.* 38 D30
Bicton Heath 38 D30
Bidborough 23 G51
Biddenden 14 D54
Biddenham 32 D46
Biddestone 20 D34
Biddisham 19 F29
Biddlesden 31 D42
Biddlestone 70 C35
Biddulph 49 G34
Biddulph Moor 49 G35
Bideford 6 C20
Bidford-on-Avon 30 C36
Bidston 48 C28
Bielby 58 E43
Bieldside 91 C34
Bierley *I.o.W.* 11 G40
Bierley *W.Y.* 57 G37
Bierton 32 G44
Bigbury 52 B46
Bigbury-on-Sea 5 F21
Bigby 52 B46
Bigert Mire 60 G27
Biggar *Cum.* 54 C27
Biggar *Str.* 75 G26
Biggin *Dby.* 50 G37
Biggin *Dby.* 40 A38
Biggin *N.Y.* 58 F41
Biggings 107 A37
Biggin Hill 23 F50
Biggleswade 32 D47
Bigholms 69 E29
Bighouse 102 B24
Bighton 11 A42
Biglands 60 D34
Bignor 12 E45
Bigrigg 60 E25
Big Sand 94 D13
Bigton 107 E39
Bilberry 4 E16
Bilborough 41 A41
Bilbrook *Stf.* 40 E34
Bilbrook *Som.* 7 A26
Bilbrough 58 E41
Bilbster 103 C28
Bildershaw 62 D37

Bildeston 34 D55
Billericay 24 B52
Billesdon 42 E43
Billesley 30 C37
Billholm 69 D28
Billingborough 42 B47
Billinge 48 B31
Billingford *Nfk* 35 A57
Billingford *Nfk* 44 C55
Billingham 62 D40
Billinghay 52 G47
Billingley 51 B40
Billingshurst 12 D46
Billingsley 39 G32
Billington *Bfd.* 32 F45
Billington *Lan.* 56 F32
Billockby 45 D60
Billy Row 62 C37
Bilsborrow 55 E30
Bilsby 53 E50
Bilsdean 77 C33
Bilsham 12 F45
Bilsington 15 D56
Bilson *W.M.* 40 F35
Bilson *Ltn* 76 D28
Bilstone 41 E39
Bilting 15 C56
Bilton *Hum.* 59 F47
Bilton *N.Y.* 57 D39
Bilton *N.Y.* 57 D40
Bilton *War.* 31 A40
Bilton *Nor.* 71 B38
Bimbister 104 E29
Bincombe 9 F32
Bindal 97 C25
Binegar 19 G31
Bines Green 12 E47
Binfield 22 D44
Binfield Heath 22 D43
Bingfield 70 F35
Bingham 41 B42
Bingham's Melcombe 9 D33
Bingley 57 F37
Binham 44 B55
Binley *Ham.* 21 F40
Binley *War.* 30 A39
Binniehill 75 C24
Binsness 97 E26
Binsoe 57 A38
Binstead 11 E41
Binsted *W.S.* 12 F45
Binsted *Ham.* 22 G43
Binton 30 C37
Bintree 44 C56
Binweston 38 E28
Birch *Esx* 34 G55
Birch *G.M.* 49 B34
Birchanger 33 F50
Bircher 28 B30
Birchfield 96 B20
Birchgrove *W.G.* 18 B23
Birchgrove *S.G.* 18 C27
Birch Heath 48 F31
Birchington 25 E58
Birchover 50 F38
Birch Vale 50 D36
Bircotes 51 C42
Birdbrook 33 D52
Bird End 40 F36
Birdfield 73 A15
Birdham 12 G44
Birdingbury 31 B40
Birdlip 29 G35
Birdsall 58 C44
Birdsgreen 39 G33
Birdsmoor Gate 8 D29
Birdwell 51 B39
Birdwood 29 G33
Birgham 77 G33
Birichen 96 B23
Birkby 62 F39
Birkdale *Mer.* 48 A29
Birkdale *N.Y.* 61 F34
Birkenhead 48 D28
Birkenhills 99 E33
Birkenshaw 57 G37
Birkhall 90 D29
Birkhill *Tay.* 82 D29
Birkhill *Bor.* 69 B27
Birkhill *Bor.* 76 F31
Birkin 58 G41
Birkwood 75 G23
Birley 28 C30
Birley Carr 51 C39
Birling *Nor.* 71 C38
Birling *Kent* 24 E52
Birling Gap 13 G51
Birlingham 29 D35
Birmingham 40 G36
Birmingham Airport 40 G37
Birnam 82 C26
Birsay 104 D28
Birse 90 D31
Birsemore 90 D31

Birstall 41 E41
Birstall Smithies 57 G38
Birstwith 57 D38
Birthorpe 42 B46
Birtley *Drm* 62 A38
Birtley *H.&W.* 28 B29
Birtley *Nor.* 70 F34
Birts Street 29 E33
Bisbrooke 42 F44
Bisham 22 C44
Bishampton 29 C35
Bish Mill 7 C23
Bishop Auckland 62 D38
Bishopbridge 52 C46
Bishopbriggs 74 C21
Bishop Burton 59 F45
Bishop Middleham 62 C39
Bishopmill 97 E27
Bishop Monkton 57 C39
Bishop Norton 52 C45
Bishopsbourne 15 B57
Bishops Cannings 20 E36
Bishop's Castle 38 G28
Bishop's Caundle 9 C32
Bishop's Cleeve 29 F35
Bishop's Frome 29 D32
Bishop's Green 33 G52
Bishop's Hull 7 C27
Bishop's Itchington 30 C39
Bishop's Lydeard 7 C27
Bishop's Nympton 7 C23
Bishop's Offley 39 C33
Bishop's Stortford 33 F50
Bishop's Sutton 11 A42
Bishop's Tachbrook 30 B39
Bishop's Tawton 6 B21
Bishopsteignton 5 C25
Bishopstoke 11 C40
Bishopston 17 F21
Bishopstone *Wts.* 21 C38
Bishopstone *E.S.* 13 F50
Bishopstone *H.&W.* 28 D29
Bishopstone *Bkh.* 31 G43
Bishopstone *Wts.* 10 B36
Bishopstrow 20 G34
Bishop Sutton 19 F31
Bishop's Waltham 11 C41
Bishop's Wood 40 E34
Bishopswood 8 C28
Bishopsworth 19 E31
Bishop Thornton 57 C38
Bishopthorpe 58 E41
Bishopton *Str.* 74 C20
Bishopton *Drm* 62 D39
Bishop Wilton 58 D43
Bishton 19 C29
Bisley *Glo.* 20 A35
Bisley *Sry* 22 F45
Bispham 55 E28
Bissoe 2 D13
Bisterne 10 D37
Bisterne Close 10 D38
Bitchfield 42 C45
Bittadon 6 A21
Bittaford 5 E22
Bittering 44 D55
Bitterley 28 A31
Bitterne 11 C40
Bitteswell 41 G41
Bitton 19 E32
Bix 22 C43
Bixter 107 B39
Blaby 41 F41
Blackacre 69 D26
Blackadder 77 E34
Blackawton 5 E23
Blackborough 7 E26
Blackborough End 44 D52
Black Bourton 21 A38
Blackboys 13 D51
Blackbraes *Grm.* 91 B34
Blackbraes *Cen.* 75 C24
Blackbrook 39 B33
Blackburn *Ltn* 75 D25
Blackburn *Lan.* 56 G32
Blackburn *Grm.* 91 B34
Black Callerton 71 G37
Blackcastle 97 F24
Blackchambers 91 B33
Black Clauchrie 67 E18
Black Corries Lodge 80 B18
Blackcraig *D.&G.* 68 E22
Blackcraig *D.&G.* 64 D20
Black Cross 3 B14
Blackden Heath 49 E33
Black Dog 7 E24
Blackdog 91 B35
Blackdown *Dor.* 8 D29
Blackdown *Dev.* 5 C21
Blackfield 11 D40
Blackford *Som.* 9 B32
Blackford *Tay.* 81 G24
Blackford *Cum.* 69 G29
Blackford *Grm.* 98 F32
Blackford *Som.* 19 G29
Blackfordby 41 D39

Blackgang 11 G40
Blackhall 76 C28
Blackhall Colliery 62 B40
Blackhall Rocks 62 C40
Blackham 13 C51
Blackheath *Sry* 22 G46
Blackheath *W.M.* 40 G35
Blackheath *Sfk* 35 A59
Blackheath *Esx* 34 F55
Black Heddon 71 F36
Blackhill *Hgh.* 86 B11
Blackhill *Grm.* 99 D36
Blackhill *Grm.* 99 E36
Blackhillock 98 E30
Blackhills 98 D28
Blackland 20 E35
Blacklunans 82 A27
Black Marsh 38 F29
Blackmill 18 C25
Blackmoor *Som.* 7 D27
Blackmoor *Ham.* 11 A43
Blackmoor Gate 6 A22
Blackmore 23 A51
Blackmore End *Hfs.* 32 G47
Blackmore End *Esx* 34 E53
Black Mount 80 C18
Blackness *Cen.* 75 C26
Blackness *Hgh.* 103 E28
Blackness *Grm.* 91 D32
Blacknest 22 G43
Black Notley 34 F53
Blacko 56 E34
Black Pill 17 F22
Blackpool 55 F28
Blackpool Airport 55 F29
Blackpool Gate 69 F30
Blackridge 75 D24
Blackrock *Gwe.* 28 G27
Blackrock *Str.* 72 D8
Blackrod 48 A31
Blackshaw 69 G26
Blackshaw Head 56 G35
Blacksmith's Corner 34 E56
Blackstone 13 E48
Blackthorn 31 G41
Blackthorpe 34 B54
Blacktoft 58 G44
Blacktop 91 C34
Black Torrington 6 E20
Blacktown 19 C28
Blackwater *Cnw.* 2 D12
Blackwater *Sfk* 35 A60
Blackwater *I.o.W.* 11 F41
Blackwater *Ham.* 22 F44
Blackwaterfoot 66 A14
Blackwell *Dby.* 50 E37
Blackwell *Drm* 62 E38
Blackwell *War.* 30 D38
Blackwell *H.&W.* 29 A35
Blackwell *Dby.* 51 G40
Blackwells End 29 F33
Blackwood *Str.* 75 F23
Blackwood *D.&G.* 68 E24
Blackwood *Gwe.* 18 B27
Blackwood Hill 49 G35
Blacon 48 F29
Bladbean 15 C57
Blades 62 G35
Bladnoch 64 E20
Bladon 31 G40
Blaenannerch 26 D18
Blaenau Dolwyddelan 46 G22
Blaenau Ffestiniog 37 A23
Blaenavon 19 A28
Blaenawey 28 G28
Blaencwm 18 A24
Blaen Dyryn 27 E25
Blaenffos 16 A17
Blaengarw 18 B24
Blaengweche 17 C22
Blaengwrach 18 A24
Blaengwynfi 18 B24
Blaenos 27 E23
Blaenpennal 27 B22
Blaenplwyf 26 A21
Blaenporth 26 D18
Blaenrhondda 18 A25
Blaenwaun 17 B18
Blaen-y-coed 17 B19
Blagdon *Avon* 19 F30
Blagdon *Dev.* 5 D24
Blagdon Hill 8 C28
Blaich 87 G16
Blaina 18 A27
Blair 74 F18
Blairannaich 80 G18
Blair Atholl 81 A24
Blairbuie 73 C16
Blair Drummond 75 A23
Blairgowrie 82 C27
Blairhall 75 B25
Blairhoyle 81 G21
Blairhullichan 81 G20
Blairingone 75 A25
Blairkip 74 G21
Blairlogie 75 A24

Blairmore *Hgh.* 101 B17
Blairmore *Str.* 73 B17
Blairmore *Hgh.* 96 A23
Blairnairn 74 B19
Blairnamarrow 90 B27
Blairpark 74 E18
Blairquhan 67 C19
Blairquhosh 74 B21
Blairshinnoch 98 C32
Blairuskinmore 81 G20
Blairvadach 74 B18
Blairydryne 91 D33
Blairythan 91 A35
Blaisdon 29 G32
Blakebrook 29 A33
Blakedown 29 A34
Blake End 33 F52
Blakelaw *Bor.* 77 G33
Blakelaw *T.&W.* 71 G38
Blakemere 28 D29
Blakeney *Nfk* 44 A56
Blakeney *Glo.* 19 A32
Blakenhall *Che.* 39 A33
Blakenhall *Stf.* 40 F34
Blakeshall 40 G34
Blakesley 31 C42
Blanchland 61 A35
Blandford Camp 9 D35
Blandford Forum 9 D34
Blandford St Mary 9 D34
Bland Hill 57 D38
Blanefield 74 C21
Blankney 52 F46
Blar a'Chaorainn 80 A16
Blargie 88 E21
Blarglas 74 B19
Blarmachfoldach 80 A16
Blarnalevoch 95 B17
Blashford 10 D37
Blaston 42 F43
Blathaisbhal 92 D4
Blatherwycke 42 F45
Blawith 55 A28
Blaxhall 35 C59
Blaxton 51 B42
Blaydon 71 G37
Bleadney 19 G30
Bleadon 19 F29
Bleak Hey Nook 49 B35
Blean 25 E57
Bleasby 42 A43
Bleasdale 56 E31
Blebocraigs 83 F30
Bleddfa 28 B27
Bledington 30 F38
Bledlow 22 A43
Bledlow Ridge 22 B43
Blencarn 61 C32
Blencogo 60 B27
Blencow 60 C30
Blendworth 11 C43
Blennerhasset 60 B27
Blervie Castle 97 F26
Bletchingdon 31 G40
Bletchingley 23 F49
Bletchley *Bkh.* 32 E44
Bletchley *Shr.* 39 B32
Bletherston 16 B16
Bletsoe 32 C46
Blewbury 21 C41
Blickling 45 C57
Blidworth 51 G41
Blindburn *Grm.* 99 F35
Blindburn *Nor.* 70 B34
Blindcrake 60 C27
Blindley Heath 23 G49
Blisland 4 C17
Blissford 10 C37
Bliss Gate 29 A33
Blisworth 31 C43
Blithbury 40 C36
Blitterlees 60 A26
Blockley 30 E37
Blofield 45 E59
Blo Norton 34 A56
Blore 40 A37
Blossomfield 30 A37
Blount's Green 40 B36
Bloxham 31 E40
Bloxholm 52 G46
Bloxwich 40 E36
Bloxworth 9 E34
Blubberhouses 57 D37
Blue Anchor *Cnw.* 3 C15
Blue Anchor *Som.* 7 A26
Blue Bell Hill 24 E53
Blundeston 45 F60
Blunham 32 C47
Blunsdon St Andrew 20 B37
Bluntisham 33 A49
Blunts 4 D19
Blyborough 52 C45
Blyford 35 A60
Blymhill 40 D34
Blyth *Not.* 51 D42

Blyth *Nor.* 71 E39
Blyth Bridge 75 F27
Blythburgh 35 A60
Blythe Bridge 40 A35
Blythe Marsh 40 A35
Blyton 52 C44
Boarhills 83 F31
Boarhunt 11 D41
Boars Hill 21 A40
Boarshead 13 C51
Boarstall 31 G42
Boarzell 14 E53
Boasley Cross 6 F20
Boath 96 D21
Boat o' Brig 98 D28
Boat of Garten 89 C25
Bobbing 24 E54
Bobbington 39 F33
Bobbingworth 23 A51
Bocaddon 4 E17
Bochastle 81 G21
Bockhampton 21 D39
Bocking 34 F53
Bocking Churchstreet 34 F53
Boconnoc 4 D17
Boddam *She.* 107 D37
Boddam *Grm.* 99 E37
Boddington 29 F34
Bodedern 46 D19
Bodelwyddan 47 E26
Bodenham *Wts.* 10 B37
Bodenham *H.&W.* 28 C31
Bodenham Moor 28 C31
Bodesbeck 69 C27
Bodewryd 46 C19
Bodfari 47 E26
Bodffordd 46 E20
Bodfuan 36 B19
Bodham Street 45 A57
Bodiam 14 E53
Bodicote 31 E40
Bodieve 42 A15
Bodinnick 4 E17
Bodior 46 E18
Bodle Street Green 13 E52
Bodmin 4 D16
Bodney 44 F54
Bodorgan 46 F19
Bodsham Green 15 C56
Bodwen 4 D16
Bogallan 96 F22
Bogbain 96 G22
Bogbrae 99 F36
Bogbuie 96 F21
Bogend 74 G19
Bogfern 90 C31
Bogfields 90 C31
Bogfold 99 D34
Boghead *Str.* 75 F23
Boghead *Grm.* 98 D32
Boghead *Str.* 68 A22
Boghole Fm 97 F25
Bogmoor 98 C29
Bogniebrae 98 E31
Bognor Regis 12 G45
Bograxie 91 B32
Bogroy 89 B24
Bogside 75 A25
Bogston 90 C29
Bogton 98 D32
Bogue 68 E22
Bohenie 87 F18
Bohortha 3 E14
Bohuntine 87 F18
Boirseam 92 C6
Bojewyan 2 E9
Bolam 62 D37
Bolberry 5 G22
Bolderwood 10 D38
Bold Heath 48 D31
Boldon 71 G39
Boldre 10 E38
Boldron 62 E36
Bole 51 D43
Bolehill 50 G38
Boleigh 2 F10
Boleside 76 G30
Bolfracks 81 C23
Bolgoed 17 D21
Bolham 7 D25
Bolham Water 7 D27
Bolingey 2 C13
Bollington *Che.* 49 E35
Bollington *Che.* 49 D33
Bolney 13 D48
Bolnhurst 32 C46
Bolshan 83 B32
Bolsover 51 E40
Bolsterstone 50 C38
Bolstone 28 E31
Boltby 57 A40
Bolter End 22 B43
Bolton *Cum.* 61 D32
Bolton *Hum.* 58 D43
Bolton *G.M.* 49 B32
Bolton *Ltn* 76 C31

Bolton *Nor.* 71 B36
Bolton Abbey 57 D36
Bolton Bridge 57 D36
Bolton by Bowland 56 E33
Boltonfellend 69 G30
Boltongate 60 B28
Bolton-le-Sands 55 C30
Bolton Low Houses 60 B28
Bolton-on-Swale 62 G38
Bolton Percy 58 E41
Bolton upon Dearne 51 B40
Bolventor 4 C17
Bombie 65 F23
Bomere Heath 38 D30
Bonar Bridge 96 B21
Bonawe 80 D15
Bonawe Quarries 80 D16
Bonby 52 A46
Boncath 16 A17
Bonchester Bridge 70 B31
Bonchurch 11 G41
Bondleigh 6 E22
Bonehill 40 E37
Bo'ness 75 B25
Bonhill 74 C19
Boningale 39 E33
Bonjedward 70 A32
Bonkle 75 E24
Bonnington *Kent* 15 D56
Bonnington *Tay.* 83 D31
Bonnybank 82 G30
Bonnybridge 75 B24
Bonnykelly 99 D34
Bonnyrigg 76 D28
Bonnyton *Grm.* 98 F32
Bonnyton *Tay.* 82 D29
Bonnyton *Tay.* 83 B32
Bonsall 50 G38
Bont 28 G29
Bontddu 37 D22
Bont dolgadfan 37 F24
Bont-goch (Elerch) 37 G22
Bont Newydd 37 C23
Bontnewydd 46 F20
Bontuchel 47 G26
Bonvilston 18 D26
Bon-y-maen 17 E22
Boohay 5 E25
Booker 22 B44
Booley 38 C31
Boor 94 C14
Boosbeck 63 E42
Boot 60 F27
Boothby Graffoe 52 G45
Boothby Pagnell 42 B45
Boothstown 49 B33
Boothtown 57 G36
Boothville 31 B43
Booth Wood 50 A36
Bootle *Mer.* 48 C29
Bootle *Cum.* 54 A27
Booton 45 C57
Boquhan 74 B21
Boraston 28 A31
Bordeaux 3 E17
Borden 24 E54
Bordley 56 C35
Bordon 11 A43
Boreham *Esx* 24 A53
Boreham *Wts.* 20 G34
Boreham Street 13 E52
Borehamwood 22 B47
Boreland *Cen.* 81 D21
Boreland *D.&G.* 69 D27
Boreland *D.&G.* 64 D19
Boreraig 93 F7
Borgh *W.I.* 84 D2
Borgh *W.I.* 92 C4
Borghaston 100 C7
Borgie 102 C22
Borgue *D.&G.* 65 F22
Borgue *Hgh.* 103 F27
Borley 34 D54
Bornais 84 B3
Borness 65 F22
Boroughbridge 57 C39
Borough Green 23 F51
Borras Head 48 G29
Borrowash 41 B39
Borrowby *N.Y.* 63 E43
Borrowby *N.Y.* 57 A40
Borrowdale 60 E28
Borrowfield 91 D34
Borstal 24 E53
Borth 36 G21
Borthwick 76 E28
Borthwickbrae 69 B29
Borthwickshiels 69 B30
Borth-y-Gest 36 B21
Borve 93 G10
Borwick 55 B31
Bosavern 2 E9
Bosbury 29 D32
Boscastle 4 A16
Boscombe *Wts.* 10 A37
Boscombe *Dor.* 10 E37

Boscoppa 4 E16
Bosham 12 F44
Bosherston 16 E15
Bosley 49 F35
Bossa I 58 C43
Bossiney 4 B16
Bossingham 15 C57
Bossington Ham. 10 A39
Bossington Som. 7 A24
Bostock Green 49 F32
Boston 43 A48
Boston Spa 57 E40
Boswinger 3 D15
Botallack 2 E9
Botany Bay 23 B49
Botarua 92 D3
Botcheston 41 E40
Botesdale 34 A56
Bothal 71 E38
Bothamsall 51 E42
Bothel 60 C27
Bothenhampton 8 E30
Bothwell 75 E23
Botley Oxf. 21 A40
Botley Ham. 11 C41
Botley Bkh. 22 A45
Botloe's Green 29 F32
Botolph 44 E56
Botolph Claydon 31 F43
Botolphs 12 F47
Bottacks 96 E20
Bottesford Hum. 52 B45
Bottesford Lei. 42 B43
Bottisham 33 B51
Bottomcraig 82 E29
Bottom Head 56 C32
Botusfleming 4 D19
Botwnnog 36 B18
Bough Beech 23 G50
Boughrood 28 E27
Boughspring 19 B31
Boughton Nmp. 31 B43
Boughton Not. 51 F42
Boughton Nfk 44 E52
Boughton Aluph 14 C55
Boughton Green 14 B53
Boughton Lees 15 C56
Boughton Malherbe 14 C54
Boughton Street 15 B56
Boulby 63 E43
Bouldon 38 G31
Boulmer 71 B38
Boulston 16 C15
Boultenstone 90 B29
Boultham 52 F45
Bourn 33 C49
Bournbrook 40 G36
Bourne 42 C47
Bournebridge 23 B51
Bourne End Bkh. 22 C44
Bourne End Hfs. 22 A46
Bourne End Bfd. 32 D45
Bournemouth 10 F36
Bournemouth (Hurn) Airport 10 E37
Bournes Green 20 A35
Bournheath 29 A35
Bournmoor 62 A38
Bournville 40 G36
Bourton Oxf. 21 C38
Bourton Shr. 38 F31
Bourton Avon 19 E29
Bourton Dor. 9 A33
Bourton on Dunsmore 31 A40
Bourton-on-the-Hill 30 E37
Bourton-on-the-Water 30 F37
Bousd 78 A8
Boustead Hill 60 A28
Bouth 55 A29
Bouthwaite 57 B37
Bovain 81 D21
Boveney 22 D45
Boveridge 10 C36
Boverton 18 E25
Bovey Tracey 5 C24
Bovingdon 22 A45
Bovinger 23 A51
Bovington Camp 9 F34
Bow Ork. 105 B29
Bow Dev. 7 E23
Bowbank 61 D35
Bow Brickhill 32 E45
Bowburn 62 C38
Bowcombe 11 F40
Bowd 7 G27
Bowden Dev. 5 F24
Bowden Bor. 76 G31
Bowden Hill 20 E35
Bowdon 49 D33
Bower 70 E33
Bowerchalke 10 B36
Bower Hinton 8 F29
Bowermadden 103 B28
Bowers Gifford 24 C53
Bowershall 75 A26
Bowertower 103 B28

Bowes 62 E35
Bowgreave 55 E30
Bowland Bridge 55 A30
Bowley 28 C31
Bowlhead Green 12 C45
Bowling 74 C20
Bowling Bank 38 A29
Bowlish 19 G31
Bowmanstead 60 G29
Bowmore 72 E8
Bowness-on-Solway 69 G27
Bowness-on-Windermere 60 G30
Bow of Fife 82 F29
Bowsden 77 F35
Bowside Lodge 102 B24
Bow Street 37 G22
Bowthorpe 45 E57
Bowtrees 75 B24
Box Wts. 20 E34
Box Glo. 20 A34
Boxbush 29 G33
Box End 32 D45
Boxford Sfk 34 D55
Boxford Brk. 21 D40
Boxgrove 12 F45
Boxley 14 B53
Boxmoor 22 A46
Boxted Esx 34 E55
Boxted Sfk 34 C54
Boxted Cross 34 E55
Boxworth 33 B49
Boxworth End 33 B49
Boyden Gate 25 E58
Boydston 74 G20
Boylestone 40 B37
Boyndie 98 C32
Boynton 59 C47
Boysack 83 C31
Boyton Wts. 9 A35
Boyton Cnw. 6 F19
Boyton Sfk 35 D59
Boyton Cross 24 A52
Bozeat 32 C44
Braaid 54 F25
Braal Castle 103 B27
Brabling Green 35 B58
Brabourne 15 C56
Brabourne Lees 15 C56
Brabster 103 B28
Bracadale 85 A9
Braceborough 42 D46
Bracebridge 52 F45
Bracebridge Heath 52 F45
Braceby 42 B46
Bracewell 56 E34
Brachla 88 A21
Brackenber 61 D32
Brackenfield 51 G39
Brackens 99 D33
Bracklach 90 A29
Bracklamore 99 D34
Brackletter 87 F17
Brackley Nmp. 31 E41
Brackley Hgh. 97 F24
Brackly 73 B14
Bracknell 22 E44
Braco 81 G24
Bracobrae 98 D30
Bracon Ash 45 F57
Bracora 86 E13
Bracorina 86 E13
Bradbourne 50 G37
Bradbury 62 D38
Bradda 54 F23
Bradda East 54 F23
Bradden 31 D42
Bradenham 22 B44
Bradenstoke 20 D35
Bradfield Dev. 7 E26
Bradfield Esx 35 E57
Bradfield Nfk 45 B58
Bradfield Brk. 21 D42
Bradfield Combust 34 C54
Bradfield Green 49 G32
Bradfield Heath 35 F57
Bradfield St Clare 34 C55
Bradfield St George 34 C55
Bradford Dev. 6 E20
Bradford Nor. 77 G37
Bradford N.Y. 57 F37
Bradford Abbas 8 C31
Bradford Leigh 20 E34
Bradford-on-Avon 20 E33
Bradford-on-Tone 7 C27
Bradford Peverell 9 E32
Brading 11 F42
Bradley Hum. 53 B48
Bradley Ham. 21 G42
Bradley N.Y. 57 A36
Bradley W.M. 40 F35
Bradley Dby. 40 A38
Bradley Stf. 40 D34
Bradley Green 29 B35
Bradley in the Moors 40 A36
Bradley Stoke 19 C32

Bradmore Not. 41 B41
Bradmore W.M. 40 F34
Bradninch 7 E25
Bradnop 49 G35
Bradpole 8 E30
Bradshaw 49 A33
Bradstone 6 G19
Bradwall Green 49 F33
Bradwell Dby. 50 D37
Bradwell Bkh. 32 E44
Bradwell Esx 34 F53
Bradwell Nfk 45 E60
Bradwell Grove 20 A37
Bradwell Bridge 29 C34
Bradwell-on-Sea 25 A55
Bradwell Waterside 25 A55
Bradworthy 6 D19
Brae D.&G. 65 C24
Brae She. 107 A39
Brae Hgh. 96 A20
Braeantra 96 D21
Braedownie 90 F28
Braefoot 98 E32
Braegrum 82 E25
Braehead Tay. 83 B32
Braehead Ork. 105 A31
Braehead Grm. 98 E29
Braehead Ork. 104 B30
Braehead Str. 75 E25
Braehead Str. 75 G24
Braehoulland 106 E38
Braeleny 81 F22
Braemar 90 D27
Braemore Hgh. 95 D17
Braemore Hgh. 96 A21
Braemore Hgh. 103 E26
Braeswick 104 C31
Braeval 81 G21
Brafferton N.Y. 57 B40
Brafferton Drm 62 D38
Brafield-on-the-Green 32 C44
Bragar 100 C8
Bragbury End 33 F48
Bragleenbeg 79 E14
Braichmelyn 46 F21
Braides 55 D30
Braidwood 75 F24
Braigo 72 D8
Brailsford 40 A38
Braintree 34 F53
Braiseworth 35 A57
Braishfield 10 B39
Braithwaite S.Y. 51 A42
Braithwaite Cum. 60 D28
Braithwell 51 C41
Bramber 12 E47
Brambletye 13 C49
Bramcote 41 B40
Bramdean 11 B42
Bramerton 45 E58
Bramfield Sfk 35 A59
Bramfield Hfs. 33 G48
Bramford 34 D56
Bramhall 49 D34
Bramham 57 E40
Bramhope 57 E38
Bramley Sry 22 G46
Bramley Ham. 21 F42
Bramley S.Y. 51 C40
Bramling 15 B58
Brampford Speke 7 F25
Brampton Lcn. 52 D44
Brampton S.Y. 51 B39
Brampton Dby. 51 E39
Brampton Cbs. 32 A47
Brampton Sfk 45 G60
Brampton Cum. 70 G31
Brampton Nfk 45 C58
Brampton Abbotts 28 F31
Brampton Ash 42 G43
Brampton Bryan 28 A29
Brampton-en-le-Morthen 51 D40
Bramshall 40 B36
Bramshaw 10 C38
Bramshill 22 E43
Bramshott 12 C44
Bramwell 8 B30
Branault 79 A11
Brancaster 44 A53
Brancepeth 62 C37
Branchill 97 F26
Branderburgh 98 B28
Brandesburton 59 E47
Brandeston 35 B58
Brand Green 29 F33
Brandis Corner 6 E20
Brandiston 45 C57
Brandon Sfk 44 G53
Brandon Drm 62 C38
Brandon War. 30 A39
Brandon Lcn. 42 A44
Brandon Nor. 71 B36

Brandon Bank 43 G51
Brandon Creek 44 F52
Brandon Parva 44 E56
Brandsby 58 B41
Brandy Wharf 52 C45
Brane 2 F9
Bran End 33 F52
Branksome 10 E36
Branksome Park 10 E36
Bransby 52 E44
Branscombe 7 G27
Bransford 29 C33
Bransford Bridge 29 C34
Bransgore 10 E37
Branson's Cross 30 A36
Branston Lcn. 52 F46
Branston Lei. 42 C43
Branston Stf. 40 C38
Branston Booths 52 F46
Branstone 11 F41
Brant Broughton 52 G44
Brantham 35 E57
Branthwaite Cum. 60 C28
Branthwaite Cum. 60 D26
Brantingham 59 G45
Branton S.Y. 51 B42
Branton Nor. 71 B36
Brantwood 60 G29
Branxholm Bridgend 69 B30
Branxholme 69 B30
Branxton 77 G34
Brassington 50 G38
Brasted 23 F50
Brasted Chart 23 F50
Brathens 91 D32
Bratoft 53 F50
Brattleby 52 D45
Bratton 20 F34
Bratton Clovelly 6 F20
Bratton Fleming 6 B22
Bratton Seymour 9 B32
Braughing 33 F49
Braunston Nmp. 31 B41
Braunston Lei. 42 E44
Braunstone 41 E41
Braunton 6 B20
Brawby 58 B43
Brawdy 16 B14
Brawl 102 B23
Brawlbin 103 C26
Bray 22 D45
Braybrooke 42 G43
Brayford 6 B22
Brayshaw 56 D33
Bray Shop 4 C19
Brayton 58 F41
Bray Wick 22 C44
Brazacott 4 A18
Breach 15 C57
Breachwood Green 32 F47
Breacleit 100 D7
Breadsall 41 A39
Breadstone 19 A32
Breage 2 F12
Breakon 106 B41
Bream 19 A31
Breamore 10 C37
Brean 19 F28
Breanais 100 E6
Brearton 57 C39
Breascleit 100 D8
Breaston 41 B40
Brechfa 17 A21
Brechin 83 A31
Brecklate 66 B12
Breckles 44 F55
Breckonside 68 C23
Brecon 27 F26
Bredbury 49 C35
Brede 14 F54
Bredenbury 28 C31
Bredfield 35 C58
Bredgar 24 E54
Bredhurst 24 E53
Bredicot 29 C35
Bredon 29 E35
Bredon's Hardwick 29 E34
Bredon's Norton 29 E34
Bredwardine 28 D29
Breedon on the Hill 41 C39
Breibhig 100 D10
Breich 75 D25
Breighton 58 F43
Breinton 28 E30
Bremhill 20 D35
Brenachoil 80 G15
Brenchley 23 G52
Brendon Dev. 7 A23
Brendon Dev. 6 D19
Brenkley 71 F37
Brent 22 C47
Brent Eleigh 34 D55
Brentford 22 D47
Brentingby 42 D43
Brent Knoll 19 F29
Brent Pelham 33 E49

Brentwood 24 B52
Brenzett 14 E55
Breoch 65 E23
Brereton 40 D36
Brereton Green 49 F33
Brereton Heath 49 F34
Bressingham 44 G56
Bretabister 107 B40
Bretby 40 C38
Bretford 31 A40
Bretforton 30 D36
Bretherdale Head 61 F31
Bretherton 55 G30
Brettenham Nfk 44 G55
Brettenham Sfk 34 C55
Bretton 48 F29
Brewood 40 E34
Briach 97 F26
Briantspuddle 9 E33
Bricket Wood 22 A47
Bricklehampton 29 D35
Bride 54 C26
Bridekirk 60 C26
Bridell 26 D17
Bridestones 49 F35
Bridestowe 6 G20
Brideswell 98 F31
Bridford 7 G23
Bridge Cnw. 2 D12
Bridge Kent 15 B57
Bridge End Bfd. 32 C45
Bridge End Lcn. 42 B47
Bridge End She. 107 D39
Bridgefoot Cum. 60 D26
Bridgefoot Cbs. 33 D50
Bridgehampton 8 B31
Bridge Hewick 57 B39
Bridgemary 11 D41
Bridgemere 39 A32
Bridgend Str. 73 A14
Bridgend Str. 72 D9
Bridgend Ltn 75 C26
Bridgend M.G. 18 D25
Bridgend Grm. 98 F29
Bridgend Grm. 98 F30
Bridgend Tay. 82 E27
Bridgend Tay. 83 A31
Bridgend Grm. 90 D29
Bridgend Fife 82 F29
Bridgend Cum. 60 E29
Bridgend Cnw. 4 E17
Bridgend of Lintrathen 82 B28
Bridge of Alford 90 B31
Bridge of Allan 75 A23
Bridge of Balgie 81 C21
Bridge of Bogendreip 91 D32
Bridge of Brewlands 82 A27
Bridge of Brown 89 B26
Bridge of Cally 82 B27
Bridge of Canny 91 D32
Bridge of Craigisla 82 B28
Bridge of Dee Grm. 90 D27
Bridge of Dee Grm. 91 D32
Bridge of Dee D.&G. 65 D23
Bridge of Don 91 C35
Bridge of Dun 83 B32
Bridge of Dye 91 E32
Bridge of Earn 82 F26
Bridge of Ericht 81 B20
Bridge of Ess 90 D30
Bridge of Feugh 91 D32
Bridge of Forss 103 B26
Bridge of Gairn 90 D29
Bridge of Gaur 81 B20
Bridge of Muchalls 91 D34
Bridge of Orchy 80 D18
Bridge of Tilt 81 A24
Bridge of Tynet 98 C29
Bridge of Walls 107 B38
Bridge of Weir 74 D19
Bridgerule 6 E18
Bridges 38 F29
Bridge Sollers 28 D30
Bridge Street 34 D54
Bridgeton 90 B31
Bridgetown Som. 7 B25
Bridgetown Cnw. 6 G19
Bridge Trafford 48 E30
Bridgeyate 19 D32
Bridgham 44 G55
Bridgnorth 39 F32
Bridgtown 40 E35
Bridgwater 8 A28
Bridlington 59 C47
Bridport 8 E30
Bridstow 28 F31
Brierfield 56 F34
Brierley S.Y. 51 A40
Brierley H.&W. 28 C30
Brierley Glo. 29 G32
Brierley Hill 40 G34
Brierton 62 D40
Brigehaugh 98 F29
Brigg 52 B46
Brigham Cum. 60 C26
Brigham Hum. 59 D46

Brighouse 57 G37
Brighstone 10 F39
Brightgate 50 G38
Brighthampton 21 A39
Brightling 13 D52
Brightlingsea 34 G56
Brighton Cnw. 3 C14
Brighton E.S. 13 F49
Brightons 75 C24
Brightwalton 21 D39
Brightwell Sfk 35 D58
Brightwell Oxf. 21 B41
Brightwell Baldwin 21 B42
Brignall 62 E36
Brig o'Turk 81 G21
Brigsley 53 B48
Brigsteer 55 A30
Brigstock 42 G45
Brill Bkh. 31 G42
Brill Cnw. 2 F13
Brilley 8 D28
Brilley Mountain 28 C28
Brimfield 28 B31
Brimington 51 E39
Brimington Common 51 E39
Brimley 5 C23
Brimpsfield 29 G35
Brimpton 21 E41
Brimstage 48 D28
Brind 58 F43
Brindister She. 107 D40
Brindister She. 107 B38
Brindle 55 G31
Brindley Ford 49 G34
Brineton 40 D34
Bringhurst 42 F44
Brington 32 A46
Briningham 44 B56
Brinkhill 53 E49
Brinkley 33 C51
Brinklow 31 A40
Brinkworth 20 C36
Brinmore 88 B22
Brinscall 56 G32
Brinsley 41 A40
Brinsop 28 D30
Brinsworth 51 D39
Brinton 44 B56
Brinyan 104 D30
Brisco 60 A30
Brisley 44 C55
Brislington 19 D31
Bristol 19 D31
Bristol (Lulsgate) Airport 19 E30
Briston 44 B56
Britannia 56 G34
Britford 10 B37
Brithdir 37 D23
Brithem Bottom 7 D26
Briton Ferry 18 B23
Britwell Salome 21 B42
Brixham 5 E25
Brixton 5 E21
Brixton Deverill 9 A34
Brixworth 31 A43
Brize Norton 21 A38
Broad Blunsdon 20 B37
Broadbottom 49 C35
Broadbridge 11 D43
Broadbridge Heath 12 C47
Broad Campden 30 E37
Broad Chalke 10 B36
Broad Clyst 7 F25
Broadford 86 B12
Broadford Bridge 12 D46
Broadgate 54 A27
Broad Green Bfd. 32 D45
Broad Green H.&W. 29 C33
Broad Green Esx 34 F54
Broadgroves 33 G52
Broadhaugh 69 C30
Broad Haven 16 C14
Broadheath 49 D33
Broad Heath 29 B32
Broadhembury 7 E26
Broadhempston 5 D23
Broad Hill 33 A51
Broad Hinton 20 D36
Broadholme 52 E44
Broadland Row 14 F54
Broadlay 17 D19
Broad Laying 21 E40
Broadley Lan. 49 A34
Broadley Grm. 98 C29
Broadley Common 23 A50
Broad Marston 30 D37
Broadmayne 9 F33
Broadmeadows 76 G29
Broadmere 21 G42
Broadnymet 7 E23
Broadoak Dor. 8 E30
Broad Oak H.&W. 28 F30
Broadoak Kent 25 E57
Broad Oak E.S. 14 E54
Broad Oak E.S. 13 D52
Broad Oak Cum. 60 G27

Broadoak Dyf. 17 B21
Broadrashes 98 D29
Broadsea 99 C35
Broadstairs 25 E59
Broadstone Dor. 9 E35
Broadstone Shr. 38 G31
Broad Street 14 B54
Broadstreet Common 19 C29
Broad Street Green 24 A54
Broad Town 20 D36
Broadwas 29 C33
Broadwater Hfs. 33 F48
Broadwater W.S. 12 F47
Broadway Dyf. 17 D19
Broadway Dyf. 17 C18
Broadway Dyf. 16 C14
Broadway Sfk 35 A59
Broadway H.&W. 30 E36
Broadway Som. 8 C28
Broadwell Oxf. 21 A38
Broadwell War. 31 B40
Broadwell Glo. 30 F37
Broadwell Glo. 28 G31
Broadwell House 61 A34
Broadwey 9 F32
Broadwindsor 8 D30
Broadwood Kelly 6 E22
Broadwoodwidger 6 G20
Brobury 28 D29
Brochel 94 G11
Brochloch 67 D21
Brock 78 C6
Brockbridge 11 C42
Brockdish 35 A58
Brockenhurst 10 D38
Brockfield 58 D42
Brockford Street 34 B56
Brockhall 31 B42
Brockham 22 G47
Brockhampton 28 E31
Brockholes 50 A37
Brockhurst 13 C50
Brocklebank 60 B28
Brocklesby 52 A47
Brockley 19 E30
Brockley Green 34 C54
Brockton Shr. 38 G29
Brockton Shr. 38 F31
Brockton Shr. 38 E28
Brockton Shr. 39 E33
Brockweir 19 A31
Brockwood Park 11 B42
Brockworth 29 G34
Brocton 40 D35
Brodick 73 G16
Brodsworth 51 B40
Brogborough 32 E45
Brogyntyn 38 B28
Brokenborough 20 C34
Broken Cross Che. 49 E34
Broken Cross Che. 49 E32
Bromborough 48 D29
Brome 35 A57
Brome Street 35 A57
Bromeswell 35 C58
Bromfield Cum. 60 B27
Bromfield Shr. 28 A30
Bromham Bfd. 32 C45
Bromham Wts. 20 E35
Bromley 23 E50
Bromley Green 14 D55
Brompton N.Y. 59 A45
Brompton Kent 24 E53
Brompton N.Y. 62 G39
Brompton on Swale 62 F37
Brompton Ralph 7 B26
Brompton Regis 7 B25
Bromsash 29 F33
Bromsberrow Heath 29 E33
Bromsgrove 29 A35
Bromstead Heath 40 D34
Bromyard 29 C32
Bromyard Downs 29 C32
Bronaber 37 B22
Brongest 26 D19
Bronington 38 B30
Bronllys 28 E27
Bronnant 27 B22
Bronydd 28 D28
Bron-y-Gaer 17 C18
Bronygarth 38 B28
Brook Dyf. 17 D18
Brook Kent 15 C56
Brook Sry 12 C45
Brook I.o.W. 10 F39
Brook Ham. 10 C38
Brook Ham. 10 B39
Brooke Lei. 42 E44
Brooke Nfk 45 F58
Brookend 19 B31
Brookhouse 55 C31
Brookhouse Green 49 F33
Brookland 14 E55
Brooklands 65 C23
Brookmans Park 23 A48
Brooks 38 F27

Brooksby 41 D42
Brooks Green 12 D47
Brook Street W.S. 13 D48
Brook Street Esx 23 B51
Brook Street Kent 14 D55
Brook Street Sfk 34 D54
Brookthorpe 29 G34
Brookwood 22 F45
Broom Bfd. 32 D47
Broom War. 30 C36
Broomcroft 38 E31
Broome Shr. 38 G29
Broome H.&W. 29 A34
Broome Nfk 45 F59
Broomedge 49 D33
Broomer's Corner 12 D47
Broome Wood 71 B37
Broomfield Kent 25 E57
Broomfield Esx 24 A52
Broomfield Kent 14 B54
Broomfield Som. 7 B27
Broomfield Grm. 99 F35
Broomfleet 58 G44
Broomhaugh 71 G36
Broomhead 99 C35
Broomhill 71 C38
Broom Hill 10 D36
Broom of Dalreach 82 F25
Broom's Green 29 E32
Brora 97 A24
Broseley 39 E32
Brotherlee 61 C35
Brothertoft 43 A48
Brotherton 57 G40
Brotton 63 D42
Broubster 103 B26
Brough Ork. 104 E29
Brough Dby. 50 D37
Brough She. 106 E40
Brough She. 106 E41
Brough She. 107 C41
Brough Not. 52 G44
Brough Cum. 61 E33
Brough Hum. 59 G45
Brough She. 107 A41
Broughall 38 A31
Brougham 61 D31
Brough Lodge 106 C41
Brough Sowerby 61 E33
Broughton N.Y. 58 B43
Broughton N.Y. 56 D35
Broughton Lcn. 52 B45
Broughton Cbs. 33 A48
Broughton Bkh. 32 D44
Broughton Oxf. 31 E40
Broughton Nmp. 32 A44
Broughton G.M. 49 C34
Broughton Clw. 48 F29
Broughton M.G. 18 D24
Broughton Bor. 75 D24
Broughton Ork. 104 B30
Broughton Ham. 10 A39
Broughton Astley 41 F41
Broughton Beck 55 A28
Broughton Gifford 20 E34
Broughton Hackett 29 C35
Broughton in Furness 55 A28
Broughton Mills 60 G27
Broughton Moor 60 C26
Broughton Poggs 21 A38
Broughtown 104 B32
Broughty Ferry 83 D30
Browland 107 B38
Brown Candover 11 A41
Brown Edge Stf. 49 G35
Brown Edge Lan. 48 A29
Brownhill 99 E34
Brownhills W.M. 40 E36
Brownhills Fife 83 F31
Brownieside 71 A37
Brown Lees 49 G34
Brownlow Heath 49 F34
Brownshill Green 40 G38
Brownston 5 E22
Broxa 63 G45
Broxbourne 23 A49
Broxburn Ltn 75 C26
Broxburn Ltn 76 C32
Broxholme 52 E44
Broxted 33 F51
Broxton 48 G30
Broxwood 28 C29
Bru 100 C9
Bruachmary 97 G24
Bruan 103 E28
Bruera 48 F30
Bruichladdich 72 D8
Bruisyard 35 B59
Bruisyard Street 35 B59
Brund 50 F36
Brundall 45 E59
Brundish 35 B58
Brundish Street 35 A58
Bruntingthorpe 41 G41
Bruntland 90 A30

Brunton Fife 82 E29
Brunton Nor. 71 A37
Brushford 7 C24
Brushford Barton 6 E22
Bruton 9 A32
Bryanston 9 D34
Brydekirk 69 F27
Brymbo 48 G28
Bryn G.M. 48 B31
Bryn Shr. 38 G28
Bryn W.G. 18 B24
Bryn Dyf. 17 D21
Brynamman 17 C22
Brynberian 16 A16
Bryncae 18 C25
Bryncethin 18 C25
Bryncir 36 A20
Bryn-Coch 18 B23
Bryncroes 36 B17
Bryncrug 36 E21
Bryneglwys 38 A27
Brynford 47 E27
Bryn Gates 48 B31
Bryngwran 46 E19
Bryngwyn Gwe. 19 A29
Bryngwyn Pow. 28 D27
Bryn-henllan 16 A15
Brynhoffnant 26 C19
Brynmawr 28 G27
Brynmelyn 28 A27
Brynmenyn 18 C25
Brynna 18 C25
Brynog 26 C21
Brynrefail Gwy. 46 D20
Brynrefail Gwy. 46 F21
Brynsadler 18 D25
Brynsiencyn 46 F20
Brynteg 46 D20
Bryn-y-maen 47 E24
Buaile Nam Bodach 84 D3
Bualintur 85 B9
Bualnaluib 94 C14
Bubbenhall 30 A39
Bubwith 58 F42
Buccleuch 69 B29
Buchan 65 D23
Buchanan Castle 74 B20
Buchanhaven 99 E36
Buchanty 82 E25
Buchlyvie 74 A21
Buckabank 60 B29
Buckby Wharf 31 B41
Buckden Cbs. 32 B46
Buckden N.Y. 56 B35
Buckenham 45 E59
Buckerell 7 E27
Buckfast 5 D23
Buckfastleigh 5 D22
Buckhaven 76 A29
Buckholm 76 G30
Buckhorn Weston 9 B33
Buckhurst Hill 23 B50
Buckie 98 C29
Buckies 103 B26
Buckingham 31 E42
Buckland Bkh. 32 G44
Buckland Glo. 30 E36
Buckland Dev. 5 F22
Buckland Sry 23 F48
Buckland Oxf. 21 B39
Buckland Hfs. 33 E49
Buckland Kent 15 C58
Buckland Brewer 6 C20
Buckland Common 22 A45
Buckland Dinham 20 F33
Buckland Filleigh 6 E20
Buckland in the Moor 5 C23
Buckland Monachorum 4 D20
Buckland Newton 9 D32
Buckland St Mary 8 C28
Buckland-tout-Saints 5 F23
Bucklebury 21 D41
Bucklerheads 83 D30
Bucklers Hard 10 D39
Bucklesham 35 D58
Buckley 48 F28
Buckman Corner 12 D46
Buckminster 42 C44
Bucknall Stf. 40 A35
Bucknall Lcn. 52 F47
Bucknell Oxf. 31 F41
Bucknell Shr. 28 A29
Bucksburn 91 C34
Buck's Cross 6 C19
Bucks Green 12 C46
Bucks Hill 22 A46
Bucks Horn Oak 22 G44
Buck's Mills 6 C19
Buckspool 16 E15
Buckton H.&W. 28 A29
Buckton Hum. 59 B47
Buckton Nor. 77 G36
Buckworth 32 A47
Budbrooke 30 B38
Budby 51 F42
Buddon 83 D31

Bude 6 E18
Budlake 7 E25
Budle 77 G37
Budleigh Salterton 7 G26
Budock Water 2 E13
Buerton 39 A32
Bugbrooke 31 C42
Bugle 3 C15
Bugthorpe 58 D43
Buildwas 39 E32
Builth Road 27 C26
Builth Wells 27 D26
Buirgh 92 B6
Bulby 42 C46
Buldoo 103 B25
Bulford 20 G37
Bulford Camp 20 G37
Bulkeley 48 G31
Bulkington Wts. 20 F35
Bulkington War. 41 G39
Bulkworthy 6 D19
Bull Bay 46 C20
Bulley 29 F33
Bull Green 14 D55
Bullington 21 G40
Bullpot Farm 56 A32
Bull's Green 33 G48
Bullwood 73 C17
Bulmer Esx 34 D54
Bulmer N.Y. 58 C42
Bulmer Tye 34 E54
Bulphan 24 C52
Bulverhythe 14 G53
Bulwark 99 E35
Bulwell 41 A41
Bulwick 42 F45
Bumble's Green 23 A50
Bun Abhainn Eadarra 100 G7
Bunarkaig 87 F17
Bunbury 48 G31
Bunchrew 96 G22
Bundalloch 86 B14
Buness 106 B42
Bunessan 78 E9
Bungay 45 G59
Bunlarie 73 G13
Bunloit 88 B20
Bun Loyne 87 D17
Bunnahabhainn 72 C9
Bunny 41 C41
Buntait 88 A19
Buntingford 33 F49
Bunwell 45 F57
Bunwell Street 45 F57
Burbage Wts. 21 E38
Burbage Lei. 41 F40
Burbage Dby. 50 E36
Burchett's Green 22 C44
Burcombe 10 A36
Burcot 21 B41
Burcott 32 F44
Burdale 58 C44
Burdocks 12 D46
Bures 34 E54
Bures Green 34 E54
Burford 30 G38
Burgate 34 A56
Burgess Hill 13 E49
Burgh 35 C58
Burgh by Sands 60 A29
Burgh Castle 45 E60
Burghclere 21 E40
Burghead 97 E26
Burghfield 21 E42
Burghfield Common 21 E42
Burghfield Hill 21 E42
Burgh Heath 23 F48
Burghill 28 D30
Burgh le Marsh 53 F51
Burgh next Aylsham 45 C58
Burgh on Bain 53 D48
Burgh St Margaret 45 D59
Burgh St Peter 45 F60
Burghwallis 51 A41
Burham 24 E53
Buriton 11 B43
Burland 49 G31
Burlawn 3 A15
Burleigh 22 D45
Burlescombe 7 D26
Burleston 9 E33
Burley Ham. 10 D37
Burley Lei. 42 D44
Burleydam 39 A32
Burley Gate 28 D31
Burley in Wharfedale 57 E37
Burley Street 10 D38
Burlingjobb 28 C28
Burlow 13 E51
Burlton 38 C30
Burmarsh 15 D56
Burmington 30 E38
Burn 58 G41
Burnage 49 C34
Burnaston 40 B38
Burnby 58 E44

Burndell 12 F45
Burnend 99 E34
Burneside 61 G31
Burness 104 B32
Burneston 57 A39
Burnett 19 E32
Burnfoot *Bor.* 69 B30
Burnfoot *Bor.* 69 B30
Burnfoot *Hgh.* 102 E24
Burnfoot *Tay.* 82 G25
Burnham *Bkh.* 22 C45
Burnham *Hum.* 52 A46
Burnham Deepdale 44 A54
Burnham Green 33 G48
Burnham Market 44 A53
Burnham Norton 44 A54
Burnham-on-Crouch 25 B55
Burnham-on-Sea 19 G28
Burnham Overy 44 A54
Burnham Thorpe 44 A54
Burnhaven 99 E37
Burnhead *D.&G.* 68 D24
Burnhead *D.&G.* 67 E21
Burnhervie 91 B33
Burnhill Green 39 E33
Burnhope 62 B37
Burnhouse 74 E19
Burniston 63 G46
Burnley 56 F34
Burnmouth 77 D35
Burn Naze 55 E29
Burn of Cambus 81 G23
Burnopfield 62 A37
Burnsall 57 C36
Burnside *Grm.* 91 B33
Burnside *Fife* 82 G27
Burnside *Tay.* 83 C30
Burnside *Str.* 67 B21
Burnside *Ltn* 75 C26
Burnside *She.* 106 E38
Burnside of Duntrune 83 D30
Burnstones 61 A32
Burnswark 69 F27
Burntcliff Top 49 F35
Burnt Houses 62 D37
Burntisland 76 B28
Burnton *Str.* 67 C20
Burnton *Str.* 67 B20
Burntwood 40 D36
Burntwood Green 40 E36
Burnt Yates 57 C38
Burpham *W.S.* 12 F46
Burpham *Sry* 22 F46
Burradon *T.&W.* 71 F38
Burradon *Nor.* 70 C35
Burrafirth 106 A41
Burraland 106 E39
Burras 2 E12
Burravoe *She.* 107 A39
Burravoe *She.* 106 D41
Burrells 61 E32
Burrelton 82 D27
Burridge 11 C41
Burrill 57 A38
Burringham 52 B44
Burrington *Som.* 19 F30
Burrington *Dev.* 6 D21
Burrington *H.&W.* 28 A30
Burrough End 33 C52
Burrough Green 33 C52
Burrough on the Hill 42 D43
Burrow Bridge 8 B29
Burrowhill 22 E45
Burry Port 17 D20
Burscough 48 A30
Burscough Bridge 48 A30
Bursea 58 F44
Burshill 59 E46
Bursledon 11 D40
Burslem 40 A34
Burstall 34 D56
Burstock 8 D30
Burston *Stf.* 40 B35
Burston *Nfk* 45 G57
Burstow 23 G49
Burstwick 59 G48
Burtersett 56 A34
Burtle 19 G29
Burton *Wts.* 20 D34
Burton *Nor.* 77 G37
Burton *Som.* 7 A27
Burton *Mer.* 48 E29
Burton *Che.* 48 F30
Burton *Lcn.* 52 E45
Burton *Dyf.* 16 D15
Burton *Dor.* 10 E37
Burton *Dor.* 9 E32
Burton Agnes 59 C47
Burton Bradstock 8 F30
Burton Coggles 42 C45
Burton Green *Clw.* 48 G29
Burton Green *W.M.* 30 A38
Burton Hastings 41 F40
Burton-in-Kendal 55 B31
Burton in Lonsdale 56 B32
Burton Joyce 41 A42

Burton Latimer 32 A44
Burton Lazars 42 D43
Burton Leonard 57 C39
Burton on the Wolds
  41 C41
Burton Overy 41 F42
Burton Pedwardine 42 A47
Burton Pidsea 59 F48
Burton Salmon 57 G40
Burton upon Stather
  52 A44
Burton upon Trent 40 C38
Burtonwood 48 C31
Burwardsley 48 G30
Burwarton 38 G31
Burwash 13 D52
Burwash Common 13 D52
Burwash Weald 13 D52
Burwell *Lcn.* 53 E49
Burwell *Cbs.* 33 B51
Burwen 46 C20
Burwick *Ork.* 105 C30
Burwick *She.* 107 C39
Bury *Som.* 7 C25
Bury *G.M.* 49 A33
Bury *W.S.* 12 E46
Bury *Cbs.* 43 G48
Buryas Bridge 2 F10
Bury Green 33 F50
Bury St Edmunds 34 B54
Burythorpe 58 C43
Busbridge 22 G45
Busby *Tay.* 82 E26
Busby *Str.* 74 E21
Buscot 21 B38
Bush Bank 28 C30
Bushbury 40 E35
Bushby 41 E42
Bush Crathie 90 D28
Bushey 22 B46
Bushey Heath 22 B47
Bush Green 45 G58
Bushley 29 E34
Bushton 20 D36
Bussage 20 A34
Busta 107 A39
Butcher's Cross 13 D51
Butcher's Pasture 33 F52
Butcombe 19 E30
Buthill 97 E27
Butleigh 8 A31
Butleigh Wootton 8 A31
Butler's Cross 22 A44
Butler's Hill 41 A41
Butlers Marston 30 C38
Butley 35 C59
Butsfield 62 B36
Butterburn 70 F32
Buttercrambe 58 D43
Butterknowle 62 D36
Butterleigh 7 E25
Butterley 51 G39
Buttermere *Wts.* 21 E39
Buttermere *Cum.* 60 E27
Butters Green 49 G34
Buttershaw 57 G37
Butterstone 82 C26
Butterton 50 G36
Butterwick *Lcn.* 43 A49
Butterwick *N.Y.* 59 B45
Butterwick *N.Y.* 58 B43
Butt Green 49 G32
Buttington 38 E28
Butt Lane 49 G34
Buttonoak 29 A33
Buxhall 34 C55
Buxted 13 D50
Buxton *Nfk* 45 C58
Buxton *Dby.* 50 E36
Buxton Heath 45 C57
Bwlch 28 F27
Bwlch-clawdd 17 A19
Bwlch Derwin 36 A20
Bwlchgwyn 48 G28
Bwlch-llan 26 C21
Bwlchnewydd 17 B18
Bwlchtocyn 36 C18
Bwlch-y-cibau 38 D27
Bwlch-y-ddar 38 C27
Bwlch-y-ffridd 37 F26
Bwlch-y-groes 17 A18
Bwlch-y-sarnau 27 A25
Byers Green 62 C38
Byfield 31 C41
Byfleet 22 E46
Byford 28 D29
Bygrave 33 E48
Byker 71 G38
Bylane End 4 E18
Bylchau 47 F25
Byley 49 F33
Bynea 17 E21
Byness 70 C33
Bythorn 32 A46
Byton 28 B29
Byworth 12 D45

C

Cabharstadh 100 E9
Cabourne 52 B47
Cabrach *Str.* 72 D10
Cabrach *Grm.* 90 A29
Cackle Street 14 F54
Cacrabank 69 B28
Cadbury 7 E25
Cadbury Barton 6 D22
Cadbury Heath 19 D32
Cadder 74 C21
Cadderlie 80 D16
Caddington 32 G46
Caddletown 79 F13
Caddonfoot 76 G30
Cadeby *S.Y.* 51 B41
Cadeby *Lei.* 41 E40
Cadeleigh 7 E24
Cade Street 13 D51
Cadgwith 2 G13
Cadham 82 G28
Cadishead 49 C32
Cadle 17 E22
Cadley 21 E38
Cadmore End 22 B43
Cadnam 10 C39
Cadney 52 B46
Cadole 48 F28
Cadover Bridge 5 D21
Cadoxton *S.G.* 18 E27
Cadoxton *W.G.* 18 B23
Caeathro 46 F20
Cae Ddafydd 36 A21
Caehopkin 27 G23
Caen 103 G26
Caenby 52 D46
Caenby Corner 52 D45
Caeo 17 A22
Caerau *M.G.* 18 B24
Caerau *S.G.* 18 D27
Caerdeon 37 D22
Caer Farchell 16 B13
Caergeiliog 46 E18
Caergwrle 48 G29
Caerhun 47 E23
Caer-Lan 27 G23
Caerleon 19 B29
Caer Llan 19 A30
Caernarfon 46 F20
Caerphilly 18 C27
Caersws 37 F26
Caerwent 19 B30
Caerwys 47 E27
Caethle 38 F21
Caggan 89 C24
Cairinis 92 F4
Cairisiadar 100 D6
Cairminis 92 C5
Cairnargat 98 F30
Cairnbaan 73 A14
Cairnbeathie 90 C31
Cairnbrogie 91 A34
Cairnbulg 92 E37
Cairncross 77 D34
Cairncurran 74 D19
Cairndoon 64 G19
Cairndow 80 F17
Cairne 91 C33
Cairness 99 C36
Cairneyhill 75 B26
Cairney Lodge 82 F29
Cairnhill *Grm.* 91 A35
Cairnhill *Grm.* 98 F32
Cairnie 98 E30
Cairnorrie 99 E34
Cairnryan 64 D16
Cairnsmore 64 D20
Caister-on-Sea 45 D61
Caistor 52 B46
Caistor St Edmund 45 E58
Caistron 70 C35
Cake Street 44 F56
Calanais 100 D8
Calbost 100 F10
Calbourne 11 F40
Calcot 21 D42
Calcott 25 E57
Caldarvan 74 B20
Caldback 106 B41
Caldbeck 60 C29
Caldbergh 57 A36
Caldecote *Cbs.* 42 G47
Caldecote *Cbs.* 33 C49
Caldecote *Hfs.* 33 E48
Caldecote *War.* 41 F39
Caldecott *Lei.* 42 F44
Caldecott *Nmp.* 32 B45
Calderbank 75 D23
Calder Bridge 60 F26
Calderbrook 49 A35
Caldercruix 75 D23
Calderglen 74 E22
Calder Mains 103 C26
Caldermill 74 F22

Calder Vale 55 E31
Caldhame 83 C30
Caldicot 19 C30
Caldwell *Str.* 74 E19
Caldwell *N.Y.* 62 E37
Caldwell *Dby.* 40 D38
Caldy 48 D28
Caledrhydiau 26 C20
Calfsound 104 C31
Calgary 78 B9
Califer 97 F26
California *Cen.* 75 C24
California *Nfk* 45 D61
Calke 41 C39
Callaly 71 C36
Callander 81 G22
Callerton Lane End 71 G37
Callestick 2 C13
Calligarry 86 F12
Callington 4 D19
Callisterhall 69 E28
Callow 28 E30
Callow End 29 D34
Callow Hill *H.&W.* 29 A33
Callow Hill *Wts.* 20 C36
Callows Grave 28 B31
Callyburn 66 A13
Calmore 10 C39
Calmsden 20 A36
Calne 20 D35
Calow 51 E40
Calrossie 96 D23
Calshot 11 D40
Calstock 4 D20
Calstone Wellington 20 E36
Calthorpe 45 B57
Calthwaite 60 B30
Calton *Stf.* 50 G36
Calton *N.Y.* 56 D35
Calveley 48 G31
Calver 50 E38
Calverhall 39 B32
Calver Hill 28 D29
Calverleigh 7 D24
Calverley 57 F37
Calvert 31 F42
Calverton *Bkh.* 31 E43
Calverton *Not.* 41 A41
Calvine 81 A23
Calvo 60 A27
Cam 20 B33
Camasnacroise 79 B14
Camasterach 94 G13
Camastianavaig 85 A10
Camasunary 86 C11
Camault Muir 96 G20
Camb 106 C41
Camber 14 F55
Camberley 22 E44
Camberwell 23 D49
Camblesforth 58 G42
Cambo 71 E36
Cambois 71 E38
Camborne 2 E12
Cambridge *Cbs.* 33 C50
Cambridge *Glo.* 20 A33
Cambridge Airport 33 C50
Cambus 75 A24
Cambusbarron 75 A23
Cambuskenneth 75 A24
Cambuslang 74 D22
Cambusnethan 75 E23
Cambus o'May 90 D29
Camchuart 73 B15
Camden 23 C48
Cameley 19 F31
Camelford 4 B17
Camelon 75 B24
Camelsdale 12 C44
Camer 24 E52
Cameron 74 B19
Camerory 89 A25
Camer's Green 29 E33
Camerton *Som.* 19 F32
Camerton *Cum.* 60 C26
Camghouran 81 B21
Camis Eskan 74 B19
Cammachmore 91 D34
Cammeringham 52 D45
Campbeltown 66 A12
Camperdown 71 F38
Camphouse 79 A10
Campmuir 82 D27
Campsall 51 A41
Camps End 33 D51
Campsey Ash 35 C59
Camps Heath 45 F60
Campton 32 E47
Camptown 70 B32
Camrose 16 C14
Camsail 74 B18
Camserney 81 C23
Camstraddan 74 A19
Camus Croise 86 C12
Camus-luinie 86 B15
Camusnagaul *Hgh.* 87 G16

Camusnagaul *Hgh.* 95 C16
Camusrory 86 E14
Camusteel 94 G13
Camusurich 81 D22
Camusvrachan 81 C21
Canada 10 C38
Candacraig 90 D29
Candlesby 53 F50
Candy Mill 75 F26
Cane End 21 D42
Canewdon 24 B54
Canford Bottom 10 D36
Canford Cliffs 10 F36
Canford Magna 10 E36
Canisbay 103 A29
Cann 9 B34
Cannard's Grave 19 G32
Cann Common 9 B34
Cannich 88 A19
Cannington 8 A28
Cannock 40 D35
Cannock Wood 40 D36
Cannop 28 G31
Canonbie 69 F29
Canon Bridge 28 D30
Canon Frome 29 D32
Canon Pyon 28 D30
Canons Ashby 31 C41
Canon's Town 2 E10
Canterbury *Kent* 15 B57
Canterbury *Grm.* 98 D31
Cantley *S.Y.* 51 B42
Cantley *Nfk* 45 E59
Cantlop 38 E31
Canton 18 D27
Cantray 96 G23
Cantraydoune 96 G23
Cantraywood 96 G23
Cantsfield 56 B32
Canvey Island 24 C53
Canwell Hall 40 E37
Canwick 52 F45
Canworthy Water 4 A17
Caol 87 G16
Caolas 78 C6
Caolasnacon 80 A17
Caolas Scalpaigh 93 B8
Capel *Kent* 23 G52
Capel *Sry* 22 G47
Capel Bangor 37 G22
Capel Betws Lleucu 27 C22
Capel Carmel 36 C17
Capel Coch 46 D20
Capel Curig 46 G22
Capel Cynon 26 D19
Capel Dewi *Dyf.* 26 D20
Capel Dewi *Dyf.* 17 B20
Capel Dewi *Dyf.* 37 G22
Capel Garmon 47 G24
Capel Gwyn *Gwy.* 46 E19
Capel Gwyn *Dyf.* 17 B20
Capel Gwynfe 27 F23
Capel Hendre 17 C21
Capel Isaac 17 B21
Capel Iwan 17 A18
Capel le Ferne 15 D58
Capel Parc 46 D20
Capel Seion 37 G22
Capel St Andrew 35 D59
Capel St Mary 34 E56
Capel St Silin 26 C21
Capel Tygwydd 26 D18
Capeluchaf 36 A19
Capelulo 47 E23
Capel-y-ffin 28 E28
Capenhurst 48 E29
Capernwray 55 B31
Capheaton 71 E36
Caplaw 74 E20
Cappercleuch 69 A28
Capplegill 69 C27
Capstone 24 E53
Capton 5 E24
Caputh 82 C26
Carbellow 68 A22
Carbeth 74 C21
Carbis Bay 2 E11
Carbost *Hgh.* 85 A9
Carbost *Hgh.* 93 G10
Carbrooke 44 E55
Carburton 51 E41
Carcary 83 B32
Carclew 2 E13
Carco 68 B23
Car Colston 42 A43
Carcroft 51 B41
Cardenden 76 A28
Cardeston 38 D29
Cardiff 18 D27
Cardiff Airport 18 E26
Cardigan 26 D17
Cardington *Shr.* 38 F30
Cardington *Bfd.* 32 D46
Cardinham 4 D16
Cardno 99 C35
Cardoness 65 E21

Cardow 97 G27
Cardrona 76 G28
Cardross 74 C19
Cardurnock 60 A27
Careby 42 D46
Careston 83 B31
Carew 16 D16
Carew Cheriton 16 D16
Carew Newton 16 D16
Carey 28 E31
Carfrae 76 D31
Cargen 65 C25
Cargenbridge 65 C25
Cargill 82 D27
Cargo 60 A29
Cargo Fleet 63 D41
Cargreen 4 D20
Carham 77 G33
Carhampton 7 A25
Carharrack 2 D13
Carie *Tay.* 81 D22
Carie *Tay.* 81 B22
Carines 2 C13
Carisbrooke 11 F40
Cark 55 B29
Carkeel 4 D20
Carland Cross 3 C14
Carlby 42 D46
Carlecotes 50 B37
Carleton *Cum.* 60 A30
Carleton *W.Y.* 57 G40
Carleton *N.Y.* 56 E35
Carleton *Lan.* 55 E29
Carleton Fishery 66 E16
Carleton Forehoe 44 E56
Carleton Rode 44 F56
Carlingcott 19 F32
Carlin How 63 E42
Carlisle 60 A29
Carlops 75 E27
Carlton *Drm* 62 D39
Carlton *Lei.* 41 E39
Carlton *Not.* 41 A41
Carlton *S.Y.* 51 B38
Carlton *Sfk* 35 B59
Carlton *Cbs.* 33 C52
Carlton *Bfd.* 32 C45
Carlton *N.Y.* 58 G42
Carlton *W.Y.* 57 G39
Carlton *N.Y.* 57 A36
Carlton *N.Y.* 58 A42
Carlton Colville 45 G61
Carlton Curlieu 41 F42
Carlton Husthwaite 57 B40
Carlton in Cleveland 63 F41
Carlton in Lindrick 51 D41
Carlton-le-Moorland 52 G44
Carlton Miniott 57 A39
Carlton-on-Trent 51 F43
Carlton Scroop 42 A45
Carluke 75 E24
Carlyon Bay 4 E16
Carmacoup 68 A23
Carmarthen 17 B19
Carmel *Dyf.* 17 C21
Carmel *Clw.* 47 E35
Carmel *Gwy.* 46 D19
Carmel *Gwy.* 46 G20
Carmont 91 E33
Carmore 96 B23
Carmunnock 74 E22
Carmyle 74 D22
Carmyllie 83 C31
Carn 72 E8
Carnaby 59 C47
Carnach 87 B16
Carnassarie 79 G14
Carnbee 83 G31
Carnbo 82 G26
Carn Brea 2 D12
Carn Dearg 94 D13
Carnduncan 72 D8
Carne 3 E15
Carnforth 55 B30
Carnichal 99 D35
Carnmore 72 F9
Carno 37 F25
Carnoch *Hgh.* 97 G24
Carnoch *Hgh.* 88 A13
Carnoch *Hgh.* 95 F18
Carnock 75 B26
Carnon Downs 3 D14
Carnousie 98 D32
Carnoustie 83 D31
Carnwath 75 F25
Carnyorth 2 E9
Carperby 62 G36
Carradale 73 G13
Carragrich 93 B7
Carrbridge 89 B24
Carrefour Selous 3 G17
Carreglefn 46 D19
Carrick *Str.* 73 B14
Carrick *Str.* 73 A17

Carrick *Fife* 83 E30
Carriden 75 B25
Carrine 66 C12
Carrington *G.M.* 49 C33
Carrington *Lcn.* 53 G49
Carrington *Ltn* 76 D28
Carroch 68 D22
Carrog 38 A27
Carroglen 81 E23
Carrol 97 A24
Carron *Grm.* 98 E28
Carron *Cen.* 75 B24
Carron *Str.* 73 A15
Carron Bridge 75 B23
Carronbridge 68 D24
Carronshore 75 B24
Carrot 83 C30
Carr Shield 61 B33
Carrutherstown 69 F26
Carruthmuir 74 D19
Carr Vale 51 F40
Carrville 62 B38
Carry 73 D15
Carsaig 79 E11
Carscreugh 64 D18
Carse 73 D13
Carsegowan 64 E19
Carse of Ardesier 97 F24
Carseriggan 64 D18
Carsethorn 65 E25
Carsgoe 103 B27
Carshalton 23 E48
Carsington 50 G38
Carsluith 64 E20
Carsphairn 67 D21
Carstairs 75 F25
Carstairs Junction 75 F25
Carswell Marsh 21 B39
Carter's Clay 10 B38
Carterton 21 A38
Carterway Heads 62 A36
Carthew 3 C15
Carthorpe 57 A38
Cartington 71 C36
Cartmel 55 B29
Cartmel Fell 55 A30
Carway 17 D20
Cascob 28 B28
Cashel 74 A20
Cashlie 81 C20
Cashmoor 9 C35
Cassencarie 64 E20
Cassington 31 G40
Cassop 62 C39
Castellau 18 C26
Castell Gorfod 17 B18
Castell Howell 26 D20
Castell-y-bwch 19 B28
Casterton 56 A32
Castle Acre 44 D54
Castle Ashby 32 C44
Castle Bank 40 C35
Castlebay (Bagh A Chaisteil) 84 E2
Castle Bolton 62 G35
Castle Bromwich 40 G37
Castle Bytham 42 D45
Castlebythe 16 B16
Castle Caereinion 38 E27
Castle Camps 33 D52
Castle Carrock 61 A31
Castle Cary 9 A32
Castlecary 75 C23
Castle Combe 20 D34
Castlecraig *Hgh.* 97 E24
Castlecraig *Bor.* 75 F27
Castle Donington 41 C40
Castle Douglas 65 D23
Castle Eaton 20 B37
Castle Eden 62 C40
Castle End 30 A38
Castlefairn 68 E23
Castleford 57 G40
Castle Frome 29 D32
Castle Gresley 40 D38
Castle Heaton 77 F35
Castle Hedingham 34 E53
Castle Hill 35 D57
Castle Kennedy 64 E16
Castle Leod 96 F20
Castle Levan 74 C18
Castle Madoc 27 E25
Castlemartin 16 E15
Castlemilk *Str.* 74 E21
Castlemilk *D.&G.* 69 F27
Castle Morris 16 A14
Castlemorton 29 E33
Castle O'er 69 D28
Castle Rising 44 C52
Castleside 62 B36
Castle Stuart 96 F23
Castlethorpe 31 D43
Castleton *Dby.* 50 D37
Castleton *Str.* 73 B14
Castleton *N.Y.* 63 F42
Castleton *Grm.* 98 D32

Castleton *Gwe.* 19 C28
Castleton *Lan.* 49 A34
Castleton *Bor.* 70 D31
Castleton *Tay.* 82 C29
Castletown *Hgh.* 96 G23
Castletown *Hgh.* 103 B27
Castletown *I.o.M.* 54 G24
Castleweary 69 C29
Castlewigg 64 F20
Caston 44 F55
Castor 42 F47
Castramont 65 D21
Cat and Fiddle Inn 49 E35
Catbrain 19 C31
Catchall 2 F10
Catcleugh 70 C33
Catcliffe 51 D40
Catcott 8 A29
Caterham 23 F49
Catesby 31 C41
Catfield 45 C59
Catford 23 D49
Catforth 55 F30
Cathedine 28 F27
Catherington 11 C42
Catherton 29 A32
Catlow 56 F34
Catlowdy 69 F30
Catmore 21 D40
Caton *Lan.* 55 C31
Caton *Dev.* 5 C23
Cator Court 5 C22
Catrine 67 A21
Catsfield 14 F53
Catshill 29 A35
Cattadale 72 E9
Cattal 57 D40
Cattawade 35 E57
Catterall 55 E30
Catterick 62 G38
Catterick Camp 62 G37
Catterlen 61 C30
Catterline 91 F34
Catterton 57 E40
Catthorpe 31 A41
Cattistock 8 D31
Catton *Nor.* 61 A34
Catton *Nfk* 45 D58
Catton *N.Y.* 57 B39
Catton Hall 40 D38
Catwick 59 E47
Catworth 32 A46
Caudworthy 4 A18
Caulcott 31 F40
Cauldcots 83 C32
Cauldhame *Cen.* 81 G24
Cauldhame *Cen.* 74 A22
Cauldon 40 A36
Cauldside 69 E30
Caulkerbush 65 E25
Caundle Marsh 9 C32
Caunsall 40 G34
Caunton 51 F43
Causeway End *D.&G.* 64 D19
Causeway End *Esx* 33 G32
Causewayhead *Cen.* 75 A24
Causewayhead *Cum.* 60 A26
Causeyend 91 B35
Causey Park 71 D37
Cautley 61 G32
Cavendish 34 D53
Cavenham 34 B53
Cavens 65 E25
Caversfield 31 F41
Caversham 22 D43
Caverswall 40 A35
Cawdor 97 F24
Cawkwell 53 D48
Cawood 58 F41
Cawsand 4 F20
Cawston 45 C57
Cawthorne 50 B38
Cawthorpe 42 C46
Cawton 58 B42
Caxton 33 C48
Caxton Gibbet 33 C48
Caynham 28 A31
Caythorpe *Lcn.* 42 A45
Caythorpe *Not.* 41 A42
Cayton 59 A46
Ceallan 92 F4
Ceann A Bhaigh *W.I.* 92 C6
Ceann A Bhaigh *W.I.* 92 E3
Ceann Loch Shiophoirt 100 F8
Cearsiadar 100 E9
Ceathramh Meadhanach 92 D3
Cedig 37 C25
Cefn-brith 47 G25
Cefn-caer-Ferch 36 A19
Cefn Cantref 27 F26
Cefn Coch 47 G27
Cefn-coch 37 C26
Cefn-coed-y-cymmer 18 A26
Cefn Cribwr 18 C24

Cefn Cross 18 C24
Cefn-ddwysarn 37 B25
Cefndeuddwr 37 C23
Cefn Einion 38 G28
Cefneithin 17 C21
Cefn-gorwydd 27 D24
Cefn-gwyn 38 G27
Cefn Hengoed 18 B27
Cefn-mawr 38 A28
Cefn-y-bedd 48 G29
Cefn-y-pant 16 B17
Ceidio 46 D19
Ceidio Fawr 36 B18
Ceint 46 E20
Cellan 27 D22
Cellardyke 83 G31
Cellarhead 40 A35
Cemaes 46 C19
Cemmaes 37 E24
Cenarth 26 D18
Cennin 36 A20
Ceos 100 E9
Ceres 82 F29
Cerne Abbas 9 D32
Cerney Wick 20 B36
Cerrigceinwen 46 E19
Cerrigydrudion 37 A25
Cessford 70 A33
Chaceley 29 E34
Chacewater 2 D13
Chackmore 31 E42
Chacombe 31 D40
Chadderton 49 B34
Chaddesden 41 B39
Chaddesley Corbett 29 A34
Chaddleworth 21 D40
Chadlington 30 F38
Chadshunt 30 C39
Chad Valley 40 G36
Chadwell 42 C43
Chadwell St Mary 24 D52
Chadwick End 30 A38
Chaffcombe 8 D29
Chagford 7 G23
Chailey 13 E49
Chainhurst 14 C53
Chalbury Common 10 D36
Chaldon 23 F49
Chaldon Herring or East
  Chaldon 9 F33
Chale 11 G40
Chale Green 11 F40
Chalfont Common 22 B46
Chalfont St Giles 22 B45
Chalfont St Peter 22 B46
Chalford 20 A34
Chalgrove 21 B42
Chalk 24 D52
Challacombe 6 A22
Challoch 64 D19
Challock 14 B55
Chalmington 8 D31
Chalton *Bfd.* 32 F46
Chalton *Ham.* 11 C43
Chalvington 13 F51
Champany 75 C26
Chandler's Cross 22 B46
Chandler's Ford 11 B40
Channerwick 107 E39
Chantry *Sfk* 35 D57
Chantry *Som.* 20 G33
Chapel 76 A28
Chapel Allerton *Som.* 19 F29
Chapel Allerton *W.Y.* 57 F39
Chapel Amble 3 A15
Chapelbank 82 F25
Chapel Brampton 31 B43
Chapel Chorlton 39 B33
Chapel Cross 13 E52
Chapeldonan 67 C17
Chapel End 41 F39
Chapel-en-le-Frith 50 D36
Chapel Fields 30 A39
Chapelgate 43 C50
Chapel Haddlesey 58 G41
Chapelhall 75 D23
Chapel Hill *Gwe.* 19 B31
Chapelhill *Hgh.* 97 D24
Chapel Hill *Grm.* 99 F36
Chapel Hill *Lcn.* 52 G47
Chapelhill *Tay.* 82 D26
Chapelhill *Tay.* 82 F28
Chapelknowe 69 F28
Chapel Lawn 28 A29
Chapel-le-Dale 56 B33
Chapel of Garioch 91 A33
Chapel Rossan 64 F16
Chapel Row 21 E41
Chapel Stile 60 F29
Chapel St Leonards 53 E51
Chapelton *Tay.* 83 C32
Chapelton *Grm.* 91 E34
Chapelton *Str.* 74 F22
Chapeltown *Lan.* 49 A33
Chapeltown *Cum.* 69 F30
Chapeltown *S.Y.* 51 C39

Chapeltown *Grm.* 90 A28
Chapel Town 3 C14
Chapmanslade 20 G33
Chapman's Well 6 F19
Chapmore End 33 G49
Chappel 34 F54
Chard 8 D29
Chard Junction 8 D29
Charfield 19 B32
Charing 14 C55
Charing Heath 14 C55
Charingworth 30 D37
Charlbury 30 G39
Charlcombe 20 E33
Charlcutt 20 D35
Charlecote 30 C38
Charles 6 B22
Charleshill 22 G44
Charleston 82 C29
Charlestown *Dor.* 9 G32
Charlestown *Grm.* 91 C35
Charlestown *Hgh.* 94 D14
Charlestown *Fife* 75 B26
Charlestown *Hgh.* 96 G22
Charlestown *Cnw.* 4 E16
Charlestown *Grm.* 99 C36
Charlestown of Aberlour 98 E28
Charles Tye 34 C55
Charlesworth 49 C35
Charlinch 8 A28
Charlton *Nor.* 70 E33
Charlton *Wts.* 20 F37
Charlton *Som.* 19 F32
Charlton *Wts.* 20 C35
Charlton *Hfs.* 32 F47
Charlton *H.&W.* 29 D36
Charlton *Nmp.* 31 E41
Charlton *G.L.* 23 D50
Charlton *Oxf.* 21 C40
Charlton *Ham.* 21 G39
Charlton *W.S.* 12 E44
Charlton *Wts.* 9 B34
Charlton Abbots 30 F36
Charlton Adam 8 B31
Charlton-All-Saints 10 B37
Charlton Horethorne 9 B32
Charlton Kings 29 F35
Charlton Mackrell 8 B31
Charlton Marshall 9 D34
Charlton Musgrove 9 A33
Charlton-on-Otmoor 31 G41
Charlwood 23 G48
Charminster 9 E32
Charmouth 8 E29
Charndon 31 F42
Charney Bassett 21 B39
Charnock Richard 48 A31
Charsfield 35 C58
Chart Corner 14 C53
Charter Alley 21 F41
Charterhouse 19 F30
Charterville Allotments 30 G39
Chartham 15 B56
Chartham Hatch 15 B56
Chartridge 22 A45
Chart Sutton 14 C53
Charwelton 31 C41
Chase End Street 29 E33
Chase Terrace 40 D36
Chasetown 40 E36
Chastleton 30 F38
Chasty 6 E19
Chatburn 56 E33
Chatcull 39 B33
Chatham 24 E53
Chathill 71 A37
Chattenden 24 D53
Chatteris 43 G49
Chattisham 34 D56
Chatto 70 B33
Chatton 71 A36
Chawleigh 7 D23
Chawley 21 A40
Chawston 32 C47
Chawton 11 A43
Cheadle *Stf.* 40 A35
Cheadle *G.M.* 49 D34
Cheadle Hulme 49 D34
Cheam 23 E48
Cheapside 22 E45
Chearsley 21 A42
Chebsey 40 C34
Checkendon 21 C42
Checkley *Stf.* 40 B36
Checkley *Che.* 39 A33
Checkley *H.&W.* 28 E31
Chedburgh 34 C53
Cheddar 19 F30
Cheddington 32 G44
Cheddleton 49 G35
Cheddon Fitzpaine 8 B28
Chedglow 20 B35
Chedgrave 45 F59
Chedington 8 D30
Chediston 35 A59

Chedworth **30 G36**
Chedzoy **8 A29**
Cheeklaw **77 E33**
Cheesden **49 A34**
Cheeseman's Green **15 D56**
Cheetham Hill **49 B34**
Cheldon **7 D23**
Chelford **49 E34**
Chellaston **41 B39**
Chellington **32 C45**
Chelmarsh **39 G32**
Chelmondiston **35 E58**
Chelmorton **50 F36**
Chelmsford **24 A52**
Chelsfield **23 E50**
Chelsham **23 F49**
Chelsworth **34 D55**
Cheltenham **29 F35**
Chelveston **32 B45**
Chelvey **19 E30**
Chelwood **19 E32**
Chelwood Gate **13 D49**
Chelworth **20 B35**
Cheney Longville **38 G29**
Chenies **22 B46**
Chepstow **19 B31**
Cherhill **20 D36**
Cherington *Glo.* **20 B34**
Cherington *War.* **30 E38**
Cheriton *Dev.* **7 A23**
Cheriton *W.G.* **17 E20**
Cheriton *Kent* **15 D57**
Cheriton *Dyf.* **16 E15**
Cheriton *Ham.* **11 B41**
Cheriton Bishop **7 F23**
Cheriton Cross **7 F23**
Cheriton Fitzpaine **7 E24**
Cherrington **39 D32**
Cherry Burton **59 E45**
Cherry Hinton **33 C50**
Cherry Willingham **52 E46**
Chertsey **22 E46**
Cheselbourne **9 E33**
Chesham **22 A45**
Chesham Bois **22 B45**
Cheshunt **23 A49**
Cheslyn Hay **40 E35**
Chessington **22 E47**
Chester **48 F29**
Chesterblade **19 G32**
Chesterfield *Dby.* **51 E39**
Chesterfield *Stf.* **40 E36**
Chester-le-Street **62 A38**
Chesters *Bor.* **70 B32**
Chesters *Bor.* **70 A31**
Chesterton *Shr.* **39 F33**
Chesterton *Oxf.* **31 F41**
Chesterton *Cbs.* **42 F47**
Chesterton *Stf.* **40 A34**
Chesterton *Cbs.* **33 C50**
Chesterton Green **30 C39**
Chestfield **25 E57**
Cheswardine **39 C33**
Cheswick **77 F36**
Chetnole **8 D31**
Chettiscombe **7 D25**
Chettisham **43 G51**
Chettle **8 C35**
Chetton **39 F32**
Chetwode **31 F42**
Chetwynd Aston **39 D33**
Cheveley **33 B52**
Chevening **23 F50**
Cheverell's Green **32 G46**
Chevington **34 C53**
Chevington Drift **71 D38**
Chevithorne **7 D25**
Chew Magna **19 E31**
Chew Stoke **19 E31**
Chewton Keynsham **19 E32**
Chewton Mendip **19 F31**
Chicheley **32 D44**
Chichester **11 D43**
Chickerell **9 F32**
Chickering **35 A58**
Chicklade **9 A34**
Chickney **33 F51**
Chicksands **32 E47**
Chidden **11 C42**
Chiddingfold **12 C45**
Chiddingly **13 E51**
Chiddingstone **23 G50**
Chiddingstone Causeway **23 G51**
Chiddingstone Hoath **23 G51**
Chideock **8 E29**
Chidham **11 D43**
Chieveley **21 D40**
Chignall Smealy **33 G52**
Chignall St James **33 G52**
Chigwell **23 B50**
Chigwell Row **23 B50**
Chilbolton **21 G39**
Chilcomb **11 B40**
Chilcombe **8 E31**
Chilcompton **19 F32**

Chilcote **40 D38**
Childerditch **24 C52**
Childer Thornton **48 E29**
Child Okeford **9 C34**
Childrey **21 C39**
Child's Ercall **39 C32**
Childswickham **30 E36**
Childwall **48 D30**
Childwick Green **32 G47**
Chilfrome **8 E31**
Chilgrove **12 E44**
Chilham **15 B56**
Chillaton **6 G20**
Chillenden **15 B58**
Chillerton **11 F40**
Chillesford **24 C52**
Chillingham **71 A36**
Chillington *Dev.* **5 F23**
Chillington *Som.* **8 C29**
Chilmark **9 A35**
Chilson **30 G39**
Chilsworthy *Cnw.* **4 C20**
Chilsworthy *Dev.* **6 E19**
Chilthorne Domer **8 C31**
Chilton *Drm* **62 C38**
Chilton *Bkh.* **31 G42**
Chilton *Oxf.* **21 C40**
Chilton Candover **11 A41**
Chilton Cantelo **8 B31**
Chilton Foliat **21 D39**
Chilton Polden **8 A29**
Chilton Street **34 D53**
Chilton Trinity **8 A28**
Chilvers Coton **41 F39**
Chilworth *Sry* **22 G46**
Chilworth *Ham.* **11 C40**
Chimney **21 A39**
Chineham **21 F42**
Chingford **23 B49**
Chinley **50 D36**
Chinley Head **50 D36**
Chinnor **22 A43**
Chipchase Castle **70 F34**
Chipley Park **7 C27**
Chipnall **39 B33**
Chippenham *Cbs.* **33 B52**
Chippenham *Wts.* **20 D34**
Chipperfield **22 A46**
Chipping *Lan.* **56 E32**
Chipping *Hfs.* **33 E49**
Chipping Campden **30 E37**
Chipping Hill **34 G53**
Chipping Norton **30 F39**
Chipping Ongar **23 A51**
Chipping Sodbury **20 C33**
Chipping Warden **31 D40**
Chipstable **7 C26**
Chipstead *Sry* **23 F48**
Chipstead *Kent* **23 F50**
Chirbury **38 F28**
Chirk **38 B28**
Chirmorrie **64 C17**
Chirnside **77 E34**
Chirnsidebridge **77 E34**
Chirton **37 F36**
Chisbury **21 E38**
Chiscan **66 B12**
Chiselborough **8 C30**
Chiseldon **20 D37**
Chislehampton **21 B41**
Chislehurst **23 D50**
Chislet **25 E57**
Chiswell Green **22 A47**
Chiswick **23 D48**
Chisworth **49 C35**
Chithurst **12 D44**
Chittering **33 B50**
Chitterne **20 G35**
Chittlehamholt **6 C22**
Chittlehampton **6 C22**
Chittoe **20 E35**
Chivelstone **5 G23**
Chobham **22 E45**
Choicelee **77 E33**
Cholderton **21 G38**
Cholesbury **22 A45**
Chollerton **70 F35**
Cholsey **21 C41**
Cholstrey **28 C30**
Cholwell *Dev.* **4 C20**
Cholwell *Avon* **19 F32**
Chop Gate **63 F41**
Chopwell **62 A36**
Chorley *Che.* **48 G31**
Chorley *Lan.* **48 A31**
Chorley *Stf.* **40 D36**
Chorley *Shr.* **39 G32**
Chorleywood **22 B45**
Chorlton **49 G33**
Chorlton-cum-Hardy **49 C34**
Chorlton Lane **38 A30**
Chowley **48 G30**
Chrishall **33 E50**
Chrishall Grange **33 D50**
Chrisswell **74 C18**
Christchurch *Gwe.* **19 C29**

Christchurch *Glo.* **28 G31**
Christchurch *Dor.* **10 E37**
Christchurch *Cbs.* **43 F50**
Christian Malford **20 D35**
Christleton **48 F30**
Christmas Common **22 B43**
Christon **19 F29**
Christon Bank **71 A37**
Christow **7 G23**
Chryston **74 C22**
Chudleigh **5 C24**
Chudleigh Knighton **5 C24**
Chulmleigh **6 D22**
Chunal **50 C36**
Church **56 G33**
Church Aston **39 D33**
Church Brampton **31 B43**
Church Broughton **40 B37**
Church Common **35 C59**
Church Crookham **22 F43**
Churchdown **29 F34**
Church Eaton **40 D34**
Churchend *Avon* **20 B33**
Church End *Ham.* **21 F42**
Churchend *Esx* **25 B55**
Church End *Hum.* **59 D46**
Church End *Bed.* **32 E45**
Church End *Hfs.* **32 G47**
Church End *Bfd.* **32 F45**
Church End *Bfd.* **32 E47**
Churchend *Esx* **33 F51**
Church End *Esx* **33 F52**
Church End *Cbs.* **33 C50**
Church End *Esx* **33 D51**
Church End *Cbs.* **43 E49**
Church End *Lcn.* **43 B48**
Church End *War.* **40 F38**
Church End *Lcn.* **53 C50**
Church End *Wts.* **20 D36**
Church Enstone **30 F39**
Church Fenton **58 F41**
Churchgate **23 A49**
Churchgate Street **33 G50**
Church Green **7 F27**
Church Gresley **40 D38**
Church Hanborough **31 G40**
Church Houses **63 G42**
Churchill *Avon* **19 F30**
Churchill *Oxf.* **30 F38**
Churchill *H.&W.* **29 A34**
Churchill *H.&W.* **29 C35**
Churchingford **7 D27**
Church Knowle **9 F35**
Church Langton **42 F43**
Church Lawford **31 A40**
Church Lawton **49 G34**
Church Leigh **40 B36**
Church Lench **30 C36**
Church Minshull **49 F32**
Church Norton **12 G44**
Churchover **41 G40**
Church Preen **38 F31**
Church Pulverbatch **38 E30**
Churchstanton **7 D27**
Church Stoke **38 F28**
Churchstow **5 F23**
Church Stowe **31 C42**
Church Street **24 D53**
Church Stretton **38 F30**
Churchthorpe **53 C49**
Churchtown *I.o.M.* **54 D25**
Churchtown *Dev.* **6 A22**
Churchtown *Mer.* **48 A29**
Churchtown *Lan.* **55 E30**
Church Village **18 C26**
Church Warsop **51 F41**
Churnsike Lodge **70 F32**
Churston Ferrers **5 E24**
Churt **12 C44**
Churton **48 G30**
Churwell **57 G38**
Chute Cadley **21 F39**
Chute Standen **21 F39**
Chwilog **36 B20**
Chyandour **2 E10**
Cilan Uchaf **36 C18**
Cilcain **47 F27**
Cilcennin **26 B21**
Cilfrew **18 A23**
Cilgerran **26 D17**
Cilgwyn *Dyf.* **27 F23**
Cilgwyn *Dyf.* **16 A16**
Ciliau-Aeron **26 C20**
Cille Bhrighde **84 C3**
Cille Pheadair **84 C3**
Cilmery **27 C25**
Cilrhedyn **17 A18**
Cilrhedyn Bridge **16 A15**
Ciltalgarth **37 A24**
Cilwendeg **17 A18**
Cilybebyll **18 A23**
Cilycwm **27 D23**
Cinderford **29 G32**
Cippyn **26 D17**
Cirbhig **100 C7**

Cirencester **20 A35**
City Dulas **46 D20**
City of London **23 D49**
City of Westminster **23 C48**
Clabhach **78 B7**
Clachaig **73 B17**
Clachan *Str.* **73 E13**
Clachan *W.I.* **92 G3**
Clachan *Hgh.* **86 A11**
Clachan *Str.* **80 F17**
Clachan *Str.* **79 C14**
Clachandhu **79 D10**
Clachaneasy **64 C19**
Clachanmore **64 F16**
Clachan of Campsie **74 C21**
Clachan of Glendaruel **73 B15**
Clachan-Seil **79 F13**
Clachanturn **90 D28**
Clach-bhreac **73 C13**
Clachnabrain **82 A29**
Clachnaharry **96 G22**
Clachtoll **101 F16**
Clackmannan **75 A24**
Clacton-on-Sea **35 G57**
Cladach A Chaolais **92 E3**
Cladach Chirceboist **92 E3**
Cladich **80 E16**
Claggan *Hgh.* **87 G17**
Claggan *Hgh.* **79 C12**
Claigan **93 F8**
Claines **29 C34**
Clandown **19 F32**
Clanfield *Ham.* **11 C42**
Clanfield *Oxf.* **21 A38**
Clannaborough Barton **7 E23**
Clanville **21 G38**
Claonaig **73 E14**
Claonairigh **80 G16**
Claonel **96 A21**
Clapgate **10 D36**
Clap Gate **57 E39**
Clapham *N.Y.* **56 C33**
Clapham *Bfd.* **32 C46**
Clapham *W.S.* **12 F46**
Clapham *G.L.* **23 D48**
Clapham Hill **25 E56**
Clappers **77 E35**
Clappersgate **60 F29**
Clapton **8 D29**
Clapton-in -Gordano **19 D30**
Clapton-on-the-Hill **30 G37**
Clapworthy **6 C22**
Clarbeston **16 B16**
Clarbeston Road **16 B16**
Clarborough **51 D43**
Clardon **103 B27**
Clare **34 D53**
Clarebrand **65 D23**
Clarencefield **69 G26**
Clareton **57 E39**
Clarilaw **70 B31**
Clarkston **71 G40**
Clashban **96 B22**
Clashcoig **96 B22**
Clashgour **80 C18**
Clashindarroch **98 F30**
Clashmore **96 B23**
Clashnessie **101 E16**
Clashnoir **90 A28**
Clathy **82 E25**
Clatt **90 A31**
Clatter **37 F25**
Clatterford End **23 A51**
Clatterin Brig **91 F32**
Clatteringshaws **65 C21**
Clatworthy **7 B26**
Claughton *Lan.* **55 C31**
Claughton *Lan.* **55 E31**
Claverdon **30 B37**
Claverham **19 E30**
Clavering **33 E50**
Claverley **39 F33**
Claverton **20 E33**
Clawdd-newydd **47 G26**
Clawfin **67 C21**
Clawthorpe **55 B31**
Clawton **6 F19**
Claxby *Lcn.* **52 C47**
Claxby *Lcn.* **53 E50**
Claxby Pluckacre **53 F48**
Claxton *N.Y.* **58 C42**
Claxton *Nfk* **45 E59**
Clay Common **45 G60**
Clay Coton **31 A41**
Clay Cross **51 F39**
Claydene **23 G50**
Claydon *Oxf.* **31 C40**
Claydon *Sfk* **35 D57**
Claygate *Kent* **14 C52**
Claygate *Sry* **22 E47**
Claygate Cross **23 F51**
Clayhanger *W.M.* **40 E36**
Clayhanger *Dev.* **7 C25**
Clayhidon **7 D27**

Clayock **103 C27**
Clay of Allan **97 D24**
Claypole **42 A44**
Claythorpe **53 E50**
Clayton *S.Y.* **51 B40**
Clayton *Stf.* **40 A34**
Clayton *W.S.* **13 E48**
Clayton *W.Y.* **57 F37**
Clayton-le-Moors **56 F32**
Clayton-le-Woods **55 G31**
Clayton West **50 A38**
Clayworth **51 D43**
Cleadale **85 F10**
Cleadon **71 G39**
Clearbrook **5 D21**
Clearwell **19 A31**
Cleasby **62 E38**
Cleat **105 C30**
Cleatlam **62 E36**
Cleatop **56 C34**
Cleator **60 E26**
Cleator Moor **60 E26**
Cleckheaton **57 G37**
Cleedownton **38 G31**
Cleehill **28 A31**
Clee St Margaret **38 G31**
Cleethorpes **53 B49**
Cleeton St Mary **29 A32**
Cleeve *Avon* **19 E30**
Cleeve *Oxf.* **21 C42**
Cleeve Hill **29 F35**
Cleeve Prior **30 D36**
Cleghorn **75 F24**
Clehonger **28 E30**
Cleigh **79 E14**
Cleish **75 A26**
Cleland **75 E23**
Clench Common **20 E37**
Clenchwarton **43 C51**
Clent **40 G35**
Cleobury Mortimer **29 A32**
Cleobury North **39 G32**
Clephanton **96 F23**
Clerklands **69 A30**
Clestrain **105 A28**
Cleuchbrae **69 F26**
Cleuch Head **70 C31**
Clevancy **20 D36**
Clevedon **19 D29**
Cleveland Tontine **62 G40**
Cleveleys **55 E28**
Clevelode **29 D34**
Cleverton **20 C35**
Clewer **19 F30**
Clewer Village **22 D45**
Cley next the Sea **44 A56**
Cliburn **61 D31**
Cliddesden **21 G42**
Cliff *Dyf.* **17 D19**
Cliff *Hgh.* **79 A12**
Cliff End **14 F54**
Cliffe *N.Y.* **58 F42**
Cliffe *Kent* **24 D53**
Cliff End **25 E59**
Cliffe Woods **24 D53**
Clifford *H.&W.* **28 D28**
Clifford *W.Y.* **57 E40**
Clifford Chambers **30 C37**
Clifford's Mesne **29 F33**
Cliffs End **25 E59**
Clifton *Cum.* **61 D31**
Clifton *Lan.* **55 F30**
Clifton *Bfd.* **32 E47**
Clifton *Oxf.* **31 E40**
Clifton *H.&W.* **29 D34**
Clifton *Not.* **41 B41**
Clifton *Dby.* **40 A37**
Clifton *Nor.* **71 E37**
Clifton *Avon* **19 D31**
Clifton *Cen.* **80 D19**
Clifton Campville **40 D38**
Clifton Hampden **21 B41**
Clifton Reynes **32 C45**
Clifton upon Dunsmore **31 A41**
Clifton upon Teme **29 B33**
Cliftonville **25 D59**
Clifynydd **18 B26**
Climping **12 F46**
Climpy **75 E25**
Clint **57 C38**
Clinterty **91 B34**
Clint Green **44 D56**
Clintmains **76 G31**
Clippesby **45 D60**
Clipsham **42 D45**
Clipston *Nmp.* **41 G42**
Clipston *Not.* **41 B42**
Clipstone **51 F41**
Clitheroe **56 E33**
Clive **38 C30**
Clivocast **106 B41**
Clocaenog **47 G26**
Clochan **98 C29**
Clochtow **99 F36**
Clock Face **48 C31**
Clockhill **99 E34**
Cloddach **97 F27**

Clodock 28 F29
Cloford 20 G33
Cloichran 81 D22
Clola 99 E36
Clonrae 68 D24
Clophill 32 E46
Clopton 42 G46
Clopton Green 34 C53
Closeburn 68 D24
Close Clark 54 F24
Closworth 8 C31
Clothall 33 E48
Clothan 106 D40
Clotton 48 F31
Clough *G.M.* 49 A35
Clough *Cum.* 61 G33
Clough Foot 56 G34
Cloughton 63 G46
Cloughton Newlands 63 G46
Clounlaid 79 B13
Clousta 107 B38
Clouston 104 E28
Clova *Grm.* 90 A30
Clova *Tay.* 90 F29
Clovelly 6 C19
Clovelly Cross 6 C19
Clove Lodge 61 E35
Clovenfords 76 G30
Clovenstone 91 B33
Cloverhill 91 B35
Cloves 97 E27
Clovullin 80 A15
Clowne 51 E40
Clows Top 29 A32
Cloyntie 67 C19
Cluanach 72 E9
Clubworthy 4 A18
Cluer 93 B7
Clun 38 G28
Clunas 97 G24
Clunbury 38 G29
Clune *Grm.* 98 C31
Clune *Hgh.* 88 B23
Clunes 87 F17
Clungunford 28 A29
Clunie *Tay.* 82 C27
Clunie *Grm.* 98 D32
Clunton 38 G29
Cluny 76 A28
Clutton *Che.* 48 G30
Clutton *Avon* 19 F32
Clwt-y-bont 46 F21
Clydach *W.G.* 17 D22
Clydach *Gwe.* 28 G28
Clydach Vale 18 B25
Clydebank 74 D21
Clydey 17 A18
Clyffe Pypard 20 D36
Clynder 74 B18
Clynderwen 16 C16
Clynelish 97 A24
Clynfyw 17 A18
Clynnog-fawr 36 A19
Clyro 28 D28
Clyst Honiton 7 F25
Clyst Hydon 7 E26
Clyst St George 7 G25
Clyst St Lawrence 7 E26
Clyst St Mary 7 F25
Cnewr 27 F24
Cnoc 100 D10
Cnoc nan Sltheag 81 G20
Cnwch Coch 27 A22
Coachford 98 E30
Coad's Green 4 C18
Coal Aston 51 D39
Coalbrookdale 39 E32
Coalbrookvale 18 A27
Coalburn 75 G23
Coalburns 71 G37
Coalcleugh 61 B33
Coaley 20 A33
Coalpit Heath 19 C32
Coalpit Hill 49 G33
Coalport 39 E32
Coalsnaughton 75 A25
Coaltown of Balgonie 76 A28
Coaltown of Wemyss 76 A29
Coalville 41 D40
Coat 8 B30
Coatbridge 74 D22
Coate *Wts.* 20 E36
Coate *Wts.* 20 C37
Coates *Glo.* 20 A35
Coates *Cbs.* 43 F48
Coates *W.S.* 12 E45
Coatham 63 D41
Coatham Mundeville 62 D38
Cobairdy 98 E31
Cobbaton 6 C22
Coberley 29 G35
Cobham *Kent* 24 E52
Cobham *Sry* 22 F47
Cobleland 74 A20
Cobler's Green 33 G52
Cobnash 28 B30

Coburty 99 C35
Cochno 74 C20
Cock Alley 51 E40
Cockayne 63 G42
Cockayne Hatley 33 D48
Cock Bridge 90 C28
Cockburnspath 77 C33
Cock Clarks 24 A53
Cockenzie and Port Seton 76 C29
Cockerham 55 D30
Cockermouth 60 C26
Cockernhoe 32 F47
Cockett 17 E22
Cockfield *Drm* 62 D37
Cockfield *Sfk* 34 C54
Cockfosters 23 B48
Cocking 12 E44
Cockington 5 D24
Cocklake 19 G30
Cockley Beck 60 F28
Cockley Cley 44 E53
Cockpole Green 22 C43
Cockshutt 38 C30
Cockthorpe 44 A55
Cockwood 7 G25
Codda 4 C17
Coddenham 35 C57
Coddington *H.&W.* 29 D33
Coddington *Not.* 52 G44
Coddington *Che.* 48 G30
Codford St Mary 20 G35
Codford St Peter 20 G35
Codicote 32 G47
Codmore Hill 12 D46
Codnor 41 A40
Codrington 19 D32
Codsall 40 E34
Codsall Wood 40 E34
Coedcae 19 A28
Coedely 18 C26
Coedkernew 19 C28
Coed Morgan 28 G29
Coedpoeth 48 G28
Coed-y-paen 19 B29
Coed-yr-ynys 28 F27
Coed Ystumgwern 36 C21
Coelbren 27 G24
Cofcott Green 6 F19
Coffinswell 5 D24
Cofton Hackett 30 A36
Cogan 18 D27
Cogenhoe 32 C44
Coggeshall 34 F54
Coggeshall Hamlet 34 F54
Coggins Mill 13 D51
Coig Peighinnean *W.I.* 101 A11
Coig Peighinnean *W.I.* 100 B9
Coilantogle 81 G21
Coileitir 80 C17
Coilesan 80 G18
Coillaig 80 E16
Coille Mhorgil 87 D16
Coille -righ 86 B15
Coillore 85 A9
Coity 18 C25
Col 100 C10
Colaboll 102 G21
Colan 3 B14
Colaton Raleigh 7 G26
Colbost 93 G7
Colbury 10 C39
Colby *Nfk* 45 B58
Colby *Cum.* 61 D32
Colby *I.o.M.* 54 F24
Colchester 34 F55
Colcot 18 D27
Cold Ash 21 E41
Cold Ashby 31 A42
Cold Ashton 20 D33
Cold Aston 30 F37
Coldbackie 102 B21
Cold Blow 16 C17
Cold Brayfield 32 C45
Cold Chapel 68 A25
Coldean 13 F49
Coldeast 5 C23
Colden Common 11 B40
Coldfair Green 35 B60
Coldham 43 E50
Cold Hanworth 52 D46
Coldharbour 22 G47
Coldhayes 11 B43
Cold Hesledon 62 B39
Cold Higham 31 C42
Coldingham 77 D34
Cold Kirby 58 A41
Cold Newton 42 E43
Cold Norton 24 B54
Cold Overton 42 E43
Coldrain 82 G26
Coldred 15 C58
Coldridge 6 E22
Coldrey 22 G43
Coldrife 71 D36

Coldstream 77 G34
Coldwaltham 12 E46
Coldwells 99 E37
Cole 9 A32
Colebatch 38 G28
Colebrook 7 E25
Coleby *Lcn.* 52 F45
Coleby *Hum.* 52 A45
Coleford *Glo.* 28 G31
Coleford *Som.* 19 G32
Coleford *Dev.* 7 E23
Cole Green 33 G48
Colehill 10 D36
Coleman's Hatch 13 C50
Colemere 38 B30
Colemore 11 A43
Colenden 82 E26
Coleorton 41 D39
Colerne 20 D33
Colesbourne 29 G35
Cole's Cross 5 F23
Colesden 32 C47
Coleshill *War.* 40 G37
Coleshill *Bkh.* 22 B45
Coleshill *Oxf.* 21 B38
Colestocks 7 E26
Colfin 64 E16
Colgate 13 C48
Colgrain 74 B19
Colinsburgh 83 G30
Colinton 76 D28
Colintraive 73 C16
Colkirk 44 C55
Collace 82 D27
Collafirth *She.* 107 A40
Collafirth *She.* 106 D39
Collamoor Head 4 A17
Collaton St Mary 5 E24
Collessie 82 F28
Colleton Mills 6 D22
Collett's Green 29 C33
Collier Row 23 B50
Collier's End 33 F49
Collier Street 14 C53
Colliery Row 62 B39
Collieston 91 A36
Collin 69 F26
Collingbourne Ducis 21 F38
Collingbourne Kingston 21 F38
Collingham *S.Y.* 57 E39
Collingham *Not.* 52 F44
Collington 29 B32
Collingtree 31 C43
Collins Green 48 C31
Colliston 83 C31
Colliton 7 E26
Collmuir 90 C31
Collycroft 41 G39
Collynie 99 F34
Collyweston 42 E46
Colmonell 67 E17
Colmworth 32 C46
Coln 30 G36
Colnabaichin 90 C28
Colnbrook 22 D46
Colne *Lan.* 56 F34
Colne *Cbs.* 33 A49
Colne Engaine 34 E54
Colney 45 E57
Colney Heath 22 A47
Colney Street 22 A47
Coln Rogers 20 A36
Coln St Aldwyns 20 A37
Colonsay 72 A9
Colpy 98 F32
Colquhar 76 F29
Colsterdale 57 A37
Colsterworth 42 C45
Colston Bassett 41 B42
Coltfield 97 E26
Coltishall 45 C58
Colton *Nfk* 45 D57
Colton *N.Y.* 58 E41
Colton *Stf.* 40 C36
Colton *Cum.* 55 A29
Colva 28 C27
Colvend 65 E24
Colvister 106 C40
Colwall Green 29 D33
Colwall Stone 29 D33
Colwell 70 F35
Colwich 40 C35
Colwick 41 A41
Colwinston 18 D25
Colworth 12 F45
Colwyn Bay 47 E24
Colyford 8 E28
Colyton 8 E28
Combe *Brk.* 21 E39
Combe *Oxf.* 30 G39
Combe *H.&W.* 28 B29
Combe Cross 5 C23
Combe Down 20 E33
Combe Florey 7 B27
Combe Hay 20 E33
Combeinteignhead 5 C25

Combe Martin 6 A21
Combe Moor 28 B29
Combe Raleigh 7 E27
Comberbach 49 E32
Comberford 40 E37
Comberton *H.&W.* 28 B30
Comberton *Cbs.* 33 C49
Combe St Nicholas 8 C29
Combpyne 8 E28
Combrook 30 C38
Combs *Sfk* 34 C56
Combs *Dby.* 50 E36
Combs Ford 34 C56
Combwich 19 G28
Comer 80 G19
Comers 91 C32
Commercial End 33 B51
Commins Coch 37 E24
Commondale 63 E42
Common Edge 55 F29
Common Moor 4 D18
Commonside 40 A38
Common Side 51 E39
Compstall 49 C35
Compton *Dev.* 5 D24
Compton *W.S.* 11 C43
Compton *Ham.* 11 B40
Compton *Sry* 22 G45
Compton *Brk.* 21 D41
Compton Abbas 9 C34
Compton Abdale 30 G36
Compton Bassett 20 D36
Compton Beauchamp 21 C38
Compton Bishop 19 F29
Compton Chamberlayne 10 B36
Compton Dando 19 E32
Compton Dundon 8 A30
Compton Martin 19 F31
Compton Pauncefoot 9 B32
Compton Valence 8 E31
Comra 88 E21
Comrie 81 E23
Conchra *Hgh.* 86 B14
Conchra *Str.* 73 B16
Concraigie 82 C26
Conder Green 55 D30
Conderton 29 E35
Condicote 30 F37
Condorrat 75 C23
Condover 30 E30
Coneyhurst Common 12 D47
Coneysthorpe 58 B43
Coneythorpe 57 D39
Coney Weston 34 A55
Conford 12 C44
Congash 89 B26
Congdon's Shop 4 C18
Congerstone 41 E39
Congham 44 C52
Congleton 49 F34
Congresbury 19 E30
Conicavel 97 F25
Coningsby 53 G48
Conington *Cbs.* 42 G47
Conington *Cbs.* 33 B49
Conisbrough 51 C40
Conisby 72 D8
Conisholme 53 C49
Coniston *Cum.* 60 G28
Coniston *Hum.* 59 F47
Coniston Cold 56 D34
Conistone 56 C35
Conland 98 E31
Connah's Quay 48 F28
Connel 80 D15
Connel Park 67 B21
Connor Downs 2 E11
Conon Bridge 96 F21
Cononish 80 E18
Cononley 56 E35
Cononsyth 83 C31
Consall 40 A35
Consett 62 A36
Constable Burton 62 G37
Constantine 2 F13
Contin 96 F20
Contlaw 91 C34
Contullich 96 D22
Conwy 47 E23
Conyer 25 E55
Cooden 13 F52
Coodham 74 G19
Cookbury 6 E19
Cookham 22 C44
Cookham Dean 22 C44
Cookham Rise 22 C44
Cookhill 30 C36
Cookley *Sfk* 35 A59
Cookley *H.&W.* 40 G34
Cookley Green 21 C42
Cookney 91 D34
Cooksbridge 13 E50
Cookshill 40 A35
Cooksmill Green 24 A52
Cookston 99 F35
Coolham 12 D47

Cooling 24 D53
Coombe *Cnw.* 2 D12
Coombe *Cnw.* 3 C15
Coombe *Dev.* 7 G24
Coombe *Cnw.* 6 D18
Coombe *Dev.* 5 F23
Coombe Bissett 10 B37
Coombe Hill 29 F34
Coombe Keynes 9 F34
Coombes 12 F47
Coopersale Common 23 A50
Cooper's Corner *E.S.* 14 E53
Cooper's Corner *Kent* 23 G50
Cooper's Hill 22 D45
Cootham 12 E46
Copdock 35 D57
Copford Green 34 F55
Copgrove 57 C39
Copister 106 E40
Cople 32 D46
Copley 62 D36
Coplow Dale 50 E37
Copmanthorpe 58 E41
Coppathorne 6 E18
Coppenhall 40 D34
Coppenhall Moss 49 G33
Coppingford 32 A47
Coppleridge 9 B34
Copplestone 7 E23
Coppull 48 A31
Coppull Moor 48 A31
Copsale 12 D47
Copster Green 56 F32
Copston Magna 41 G40
Cop Street 15 B58
Copt Heath 30 A37
Copt Hewick 57 B39
Copthorne 13 C49
Copt Oak 41 D40
Copy Lake 6 D22
Copythorne 10 C39
Coralhill 99 C36
Corbiegoe 103 D29
Corbridge 70 G35
Corby 42 G44
Corby Glen 42 C46
Cordach 90 D31
Coreley 29 A32
Corfe 8 C28
Corfe Castle 9 F35
Corfe Mullen 9 E35
Corfton 38 G30
Corgarff 90 C28
Corhampton 11 B42
Corley 40 G38
Corley Ash 40 G38
Corley Moor 40 G38
Cornabus 72 F9
Corney 60 G27
Cornforth 62 C38
Cornhill 98 D31
Cornhill on Tweed 77 G34
Cornholme 56 G35
Cornish Hall End 33 E52
Cornquoy 105 D30
Cornriggs 61 B34
Cornsay 62 B37
Cornsay Colliery 62 B37
Corntown *Hgh.* 96 F21
Corntown *M.G.* 18 D25
Cornwell 30 F38
Cornwood 5 E22
Cornworthy 5 E24
Corpach 87 G16
Corpusty 45 C57
Corrachree 90 C30
Corran *Hgh.* 86 D14
Corran *Hgh.* 80 A15
Corran *Str.* 74 A18
Corranbuie 73 D14
Corranmore 79 G13
Corrany 54 E26
Corrie 73 F16
Corriechrevie 73 E13
Corrie Common 69 E28
Corriecravie 66 A14
Corriedoo 68 E22
Corrielorne 79 F14
Corrievorrie 88 B23
Corrimony 88 A19
Corringham *Lcn.* 52 C44
Corringham *Esx* 24 C53
Corris 37 E23
Corris Uchaf 37 E23
Corrlarach 86 G15
Corrour Shooting Lodge 80 A19
Corrow 80 G17
Corry 86 B12
Corrychurrachan 80 A16
Corrykinloch 101 F19
Corrylach 72 G12
Corrymuckloch 81 D24
Corsback 103 B27
Corscombe 8 D30
Corse 98 E31
Corsebank 68 B23

Corsehill 69 E27
Corse Lawn 29 E34
Corsemalzie 64 E19
Corse of Kinnoir 98 E31
Corsewall 64 D16
Corsham 20 D34
Corsindae 91 C32
Corsley 20 G34
Corsley Heath 20 G34
Corsock 65 C23
Corston *Wts.* 20 C35
Corston *Avon* 19 E32
Corstorphine 75 C27
Cortachy 82 B29
Corton *Wts.* 20 G35
Corton *Sfk* 45 F61
Corton Denham 9 B32
Corunna 92 E4
Corwar House 67 E18
Corwen 37 A26
Coryton *Dev.* 6 G20
Coryton *Esx* 24 C53
Cosby 41 F41
Coseley 40 F35
Cosford 39 E33
Cosgrove 31 D43
Cosham 11 D42
Cosheston 16 D15
Coshieville 81 C23
Cossall 41 A40
Cossington *Lei.* 41 D41
Cossington *Som.* 19 G29
Costa 104 D29
Costessey 45 D57
Costock 41 C41
Coston *Lei.* 42 C44
Coston *Nfk* 44 E56
Cote *Oxf.* 21 A39
Cote *Som.* 19 G29
Cotebrook 48 F31
Cotehill 61 A30
Cotes *Lei.* 41 C41
Cotes *Stf.* 40 B34
Cotes *Cum.* 55 A30
Cotesbach 41 G41
Cotgrave 41 B42
Cothall 91 B34
Cotham 42 A43
Cothelstone 7 B27
Cothercott 40 E30
Cotheridge 29 C33
Cotherstone 62 E35
Cothill 21 B40
Cotleigh 7 E27
Coton *Cbs.* 33 C49
Coton *Stf.* 40 E37
Coton *Stf.* 40 B35
Coton *Nmp.* 31 A42
Coton Clanford 40 C34
Coton in the Clay 40 C37
Coton in the Elms 40 D38
Cottam *Not.* 52 D44
Cottam *Hum.* 59 C45
Cottam *Lan.* 55 F30
Cottartown 89 A26
Cottenham 33 B50
Cotterdale 61 G34
Cottered 37 F49
Cotteridge 40 G36
Cotterstock 42 F46
Cottesbrooke 31 A42
Cottesmore 42 D44
Cottingham *Nmp.* 42 F44
Cottingham *Hum.* 59 F46
Cottisford 31 E41
Cotton 34 B56
Cotton End 32 D46
Cot-town *Grm.* 99 E33
Cot-town *Grm.* 90 A31
Cottown 91 B33
Cotwalton 40 B35
Couch's Mill 4 E17
Coughton *War.* 30 B36
Coughton *H.&W.* 28 F31
Cougie 87 B18
Coulaghailtro 72 D12
Coulags 94 G15
Coulby Newham 63 E41
Coull 90 C31
Coulport 73 B17
Coulsdon 23 F48
Coulston 20 F35
Coulter 75 G26
Coultershaw Bridge 12 E45
Coultings 19 G28
Coulton 58 B42
Coultra 82 E29
Cound 38 E31
Coundon 62 C38
Coundon Grange 62 D37
Countersett 56 A35
Countess 20 G37
Countess Wear 7 F25
Countesthorpe 41 F41
Countisbury 7 A23
County Oak 13 C48

Coupar Angus 82 C28
Coupland *Cum.* 61 E32
Coupland *Nor.* 77 G35
Cour 73 F14
Court-at-Street 15 D56
Court Barton 7 F23
Courteenhall 31 C43
Court Henry 17 B21
Court House Green 41 G39
Courtsend 25 B56
Courtway 7 B27
Cousland 76 D29
Cousley Wood 13 C52
Coustonn 73 C16
Cove *Dev.* 7 D25
Cove *Str.* 74 B18
Cove *Hgh.* 94 B14
Cove *Ham.* 22 F44
Cove Bay 91 C35
Covehithe 45 G61
Coven 40 E34
Coveney 43 G50
Covenham St Bartholomew
53 C49
Covenham St Mary 53 C49
Coventry 30 A39
Coventry Airport 30 A39
Coverack 2 G13
Coverham 57 A36
Covesea 97 D27
Covington *Str.* 75 G25
Covington *Cbs.* 32 A46
Cowan Bridge 56 B32
Cowbeech 13 E52
Cowbit 43 D48
Cowbridge 18 D25
Cowden 23 G50
Cowdenbeath 75 A27
Cowden Pound 23 G50
Cowes 11 E40
Cowesby 62 G40
Cowfold 13 D48
Cowgill 56 A33
Cowie *Grm.* 91 E34
Cowie *Cen.* 75 B24
Cowlam Manor 59 C45
Cowley *G.L.* 22 C46
Cowley *Oxf.* 21 A41
Cowley *Glo.* 29 G35
Cowley *Dev.* 7 F24
Cowling *N.Y.* 57 A38
Cowling *N.Y.* 56 E35
Cowlinge 33 C52
Cowmes 50 A37
Cowpen 71 E38
Cowpen Bewley 62 D40
Cowplain 11 C42
Cowshill 61 B34
Cowthorpe 57 D40
Coxbank 39 A32
Coxbench 41 A39
Cox Common 45 G59
Coxheath 14 B53
Coxhoe 62 C38
Coxley 19 G31
Coxtie Green 23 B51
Coxwold 58 B41
Coychurch 18 D25
Coylet 73 B17
Coylton 67 B20
Coylumbridge 89 C24
Coynach 90 C30
Coynachie 98 F30
Coytrahen 18 C24
Crabbet Park 13 C49
Crabbs Cross 30 B36
Crabtree *Dev.* 4 E20
Crabtree *W.S.* 12 D47
Crackaig 72 D11
Crackenthorpe 61 D32
Crackington 4 A17
Crackington Haven 4 A16
Crackleybank 39 D33
Crackpot 62 G35
Cracoe 56 C35
Craddock 7 D26
Cradhlastadh 100 D6
Cradley *W.M.* 40 G35
Cradley *H.&W.* 29 D33
Crafthole 4 E19
Cragg 56 G35
Craggan 81 F23
Cragganruar 81 C22
Craggie *Hgh.* 88 A23
Craggie *Hgh.* 102 F24
Craghead 62 A37
Craibstone *Grm.* 91 B34
Craibstone *Grm.* 98 D30
Craichie 83 C30
Craig *Str.* 67 C19
Craig *D.&G.* 65 D22
Craig *Str.* 80 D16
Craig *Str.* 79 E11
Craig *Hgh.* 95 G16
Craig *Hgh.* 94 E13
Craigandaive 73 B16

Craigans 73 A14
Craigbeg 88 F19
Craigcefnparc 17 D22
Craigcleuch 69 E29
Craigculter 99 D34
Craigdam 99 F34
Craigdarroch *D.&G.* 68 D23
Craigdarroch *Str.* 68 C22
Craigdhu *D.&G.* 64 F19
Craigdhu *Hgh.* 96 G20
Craigearn 91 B32
Craigellachie 98 E28
Craigellie 99 C36
Craigencallie 64 C20
Craigend *Grm.* 97 F27
Craigend *Tay.* 82 F26
Craigendoran 74 B19
Craigengillan 67 C20
Craigenputtock 68 E23
Craigens 72 D8
Craighall 82 F29
Craighat 74 B20
Craighead *Fife* 83 G32
Craighead *Hgh.* 96 E23
Craighlaw 64 D18
Craighouse 72 D11
Craigie *Str.* 74 G20
Craigie *Tay.* 82 C27
Craigie *Grm.* 91 B35
Craigie Brae 99 F34
Craigieburn 69 C26
Craigieholm 82 D27
Craiglockhart 75 C27
Craiglug 91 D33
Craigmaud 99 D34
Craigmillar 76 C28
Craigmore 73 D17
Craigmyle Ho. 91 C32
Craignafeich 73 C15
Craignant 38 B28
Craignavie 81 D21
Craigneil 67 E17
Craignure 79 D13
Craigo 91 G32
Craigoch 67 C19
Craigow 82 G26
Craig Penllyn 18 D25
Craigrothie 82 F29
Craigroy 97 F27
Craigruie 81 E20
Craigsanquhar 82 F29
Craigton *Grm.* 91 C34
Craigton *Cen.* 74 B22
Craigton *Tay.* 82 B29
Craigton *Tay.* 83 D31
Craigtown 102 C24
Craig-y-nos 27 G24
Craik *Grm.* 90 A30
Craik *Bor.* 69 C29
Crail 83 G32
Crailing 70 A32
Crailinghall 70 A32
Craiselound 51 C43
Crakehill 57 B40
Crambe 58 C43
Cramlington 71 F38
Cramond 75 C27
Cranage 49 F33
Cranberry 39 B33
Cranborne 10 C36
Cranbourne 22 D45
Cranbrook 14 D53
Cranbrook Common 14 D53
Cranfield 32 D45
Cranford *Dev.* 6 C19
Cranford *G.L.* 22 D47
Cranford St Andrew 32 A45
Cranford St John 32 A45
Cranham *Glo.* 29 G34
Cranham *Esx* 23 C51
Crank 48 B30
Cranleigh 12 C46
Cranmer Green 34 A56
Cranmore *Som.* 19 G32
Cranmore *I.o.W.* 10 E39
Cranna 98 D32
Crannach 98 D30
Cranoe 42 F43
Cransford 35 B59
Cranshaws 76 D32
Cranstal 54 C26
Crantock 2 B13
Cranwell 52 G46
Cranwich 44 F53
Cranworth 44 E55
Craobh Haven 79 G13
Crapstone 4 D20
Crarae 73 A15
Crask Inn 102 F21
Craskins 90 C30
Crask of Aigas 96 G20
Craster 71 A38
Craswall 28 E28
Cratfield 35 A59

Crathes 91 D33
Crathie *Grm.* 90 D28
Crathie *Hgh.* 88 E21
Crathorne 62 F40
Craven Arms 38 G30
Craw 73 F14
Crawcrook 71 G37
Crawford *Lan.* 48 B31
Crawford *Str.* 68 A25
Crawfordjohn 68 A24
Crawfordton 68 D23
Crawick 68 B23
Crawley *Oxf.* 30 G39
Crawley *W.S.* 13 C48
Crawley *Ham.* 11 A40
Crawley Down 13 C49
Crawleyside 62 B35
Crawshawbooth 56 G33
Crawton 91 F34
Crawyn 54 D25
Cray *Tay.* 82 A27
Cray *Pow.* 27 F24
Cray *N.Y.* 56 B35
Crayford 23 D51
Crayke 58 B41
Crays Hill 24 B53
Cray's Pond 21 C42
Crazies Hill 22 D43
Creacombe 7 D24
Creagbheitheachain 80 A15
Creag Ghoraidh 92 G3
Creaton 31 A42
Creca 69 F28
Credenhill 28 D30
Crediton 7 E24
Creech St Michael 8 B28
Creed 3 D15
Creedy Park 7 E24
Creekmouth 23 C50
Creeting St Mary 34 C56
Creeton 42 C46
Creetown 64 E20
Creggans 80 G16
Cregneish 54 G23
Cregrina 28 C27
Creich 82 E29
Creigiau 18 C26
Crelevan 88 A19
Cremyll 4 E20
Cressage 38 E31
Cresselly 16 D16
Cressing 34 F53
Cresswell *Stf.* 40 B35
Cresswell *Nor.* 71 D38
Cresswell *Dyf.* 16 D16
Creswell 51 E41
Cretingham 35 B58
Cretshengan 72 D12
Crewe *Che.* 48 G30
Crewe *Che.* 49 G33
Crewgreen 38 D29
Crewkerne 8 D30
Crewton 41 B39
Crianlarich 80 E19
Cribyn 26 C21
Criccieth 36 B20
Crich 51 G39
Crich Carr 51 G39
Crichie 99 E35
Crichton 76 D29
Crick *Gwe.* 19 C30
Crick *Nmp.* 31 A41
Crickadarn 27 D26
Cricket Malherbie 8 C29
Cricket St Thomas 8 D29
Crickheath 38 C28
Crickhowell 28 G27
Cricklade 20 B36
Cricklewood 23 F39
Cridling Stubbs 58 G41
Crieff 81 E24
Criggion 38 D28
Crigglestone 51 A39
Crimdon Park 62 C40
Crimond 99 D36
Crimonmogate 99 D36
Crimplesham 44 E52
Crinan 73 A13
Cringleford 45 E57
Cringletie 76 F28
Crinow 16 C17
Cripplesease 2 E10
Cripp's Corner 14 E53
Crix 34 G53
Croalchapel 68 D24
Croasdale 60 E26
Crockenhill 23 E50
Crockernwell 7 F23
Crockerton 20 G34
Crocketford or Ninemile Bar
65 C24
Crockey Hill 58 E42
Crockham Hill 23 F50
Crockhurst Street 23 G52
Crockleford Heath 34 F56
Crock Street 8 C29
Croesau Bach 38 C28

Croeserw 18 B24
Croesgoch 16 B14
Croes Hywel 28 G29
Croes-lan 26 D19
Croesor 37 A22
Croespenmaen 18 B27
Croesyceiliog *Gwe.* 19 B29
Croesyceiliog *Dyf.* 17 C20
Croes-y-mwyalch 19 B28
Croes y pant 19 A28
Croft *Che.* 49 C32
Croft *Lcn.* 53 F51
Croft *Lei.* 41 F41
Crofthead 69 F29
Croftmore 81 A24
Crofton *W.Y.* 51 A39
Crofton *Wts.* 21 E38
Croft-on-Tees 62 E38
Crofts 65 C23
Crofts of Benachielt 103 E27
Crofts of Buinach 97 F27
Crofts of Haddo 99 F34
Crofty 17 E21
Crogen 37 B26
Croggan 79 E12
Croglin 61 B31
Croick *Hgh.* 102 C24
Croick *Hgh.* 96 B20
Croig 78 B9
Crois Dughaill 84 C3
Croit e Caley 54 G24
Cromarty 96 E23
Crombie Mill 83 C31
Cromblet 99 F33
Cromdale 89 B26
Cromer *Nfk* 45 A58
Cromer *Hfs.* 33 F48
Cromer Hyde 32 G47
Cromford 50 G38
Cromhall 19 B32
Cromhall Common 19 C32
Crompton Fold 49 B35
Cromwell 51 F43
Cronberry 67 A21
Crondall 22 G43
Cronk-y-Voddy 54 E24
Cronton 48 D30
Crook *Drm* 62 C37
Crook *Cum.* 61 G30
Crookedholm 74 G20
Crookham *Nor.* 77 G34
Crookham *Brk.* 21 E41
Crookham Village 22 F43
Crooklands 55 A31
Crook of Devon 82 G26
Cropredy 31 D40
Cropston 41 D41
Cropthorne 29 D35
Cropton 58 A43
Cropwell Bishop 41 B42
Cropwell Butler 41 B42
Cros 101 A11
Crosbie 74 F18
Crosbost 100 E9
Crosby *I.o.M.* 54 F24
Crosby *Cum.* 60 C26
Crosby *Mer.* 48 B28
Crosby *Hum.* 52 A44
Crosby Court 62 G39
Crosby Garrett 61 F33
Crosby Ravensworth 61 E32
Croscombe 19 G31
Cross 19 F29
Crossaig 73 E14
Crossapol 78 B7
Crossapoll 78 C5
Cross Ash 28 F29
Cross Bush 12 F46
Crosscanonby 60 C26
Crossdale Street 45 B58
Crossens 55 G29
Crossford *D.&G.* 68 E24
Crossford *Str.* 75 F24
Crossford *Fife* 75 B26
Cross Foxes Inn 37 D23
Crossgate 43 C48
Crossgatehall 76 D29
Crossgates *Tay.* 82 E26
Cross Gates 57 F39
Crossgates *Pow.* 27 B26
Crossgates *Fife* 75 B27
Crossgill 55 C31
Cross Green *Sfk* 34 C55
Cross Green *Sfk* 34 C54
Cross Green *Cnw.* 6 G19
Crosshands 74 G20
Cross Hands *Dyf.* 16 C16
Cross Hands *Dyf.* 17 C21
Cross Hill 41 A39
Crosshill *Fife* 75 A27
Crosshill *Str.* 67 C19
Crosshouse 74 G19
Cross Houses 38 E31
Cross in Hand 13 D51
Cross Inn *Dyf.* 26 B21

Cross Inn *Dyf.* 26 C19
Cross Inn *M.G.* 18 C26
Cross Keys 20 D34
Crosskeys 18 B27
Crosskirk 103 A26
Cross Lane Head 39 F32
Crosslanes *Shr.* 38 D29
Cross Lanes *N.Y.* 58 C41
Crosslanes *Cnw.* 2 F12
Cross Lanes *Cnw.* 2 D13
Crosslee *Str.* 74 D20
Crosslee *Bor.* 69 B28
Crosslet 74 C20
Crossmichael 65 D23
Crossmoor 55 F30
Cross of Jackson 99 F33
Cross o' the Hands 40 A38
Crossroads *Str.* 74 G20
Crossroads *Grm.* 91 D33
Cross Street 35 A57
Crossway *Gwe.* 28 G30
Crossway *Pow.* 27 C26
Crossway Green 29 B34
Crossways 28 G31
Crosswell 16 A17
Crosthwaite 60 G30
Croston 48 A30
Crostwick 45 D58
Crostwight 45 C59
Crouch 23 F52
Crouch Hill 9 C32
Croughton 31 E41
Crovie 99 C33
Crow 10 D37
Crowan 2 E12
Crowborough 13 C51
Crowcombe 7 B27
Crowdecote 50 F36
Crowdhill 11 B40
Crowfield *Sfk* 35 C57
Crowfield *Nmp.* 31 D41
Crow Hill 29 F32
Crowhurst *E.S.* 14 F53
Crowhurst *Sry* 23 G49
Crowhurst Lane End 23 G49
Crowland *Sfk* 34 A56
Crowland *Lcn.* 43 D48
Crowlas 2 E11
Crowle *H.&W.* 29 C35
Crowle *Hum.* 51 A43
Crowle Green 29 C34
Crowmarsh Gifford 21 C42
Crownhill 4 E20
Crownthorpe 44 E56
Crowntown 2 E12
Crows-an-wra 2 F9
Crowthorne 22 E44
Crowton 48 E31
Croxall 40 D37
Croxdale 62 C38
Croxden 40 B36
Croxley Green 22 B46
Croxton *Cbs.* 33 C48
Croxton *Nfk* 44 G54
Croxton *Stf.* 39 B33
Croxton *Hum.* 52 A47
Croxtonbank 39 B33
Croxton Green 48 G31
Croxton Kerrial 42 C44
Croy *Str.* 75 C23
Croy *Hgh.* 96 G23
Croyde 6 B20
Croydon *Cbs.* 33 C48
Croydon *Sry* 23 E49
Cruach 72 E9
Cruchie 98 E31
Cruckmeole 38 E30
Cruckton 38 D30
Cruden Bay 99 F36
Crudgington 39 D32
Crudwell 20 B35
Crug 28 A27
Crugmeer 3 A15
Crugybar 17 A22
Crulabhig 100 D7
Crumlin 18 B27
Crundale *Dyf.* 16 C15
Crundale *Kent* 15 C56
Crutherland 74 E22
Cruwys Morchard 7 D24
Crux Easton 21 F40
Crwbin 17 C20
Cryers Hill 22 B44
Crymlyn 46 E22
Crymych 16 A17
Crynant 18 A23
Crystal Palace 23 D49
Cuaig 94 F13
Cubbington 30 B39
Cubert 2 C13
Cublington 32 F44
Cuckfield 13 D49
Cucklington 9 B33
Cuckney 51 E41
Cuckoo's Nest 48 F29
Cuddesdon 21 A41

Cuddington *Che.* 48 E31
Cuddington *Bkh.* 31 G43
Cuddington Heath 38 A30
Cuddy Hill 55 F30
Cudham 23 F50
Cudliptown 5 C21
Cudworth *S.Y.* 51 B39
Cudworth *Som.* 8 C29
Cuffley 23 A48
Cuidhaseadair 101 B11
Cuidhir 84 D2
Cuidhtinis 92 C6
Cuidrach 93 F9
Cuilmuich 73 A17
Cuil-uaine 79 D14
Culag 74 A19
Culbo 96 E22
Culbokie 96 F21
Culbone 7 A24
Culburnie 96 G20
Culcabock 96 G22
Culcharan 79 D14
Culcharry 97 F24
Culcheth 49 C32
Culdrain 98 F30
Culduie 94 G13
Culford 34 B54
Culgaith 61 D31
Culgower 103 G25
Culham 21 B41
Culindrach 73 E14
Culkein 101 E16
Culkerton 20 B35
Cullachie 89 B25
Cullen 98 C31
Cullercoats 71 F39
Cullicudden 96 E22
Culligran 96 G19
Cullingworth 57 F36
Cullipool 79 F13
Cullivoe 106 B41
Culloch 81 F23
Culloden 96 G23
Cullompton 7 E25
Culmaily 96 B23
Culmington 38 G30
Culmstock 7 D26
Culnacraig 95 A16
Culnadalloch 80 D15
Culnaknock 94 E11
Culnamean 85 B10
Culpho 35 D57
Culquhirk 64 E20
Culrain 96 B21
Culross 75 B25
Culroy 67 B19
Culsh 90 D29
Culshabbin 64 E18
Culswick 107 C38
Culter Allers Farm 75 G26
Cultercullen 91 A34
Cults *Grm.* 91 C34
Cults *D.&G.* 64 F20
Cults *Grm.* 98 F31
Cultybraggan Camp 81 E23
Culverstone Green 24 E52
Culverthorpe 42 A45
Culvie 98 D31
Culworth 31 D41
Cumberhead 75 G23
Cumbernauld 75 C23
Cumberworth 53 E50
Cuminestown 99 D33
Cumloden 64 D20
Cummersdale 60 A29
Cummertrees 69 G27
Cummingstown 97 E26
Cumnock 67 B21
Cumnor 21 A40
Cumrew 61 A31
Cumrue 69 E26
Cumstoun 65 E22
Cumwhinton 60 A30
Cumwhitton 61 A30
Cundall 57 B40
Cunninghamhead 74 F19
Cunnister 106 C41
Cunnoquhie 82 F28
Cupar 82 F29
Cupar Muir 82 F29
Curbar 50 E38
Curbridge *Oxf.* 21 A39
Curbridge *Ham.* 11 C41
Curdridge 11 C41
Curdworth 40 F37
Curland 8 C28
Curload 8 B29
Curridge 21 D40
Currie 75 D27
Curry Mallet 8 B29
Curry Rivel 8 B29
Curteis' Corner 14 D54
Curtisden Green 14 C53
Cury 2 F12
Cushnie 99 C33
Cushuish 7 B27

Cusop 28 D28
Cutcloy 64 G20
Cutcombe 7 B25
Cuthill 96 C23
Cutiau 37 D22
Cutnall Green 29 B34
Cutsdean 30 E36
Cutthorpe 51 E39
Cutts 107 D39
Cuttyhill 99 D36
Cuxham 21 B42
Cuxton 24 E52
Cuxwold 52 B47
Cwm *Clw.* 47 E26
Cwm *W.G.* 17 E22
Cwm *Gwe.* 18 A27
Cwmafan 18 B23
Cwmaman 18 B25
Cwmann 26 D21
Cwmbach *Pow.* 27 C26
Cwmbach *Dyf.* 17 B18
Cwmbach *M.G.* 18 A25
Cwmbach *Pow.* 28 D27
Cwmbelan 37 G25
Cwmbran 19 B28
Cwmbrwyno 37 G22
Cwmcarn 18 B27
Cwmcarvan 19 A30
Cwm-Cewydd 37 D24
Cwmcoy 26 D18
Cwmdare 18 A25
Cwmdu *Pow.* 28 F27
Cwmdu *Dyf.* 17 A22
Cwmduad 17 A19
Cwmfelin Boeth 16 C17
Cwmfelinfach 18 B27
Cwmfelin Mynach 16 B17
Cwmffrwd 17 C20
Cwm Frrwd-oer 19 A28
Cwmgiedd 27 G23
Cwmgors 17 C22
Cwmgwrach 18 A24
Cwm Irfon 27 D24
Cwmisfael 17 C20
Cwm-Llinau 37 E24
Cwmllyfri 17 C19
Cwmllynfell 27 G23
Cwm-Morgan 17 A18
Cwm Owen 27 D25
Cwm-parc 18 B25
Cwmpengraig 17 A19
Cwmsychbant 26 D20
Cwmsymlog 37 G22
Cwmtillery 18 A27
Cwm-twrch Isaf 27 G23
Cwm-y-glo 46 F21
Cwmyoy 28 F28
Cwmystwyth 27 A23
Cwrt 37 E22
Cwrt-newydd 26 D20
Cwrt-y-gollen 28 G28
Cydwelli (Kidwelly) 17 D20
Cyffylliog 47 G26
Cymmer *M.G.* 18 B26
Cymmer *W.G.* 18 B24
Cynghordy 27 E23
Cynheidre 17 D20
Cynwyd 37 A26
Cynwyl Elfed 17 B19

D

Dabton 68 D24
Daccombe 5 D24
Dacre *Cum.* 60 D30
Dacre *N.Y.* 57 C37
Dacre Banks 57 C37
Daddry Shield 61 C34
Dadford 31 E42
Dadlington 41 F39
Dafen 17 D21
Daffy Green 44 E55
Dagenham 23 C51
Daggons 10 C36
Daglingworth 20 A35
Dagnall 32 G45
Dail 80 D16
Dail Beag 100 C8
Dail Bho Dheas 100 A10
Dail Bho Thuath 100 A10
Dailly 67 C18
Dail Mor 100 C7
Dailnamac 80 D15
Dairsie or Osnaburgh 82 F29
Dalabrog 84 B3
Dalavich 80 F15
Dalballoch 88 E22
Dalbeattie 65 D24
Dalblair 68 B22
Dalbog 90 F31
Dalbreck 102 G23
Dalbury 40 B38
Dalby 54 F24
Dalcairnie 67 C20
Dalchalloch 81 A23
Dalchalm 97 A24

Dalchenna 80 G16
Dalchork 102 G21
Dalchreichart 87 C18
Dalchruin 81 F22
Dalcross 96 G23
Dalderby 53 F48
Daldownie 90 C28
Dale *Dyf.* 16 D14
Dale *Dby.* 41 B40
Dale *She.* 107 B37
Dale Head 60 E30
Dalehouse 63 E43
Dalelia 79 A13
Dale Park 12 F45
Daless 89 A24
Dalestie 90 B27
Dalfad 90 C29
Dalganachan 103 D25
Dalgarven 74 F18
Dalgety Bay 75 B27
Dalgig 67 B21
Dalginross 81 E23
Dalgonar 68 C22
Dalguise 82 C25
Dalhalvaig 102 C24
Dalham 34 B53
Daligan 74 B18
Dalivaddy 66 B12
Daljarrock 67 E17
Dalkeith 76 D29
Dallas 97 F27
Dallaschyle 96 G23
Dallash 64 D20
Dallinghoo 35 C58
Dallington *E.S.* 13 E52
Dallington *Nmp.* 31 B43
Dalmadilly 91 B33
Dalmally 80 E17
Dalmarnock 82 C25
Dalmary 74 A21
Dalmellington 67 C20
Dalmeny 75 C27
Dalmichy 102 G21
Dalmigavie 88 C23
Dalmore 96 E22
Dalmunzie Hotel 89 G26
Dalnabreck 79 A12
Dalnacarn 82 A25
Dalnaglar Castle 82 A27
Dalnaha 79 E12
Dalnahaitnach 89 C24
Dalnamain 96 B23
Dalnatrat 80 B15
Dalnavie 96 D22
Dalness 80 B17
Dalnessie 102 G22
Dalnigap 64 C17
Dalqueich 82 G26
Dalreoch 67 E17
Dalriech 81 D23
Dalroy 96 G23
Dalrulzian 82 B27
Dalry 74 F18
Dalrymple 67 B19
Dalserf 75 E24
Dalshangan 67 E21
Dalskairth 65 C25
Dalston 60 A29
Dalswinton 68 E25
Daltomach 88 B23
Dalton *D.&G.* 69 F26
Dalton *N.Y.* 57 F36
Dalton *Nor.* 61 A35
Dalton *Nor.* 71 F36
Dalton *Lan.* 48 B30
Dalton *S.Y.* 51 C40
Dalton *N.Y.* 57 B40
Dalton-in-Furness 54 B27
Dalton-le-Dale 62 B39
Dalton-on-Tees 62 F38
Dalton Piercy 62 C40
Daltot 73 B13
Daltra 97 G25
Dalveich 81 E22
Dalvennan 67 B19
Dalvourn 88 A22
Dalwhinnie 88 F22
Dalwood 8 D28
Damerham 10 C37
Damgate 45 E60
Damnaglaur 64 G16
Damside 82 F25
Danbury 24 A53
Danby 63 F42
Danby Wiske 62 G39
Dandaleith 98 E28
Danderhall 76 D28
Danebridge 49 F35
Dane End 33 F49
Danehill 13 D50
Dane Hills 41 E41
Danesmoor 51 F39
Danestone 91 B34
Danskine 76 D31
Darby Green 22 E44
Darenth 23 D51

Daresbury 48 D31
Darfield 51 B39
Dargate 25 E56
Dargues 70 D34
Darite 4 D18
Darlaston 40 F35
Darley 57 D38
Darley Dale 50 F38
Darlingscott 30 D38
Darlington 62 E38
Darliston 38 B31
Darlton 51 E43
Darnabo 99 E33
Darnall 51 D39
Darnconner 67 A21
Darnford 91 D33
Darngarroch 65 D22
Darnick 76 G31
Darowen 37 E24
Darra 99 E33
Darras Hall 71 F37
Darrington 51 A40
Darsham 35 B60
Dartfield 99 D36
Dartford 23 D51
Dartington 5 D23
Dartmeet 5 C22
Dartmouth 5 E24
Darton 51 B39
Darvel 74 G21
Darwell 14 E53
Darwen 56 G32
Datchet 22 D45
Datchworth 33 G48
Datchworth Green 33 G48
Daubhill 49 B33
Daugh of Kinermony 98 E28
Dauntsey 20 C35
Dava 89 A25
Davaar 66 B13
Davan 90 C30
Davenham 49 E32
Daventry 31 B41
Davidstow 4 B17
Davington 69 C28
Daviot *Hgh.* 88 A23
Daviot *Hgh.* 91 A33
Davoch of Grange 98 D30
Dawley 39 E32
Dawlish 5 C25
Dawn 47 E24
Daws Heath 24 C54
Dawsmere 43 B50
Daylesford 30 F38
Ddol 47 E27
Deadwaters 75 F23
Deal 15 B59
Deal Hall 25 B55
Dean *Ham.* 11 C41
Dean *Dor.* 9 C35
Dean *Dev.* 5 D23
Dean *Cum.* 60 D26
Dean *Som.* 19 G32
Dean *Oxf.* 30 F39
Dean Bank 62 C38
Deanburnhaugh 69 B29
Deane 21 F41
Deanland 9 C35
Dean Prior 5 D22
Dean Row 49 D34
Deanscales 60 D26
Deanshanger 31 D43
Deanston 81 G22
Dean Street 14 B53
Dearham 60 C26
Debach 35 C58
Debate 69 E28
Debden 33 E51
Debden Green 33 E51
Debenham 35 B57
Dechmont 75 C26
Deddington 31 E40
Dedham 34 E56
Deecastle 90 D30
Deene 42 F45
Deenethorpe 42 F45
Deepcar 50 C38
Deepcut 22 F45
Deepdale *Cum.* 56 A33
Deepdale *N.Y.* 56 A34
Deeping Gate 42 E47
Deeping St James 42 D47
Deeping St Nicholas 43 D48
Deerhill 98 D30
Deerhurst 29 E34
Defford 29 D35
Defynnog 27 F25
Deganwy 47 E23
Degnish 79 F13
Deighton *N.Y.* 62 F39
Deighton *N.Y.* 58 E42
Deiniolen 46 F21
Delabole 4 B16
Delamere 48 F31
Delavorar 90 B27
Delfrigs 91 A35

Delliefure 89 A26
Dell Lodge 89 C25
Delnabo 90 B27
Delny 96 D23
Delph 49 B35
Delphorie 90 B30
Delves 62 A37
Delvine 82 C27
Dembleby 42 B46
Denaby 51 C40
Denaby Main 51 C40
Denbigh 47 F26
Denbury 5 D23
Denby 41 A39
Denby Dale 50 B38
Denchworth 21 B39
Dendron 55 B28
Denend 98 F31
Denford 32 A45
Dengie 25 A55
Denham *Bkh.* 22 C46
Denham *Sfk* 35 A57
Denham *Sfk* 34 B53
Denham Green 22 C46
Denhead *Grm.* 91 B33
Denhead *Grm.* 99 D36
Denhead *Tay.* 82 D29
Denhead *Tay.* 83 C31
Denhead *Fife* 83 F30
Denholm 70 B31
Denholme 57 F36
Denholme Clough 57 F36
Denio 36 B19
Denmead 11 C42
Denmill 91 B34
Denmoss 98 E32
Dennington 35 B58
Denny 75 B24
Dennyloanhead 75 B23
Denshaw 49 A35
Denside 91 D33
Densole 15 C57
Denston 34 C53
Denstone 40 A36
Dent 56 A32
Denton *N.Y.* 57 E37
Denton *Kent* 15 C57
Denton *E.S.* 13 F50
Denton *Cbs.* 42 G47
Denton *Lcn.* 42 B44
Denton *Nmp.* 32 C44
Denton *G.M.* 49 C35
Denton *Nfk* 45 G58
Denton *Oxf.* 21 A41
Denton *Drm* 62 E37
Denver 43 E51
Denvilles 11 D43
Denwick 71 B37
Deopham 44 E56
Deopham Green 44 F56
Depden 34 C53
Deptford *Wts.* 10 A36
Deptford *G.L.* 23 D49
Derby 41 B39
Derbyhaven 54 G24
Dererach 79 E10
Deri 18 A27
Derringstone 15 C57
Derrington 40 C34
Derry 81 E22
Derry Hill 20 D35
Derrythorpe 52 B44
Dervaig 79 B10
Derwen 47 G26
Derwenlas 37 F22
Derwydd 17 C21
Derybruich 73 C15
Desborough 42 G43
Desford 41 E40
Detchant 77 G36
Detling 14 B53
Deuddwr 38 D28
Deunant 47 F25
Deuxhill 39 G32
Devauden 19 B30
Devil's Bridge 27 A23
Devizes 20 E36
Devonport 4 E20
Devonside 75 A25
Devoran 2 E13
Dewar 76 F29
Dewlish 9 E33
Dewsall Court 28 E30
Dewsbury 57 G38
Dhoon 54 E26
Dhoor 54 D26
Dhowin 54 C25
Dhuhallow 88 B21
Dial Post 12 E47
Dibden 11 D40
Dibden Purlieu 10 D39
Dickleburgh 45 G57
Didbrook 30 E36
Didcot 21 C41
Diddington 32 B47
Diddlebury 38 G30

Didley 28 E30
Didling 12 E44
Didmarton 20 C33
Didsbury 49 C34
Didworthy 5 D22
Digby 52 G46
Digg 93 E10
Diggle 50 B36
Digmoor 48 B30
Digswell 33 G48
Dihewyd 26 C20
Dilham 45 C59
Dilhorne 40 A35
Dilston 70 G35
Dilton Marsh 20 G34
Dilwyn 28 C29
Dilwyn Common 28 C30
Dinas *Dyf.* 17 B18
Dinas *Dyf.* 16 A16
Dinas *Gwy.* 36 B18
Dinas *Gwy.* 46 G20
Dinas-Mawddwy 37 D24
Dinas Powys 18 D27
Dinder 19 G31
Dinedor 28 E31
Dingestow 28 G28
Dingley 42 G43
Dingwall 96 F21
Dinlabyre 70 D31
Dinnet 90 D30
Dinnington *Som.* 8 C29
Dinnington *S.Y.* 51 D41
Dinnington *T.&W.* 71 F37
Dinorwic 46 F21
Dinton *Bkh.* 31 G43
Dinton *Wts.* 10 A36
Dinwoodie Mains 69 D26
Dinworthy 6 D19
Dippen 73 G13
Dippenhall 22 G43
Dippin 66 A16
Dipple *Grm.* 98 D29
Dipple *Str.* 67 C18
Diptford 5 E23
Dipton 62 A37
Dirdhu 89 B26
Dirleton 76 B30
Discoed 28 B28
Diseworth 41 C40
Dishes 104 D32
Dishforth 57 B39
Dishig 79 D10
Disley 49 D35
Diss 45 G57
Disserth 27 C26
Distington 60 D25
Ditcheat 9 A32
Ditchingham 45 F59
Ditchley 30 F39
Ditchling 13 E49
Ditteridge 20 E33
Dittisham 5 E24
Ditton *Che.* 48 D30
Ditton *Kent* 23 F52
Ditton Green 33 C52
Ditton Priors 39 G32
Dixton *Glo.* 29 E35
Dixton *H.&W.* 28 G31
Dobwalls 4 D18
Doccombe 7 G23
Dochgarroch 96 G21
Docklow 28 C31
Dockray 60 D29
Doddinghurst 23 B51
Doddington *Cbs.* 43 G49
Doddington *Shr.* 28 A31
Doddington *Kent* 14 B55
Doddington *Nor.* 77 G35
Doddington *Lcn.* 52 E44
Doddiscombsleigh 7 G24
Dodford *Nmp.* 31 B42
Dodford *H.&W.* 29 A35
Dodington *Som.* 7 A27
Dodington *Avon* 20 C33
Dodington Ash 20 D33
Dodleston 48 F29
Dodworth 50 B38
Doe Lea 51 F40
Dogdyke 52 G47
Dogmersfield 22 F43
Dog Village 7 F25
Dolanog 37 D26
Dolau Honddu 27 D25
Dolbenmaen 36 A20
Dolfach 27 A24
Dol Fawr 37 E24
Dolfor 37 G26
Dolgarreg 27 E23
Dolgarrog 47 F23
Dolgellau 37 D23
Dolgoch 37 E22
Dol-gran 17 A20
Doll 97 A24
Dollar 75 A25

Dollarbeg 75 A25
Dolleycanney 28 D27
Dolphinholme 55 D31
Dolphinton 75 F26
Dolton 6 D21
Dolwen *Clw.* 47 E24
Dolwen *Pow.* 37 E25
Dolwyddelan 47 G23
Dolybont 37 G22
Dolyhir 28 C28
Dolywern 38 B28
Domgay 38 D28
Doncaster 51 B41
Donhead St Andrew 9 B35
Donhead St Mary 9 B34
Donibristle 75 B27
Doniford 7 A26
Donington 43 B48
Donington le Heath 41 D40
Donington on Bain 53 D48
Donisthorpe 40 D38
Donkey Town 22 E45
Donnington *Brk.* 21 E40
Donnington *W.S.* 12 F44
Donnington *Shr.* 38 E31
Donnington *Shr.* 39 D33
Donnington *Glo.* 30 F37
Donnington *H.&W.* 29 E33
Donyatt 8 C29
Dorchester *Dor.* 9 E32
Dorchester *Oxf.* 21 B41
Dordon 40 E38
Dore 50 D38
Dores 88 A21
Dorket Head 41 A41
Dorking 22 G47
Dormansland 23 G50
Dormans Park 23 G49
Dormanstown 63 D41
Dormington 28 D31
Dorney 22 D45
Dornie 86 B14
Dornoch 96 C23
Dornock 69 G28
Dorrery 103 C26
Dorridge 30 A37
Dorrington *Lcn.* 52 G46
Dorrington *Shr.* 38 E30
Dorsell 90 B31
Dorsington 30 C37
Dorstone 28 D28
Dorton 31 G42
Dorusduain 86 B15
Dosthill 40 F38
Dotland 61 A35
Dottery 8 E30
Doublebois 4 D17
Dougalston 74 C21
Dougarie 73 G14
Doughton 20 B34
Douglas *Str.* 75 G24
Douglas *I.o.M.* 54 F25
Douglas and Angus 83 D30
Douglas Hall 65 E24
Douglas Hill 46 F22
Douglastown 82 C29
Douglas Water 75 G24
Doulting 19 G32
Dounby 104 D28
Doune *Str.* 81 G23
Doune *Str.* 80 F19
Doune *Str.* 74 A18
Doune *Hgh.* 89 C24
Doune *Hgh.* 96 A20
Doune Park 98 C32
Douneside 90 C30
Dounie *Hgh.* 96 B21
Dounie *Hgh.* 96 C22
Dounreay 103 B25
Dousland 5 D21
Dovaston 38 C29
Dove Holes 50 E36
Dovenby 60 C26
Dover 15 C59
Doverdale 29 B34
Doveridge 40 B36
Doversgreen 23 G48
Dowally 82 C25
Dowdeswell 29 F35
Dowhill 67 C18
Dowland 6 D21
Dowlands 8 E28
Dowlish Wake 8 C29
Down Ampney 20 B37
Downderry 4 E18
Downe 23 E50
Downend *Brk.* 21 D40
Downend *I.o.W.* 11 F41
Downend *Avon* 19 D32
Down End 19 G28
Downfield 82 D29
Down Field 33 A51
Downgate 4 C19
Downham *Nor.* 77 G34
Downham *Lan.* 56 E33
Downham *Esx* 24 B53

Downham Market 44 E52
Down Hatherley 29 F34
Downhead *Cnw.* 4 B18
Downhead *Som.* 19 G32
Downholland Cross 48 B29
Downholme 62 G37
Downies 91 D35
Downing 47 E27
Downley 22 B44
Downside *Sry* 22 F47
Downside *Som.* 19 G32
Downside *Avon* 19 E30
Down St Mary 7 E23
Down Thomas 5 F21
Downton *Dby.* 6 G21
Downton *Dev.* 5 E24
Downton *Ham.* 10 E38
Downton *Wts.* 10 B37
Downton on the Rock 28 A30
Dowsby 42 B47
Dowthwaitehead 60 D29
Doynton 19 D32
Draethen 18 C27
Draffan 75 F23
Drakeland Corner 5 E21
Drakes Broughton 29 D34
Drakes Cross 30 A36
Drambuie 68 B23
Draughton *Nmp.* 31 A43
Draughton *N.Y.* 57 D36
Drax 58 G42
Draycote 31 A40
Draycott *Glo.* 30 E37
Draycott *Dby.* 41 B40
Draycott *Som.* 19 F30
Draycott *H.&W.* 29 D34
Draycott in the Clay 40 C37
Draycott in the Moors 40 A35
Drayton *Nfk* 45 D57
Drayton *Lcn.* 43 B48
Drayton *Lei.* 42 F44
Drayton *Oxf.* 31 D40
Drayton *H.&W.* 29 A35
Drayton *Oxf.* 21 B40
Drayton *Som.* 8 B29
Drayton Bassett 40 E37
Drayton Beauchamp 32 G45
Drayton Parslow 32 F44
Drayton St Leonard 21 B41
Drebley 57 D36
Dreemskerry 54 D26
Dreenhill 16 C14
Dre-fach 26 D20
Drefach *Dyf.* 17 C21
Drefach *Dyf.* 17 A19
Dreghorn 74 G19
Drellingore 15 C58
Drem 76 B30
Drewsteignton 7 F23
Driby 53 E49
Driffield 20 B36
Drigg 60 G26
Drighlington 57 G37
Drimfern 80 F16
Drimlee 80 F17
Drimnin 79 B11
Drimore 92 G3
Drimpton 8 D29
Drimsynie 80 G17
Drimvore 73 A14
Drinan 86 C11
Drinkstone 34 B55
Drinkstone Green 34 C55
Drishaig 80 F17
Drissaig 80 F15
Drointon 40 C36
Droitwich 29 B34
Dron 82 F27
Dronfield 51 E39
Dronfield Woodhouse 51 E39
Drongan 67 B20
Dronley 82 D29
Dropmore 22 C45
Droxford 11 C41
Droylsden 49 C34
Druid 37 A26
Druidston 16 C14
Druimarbin 87 G16
Druimavuic 80 C15
Druimdrishaig 73 C13
Druimindarroch 86 F12
Druimkinnerras 88 A20
Drum *Str.* 73 C15
Drum *Tay.* 82 G26
Drumachloy 73 D16
Drumbeg 101 E17
Drumblade 98 E31
Drumblair 98 E32
Drumbuie 86 A13
Drumburgh 60 A28
Drumchapel 74 C21
Drumchardine 96 G21
Drumchork 94 C14
Drumclog 74 G22
Drumdelgie 98 E30

Drumderfit 96 F22
Drumeldrie 83 G30
Drumelzier 75 G27
Drumfearn 86 C12
Drumfern 86 G15
Drumgarve 66 A13
Drumgley 82 B29
Drumguish 88 E23
Drumhead 90 D31
Drumine 91 C32
Drumjohn 67 D21
Drumlamford Ho. 64 C18
Drumlasie 90 C30
Drumlemble 66 B12
Drumlithie 91 E33
Drummond *Hgh.* 96 E22
Drummond *Cen.* 81 G22
Drummore 64 G17
Drummuir Castle 98 E29
Drumnadrochit 88 A20
Drumna-gorrach 98 D31
Drumnatorran 79 A13
Drumoak 91 D33
Drumore 66 A12
Drumour 82 C25
Drumrash 65 C22
Drumrunie 95 A17
Drums 91 A35
Drumsturdy 83 D30
Drumuie 93 G10
Drumuillie 89 B25
Drumvaich 81 G22
Drumwhindle 99 F34
Drumwhirn 68 E23
Drunkendub 83 C32
Drury 48 F28
Drybeck 61 E32
Drybridge *Grm.* 98 C30
Drybridge *Str.* 74 G19
Drybrook 29 G32
Dry Doddington 42 A44
Dry Drayton 33 B49
Drygrange 76 G31
Dry Harbour 94 F11
Dryhope 69 A28
Drymen 74 B20
Drymuir 99 E34
Drynoch 85 A9
Dry Sandford 21 B40
Dryslwyn 17 B21
Dry Street 24 C52
Dryton 38 E31
Duachy 79 E13
Dubford 99 C33
Dubhchladach 73 D14
Dubheads 82 E25
Dubton 83 B31
Duchal 74 D19
Duchally 101 G19
Duchray 74 A20
Duck End 33 F52
Duckington 48 G30
Ducklington 21 A39
Duck's Cross 32 C47
Duddenhoe End 33 E50
Duddingston 76 C28
Duddington 42 E45
Duddleswell 13 D50
Duddo 77 F35
Duddon 48 F30
Duddon Bridge 54 A27
Dudleston Heath 38 B29
Dudley *W.M.* 40 F35
Dudley *T.&W.* 71 F38
Dudley Hill 57 F37
Dudley Port 40 F35
Dudsbury 10 E36
Duffield 41 A39
Duffryn 18 B24
Dufftown 98 E28
Duffus 97 E27
Dufton 61 D32
Duggleby 58 C44
Duible 103 F25
Duiletter 80 E17
Duinish 81 A21
Duirinish 86 A13
Duisdealmor 86 C12
Duisky 86 G15
Dukestown 28 G27
Dukinfield 49 C35
Dulas 46 D20
Dulax 90 B29
Dulcote 19 G31
Dulford 7 E26
Dull 81 C23
Dullatur 75 C23
Dullingham 33 C51
Dulnain Bridge 89 B25
Duloe *Cnw.* 4 E18
Duloe *Bfd.* 32 B47
Dulsie 97 G25
Dulverton 7 C24
Dulwich 23 D49
Dumbarton 74 C20
Dumbleton 29 E35

Dumcrieff 69 C26
Dumeath 98 F30
Dumfin 74 B19
Dumfries 65 C25
Dumgoyne 74 B21
Dummer 21 G41
Dun 83 B32
Dunach 79 E14
Dunalastair 81 B22
Dunan *Str.* 73 C17
Dunan *Hgh.* 86 B11
Dunans 73 A16
Dunball 19 G28
Dunbar 76 C32
Dunbeath 103 F27
Dunbeg 79 D14
Dunblane 81 G23
Dunbog 82 F28
Duncanston *Grm.* 90 A31
Duncanston *Hgh.* 96 F21
Dunchideock 7 G24
Dunchurch 31 A40
Duncote 31 C42
Duncow 68 E25
Duncraggan 81 G21
Duncrievie 82 G27
Duncroist 81 D21
Duncrub 82 F25
Duncryne 74 B20
Duncton 12 E45
Dundee 82 D29
Dundee Airport 82 E29
Dundon 8 A30
Dundonald 74 G19
Dundonnell 95 C16
Dundraw 60 B27
Dundreggan 88 C19
Dundrennan 65 F23
Dundry 19 E31
Dunearn 75 B27
Dunecht 91 C33
Dunfermline 75 B26
Dunfield 20 B37
Dunford Bridge 50 B37
Dungavel 74 G22
Dunham 51 E43
Dunham-on-the-Hill 48 E30
Dunhampton 29 B34
Dunham Town 49 D33
Dunholme 52 E46
Dunino 83 F31
Dunipace 75 B24
Dunira 81 E23
Dunkeld 82 C26
Dunkerton 19 F32
Dunkeswell 7 E27
Dunkeswick 57 E39
Dunkirk 15 B56
Dunk's Green 23 F52
Dunlappie 83 A31
Dunley 29 B33
Dunlop 74 F19
Dunloskin 73 C17
Dunmere 4 D16
Dunmore *Str.* 73 D13
Dunmore *Cen.* 75 B24
Dunn 103 C27
Dunnabie 69 E28
Dunnet 103 A28
Dunnichen 83 C30
Dunning 82 F26
Dunnington *N.Y.* 58 D42
Dunnington *War.* 30 C36
Dunnington *Hum.* 59 D47
Dunnockshaw 56 G33
Dunoon 73 C17
Dunragit 64 E17
Dunrostan 73 B13
Duns 77 E33
Dunsby 42 C47
Dunscore 68 E24
Dunscroft 51 B42
Dunsdale 63 E41
Dunsden Green 22 D43
Dunsfold 12 C46
Dunsford 7 G23
Dunshelt 82 F28
Dunsinnan 82 D27
Dunsland Cross 6 E20
Dunsley 63 E44
Dunsmore 22 A44
Dunsop Bridge 56 E32
Dunstable 32 F45
Dunstall 40 C37
Dunstall Green 34 B53
Dunstan 71 A38
Dunster 7 A25
Duns Tew 31 F40
Dunston *Stf.* 40 D35
Dunston *Lcn.* 52 F46
Dunston *T.&W.* 71 G38
Dunston *Nfk* 45 E58
Dunstone *Dev.* 5 F23
Dunstone *Dev.* 5 E21
Dunstone *Dev.* 5 C23
Dunsville 51 B42
Dunswell 59 F46
Dunsyre 75 F26
Dunterton 4 C19
Duntisbourne Abbots 20 A35
Duntisbourne Leer 20 A35
Duntisbourne Rouse 20 A35
Duntish 9 D32
Duntocher 74 C20
Dunton *Bfd.* 33 D48
Dunton *Bkh.* 32 F44
Dunton Bassett 41 F41
Dunton Green 23 F51
Dunton Wayletts 24 B52
Duntulm 93 D9
Dunure 67 B18
Dunure Mains 67 B18
Dunvant 17 E21
Dunvegan 93 G8
Dunwich 35 A60
Dura 83 F30
Durdar 60 A29
Durgates 13 C52
Durham 62 B38
Durinemast 79 B12
Durisdeer 68 C24
Durleigh 8 A28
Durley *Ham.* 11 C41
Durley *Wts.* 21 E38
Durnamuck 94 B15
Durness 101 B19
Durno 91 A33
Duror 80 B15
Durran *Str.* 80 G15
Durran *Hgh.* 103 B27
Durrington *Wts.* 20 G37
Durrington *W.S.* 12 F46
Dursley 20 B33
Durston 8 B28
Durweston 9 D34
Dury 107 A40
Duston 31 B43
Duthil 89 B25
Dutlas 28 A27
Duton Hill 33 F51
Dutton 48 E31
Duxford 33 D50
Dwygyfylchi 47 E23
Dwyran 46 F20
Dyce 91 B34
Dyfatty 17 D20
Dyffryn *M.G.* 18 B24
Dyffryn *Dyf.* 16 A15
Dyffryn Ardudwy 36 C21
Dyffryn Castell 37 G23
Dyffryn Ceidrych 17 B22
Dyffryn Cellwen 18 A24
Dyke *Grm.* 97 F25
Dyke *Dev.* 6 C19
Dyke *Lcn.* 42 C47
Dykehead *Str.* 75 E24
Dykehead *Tay.* 82 A29
Dykehead *Cen.* 74 A22
Dykelands 91 G33
Dykends 82 B28
Dykeside 99 E33
Dylife 37 F24
Dymchurch 15 E56
Dymock 29 E32
Dyrham 20 D33
Dysart 76 A28
Dyserth 47 E26

E

Eadar Dha Fhadhail 100 D6
Eagland Hill 55 E30
Eagle 52 F44
Eaglescliffe 62 E39
Eaglesfield *D.&G.* 69 F28
Eaglesfield *Cum.* 60 D26
Eaglesham 74 E21
Eaglethorpe 42 F46
Eagley 49 A33
Eairy 54 F24
Eakley 32 C44
Eakring 51 F42
Ealand 51 A43
Ealing 22 C47
Eamont Bridge 61 D30
Earby 56 E35
Earcroft 56 G32
Eardington 39 F32
Eardisland 28 C29
Eardisley 28 D28
Eardiston *H.&W.* 29 B32
Eardiston *Shr.* 38 C29
Earith 33 A49
Earle 70 A35
Earlestown 48 C31
Earlham 45 E57
Earlish 93 E9
Earls Barton 32 B44
Earls Colne 34 F54
Earl's Common 29 B35
Earl's Croome 29 D34
Earlsdon 30 A38
Earlsferry 83 G30
Earlsford 99 F34
Earl's Green 34 B56
Earl Shilton 41 F40
Earl Soham 35 B58
Earl Sterndale 50 F36
Earlston 76 G31
Earl Stonham 35 C57
Earlswood *War.* 30 A36
Earlswood *Gwe.* 19 B30
Earnley 12 G44
Earsairidh 84 E3
Earsdon 71 F39
Earsdon Moor 71 D37
Earsham 45 G59
Earswick 58 D42
Eartham 12 F45
Earthcote Green 19 C32
Easby 63 F41
Eascairt 73 E14
Easdale 79 F13
Easebourne 12 D44
Easenhall 41 G40
Eashing 22 G45
Easington *Oxf.* 21 B42
Easington *Hum.* 53 A50
Easington *Cle.* 63 E43
Easington *Nor.* 77 G36
Easington *Bkh.* 21 A42
Easington *Drm* 62 B39
Easington Colliery 62 B39
Easington Lane 62 B39
Easingwold 58 C41
Easole Street 15 B58
Eassie and Nevay 82 C29
East Aberthaw 18 E26
East Allington 5 F23
East Anstey 7 C24
East Appleton 62 G38
East Ardsley 57 G38
East Ashey 11 F41
East Ashling 12 F44
East Auchronie 91 C33
East Ayton 59 A45
East Barkwith 52 D47
East Barming 14 B53
East Barnby 63 E44
East Barnet 23 B48
East Barsham 44 B55
East Beckham 45 B57
East Bedfont 22 D46
East Bergholt 34 E56
East Bilney 44 C55
East Blatchington 13 F50
East Boldon 71 G39
East Boldre 10 D39
East Bolton 71 B37
Eastbourne *Drm* 62 E38
Eastbourne *E.S.* 13 G52
East Bradenham 44 E55
East Brent 19 F29
East Bridge 35 B60
East Bridgford 41 A42
East Brora 97 A24
East Buckland 6 B22
East Budleigh 7 G26
Eastburn 59 D45
East Burrafirth 107 B39
East Burton 9 F34
Eastbury *G.L.* 22 B47
Eastbury *Brk.* 21 D39
Eastby 57 D36
East Cairnbeg 91 F32
East Calder 75 D26
East Carleton 45 E57
East Carlton 42 G44
East Challow 21 C39
East Charleton 5 F23
East Chelborough 8 D31
East Chiltington 13 E49
East Chinnock 8 C30
East Chisenbury 20 F37
Eastchurch 25 D55
East Clandon 22 F46
East Claydon 31 F43
East Clyth 103 E28
East Coker 8 C31
Eastcombe 20 A34
East Combe 7 B27
East Cornworthy 5 E23
Eastcote *G.L.* 22 C47
Eastcote *Nmp.* 31 C42
Eastcote *W.M.* 30 A37
Eastcott *Cnw.* 6 D18
Eastcott *Wts.* 20 F36
East Cottingwith 58 E43
Eastcourt 20 B35
East Cowes 11 E41
East Cowick 58 G42
East Cowton 62 F39
East Cranmore 19 G32
East Creech 9 F35
East Croachy 88 B22
East Darlochan 66 A12
East Davoch 90 C30
East Dean *E.S.* 13 G51
East Dean *Ham.* 10 B38
East Dean *W.S.* 12 E45
East Dereham 44 D55
East Down 6 A21
East Drayton 51 E43
East End *Kent* 14 D54
East End *Ham.* 10 E39
East End *Ham.* 21 E40
East End *Avon* 19 D30
East End *Dor.* 9 E35
East End *Oxf.* 30 G39
Eastend 30 F39
East End *Sfk* 35 E57
East End *Cbs.* 33 F50
Easter Ardross 96 D22
Easter Balmoral 90 D28
Easter Boleskine 88 B21
Easter Borland 81 G22
Easter Brae 96 E22
Easter Buckieburn 75 B23
Easter Compton 19 C31
Easter Drummond 88 C20
Easter Dullater 81 G21
Easter Ellister 72 E8
Easter Fearn 96 C22
Easter Galcantray 97 G24
Eastergate 12 F45
Easter Howlaws 77 F33
Easter Kinkell 96 F21
Easter Knox 83 D31
Easter Lednathie 82 A29
Easter Moniack 96 G21
Easter Ord 91 C34
Easter Poldar 74 A22
Easter Quarff 107 D40
Easter Skeld 107 C38
Easter Suddie 96 F22
Easterton 20 F35
Eastertown 19 F29
Easter Tulloch 91 F33
Easter Whyntie 98 C32
East Farleigh 14 B53
East Farndon 42 G43
East Ferry 51 C43
Eastfield *Str.* 75 D24
Eastfield *N.Y.* 59 A46
Eastfield Hall 71 C38
East Fortune 76 B31
East Garston 21 D39
Eastgate *Drm* 61 C35
Eastgate *Nfk* 45 C57
Eastgate *Lcn.* 42 D47
East Ginge 21 C40
East Goscote 41 D42
East Grafton 21 E38
East Grimstead 10 B38
East Grinstead 13 C49
East Guldeford 14 E55
East Haddon 31 B42
East Hagbourne 21 C41
East Halton 52 A47
East Ham 23 C50
Eastham 48 D29
Easthampstead 22 E44
East Hanney 21 B40
East Hanningfield 24 A53
East Hardwick 51 A40
East Harling 44 G55
East Harlsey 62 F40
East Harptree 19 F31
East Hartford 71 F38
East Harting 12 E44
East Hatch 9 B35
East Hatley 33 C48
East Hauxwell 62 G37
East Haven 83 D31
Eastheath 22 E44
East Heckington 42 A47
East Hedleyhope 62 B37
East Helmsdale 103 G26
East Hendred 21 C40
East Heslerton 59 B45
East Hoathly 13 E51
Easthope 38 F31
East Horndon 24 C52
Easthorpe *Lei.* 42 B43
Easthorpe *Not.* 51 G43
Easthorpe *Esx* 34 F55
East Horrington 19 G31
East Horsley 22 F46
East Horton 77 G36
Easthouses 76 D29
East Huntspill 19 G29
East Hyde 32 G47
East Ilsley 21 C40
Eastington *Glo.* 20 A33
Eastington *Dev.* 7 E23
Eastington *Glo.* 30 G37
East Keal 53 F49
East Kennett 20 E37
East Keswick 57 E39
East Kilbride 74 E22
East Kirkby 53 F49
East Knapton 58 B44
East Knighton 9 F34
East Knoyle 9 A34
East Lambrook 8 C30
East Langdon 15 C59
East Langton 42 F43
East Langwell 96 A23
East Lavant 12 F44
East Lavington 12 E45
East Layton 62 E37
Eastleach Martin 21 A38
Eastleach Turville 20 A37
East Leake 41 C41
East Learmouth 77 G34
East Learney 91 C32
Eastleigh *Ham.* 11 C40
Eastleigh *Dev.* 6 C20
East Leigh 7 E23
East Lexham 44 D54
East Lilburn 71 A36
Eastling 14 B55
East Linton 76 C31
East Liss 11 B43
East Looe 4 E18
East Lound 51 C43
East Lulworth 9 F34
East Lutton 59 C45
East Lydford 8 A31
East Mains 91 D32
East Malling 14 B53
East March 83 D30
East Marden 12 E44
East Markham 51 E43
East Marton 56 D34
East Meon 11 B42
East Mere 7 D25
East Mersea 34 G56
East Mey 103 A28
East Midlands Airport 41 C40
East Molesey 22 E47
East Morden 9 E34
East Morton 57 E36
East Ness 58 B42
Eastney 11 E42
Eastnor 29 E33
East Norton 42 E43
East Oakley 21 G41
Eastoft 51 A43
East Ogwell 5 D24
Eastoke 11 E43
Easton *Ham.* 11 A41
Easton *I.o.W.* 10 F39
Easton *Wts.* 20 D34
Easton *Nfk* 45 D57
Easton *Cum.* 60 A28
Easton *Som.* 19 G30
Easton *Dev.* 9 G32
Easton *Dev.* 7 G23
Easton *Cum.* 69 F30
Easton *Lcn.* 42 C45
Easton *Cbs.* 32 A47
Easton *Sfk* 35 C58
Easton Grey 20 C34
Easton-in -Gordano 19 D31
Easton Maudit 32 C44
Easton on the Hill 42 E46
Easton Royal 21 E38
East Orchard 9 C34
East Ord 77 E35
East Panson 6 F19
East Peckham 23 G52
East Pennard 8 A31
East Poringland 45 E58
East Portlemouth 5 G23
East Prawle 5 G23
East Preston 12 F46
East Putford 6 D19
East Quantoxhead 7 A27
East Rainton 62 B39
East Ravendale 53 C48
East Raynham 44 C54
Eastrea 43 F48
East Retford (Retford) 51 D42
Eastriggs 69 G28
East Rigton 57 E39
Eastrington 58 F43
East Rolstone 19 E29
East Rounton 62 F40
East Rudham 44 C54
East Runton 45 A57
East Ruston 45 C59
Eastry 15 B58
East Saltoun 76 D30
East Shefford 21 D39
Eastside 105 B30
East Sleekburn 71 E38
East Somerton 45 C60
East Stockwith 51 C43
East Stoke *Not.* 42 A43
East Stoke *Dor.* 9 F34
East Stour 9 B33
East Stourmouth 25 E58
East Stratton 11 A41
East Studdal 15 B59
East Suisnish 86 A11
East Taphouse 4 D17
East-the-Water 6 C20
East Thirston 71 D37
East Tilbury 24 D52

East Tisted 11 A43
East Torrington 52 D47
East Tuddenham 44 D56
East Tytherley 10 B39
East Tytherton 20 D35
East Village 7 E24
Eastville 53 G50
East Wall 38 F31
East Walton 44 D53
Eastwell 42 C43
East Wellow 10 B39
East Wemyss 76 A29
East Whitburn 75 D25
Eastwick 33 G50
East Wickham 23 D50
East Williamston 16 D16
East Winch 44 D52
East Wittering 11 E43
East Witton 57 A37
Eastwood *W.Y.* 56 G35
Eastwood *Esx* 24 C54
Eastwood *Not.* 41 A40
East Woodhay 21 E39
East Worldham 11 A43
East Worlington 7 D23
Eathorpe 30 B39
Eaton *Lei.* 42 C43
Eaton *Shr.* 38 F31
Eaton *Shr.* 38 G29
Eaton *Not.* 51 E42
Eaton *Oxf.* 21 A40
Eaton *Che.* 49 F34
Eaton *Nfk* 45 E58
Eaton *Che.* 48 F31
Eaton Bishop 28 E30
Eaton Bray 32 F45
Eaton Constantine 39 E32
Eaton Ford 32 C47
Eaton Green 32 F45
Eaton Hall 48 F30
Eaton Hastings 21 B38
Eaton Socon 32 C47
Eaton upon Tern 39 C32
Eavestone 57 C37
Ebberston 58 A44
Ebbesborne Wake 9 B35
Ebbw Vale 18 A27
Ebchester 62 A36
Ebford 7 G25
Ebrington 30 D37
Ecchinswell 21 F40
Ecclaw 77 D33
Ecclefechan 69 F27
Eccles *Bor.* 77 F33
Eccles *G.M.* 49 C33
Eccles *Kent* 24 E53
Ecclesfield 51 C39
Ecclesgreig 83 A33
Ecclesgrieg 91 G33
Eccleshall 40 C34
Ecclesmachan 75 C26
Eccles Road 44 F56
Eccleston *Che.* 48 F30
Eccleston *Mer.* 48 C30
Eccleston *Lan.* 48 A30
Eccup 57 E38
Echt 91 C33
Eckford 70 A32
Eckington *Dby.* 51 E40
Eckington *H.&W.* 29 D35
Ecton *Nmp.* 32 B44
Ecton *Stf.* 50 G37
Edale 50 D37
Eday Airport 104 C31
Edburton 13 E48
Edderside 60 B26
Edderton 96 C22
Eddington 21 E39
Eddleston 76 F28
Eddlewood 75 E23
Edenbridge 23 G50
Edendonich 80 E17
Edenfield 49 A34
Edenhall 61 C31
Edenham 42 C46
Eden Park 23 E49
Edensor 50 F38
Edentaggart 74 A18
Edenthorpe 51 B42
Edern 36 B18
Edgarley 8 A30
Edgbaston 40 G36
Edgcott 31 F42
Edgcumbe 2 E13
Edge *Shr.* 38 E29
Edge *Glo.* 20 A34
Edgebolton 38 C31
Edge End 28 G31
Edgefield 45 B57
Edgeley 38 A31
Edgerley 38 D29
Edgeworth 20 A34
Edginswell 5 D24
Edgmond 39 D32
Edgmond Marsh 39 C33
Edgton 38 G29

Edgware 22 B47
Edgworth 49 A33
Edial 40 E36
Edinample 81 E21
Edinbain 93 F9
Edinbanchory 90 B30
Edinbarnet 74 C21
Edinburgh 76 C28
Edinburgh (Turnhouse) Airport 75 D27
Edinchip 81 E21
Edingale 40 D37
Edingley 51 G42
Edingthorpe 45 B59
Edington *Som.* 8 A29
Edington *Wts.* 20 F35
Edintore 98 E30
Edinvale 97 F26
Edistone 6 C18
Edithmead 19 G29
Edith Weston 42 E45
Edlaston 40 A37
Edlesborough 32 G45
Edlingham 71 C36
Edlington 53 E48
Edmondsham 10 C36
Edmondsley 62 B38
Edmondthorpe 42 D44
Edmonstone 104 D31
Edmonton 23 B49
Edmundbyres 62 A36
Ednam 77 G33
Ednaston 40 A37
Edney Common 24 A52
Edra 81 F20
Edradynate 81 B24
Edrom 77 E34
Edstaston 38 B31
Edstone 30 B37
Edvin Loach 29 C32
Edwalton 41 B41
Edwardstone 34 D55
Edwinsford 17 A22
Edwinstowe 51 F41
Edworth 33 D48
Edwyn Ralph 29 C32
Edzell 83 A31
Efail Isaf 18 C26
Efailnewydd 36 B19
Efailwen 16 B17
Efenechtyd 47 G26
Effingham 22 F46
Effirth 107 B38
Egbury 21 F40
Egdean 12 D45
Egerton *Kent* 14 C55
Egerton *G.M.* 49 A33
Egerton Forstal 14 C54
Egerton Green 48 G31
Egg Buckland 5 E21
Eggerness 64 F20
Eggesford Barton 6 D22
Eggington 32 F45
Egginton 40 C38
Egglescliffe 62 E39
Eggleston 62 D35
Egham 22 D46
Egleton 42 E44
Eglingham 71 B36
Egloshayle 4 C16
Egloskerry 4 B18
Eglwysbach 47 E23
Eglwys-Brewis 18 E25
Eglwys Cross 38 A30
Eglwys Fach 37 F22
Eglwyswrw 16 A17
Egmanton 51 F43
Egremont 60 E25
Egton 63 F43
Egton Bridge 63 F44
Egypt 21 G40
Eight Ash Green 34 F55
Eignaig 79 C13
Eil 89 C24
Eilanreach 86 C14
Eilean Darach 95 C16
Eilean Iarmain (Isleornsay) 86 C12
Einacleit 100 E7
Eisgean 100 F9
Eisingrug 36 B21
Eisteddfa Gurig 37 G23
Elan Village 27 B25
Elberton 19 C31
Elburton 5 E21
Elcho 82 E27
Elcombe 20 C36
Eldernell 43 F48
Eldersfield 29 E33
Elderslie 74 D20
Eldrick 67 E18
Eldroth 56 C33
Eldwick 57 E37
Elerch (Bont-goch) 37 G22
Elford *Stf.* 40 D37

Elford *Nor.* 77 G37
Elgin 97 E27
Elgol 86 C11
Elham 15 C57
Elie 83 G30
Elilaw 70 C35
Elim 46 D19
Eling 10 C39
Eliock 68 C23
Elishader 94 E11
Elishaw 70 D34
Elkesley 51 E42
Elkstone 29 G35
Elland 57 G36
Ellary 73 C13
Ellastone 40 A38
Ellemford 77 D33
Ellenborough 60 C26
Ellenhall 40 C34
Ellen's Green 12 C47
Ellerbeck 62 G40
Ellerby 63 E43
Ellerdine Heath 39 C32
Elleric 80 C16
Ellerker 59 G45
Ellerton *Hum.* 58 E42
Ellerton *N.Y.* 62 G38
Ellerton *Shr.* 39 C33
Ellesborough 22 A44
Ellesmere 38 B29
Ellesmere Port 48 E30
Ellingham *Nfk* 45 F59
Ellingham *Nor.* 71 A37
Ellingham *Ham.* 10 D36
Ellingstring 57 A37
Ellington *Nor.* 71 D38
Ellington *Cbs.* 32 A47
Ellisfield 21 G42
Ellistown 41 D40
Ellon 99 F35
Ellonby 60 C30
Ellough 45 G60
Elloughton 59 G45
Ellwood 19 A31
Elm 43 E50
Elmbridge 29 B34
Elmdon *Esx* 33 E50
Elmdon *W.M.* 40 G37
Elmdon Heath 40 G37
Elmesthorpe 41 F40
Elmhurst 40 D36
Elmley Castle 29 D35
Elmley Lovett 29 B34
Elmore 29 G33
Elmore Back 29 G33
Elm Park 23 C51
Elmscott 6 C18
Elmsett 34 D56
Elmstead Market 34 F56
Elmstone 25 E58
Elmstone Hardwicke 29 F35
Elmswell *Sfk* 34 B55
Elmswell *Hum.* 59 D45
Elmton 51 E40
Elphin 101 G18
Elphinstone 76 C29
Elrick *Grm.* 90 A30
Elrick *Grm.* 91 C34
Elrig 64 F19
Elrigbeag 80 F17
Elsdon 70 D35
Elsecar 51 C39
Elsenham 33 F51
Elsfield 21 A41
Elsham 52 A46
Elsing 44 D56
Elslack 56 E35
Elson 38 B29
Elsrickle 75 F26
Elstead 22 G44
Elsthorpe 42 C46
Elstob 62 D39
Elston *Not.* 42 A43
Elston *Lan.* 55 F31
Elstone 6 D22
Elstow 32 D46
Elstree 22 B47
Elstronwick 59 F48
Elswick 55 F30
Elsworth 33 B48
Elterwater 60 F29
Eltham 23 D50
Eltisley 33 C48
Elton *Glo.* 29 G33
Elton *H.&W.* 28 A30
Elton *Cbs.* 42 F46
Elton *Dby.* 50 F38
Elton *Che.* 48 E30
Elton *Cle.* 62 E39
Elton *Not.* 42 B43
Elvanfoot 68 B25
Elvaston 41 B39
Elveden 34 A54
Elvingston 76 C30
Elvington *N.Y.* 58 E43

Elvington *Kent* 15 B58
Elwick *Nor.* 77 G36
Elwick *Cle.* 62 C40
Elworth 49 F33
Elworthy 7 B26
Ely *S.G.* 18 D27
Ely *Cbs.* 33 A51
Emberton 32 D44
Embleton *Nor.* 71 A38
Embleton *Cum.* 60 C27
Embo 97 B24
Emborough 19 F31
Embo Street 96 B23
Embsay 56 D35
Emery Down 10 D38
Emley 50 A38
Emmer Green 22 D43
Emmington 22 A43
Emneth 43 E50
Emneth Hungate 43 E51
Empingham 42 E45
Empshott 11 A43
Emsworth 11 D43
Enborne 21 E40
Enchmarsh 38 F30
Enderby 41 F41
Endmoor 55 A31
Endon 49 G35
Enfield 23 B49
Enford 20 F37
Engine Common 19 C32
Englefield 21 D42
Englefield Green 22 D45
Englesea-brook 49 G33
English Bicknor 28 G31
Englishcombe 19 E32
English Frankton 38 B30
Enham Alamein 21 F39
Enmore 8 A28
Ennerdale Bridge 60 E26
Enochdu 82 A26
Enterkinfoot 68 C24
Enterpen 62 F40
Enville 40 G34
Eolaigearraidh 84 D3
Eorabus 78 E9
Eorodal 101 A11
Eoropaidh 100 A10
Epperstone 41 A42
Epping 23 A50
Epping Green *Esx* 23 A50
Epping Green *Hfs.* 23 A48
Epping Upland 23 A50
Eppleby 62 E37
Eppleworth 59 F46
Epsom 22 E47
Epwell 30 D39
Epworth 51 B43
Erbistock 38 A29
Erbusaig 86 B13
Erchless Castle 96 G20
Erdington 40 F36
Eredine 80 G15
Eriboll 102 C20
Ericstane 69 B26
Eridge Green 13 C51
Eriff 67 C21
Erines 73 C14
Eriswell 33 A52
Erith 23 D50
Erlestoke 20 F35
Ermington 5 E22
Erpingham 45 B57
Errogie 88 B21
Errol 82 E28
Errollston 99 F36
Erskine 74 C20
Erwarton 35 E58
Erwood 27 D26
Eryholme 62 F39
Eryrys 48 G28
Escart 73 D14
Escomb 62 D37
Escrick 58 E42
Esgair 17 B19
Esgairgeiliog 37 E23
Esh 62 B37
Esher 22 E47
Eshott 71 D37
Eshton 56 D35
Esh Winning 62 B37
Eskadale 88 A20
Eskbank 76 D29
Eskdale Green 60 F27
Eskdalemuir 69 D28
Eskham 53 C49
Esknish 72 D9
Espley Hall 71 D37
Esprick 55 F30
Essendine 42 D46
Essendon 23 A48
Essich 88 A22
Essington 40 E35

Esslemont 91 A35
Eston 63 E41
Etal 77 G35
Etchilhampton 20 E36
Etchingham 13 D52
Etchinghill *Kent* 15 D57
Etchinghill *Stf.* 40 D35
Ethie Mains 83 C32
Eton 22 D45
Eton Wick 22 D45
Etteridge 88 E22
Ettingshall 40 F35
Ettington 30 D38
Etton *Cbs.* 42 E47
Etton *Hum.* 59 E45
Ettrick 69 B28
Ettrickbridge 69 A29
Ettrickhill 69 B28
Etwall 40 B38
Eurach 79 G14
Euston 34 A54
Euxton 55 G31
Evanton 96 E21
Evedon 42 A46
Evelix 96 B23
Evenjobb 28 B28
Evenley 31 E41
Evenlode 30 F37
Evenwood 62 D37
Everbay 104 D32
Evercreech 9 A32
Everdon 31 C41
Everingham 58 E44
Everleigh 20 F37
Everley *N.Y.* 59 A45
Everley *Hgh.* 103 B29
Eversholt 32 E45
Evershot 8 D31
Eversley 22 E43
Eversley Cross 22 E43
Everthorpe 58 F44
Everton *Bfd.* 32 C47
Everton *Not.* 51 C42
Everton *Ham.* 10 E38
Evertown 69 F29
Evesbatch 29 D32
Evesham 30 D36
Evie 104 D29
Evington 41 E42
Ewart Newtown 77 G35
Ewden Village 50 C38
Ewell 22 E47
Ewell Minnis 15 C58
Ewelme 21 B42
Ewen 20 B36
Ewenny 18 D24
Ewerby 42 A47
Ewerby Thorpe 42 A47
Ewhurst *Sry* 22 G46
Ewhurst *E.S.* 14 E53
Ewhurst Green 12 C46
Ewloe 48 F28
Ewood 56 G32
Eworthy 6 F20
Ewshot 22 G44
Ewyas Harold 28 F29
Exbourne 6 E22
Exbury 11 D40
Exebridge 7 C24
Exelby 57 A38
Exeter 7 F24
Exford 7 B24
Exfords Green 38 E30
Exhall 30 C36
Exlade Street 21 C42
Exminster 7 G25
Exmouth 7 G25
Exnaboe 107 E37
Exning 33 B51
Exton *Lei.* 42 D45
Exton *Dev.* 7 G25
Exton *Som.* 7 B25
Exton *Ham.* 11 B41
Exwick 7 F24
Eyam 50 E38
Eydon 31 C41
Eye *H.&W.* 28 B30
Eye *Sfk* 35 A57
Eye *Cbs.* 43 E48
Eye Green 43 E48
Eyemouth 77 D35
Eyeworth 33 D48
Eyhorne Street 14 B54
Eyke 35 C59
Eynesbury 32 C47
Eynort 85 B9
Eynsford 23 E51
Eynsham 21 A40
Eype 8 E30
Eyre 93 F10
Eythorne 15 C58
Eyton *H.&W.* 28 B30
Eyton *Clw.* 38 A29
Eyton *Shr.* 38 G29
Eyton upon the Weald Moors 39 D32

Eywood 28 C28

F

Faccombe 21 F39
Faceby 62 F40
Fachwen 46 F21
Faddiley 48 G31
Fadmoor 58 A42
Faebait 96 F20
Faifley 74 C21
Fail 67 A20
Failand 19 D30
Failford 67 A20
Failsworth 49 B34
Fain 95 D17
Fairbourne 36 D21
Fairburn 57 G40
Fairfield Dby. 50 E36
Fairfield H.&W. 29 A35
Fairford 20 A37
Fairgirth 65 E24
Fairholm 75 E23
Fairley 91 C34
Fairlie 73 E17
Fairlight 14 F54
Fairlight Cove 14 F54
Fairmile 7 F26
Fairmilehead 76 D28
Fairnington 70 A32
Fairoak 39 B33
Fair Oak Ham. 11 C40
Fair Oak Ham. 21 E41
Fairseat 24 E52
Fairstead Esx 34 G53
Fairstead Nfk 45 C58
Fairwarp 13 D50
Fairy Cross 6 C19
Fairyhill 17 E20
Fakenham 44 C55
Fala 76 D30
Fala Dam 76 D30
Falahill 76 E29
Faldingworth 52 D46
Falfield Avon 19 B32
Falfield Fife 83 G30
Falkenham 35 E58
Falkirk 75 B24
Falkland 82 G28
Falla 70 B32
Fallgate 51 F39
Fallin 75 A24
Falmer 13 F49
Falmouth 2 E13
Falsgrave 59 A46
Falstone 70 E33
Fanagmore 101 C17
Fanans 80 E16
Fancott 32 F46
Fangdale Beck 63 G41
Fangfoss 58 D43
Fanmore 79 C10
Fans 76 F32
Farcet 42 F47
Far Cotton 31 C43
Farden 28 A31
Fareham 11 D41
Farewell 40 D36
Far Forest 29 A33
Farforth 53 E49
Far Gearstones 56 A33
Faringdon 21 B38
Farington 55 G31
Farlam 61 A31
Farlary 96 A23
Farleigh Sry 23 E49
Farleigh Avon 19 E30
Farleigh Hungerford 20 F33
Farleigh Wallop 21 G42
Farlesthorpe 53 E50
Farleton 55 A31
Farley Stf. 40 A36
Farley Shr. 38 E29
Farley Wts. 10 B38
Farley Green 22 G46
Farley Hill 22 E43
Farleys End 29 G33
Farlington 58 C42
Farlow 39 G32
Farmborough 19 E32
Farmcote 30 F36
Farmington 30 G37
Farmoor 21 A40
Farmtown 98 D30
Farnborough Ham. 22 F43
Farnborough War. 31 C40
Farnborough Sry 23 E50
Farnborough Brk. 21 C40
Farnborough Green 22 F44
Farncombe 22 G45
Farndish 32 B45
Farndon Not. 51 G43
Farndon Che. 48 G30
Farnell 83 B32
Farnham Sfk 35 C59
Farnham Esx 33 F50

Farnham Sry 22 G44
Farnham N.Y. 57 C39
Farnham Dor. 9 C35
Farnham Common 22 C45
Farnham Green 33 F50
Farnham Royal 22 C45
Farningham 23 E51
Farnley 57 E37
Farnley Tyas 50 A37
Farnsfield 51 G42
Farnworth G.M. 49 B33
Farnworth Che. 48 D31
Farr Hgh. 88 A22
Farr Hgh. 89 D24
Farr Hgh. 102 B23
Farraline 88 B21
Farr Ho. 88 A22
Farringdon 7 F26
Farrington Gurney 19 F32
Farsley 57 F38
Farthinghoe 31 E41
Farthingloe 15 D58
Farthingstone 31 C41
Farway 7 F27
Fasag 94 F14
Fasagrianach 95 C17
Fascadale 79 A10
Faslane 74 B18
Fasnacloich 80 C16
Fasnakyle 87 B18
Fassfern 87 G16
Fatfield 62 A38
Fattahead 98 D32
Faugh 61 A30
Fauldhouse 75 D24
Faulkbourne 34 G53
Faulkland 20 F33
Fauls 38 B31
Faversham 25 E55
Favillar 98 F28
Fawdington 57 B40
Fawdon 71 G38
Fawfieldhead 50 F36
Fawkham Green 23 E51
Fawler 30 G39
Fawley Bkh. 22 C43
Fawley Brk. 21 C39
Fawley Ham. 11 D40
Fawley Chapel 28 F31
Fawsyde 91 F34
Faxfleet 58 G44
Faxton 31 A43
Faygate 12 C47
Fazeley 40 E37
Fearby 57 A37
Fearn 57 D24
Fearnach 73 C16
Fearnan 81 C23
Fearnbeg 94 F13
Fearnhead 49 C32
Fearnmore 94 E13
Fearnoch 73 B15
Featherstone W.Y. 57 G39
Featherstone Stf. 40 E35
Featherstone Castle 70 G32
Feckenham 29 B35
Feering 34 F54
Feetham 62 G35
Feith-hill 98 E32
Feizor 56 C33
Felbridge 13 C49
Felbrigg 45 B58
Felcourt 23 G49
Felden 22 A46
Felindre Dyf. 17 B21
Felindre Dyf. 27 F23
Felindre Dyf. 17 A19
Felindre Pow. 38 G27
Felindre W.G. 17 D22
Felinfach 27 E26
Felinfoel 17 D21
Felingwmuchaf 17 B20
Felixkirk 57 A40
Felixstowe 35 E59
Felixstoweferry 35 E59
Felkington 77 F35
Felldownhead 6 G19
Felling 71 G38
Fellonmore 79 E12
Felmersham 32 C45
Felmingham 45 C58
Felpham 12 G45
Felsham 34 C55
Felsted 33 F52
Feltham 22 D46
Felthorpe 45 D57
Felton Avon 19 E31
Felton H.&W. 28 D31
Felton Nor. 71 C37
Felton Butler 38 D29
Feltwell 44 G52
Fence 56 F34
Fence Houses 62 A38
Fencott 31 G41
Fendike Corner 53 F50
Fen Ditton 33 C50

Fen Drayton 33 B49
Fen End 30 A38
Fenhouses 43 A48
Feniscowles 56 G32
Feniton 7 F26
Fenny Bentley 40 A37
Fenny Bridges 7 F26
Fenny Compton 31 C40
Fenny Drayton 41 F39
Fenny Stratford 32 E44
Fenrother 71 D37
Fenstanton 33 B49
Fen Street 34 A55
Fenton Cbs. 33 A49
Fenton Stf. 40 A34
Fenton Lcn. 52 G44
Fenton Lcn. 52 E44
Fenton Nor. 77 F35
Fenwick Nor. 77 F36
Fenwick Str. 74 F20
Fenwick S.Y. 51 A41
Fenwick Nor. 71 F36
Feochaig 66 B13
Feock 3 E14
Feolin 72 D11
Feolin Ferry 72 D10
Feorlan 66 C12
Feorlin 73 A15
Feriniquarrie 93 F7
Fern 83 A30
Ferndale 18 B25
Ferndown 10 D36
Ferness 98 D29
Fernham 21 B38
Fernhill Heath 29 C34
Fernhurst 12 D44
Fernie 82 F29
Fernilea 85 A9
Fernilee 49 E35
Fernybank 90 F31
Ferrensby 57 C39
Ferring 12 F46
Ferrybridge 57 G40
Ferryden 83 B32
Ferryhill 62 C38
Ferryside 17 C19
Fersfield 44 G56
Fersit 88 G19
Feshiebridge 89 D24
Fetcham 22 F47
Fetterangus 99 D35
Fettercairn 91 F32
Fetternear Ho. 91 B32
Feus of Caldhame 91 G32
Fewcott 31 F41
Fewston 57 D37
Ffairfach 17 B22
Ffair-Rhos 27 B23
Ffarmers 27 D22
Ffawyddog 28 G27
Ffestiniog 37 A22
Ffordd-las 47 F27
Fforest 17 D21
Fforest-fach 17 E21
Ffostrasol 26 D19
Ffos-y-ffin 26 B20
Ffridd Uchaf 46 G21
Ffrith 48 G28
Ffrwdgrech 27 F26
Ffynnon-ddrain 17 B19
Ffynnongroyw 47 D27
Fibhig 100 C8
Fichlie 90 B30
Fidden 78 E8
Fiddington Som. 19 G28
Fiddington Glo. 29 E34
Fiddler's Green 28 E31
Fiddlers Hamlet 23 A50
Field 40 B36
Field Broughton 55 A29
Field Dalling 44 B56
Field Head 41 E40
Fifehead Magdalen 9 B33
Fifehead Neville 9 C33
Fife Keith 98 D29
Fifield Brk. 22 D45
Fifield Oxf. 30 G38
Fifield Bavant 10 B38
Figheldean 20 G37
Filby 45 D60
Filey 59 B47
Filgrave 32 D44
Filkins 21 A38
Filleigh Dev. 6 C22
Filleigh Dev. 7 D23
Fillingham 52 D45
Fillongley 40 G38
Filmore Hill 11 B42
Filton 19 D31
Fimber 58 C44
Finavon 83 B30
Fincham 44 E52
Finchampstead 22 E43
Finchdean 11 C43
Finchingfield 33 E52
Finchley 23 B48

Findern 40 B38
Findhorn 97 E26
Findhorn Bridge 88 B23
Findhuglen 81 F23
Findochty 98 C30
Findo Gask 82 E26
Findon W.S. 12 F44
Findon Grm. 91 D35
Findon Mains 96 E21
Findrassie 97 E27
Findron 90 B27
Finedon 32 A45
Fingal Street 35 A58
Fingask 91 A33
Fingerpost 29 A33
Fingest 22 B43
Finghall 57 A37
Fingland Cum. 60 A28
Fingland D.&G. 69 C28
Fingland D.&G. 68 B23
Finglesham 15 B58
Fingringhoe 34 G56
Finlarig 81 D21
Finmere 31 E42
Finnart Tay. 81 B21
Finnart Str. 74 A18
Finningham 34 B56
Finningly 51 C42
Finnygaud 98 D31
Finsbury 23 C48
Finstall 29 A35
Finsthwaite 55 A29
Finstock 30 G39
Finstown 104 E29
Fintry Cen. 74 B21
Fintry Grm. 99 D33
Finzean 90 D31
Fionnphort 78 E8
Firbank 61 G32
Firbeck 51 D41
Firgrove 49 A35
Firsby 53 F50
Firs Road 10 A38
First Coast 94 B14
Firth 106 E40
Fir Tree 62 C37
Fir Vale 51 D39
Fishbourne W.S. 12 F44
Fishbourne I.o.W. 11 E41
Fishburn 62 C39
Fisherford 98 F32
Fisher's Pond 11 B40
Fisher's Row 55 E30
Fisherstreet 12 C45
Fisherton Hgh. 96 F23
Fisherton Str. 67 B18
Fisherton de la Mere 20 G35
Fishguard 16 A15
Fishlake 51 A42
Fishley Barton 6 C21
Fishpond Bottom 8 E29
Fishponds 19 D32
Fishpool 49 B33
Fishtoft 43 A49
Fishtoft Drove 43 A48
Fishtown of Usan 83 B32
Fishwick Bor. 77 E34
Fishwick Lan. 55 F31
Fiskerton Lcn. 52 E46
Fiskerton Not. 51 G43
Fittleton 20 F37
Fittleworth 12 E46
Fitton End 43 D50
Fitz 38 D30
Fitzhead 7 C27
Fitzwilliam 51 A39
Fiunary 79 C12
Five Ash Down 13 D50
Five Ashes 13 D51
Five Bridges 29 D32
Fivehead 8 B29
Fivelanes 4 B17
Five Oak Green 23 G52
Five Oaks W.S. 12 D46
Five Oaks C.I. 3 G17
Five Roads 17 D20
Five Turnings 28 A28
Five Wents 14 B53
Flackwell Heath 22 C44
Fladbury 29 D35
Fladdabister 107 D40
Flagg 50 F37
Flamborough 59 B47
Flamstead 32 G46
Flamstead End 23 A49
Flansham 12 F45
Flasby 56 D35
Flash 50 F36
Flashader 93 F9
Flask Inn 63 F45
Flaunden 22 A46
Flawborough 42 A43
Flawith 57 C40
Flax Bourton 19 E30
Flaxby 57 D39

Flaxley 29 G32
Flaxpool 7 B27
Flaxton 58 C42
Fleckney 41 F42
Flecknoe 31 B40
Fleet Lcn. 43 C49
Fleet Ham. 22 F43
Fleet Hargate 43 C49
Fleetwood 55 E28
Flemingston 18 E25
Flemington 74 E22
Flempton 34 B53
Fleoideabhagh 92 C6
Fletchertown 60 B27
Fletching 13 D50
Flete 5 E22
Fleuchats 90 C29
Fleur-de-lis 18 B27
Flexbury 6 E18
Flexford 22 F45
Flimby 60 C26
Flimwell 14 D53
Flint 48 E28
Flint Cross 33 D49
Flintham 42 A43
Flint Mountain 48 E28
Flinton 59 F48
Flishinghurst 14 D53
Flitcham 44 C53
Flitton 32 E46
Flitwick 32 E46
Flixborough 52 A44
Flixton G.M. 49 C33
Flixton Sfk 45 G59
Flockton 50 A38
Flockton Green 50 A38
Flodden 77 G34
Flodigarry 93 D10
Flookburgh 55 B29
Floors 98 D30
Flordon 45 F57
Flore 31 B42
Flotterton 70 C35
Flowton 34 D56
Flushing Grm. 99 E36
Flushing Cnw. 3 E14
Flyford Flavell 29 C35
Fobbing 24 C53
Fochabers 98 D29
Fochriw 18 A26
Fockerby 52 A44
Fodderletter 90 A27
Fodderty 96 E20
Foel 37 D25
Foffarty 82 C29
Foggathorpe 58 F43
Fogo 77 F33
Fogorig 77 F33
Foindle 101 D17
Folda 82 A27
Fole 40 B36
Foleshill 41 G39
Folke 9 C32
Folkestone 15 D58
Folkingham 42 B46
Folkington 13 F51
Folksworth 42 G46
Folla Rule 99 F33
Follifoot 57 D39
Folly Dyf. 16 B15
Folly Dor. 9 D33
Folly Gate 6 F21
Fonthill Bishop 9 A35
Fonthill Gifford 9 A35
Fontmell Magna 9 C34
Fontwell 12 F45
Foolow 50 E37
Foots Cray 23 D50
Forbestown 90 B29
Force Forge 60 G29
Forcett 62 E37
Forches Cross 7 E23
Ford Str. 79 G14
Ford Dev. 5 E22
Ford Dev. 6 C20
Ford Mer. 48 B29
Ford Dev. 5 F23
Ford Ltn 20 D34
Ford Wts. 20 D34
Ford Nor. 77 G35
Ford Shr. 38 D30
Ford Glo. 30 F36
Ford Som. 7 C26
Ford Dyf. 16 B15
Ford Bkh. 22 A43
Ford W.S. 12 F45
Fordcombe 23 G51
Fordell 75 B27
Forden 38 E28
Ford End 33 G52
Forder Green 5 D23
Fordham Esx 34 F55
Fordham Cbs. 33 A52
Fordham Nfk 43 F51
Fordham Abbey 33 B52
Fordingbridge 10 C37

Fordoun 91 F33
Fordstreet 34 F54
Ford Street 7 D27
Fordwells 30 G38
Fordwich 15 B57
Fordyce 98 C31
Forebrae 82 E25
Foreland 72 D8
Forest Gate 23 C50
Forest Green 22 G46
Forest Hall *Cum.* 61 F31
Forest Hall *T.&W.* 71 G38
Forest Head 61 A31
Forest Hill 21 A41
Forest-in-Teesdale 61 D34
Forest Lodge *Str.* 80 C18
Forest Lodge *Tay.* 89 G25
Forest Mill 75 A25
Forest Row 13 C50
Forestside 11 C43
Forest Town 51 F41
Forfar 83 C30
Forgandenny 82 F26
Forgie 98 D29
Formby 48 B28
Forncett End 45 F57
Forncett St Mary 45 F57
Forncett St Peter 45 F57
Forneth 82 C26
Fornham All Saints 34 B53
Fornham St Martin 34 B54
Fornighty 97 F25
Forres 97 F26
Forrest 75 D24
Forrest Lodge 67 E21
Forsbrook 40 A35
Forse 103 E28
Forsie 103 B26
Forsinain 102 D24
Forsinard 102 D24
Forston 9 E32
Fort Augustus 88 D19
Forter 82 A27
Forteviot 82 F26
Fort George 96 F23
Forth 75 E25
Forthampton 29 E34
Fortingall 81 C23
Forton *Som.* 8 D29
Forton *Stf.* 39 C33
Forton *Shr.* 38 D30
Forton *Ham.* 21 G40
Forton *Lan.* 55 D30
Fortrie 98 E32
Fortrose 96 F23
Fortuneswell 9 G32
Fort William 87 G16
Forty Green 22 B45
Forty Hill 23 B49
Forward Green 34 C56
Fosbury 21 F39
Foscot 30 F38
Fosdyke 43 B49
Foss 81 B23
Foss Cross 30 G36
Fossdale 61 G34
Fossebridge 30 G36
Foster's Booth 31 C42
Foster Street 23 A50
Foston *N.Y.* 58 C42
Foston *Lcn.* 42 A44
Foston *Dby.* 40 B37
Foston on the Wolds 59 D47
Fotherby 53 C48
Fotheringhay 42 F46
Foubister 105 A31
Foulbog 69 C28
Foulden *Bor.* 77 E35
Foulden *Nfk* 44 F53
Foul Mile 13 E52
Foulridge 56 E34
Foulsham 44 C56
Foulzie 99 C33
Fountainhall 76 F30
Four Ashes *Sfk* 34 A55
Four Ashes *Stf.* 40 E35
Four Crosses *Stf.* 40 E35
Four Crosses *Pow.* 38 D28
Four Crosses *Clw.* 37 A26
Four Crosses *Pow.* 37 E26
Four Elms 23 G50
Four Forks 8 A28
Four Gotes 43 D50
Fourlane Ends 51 G39
Four Lanes 2 E12
Fourlanes End 49 G34
Four Marks 11 A42
Four Mile Bridge 46 E18
Four Oaks *W.M.* 40 G38
Four Oaks *W.M.* 40 F36
Four Oaks *E.S.* 14 E54
Fourpenny 96 B23
Four Roads 17 D20
Fourstones 70 G34
Four Throws 14 E53

Fovant 10 B36
Foveran 91 A35
Fowey 4 E16
Fowlis 82 D29
Fowlis Wester 82 E25
Fowlmere 33 D49
Fownhope 28 E31
Foxcote 29 G35
Foxdale 54 F24
Foxearth 34 D54
Foxfield 55 A28
Foxham 20 D35
Foxhole *Hgh.* 88 A21
Foxhole *Cnw.* 3 C15
Foxhunt Green 13 E51
Fox Lane 22 F44
Foxley *Wts.* 20 C34
Foxley *Nmp.* 31 C42
Foxley *H.&W.* 28 D30
Foxley *Nfk* 44 C56
Fox Street 34 F56
Foxt 40 A36
Foxton *Cbs.* 33 D49
Foxton *Lei.* 41 G43
Foxton *N.Y.* 62 D39
Foxup 56 B34
Foxwist Green 49 F32
Foy 28 F31
Foyers 88 B20
Frachadil 78 B9
Fraddam 2 E11
Fraddon 3 C15
Fradley 40 D37
Fradswell 40 B35
Fraisthorpe 59 C47
Framfield 13 D50
Framingham Earl 45 E58
Framingham Pigot 45 E58
Framlingham 35 B58
Frampton *Lcn.* 43 B49
Frampton *Dor.* 9 E32
Frampton Cotterell 19 C32
Frampton Mansell 20 A34
Frampton on Severn 20 A33
Frampton West End 43 A49
Framsden 35 C58
Framwellgate Moor 62 B38
Franche 29 A34
Frankby 48 D28
Frankley 40 G35
Frankton 31 A40
Frant 13 C51
Fraserburgh 99 C35
Frating Green 34 F56
Fratton 11 D42
Freathy 4 E19
Freckenham 33 A52
Freckleton 55 G30
Freeby 42 C43
Freefolk 21 G40
Freeland 30 G39
Freemantle 11 C40
Freester 107 B40
Freethorpe 45 E60
Freethorpe Common 45 E59
Freiston *Lcn.* 43 A49
Freiston *Lcn.* 42 A45
Freiston Shore 43 A50
Fremington *Dev.* 6 B21
Fremington *N.Y.* 62 G36
Frenchay 19 D32
Frenchbeer 6 G22
Frendraught 98 E31
Frenich 80 G19
Frensham 22 G44
Fresgoe 103 B25
Freshfield 48 B28
Freshford 20 F33
Freshwater 10 F39
Freshwater East 16 E16
Fressingfield 35 A58
Freston 35 E57
Freswick 103 B29
Frettenham 45 D58
Freuchie 82 G28
Freystrop Cross 16 C15
Friars Carse 68 E25
Friar's Gate 13 C50
Friarton 82 E26
Friday Bridge 43 E50
Friday Street *E.S.* 13 F52
Friday Street *Sry* 22 G47
Fridaythorpe 58 D44
Friern Barnet 23 B48
Friesthorpe 52 D46
Frieth 22 B43
Frilford 21 B40
Frilsham 21 D41
Frimley 22 F44
Frimley Green 22 F44
Frindsbury 24 E53
Fringford 31 F41
Frinsted 14 B54
Frinton-on-Sea 35 G58
Friockheim 83 C31
Friog 37 D22

Frisby on the Wreake 41 D42
Friskney 53 G50
Friskney Eaudike 53 G50
Friston *E.S.* 13 G51
Friston *Sfk* 35 C60
Fritchley 51 F39
Frith 14 B55
Fritham 10 C38
Frith Bank 43 A49
Frith Common 29 A32
Frithelstock 6 D20
Frithelstock Stone 6 D20
Frithville 53 G49
Frittenden 14 C53
Fritton *Nfk* 45 E60
Fritton *Nfk* 45 F58
Fritwell 31 F41
Frizington 60 E26
Frocester 20 A33
Frochas 38 E28
Frodesley 38 E30
Frodingham 52 A44
Frodsham 48 E31
Frogden 70 A33
Frog End 33 C50
Froggatt 50 E38
Froghall 40 A36
Frogham 10 C37
Frogmore *Ham.* 22 F44
Frogmore *Hfs.* 22 A47
Frogmore *Dev.* 5 F23
Frog Pool 29 B33
Frolesworth 41 F40
Frome 20 G33
Fromes Hill 29 D32
Frome St Quentin 8 D31
Fron *Pow.* 38 E28
Fron *Gwy.* 36 B19
Fron *Pow.* 27 B26
Froncysyllte 38 A28
Fron-goch 37 B24
Frostenden 45 G60
Frosterley 62 C36
Froxfield 21 E38
Froxfield Green 11 B43
Fryerning 24 A52
Fryton 58 B42
Fugglestone St Peter 10 A37
Fulbeck 52 G45
Fulbourn 33 C50
Fulbrook 30 G38
Fulford *Stf.* 40 B35
Fulford *Som.* 7 C27
Fulford *N.Y.* 58 E42
Fulham 23 D48
Fulking 13 E48
Fuller's Moor 48 G30
Fuller Street 34 G53
Fullerton 10 A39
Fulletby 53 E48
Full Sutton 58 D43
Fullwood 74 F20
Fulmer 22 C45
Fulmodeston 44 B55
Fulnetby 52 E47
Fulready 30 D38
Fulstow 53 C49
Fulwell *Oxf.* 30 F39
Fulwell *T.&W.* 62 A39
Fulwood *S.Y.* 51 D39
Fulwood *Lan.* 55 F31
Fundenhall 45 F57
Funtington 11 D43
Funtley 11 D41
Funzie 106 C42
Furley 8 D28
Furnace *Str.* 80 G16
Furnace *Dyf.* 37 F22
Furnace *Hgh.* 94 D15
Furneux Pelham 33 F50
Furzehill 7 A23
Furze Platt 22 C44
Fyfett 8 C28
Fyfield *Oxf.* 21 B40
Fyfield *Wts.* 20 E37
Fyfield *Glo.* 21 A38
Fyfield *Esx* 23 A51
Fyfield *Ham.* 21 G38
Fylingthorpe 63 F45
Fyvie 99 F33

G

Gabhsunn Bho Dheas 100 A10
Gabhsunn Bho Thuath 100 B10
Gablon 96 B22
Gabroc Hill 74 E20
Gaddesby 41 D42
Gaddesden Row 32 G46
Gaer 28 F27
Gaerllwyd 19 B30
Gaerwen 46 E20
Gagingwell 30 F39
Gaich 89 B26
Gaick 88 A22
Gaick Lodge 88 F23

Gailey 40 D34
Gainford 62 E37
Gainsborough 51 C43
Gairloch 94 D13
Gairlochy 87 F17
Gairney Bank 75 A27
Gairnshiel Lodge 90 C28
Gaitsgill 60 B29
Galabank 76 F30
Galashiels 76 G30
Galby 41 E42
Galdenoch 64 D17
Galgate 55 D30
Galhampton 9 B32
Gallanach 79 E14
Gallantry Bank 48 G31
Gallatown 76 A28
Gallchoille 73 B13
Gallery 91 G32
Galley Common 41 F39
Galleyend 24 A52
Galleywood 24 A52
Gallowfauld 83 C30
Gallowstree Common 21 C42
Gallowstree Elm 39 G33
Galltair 86 C14
Galmisdale 85 F10
Galmpton *Dev.* 5 E24
Galmpton *Dev.* 5 F22
Galphay 57 B38
Galston 74 G21
Galtrigill 93 F7
Gamblesby 61 C31
Gamble's Green 34 G53
Gamelsby 60 A28
Gamlingay 33 C48
Gammaton Moor 6 C20
Gammersgill 57 A36
Gamrie 99 C33
Gamston *Not.* 41 B41
Gamston *Not.* 51 E42
Ganarew 28 G31
Ganllwyd 37 C23
Gannochy 90 F31
Ganstead 59 F47
Ganthorpe 58 B42
Ganton 59 B45
Gaodhail 79 D11
Gara Bridge 5 E23
Garadheancal 94 A15
Garbat 96 E20
Garbhallt 73 A16
Garboldisham 44 G56
Garden 74 A21
Garden City 48 F29
Gardenstown 99 C33
Garderhouse 107 C38
Gardham 59 E45
Gare Hill 20 G33
Garelochhead 73 A17
Garford 21 B40
Garforth 57 F40
Gargrave 56 D35
Gargunnock 74 A22
Gariob 73 B13
Garlies Castle 64 D20
Garlieston 64 F20
Garlogie 91 C33
Garmond 99 D33
Garmony 79 C12
Garmouth 98 C28
Garn 36 B18
Garnant 17 C22
Garn-Dolbenmaen 36 A20
Garneddwen 37 E23
Garnett Bridge 61 G31
Garnswllt 17 D22
Garrabost 100 D10
Garrachra 73 B16
Garralburn 98 D30
Garras 2 F12
Garreg 36 A21
Garreg Bank 38 D28
Garrick 81 F24
Garrigill 81 B33
Garroch 67 E21
Garrochty 73 E16
Garros 93 E10
Garrow 81 D24
Garryhorn 67 D21
Garsdale Head 61 G33
Garsdon 20 C35
Garshall Green 40 B35
Garsington 21 A41
Garstang 55 E30
Garston 48 C31
Garswood 48 C31
Gartachoil 74 A21
Gartally 88 A20
Gartavaich 73 E14
Gartbreck 72 E8
Gartcosh 74 D22
Garth *M.G.* 18 B24
Garth *Gwy.* 46 E21
Garth *I.o.M.* 54 F25

Garth *She.* 107 B38
Garth *Clw.* 38 A28
Garth *Pow.* 27 D25
Garthbrengy 27 E26
Gartheli 26 C21
Garthmyl 38 F27
Garthorpe *Lei.* 42 C44
Garthorpe *Hum.* 52 A44
Garths 61 G31
Garthynty 27 D22
Gartincaper 81 G22
Gartly 98 F31
Gartmore 74 A20
Gartnagrenach 73 E13
Gartnatra 72 E9
Gartness 74 B20
Gartocharn 74 B19
Garton 59 F48
Garton-on-the-Wolds 59 C45
Gartymore 103 G25
Garvald 76 C31
Garvamore 88 E21
Garvan 86 G15
Garvard 72 A9
Garve 96 E19
Garveld 66 C12
Garvestone 44 E55
Garvie 73 B16
Garvock *Str.* 74 C18
Garvock *Tay.* 82 F26
Garvock *Grm.* 91 F33
Garwald 69 D27
Garwaldwaterfoot 69 C28
Garway 28 F30
Garway Hill 28 F30
Gask *Grm.* 99 E33
Gask *Grm.* 99 F36
Gask *Tay.* 82 F25
Gaskan 86 G13
Gass 67 C20
Gastard 20 E34
Gasthorpe 44 G55
Gatcombe 11 F40
Gateacre 48 D30
Gatebeck 55 A31
Gate Burton 52 D44
Gateford 51 D41
Gateforth 58 G41
Gatehead 74 G19
Gate Helmsley 58 D42
Gatehouse *Tay.* 81 C24
Gatehouse *Str.* 72 C11
Gatehouse of Fleet 65 E22
Gatelawbridge 68 D24
Gateley 44 C55
Gatenby 57 A39
Gateshaw 70 A33
Gateshead 71 G38
Gatesheath 48 F30
Gateside *Str.* 74 E19
Gateside *Fife* 82 G27
Gateside *Tay.* 83 C30
Gateside *Grm.* 91 B32
Gateslack 68 C24
Gathurst 48 B31
Gatley 49 D34
Gattonside 76 G31
Gatwick (London) Airport 23 G48
Gaufron 27 B25
Gauldry 82 E29
Gaunt's Common 10 D36
Gautby 52 E47
Gavinton 77 E33
Gawber 51 B39
Gawcott 31 E42
Gawsworth 49 E34
Gawthrop 56 A32
Gawthwaite 55 A28
Gaydon 30 C39
Gayhurst 32 D44
Gayles 62 F37
Gay Street 12 D46
Gayton *Nfk* 44 D53
Gayton *Mer.* 48 D28
Gayton *Nmp.* 31 C42
Gayton *Stf.* 40 C35
Gayton le Marsh 53 D50
Gayton le Wold 53 D48
Gayton Thorpe 44 D53
Gaywood 44 C52
Gazeley 34 B53
Geanies Ho. 97 D24
Gearach 72 E8
Gearnsary 102 E23
Gearradh 80 A15
Gearraidh Bhaird 100 F9
Gearraidh Na H-Aibhne 100 D8
Gearraidh Na Monadh 84 C2
Gearrannan 100 C7
Geary 93 E8
Geavraidh Bhailteas 84 B2
Gedding 34 C55
Geddington 42 G44
Gedgrave Hall 35 D60
Gedling 41 A42

Gedney 43 C49
Gedney Broadgate 43 C49
Gedney Drove End 43 C50
Gedney Dyke 43 C50
Gedney Hill 43 D49
Gee Cross 49 C35
Geirninis 92 G3
Geisiadar 100 D7
Geldeston 45 F59
Gell *Clw.* 47 F24
Gell *Gwy.* 36 B20
Gelligaer 18 B26
Gelli Gynan 47 G27
Gellilydan 37 B22
Gellioedd 37 A25
Gelly 16 C16
Gellyburn 82 D26
Gellywen 17 B18
Gelston 65 E23
Gembling 59 D47
Gemmil 79 G13
Genoch 64 E17
Genoch Square 64 E17
Gentleshaw 40 D36
George Green 22 C46
Georgeham 6 B20
George Nympton 7 C23
Georgetown 74 D20
Gerlan 46 F22
Germansweek 6 F19
Germoe 2 F11
Gerrans 3 E14
Gerrards Cross 22 C45
Gerston 103 C27
Gestingthorpe 34 E53
Geuffordd 38 D28
Geufron 37 G24
Gibbshill 65 C23
Gibraltar 53 G51
Gidea Park 23 C51
Gidleigh 6 G22
Giffnock 74 E21
Gifford 76 D31
Giffordland 74 F18
Giggleswick 56 C33
Gilberdyke 58 G44
Gilchriston 76 D30
Gilcrux 60 C27
Gildersome 57 G38
Gildingwells 51 D41
Gileston 18 E25
Gilfach 18 B27
Gilfach Goch 18 C25
Gilfachrheda 26 C19
Gilgarran 60 D26
Gillamoor 63 G42
Gillen 93 F8
Gillenbie 69 E27
Gillfoot 65 C25
Gilling East 58 B42
Gillingham *Nfk* 45 F60
Gillingham *Dor.* 9 B33
Gillingham *Kent* 24 E53
Gilling West 62 F37
Gillivoan 103 E27
Gillock 103 C27
Gillow Heath 49 G34
Gills 103 A29
Gill's Green 14 D53
Gilmanscleuch 69 A29
Gilmerton *Tay.* 81 E24
Gilmerton *Ltn* 76 D28
Gilmilnscroft 67 A21
Gilmonby 62 E35
Gilmorton 41 G41
Gilsland 70 G32
Gilsland Spa 70 G32
Gilston 76 E30
Gilston Park 33 G50
Gilwern 28 G28
Gimingham 45 B58
Giosla 100 E7
Gipping 34 B56
Gipsey Bridge 53 G48
Girlsta 107 B40
Girsby 62 F39
Girtford 32 D47
Girthon 65 E21
Girton *Cbs.* 33 B50
Girton *Not.* 52 F44
Girvan 67 D17
Gisburn 56 E34
Gisleham 45 G60
Gislingham 34 A56
Gissing 45 G57
Gittisham 7 F27
Givons Grove 22 F47
Glack 91 A33
Glackour 95 C17
Gladestry 28 C28
Gladsmuir 76 C30
Glaic 73 C16
Glais 17 D22
Glaisdale 63 F43
Glame 94 G11

Glamis 82 C29
Glanaber Terrace 37 A23
Glan Adda 46 E21
Glanaman 17 C22
Glanbran 27 E23
Glan-Conwy 47 G24
Glanderston 90 A31
Glandford 44 A56
Glandwr *Gwe.* 19 A28
Glandwr *Dyf.* 16 B17
Glan-Dwyfach 36 A20
Glangrwyne 28 G28
Glan Honddu 27 E25
Glan-llynfi 18 B24
Glanmule 38 G27
Glanrhyd 26 D17
Glanton 71 B36
Glantwymyn 37 E23
Glanvilles Wootton 9 D32
Glan-y-don 47 E27
Glan-y-llyn 18 C27
Glan-yr-afon *Clw.* 37 A26
Glan-yr-afon *Gwy.* 37 A25
Glapthorn 42 G46
Glapwell 51 F40
Glasahoile 81 G20
Glasbury 28 E27
Glaschoil 89 A26
Glascoed 19 A29
Glascorrie 90 D29
Glascote 40 E38
Glascwm 28 C27
Glasdrum 80 C15
Glasfryn 47 G25
Glasgow 74 D21
Glasgow Airport 74 D20
Glashmore 91 C33
Glasinfryn 46 F21
Glasnacardoch 86 E12
Glasnakille 86 C11
Glaspant 17 A18
Glaspwll 37 F23
Glassaugh 98 C31
Glassburn 88 A19
Glassel 91 D32
Glassenbury 14 D53
Glasserton 64 G19
Glassford 75 F23
Glasshouse Hill 29 F33
Glasshouses 57 C37
Glassingall 81 G23
Glasslie 82 G28
Glasson *Cum.* 69 G28
Glasson *Lan.* 55 D30
Glassonby 61 C31
Glasterlaw 83 B31
Glaston 42 E44
Glastonbury 8 A30
Glatton 42 G47
Glazebury 49 C32
Glazeley 39 G32
Gleadless 51 D39
Gleadsmoss 49 F34
Gleann Ghrabhair 100 E10
Gleann Tholastaidh 101 C11
Gleaston 55 B28
Glecknabae 73 D16
Gledhow 57 F39
Gledrid 38 B28
Glemsford 34 D54
Glen *D.&G.* 65 E21
Glen *D.&G.* 65 C24
Glenae 68 E25
Glenaladale 86 G14
Glenald 74 A18
Glenamachrie 79 E14
Glenapp Castle 66 E16
Glenarm 82 A29
Glen Auldyn 54 D26
Glenbarr 72 G12
Glenbatrick 72 C10
Glenbeg *Hgh.* 79 A11
Glenbeg *Hgh.* 89 B25
Glenbeg *Hgh.* 95 C18
Glenbeich 81 E21
Glenbervie *Grm.* 91 E33
Glenbervie *Cen.* 75 B24
Glenboig 75 D23
Glenborrodale 79 A11
Glenbranter 73 A16
Glenbreck 69 A26
Glenbrittle 85 B9
Glenbuck 68 A23
Glenbyre 79 E11
Glencaird 64 C19
Glencaple 65 D25
Glencarse 82 E27
Glencat 90 D31
Glenceitlein 80 C17
Glencloy 73 G15
Glencoe 80 B16
Glenconglass 90 A27
Glencraig 75 A24
Glencripesdale 79 B12
Glencrosh 68 E23
Glencruittein 79 E14

Glencuie 90 B30
Glendearg *D.&G.* 69 C28
Glendearg *Bor.* 76 G30
Glendessary 86 E15
Glendevon 82 G25
Glendoebeg 88 D19
Glendoick 82 E27
Glendoll Lodge 90 F28
Glendoune 67 D17
Glendrissaig 67 D17
Glenduckie 82 F28
Glenduisk 67 E17
Glendye Lodge 91 E32
Gleneagles 82 G25
Gleneagles Hotel 81 F24
Glenearn 82 E27
Glenegedale 72 E9
Glenelg 86 C14
Glenfarg 82 F27
Glenfeochan 79 E14
Glenfield 41 E41
Glenfinnan 86 F14
Glenfoot 82 F27
Glengalmadale 79 B14
Glengap 65 E22
Glengarnock 74 E18
Glengarrisdale 72 A12
Glengennet 67 D18
Glengolly 103 B26
Glengrasco 93 G10
Glengyle 80 F19
Glenhead 68 E24
Glenhead Farm 82 A28
Glenhurich 79 A14
Glenkerry 69 B28
Glenkiln 73 G16
Glenkin 73 C17
Glenkindie 90 B30
Glenlair 65 C23
Glenlatterach 97 F27
Glenlean 73 B16
Glenlee *D.&G.* 67 E21
Glenlee *Tay.* 90 E30
Glenlichorn 81 F23
Glenlivet 90 A27
Glenlochar 65 D23
Glenluce 64 E17
Glenmallan 74 A18
Glenmanna 68 C23
Glenmavis 75 D23
Glenmaye 54 E24
Glenmeanie 95 F18
Glenmore *Hgh.* 93 G10
Glenmore *Str.* 73 D16
Glenmore Lodge 89 D25
Glenmoy 82 A29
Glenmuick 101 G19
Glennoe 80 D16
Glenochar 68 B25
Glenogil 83 A30
Glen Parva 41 F41
Glenprosen 82 A29
Glenquiech 82 A29
Glenramskill 66 B13
Glenrazie 64 D19
Glenridding 60 E29
Glenrisdell 73 E14
Glenrossal 96 A20
Glenrothes 82 G28
Glensanda 79 C14
Glensaugh 91 F32
Glensgaich 96 E20
Glenshalg 90 C31
Glenshee 82 D25
Glenshellish 73 A16
Glensluan 73 A16
Glentaggart 68 A24
Glentham 52 C45
Glenton 91 A32
Glentress 76 G28
Glen Trool Lodge 67 E19
Glentruan 54 C26
Glentworth 52 D45
Glenuachdarach 93 F10
Glenure 80 C16
Glenurquhart 96 E23
Glen Vine 54 F25
Glenwhilly 64 C17
Glespin 68 A23
Gletness 107 B40
Glewstone 28 F31
Glinton 42 E47
Glooston 42 F43
Glororum 77 G37
Glossop 50 C36
Gloster Hill 71 C38
Gloucester 29 G33
Gloucester (Staverton) Airport
   29 F34
Gloup 106 B40
Gloweth 2 D13
Glusburn 56 E35
Gluss 106 E39
Glympton 31 F40
Glyn 47 G23
Glynarthen 26 D18

Glyn Ceiriog 38 B27
Glyncoch 18 B26
Glyncorrwg 18 B24
Glyn-Cywarch 36 B21
Glynde 13 F50
Glyndebourne 13 E50
Glyndyfrdwy 38 A27
Glyn-Neath 18 A24
Glynogwr 18 C25
Glyntaff 18 C26
Glynteg 17 A19
Gnosall 40 C34
Gnosall Heath 40 D34
Goadby 42 F43
Goadby Marwood 42 C43
Goatacre 20 D36
Goatfield 80 G15
Goathill 9 C32
Goathland 63 F44
Goathurst 8 A28
Gobernuisgeach 103 E25
Gobhaig 100 G6
Gobowen 38 B29
Godalming 22 G45
Godford Cross 7 E27
Godmanchester 33 B48
Godmanstone 9 E32
Godmersham 15 B56
Godolphin Cross 2 E12
Godor 38 D27
Godre'r-graig 18 A23
Godshill *I.o.W.* 11 F41
Godshill *Ham.* 10 C37
Godstone 23 F49
Goetre 19 A29
Goff's Oak 23 A49
Gogar 75 C27
Gogarth 47 D23
Goginan 37 G22
Goirtean a'Chladaich 87 G16
Goirtein 73 B15
Golan 36 A21
Golant 4 E17
Golberdon 4 C18
Golborne 48 C31
Golcar 50 A36
Goldcliff 19 C29
Golden Cross 13 E51
Golden Green 23 G52
Golden Grove 17 C21
Goldenhill 49 G34
Golden Pot 22 G43
Golden Valley 29 F34
Golders Green 23 C48
Goldhanger 24 A54
Gold Hill 43 F51
Goldielea 65 C25
Golding 38 E31
Goldington 32 C46
Goldsborough *N.Y.* 63 E44
Goldsborough *N.Y.* 57 D39
Goldsithney 2 E11
Goldthorpe 51 B40
Goldworthy 6 C19
Gollanfield 96 F23
Golspie 97 B24
Golval 102 B24
Gomeldon 10 A37
Gomersal 57 G37
Gometra Ho. 78 C9
Gomshall 22 G46
Gonachan 74 B22
Gonalston 41 A42
Gonfirth 107 A39
Good Easter 33 G51
Gooderstone 44 E53
Goodleigh 6 B21
Goodmanham 58 E44
Goodnestone *Kent* 25 E56
Goodnestone *Kent* 15 B58
Goodrich 28 G31
Goodrington 5 E24
Goodwick 16 A15
Goodworth Clatford 21 G39
Goodyers End 41 G39
Goole 58 G43
Goonbell 2 D13
Goonhavern 2 C13
Goose Green 23 F52
Gooseham 6 D18
Goosewell 5 E21
Goosey 21 B39
Goosnargh 55 F31
Goostrey 49 F33
Gorcott Hill 30 B36
Gorddinog 46 E22
Gordon 76 F32
Gordonbush 97 A24
Gordonstoun 97 E27
Gordonstown *Grm.* 98 D31
Gordonstown *Grm.* 99 F33
Gorebridge 76 D29
Gore Cross 20 B36
Gorefield 43 D50
Gore Street 25 E58
Gorey 3 G18

Goring 21 C42
Goring-by-Sea 12 F47
Gorleston on Sea 45 E61
Gorllwyn 17 A19
Gornalwood 40 F34
Gorrachie 99 D33
Gorran Churchtown 3 D15
Gorran Haven 4 F16
Gors 27 A22
Gorsedd 47 E27
Gorseinon 17 E21
Gorseness 104 E29
Gorsgoch 26 C20
Gorslas 17 C21
Gorsley 29 F32
Gorsley Common 29 F32
Gorstan 26 E19
Gorstanvorran 86 G13
Gorten 79 D13
Gortenbuie 79 D11
Gorteneorn 79 A12
Gorton *G.M.* 49 C34
Gorton *Str.* 78 B7
Gosbeck 35 C57
Gosberton 43 B48
Goseley Dale 41 C39
Gosfield 34 F53
Gosforth *Cum.* 60 F26
Gosforth *T.&W.* 71 G38
Gosmore 32 F47
Gospel End 40 F35
Gossabrough 106 D41
Gossops Green 13 C48
Goswick 77 F36
Gotham 41 B41
Gotherington 29 F35
Gott 107 C40
Goudhurst 13 C52
Goulceby 53 E48
Gourdas 99 E33
Gourdon 91 F34
Gourock 74 C18
Govan 74 D21
Goveton 5 F23
Govilon 28 G28
Gowanhill 99 C36
Gowdall 58 G42
Gowerton 17 E21
Gowkhall 75 B26
Gowthorpe 58 D43
Goxhill *Hum.* 59 G47
Goxhill *Hum.* 59 E47
Goytre 18 C23
Grabhair 100 F9
Gradbach 49 F35
Grade 2 G12
Graffham *Sry* 22 G46
Grafham *Cbs.* 32 B47
Grafton *H.&W.* 28 E30
Grafton *H.&W.* 28 B31
Grafton *Shr.* 38 D30
Grafton *Oxf.* 21 A38
Grafton *N.Y.* 57 C39
Grafton Flyford 29 C35
Grafton Regis 31 D43
Grafton Underwood 42 G45
Grafty Green 14 C54
Graianfryd 47 G27
Graig *Clw.* 47 E26
Graig *Gwy.* 47 E24
Graig-fechan 47 G27
Grain 24 D54
Grainel 72 D8
Grainhow 99 E34
Grainsby 53 C48
Grainthorpe 53 C49
Grampound 3 D15
Grampound Road 3 C15
Gramsdal 92 F4
Granborough 31 F43
Granborough 31 F43
Grandborough 31 B40
Grandtully 81 B24
Grange *Mer.* 48 D28
Grange *Cum.* 60 E28
Grange *N.Y.* 63 F47
Grange *Tay.* 82 E28
Grange *Hgh.* 88 A19
Grange *Kent* 24 E53
Grange Crossroads 98 D30
Grange Hall 97 E26
Grange Hill 23 B50
Grangemill 50 G38
Grange Moor 50 A38
Grangemouth 75 B25
Grangemuir 83 G31
Grange of Lindores 82 F28
Grange-over-Sands 55 B30
Grangeston 67 D17
Grangetown *Cle.* 63 D41
Grangetown *S.G.* 18 D27
Grange Villa 62 A38
Granish 89 C24
Gransmoor 59 D47

Granston 16 A14
Grantchester 33 C49
Grantham 42 B44
Grantley 57 B38
Grantlodge 91 B32
Granton House 69 C26
Grantown-on-Spey 89 B25
Grantshouse 77 D33
Grappenhall 49 D32
Grasby 52 B46
Grasmere 60 F29
Grasscroft 49 B35
Grassendale 48 D29
Grassholme 61 D34
Grassington 57 C36
Grassmoor 51 C39
Grassthorpe 51 F43
Grateley 21 G38
Gratwich 40 B36
Graveley Hfs. 33 F48
Graveley Cbs. 33 B48
Gravelly Hill 40 F37
Gravels 38 F29
Graven 106 E39
Graveney 25 E56
Gravesend 24 D52
Grayingham 52 C45
Grayrigg 61 G31
Grays 24 D52
Grayshott 12 C44
Grayswood 12 C45
Grazeley 21 E42
Greasbrough 51 C39
Greasby 48 D28
Great Abington 33 D51
Great Addington 32 A45
Great Alne 30 C36
Great Altcar 48 B29
Great Amwell 33 G49
Great Asby 61 E32
Great Ashfield 34 B55
Great Ayton 63 E41
Great Baddow 24 A53
Great Bardfield 33 E52
Great Barford 32 C47
Great Barr 40 F36
Great Barrington 30 G38
Great Barrow 48 F30
Great Barton 34 B54
Great Barugh 58 B43
Great Bavington 70 E35
Great Bealings 35 D58
Great Bedwyn 21 E38
Great Bentley 35 F57
Great Billing 31 B43
Great Blakenham 34 C56
Great Bolas 39 C32
Great Bookham 22 F47
Great Bourton 31 D40
Great Bowden 42 G43
Great Bradley 33 C52
Great Braxted 34 G54
Great Bricett 34 C56
Great Brickhill 32 E45
Great Bridgeford 40 C34
Great Brington 31 B42
Great Bromley 34 F56
Great Broughton N.Y. 63 F41
Great Broughton Cum. 60 C26
Great Budworth 49 E32
Great Burdon 62 E39
Great Burstead 24 B52
Great Busby 63 F41
Great Canfield 33 G51
Great Canney 24 A53
Great Carlton 53 D50
Great Casterton 42 E46
Great Chart 14 C55
Great Chatwell 39 D33
Great Chesterford 33 D50
Great Cheverell 20 F35
Great Chishill 33 E50
Great Clacton 35 G57
Great Clifton 60 C26
Great Coates 53 B48
Great Comberton 29 D35
Great Corby 61 A30
Great Cornard 34 D54
Great Cowden 59 E48
Great Coxwell 21 B38
Great Crakehall 62 G38
Great Cransley 32 A44
Great Cressingham 44 E54
Great Crosby 48 C29
Great Cubley 40 B37
Great Dalby 42 D43
Great Doddington 32 B44
Great Driffield 59 D46
Great Dunham 44 D54
Great Dunmow 33 F52
Great Durnford 10 A37
Great Easton Esx 33 F51
Great Easton Lei. 42 D45
Great Eccleston 55 E29
Great Edstone 58 A43
Great Ellingham 44 F56

Great Elm 20 G33
Great Eversden 33 C49
Great Fencote 62 G38
Great Finborough 34 C56
Greatford 32 D46
Great Fransham 44 D54
Great Gaddesden 32 G46
Greatgate 40 A36
Great Gidding 42 G47
Great Givendale 58 D44
Great Glemham 35 B58
Great Glen 41 F42
Great Gonerby 42 B44
Great Gransden 33 C48
Great Green Nfk 45 F58
Green Green Sfk 34 C55
Great Habton 58 B43
Great Hale 42 A47
Great Hallingbury 33 G51
Greatham Cle. 62 D40
Greatham W.S. 12 E46
Greatham Ham. 11 A43
Great Hanwood 38 E30
Great Harrowden 32 A44
Great Harwood 56 F33
Great Haseley 21 A42
Great Hatfield 59 E47
Great Haywood 40 C35
Great Heath 41 G39
Great Heck 58 G41
Great Henny 34 E54
Great Hinton 20 F35
Great Hockham 44 F55
Great Holland 35 G58
Great Horkesley 34 E55
Great Hormead 33 F49
Great Horwood 31 E43
Great Houghton Nmp. 31 C43
Great Houghton S.Y. 51 B40
Great Hucklow 50 E37
Great Kelk 59 D47
Great Kimble 22 A43
Great Kingshill 22 B44
Great Langton 62 G38
Great Leighs 34 G53
Great Limber 52 B47
Great Linford 32 D44
Great Livermere 34 A54
Great Longstone 50 E38
Great Lumley 62 B38
Great Lyth 38 E30
Great Malvern 29 D33
Great Maplestead 34 E54
Great Marton 55 F29
Great Massingham 44 C54
Great Melton 45 E57
Great Milton 21 A42
Great Missenden 22 A44
Great Mitton 56 F33
Great Mongeham 15 B59
Great Moulton 45 F57
Great Musgrave 61 E33
Great Ness 38 D29
Great Oak 28 G29
Great Oakley Esx 35 F57
Great Oakley Nmp. 42 G44
Great Offley 32 F47
Greatoften 61 E33
Great Orton 60 A29
Great Ouseburn 57 C40
Great Oxendon 42 G43
Great Oxney Green 24 A52
Great Palgrave 44 D54
Great Parndon 23 A50
Great Paxton 33 B48
Great Plumpton 55 F29
Great Plumstead 45 D59
Great Ponton 42 B44
Great Preston 57 G40
Great Raveley 43 G48
Great Rissington 30 G37
Great Rollright 30 E39
Great Ryburgh 44 C55
Great Ryle 71 B36
Great Ryton 38 E30
Great Saling 33 F52
Great Salkeld 61 C31
Great Sampford 33 E52
Great Sankey 48 D31
Great Saxham 34 B53
Great Shefford 21 D39
Great Shelford 33 C50
Great Smeaton 62 F39
Great Snoring 44 B55
Great Somerford 20 C35
Great Stainton 62 D39
Great Stambridge 24 B54
Great Staughton 32 B47
Great Steeping 53 F50
Great Stonar 15 B59
Greatstone-on-Sea 15 E56
Great Strickland 61 D31
Great Stukeley 33 A48
Great Sturton 53 E48
Great Sutton Shr. 38 G31
Great Sutton Che. 48 E29

Great Swinburne 70 F35
Great Tew 30 F39
Great Tey 34 F54
Great Thurlow 33 D52
Great Torrington 6 D21
Great Tosson 71 C36
Great Totham Esx 34 G54
Great Totham Esx 34 G54
Great Urswick 55 B28
Great Wakering 25 C53
Great Waldingfield 34 D55
Great Walsingham 44 B55
Great Waltham 33 G52
Great Warley 23 B51
Great Washbourne 29 E35
Great Welnetham 34 C54
Great Wenham 34 E56
Great Whittington 70 F35
Great Wigborough 34 G55
Great Wilbraham 33 C51
Great Wishford 10 A36
Great Witcombe 29 G35
Great Witley 29 B33
Great Wolford 30 E38
Great Woolstone 32 E44
Greatworth 31 D41
Great Wratting 33 D52
Great Wymondley 33 F48
Great Wyrley 40 E35
Great Wytheford 38 D31
Great Yarmouth 45 E61
Great Yeldham 34 E53
Greenburn 83 D30
Greencroft Hall 62 B37
Greendams 91 D32
Greendykes 71 A36
Green End Hfs. 33 F49
Green End Bfd. 32 C47
Greenfield Bfd. 32 E46
Greenfield G.M. 50 B36
Greenfield Clw. 48 E28
Greenfield Oxf. 22 B43
Greenfield Hgh. 87 D18
Greenford 22 C47
Greengairs 75 C23
Greenhalgh 55 F30
Greenhall 91 A32
Greenham Brk. 21 E40
Greenham Som. 7 C26
Green Hammerton 57 D40
Greenhaugh 70 E33
Greenhead 70 G32
Greenheads 99 F36
Greenhill Hgh. 97 A25
Greenhill S.Y. 51 D39
Greenhill G.L. 22 C47
Greenhithe 23 D51
Greenholm 74 G21
Greenholme 56 F31
Greenhow Hill 57 C37
Greenigo 105 A29
Greenland 103 B28
Greenlands 22 C43
Greenlaw Grm. 98 D32
Greenlaw Bor. 76 F32
Greenloaning 81 G24
Greenmount 49 A33
Greenmyre 99 F33
Greenock 74 C18
Greenodd 55 A29
Green Ore 19 F31
Greenscares 81 F23
Greenside 71 G37
Greenskares 99 C33
Greens Norton 31 C42
Greenstead Green 34 F54
Greensted 23 A51
Green Street 22 B47
Green Street Green G.L. 23 E50
Green Street Green Kent 23 D51
Green Tye 33 G50
Greenway Som. 8 B29
Greenway Dyf. 16 A16
Greenwich 23 D49
Greet 30 E36
Greete 28 A31
Greetham Lcn. 53 E49
Greetham Lei. 42 D45
Greetland 57 G36
Greinetobht 92 D4
Greinton 8 A29
Grenaby 54 F24
Grendon War. 40 E38
Grendon Nmp. 32 B44
Grendon Common 40 F38
Grendon Green 28 C31
Grendon Underwood 31 F42
Grenoside 51 C39
Greosabhagh 93 B7
Gresford 38 G29
Gresham 45 B57
Greshornish 93 F9
Gressenhall 44 D55
Gressingham 55 B31
Greta Bridge 62 E36
Gretna 69 G29

Gretna Green 69 G28
Gretton Nmp. 42 F44
Gretton Shr. 38 F31
Gretton H.&G. 29 E35
Grewelthorpe 57 B37
Greygarth 57 B37
Greylake 8 A29
Greys Green 22 C43
Greysouthen 60 D26
Greystoke 60 C30
Greystone Tay. 83 C31
Greystone Grm. 90 D28
Greystone Lan. 56 E34
Greywell 22 F43
Griais 100 C10
Gribthorpe 58 F43
Gribton 68 E25
Gridley Corner 6 F19
Griff 41 G39
Griffithstown 19 B28
Grigadale 79 A10
Grigghall 60 G30
Grimeford Village 49 A32
Grimethorpe 51 B40
Griminis 92 F3
Grimister 106 C40
Grimley 29 B34
Grimmet 67 B19
Grimness 105 B30
Grimoldby 53 D49
Grimpo 38 C29
Grimsargh 55 F31
Grimsbury 31 D40
Grimsby 53 B48
Grimscote 31 C42
Grimscott 6 E18
Grimsiadar 100 E9
Grimsthorpe 42 C46
Grimston Lei. 41 C42
Grimston Nfk 44 C53
Grimstone 9 E32
Grindale 59 B47
Grindiscol 107 C40
Grindle 39 E33
Grindleford 50 E38
Grindleton 56 E33
Grindley 40 C36
Grindlow 50 E37
Grindon Stf. 50 G36
Grindon Nor. 77 F34
Gringley on the Hill 51 C43
Grinsdale 60 A29
Grinshill 38 C31
Grinton 62 G36
Griomarstaidh 100 D7
Grishipoll 78 B7
Gristhorpe 59 A46
Griston 44 F55
Gritley 105 A31
Grittenham 20 C36
Grittleton 20 C34
Grizebeck 54 A29
Grizedale 60 G29
Grobister 104 D32
Groby 41 E41
Groes 47 F26
Groes-faen 18 C26
Groesffordd 36 B18
Groesffordd Marli 47 E26
Groeslon 46 G20
Groes-lwyd 38 D27
Grogport 73 F13
Groigearraidh 84 A3
Gromford 35 C59
Gronant 47 D26
Groombridge 13 C51
Grosmont N.Y. 63 F44
Grosmont Gwe. 28 F29
Grotaig 88 B22
Groton 34 D55
Grouville 3 G18
Grove Dor. 9 G32
Grove Oxf. 21 B39
Grove Not. 51 E43
Grove Kent 25 E58
Grove Park 23 D50
Grovesend 17 D21
Gruids 96 A21
Gruinart Flats 72 D8
Gruline 79 D11
Grundcruie 82 E26
Grundisburgh 35 C57
Gruting 107 C38
Grutness 107 B38
Gualachulain 80 C16
Guardbridge 83 F30
Guarlford 29 D33
Guay 82 C25
Gubbergill 60 G26
Guestling Green 14 F54
Guestling Thorn 14 F54
Guestwick 44 C55
Guide Post 71 E38
Guilden Morden 33 D48
Guilden Sutton 48 F30
Guildford 22 G46

Guildtown 82 D27
Guilsborough 31 A42
Guilsfield 38 D28
Guisborough 63 E41
Guiseley 57 E37
Guist 44 C55
Guith 104 C31
Guiting Power 30 F36
Gulberwick 107 D40
Gullane 76 B30
Gulval 2 E10
Gulworthy 4 C20
Gumfreston 16 D16
Gumley 41 F42
Gunby Lcn. 42 C45
Gunby Hum. 58 F43
Gundleton 11 A42
Gunn 6 B22
Gunnerside 61 G35
Gunnerton 70 F34
Gunness 52 A44
Gunnislake 4 C20
Gunnista 107 C40
Gunter's Bridge 12 D45
Gunthorpe Nfk 44 B56
Gunthorpe Not. 41 A42
Gunville 11 F40
Gunwalloe 2 F12
Gurnard 11 E40
Gurney Slade 19 G32
Gurnos 18 A23
Gussage All Saints 9 C35
Gussage St Michael 9 C35
Guston 15 C58
Gutcher 106 C41
Guthrie 83 B31
Guyhirn 43 E50
Guynd 83 C31
Guy's Head 43 C50
Guy's Marsh 9 B34
Guyzance 71 C37
Gwaelod-y-garth 18 C26
Gwaenysgor 47 D26
Gwaithla 28 C27
Gwalchmai 46 E19
Gwaun-Cae-Gurwen 27 G23
Gwaun-leision 17 C22
Gwaynynog 47 F26
Gwbert 26 C17
Gweek 2 F13
Gwehelog 19 A29
Gwenddwr 27 D26
Gwennap 2 D13
Gwenter 2 G13
Gwernaffield 47 F27
Gwernesney 19 A29
Gwernogle 17 A21
Gwernymynydd 48 F28
Gwersyllt 48 G29
Gwespyr 47 D26
Gwinear 2 E11
Gwithian 2 D11
Gwyddelwern 37 A26
Gwyddgrug 17 A20
Gwystre 27 B26
Gwytherin 47 F24
Gyfelia 38 A29
Gyffin 47 E23
Gyre 105 A29
Gyrn Goch 36 A19

H

Habberley 38 E29
Habrough 52 A47
Haccombe 5 D24
Hacconby 42 C47
Haceby 42 B46
Hacheston 35 C59
Hackenthorpe 51 D39
Hackford 44 E56
Hackforth 62 G38
Hackland 104 D29
Hackleton 31 C43
Hacklinge 15 B59
Hackness Ork. 105 B29
Hackness N.Y. 63 G45
Hackney 23 C49
Hackthorn 52 D45
Hackthorpe 61 D31
Hadden 77 G33
Haddenham Cbs. 33 A50
Haddenham Bkh. 22 A43
Haddington Ltn. 76 C30
Haddington Lcn. 52 F44
Haddiscoe 45 F60
Haddon 42 F47
Hademore 40 E37
Hadfield 50 C36
Hadham Cross 33 G50
Hadham Ford 33 F50
Hadleigh Sfk 34 D56
Hadleigh Esx 24 C54
Hadley 39 D32
Hadley End 40 C37
Hadley Wood 23 B48

Hadlow 23 G52
Hadlow Down 13 D51
Hadnall 38 C31
Hadstock 33 D51
Hadzor 29 B35
Haffenden Quarter 14 C54
Hafod-Dinbych 47 G24
Hafodunos 47 F24
Haggate 56 F34
Haggbeck 69 F30
Haggs 75 C23
Hagley H.&W. 28 D31
Hagley H.&W. 40 G34
Hagnaby 53 F49
Hagworthingham 53 F49
Haigh 49 B32
Haighton Green 55 F31
Haile 60 F26
Hailes 30 E36
Hailey Oxf. 30 G39
Hailey Hfs. 23 A49
Hailey Oxf. 21 C42
Hailsham 13 F51
Hail Weston 32 B47
Haimer 103 B27
Hainault 23 B50
Hainford 45 D58
Hainton 52 D47
Haisthorpe 59 C47
Halam 51 G42
Halbeath 75 B27
Halberton 7 D25
Halcro 103 B28
Hale G.M. 49 D33
Hale Sry 22 G44
Hale Ham. 10 C37
Hale Bank 48 D30
Halebarns 49 D33
Hales Nfk 45 F59
Hales Stf. 39 B33
Halesowen 40 G35
Hales Place 15 B57
Hale Street 23 G52
Halesworth 35 A59
Halewood 48 D30
Halford War. 30 D38
Halford Shr. 38 G30
Halfpenny Green 40 F34
Halfway S.Y. 51 D40
Halfway Dyf. 27 E24
Halfway Brk. 21 E39
Halfway Dyf. 17 A22
Halfway House 38 D29
Halfway Houses 25 D55
Half Way Inn 7 G26
Halghton Mill 38 A29
Halifax 57 G36
Halistra 93 E8
Halkirk 103 C27
Halkyn 47 E27
Hall 74 E20
Halland 13 E51
Hallaton 42 F43
Hallatrow 19 F32
Hallbankgate 61 A31
Hall Dunnerdale 60 G28
Hallen 19 C31
Hall Green 40 G37
Hallin 93 F8
Halling 24 E52
Hallington Lcn. 53 D48
Hallington Nor. 70 F35
Hall of the Forest 38 G28
Halloughton 51 G42
Hallow 29 C34
Hallow Heath 29 C34
Hallrule 70 B31
Halls 76 C32
Hallsands 5 G24
Hall's Green 33 F48
Hall's Tenement 61 A31
Halltoft End 43 A49
Hallworthy 4 B17
Halmer End 39 A33
Halmore 19 A32
Halmyre Mains 75 F27
Halnaker 12 F45
Halsall 48 A29
Halse Nmp. 31 D41
Halse Som. 7 C27
Halsetown 2 E10
Halsham 59 G48
Halsinger 6 B21
Halstead Lei. 42 E43
Halstead Esx 34 E53
Halstead Kent 23 E50
Halstock 8 D31
Haltham 53 F48
Halton Lan. 55 C31
Halton Clw. 38 B29
Halton Bkh. 32 G44
Halton Nor. 70 G35
Halton Che. 48 D31
Halton Gill 56 B34
Halton East 57 D36
Halton Holegate 53 F50

Halton Lea Gate 61 A32
Halton West 56 D34
Haltwhistle 70 G32
Halvergate 45 E60
Halwell 5 E23
Halwill 6 F19
Halwill Junction 6 F20
Ham Glo. 19 B32
Ham Som. 8 B28
Ham Hgh. 103 A28
Ham She. 106 A38
Ham G.L. 22 D47
Ham Wts. 21 E39
Ham Kent 15 B59
Hamble 11 D40
Hambleden 22 C43
Hambledon Sry 12 C45
Hambledon Ham. 11 C42
Hambleton Lan. 55 E29
Hambleton N.Y. 58 F41
Hambleton Moss Side 55 E29
Hambridge 8 B29
Hambrook Avon 19 D32
Hambrook W.S. 11 D43
Hameringham 53 F49
Hamerton 32 A47
Ham Green H.&W. 29 B35
Ham Green Avon 19 D31
Ham Hill 24 E52
Hamilton 74 E22
Hamlet 7 F27
Hammer 12 C44
Hammerpot 12 F46
Hammersmith & Fulham 22 D47
Hammerwich 40 E36
Hammerwood 13 C50
Hammond Street 23 A49
Hammoon 9 C33
Hamnavoe She. 106 E40
Hamnavoe She. 106 D40
Hamnavoe She. 107 D39
Hamnavoe She. 106 D38
Hampden Park 13 F52
Hampnett 30 G36
Hampole 51 B40
Hampreston 10 E36
Hampstead 23 C48
Hampstead Norreys 21 D41
Hampsthwaite 57 D38
Hamptom Heath 48 B46
Hampton H.&W. 30 D36
Hampton Shr. 39 G33
Hampton G.L. 22 E47
Hampton Bishop 28 E31
Hampton in Arden 40 G38
Hampton Lovett 29 B34
Hampton Lucy 30 C38
Hampton on the Hill 30 B38
Hampton Poyle 31 G40
Hamptworth 10 B38
Hamsey 13 E50
Hamstall Ridware 40 D36
Hamstead W.M. 40 F36
Hamstead I.o.W. 10 E39
Hamstead Marshall 21 E39
Hamsterley Drm 62 C37
Hamsterley Drm 62 A36
Ham Street 8 A31
Hamstreet 14 D55
Hamworthy 9 E35
Hanbury Stf. 40 C37
Hanbury H.&W. 29 B35
Hanbury Woodend 40 C37
Hanchurch 40 A34
Handbridge 48 F30
Handcross 13 D48
Handforth 49 D34
Handley 48 G30
Handsacre 40 D36
Handsworth W.M. 40 F36
Handsworth S.Y. 51 D39
Handy Cross 22 B44
Hanford 40 A34
Hanging Bridge 40 A37
Hanging Langford 9 A35
Hangingshaw 69 E26
Hangleton 13 F48
Hanham 19 D32
Hankelow 39 A32
Hankerton 20 B35
Hankham 13 F52
Hanley 40 A34
Hanley Castle 29 D34
Hanley Child 29 B32
Hanley Swan 29 D34
Hanley William 29 B32
Hanlith 56 C35
Hanmer 38 B30
Hannah 53 E51
Hannington Nmp. 31 A43
Hannington Ham. 21 F41
Hannington Wts. 20 B37
Hannington Wick 20 B37
Hanslope 31 D43
Hanthorpe 42 C46
Hanwell Oxf. 31 D40

Hanwell G.L. 22 D47
Hanworth G.L. 22 D47
Hanworth Nfk. 45 B57
Happisburgh 45 B59
Happisburgh Common 45 C59
Hapsford 48 E30
Hapton Nfk. 45 F57
Hapton Lan. 56 F34
Harberton 5 E23
Harbertonford 5 E23
Harbledown 15 B56
Harborne 40 G36
Harborough Magna 31 A40
Harbottle 70 C35
Harbourneford 5 D22
Harbridge 10 D34
Harbury 30 C39
Harby Lei. 42 B43
Harby Not. 52 E44
Harcombe 7 F27
Harden 57 F36
Hardenhuish 20 D34
Hardgate 91 C33
Hardham 12 E46
Hardingham 44 E56
Hardingstone 31 C43
Hardings Wood 49 G33
Hardington 20 F33
Hardington Mandeville 8 C31
Hardington Marsh 8 D31
Hardley 11 D40
Hardley Street 45 E59
Hardmead 32 D45
Hardraw 61 G34
Hardstoft 51 F40
Hardway Ham. 11 D41
Hardway Som. 9 A33
Hardwick Cbs. 33 C49
Hardwick Nmp. 32 B44
Hardwick Bkh. 31 G44
Hardwick Oxf. 31 F41
Hardwick Nfk. 45 F58
Hardwick Oxf. 21 A39
Hardwicke Glo. 29 F34
Hardwicke Glo. 29 G33
Hardwicke H.&W. 28 D28
Hardy's Green 34 G55
Hareby 53 F49
Hareden 56 D32
Harefield 22 B46
Hare Green 34 F56
Hare Hatch 22 D44
Harehills 57 F39
Harelaw 75 F25
Haresceugh 61 B31
Harescombe 29 G34
Haresfield 29 G33
Hareshaw 74 F22
Hare Street Hfs. 33 F49
Hare Street Hfs. 33 F49
Harewood 57 E39
Harewood End 28 F31
Harford 5 E22
Hargate 45 F57
Hargrave Che. 48 F30
Hargrave Sfk 34 C53
Hargrave Nmp. 32 A46
Haringey 23 C49
Harker 69 G29
Harkstead 35 E57
Harlaston 40 D37
Harlaxton 42 B44
Harlech 36 B21
Harlesden 23 C48
Harleston Sfk 34 C56
Harleston Nfk 45 G58
Harlestone 31 B42
Harle Syke 56 F34
Harley 38 E31
Harleyholm 75 G25
Harlington 32 E46
Harlosh 93 G8
Harlow 33 G50
Harlow Hill 71 G36
Harlthorpe 58 F43
Harlton 33 C49
Harman's Cross 9 F35
Harmby 62 G37
Harmer Green 33 G48
Harmer Hill 38 C30
Harmondsworth 22 D46
Harmston 52 F45
Harnham 10 B37
Harnhill 20 A36
Harold Hill 23 B51
Haroldston West 16 C14
Haroldswick 106 A42
Harold Wood 23 C51
Harome 58 A42
Harpenden 32 G47
Harpford 7 F26
Harpham 29 F34
Harpley H.&W. 29 B32
Harpley Nfk 44 C53
Harpole 31 B42
Harprigg 55 A31

Harpsdale 103 C27
Harpsden 22 C43
Harpswell 52 D45
Harpurhey 49 B34
Harpur Hill 50 E36
Harrapool 86 B12
Harrietfield 82 D25
Harrietsham 14 B54
Harrington Nmp. 31 A43
Harrington Lcn. 53 E49
Harringworth 42 F44
Harris 85 E9
Harriseahead 49 G34
Harrogate 57 D38
Harrold 32 C45
Harrow Hgh. 103 A28
Harrow G.L. 22 C47
Harrowbarrow 4 C19
Harrowden 32 D46
Harrow on the Hill 22 C47
Harrow Weald 22 B47
Harston Cbs. 33 C49
Harston Lei. 42 B44
Hart 62 C40
Hartburn Nor. 62 E40
Hartburn Cle. 71 E36
Hartest 34 C54
Hartfield E.S. 13 C50
Hartfield Hgh. 94 G13
Hartford Cbs. 33 A48
Hartford Che. 49 E32
Hartfordbridge 22 F43
Hartford End 33 G52
Harthill Che. 48 G30
Harthill S.Y. 51 D40
Harthill Ltn 75 D25
Hartington 50 F37
Hartland 6 C18
Hartlebury 29 A34
Hartlepool 62 C40
Hartley Kent 14 D53
Hartley Kent 23 E51
Hartley Cum. 61 F33
Hartley T.&W. 71 F39
Hartley Wespall 21 F42
Hartley Wintney 22 F43
Hartlip 24 E54
Harton T.&W. 71 G39
Harton N.Y. 58 C43
Harton Shr. 38 G30
Hartpury 29 F33
Hartrigge 70 A32
Hartshill 41 F39
Hartshorne 40 C38
Hartsop 60 E29
Hartwell Bkh. 31 G43
Hartwell Nmp. 31 D43
Hartwell E.S. 13 C50
Hartwood 75 E24
Harvel 24 E52
Harvington H.&W. 30 D36
Harvington H.&W. 29 A34
Harwell 21 C40
Harwich 35 E58
Harwood Drm 61 C34
Harwood G.M. 49 A33
Harwood Dale 63 G45
Harwood on Teviot 69 C30
Harworth 51 C41
Hasbury 40 G35
Hascombe 12 C46
Haselbech 31 A42
Haselbury Plucknett 8 C30
Haseley 30 B38
Haselor 30 C37
Hasfield 29 F34
Hasguard 16 D14
Haskayne 48 B29
Hasketon 35 C58
Hasland 51 F39
Haslemere 12 C44
Haslingden 56 G33
Haslingden Grane 56 G33
Haslingfield 33 C49
Haslington 49 G33
Hassall 49 G33
Hassall Green 49 G33
Hassall Street 15 C56
Hassendean 70 A31
Hassingham 45 E59
Hassocks 13 E48
Hassop 50 E38
Haster 103 C29
Hastigrow 103 B28
Hastingleigh 15 C56
Hastings 14 G54
Hastingwood 23 A50
Hastoe 22 A45
Haswell 62 B39
Hatch Bfd. 32 D47
Hatch Ham. 21 F42
Hatch Beauchamp 8 B28
Hatch End 22 B47
Hatch Green 8 C28
Hatching Green 32 G47
Hatchmere 48 E31

Hatcliffe 53 B48
Hatfield Hfs. 23 A48
Hatfield H.&W. 28 C31
Hatfield S.Y. 51 B42
Hatfield Broad Oak 33 G51
Hatfield Heath 33 G50
Hatfield Hyde 33 G48
Hatfield Peverel 34 G53
Hatfield Woodhouse 51 B42
Hatford 21 B39
Hatherden 21 F39
Hatherleigh 6 E21
Hathern 41 C40
Hatherop 20 A37
Hathersage 50 D38
Hatherton Stf. 40 D35
Hatherton Che. 39 A32
Hatley St George 33 C48
Hatt 4 D19
Hattingley 11 A42
Hatton G.L. 22 D47
Hatton War. 30 B38
Hatton Shr. 38 F30
Hatton Lcn. 52 E47
Hatton Che. 48 D31
Hatton Grm. 99 F36
Hatton Dby 40 B37
Hatton Castle 99 E33
Hattoncrook 91 A34
Hatton Heath 48 F30
Hatton of Fintray 91 B34
Haugham 53 D49
Haugh Head 71 A36
Haughhead 74 C21
Haughley 34 B56
Haughley Green 34 B56
Haughley New Street 34 B55
Haugh of Glass 98 F29
Haugh of Urr 65 D23
Haughs 98 E30
Haughton Not. 51 E42
Haughton Stf. 40 C34
Haughton Shr. 38 D31
Haughton Shr. 38 C29
Haughton Shr. 39 F32
Haughton Green 49 C35
Haughton Le Skerne 62 E38
Haughton Moss 48 G31
Haultwick 33 F49
Haunn 84 C3
Haunton 40 D38
Hauxley 71 C38
Hauxton 33 C50
Havant 11 D42
Haven 28 C29
Haven Side 59 G49
Havenstreet 11 E41
Haverfordwest 16 C14
Haverhill 33 D52
Haverigg 54 B27
Havering 23 C51
Havering-atte-Bower 23 B51
Haversham 32 D44
Haverthwaite 55 A29
Haverton Hill 62 D40
Hawarden 48 F29
Hawbridge 29 D34
Hawbush Green 34 G53
Hawcoat 54 B27
Hawen 26 D19
Hawes 56 A34
Hawford 29 B34
Hawick 68 B30
Hawkchurch 8 D29
Hawkedon 34 C53
Hawkenbury 13 C51
Hawkeridge 20 F34
Hawkerland 7 G26
Hawkesbury 20 C33
Hawkesbury Upton 20 C33
Hawkes End 40 G38
Hawkhill 71 B38
Hawkhurst 14 D53
Hawkinge 15 C57
Hawkley 11 B43
Hawkridge 7 B24
Hawkshead 60 G29
Hawksland 75 G24
Hawkswick 56 B35
Hawksworth W.Y. 57 E37
Hawksworth Not. 42 A43
Hawkwell Nor. 71 F36
Hawkwell Esx 24 B54
Hawley Ham. 22 F44
Hawley Kent 23 D51
Hawling 30 F36
Hawnby 63 G41
Haworth 57 F36
Hawstead 34 C54
Hawthorn Drm 62 B40
Hawthorn Wts. 20 E34
Hawthorn Hill Brk. 22 D44
Hawthorn Hill Lcn. 53 G48
Hawthorpe 42 C46
Hawton 51 G43
Haxby 58 D42

Haxey 51 C43	Hebden Bridge 56 G35	Heniarth 37 E26	Heversham 55 A30	High Garrett 34 F53
Haxted 23 G50	Hebden Green 49 F32	Henlade 8 B28	Hevingham 45 C57	High Gate 56 G35
Haydock 48 C31	Hebing End 33 F49	Henley Som. 8 A30	Hewas Water 3 D15	High Grange 62 C37
Haydon 9 C32	Hebron Nor. 71 E37	Henley Shr. 28 A31	Hewell Grange 30 B36	High Green Nfk 45 E57
Haydon Bridge 70 G34	Hebron Dyf. 16 B17	Henley Sfk 35 C57	Hewell Lane 29 B35	High Green H.&W. 29 D34
Haydon Wick 20 C37	Heck 69 E26	Henley W.S. 12 D44	Hewelsfield 19 A31	High Green S.Y. 51 C39
Haye 4 C19	Heckfield 22 E43	Henley Corner 8 A30	Hewelsfield Common 19 A31	Highgreen Manor 70 D33
Hayes G.L. 23 E49	Heckfield Green 35 A57	Henley-in-Arden 30 B37	Hewish Avon 19 E29	High Halden 14 D54
Hayes G.L. 22 C46	Heckfordbridge 34 F55	Henley-on-Thames 22 C43	Hewish Som. 8 D30	High Halstow 24 D53
Hayfield Dby 50 D36	Heckingham 45 F59	Henley Park 22 F45	Hewton 6 F20	High Ham 8 A30
Hayfield Hgh. 103 B27	Heckington 42 A47	Henley's Down 14 F53	Hexham 70 G35	High Harrington 60 D25
Hayfield Str. 80 E16	Heckmondwike 57 G38	Henllan Dyf. 26 D19	Hextable 23 D51	High Harrogate 57 D39
Hayhillock 83 C30	Heddington 20 E35	Henllan Clw. 47 F26	Hexton 32 E47	High Hatton 39 C32
Haylands 11 E41	Heddle 104 E29	Henllan Amgoed 16 B17	Hexworthy 5 C22	High Hawsker 63 F44
Hayle 2 E11	Heddon-on-the-Wall 71 G37	Henllys 19 B28	Heybridge Esx 24 B52	High Heath 39 C32
Hay Mills 40 G37	Hedenham 45 F59	Henlow 32 E47	Heybridge Esx 24 A54	High Hesket 61 B30
Haynes 32 D46	Hedge End 11 C40	Hennock 7 G24	Heybridge Basin 24 A54	High Hoyland 50 B38
Haynes Church End 32 D46	Hedgerley 22 C45	Henny Street 34 E54	Heybrook Bay 4 F20	High Hunsley 59 F45
Hay-on-Wye 28 D28	Hedging 8 B28	Henryd 47 E23	Heydon Cbs. 33 D50	High Hurstwood 13 D50
Hayscastle 16 B14	Hedley on the Hill 62 A36	Henry's Moat 16 B16	Heydon Nfk 45 C57	High Hutton 58 C43
Hayscastle Cross 16 B15	Hednesford 40 D35	Hensall 58 G41	Heydour 42 B45	High Ireby 60 C28
Hay Street 33 F49	Hedon 59 G48	Henshaw 70 G33	Heylipoll 78 C5	High Kilburn 57 A40
Hayton Not. 51 D43	Hedsor 22 C45	Hensingham 60 E25	Heylor 106 D38	Highlane Dby 51 D39
Hayton Cum. 61 A40	Heeley 51 D39	Henstead 45 G60	Heysham 55 C29	Highlane Che. 49 F34
Hayton Hum. 58 E44	Heglibister 107 B39	Henstridge 9 C32	Heyshaw 57 C37	High Lane Dby 41 A40
Hayton Cum. 60 B26	Heighington Lcn. 52 F46	Henstridge Ash 9 B32	Heyshott 12 E44	High Lane H.&W. 29 B32
Hayton's Bent 38 G31	Heighington Drm 62 D38	Henstridge Marsh 9 B33	Heyside 48 B35	High Laver 23 A51
Haytor Vale 5 C23	Heights of Brae 96 E20	Henton Oxf. 22 A43	Heytesbury 20 G34	Highlaws 60 B27
Haywards Heath 13 D49	Heilam 102 B20	Henton Som. 19 G30	Heythrop 30 F39	Highleadon 29 F33
Haywood Oaks 51 G41	Heithat 69 E27	Henwick 29 C34	Heywood G.M. 49 A34	High Legh 49 D33
Hazelbank Str. 80 G17	Heiton 76 G32	Henwood 4 C18	Heywood Wts. 20 F34	Highleigh 12 G44
Hazelbank Str. 75 F24	Hele Dev. 6 A21	Heogan 107 C40	Hibaldstow 52 B45	High Leven 62 E40
Hazelbury Bryan 9 D33	Hele Dev. 7 E25	Heol-ddu 17 C21	Hickleton 51 B40	Highley 39 G33
Hazeleigh 24 A53	Helebridge 6 E18	Heol Lly Goden 28 F27	Hickling Not. 41 C42	High Littleton 19 F32
Hazel End 33 F50	Hele Bridge 6 E21	Heol Senni 27 F25	Hickling Nfk 45 C60	High Lorton 60 D27
Hazeley 22 F43	Hele Lane 7 D23	Heol-y-Cyw 18 C25	Hickling Green 45 C60	Highmead 26 D20
Hazel Grove 49 D35	Helensburgh 74 B19	Hepburn 71 A36	Hickling Heath 45 C60	High Melton 51 B41
Hazelhead 91 C34	Helford 2 F13	Hepple 70 C35	Hickstead 13 D48	Highmoor Cross 21 C42
Hazelside 68 A23	Helhoughton 44 C54	Hepscott 71 E38	Hidcote Boyce 30 D37	Highmoor Hill 19 C30
Hazelslade 40 D36	Helions Bumpstead 33 D52	Heptonstall 56 G35	High Ackworth 51 A40	Highnam 29 G33
Hazelton Walls 82 E29	Helland 4 C16	Hepworth Sfk 34 A55	Higham Dby 51 G39	High Newton 55 A30
Hazelwood G.L. 23 E50	Hellandbridge 4 C16	Hepworth W.Y. 50 B37	Higham Sfk 34 E56	High Newton by-the-Sea 71 A38
Hazelwood Dby 41 A39	Hellesdon 45 D58	Herbrandston 16 D14	Higham Sfk 34 B53	High Nibthwaite 60 G28
Hazlefield 65 F23	Hellidon 31 C40	Herdicott 6 F19	Higham Kent 24 D53	High Offley 39 C33
Hazlemere 22 B44	Hellifield 56 D34	Hereford 28 E30	Higham Lan. 56 F34	High Ongar 23 A51
Hazlerigg 71 F38	Hellingly 13 E51	Heriot 76 E29	Higham Dykes 71 F37	High Onn 40 D34
Hazleton 30 G36	Hellington 45 E59	Hermiston 75 C27	Higham Ferrers 32 B45	High Risby 52 A45
Headbourne Worthy 11 A40	Hellister 107 C39	Hermitage Bor. 69 D30	Higham Gobion 32 E46	High Roding 33 G51
Head Bridge 6 D22	Helmdon 31 D41	Hermitage D.&G. 65 D24	Higham on the Hill 41 F39	High Salvington 12 F47
Headcorn 14 C54	Helmingham 35 C57	Hermitage Dor. 9 D32	Highampton 6 E20	High Shaw 61 G34
Headington 21 A41	Helmsdale 103 G26	Hermitage Brk. 21 D41	Higham Wood 23 G52	High Spen 71 G37
Headlam 62 D37	Helmshore 56 G33	Hermitage W.S. 11 D43	High Balantyre 80 F16	Highstead 25 E57
Headless Cross 29 B35	Helmsley 58 A42	Hermon Dyf. 17 A18	High Beach 28 B49	Highsted 28 E54
Headley Ham. 12 C44	Helperby 57 C40	Hermon Dyf. 17 A19	High Bentham 56 C32	High Street Cnw. 3 C15
Headley Sry 22 F47	Helperthorpe 59 B45	Hermon Gwy. 46 F19	High Bickington 6 C22	High Street Kent 14 D53
Headley Ham. 21 E40	Helpringham 42 A47	Herne 25 E57	High Birkwith 56 B34	High Street Sfk 35 C60
Headley Down 12 C44	Helpston 42 E47	Herne Bay 25 E57	High Blantyre 74 E22	Highstreet Green 34 E53
Headon 51 E43	Helsby 48 E30	Herne Common 25 E57	High Bonnybridge 75 C24	High Street Green 34 C56
Heads Nook 61 A30	Helston 2 F12	Herner 6 C21	High Borgue 65 E22	Hightae 69 F26
Heage 51 G39	Helstone 4 B16	Hernhill 25 E56	High Bradfield 50 C38	High Throston 62 C40
Healaugh N.Y. 62 G36	Helton 61 D30	Herodsfoot 4 D17	High Bray 6 B22	Hightown Mer. 48 B28
Healaugh N.Y. 57 E40	Helwith Bridge 56 C34	Herongate 24 B52	Highbridge 19 G28	Hightown Che. 49 F34
Heald Green 49 D34	Hemblington 45 D59	Heronsgate 22 B45	Highbrook 13 C49	High Toynton 53 F48
Heale 6 A22	Hemborough Post 5 E24	Heron's Ghyll 13 D50	High Brooms 23 G51	High Trewhitt 71 C36
Healey G.M. 49 A34	Hemel Hempstead 22 A46	Herriard 21 G42	High Bullen 6 C20	Highway 20 D36
Healey Drm 62 A36	Hemingbrough 58 F42	Herringfleet 45 F60	Highburton 50 A37	Highweek 5 C24
Healey N.Y. 57 A37	Hemingby 53 E48	Herring's Green 32 D46	High Burton 57 A38	High Wollaston 19 B31
Healeyfield 62 B36	Hemingford Abbots 33 A48	Herringswell 33 B52	Highbury 19 G32	Highworth 20 B37
Healing 52 A47	Hemingford Grey 33 B48	Herrington 62 A39	Highbury Vale 41 A41	High Wray 60 G29
Heamoor 2 E10	Hemingstone 35 C57	Hersden 25 E57	High Buston 71 C38	High Wych 33 G50
Heanish 78 C6	Hemington Nmp. 42 G46	Hersham Sry 22 E46	High Callerton 71 F37	High Wycombe 22 B43
Heanor 41 A40	Hemington Lei. 41 C40	Hersham Cnw. 6 E18	High Catton 58 D43	Hilborough 44 E53
Heanton Punchardon 6 B21	Hemington Som. 20 F33	Herstmonceux 13 E52	Highclere 21 E40	Hilcott 20 F37
Heanton Satchville 6 D21	Hemley 35 D58	Herston Ork. 105 B30	Highcliffe 10 E38	Hildenborough 23 G51
Heapey 56 G32	Hemlington 62 E40	Herston Dor. 10 G36	High Cogges 21 A39	Hilden Park 23 G51
Heapham 52 D44	Hempholme 59 E46	Hertford 33 G49	High Coniscliffe 62 E38	Hildersham 33 D51
Hearthstane 69 A26	Hempnall 45 F58	Hertford Heath 33 G49	High Cross Hfs. 33 G49	Hilderstone 40 B35
Heasley Mill 6 B22	Hempnall Green 45 F58	Hertingfordbury 33 G48	High Cross Ham. 11 B43	Hilderthorpe 59 C47
Heaste 86 C12	Hempriggs 97 E26	Hesketh Bank 55 G30	High Cross Bank 40 D38	Hilfield 9 D32
Heath 51 F40	Hempriggs House 103 D29	Hesketh Lane 56 E32	High Easter 33 G52	Hilgay 44 F52
Heath and Reach 32 F45	Hempstead Nfk 45 C60	Hesket Newmarket 60 C29	High Ellington 57 A37	Hill 19 B32
Heathcot 91 C34	Hempstead Nfk 45 B57	Heskin Green 48 A31	High Entercommon 62 F39	Hillam 58 G41
Heathcote Dby 50 F37	Hempstead Esx 33 E52	Hesleden 62 C40	Higher Ansty 9 D33	Hillbeck 61 E33
Heathcote Stf. 39 C32	Hempsted 29 G33	Hesleyside 70 E33	Higher Ashton 7 G24	Hillberry 54 E25
Heath End Ham. 22 G44	Hempton Oxf. 31 E40	Heslington 58 D42	Higher Ballam 55 F29	Hillborough 25 E57
Heath End Ham. 21 E41	Hempton Nfk 44 C54	Hessay 58 D41	Higher Blackley 49 B34	Hillbrae Grm. 98 E31
Heather 41 D39	Hemsby 45 D60	Hessenford 4 E18	Higher Brixham 5 E25	Hillbrae Grm. 99 F34
Heathfield Dev. 5 C23	Hemswell 52 C45	Hessett 34 B55	High Ercall 38 D31	Hillbrae Grm. 91 A33
Heathfield Som. 7 C27	Hemsworth 51 A40	Hessle 59 G46	Higher Cheriton 7 E26	Hill Brow 11 B43
Heathfield E.S. 13 D51	Hemyock 7 D27	Hest Bank 55 C30	Higher Gabwell 5 D25	Hill Chorlton 39 B33
Heath Hayes 40 D35	Henbury Che. 49 E34	Heston 22 D47	Higher Green 49 B33	Hill Dyke 43 A49
Heath Hill 39 D33	Henbury Avon 19 D31	Heswall 48 D28	Higher Kingcombe 8 D31	Hillend Grm. 98 E30
Heath House 19 G30	Henderland 65 C24	Hethe 31 F41	Higher Tale 7 E26	Hill End Drm 62 C36
Heathrow (London) Airport 22 D46	Hendersyde Park 77 G33	Hetherington 70 F33	Higher Thrushgill 56 C32	Hill End N.Y. 57 D36
Heathton 39 F33	Hendon T.&W. 62 A39	Hethersett 45 E57	Higher Town 2 A11	Hillend Ltn. 76 D28
Heath Town 40 F35	Hendon G.L. 23 C48	Hethersgill 69 G30	Higher Walreddon 4 C20	Hillend Fife 75 B27
Heatley 49 D32	Hendy 17 D21	Hethpool 70 A34	Higher Walton Che. 49 D32	Hill End Fife 75 A26
Heaton T.&W. 71 G38	Heneglwys 46 E20	Hett 62 C38	Higher Walton Lcn. 55 G31	Hillesden 31 F42
Heaton Stf. 49 F35	Henfield 12 E47	Hetton 56 D35	Higher Whatcombe 9 D34	Hillesley 20 C33
Heaton Lan. 55 C30	Henford 6 F19	Hetton-le-Hole 62 B39	Higher Whitley 49 D32	Hillfarrance 7 C27
Heaton Moor 49 C34	Hengherst 14 D55	Heugh 71 F36	Higher Wych 38 A30	Hillhead 5 E25
Heaverham 23 F51	Hengoed M.G. 18 B27	Heugh-head Grm. 90 D30	High Etherley 62 D37	Hill Head 11 D41
Heaviley 49 D34	Hengoed Pow. 28 C28	Heugh-head Grm. 90 B29	Highfield T.&W. 62 A37	Hillhead of Auchentumb 99 D35
Hebburn 71 G38	Hengoed Clw. 38 B28	Heveningham 35 A59	Highfield Hum. 58 F43	Hillhead of Cocklaw 99 E36
Hebden 57 C36	Hengrave 34 B54	Hever 23 G50	Highfield Str. 74 E19	Hilliard's Cross 40 D37
	Henham 33 F51		Highfields 33 C49	Hilliclay 103 B27

Hillingdon 22 C46
Hillington 44 C53
Hillmorton 31 A41
Hillockhead *Grm.* 90 B30
Hillockhead *Grm.* 90 C29
Hill of Beath 75 A27
Hill of Fearn 97 D24
Hillowton 65 D23
Hillpound 11 C41
Hill Ridware 40 D36
Hillsford Bridge 7 A23
Hillside *Grm.* 97 E27
Hillside *Tay.* 91 G32
Hillside *She.* 107 A39
Hillside *Grm.* 91 D35
Hills Town 51 F40
Hillswick 106 E38
Hill Top *W.Y.* 51 A39
Hill Top *Ham.* 11 D40
Hill View 9 E35
Hillway 11 F42
Hillwell 107 D37
Hilmarton 20 D36
Hilperton 20 F34
Hilsea 11 D42
Hilton *Dor.* 9 D33
Hilton *Cum.* 61 D33
Hilton *Hgh.* 97 C25
Hilton *Grm.* 99 F35
Hilton *Cle.* 62 E40
Hilton *Drm* 62 D37
Hilton *Dby.* 40 B38
Hilton *Shr.* 39 F33
Hilton *Cbs.* 33 B48
Hilton of Cadboll 97 D24
Hilton of Delnies 97 F24
Himbleton 29 C35
Himley 40 F34
Hincaster 55 A31
Hinckley 41 F40
Hinderclay 34 A56
Hinderwell 63 E43
Hindford 38 B29
Hindhead 12 C44
Hindley 49 B32
Hindley Green 49 B32
Hindlip 29 C34
Hindolveston 44 C56
Hindon 9 A34
Hindringham 44 B55
Hingham 44 E56
Hinstock 39 C32
Hintlesham 34 D56
Hinton *Nmp.* 31 C41
Hinton *H.&W.* 28 E29
Hinton *Shr.* 38 E30
Hinton *Avon* 20 D33
Hinton *Ham.* 10 E38
Hinton Admiral 10 E37
Hinton Ampner 11 B42
Hinton Blewett 19 F31
Hinton Charterhouse 20 F33
Hinton-in-the-Hedges 31 E41
Hinton Martell 9 D35
Hinton on the Green 29 D35
Hinton Parva 21 C38
Hinton St George 8 C30
Hinton St Mary 9 C33
Hinton Waldrist 21 B39
Hints *Shr.* 29 A32
Hints *Stf.* 40 E37
Hinwick 32 B45
Hinxhill 15 C56
Hinxton 33 D50
Hinxworth 33 D48
Hipperholme 57 G37
Hirn 91 D33
Hirnant 37 C26
Hirst 71 E38
Hirst Courtney 58 G42
Hirwaen 47 F27
Hirwaun 18 A25
Hiscott 6 C21
Histon 33 B50
Hitcham *Sfk* 34 C55
Hitcham *Bkh.* 22 C45
Hitchin 32 E47
Hither Green 23 D49
Hittisleigh 7 F23
Hixon 40 C35
Hoaden 15 B58
Hoaldalbert 28 F29
Hoar Cross 40 C37
Hoarwithy 28 F31
Hoath 25 E57
Hobarris 28 A28
Hobbister 105 A29
Hobbs Lots Bridge 43 E49
Hobkirk 70 B31
Hobland Hall 45 E61
Hobson 62 A37
Hoby 41 D42
Hockering 44 D56
Hockerton 51 G42
Hockley 24 B54
Hockley Heath 30 A37

Hockliffe 32 F45
Hockwold cum Wilton 44 G53
Hockworthy 7 D26
Hoddesdon 23 A49
Hoddlesden 56 G33
Hodgeston 16 E16
Hodnet 39 C32
Hodthorpe 51 E41
Hoe 44 D55
Hoe Gate 11 C42
Hoff 61 E32
Hoffleet Stow 43 B48
Hoggeston 31 F43
Hoggie 98 C31
Hogha Gearraidh 92 D2
Hoghton 55 G31
Hognaston 50 G38
Hogsthorpe 53 E51
Holbeach 43 C49
Holbeach Bank 43 C49
Holbeach Clough 43 C49
Holbeach Drove 43 D49
Holbeach Hurn 43 C49
Holbeach St Johns 43 D49
Holbeach St Marks 43 B49
Holbeach St Matthew 43 B50
Holbeck 51 E41
Holberrow Green 29 B35
Holbeton 5 F22
Holborn 23 C49
Holborough 24 E53
Holbrook *Sfk* 35 E57
Holbrook *Dby.* 41 A39
Holburn 77 G36
Holbury 11 D40
Holcombe *Som.* 19 G32
Holcombe *Dev.* 5 C25
Holcombe Rogus 7 D26
Holcot 31 B43
Holden 56 E33
Holdenby 31 B42
Holdenhurst 10 E37
Holdgate 38 G31
Holdingham 42 A46
Holditch 8 D29
Hole-in-the-Wall 28 F31
Hole Park 14 D54
Hole Street 12 E47
Holford 7 A27
Holker 55 B29
Holkham 44 A54
Hollacombe 6 E19
Holland *Ork.* 104 A30
Holland *Ork.* 104 D32
Holland *Sry* 23 F50
Holland-on-Sea 35 G58
Hollandstoun 104 A33
Hollee 69 G28
Hollesley 35 D59
Hollingbourne 14 B54
Hollingbury 13 F49
Hollington *E.S.* 14 F53
Hollington *Stf.* 40 B36
Hollington *Dby.* 40 B38
Hollingworth 49 C35
Hollins 49 B33
Hollinsclough 50 F36
Hollins Green 49 C32
Hollinswood 39 E33
Hollinwood 38 B31
Hollocombe 6 D21
Holloway 51 G39
Hollowell 31 A42
Hollybush *H.&W.* 29 E33
Hollybush *Gwe.* 18 A27
Hollybush *Str.* 67 B19
Holly End 43 E51
Holly Green 29 D34
Hollym 59 G49
Holm 69 D28
Holmbury St Mary 22 G47
Holmbush *W.S.* 13 C48
Holmbush *Cnw.* 4 E16
Holme *Cbs.* 42 G47
Holme *Cum.* 55 B31
Holme *W.Y.* 50 B36
Holme *Not.* 52 G44
Holmebridge 9 F34
Holme Chapel 56 G34
Holme Hale 44 E54
Holme Lacy 28 E31
Holme Marsh 28 C29
Holme next the Sea 44 A52
Holme-on-Spalding-Moor
58 F43
Holme on the Wolds 59 E45
Holme Pierrepont 41 B42
Holmer 28 D30
Holmer Green 22 B45
Holmes Chapel 49 F33
Holmesfield 50 E38
Holme's Hill 13 E51
Holmeswood 48 A29
Holmewood 51 F40
Holmfield 57 G36
Holmfirth 50 B37

Holmhead *D.&G.* 68 E23
Holmhead *Str.* 67 A21
Holm of Drumlanrig 68 D24
Holmpton 59 G49
Holmrook 60 F26
Holmsgarth 107 C40
Holmside 62 B37
Holmston 67 A19
Holmwrangle 61 B30
Holne 5 D23
Holnest 9 D32
Holsworthy 6 E19
Holsworthy Beacon 6 E19
Holt *Clw.* 48 G29
Holt *Wts.* 20 E34
Holt *H.&W.* 29 B34
Holt *Nfk* 44 B56
Holt *Dor.* 10 D36
Holtby 58 D42
Holt End *H.&W.* 30 B36
Holt End *Ham.* 11 A42
Holt Fleet 29 B34
Holt Heath *H.&W.* 29 B34
Holt Heath *Dor.* 10 D36
Holton *Som.* 9 B32
Holton *Oxf.* 21 A41
Holton *Sfk* 35 A59
Holton *Lcn.* 52 D47
Holton Heath 9 E35
Holton le Clay 53 B48
Holton le Moor 52 C46
Holton St Mary 34 E56
Holtspur 22 B45
Holtye Common 13 C50
Holwell *Dor.* 9 C32
Holwell *Hfs.* 32 E47
Holwell *Lei.* 42 C43
Holwell *Oxf.* 21 A38
Holwell *Som.* 20 G33
Holwick 61 D34
Holworth 9 F33
Holybourne 22 G43
Holy Cross 29 A34
Holymoorside 51 F39
Holyport 22 D44
Holystone 70 C35
Holytown 75 D23
Holywell *Cnw.* 2 C13
Holywell *Dor.* 8 D31
Holywell *Clw.* 47 E27
Holywell *Cbs.* 33 A49
Holywell *E.S.* 13 G52
Holywell Green 50 A36
Holywell Lake 7 D27
Holywell Row 34 A53
Holywood 68 E25
Homer 39 E32
Homersfield 45 G58
Hom Green 28 F31
Homington 10 B37
Honeyborough 16 D15
Honeybourne 30 D36
Honeychurch 6 E22
Honey Hill 25 C23
Honey Tye 34 E55
Honiley 30 A38
Honing 45 C59
Honingham 45 D57
Honington *War.* 30 D38
Honington *Sfk* 34 A54
Honington *Lcn.* 42 A45
Honiton 7 E27
Honley 50 A37
Hoo *Sfk* 35 C58
Hoo *Kent* 24 D53
Hooe *E.S.* 13 F52
Hooe *Dev.* 4 E20
Hooe Common 13 E52
Hook *G.L.* 22 E47
Hook *Ham.* 22 F43
Hook *Dyf.* 16 C15
Hook *Hum.* 58 G43
Hook *Wts.* 20 C36
Hook-a-Gate 38 E30
Hooke 8 D31
Hookgate 39 B33
Hook Green *Kent* 24 E52
Hook Green *Kent* 24 D52
Hook Green *Kent* 13 C52
Hook Norton 30 E39
Hookway 7 F24
Hookwood 23 G48
Hoole 48 F30
Hooley 23 F48
Hooton 48 E29
Hooton Levitt 51 C41
Hooton Pagnell 51 B40
Hooton Roberts 51 C40
Hopcrofts Holt 31 F40
Hope *Dby.* 50 D37
Hope *Shr.* 38 E29
Hope *Pow.* 38 E28
Hope *Clw.* 48 G29
Hope *Dev.* 5 G22
Hope Bagot 28 A31
Hope Bowdler 38 F30

Hope End Green 33 G51
Hopehouse 69 B28
Hopeman 97 E27
Hope Mansell 29 G32
Hopesay 38 G29
Hope's Green 24 C53
Hope under Dinmore 28 C30
Hopkinstown 18 B26
Hopton *Nfk* 45 E61
Hopton *Stf.* 40 C35
Hopton *Shr.* 38 C31
Hopton *Dby.* 50 G38
Hopton *Sfk* 34 A55
Hopton Cangeford 38 G31
Hopton Castle 28 A29
Hoptonheath 28 A29
Hopton Wafers 29 A32
Hopwas 40 E37
Hopwood 30 A36
Horam 13 E51
Horbling 42 B47
Horbury 50 A38
Horden 62 B40
Horderley 38 G29
Hordle 10 E38
Hordley 38 B29
Horeb *Dyf.* 17 D21
Horeb *Dyf.* 26 D19
Horfield 19 D31
Horham 35 A58
Horkesley Heath 34 F55
Horkstow 52 A45
Horley *Oxf.* 31 D40
Horley *W.S.* 23 G48
Hornblotton Green 8 A31
Hornby *N.Y.* 62 G38
Hornby *N.Y.* 62 F39
Hornby *Lan.* 55 C31
Horncastle 53 F48
Hornchurch 23 C51
Horncliffe 77 E35
Horndean *Bor.* 77 F34
Horndean *Ham.* 11 C42
Horndon 6 G21
Horndon on the Hill 24 C52
Horne 23 G49
Horniehaugh 82 A29
Horning 45 D59
Horninghold 42 F43
Horninglow 40 C38
Horningsea 33 B50
Horningsham 20 G33
Horningtoft 44 C55
Horningtops 4 D18
Hornsby 61 B30
Hornsby Gate 61 A31
Horns Cross *Dev.* 6 C19
Horns Cross *E.S.* 14 E54
Hornsea 59 E48
Hornsey 23 C48
Hornton 30 D39
Horrabridge 4 D20
Horridge 5 C23
Horringer 34 B54
Horsebridge *Dev.* 4 C20
Horse Bridge 49 G35
Horsebridge *Ham.* 10 A39
Horsebrook 40 D34
Horsehay 39 E32
Horseheath 33 D51
Horsehouse 57 A36
Horsell 22 F45
Horseman's Green 38 A30
Horseway 43 G50
Horsey 45 C60
Horsford 45 D57
Horsforth 57 F38
Horsham *H.&W.* 29 C33
Horsham *W.S.* 12 C47
Horsham St Faith 45 D58
Horsington *Lcn.* 52 F47
Horsington *Som.* 9 B32
Horsley *Dby.* 41 A39
Horsley *Glo.* 20 B34
Horsley *Nor.* 71 G36
Horsley *Nor.* 70 D34
Horsley Cross 35 F57
Horsleycross Street 35 F57
Horsleyhill 70 B31
Horsley Woodhouse 41 A39
Horsmonden 23 G52
Horspath 21 A41
Horstead 45 D58
Horsted Keynes 13 D49
Horton *Dor.* 10 D36
Horton *Bkh.* 22 D46
Horton *Lan.* 56 D34
Horton *Wts.* 20 E36
Horton *Avon* 20 C33
Horton *W.G.* 17 F20
Horton *Som.* 8 C29
Horton *Stf.* 49 G35
Horton *Bkh.* 32 G45
Horton *Nmp.* 32 C44
Horton Cross 8 C29

Horton-cum-Studley 31 G41
Horton Green 38 A30
Horton Heath 11 C40
Horton Inn 10 D36
Horton in Ribblesdale 56 B34
Horton Kirby 23 E51
Horwich 49 A32
Horwood 6 C21
Hose 42 C43
Hoses 60 G28
Hosh 81 E24
Hosta 92 D3
Hoswick 107 E40
Hotham 58 F44
Hothfield 14 C55
Hoton 41 C41
Houbie 106 C42
Hough 49 G33
Hougham 42 A44
Hough Green 48 D30
Hough-on-the-Hill 42 A44
Houghton *Cbs.* 33 A48
Houghton *Dev.* 5 F22
Houghton *Cum.* 60 A29
Houghton *W.S.* 12 E45
Houghton *Ham.* 10 A39
Houghton *Dyf.* 16 D15
Houghton Bank 62 D38
Houghton Conquest 32 D46
Houghton-le-Side 62 D38
Houghton le Spring 62 A39
Houghton on the Hill 41 E42
Houghton Regis 32 F46
Houghton St Giles 44 B55
Houlsyke 63 F43
Hound 11 D40
Hound Green 22 F43
Houndslow 76 F32
Houndwood 77 D34
Hounsdown 10 C39
Hounslow 22 D47
Hounslow Green 33 G52
Househill 97 F24
Housetter 106 D39
Houston 74 D19
Houstry 103 E27
Houstry of Dunn 103 C27
Houton 105 A29
Hove 13 F48
Hoveringham 41 A42
Hoveton 45 D59
Hovingham 58 B42
How 61 A31
How Caple 28 E31
Howden 58 G43
Howden-le-Wear 62 C37
Howe *N.Y.* 57 A39
Howe *Nfk* 45 E58
Howe *Hgh.* 103 B29
Howe *Cum.* 55 A30
Howe Green 24 A53
Howell 42 A47
How End 32 D46
Howe of Teuchar 99 E33
Howe Street *Esx* 33 G52
Howe Street *Esx* 33 E52
Howey 27 C26
Howgate 76 E28
Howgill 57 D36
Howick 71 B38
Howle 39 C32
Howlett End 33 E51
Howley 8 D28
How Man 60 F25
Hownam 70 B33
Hownam Mains 70 A33
Howpasley 69 C29
Howsham *N.Y.* 58 C43
Howsham *Hum.* 52 B46
Howtel 77 G34
Howton 28 F29
Howwood 74 D20
Hoxa 105 B30
Hoxne 35 A57
Hoy 103 B28
Hoylake 47 D27
Hoyland 51 B39
Hoyland Swaine 50 B38
Hubberholme 56 B34
Hubbert's Bridge 43 A48
Huby *N.Y.* 58 C41
Huby *N.Y.* 57 E38
Hucclecote 29 G34
Hucking 14 B54
Hucknall 41 A41
Huddersfield 50 A37
Huddington 29 C35
Hudscott 6 C22
Hudswell 62 F37
Huggate 58 D44
Hugglescote 41 D40
Hughenden Valley 22 B44
Hughley 38 F31
Hugh Town 2 A10
Hugmore 48 G29
Huish *Dev.* 6 D21

Huish *Wts.* 20 E37
Huish Champflower 7 C26
Huish Episcopi 8 B29
Huisinis 100 F6
Hulcott 32 G44
Hulland 40 A38
Hullavington 20 C34
Hullbridge 24 B54
Hulme End 50 G37
Hulme Walfield 49 F34
Hulver Street 45 G60
Humber Court 28 C31
Humberside Airport 52 B46
Humberston 53 B49
Humberstone 41 E42
Humbie 76 D30
Humbleton *Hum.* 59 F48
Humbleton *Nor.* 70 A35
Humby 42 B46
Hume 76 F32
Humehall 76 F32
Humshaugh 70 F34
Huna 103 A29
Huncoat 56 F33
Huncote 41 F41
Hundalee 70 B32
Hunderthwaite 62 D35
Hundleby 53 F49
Hundleton 16 D15
Hundon 34 D53
Hundred Acres 11 C41
Hundred End 55 G30
Hundred House 28 C27
Hungarton 41 E42
Hungerford *Ham.* 10 C37
Hungerford *Bkh.* 21 E39
Hungerford Newtown 21 D39
Hunglader 93 D9
Hunningham 30 B39
Hunny Hill 11 F40
Hunsdon 33 G49
Hunsingore 57 D40
Hunsonby 61 C31
Hunspow 103 A27
Hunstanton 44 A52
Hunstanworth 61 B35
Hunston *Sfk* 34 B55
Hunston *W.S.* 12 F44
Hunstrete 19 E32
Hunt End 30 B36
Huntercombe End 21 C42
Hunters Forstal 25 E57
Hunter's Quay 73 C17
Hunterston 73 E17
Huntford 70 C32
Hunt House 63 G44
Huntingdon 33 A48
Huntingfield 35 A59
Huntingford 9 B33
Huntington *H.&W.* 28 C28
Huntington *N.Y.* 58 D42
Huntington *Stf.* 40 D35
Huntingtower 82 E26
Huntley 29 G33
Huntly 98 E31
Huntlywood 76 F31
Hunton *N.Y.* 62 G37
Hunton *Kent* 14 C53
Hunton *Ham.* 11 A40
Huntonbridge 22 A46
Hunt's Cross 48 D30
Huntsham 7 C25
Huntshaw Cross 6 C21
Huntspill 19 G28
Huntworth 8 A28
Hunwick 62 C37
Hunworth 44 B56
Hurdsfield 49 E35
Hurley *War.* 40 F38
Hurley *Brk.* 22 C44
Hurley Bottom 22 C44
Hurlford 74 G20
Hurliness 105 C28
Hurn 10 E37
Hursley 11 B40
Hurst *Brk.* 22 D43
Hurst *G.M.* 49 B35
Hurst *N.Y.* 62 F34
Hurstbourne Priors 21 G40
Hurstbourne Tarrant 21 F39
Hurst Green *E.S.* 14 E53
Hurst Green *Lan.* 56 F32
Hurstpierpoint 13 E48
Hurstway Common 28 D28
Hurstwood 56 F34
Hurtmore 22 G45
Hurworth-on-Tees 62 E38
Hury 61 D35
Husabost 93 F7
Husbands Bosworth 41 G42
Husborne Crawley 32 E45
Husthwaite 58 B41
Huthwaite 51 G40
Huttoft 53 E51
Hutton *Bor.* 77 E34
Hutton *Avon* 19 F29

Hutton *Cum.* 60 D30
Hutton *Esx* 24 B52
Hutton *Lan.* 55 G30
Hutton Bonville 62 F39
Hutton Buscel 59 A45
Hutton Conyers 57 B39
Hutton Cranswick 59 D46
Hutton End 60 C30
Hutton Henry 62 C40
Hutton-le-Hole 63 G42
Hutton Magna 62 E37
Hutton Roof *Cum.* 60 C29
Hutton Roof *Cum.* 55 B31
Hutton Rudby 62 F40
Hutton Sessay 57 B40
Hutton Wandesley 58 D41
Huxley 48 F31
Huxter *She.* 107 A41
Huxter *She.* 107 B39
Huyton 48 C30
Hycemoor 54 A26
Hyde *G.M.* 49 C35
Hyde *Glo.* 20 A34
Hyde Heath 22 B45
Hyde Lea 40 D34
Hydestile 22 G45
Hyndford Bridge 75 F25
Hyndlee 70 C31
Hynish 78 D5
Hyssington 38 F28
Hythe *Ham.* 11 D40
Hythe *Kent* 15 D57
Hythe End 22 D46
Hythie 99 D36
Hyton 54 A26

I

Ianstown 98 C30
Ibberton 9 D33
Ible 50 G38
Ibsley 10 D37
Ibstock 41 D39
Ibstone 22 B43
Ibthorpe 21 F39
Ibworth 21 F41
Icelton 19 E29
Ickburgh 44 F53
Ickenham 22 C46
Ickford 21 A42
Ickham 15 B57
Ickleford 32 E47
Icklesham 14 F54
Ickleton 33 D50
Icklingham 34 A53
Ickwell Green 32 D47
Icomb 30 F37
Idbury 30 F38
Iddesleigh 6 E21
Ide 7 F24
Ideford 5 C24
Ide Hill 23 F50
Iden 14 E55
Iden Green *Kent* 14 D53
Iden Green *Kent* 14 D54
Idlicote 30 D38
Idmiston 10 A38
Idridgehay 40 A38
Idrigil 93 E9
Idstone 21 C38
Idvies 83 C31
Iffley 21 A41
Ifield 13 C48
Ifieldwood 13 C48
Ifold 12 C46
Iford 13 F50
Ifton Heath 38 B29
Ightfield 38 B31
Ightham 23 F51
Iken 35 C60
Ilam 50 G37
Ilchester 8 B31
Ilderton 70 A35
Ilford 23 C50
Ilfracombe 6 A20
Ilkeston 41 A40
Ilketshall St Andrew 45 G59
Ilketshall St Lawrence 45 G59
Ilketshall St Margaret 45 G59
Ilkley 57 E36
Illey 40 G35
Illington 44 G55
Illingworth 57 G36
Illogan 2 D12
Illston on the Hill 42 F43
Ilmer 22 A43
Ilmington 30 D37
Ilminster 8 C29
Ilsington 17 E21
Ilston 17 E21
Ilton *N.Y.* 57 B37
Ilton *Som.* 8 C29
Imachar 73 F14
Immeroin 81 F21
Immingham 52 A47
Immingham Dock 53 A48

Impington 33 B50
Ince 48 E30
Ince Blundell 48 B29
Ince-in-Makerfield 48 B31
Inch 91 F32
Inchbare 83 A31
Inchberry 98 D28
Inchbraoch 83 B32
Inchgrundle 90 F29
Inchindown 96 D22
Inchinnan 74 D20
Inchkinloch 102 D21
Inchlaggan 87 D17
Inchlumpie 96 D21
Inchmarlo 91 D32
Inchnabobart 90 E28
Inchnacardoch Hotel 88 C19
Inchnadamph 101 F18
Inchock 83 C32
Inchrory 90 C27
Inchture 82 E28
Inchvuilt 87 A18
Inchyra 82 E27
Indian Queens 3 C15
Inerval 72 F9
Ingatestone 24 A52
Ingbirchworth 50 B38
Ingerthorpe 57 C38
Ingestre 40 C35
Ingham *Lcn.* 52 D45
Ingham *Sfk* 34 A54
Ingham *Nfk* 45 C59
Ingleby 41 C39
Ingleby Arncliffe 62 F40
Ingleby Barwick 62 E40
Ingleby Cross 62 F40
Ingleby Greenhow 63 F41
Inglesbatch 19 E32
Inglesham 20 B37
Ingleton *Drm.* 62 D37
Ingleton *N.Y.* 56 B32
Inglewhite 55 F31
Ingmire Hall 61 G32
Ingoe 71 F36
Ingoldmells 53 F51
Ingoldsby 42 B45
Ingon 30 C38
Ingram 70 B35
Ingrave 24 B52
Ingrow 57 F36
Ings 60 G30
Ingst 19 C31
Ingworth 45 B57
Inistrynich 80 E16
Injebreck 54 E25
Inkberrow 29 C35
Inkhorn 99 F35
Inkpen 21 E39
Inkstack 103 A28
Innellan 73 D17
Innergellie 83 G31
Innerleithen 76 G29
Innerleven 82 G29
Innermessan 64 D16
Innerwick *Tay.* 81 C21
Innerwick *Ltn.* 76 C32
Inninbeg 79 C12
Innsworth 29 F34
Insch 91 A32
Insh 89 D24
Inshore 101 A19
Inskip 55 F30
Instow 6 B20
Intake 51 D39
Intwood 45 E57
Inver *Hgh.* 97 C24
Inver *Hgh.* 103 F27
Inver *Str.* 80 C15
Inver *Tay.* 82 C26
Inver *Grm.* 90 D28
Inverailort 86 F13
Inveralligan 94 F14
Inverallochy 99 C36
Inveran 96 B21
Inveraray 80 G16
Inverardoch Mains 81 G23
Inverardran 80 E19
Inverarish 86 A11
Inverarity 83 C30
Inverarnan 80 F18
Inverasdale 94 C13
Inverbain 94 F13
Inverbeg 74 A19
Inverbervie 91 F34
Inverbroom 95 C17
Inverbrough 88 B23
Invercassley 96 A20
Inverchaolain 73 C16
Invercharnan 80 C17
Inverchorachan 80 F17
Inverchoran 95 F18
Invercreran 80 C15
Inverdruie 89 C24
Inverebrie 99 F35
Invereen 88 A23
Invererne 97 E26

Inveresk 76 C29
Inverey 89 F26
Inverfarigaig 88 B20
Invergarry 87 D18
Invergelder 90 D28
Invergeldie 81 E23
Invergloy 87 F18
Invergordon 96 E22
Invergowrie 82 D29
Inverguseran 86 D13
Inverhadden 81 B22
Inverherive 80 E19
Inverhope 102 B20
Inverie 86 D13
Inverinan 80 F15
Inverinate 86 B15
Inverkeilor 83 C32
Inverkeithing 75 B26
Inverkeithny 98 E32
Inverkip 74 C18
Inverkirkaig 101 F16
Inverlael 95 C17
Inverlauren 74 B18
Inverliever 79 G14
Inverliver 80 D16
Inverlochlarig 81 F20
Inverlochy 80 E17
Inverlussa 72 B12
Inver Mallie 87 F17
Invermay 82 F26
Invermoriston 88 C19
Invernaver 102 B22
Inverneil 73 B14
Inverness 96 G22
Inverness (Dalcross) Airport 96 F23
Invernettie 99 E37
Invernoaden 73 A17
Inveroran Hotel 80 C18
Inverquharity 82 B29
Inverquhomery 99 E36
Inverroy 87 F18
Inversanda 80 B15
Invershiel 86 C15
Inversnaid Hotel 80 G19
Invertrossachs 81 G21
Inverugie 99 E36
Inveruglas 80 G18
Inveruglass 88 D23
Inverurie 91 A33
Invervar 81 C22
Invervegain 73 C16
Invery Ho. 91 D32
Inverythan 99 E33
Inwardleigh 6 F21
Inworth 34 G54
Iochda 92 G3
Iping 33 C46
Ipplepen 5 D24
Ipsden 21 C42
Ipstones 50 G36
Ipswich 35 D57
Irby 48 D28
Irby in the Marsh 53 F50
Irby upon Humber 52 B47
Irchester 32 B45
Ireby *Cum.* 60 C28
Ireby *Lan.* 56 B32
Ireland *Ork.* 105 A29
Ireland *She.* 107 E39
Ireleth 55 B28
Ireshopeburn 61 C34
Irlam 49 C33
Irnham 42 C46
Iron Acton 19 C32
Ironbridge 39 E32
Iron Cross 30 C36
Ironside 99 D34
Ironville 51 G40
Irstead 45 C59
Irthington 69 G30
Irthlingborough 32 B45
Irton 59 A46
Irvine 74 G18
Isauld 103 B25
Isbister *Ork.* 104 D28
Isbister *Ork.* 104 E29
Isbister *She.* 107 A41
Isbister *She.* 106 C39
Isfield 13 E50
Isham 32 A44
Ishriff 79 D12
Islay Ho. 72 D9
Isle Abbotts 8 B29
Isle Brewers 8 B29
Isleham 3 A52
Isle of Dogs 23 D49
Isle of Whithorn 64 G20
Isleornsay (Eilean Iarmain) 86 C12
Islesburgh 107 A39
Isleworth 22 D47
Isley Walton 41 C40
Islibhig 100 E6
Islington 23 C48

Islip *Nmp.* 32 A45
Islip *Oxf.* 31 G41
Isombridge 38 D31
Istead Rise 24 E52
Itchen 11 C40
Itchen Abbas 11 A41
Itchen Stoke 11 A41
Itchingfield 12 D47
Itchington 19 C32
Itteringham 45 B57
Itton 6 F22
Itton Common 19 B30
Ivegill 60 B29
Ivelet 61 G35
Iver 22 C46
Iver Heath 22 C45
Iveston 62 A37
Ivinghoe 32 G45
Ivinghoe Aston 32 G45
Ivington 28 C30
Ivington Green 28 C30
Ivybridge 5 E21
Ivychurch 15 E56
Ivy Hatch 23 F51
Ivy Todd 44 E54
Iwade 25 E55
Iwerne Courtney or Shroton 9 C34
Iwerne Minster 9 C34
Ixworth 34 B55
Ixworth Thorpe 34 A54

J

Jack Hill 57 D37
Jackstown 99 F33
Jackton 74 E21
Jacobstow 4 A18
Jacobstowe 6 E21
Jameston 16 E16
Jamestown *Hgh.* 96 F20
Jamestown *Str.* 74 B19
Jamestown *D.&G.* 69 D29
Janefield 96 F23
Janetstown 103 B26
Jarrow 71 G39
Jarvis Brook 13 D51
Jasper's Green 33 F52
Jawcraig 75 C24
Jayes Park 22 G47
Jaywick 35 G57
Jedburgh 70 B32
Jeffreyston 16 D16
Jemimaville 96 E22
Jersay 75 D24
Jerviswood 75 F24
Jesmond 71 G38
Jevington 13 F51
Jodrell Bank 49 E33
Johnby 60 C30
John 'o' Groats 103 A29
John's Cross 14 E53
Johnshaven 91 G33
Johnston 16 C15
Johnstone 74 D20
Johnstonebridge 69 D26
Johnstone Castle 74 D20
Johnston Mains 91 G33
Johnstown *Clw.* 38 A29
Johnstown *Dyf.* 17 C19
Joppa *Ltn.* 76 C29
Joppa *Str.* 67 B19
Jordans 22 B45
Jordanston 16 A14
Jordanstone 82 C28
Jump 51 B39
Juniper Green 75 D27
Jura Ho. 72 D10
Jurby East 54 D25
Jurby West 54 D25

K

Kaber 61 E33
Kaimes 76 D28
Kalnakill 94 F12
Kames *Str.* 73 C15
Kames *Str.* 79 F14
Kames *Str.* 68 A22
Kea 2 D13
Keadby 52 A44
Keal Cotes 53 F49
Kearsley 49 B33
Kearstwick 55 A31
Kearton 62 G35
Kearvaig 101 A18
Keasden 56 C33
Kebholes 98 D32
Keckwick 48 D31
Keddington 53 D49
Kedington 33 D52
Kedleston 40 A38
Keelby 52 B47
Keele 40 A34
Keeley Green 32 D46
Keeres Green 33 G51

Keeston 16 C15
Keevil 20 F35
Kegworth 41 C40
Kehelland 2 D11
Keig 91 B32
Keighley 57 E36
Keil *Hgh.* 80 B15
Keil *Str.* 66 C12
Keilhill 98 D32
Keillmore 72 B12
Keillor 82 C28
Keillour 82 E25
Keills 72 D10
Keils 72 D11
Keinton Mandeville 8 A31
Keir 75 A23
Keir Mill 68 D24
Keisby 42 C46
Keisley 61 D32
Keiss 103 B29
Keith 98 D30
Keithick 82 D27
Keithmore 98 F29
Keithock 83 A31
Kelbrook 56 E35
Kelby 42 A45
Keld *N.Y.* 61 F34
Keld *Cum.* 61 E31
Keldholme 58 A43
Keldy Castle 63 G43
Kelfield *N.Y.* 58 F41
Kelfield *Hum.* 52 B44
Kelham 51 G43
Kellan 79 C11
Kellas *Grm.* 97 F27
Kellas *Tay.* 83 D30
Kellaton 5 G24
Kelleth 61 F32
Kelleythorpe 59 D46
Kelling 44 A56
Kellington 58 G41
Kelloe 62 C39
Kelloholm 68 B23
Kelly *Dev.* 6 G19
Kelly *Cnw.* 4 C16
Kelly Bray 4 C19
Kelmarsh 31 A43
Kelmscott 21 B38
Kelsale 35 B59
Kelsall 48 F31
Kelsay 72 E8
Kelshall 33 E49
Kelsick 60 A27
Kelso 77 G33
Kelstedge 51 F39
Kelstern 53 C48
Kelston 19 E32
Keltneyburn 81 C23
Kelton 65 C25
Kelty 75 A27
Kelvedon 34 G54
Kelvedon Hatch 23 B51
Kelynack 2 E9
Kemback 83 F30
Kemberton 39 E33
Kemble 20 B35
Kemerton 29 E35
Kemeys Commander 19 A29
Kemeys Inferior 19 B29
Kemnay 91 B33
Kempley 29 F32
Kempley Green 29 F32
Kempsey 29 D34
Kempsford 20 B37
Kempshott 21 G41
Kempston 32 D46
Kempston Church End 32 D46
Kempston Hardwick 32 D46
Kempton 38 G29
Kemp Town 13 F49
Kemsing 23 F51
Kemsley 24 E54
Kenardington 14 D55
Kenchester 28 D30
Kencott 21 A38
Kendal 61 G30
Kenderchurch 28 F29
Kenfig 18 C23
Kenfig Hill 18 C24
Kenilworth 30 A38
Kenknock *Cen.* 81 D20
Kenknock *Tay.* 81 C21
Kenley *Shr.* 38 E31
Kenley *G.L.* 23 F49
Kenmore *Hgh.* 94 F13
Kenmore *Tay.* 81 C23
Kenmore *Str.* 80 G16
Kenmore *W.I.* 100 G8
Kenn *Dev.* 7 G25
Kenn *Avon* 19 E30
Kennacraig 73 D14
Kennards House 4 B18
Kennavay 93 B8
Kennerleigh 7 E23
Kennerty 91 D32
Kennet 75 A25

Kennethmont 90 A31
Kennett 33 B52
Kennford 7 G25
Kenninghall 44 G56
Kennington *Oxf.* 21 A40
Kennington *Kent* 14 C55
Kennoway 82 G29
Kennyhill 33 A52
Kensaleyre 93 F10
Kensington & Chelsea 23 D48
Kensworth 32 G46
Kensworth Common 32 G46
Kentallen 80 B15
Kentchurch 28 F29
Kentford 33 B52
Kentisbeare 7 E26
Kentisbury 6 A22
Kentisbury Ford 6 A22
Kentmere 60 F30
Kenton *T.&W.* 71 G38
Kenton *Sfk* 35 B57
Kenton *Dev.* 7 G25
Kentra 79 A12
Kents Bank 55 B30
Kent's Green 29 F33
Kent's Oak 10 B39
Kent Street *E.S.* 14 F53
Kent Street *Kent* 23 F52
Kenwick 38 B29
Kenwyn 3 D14
Keoldale 101 B19
Keppanach 80 A16
Keppoch *Str.* 74 C19
Keppoch *Hgh.* 86 B15
Keprigan 66 B12
Kepwick 62 G40
Keresley 40 G38
Kerne Bridge 28 G31
Kerridge 49 E35
Kerris 2 F10
Kerry 38 G27
Kerrycroy 73 D17
Kerrysdale 94 D14
Kerry's Gate 28 E29
Kersall 51 F43
Kersey 34 D55
Kershopefoot 69 E30
Kerswell 7 E26
Kerswell Green 29 D34
Kesgrave 35 D58
Kessingland 45 G61
Kessingland Beach 45 G61
Kestle Mill 3 C14
Keston 23 E49
Keswick *Nfk* 45 E58
Keswick *Nfk* 45 B59
Keswick *Cum.* 60 D28
Ketsby 53 E49
Kettering 32 A44
Ketteringham 45 E57
Kettins 82 D28
Kettlebaston 34 D55
Kettlebridge 82 G28
Kettlebrook 40 E37
Kettleburgh 35 C58
Kettleholm 69 F27
Kettleness 63 E44
Kettleshulme 49 E35
Kettlesing 57 D37
Kettlesing Bottom 57 D38
Kettlestone 44 B55
Kettlethorpe 52 E44
Kettletoft 104 C32
Kettlewell 56 B35
Ketton 42 E45
Kew 22 D47
Kewstoke 19 E29
Kexbrough 50 B38
Kexby *Lcn.* 52 D44
Kexby *N.Y.* 58 D43
Key Green 49 F34
Keyham 41 E42
Keyhaven 10 E39
Keyingham 59 G48
Keymer 13 E49
Keynsham 19 E32
Keysoe 32 B46
Keysoe Row 32 B46
Key's Toft 53 G50
Keyston 32 A46
Keyworth 41 B41
Kibblesworth 62 A38
Kibworth Beauchamp 41 F42
Kibworth Harcourt 41 F42
Kidbrooke 23 D50
Kiddal Lane End 57 F40
Kiddemore Green 40 E34
Kidderminster 29 A33
Kiddington 30 F39
Kidlington 31 G40
Kidmore End 21 D42
Kidsdale 64 G20
Kidsgrove 49 G34
Kidstones 56 A35

Kidwelly (Cydwelli) 17 D20
Kiel Crofts 79 D14
Kielder 70 D32
Kilbarchan 74 D19
Kilbeg 86 D12
Kilberry 73 D13
Kilbirnie 74 E18
Kilblaan 80 F17
Kilbraur 102 G24
Kilbrenan 79 C10
Kilbride *Hgh.* 86 B11
Kilbride *Str.* 79 E14
Kilbride *Str.* 73 D16
Kilbride Farm 73 D15
Kilbridemore 73 A15
Kilburn *Dby.* 41 A39
Kilburn *N.Y.* 57 B40
Kilby 41 F42
Kilcadzow 75 F24
Kilchattan 73 E17
Kilchenzie 66 A12
Kilcheran 79 D14
Kilchlaren 72 E8
Kilchoan *Str.* 79 A10
Kilchoan *Hgh.* 79 F13
Kilchrenan 80 E16
Kilchrist 86 B12
Kilconquhar 83 G30
Kilcot 29 F32
Kilcoy 96 F21
Kilcreggan 74 B18
Kildale 63 F41
Kildary 96 D23
Kildavie 66 B13
Kildermorie Lodge 96 D20
Kildonan 66 A16
Kildonan Lodge 103 F25
Kildonnan 85 F10
Kildrochet 64 E16
Kildrummy 90 B30
Kildwick 57 E36
Kilfinan 73 C15
Kilfinnan 87 E18
Kilgetty 16 D17
Kilgwrrwg Common 19 B30
Kilham *Hum.* 59 C46
Kilham *Nor.* 77 G34
Kilkenneth 78 C5
Kilkenny 29 G35
Kilkerran *Str.* 67 C19
Kilkerran *Str.* 66 B13
Kilkhampton 6 D18
Killamarsh 51 D40
Killay 17 E22
Killbeg 79 C11
Killean *Str.* 80 G16
Killean *Str.* 72 F12
Killearn 74 B21
Killellan 66 B12
Killen 96 F22
Killerby 62 D37
Killichonan 81 B21
Killichronan 79 C11
Killiechanate 87 F18
Killiecrankie 81 A24
Killiehuntly 88 E23
Killiemor 79 D10
Killilan 86 A15
Killimster 103 C28
Killin *Hgh.* 97 A34
Killin *Cen.* 81 D21
Killinallan 72 C8
Killinghall 57 D38
Killington 56 A32
Killingworth 71 F38
Killochyett 76 F30
Killocraw 66 A12
Killunaig 79 E10
Killundine 79 C11
Kilmacolm 74 D19
Kilmaha 80 G15
Kilmahog 81 G21
Kilmalieu 79 B14
Kilmaluag 93 D10
Kilmany 82 E29
Kilmarie 86 C11
Kilmarnock 74 G20
Kilmartin 73 A14
Kilmaurs 74 F20
Kilmelford 79 F14
Kilmersdon 19 F32
Kilmeston 11 B41
Kilmichael 66 A12
Kilmichael Glassary 73 A14
Kilmichael of Inverlussa 73 B13
Kilmington *Wts.* 9 A33
Kilmington *Dev.* 8 E28
Kilmington Street 9 A33
Kilmorack 96 G20
Kilmore *Hgh.* 86 D12
Kilmore *Str.* 79 E14
Kilmory *Hgh.* 85 D9
Kilmory *Hgh.* 86 G11
Kilmory *Str.* 73 B13
Kilmory *Str.* 72 C12
Kilmote 103 G25

Kilmuir *Hgh.* 96 G22
Kilmuir *Hgh.* 93 D9
Kilmuir *Hgh.* 96 D23
Kilmuir *Hgh.* 93 G8
Kilmun 73 B17
Kilmux 82 G29
Kilnave 72 C8
Kilndown 14 D53
Kiln Green 22 D44
Kilnhurst 51 C40
Kilninian 78 C9
Kilninver 79 E14
Kiln Pit Hill 62 A36
Kilnsea 53 A50
Kilnsey 56 C35
Kilnwick 59 E46
Kiloran 72 A9
Kilpatrick 66 A14
Kilpeck 28 E30
Kilphedir 103 G25
Kilpin 58 G43
Kilrenny 83 G31
Kilsby 31 A41
Kilspindie 82 E28
Kilstay 64 G17
Kilsyth 74 C22
Kiltarlity 96 G20
Kilton *Cle.* 63 E42
Kilton *Som.* 7 A27
Kiltyre 81 D22
Kilvaxter 93 E9
Kilve 7 A27
Kilverstone 44 G54
Kilvington 42 A43
Kilwinning 74 F18
Kimberley *Nfk* 44 E56
Kimberley *Not.* 41 A40
Kimblesworth 62 B38
Kimble Wick 22 A43
Kimbolton *H.&W.* 28 B31
Kimbolton *Cbs.* 32 B46
Kimcote 41 G41
Kimmeridge 9 F34
Kimmerston 77 G35
Kimpton *Hfs.* 32 G47
Kimpton *Ham.* 21 G38
Kinaldy 83 F30
Kinblethmont 83 C32
Kinbrace 102 E24
Kinbreack 86 E15
Kinbuck 81 G23
Kincaldrum 82 C29
Kincaple 83 F30
Kincardine *Fife* 75 B25
Kincardine *Hgh.* 96 C21
Kincardine O'Neil 90 D31
Kinclaven 82 D27
Kincorth 91 C35
Kincraig *Grm.* 91 A35
Kincraig *Hgh.* 89 D24
Kincraigie 82 C25
Kindallachan 82 C25
Kindrogan Field Centre 82 A26
Kinellar 91 B33
Kineton *Glo.* 30 F36
Kineton *War.* 30 C39
Kineton Green 40 G36
Kinfauns 82 E27
Kingarth 73 E16
Kingcoed 19 A30
Kingerby 52 C46
Kingham 30 F38
Kingholm Quay 65 C25
Kinghorn 76 B28
Kinglassie 76 A28
Kingoodie 82 E29
Kingsand 4 E20
Kingsbarns 83 F31
Kingsbridge *Dev.* 5 F23
Kingsbridge *Som.* 7 B25
King's Bromley 40 D37
Kingsburgh 93 F9
Kingsbury *G.L.* 22 C47
Kingsbury *War.* 40 F38
Kingsbury Episcopi 8 B30
Kings Caple 28 F31
Kingscavil 75 C26
Kingsclere 21 F41
King's Cliffe 42 F45
Kingscote 20 B33
Kingscott 8 D27
King's Coughton 30 C36
Kingscross 66 A16
Kingsdale 82 G29
Kingsdon 8 B30
Kingsdown 15 C59
Kingseat 75 A27
Kingsey 22 A43
Kingsfold *Dyf.* 16 E15
Kingsfold *W.S.* 12 C47
Kingsford *Grm.* 91 C34
Kingsford *Grm.* 90 B31
Kingsford *Grm.* 99 E33
Kingsford *Str.* 74 F20
Kingsford *H.&W.* 39 G33
Kingsforth 52 A46

Kingsgate 25 D59
King's Green 29 E33
Kingsheanton 6 B21
King's Heath 40 G36
King's Hill 40 F35
Kingshouse 81 E21
Kingshouse Hotel 80 B18
Kingskerswell 5 D24
Kingskettle 82 G28
Kingsland *Gwy.* 46 D18
Kingsland *H.&W.* 28 B30
Kings Langley 22 A46
Kingsley *Che.* 48 E31
Kingsley *Stf.* 40 A35
Kingsley *Ham.* 11 A43
Kingsley Green 12 C44
King's Lynn 43 C51
Kings Meaburn 61 D32
King's Mill 3 E16
Kings Muir 76 G28
Kingsmuir 83 C30
King's Newton 41 C39
Kingsnorth 14 D55
Kingsnorth Power Station 24 D54
King's Norton *Lei.* 41 E42
King's Norton *W.M.* 30 A36
King's Nympton 6 D22
King's Pyon 28 C30
Kings Ripton 33 A48
King's Somborne 10 A39
King's Stag 9 C32
King's Stanley 20 A34
King's Sutton 31 E41
Kingstanding 40 F36
Kingsteignton 5 C24
Kingsteps 97 F24
King Sterndale 50 E36
Kingsthorne 28 E30
Kingsthorpe 31 B43
Kingston *Cbs.* 33 C49
Kingston *Grm.* 98 C29
Kingston *Dor.* 9 G35
Kingston *Ltn.* 76 B31
Kingston *Dev.* 5 F22
Kingston *Dor.* 9 D33
Kingston *Ham.* 10 D37
Kingston *Kent* 15 B57
Kingston *I.o.W.* 11 F40
Kingston *W.S.* 12 F46
Kingston Bagpuize 21 B39
Kingston Blount 22 B43
Kingston by Sea 13 F48
Kingston Deverill 9 A34
Kingstone *Som.* 8 C29
Kingstone *H.&W.* 28 E30
Kingstone *Stf.* 40 C36
Kingston Lisle 21 C39
Kingston near Lewes 13 F49
Kingston on Soar 41 C40
Kingston Russell 8 E31
Kingston Seymour 19 E29
Kingston St Mary 8 B28
Kingston Upon Hull 59 G47
Kingston upon Thames 22 D47
Kingston Warren 21 C39
Kingstown 60 A29
King's Walden 32 F47
Kingswear 5 E24
Kingswell 74 F21
Kingswells 91 C34
Kingswinford 40 G34
Kingswood *Pow.* 38 E28
Kingswood *Bkh.* 31 G42
Kingswood *War.* 30 A37
Kingswood *Glo.* 20 B33
Kingswood *Avon* 19 D32
Kingswood *Kent* 14 B54
Kingswood *Sry* 23 F48
Kingswood Common 28 C28
King's Worthy 11 A40
Kingthorpe 52 E47
Kington *H.&W.* 29 C35
Kington *H.&W.* 28 C28
Kington Langley 20 D35
Kington Magna 9 B33
Kington St Michael 20 D34
Kingussie 88 D23
Kingweston 8 A31
Kinharrachie 99 F34
Kinharvie 65 D25
Kinkell 74 C22
Kinkell Bridge 82 F25
Kinknockie 99 E35
Kinlet 39 G33
Kinloch *Hgh.* 101 E19
Kinloch *Hgh.* 79 B12
Kinloch *Tay.* 82 C27
Kinloch *Fife* 82 F28
Kinloch *Hgh.* 85 E10
Kinloch *Tay.* 82 C28
Kinloch *Hgh.* 96 D21
Kinlochan 79 A14
Kinlochard 81 G20
Kinlocharkaig 86 E15
Kinlochbeoraid 86 F14

Kinlochbervie 101 C17
Kinlocheil 86 G15
Kinlochetive 80 C16
Kinlochewe 95 E16
Kinloch Hourn 86 D15
Kinloch Laggan 88 F21
Kinlochlaich 80 C15
Kinlochleven 80 A17
Kinlochmoidart 86 G12
Kinlochmorar 86 E14
Kinlochmore 80 A17
Kinloch Rannoch 81 B22
Kinlochspelve 79 E12
Kinloss 97 E26
Kinmel Bay 47 D25
Kinmuck 91 B34
Kinnadie 99 E35
Kinnaird 82 E28
Kinneff 91 F34
Kinnelhead 69 C26
Kinnell Tay. 83 B32
Kinnell Cen. 81 D21
Kinnerley 38 C29
Kinnersley H.&W. 29 D34
Kinnersley H.&W. 28 D29
Kinnerton 28 B28
Kinnesswood 82 G27
Kinnettles 83 C30
Kinninvie 62 D36
Kinnordy 82 B29
Kinoulton 41 B42
Kinrara 89 D24
Kinross 82 G26
Kinrossie 82 D27
Kinsbourne Green 32 G47
Kinsham 28 B29
Kinsley 51 A39
Kinson 10 E36
Kintarvie 100 F8
Kintbury 21 E39
Kintessack 97 E25
Kintillo 82 F27
Kintocher 90 C31
Kinton Shr. 38 D29
Kinton H.&W. 28 A30
Kintore 91 B33
Kintour 72 E10
Kintra Str. 72 F9
Kintra Str. 78 E9
Kintradwell 97 A24
Kintraw 79 G14
Kinuachdrach 72 A12
Kinveachy 89 C24
Kinver 40 G34
Kiplaw Croft 99 F36
Kiplin 62 G38
Kipp 81 F21
Kippax 57 F39
Kippen Tay. 82 F26
Kippen Cen. 74 A22
Kippenross Ho 81 G23
Kippford or Scaur 65 E24
Kipping's Cross 23 G52
Kirbister Ork. 105 A29
Kirbister Ork. 104 D32
Kirbuster 104 D28
Kirby Bedon 45 E58
Kirby Cane 45 F59
Kirby Corner 30 A38
Kirby Cross 35 F57
Kirby Grindalythe 59 C45
Kirby Hill N.Y. 57 C39
Kirby Hill N.Y. 62 F37
Kirby Knowle 57 A40
Kirby le Soken 35 F58
Kirby Misperton 58 B43
Kirby Muxloe 41 E41
Kirby Row 45 F59
Kirby Sigston 62 G39
Kirby Underdale 58 D44
Kirby Wiske 57 A39
Kirdford 12 D46
Kirk 103 C28
Kirkabister 107 D40
Kirkandrews 65 F21
Kirkandrews-upon-Eden 60 A29
Kirkbampton 60 A28
Kirkbean 65 E25
Kirk Bramwith 51 A42
Kirkbride 60 A28
Kirkbridge 62 G38
Kirkbuddo 83 C30
Kirkburn Hum. 59 D45
Kirkburn Bor. 76 G28
Kirkburton 50 A38
Kirkby Lcn. 52 C46
Kirkby Mer. 48 C30
Kirkby N.Y. 63 F41
Kirkby Bellars 41 D42
Kirkby Fleetham 62 G38
Kirkby Green 52 G46
Kirkby in Ashfield 51 G40
Kirkby la Thorpe 42 A47
Kirkby Lonsdale 55 B31
Kirkby Malham 56 C34
Kirkby Mallory 41 E40

Kirkby Malzeard 57 B38
Kirkby Mills 58 A43
Kirkbymoorside 58 A42
Kirkby on Bain 53 F48
Kirkby Overblow 57 E39
Kirkby Stephen 61 F33
Kirkby Thore 61 D32
Kirkby Underwood 42 C46
Kirkby Wharfe 58 E41
Kirkcaldy 76 A28
Kirkcambeck 70 G31
Kirkcolm 64 D16
Kirkconnel 68 B23
Kirkconnell 65 D25
Kirkcowan 64 D19
Kirkcudbright 65 E22
Kirkdale 65 E21
Kirkdean 75 F27
Kirk Deighton 57 D39
Kirk Ella 59 G46
Kirkfieldbank 75 F24
Kirkgunzeon 65 D24
Kirk Hallam 41 B40
Kirkham N.Y. 58 C43
Kirkham Lan. 55 F30
Kirkhamgate 57 G38
Kirk Hammerton 57 D40
Kirkharle 61 A32
Kirkhaugh 61 A32
Kirkheaton W.Y. 50 A37
Kirkheaton Nor. 71 F36
Kirkhill Hgh. 96 G21
Kirkhill Grm. 98 D28
Kirkhill Tay. 91 G32
Kirkhope 69 A29
Kirkibost W.I. 100 D7
Kirkibost Hgh. 86 C11
Kirkinch 82 C28
Kirkinner 64 E20
Kirkintilloch 74 C22
Kirk Ireton 50 G38
Kirkland Cum. 60 E26
Kirkland D.&G. 69 E26
Kirkland D.&G. 68 B23
Kirkland D.&G. 68 D23
Kirkland Cum. 61 C32
Kirkland of Longcastle 64 F19
Kirk Langley 40 B38
Kirkleatham 63 D41
Kirklevington 62 E39
Kirkley 45 F61
Kirklington N.Y. 57 A38
Kirklington Not. 51 G42
Kirklinton 69 G30
Kirkliston 75 C27
Kirkmaiden 64 G16
Kirk Merrington 62 C38
Kirkmichael Str. 67 C19
Kirk Michael 54 D24
Kirkmichael Tay. 82 A26
Kirkmuirhill 75 F23
Kirknewton Ltn. 75 D26
Kirknewton Nor. 70 A34
Kirkney 98 F30
Kirk of 75 D24
Kirkoswald Str. 67 C18
Kirkoswald Cum. 61 B31
Kirkpatrick Durham 65 C23
Kirkpatrick-Fleming 69 F28
Kirk Sandall 51 B42
Kirksanton 54 A27
Kirk Smeaton 51 A41
Kirkstall 57 F38
Kirkstead 52 F47
Kirkstile Grm. 98 F31
Kirkstile D.&G. 69 D29
Kirkton Grm. 91 A32
Kirkton Hgh. 96 B23
Kirkton Hgh. 96 F23
Kirkton Grm. 98 D32
Kirkton Bor. 70 B31
Kirkton Str. 79 G13
Kirkton D.&G. 68 E25
Kirkton Hgh. 102 B24
Kirkton Tay. 83 C30
Kirkton Grm. 91 B32
Kirkton Hgh. 88 A21
Kirkton Fife 82 E29
Kirkton Tay. 82 F25
Kirktonhill 91 G32
Kirkton Manor 76 G28
Kirkton of Airlie 82 B29
Kirkton of Auchterhouse 82 D29
Kirkton of Barevan 97 G24
Kirkton of Bourtie 91 A33
Kirkton of Collace 82 D27
Kirkton of Craig 83 B32
Kirkton of Culsalmond 98 F32
Kirkton of Durris 91 D33
Kirkton of Glenbuchat 90 B29
Kirkton of Glenisla 82 A28
Kirkton of Kingoldrum 82 B29
Kirkton of Lethendy 82 C27
Kirkton of Logie Buchan 91 A35
Kirkton of Maryculter 91 D34
Kirkton of Menmuir 83 A31

Kirkton of Monikie 83 D31
Kirkton of Skene 91 C33
Kirkton of Strathmartine 82 D29
Kirkton of Tealing 82 D29
Kirktown 99 D36
Kirktown of Alvah 98 C32
Kirktown of Auchterless 99 E33
Kirktown of Deskford 98 C31
Kirktown of Fetteresso 91 E34
Kirktown of Rayne 91 A32
Kirktown of Slains 91 A36
Kirkwall 104 E30
Kirkwall Airport 105 A30
Kirkwhelpington 70 E35
Kirk Yetholm 70 A33
Kirmington 52 A47
Kirmond le Mire 52 C47
Kirn 73 C17
Kirriemuir 82 B29
Kirstead Green 45 F58
Kirtlebridge 69 F28
Kirtling 33 C52
Kirtling Green 33 C52
Kirtlington 31 G40
Kirtomy 102 B23
Kirton Lcn. 43 B48
Kirton Hgh. 86 B14
Kirton Sfk 35 E58
Kirton Not. 51 F42
Kirton End 43 B48
Kirton Holme 43 A48
Kirton in Lindsey 52 C45
Kiscadale 66 A16
Kislingbury 31 C42
Kismeblon Bridge 6 D19
Kites Hardwick 31 B40
Kitley 5 E21
Kittisford 7 C26
Kitwood 11 A42
Kiveton Park 51 D40
Klibreck 102 E21
Knabbygates 98 D31
Knaith 52 D44
Knap Corner 9 B33
Knaphill 22 F45
Knapp Som. 8 B28
Knapp Tay. 82 D28
Knapton Nfk 45 B58
Knapton N.Y. 58 D41
Knapton Green 28 C30
Knapwell 33 B49
Knaresborough 57 D39
Knarsdale 61 A32
Knaven 99 E34
Knayton 57 A40
Knebworth 33 F48
Knedlington 58 G43
Kneesall 51 F42
Kneesworth 33 D49
Kneeton 41 A42
Knelston 17 F20
Knenhall 40 B36
Knettishall 44 G55
Knightacott 6 B22
Knightcote 30 C39
Knighton Pow. 28 A28
Knighton Lei. 41 E41
Knighton Stf. 39 C33
Knighton Stf. 39 B33
Knighton Dev. 5 F21
Knighton Wts. 21 D38
Knighton Som. 7 A27
Knightwick 29 C33
Knill 28 B28
Knipoch 79 E14
Knipton 42 B44
Knitsley 62 B36
Kniveton 50 G37
Knock Cum. 61 D32
Knock Grm. 98 D31
Knock Str. 79 D11
Knockalava 73 A14
Knockally 83 A14
Knockaloe Moar 54 E24
Knockan 101 G17
Knockandhu 90 A27
Knockando 97 G27
Knockbain 96 F22
Knockban 95 E17
Knockbreck 96 C23
Knockbrex 65 F21
Knockdamph 95 B18
Knockdee 103 B27
Knockdow 73 C17
Knockdown 20 C34
Knockenkelly 66 A15
Knockentiber 74 G19
Knockfin 87 B18
Knockgray 67 D21
Knockholt 23 F50
Knockholt Pound 23 F50
Knockin 38 C29
Knocklearn 65 C23
Knocknaha 66 B12
Knocknalling 67 E21
Knock of Auchnahannet 89 A26
Knockrome 72 C11

Knocksharry 54 E24
Knockville 64 C19
Knockvologan 78 F8
Knodishall 35 B60
Knolls Green 49 E34
Knolton 38 B29
Knook 20 G35
Knossington 42 E43
Knott End-on-Sea 55 E29
Knotting 32 B45
Knotting Green 32 B46
Knottingley 57 G40
Knotty Ash 48 C30
Knotty Green 22 B45
Knowbury 28 A31
Knowe 64 C19
Knowesgate 70 E35
Knoweside 67 B18
Knowes of Elrick 98 D32
Knowetownhead 70 B31
Knowhead 99 D34
Knowle Dev. 7 E23
Knowle Dev. 7 G26
Knowle Shr. 28 A31
Knowle Dev. 6 B20
Knowle Avon 19 D31
Knowle W.M. 30 A37
Knowle Green 56 F32
Knowle Hall 19 G29
Knowl Green 34 D53
Knowl Hill 22 D44
Knowlton Kent 15 B58
Knowlton Dor. 10 C36
Knowl Wall 40 B34
Knowsley 48 C30
Knowstone 7 C24
Knucklas 28 A28
Knutsford 49 E33
Knypersley 49 G34
Kuggar 2 G13
Kyleakin 86 B13
Kyle of Lochalsh 86 B13
Kylerhea 86 B13
Kylesbeg 86 G12
Kylesknoydart 86 E13
Kylesmorar 86 E13
Kylestrome 101 E17
Kyloag 96 B22
Kynnersley 39 D32
Kyre Park 29 B32

L

Labost 100 C8
Lacasaigh 100 E9
Laceby 53 B48
Lacey Green 22 B44
Lach Dennis 49 E33
Lackford 34 A53
Lacock 20 E34
Ladbroke 31 C40
Laddingford 23 G52
Lade Bank 53 G50
Ladock 3 C14
Ladybank 82 F28
Ladycross 6 G19
Ladyfield 80 F16
Lady Hall 54 A27
Ladykirk 77 F34
Ladysford 99 C34
Lady's Green 34 C53
Laga 79 A12
Lagalochan 79 F14
Lagavulin 72 F9
Lagg Str. 72 C11
Lagg Str. 67 B18
Lagg Str. 66 A15
Laggan Hgh. 87 E18
Laggan Hgh. 88 D31
Laggan Cen. 81 F21
Laggan Str. 72 E8
Laggan Grm. 98 F29
Lagganulva 79 C10
Lagganvoulin 90 B27
Laglingarten 80 G17
Lagnalean 96 G21
Lagrae 68 B22
Laguna 82 D26
Lahill 83 G30
Laid 102 C20
Laide 84 A27
Laig 85 F10
Laight 67 B21
Lainchoil 89 C26
Laindon 24 C52
Lair 82 A27
Lairg 96 A21
Lairg Lo. 96 A21
Lairigmor 80 A16
Laithers 98 E32
Laithes 60 C30
Lake 10 A37
Lakenham 45 E58
Lakenheath 44 G52
Lakesend 43 F50
Lakeside 55 A29

Laleham 22 E46
Laleston 18 D24
Lamarsh 34 E54
Lamas 45 C58
Lamb Corner 34 E56
Lamberhurst 13 C52
Lamberhurst Quarter 13 C52
Lamberton 77 E35
Lambeth 23 D48
Lambfell Moar 54 E24
Lambley Nor. 61 A32
Lambley Not. 41 A42
Lambourn 21 D38
Lambourne End 23 B50
Lambourn Woodlands 21 D39
Lambs Green 13 C48
Lambston 16 C14
Lamellion 4 D18
Lamerton 4 C20
Lamesley 62 A38
Lamington Str. 75 G25
Lamington Hgh. 96 D23
Lamlash 73 G15
Lamloch 67 D21
Lamonby 60 C29
Lamorran 3 D14
Lampert 70 F32
Lampeter 28 D21
Lampeter Velfrey 16 C17
Lamphey 16 D15
Lamplugh 60 D26
Lamport 31 A43
Lamyatt 9 A32
Lana 6 F19
Lanark 75 F24
Lancaster 55 C30
Lanchester 62 B37
Landbeach 33 B50
Landcross 6 C20
Landerberry 91 C33
Landewednack 2 G13
Landford 10 C38
Landimore 17 E20
Landkey 6 B21
Landore 17 E22
Landrake 4 D19
Landscove 5 D23
Landshipping 16 C15
Landulph 4 D20
Landwade 33 B51
Landywood 40 E35
Laneast 4 B18
Lane-end 4 D16
Lane End Dby. 51 F40
Lane End Cum. 60 G27
Lane End Kent 23 D51
Lane End Bkh. 22 B44
Lane End Dor. 9 E34
Lane Green 40 E34
Laneham 51 E43
Lane Head Dby. 50 B37
Lane Head G.M. 49 C32
Lane Head Drm. 62 E36
Lanehead 70 E33
Laneshaw Bridge 56 E35
Langais 92 B11
Langamull 78 B9
Langar 42 B43
Langbank 74 C19
Langbar 57 D36
Langcliffe 56 C34
Langdale End 63 G45
Langdon 4 A18
Langdon Beck 61 C34
Langdon Hills 24 C52
Langdon House 5 C25
Langdyke 82 G29
Langenhoe 34 G56
Langford Bfd. 32 D47
Langford Not. 52 G44
Langford Dev. 7 E25
Langford Oxf. 21 A38
Langford Esx 24 A54
Langford Budville 7 C26
Langford End 32 C47
Langham Esx 34 E56
Langham Sfk 34 B55
Langham Lei. 42 D44
Langham Nfk 44 A56
Langham Moor 34 E55
Langho 56 F33
Langholm 69 E29
Langlands 65 E22
Langlee 70 B32
Langleeford 70 A35
Langley Brk. 22 D46
Langley Kent 14 B53
Langley W.S. 12 D44
Langley Ham. 11 D40
Langley Esx 33 E49
Langley Hfs. 33 F48
Langley War. 30 B37
Langley Dby. 41 A40
Langley Che. 49 E35
Langley Burrell 20 D35
Langley Green 40 B38

Langley Heath 14 B54
Langley Marsh 7 C26
Langley Mill 41 A40
Langley Moor 62 B38
Langley Park 62 B37
Langley Street 45 E59
Langney 13 F52
Langold 51 D41
Langore 6 G19
Langport 8 B29
Langrick 43 A48
Langridge *Dev.* 6 C21
Langridge *Avon* 20 E33
Langridgeford 6 C21
Langrigg 60 B27
Langrish 11 B42
Langriville 43 A48
Langsett 50 B38
Langshaw 76 G30
Langshawburn 69 C28
Langside 81 F23
Langskaill 104 B30
Langstone 11 D42
Langthorne 62 G38
Langthorpe 57 C39
Langthwaite 62 F35
Langtoft *Hum.* 59 C46
Langtoft *Lcn.* 42 D47
Langton *Lcn.* 53 F48
Langton *N.Y.* 58 C43
Langton *Drm* 62 E37
Langton *Lcn.* 53 E49
Langton by Wragby 52 E47
Langton Green 13 C51
Langton Herring 9 F32
Langton Long Blandford 9 D35
Langton Matravers 9 G35
Langtree 6 D20
Langwathby 61 C31
Langwell 96 A19
Langwell House 103 F26
Langworth 52 E46
Lanivet 4 D16
Lanlivery 4 E16
Lanner 2 D12
Lanreath 4 E17
Lansallos 4 E17
Lansdown 20 E33
Lanteglos 4 B16
Lanton *Nor.* 77 G35
Lanton *Bor.* 70 A32
Lapford 7 E23
Laphroaig 72 F9
Lapley 40 D34
Lapworth 30 A37
Larachbeg 79 C12
Larach na Gaibhre 73 D13
Larbert 75 B24
Larden Green 48 G31
Larg 64 C19
Largie 98 F31
Largiemore 73 B15
Largoward 83 G30
Largs 73 E17
Largue 98 E32
Largybeg 66 A16
Largymore 66 A16
Larkhall 75 E23
Lark Hall 33 C51
Larkhill 20 G37
Larling 44 G55
Larriston 70 D31
Lartington 62 E35
Lary 90 C29
Lasborough 20 B33
Lasham 21 G42
Lassington 29 F33
Lassintullich 81 B22
Lassodie 75 A27
Lasswade 76 D28
Lastingham 63 G43
Latchford 48 D31
Latchingdon 24 A54
Latchley 4 C20
Lately Common 49 C32
Lathallan Mill 83 G30
Lathbury 32 D44
Latheron 103 E27
Latheronwheel 103 E27
Lathockar 83 F30
Lathones 83 G30
Lathrisk 82 G28
Latimer 22 B46
Latteridge 19 C32
Lattiford 9 B32
Latton 20 B36
Lauchentyre 65 E21
Lauchintilly 91 B33
Lauder 76 F31
Laugharne 17 C18
Laughterton 52 E44
Laughton *Lcn.* 52 C44
Laughton *Lcn.* 42 B46
Laughton *Lei.* 41 G42
Laughton *E.S.* 13 E51
Laughton-en-le-Morthen 51 D41

Launcells 6 E18
Launcells Cross 6 E18
Launceston 6 G19
Launde Abbey 42 E44
Launton 31 F41
Laurencekirk 91 F32
Laurieston *D.&G.* 65 D22
Laurieston *Cen.* 75 C25
Lavendon 32 C44
Lavenham 34 D54
Laverhay 69 D27
Lavernock 18 E27
Laversdale 69 G30
Laverstock 10 A37
Laverstoke 21 G40
Laverton *Som.* 20 F33
Laverton *N.Y.* 57 B38
Laverton *Glo.* 30 E36
Lavister 48 G29
Law 75 E24
Lawers *Tay.* 81 E23
Lawers *Tay.* 81 D22
Lawford 34 E56
Lawhitton 6 G19
Lawkland 55 C33
Lawley 39 E32
Lawnhead 40 C34
Lawrenny 16 D15
Laws 83 D30
Lawshall 34 C54
Lawton 28 C30
Laxdale 100 D10
Laxey 54 E26
Laxfield 35 A58
Laxfirth *She.* 107 C40
Laxfirth *She.* 107 B40
Laxford Bridge 101 D18
Laxo 107 A40
Laxton *Nmp.* 42 F45
Laxton *Not.* 51 F43
Laxton *Hum.* 58 G43
Laycock 47 D36
Layer Breton 34 G55
Layer de la Haye 34 G55
Layer Marney 34 G55
Layham 34 D56
Laysters Pole 28 B31
Laytham 58 F43
Lazenby 63 D41
Lazonby 61 C31
Lea *H.&W.* 29 F32
Lea *Lcn.* 52 D44
Lea *Dby.* 51 G39
Lea *Shr.* 38 G29
Lea *Shr.* 38 E30
Lea *Wts.* 20 C35
Leac A Li 93 B7
Leachkin 96 G22
Leack 73 A16
Leadburn 76 E28
Leadenham 52 G45
Leaden Roding 33 G51
Leadgate *T.&W.* 62 A37
Leadgate *Cum.* 61 B32
Leadhills 68 B24
Leafield 30 G39
Leagrave 32 F46
Leake Common Side 53 G49
Leake Hurn's End 43 A50
Lealands 13 E51
Lealholm 63 F43
Lealt *Str.* 72 A12
Lealt *Hgh.* 93 E10
Lea Marston 40 F38
Leamington Hastings 31 B40
Leanach *Str.* 73 A16
Leanach *Hgh.* 96 G23
Leanaig 96 F21
Leanoch 97 F27
Leargybreck 72 C11
Leasgill 55 A30
Leasingham 42 A46
Leask 99 F36
Leatherhead 22 F47
Leathley 57 E38
Leaton 38 D30
Lea Town 55 F30
Leaveland 14 B55
Leavening 58 C43
Leaves Green 23 E49
Lea Yeat 56 A33
Lebberston 59 A46
Lechlade 20 B37
Lechuary 73 A14
Leck 56 B32
Leckford 10 A39
Leckfurin 102 C22
Leckgruinart 72 D8
Leckhampstead *Bkh.* 31 E42
Leckhampstead *Brk.* 21 D39
Leckhampton 29 G35
Leckie *Cen.* 74 A22
Leckie *Hgh.* 95 E16
Leckmelm 95 B17
Leckroy 88 E19
Leckwith 18 D27

Leconfield 59 E46
Ledaig 79 D14
Ledard 81 G20
Ledbeg 101 G18
Ledburn 32 F44
Ledbury 29 E32
Ledcharrie 81 E20
Ledgemoor 28 C29
Ledicot 28 B29
Ledmore *Hgh.* 101 G18
Ledmore *Str.* 79 C11
Lednagullin 102 B23
Ledsham *W.Y.* 57 F40
Ledsham *Che.* 48 E29
Ledston 57 G40
Ledwell 30 F39
Lee *Shr.* 38 B29
Lee *Dev.* 6 A20
Lee *Str.* 79 E10
Lee *Ham.* 10 C39
Lee *Lan.* 55 D31
Leebotten 107 E40
Leebotwood 38 F30
Lee Brockhurst 38 C31
Leece 55 C28
Lee Clump 22 A45
Leeds *Kent* 14 B54
Leeds *W.Y.* 57 F38
Leeds & Bradford Airport 57 E38
Leedstown 2 E12
Leeford 7 A23
Leegomery 39 D32
Leek 49 G35
Leek Wootton 30 B38
Lee Mill Bridge 5 E21
Leeming *W.Y.* 57 F36
Leeming *N.Y.* 57 A38
Leeming Bar 62 G38
Lee Moor 5 D21
Lee-on-the-Solent 11 D41
Lees *G.M.* 49 B35
Lees *Dby.* 40 B38
Leeswood 48 G28
Legars 77 F33
Legbourne 53 D49
Legerwood 76 F31
Legsby 52 D47
Leicester 41 E41
Leideag 84 E2
Leigh *Kent* 23 G51
Leigh *Wts.* 20 B36
Leigh *G.M.* 49 B34
Leigh *Shr.* 38 E29
Leigh *Glo.* 29 F34
Leigh *H.&W.* 29 C33
Leigh *Sry* 23 G48
Leigh *Dor.* 9 D32
Leigh Beck 24 C54
Leigh Common 9 A33
Leigh Delamere 20 C34
Leigh Green 14 D55
Leigh-on-Sea 24 C54
Leigh Sinton 29 C33
Leighterton 20 B33
Leighton *Som.* 20 G33
Leighton *N.Y.* 57 B37
Leighton *Shr.* 38 E31
Leighton *Pow.* 38 E28
Leighton Bromswold 32 A47
Leighton Buzzard 32 F45
Leigh upon Mendip 19 G32
Leigh Woods 19 D31
Leinthall Earls 28 B30
Leinthall Starkes 28 B30
Leintwardine 28 A29
Leire 41 G41
Leirinmore 101 B19
Leiston 35 B60
Leitfie 82 C28
Leith 76 C28
Leitholm 77 F33
Lelant 2 E11
Lelley 59 F48
Lem Hill 29 A32
Lemington 71 G37
Lemnas 99 C34
Lempitlaw 77 G33
Lemsford 32 G47
Lenchwick 30 D36
Lendalfoot 67 D17
Lendrick 81 G21
Lenham 14 B54
Lenham Heath 14 C55
Lenie 88 B21
Lenimore 73 F14
Lennel 77 F34
Lennox Plunton 65 E21
Lennoxtown 74 C22
Lenton 42 B46
Lenwade 44 D56
Lenzie 74 C22
Leoch 82 D29
Leochel-Cushnie 90 B31
Leominster 28 C30
Leonard Stanley 20 A33

Leorin 72 F9
Lepe 11 E40
Lephinchapel 73 A15
Lephinmore 73 A15
Leppington 58 C43
Lepton 50 A38
Lerags 79 E14
Lerryn 4 E17
Lerwick 107 C40
Lerwick (Tingwall) Airport 107 C40
Lesbury 71 B38
Leschangie 91 B33
Lescrow 4 E17
Leslie *Fife* 82 G28
Leslie *Grm.* 90 A31
Lesmahagow 75 G23
Lesnewth 4 A17
Lessendrum 98 E31
Lessingham 45 C59
Lessonhall 60 A27
Leswalt 64 D16
Letchmore Heath 22 B47
Letchworth 33 E48
Letcombe Bassett 21 C39
Letcombe Regis 21 C39
Letham *Fife* 82 F28
Letham *Tay.* 83 C31
Lethanhill 67 B20
Lethendy 82 E27
Lethenty 99 E33
Letheringham 35 C58
Letheringsett 44 B56
Leth Meadhanach 84 C3
Lettaford 7 G23
Letterewe 94 D15
Letterfearn 86 B14
Letter Finlay 87 E18
Lettermorar 86 E13
Lettermore *Str.* 79 C11
Lettermore *Hgh.* 102 D21
Letters 95 C17
Lettershaws 68 A24
Letterston 16 B15
Lettoch *Hgh.* 89 A26
Lettoch *Hgh.* 89 C26
Letton *H.&W.* 28 D29
Letton *H.&W.* 28 A29
Letty Green 33 G48
Letwell 51 D41
Leuchars 83 E30
Leumrabhagh 100 F9
Levedale 40 D34
Leven *Fife* 82 G29
Leven *Hum.* 59 E47
Levencorroch 66 A16
Levenhall 76 C29
Levens 55 A30
Levenshulme 49 C34
Levenwick 107 E40
Leverington 43 D50
Leverstock Green 22 A46
Leverton 43 A49
Leverton Outgate 43 A50
Levington 35 E58
Levisham 63 G44
Levishie 88 C19
Lew 21 A39
Lewannick 4 B18
Lewdown 6 G20
Lewes 13 F49
Leweston 16 B15
Lewisham 23 D49
Lewiston 88 B20
Lewknor 21 B42
Leworthy 6 B22
Lewtrenchard 6 G20
Ley *Grm.* 90 B31
Ley *Cnw.* 4 D17
Leybourne 23 F52
Leyburn 62 G37
Leycett 39 A33
Ley Green 32 F47
Leyland 55 G31
Leylodge 91 B33
Leys *Tay.* 82 D28
Leys *Grm.* 90 C30
Leys *Grm.* 99 D36
Leysdown-on-Sea 25 D55
Leysmill 83 C31
Leys of Cossans 82 C29
Leyton 23 C49
Lezant 4 C19
Lhanbryde 98 C28
Liatrie 87 A18
Libanus 27 F25
Libberton 75 F25
Liberton 76 D28
Liceasto 92 B6
Lichfield 40 E37
Lickey 29 A35
Lickey End 29 A35
Lickfold 12 D45
Liddel 105 C30
Liddesdale 79 B13
Liddington 21 C38

Lidgate *Sfk* 34 C53
Lidgate *Dby.* 50 E38
Lidlington 32 E45
Lidsing 24 E53
Lidstone 30 F39
Lienassie 86 B15
Lieurary 103 B26
Liff 82 D29
Lifton 6 G19
Liftondown 6 G19
Lighthorne 30 C39
Lightwater 22 E45
Lightwood 40 A34
Lightwood Green *Che.* 39 A32
Lightwood Green *Clw.* 38 A29
Lilbourne 31 A41
Lilburn Tower 71 A36
Lilleshall 39 D33
Lilley *Bfd.* 32 F47
Lilley *Brk.* 21 D40
Lilliesleaf 70 A31
Lillingstone Dayrell 31 E43
Lillingstone Lovell 31 D43
Lillington 9 C32
Lilliput 10 E36
Lilstock 7 A27
Limbrick 48 A31
Limbury 32 F46
Limefield 49 A33
Limehillock 98 D30
Limekilnburn 74 E22
Limekilns 75 B26
Limerigg 75 C24
Limerstone 11 F40
Limington 8 B31
Limpenhoe 45 E59
Limpley Stoke 20 E33
Limpsfield 23 F50
Linbriggs 70 C34
Linby 51 G41
Linchmere 12 C44
Lincoln 52 E45
Lincomb 29 B33
Lincombe 5 E23
Lindale 55 A29
Lindal in Furness 55 B28
Lindean 76 G30
Lindertis 82 B29
Lindfield 13 D49
Lindford 11 A43
Lindifferon 82 F28
Lindley 50 A37
Lindores 82 F28
Lindridge 29 B32
Lindsaig 73 C15
Lindsell 33 F52
Lindsey 34 D55
Linford *Ham.* 10 D37
Linford *Esx* 24 D52
Lingague 54 F24
Lingdale 63 E42
Lingen 28 B29
Lingfield 23 G49
Lingwood 45 E59
Linhead 99 D32
Linhope 69 C29
Linicro 93 E9
Linkenholt 21 F39
Linkhill 14 E54
Linkinhorne 4 C18
Linklater 105 C30
Linksness *Ork.* 104 E31
Linksness *Ork.* 105 A28
Linktown 76 A28
Linley 38 F29
Linley Green 29 C32
Linlithgow 75 C26
Linlithgow Bridge 75 C25
Linnels 70 G35
Linney 16 E14
Linn of Muick Cottage 90 E28
Linshiels 70 C34
Linsiadar 100 D7
Linsidemore 96 B21
Linslade 32 F44
Linstead Parva 35 A59
Linstock 60 A30
Linthwaite 50 A37
Lintlaw 77 E34
Lintmill 98 C30
Linton *W.Y.* 57 E39
Linton *Dby.* 40 D38
Linton *Cbs.* 33 D51
Linton *H.&W.* 29 F32
Linton *Kent* 14 C53
Linton *Bor.* 70 A33
Linton *N.Y.* 56 C35
Linton-on-Ouse 57 C40
Lintzford 62 A37
Linwood *Str.* 74 D20
Linwood *Lcn.* 52 D47
Linwood *Ham.* 10 D37
Lionacleit 92 G3
Lional 101 A11
Liphook 12 C44
Liscombe 7 B24

Liskeard 4 D18
L'Islet 3 E17
Liss 11 B43
Lissett 59 D47
Liss Forest 11 B43
Lissington 52 D46
Liston 34 D54
Lisvane 18 C27
Liswerry 19 C29
Litcham 44 D54
Litchborough 31 C42
Litchfield 21 F40
Litherland 48 C28
Litlington Cbs. 33 D48
Litlington E.S. 13 F51
Little Abington 33 D51
Little Addington 32 A45
Little Alne 30 B37
Little Amwell 33 G49
Little Assynt 101 F17
Little Aston 40 E36
Little Atherfield 10 G39
Little Ayton 63 F41
Little Baddow 24 A53
Little Badminton 20 C33
Little Ballinluig 82 B25
Little Bampton 60 A28
Little Bardfield 33 E52
Little Barford 32 C47
Little Barningham 45 B57
Little Barrington 30 G38
Little Barugh 58 A43
Little Bealings 35 D58
Littlebeck 63 F44
Little Bedwyn 21 E38
Little Bentley 35 F57
Little Berkhamsted 23 A48
Little Billing 31 B43
Little Birch 28 E31
Little Bispham 55 E28
Little Blakenham 35 D57
Little Bookham 22 B45
Littleborough G.M. 49 A35
Littleborough Not. 51 D43
Littlebourne 15 B57
Little Bowden 42 G43
Little Bradley 33 C52
Little Brampton 38 G29
Little Braxted 34 G54
Little Brechin 83 A31
Littlebredy 8 F31
Little Brickhill 32 E44
Little Bridgeford 40 C34
Little Brington 31 B42
Little Bromley 34 F56
Little Broughton 60 C26
Little Budworth 48 F31
Little Burstead 24 B52
Little Burton 59 E47
Littlebury 33 E50
Littlebury Green 33 E50
Little Bytham 42 D46
Little Carlton 53 D50
Little Casterton 42 D46
Little Catwick 59 E47
Little Cawthorpe 53 D49
Little Chalfont 22 B45
Little Chart 14 C55
Little Chesterford 33 D51
Little Cheverell 20 F35
Little Chishill 33 E50
Little Clacton 35 G57
Little Clifton 60 D26
Little Comberton 29 D35
Little Common 14 G53
Little Compton 30 E38
Little Corby 61 A30
Little Cowarne 28 C31
Little Coxwell 21 B38
Little Crakehall 62 G38
Little Creich 96 C22
Little Cressingham 44 F54
Little Crosby 48 B28
Little Cubley 40 B37
Little Dalby 42 D43
Littledean 29 G32
Little Dens 99 E36
Little Dewchurch 28 E31
Little Downham 43 G51
Little Driffield 59 D45
Little Dunham 44 D54
Little Dunkeld 82 C25
Little Dunmow 33 F52
Little Easton 33 F51
Little Eaton 41 A39
Little Ellingham 44 F56
Little End 23 A51
Little Eversden 33 C49
Little Fakenham 34 A54
Little Faringdon 20 A37
Little Fencote 62 G38
Little Fenton 58 F41
Littleferry 96 B23
Little Finborough 34 C56
Little Fransham 44 D55
Little Gaddesden 32 G45

Little Garway 28 F30
Little Gidding 42 G47
Little Glemham 35 C59
Little Gorsley 29 F32
Little Gransden 33 C48
Little Green 34 A56
Little Grimsby 53 C49
Little Gruinard 94 C15
Little Habton 58 B43
Little Hadham 33 F50
Little Hale 42 A47
Little Hallingbury 33 G50
Littleham Dev. 6 C20
Littleham Dev. 7 G26
Little Hampden 22 A44
Littlehampton 12 F46
Little Harrowden 32 A44
Little Haseley 21 A42
Little Hautbois 45 C58
Little Haven 16 C14
Little Hay 40 E36
Little Hayfield 50 D36
Little Haywood 40 C36
Little Heath 41 G39
Littlehempston 5 D24
Little Hereford 28 B31
Little Holtby 62 G38
Little Horkesley 34 E55
Little Hormead 33 F49
Little Horsted 13 E50
Little Horwood 31 E43
Little Houghton 32 C44
Littlehoughton 71 D42
Little Hucklow 50 E37
Little Hulton 49 B32
Little Hungerford 21 D41
Little Idoch 99 E33
Little Kimble 22 A44
Little Kineton 30 C39
Little Kingshill 22 B44
Little Laver 23 A51
Little Lawford 31 A40
Little Leigh 48 E31
Little Leighs 34 G53
Little Lever 49 B33
Little Ley 91 B32
Little Linford 32 D44
Little London Lcn. 53 E49
Little London Ham. 21 F39
Little London I.O.M. 54 E25
Little London Nfk 44 F53
Little London Ham. 21 F42
Little London E.S. 13 E51
Little London Nfk 43 C51
Little London Lcn. 43 C48
Little London Lcn. 43 C50
Little Longstone 50 E37
Little Malvern 29 D33
Little Maplestead 34 E54
Little Marcle 29 E32
Little Marlow 22 C44
Little Massingham 44 C53
Little Melton 45 E57
Little Mill 19 A29
Littlemill Hgh. 97 F24
Littlemill Str. 67 B20
Little Milton 21 A41
Little Missenden 22 B45
Littlemore 21 A41
Little Musgrave 61 E33
Little Ness 38 D29
Little Neston 48 E28
Little Newcastle 16 B15
Little Newsham 62 E37
Little Oakley Esx 35 F58
Little Oakley Nmp. 42 G44
Little Orton 60 A29
Little Ouseburn 57 C40
Littleover 41 B39
Little Parndon 33 G50
Little Paxton 32 B47
Little Petherick 3 A15
Little Plumstead 45 D59
Little Ponton 42 B44
Littleport 43 G51
Little Raveley 33 A48
Little Ribston 57 D39
Little Rissington 30 G37
Little Rogart 96 A23
Little Ryburgh 44 C55
Little Ryle 70 B35
Little Salkeld 61 C31
Little Sampford 33 E52
Little Saxham 34 B53
Little Scatwell 96 C19
Little Shelford 33 C50
Little Smeaton 51 A41
Little Snoring 44 B55
Little Sodbury 20 C33
Little Somborne 10 A39
Little Somerford 20 C35
Little Stainton 62 D39
Little Stanney 48 E29
Little Staughton 32 B47
Little Steeping 53 F50

Littlestone-on-Sea 15 E56
Little Stonham 35 B57
Little Stretton Shr. 38 F30
Little Stretton Lei. 41 F42
Little Strickland 61 D31
Little Stukeley 33 A48
Little Sutton 48 E29
Little Swinburne 70 F35
Little Tew 30 F39
Little Tey 34 F54
Little Thetford 33 A51
Little Thirkleby 57 B40
Little Thorpe 62 B39
Littlethorpe 57 C39
Little Thurlow 33 C52
Little Thurrock 24 D52
Littleton Sry 22 E46
Littleton Ham. 11 A40
Littleton Tay. 82 D28
Littleton Che. 48 F30
Littleton Som. 8 A30
Littleton Drew 20 C34
Littleton -on-Severn 19 B31
Littleton Panell 20 F35
Little Torboll 96 B23
Little Torrington 6 D20
Little Totham 34 G54
Littletown 62 B39
Little Town 60 E28
Little Urswick 55 B28
Little Wakering 25 C55
Little Walden 33 D51
Little Waldingfield 34 D55
Little Waltham 33 G52
Little Warley 24 B52
Little Weighton 59 F45
Little Welland 29 E33
Little Welnetham 34 B54
Little Wenham 34 E56
Little Wenlock 39 E32
Little Whittingham Green 35 A58
Little Whittington 70 G35
Littlewick Green 22 D44
Little Wilbraham 33 C51
Little Witcombe 29 G35
Little Witley 29 B33
Little Wittenham 21 B41
Little Wolford 30 E38
Little Woolstone 32 E44
Littleworth Stf. 40 D36
Littleworth H.&W. 29 C34
Littleworth Oxf. 21 B38
Little Wratting 33 D52
Little Wymondley 33 F48
Little Wyrley 40 E36
Little Yeldham 34 D53
Littley Green 33 G52
Litton Dby. 50 E37
Litton Som. 19 F31
Litton N.Y. 56 B35
Litton Cheney 8 E31
Liurbost 100 E9
Liverpool 48 C29
Liversedge 57 G37
Liverton Dev. 5 C23
Liverton Cle. 63 E42
Liverton Street 14 C54
Livingston 75 D26
Livingston Village 75 D26
Lixwm 47 E27
Lizard 2 G12
Llaingoch 46 D18
Llaithddu 37 G26
Llan 37 E24
Llanaber 36 D21
Llanaelhaearn 36 A19
Llanaeron 26 B20
Llanafan 27 A22
Llanafan-fawr 27 C25
Llanafan-fechan 27 C25
Llanallgo 46 D20
Llanarmon 36 B20
Llanarmon Dyffryn Ceiriog 38 B27
Llanarmon-yn-Ial 47 G27
Llanarth Gwe. 28 G29
Llanarth Dyf. 26 C20
Llanarthney 17 B21
Llanasa 47 D27
Llanbabo 46 D19
Llanbadarn Fawr 36 G21
Llanbadarn Fynydd 27 A26
Llanbadarn-y-garreg 27 D26
Llanbadoc 19 A29
Llanbadrig 46 C19
Llanbeder 19 B29
Llanbedr Pow. 28 F28
Llanbedr Pow. 28 D27
Llanbedr Gwy. 36 C21
Llanbedr-Dyffryn-Clwyd 47 G27
Llanbedrgoch 46 D20
Llanbedrog 36 B19
Llanbedr-y-cennin 47 F23
Llanberis 46 F21
Llanbethery 18 E26

Llanbister 27 A26
Llanblethian 18 D25
Llanboidy 16 B17
Llanbradach 18 C27
Llanbrynmair 37 E24
Llancarfan 18 E26
Llancayo 19 A29
Llancynfelyn 37 F22
Llan-dafel 18 A27
Llandaff 18 D27
Llandaff North 18 D27
Llandanwg 36 C21
Llandarog 17 C20
Llandawke 17 C18
Llanddaniel Fab 46 E20
Llanddarog 17 C20
Llanddeiniol 26 A21
Llanddeiniolen 46 F21
Llandderfel 37 B25
Llanddeusant Dyf. 27 F23
Llanddeusant Gwy. 46 D19
Llanddew 27 E26
Llanddewi 17 F20
Llanddewi-Brefi 27 C22
Llanddewi'r Cwm 27 D26
Llanddewi Rhydderch 28 G29
Llanddewi Velfrey 16 C17
Llanddewi Ystradenni 27 B26
Llanddoged 47 F23
Llanddona 46 E21
Llanddowror 17 C18
Llanddulas 47 E24
Llanddwywe 36 C21
Llanddyfnan 46 E20
Llandefaelog 17 C19
Llandefaelog Fach 27 E26
Llandefaelog-tre'r-graig 27 E26
Llandefalle 27 E26
Llandegai 46 E21
Llandegfan 46 E21
Llandegla 47 G27
Llandegley 28 B27
Llandegveth 19 B29
Llandegwning 36 B18
Llandeilo 17 B22
Llandeilo Abercywyn 17 C19
Llandeilo Graban 27 D26
Llandeilo'r-Fan 27 E24
Llandeloy 16 B14
Llandenny 19 A29
Llandevenny 19 C29
Llandinabo 28 F30
Llandinam 37 G26
Llandissilio 16 B16
Llandogo 19 A31
Llandough S.G. 18 D25
Llandough S.G. 18 D27
Llandovery 27 E23
Llandow 18 D25
Llandre Dyf. 27 D22
Llandre Dyf. 37 G22
Llandre Dyf. 16 B17
Llandrillo 37 B26
Llandrillo-yn-Rhos 47 D23
Llandrindod Wells 27 B26
Llandrinio 38 D28
Llandudno 47 D23
Llandudno Junction 47 E23
Llandwrog 46 G20
Llandybie 17 C21
Llandyfriog 26 D19
Llandyfrydog 46 D20
Llandygwydd 26 D18
Llandyrnog 47 F27
Llandyry 17 D20
Llandysilio 38 D28
Llandyssil 38 F27
Llandysul 26 D19
Llanedeyrn 18 C27
Llanegryn 36 E21
Llanegwad 17 B20
Llaneilian 46 C20
Llanelian-yn-Rhos 47 E24
Llanelidan 38 A27
Llanelieu 28 E27
Llanellen 28 G28
Llanelli 17 D20
Llanelltyd 37 D22
Llanelly 28 G28
Llanelwedd 27 C26
Llanelwy (St Asaph) 47 E26
Llanenddwyn 36 C21
Llanengan 36 C18
Llanerchymedd 46 D19
Llanerfyl 37 E26
Llanfachraeth 46 D18
Llanfachreth 37 C23
Llanfaelog 46 E19
Llanfaelrhys 36 C17
Llanfaes Pow. 27 F26
Llanfaes Gwy. 46 E21
Llanfaethlu 46 D18
Llanfaglan 46 F20
Llanfair 36 C21
Llanfair Caereinion 38 E27
Llanfair Clydogau 26 C21
Llanfair Dyffryn Clwyd 47 G27

Llanfairfechan 46 E22
Llanfair-Nant-Gwyn 16 A17
Llanfair-Orllwyn 26 D19
Llanfairpwllgwyngyll 46 E20
Llanfair Talhaiarn 47 E24
Llanfair Waterdine 28 A28
Llanfairynghornwy 46 C18
Llanfair-yn-Neubwll 46 E18
Llanfallteg 16 C17
Llanfallteg West 16 C17
Llanfaredd 27 C26
Llanfarian 26 A21
Llanfechain 38 C27
Llanfechell 46 C19
Llanfendigaid 36 E21
Llanferres 47 F27
Llanfflewyn 46 D19
Llanfigael 46 D19
Llanfihangel ar-Arth 17 A20
Llanfihangel Crucorney 28 F29
Llanfihangel Glyn Myfyr 37 A25
Llanfihangel Nant Bran 27 E25
Llanfihangel-nant-Melan 28 C27
Llanfihangel Rhydithon 28 B27
Llanfihangel Rogiet 19 C30
Llanfihangel-Tal-y-llyn 28 F27
Llanfihangel uwch-gwili 17 B20
Llanfihangel-y-Creuddyn 27 A22
Llanfihangel-yng-Ngwynfa 37 D26
Llanfihangel-y-pennant Gwy. 36 A21
Llanfihangel-y-pennant Gwy. 37 E22
Llanfihangel-y-traethau 36 B21
Llanfilo 28 E27
Llanfoist 28 G28
Llanfor 37 B25
Llanfrechfa 19 B28
Llanfrothen 36 A21
Llanfrynach 27 F26
Llanfwrog Clw. 47 G26
Llanfwrog Gwy. 46 D18
Llanfyllin 38 D27
Llanfynydd Clw. 48 G28
Llanfynydd Dyf. 17 B21
Llanfyrnach 17 A18
Llangadfan 37 D25
Llangadog 17 B22
Llangadwaladr Gwy. 46 F19
Llangadwaladr Clw. 38 B27
Llangaffo 46 F20
Llangain 17 C19
Llangammarch Wells 27 D25
Llangan 18 D25
Llangarron 28 F31
Llangasty-Talyllyn 28 F27
Llangathen 17 B21
Llangattock 28 G27
Llangattock Lingoed 28 F29
Llangattock-Vibon-Avel 28 G30
Llangedwyn 38 C27
Llangefni 46 E20
Llangeinor 18 C24
Llangeitho 26 C21
Llangeler 17 A19
Llangelynin 36 E21
Llangendeirne 17 C20
Llangennech 17 D21
Llangennith 17 E19
Llangenny 28 G28
Llangernyw 47 F24
Llangian 36 C18
Llangiwg 18 A23
Llanglydwen 16 B17
Llangoed 46 D21
Llangoedmor 26 D17
Llangollen 38 A27
Llangolman 16 B16
Llangorse 28 F27
Llangorwen 36 G21
Llangovan 19 A30
Llangower 37 B24
Llangranog 26 C18
Llangristiolus 46 E19
Llangrove 28 G31
Llangua 28 F29
Llangunllo 28 A27
Llangunnor 17 B20
Llangurig 27 A24
Llangwm Clw. 37 A25
Llangwm Dyf. 16 D15
Llangwm-isaf 19 A29
Llangwnnadl 36 B17
Llangwyfan 47 F27
Llangwyllog 46 E20
Llangwyryfon 26 A21
Llangybi Gwy. 36 A20
Llangybi Gwe. 19 B29
Llangybi Dyf. 26 C21
Llangyfelach 17 E22
Llangynhafal 47 F27
Llangynidr 28 G27
Llangynin 17 C18
Llangynmyd 18 C24
Llangynog Dyf. 17 C19

Llangynog *Pow.* 37 C26
Llanhamlach 27 F26
Llanharan 18 C25
Llanharry 18 C25
Llanhennock 19 B29
Llanhilleth 18 A27
Llanidloes 37 G25
Llaniestyn 36 B18
Llanigon 28 D27
Llanilar 27 A22
Llanilid 18 C25
Llanishen *Gwe.* 19 A30
Llanishen *S.G.* 18 C27
Llanllawddog 17 B20
Llanllechid 46 F21
Llanlleonfel 27 D25
Llanllugan 37 E26
Llanllwch 17 C19
Llanllwchaiarn 37 F26
Llanllwni 26 D20
Llanllyfni 46 G20
Llanllywel 19 B29
Llanmadoc 17 E20
Llanmaes 18 E25
Llanmartin 19 C29
Llanmerewig 38 F27
Llanmihangel 18 D25
Llanmiloe 17 D18
Llanmorlais 17 E21
Llannefydd 47 E25
Llannerch 47 E26
Llannerch-y-mor 47 E27
Llannon 17 D21
Llannor 36 B19
Llanon 26 B21
Llanover 19 A28
Llanpumsaint 17 B19
Llanreithan 16 B14
Llanrhaeadr 47 F26
Llanrhaeadr-ym-Mochnant
  38 C27
Llanrhian 16 A13
Llanrhidian 17 E21
Llanrhos 47 D23
Llanrhyddlad 46 D19
Llanrhystud 26 B21
Llanrothal 28 G30
Llanrug 46 F21
Llanrumney 18 C27
Llanrwst 47 F23
Llansadurnen 17 C18
Llansadwrn *Dyf.* 17 A22
Llansadwrn *Gwy.* 46 E21
Llansaint 17 D19
Llansamlet 17 E22
Llansannan 47 F25
Llansannor 18 D25
Llansantffraed 27 F26
Llansantffraed-Cwmdeuddwr
  27 B25
Llansantffraed-in-Elvel 27 C26
Llansantffraid 28 B20
Llansantffraid Glan Conwy
  47 E24
Llansantffraid-ym-Mechain
  38 C27
Llansawel 17 A21
Llansilin 38 C28
Llansoy 19 A30
Llanspyddid 27 F25
Llanstadwell 16 D15
Llanstephan *Dyf.* 17 C19
Llanstephan *Pow.* 28 D27
Llantarnam 19 B28
Llanteg 16 C17
Llanthony 27 F28
Llantilio Crossenny 28 G30
Llantilio Pertholey 28 G29
Llantood 26 D17
Llantrisant *M.G.* 18 C26
Llantrisant *Gwe.* 19 B29
Llantrithyd 18 D26
Llantwit Fardre 18 C26
Llantwit Major 18 E25
Llantysilio 38 A27
Llanuwchllyn 37 B24
Llanvaches 19 B30
Llanvair-Discoed 19 B30
Llanvapley 28 G29
Llanvetherine 28 G29
Llanveynoe 28 E28
Llanvihangel Gobion 19 A29
Llanvihangel-Ystern-Llewern
  28 G30
Llanwarne 28 F30
Llanwddyn 37 D25
Llanwenog 26 D20
Llanwern 19 C29
Llanwinio 17 B18
Llanwnda *Dyf.* 16 A15
Llanwnda *Gwy.* 46 G20
Llanwnen 26 D21
Llanwnog 37 F25
Llanwonno 18 B26
Llanwrda 17 A22
Llanwrin 37 E23

Llanwrthwl 27 B25
Llanwrtyd 27 D24
Llanwrtyd Wells 27 D24
Llanwyddelan 37 E26
Llanyblodwel 38 C28
Llanybri 17 C19
Llanybydder 26 D21
Llanycefn 16 B16
Llanychaer Bridge 16 A15
Llanycil 37 B24
Llanycrwys 27 D22
Llanymawddwy 37 D24
Llanymynech 38 C28
Llanynghenedl 46 D18
Llanynys 47 F27
Llan-y-pwll 48 G29
Llanyre 27 B26
Llanystumdwy 36 B20
Llanywern 27 F26
Llawhaden 16 C16
Llawnt 38 B28
Llawr-y-dref 36 C18
Llawryglyn 37 F25
Llay 48 G29
Llechcynfarwy 46 D19
Llechfaen 27 F26
Llechryd *Dyf.* 26 D17
Llechryd *M.G.* 18 A26
Llechrydau 38 B27
Lledrod *Clw.* 38 C28
Lledrod *Dyf.* 27 A22
Llethr 16 B14
Llidiadnenog 17 A21
Llidiardau 37 B24
Llithfaen 36 A19
Lloc 47 E27
Llong 48 F28
Llowes 28 D27
Lloyney 28 A28
Llwyd 27 C25
Llwydcoed 18 A25
Llwydiarth 37 D26
Llwyn 38 G28
Llwyncelyn 26 C20
Llwyndafydd 26 C19
Llwynderw 38 E27
Llwyndyrys 36 A19
Llwyngwril 36 E21
Llwynhendy 17 E21
Llwyn-Madoc 27 C24
Llwynmawr 38 B28
Llwyn-onn 26 C19
Llwyn-y-brain *Dyf.* 27 E23
Llwyn-y-brain *Dyf.* 16 C17
Llwynypia 18 B25
Llynclys 38 C28
Llynfaes 46 E19
Llysfaen 47 E24
Llyswen 28 E27
Llysworney 18 D25
Llys-y-fran 16 B16
Llywel 27 E24
Loandhu 96 D23
Loanhead *Ltn* 76 D28
Loanhead *Grm.* 99 F35
Loans 74 G19
Lochailort 86 F13
Lochaline 79 C12
Lochans 64 E16
Locharbriggs 68 E25
Lochawe 80 E17
Loch Baghasdail (Lochboisdale)
  84 C3
Lochboisdale 84 C3
Lochbuie 79 E11
Lochcarron 86 A14
Loch Coire Lodge 102 E22
Lochdhu Hotel 103 D25
Lochdon 79 D13
Lochdrum 95 D18
Lochearnhead 81 E21
Lochee 82 D29
Loch Eil Centre 87 G16
Lochend *Hgh.* 88 A21
Lochend *Hgh.* 103 B28
Lochfoot 65 C24
Lochgair 73 A15
Lochgarthside 88 C20
Lochgelly 75 A27
Lochgilphead 73 B14
Lochgoilhead 80 G17
Lochgoin 74 F20
Loch Head *D.&G.* 64 F19
Loch Head *D.&G.* 67 D20
Lochhill 68 B22
Loch-hill 98 C28
Lochinch Castle 64 D16
Lochinver 101 F16
Lochlair 83 C31
Lochlane 81 E24
Lochluichart 96 E19
Lochmaben 69 E26
Lochmaddy 92 E5
Loch Na Madadh (Lochmaddy)
  92 E5

Lochore 75 A27
Lochportain 92 D5
Lochranza 73 F15
Loch Sgioport 84 A4
Lochside *Grm.* 91 G33
Lochside *Hgh.* 102 C20
Lochside *Hgh.* 102 E24
Lochside *Hgh.* 103 B28
Lochslin 97 C24
Lochton 67 E18
Lochty 83 G31
Lochuisge 79 B13
Lochurr 68 E23
Lochussie 96 F20
Lochwinnoch 74 E19
Lockengate 4 D16
Lockerbie 69 E27
Lockeridge 20 E37
Lockerley 10 B38
Locking 19 F29
Lockington *Hum.* 59 E45
Lockington *Lei.* 41 C40
Lockleywood 39 C32
Locksbottom 23 E50
Locks Heath 11 D41
Lockton 63 G44
Loddington *Nmp.* 31 A43
Loddington *Lei.* 42 E43
Loddiswell 5 F22
Loddon 45 F59
Lode 33 B51
Loders 8 E30
Lodsworth 12 D45
Lofthouse *W.Y.* 57 G39
Lofthouse *N.Y.* 57 B36
Loftus 63 E43
Logan *Str.* 67 A21
Logan *D.&G.* 64 F16
Loganlea 75 D25
Loggerheads 39 B33
Loggie 95 B17
Logie *Grm.* 97 F25
Logie *Tay.* 82 B29
Logie *Fife* 83 E30
Logie *Tay.* 91 G32
Logie Coldstone 90 C29
Logie Hill 96 D23
Logie Newton 98 F32
Logie Pert 91 G32
Logierait 82 B25
Login 16 B17
Lolworth 33 B49
Lonbain 94 F12
Londesborough 58 E44
London Beach 14 D54
London City Airport 23 C50
London Colney 22 A47
Londonderry 57 A38
Londonthorpe 42 B45
Londubh 94 C14
Lonemore 96 C23
Long Ashton 19 D31
Long Bennington 42 A44
Longbenton 71 G38
Longborough 30 E37
Long Bredy 8 E31
Longbridge *War.* 30 B38
Longbridge *W.M.* 29 A35
Longbridge Deverill 20 G34
Long Buckby 31 B42
Longburgh 60 A28
Longburton 9 C32
Long Clawson 42 C43
Longcliffe 50 G38
Long Common 11 C41
Long Compton *Stf.* 40 C34
Long Compton *War.* 30 E38
Longcot 21 B38
Long Crendon 21 A42
Long Crichel 9 C35
Longcross *Sry* 22 E45
Longcross *Dev.* 4 C20
Longden 38 E30
Long Ditton 22 E47
Longdon *H.&W.* 29 E34
Longdon *Stf.* 40 D36
Longdon upon Tern 38 D31
Longdown 7 F24
Long Downs 2 E13
Long Drax 58 G42
Longdrum 91 B35
Long Duckmanton 51 E40
Long Eaton 41 B40
Longfield 24 E52
Longfield Hill 24 E52
Longfleet 10 E36
Longford *G.L.* 22 D46
Longford *W.M.* 41 G39
Longford *Dby.* 40 B37
Longford *Shr.* 39 D33
Longford *Shr.* 39 B32
Longford *Glo.* 29 F34
Longforgan 82 D28
Longformacus 76 E32
Longframlington 71 C36
Long Gill 56 D33

Longham *Dor.* 10 E36
Longham *Nfk* 44 D55
Long Hanborough 31 G40
Longhill 99 D35
Longhirst 71 E38
Longhope *Glo.* 29 G32
Longhope *Ork.* 105 B28
Longhorsley 71 D37
Longhoughton 71 B38
Long Itchington 31 B40
Longlands *Cum.* 60 C28
Longlands *Grm.* 90 A30
Longlane *Dby.* 40 B38
Longlane *Brk.* 21 D41
Long Lawford 31 A40
Longley Green 29 C32
Long Load 8 B30
Longmanhill 99 C33
Long Marston *N.Y.* 57 D40
Long Marston *War.* 30 D37
Long Marston *Hfs.* 32 G44
Long Marton 61 D32
Long Melford 34 D54
Longmoor Camp 11 A43
Longmorn 98 D28
Long Newton 20 B35
Longnewton *Bor.* 70 A31
Longnewton *Cle.* 62 E39
Longney 29 G33
Longniddry 76 C30
Longnor *Shr.* 38 E30
Longnor *Stf.* 50 F36
Longparish 21 G40
Long Preston 56 D34
Longridge *Lan.* 56 F32
Longridge *Ltn* 75 D25
Longridge Towers 77 E35
Longriggend 75 C24
Long Riston 59 E47
Longrock 2 E11
Longsdon 49 G35
Longside 99 E36
Longslow 39 B32
Longstanton 33 B49
Longstock 10 A39
Longstowe 33 C48
Long Stratton 45 F57
Longstreet 20 F37
Long Street 31 D43
Long Sutton *Lcn.* 43 C50
Long Sutton *Ham.* 22 G43
Long Sutton *Som.* 8 B30
Longthorpe 42 F47
Long Thurlow 34 B56
Longton *Stf.* 40 A34
Longton *Lan.* 55 G30
Longtown *Cum.* 69 G29
Longtown *H.&W.* 28 F29
Longville in the Dale 38 F31
Long Waste 39 D32
Longwell Green 19 D32
Long Whatton 41 C40
Longwick 22 A43
Long Wittenham 21 B41
Longwitton 71 E36
Longwood 39 E32
Longworth 21 B39
Longyester 76 D31
Lonmore 93 G8
Loose 14 B53
Loosegate 43 C48
Loosley Row 22 A44
Lopcombe Corner 10 A38
Lopen 8 C30
Loppington 38 C30
Lorbottle 71 C36
Lorbottle Hall 71 C36
Lorgill 93 G7
Lorn 74 B19
Lornty 82 C27
Loscoe 41 A40
Losgaintir 92 B6
Lossiemouth 98 B28
Lossit 72 E8
Lostock Gralam 49 E32
Lostock Green 49 E33
Lostock Junction 49 B32
Lostwithiel 4 E16
Lothbeg 103 G25
Lothersdale 56 E35
Lothmore 103 G25
Loudwater 22 B44
Loughborough 41 C40
Loughor 17 E21
Loughton *Bkh.* 32 E44
Loughton *Shr.* 39 G32
Loughton *Esx* 23 B50
Lound *Lcn.* 42 D46
Lound *Not.* 51 D42
Lound *Sfk* 45 F61
Lount 41 D39
Lour 83 C30
Louth 53 D49
Loveacott 6 C21
Love Clough 56 G34
Lovedean 11 C42

Lover 10 B38
Loversall 51 C41
Loves Green 24 A52
Loveston 16 D16
Lovington 8 A31
Low 55 A30
Low Ballivain 66 A12
Low Bentham 56 C32
Low Bolton 62 G36
Low Bradfield 50 C38
Low Bradley 57 E36
Low Braithwaite 60 B30
Low Brunton 70 F34
Low Burnham 51 B43
Low Burton 57 A38
Low Catton 58 D42
Low Coniscliffe 62 E38
Low Craighead 67 C18
Low Crosby 69 G30
Lowdham 41 A42
Low Dinsdale 62 E39
Low Eggborough 58 G41
Low Entercommon 62 F39
Lower Aisholt 8 A28
Lower Apperley 29 F34
Lower Ashton 7 G24
Lower Assendon 22 C43
Lower Auchalick 73 C15
Lower Barewood 28 C29
Lower Beeding 13 D48
Lower Benefield 42 G45
Lower Berry Hill 28 G31
Lower Bockhampton 9 E33
Lower Boddington 31 C40
Lower Boscaswell 2 E9
Lower Bourne 22 G44
Lower Brailes 30 E38
Lower Breakish 86 B12
Lower Broadheath 29 C34
Lower Brynamman 27 G23
Lower Bullingham 28 E31
Lower Burgate 10 C37
Lower Caldecote 32 D47
Lower Cam 20 A33
Lower Camster 103 D28
Lower Chapel 27 E25
Lower Chute 21 F38
Lower Crossings 50 D36
Lower Darwen 56 G32
Lower Dean 32 B46
Lower Diabaig 94 E13
Lower Dicker 13 E51
Lower Dinchope 38 G30
Lower Down 38 G29
Lower Drift 2 F10
Lower Dunsforth 57 C40
Lower Egleton 28 D31
Lower End 32 B44
Lower Everleigh 20 F37
Lower Failand 19 D31
Lower Farringdon 11 A43
Lower Freystrop 16 C15
Lower Froyle 22 G43
Lower Gabwell 5 D25
Lower Gledfield 96 B21
Lower Godney 19 G30
Lower Green *Nfk* 44 B55
Lower Green *Stf.* 40 E34
Lower Green *Kent* 23 G52
Lower Green Bank 55 D31
Lower Halstow 24 E54
Lower Hardres 15 B57
Lower Hawthwaite 55 A28
Lower Hayton 38 G30
Lower Hergest 28 C28
Lower Heyford 31 F40
Lower Higham 24 D53
Lower Holbrook 35 E57
Lower Hordley 38 C29
Lower Horsebridge 13 E51
Lower Kilchattan 72 A9
Lower Killeyan 72 F8
Lower Kingcombe 8 E31
Lower Kinnerton 48 F29
Lower Langford 19 E30
Lower Largo 83 G30
Lower Lemington 30 E38
Lower Lydbrook 28 G31
Lower Lye 28 B29
Lower Machen 18 C27
Lower Maes-coed 28 E29
Lower Moor 29 D35
Lower Nazeing 23 A49
Lower Oakfield 75 A27
Lower Oddington 30 F38
Lower Ollach 85 A10
Lower Penarth 18 D27
Lower Penn 40 F34
Lower Pennington 10 E39
Lower Peover 49 E33
Lower Quinton 30 D37
Lower Seagry 20 C35
Lower Shelton 32 D45
Lower Shiplake 22 D43
Lower Shuckburgh 31 B40
Lower Slaughter 30 F37

Lower Stanton St Quintin 20 C35
Lower Stoke 24 D54
Lower Stondon 32 E47
Lower Street 13 E52
Lower Sundon 32 F46
Lower Swanwick 11 D40
Lower Swell 30 F37
Lower Tean 40 B35
Lower Thurlton 45 F60
Lower Thurnham 55 D30
Lower Town *Dyf.* 16 A15
Lower Town *I.o.S.* 2 A11
Lower Tysoe 30 D39
Lower Upham 11 C41
Lower Vexford 7 B27
Lower Wallop 38 E29
Lower Walton 48 D31
Lower Weare 19 F30
Lower Welson 28 C28
Lower Whitley 49 E32
Lower Wield 21 G42
Lower Winchendon 31 G43
Lower Withington 49 F34
Lower Woodend 90 C31
Lower Woodford 10 A37
Lower Wraxall 8 D31
Lower Wyche 29 D33
Lowesby 42 E43
Lowestoft 45 F61
Lowestoft End 45 F61
Loweswater 60 D27
Low Etherley 62 D37
Lowfield Heath 13 C48
Low Gate 70 G35
Lowgill *Cum.* 61 G32
Lowgill *Lan.* 56 C32
Low Habberley 29 A33
Low Ham 8 B30
Low Hawkser 63 F45
Low Haygarth 61 G32
Low Hesket 60 B30
Low Hesleyhurst 71 D36
Low Hutton 58 C43
Lowick *Nor.* 77 G35
Lowick *Cum.* 55 A28
Lowick *Nmp.* 42 G45
Low Laithe 57 C37
Low Leighton 49 D35
Low Marishes 58 B44
Low Mill 63 G42
Low Moor 56 E32
Low Newton-by-the-Sea 71 A38
Lownie Moor 83 C30
Low Redford 62 C36
Low Risby 52 A45
Low Row *Cum.* 70 G31
Low Row *N.Y.* 62 G35
Low Santon 52 A45
Lowsonford 30 B37
Low Stillaig 73 D15
Low Street 45 C59
Lowther 61 D31
Lowther Castle 61 D31
Lowthorpe 59 D46
Lowton 48 C31
Lowton Common 49 C32
Low Torry 75 B26
Low Toynton 53 E48
Low Waters 75 E23
Low Wood 55 A29
Low Worsall 62 E39
Loxbeare 7 D24
Loxhill 12 C46
Loxhore 6 B22
Loxley 30 C38
Loxton 19 F29
Loxwood 12 C46
Lubachoinnich 96 B19
Lubcroy 96 A19
Lubenham 42 G43
Lubfearn 96 D19
Lubmore 95 F16
Lubreoch 81 C20
Luccombe 7 A25
Luccombe Village 11 G41
Lucker 77 G37
Luckett 4 C19
Luckington 20 C34
Lucklawhill 82 E29
Luckwell Bridge 7 B24
Lucton 28 B30
Ludag 84 C3
Ludborough 53 C48
Ludchurch 16 C17
Luddenden 57 G36
Luddenham Court 25 E55
Luddesdown 24 E52
Luddington *Hum.* 52 A44
Luddington *War.* 30 C37
Luddington in the Brook 42 G46
Ludford 28 A31
Ludford Magna 53 D48
Ludford Parva 52 D47
Ludgershall *Bkh.* 31 G42
Ludgershall *Wts.* 21 F38

Ludgvan 2 E10
Ludham 45 D59
Ludlow 28 A30
Ludney 53 C49
Ludstock 19 E32
Ludwell 9 B34
Ludworth 62 B39
Luffincott 4 A18
Luffness 76 B30
Lugar 67 A21
Luggiebank 75 C23
Lugton 74 E20
Lugwardine 28 D31
Luib 86 B11
Luibeilt 80 A18
Lulham 57 D36
Lullington *Som.* 20 F33
Lullington *Dby.* 40 D38
Lulsgate Bottom 19 E30
Lulsley 29 C33
Lulworth Camp 9 F34
Lumb 57 G36
Lumbutts 56 G35
Lumby 57 F40
Lumphanan 90 C31
Lumphinnans 75 A27
Lumsdaine 77 D34
Lumsden 90 A30
Lunan 83 B32
Lunanhead 83 B30
Luncarty 82 E26
Lund *Hum.* 59 E45
Lund *N.Y.* 58 F42
Lund *She.* 106 B41
Lundavra 80 A16
Lunderton 99 E37
Lundie *Tay.* 82 D28
Lundie *Hgh.* 87 C17
Lundin Links 82 G29
Lunga 79 G13
Lunna 107 A40
Lunning 107 A41
Lunsford's Cross 14 F53
Lunt 48 B29
Luntley 28 C29
Luppitt 7 E27
Lupton 55 A31
Lurgashall 12 D45
Lurignich 80 B15
Lusby 53 F49
Luss 74 A19
Lussagiven 72 B12
Lusta 93 F8
Lustleigh 7 G23
Luston 28 B30
Luthermuir 91 G32
Luthrie 82 F29
Luton *Dev.* 7 E26
Luton *Bfd.* 32 F46
Luton *Kent* 24 E53
Luton *Dev.* 5 C24
Luton Airport 32 F47
Lutterworth 41 G41
Lutton *Lcn.* 43 C50
Lutton *Nmp.* 42 G47
Lutton *Dev.* 5 E21
Luxborough 7 B25
Luxulyan 4 E16
Lybster *Hgh.* 103 B26
Lybster *Hgh.* 103 E28
Lydacott 6 E20
Lydbury North 38 G29
Lydcott 6 B22
Lydd 15 E56
Lydd Airport 15 E56
Lydden 15 C58
Lyddington 42 F44
Lydeard St Lawrence 7 B27
Lydford 6 G20
Lydford-on-Fosse 8 A31
Lydgate 56 G35
Lydham 38 F29
Lydiard Millicent 20 C36
Lydiate 48 B29
Lydlinch 9 C33
Lydney 19 A32
Lydstep 16 E16
Lye 40 G35
Lye Green 22 A45
Lyford 31 B39
Lymbridge Green 15 C56
Lymekilns 74 E22
Lyme Regis 8 E29
Lyminge 15 C57
Lymington 10 E38
Lyminster 12 F45
Lymm 49 D32
Lymore 10 E39
Lympne 15 D57
Lympsham 19 F29
Lympstone 7 G25
Lynaberack 88 E23
Lynchat 88 D23
Lyndhurst 10 D39
Lyndon 42 E44

Lyne *Sry* 22 E45
Lyne *Grm.* 91 C33
Lyneal 38 B30
Lynedale Ho 93 F9
Lynegar 103 C28
Lyneham *Wts.* 20 C36
Lyneham *Oxf.* 30 F38
Lyneholmeford 69 F30
Lynemore 89 B26
Lynemouth 71 D38
Lyne of Gorthleck 88 B20
Lyne of Skene 91 B33
Lyness 105 B28
Lynford 44 F54
Lyng *Nfk* 44 D56
Lyng *Som.* 8 B29
Lynmouth 7 A23
Lynsted 25 E55
Lynton 7 A23
Lyon's Gate 9 D32
Lyonshall 28 C29
Lyrabus 72 D8
Lytchett Matravers 9 E35
Lytchett Minster 9 E35
Lyth 103 B28
Lytham 55 G29
Lytham St Anne's 55 G28
Lythe 63 E44
Lythe Hill 12 C45
Lythes 105 C30
Lythmore 103 B26

M

Mabe Burnthouse 2 E13
Mabie 65 C25
Mablethorpe 53 D51
Macclesfield 49 E35
Macclesfield Forest 49 E35
Macduff 98 C32
Machan 75 E23
Machany 81 F24
Macharioch 66 C13
Machen 18 C27
Machrie *Str.* 73 G14
Machrie *Str.* 72 F9
Machrihanish 66 A12
Machrins 72 A9
Machynlleth 37 E23
Mackworth 40 B38
Macmerry 76 C30
Macterry 99 E33
Madderty 82 E25
Maddiston 75 C25
Madehurst 12 E45
Madeley *Shr.* 39 E33
Madeley *Stf.* 39 A33
Madeley Heath 39 A33
Madford 7 D27
Madingley 33 C49
Madjeston 9 B34
Madley 28 E30
Madresfield 29 D33
Madron 2 E10
Maenaddwyn 46 D20
Maenclochog 16 B16
Maendy 18 D25
Maentwrog 37 A22
Maer 39 B33
Maerdy *Clw.* 37 A26
Maerdy *Gwe.* 19 A29
Maerdy *M.G.* 18 B25
Maerdy *Dyf.* 17 B22
Maerdy *Dyf.* 17 B22
Maesbrook 38 C28
Maesbury Marsh 38 C28
Maes-glas 19 C28
Maesgwynne 16 B17
Maeshafn 47 F27
Maesllyn 26 D19
Maesmynis 27 D25
Maesteg 18 B24
Maes-Treylow 28 B28
Maesybont 17 C21
Maesycrugiau 26 D20
Maes-y-cwmmer 18 B27
Magdalen Laver 23 A51
Maggieknockater 98 E28
Magham Down 13 E51
Maghull 48 B29
Magor 19 C30
Maiden Bradley 9 A34
Maidencombe 5 D25
Maidenhead 22 C44
Maiden Law 62 A37
Maiden Newton 8 E31
Maidens 67 C17
Maiden's Green 22 D45
Maidenwell *Cnw.* 4 C17
Maidenwell *Lcn.* 53 E49
Maiden Wells 16 E15
Maidford 31 C41
Maids' Moreton 31 E43
Maidstone 14 B53
Maidwell 31 A43
Mail 107 E40

Mains of Ardestie 83 D31
Mains of Balhall 83 A30
Mains of Ballindarg 82 B29
Mains of Burgie 97 F26
Mains of Culsh 99 F35
Mains of Dillavaird 91 E33
Mains of Drum 91 C34
Mains of Dudwick 99 F35
Mains of Faillie 88 A22
Mains of Fedderate 99 E34
Mains of Glenbuchat 90 B29
Mains of Linton 91 C32
Mains of Melgund 83 B31
Mains of Pitfour 99 E35
Mains of Pittrichie 91 A34
Mains of Sluie 97 F25
Mains of Tannachy 98 C29
Mains of Thornton 91 F32
Mains of Tig 66 E16
Mains of Watten 103 C28
Mainsriddle 65 E25
Mainstone 38 G28
Maisemore 29 F33
Makendon 70 C33
Makerstoun 76 G32
Malacleit 92 D3
Malborough 5 G23
Malden 23 E48
Malden Rushett 22 E47
Maldon 24 A54
Malham 56 C34
Maligar 93 E10
Mallaig 86 E12
Mallaigmore 86 E12
Mallaigvaig 86 E12
Malleny Mills 75 D27
Malletsheugh 74 E20
Malling 81 G21
Malltraeth 46 F19
Mallwyd 37 D24
Malmesbury 20 C35
Malmsmead 7 A23
Malpas *Gwe.* 19 B28
Malpas *Che.* 38 A30
Malpas *Cnw.* 3 D14
Maltby *S.Y.* 51 C41
Maltby *Cle.* 62 E40
Maltby le Marsh 53 D50
Maltman's Hill 14 C54
Malton 58 B43
Malvern Link 29 D33
Malvern Wells 29 D33
Mambeg 74 B18
Mamble 29 A32
Mamhead 7 G25
Manaccan 2 F13
Manafon 38 E27
Manais 92 C6
Manaton 7 G23
Manby 53 D50
Mancetter 40 F38
Manchester 49 C34
Mancot Royal 48 F29
Mandally 87 D18
Manea 43 G50
Maneight 67 C21
Manfield 62 E37
Mangaster 106 E39
Mangotsfield 19 D32
Mangurstadh 100 D6
Mankinholes 56 G35
Manley 48 E30
Manmoel 18 A27
Mannel 78 C5
Manningford Abbots 20 F37
Manningford Bohune 20 F37
Manningford Bruce 20 E37
Mannings Heath 13 D48
Mannington 10 D36
Manningtree 34 E56
Mannofield 91 C34
Manorbier 16 E16
Manordeifi 26 D18
Manordeilo 17 B22
Manorowen 16 A14
Mansell Gamage 28 D29
Mansell Lacy 28 D30
Mansergh 55 A31
Mansfield 51 F41
Mansfield Woodhouse 51 F41
Mansriggs 55 A28
Manston *Kent* 25 E59
Manston *Dor.* 9 C33
Manston Airport 25 E59
Manswood 9 D35
Manthorpe *Lcn.* 42 D46
Manthorpe *Lcn.* 42 B45
Manton *Hum.* 52 B45
Manton *Wts.* 20 E37
Manton *Lei.* 42 E44
Manuden 33 F50
Maolachy 79 F14
Maperton 9 B32
Maplebeck 51 F42
Maple Cross 22 B46
Mapledurham 21 D42

Mapledurwell 21 F42
Maplehurst 12 D47
Mapleton 40 A37
Mapperley 41 A40
Mapperton 8 E30
Mappleborough Green 30 B36
Mappleton 59 E48
Mapplewell 51 B39
Mappowder 9 D33
Marazion 2 E11
Marbury 38 A31
March 43 F50
Marcham 21 B40
Marchamley 38 C31
Marchington 40 B37
Marchington Woodlands 40 C37
Marchwiel 38 A29
Marchwood 10 C39
Marcross 18 E24
Marcus 83 B30
Marden *H.&W.* 28 D31
Marden *Wts.* 20 F36
Marden *T.&W.* 71 F39
Marden *Kent* 14 C53
Marden Beech 14 C53
Marden Thorn 14 C53
Mardy 28 G28
Marefield 42 E43
Mare Green 8 B29
Mareham le Fen 53 F48
Mareham on the Hill 53 F48
Maresfield 13 D50
Marfleet 59 G47
Marford 48 G29
Margam 18 C23
Margaret Marsh 9 C34
Margaret Roding 33 G51
Margaretting 24 A52
Margate 25 D59
Margnaheglish 73 G16
Margreig 65 C24
Margrove Park 63 E42
Marham 44 E53
Marhamchurch 6 E18
Marholm 42 E47
Marian Cwm 47 E26
Marian-glas 46 D20
Mariansleigh 7 C23
Marishader 93 E10
Maristow 4 D20
Mark 19 G29
Markbeech 23 G50
Markby 53 E50
Mark Causeway 19 G29
Mark Cross 13 C51
Markdu 64 C17
Market Bosworth 41 E39
Market Deeping 42 D47
Market Drayton 39 B32
Market Harborough 42 G43
Markethill 82 D28
Market Lavington 20 F36
Market Overton 42 D44
Market Rasen 52 D47
Market Stainton 53 D48
Market Street 45 C58
Market Weighton 58 E44
Market Weston 34 A55
Markfield 41 D40
Markham 18 A27
Markham Moor 51 E42
Markinch 82 G28
Markington 57 C38
Marksbury 19 E32
Marks Gate 23 B50
Marks Tey 34 F54
Markwell 4 E19
Markyate 32 G46
Marlborough 20 D37
Marldon 5 D24
Marlesford 35 C59
Marley Green 38 A31
Marley Hill 62 A37
Marlingford 45 E57
Mar Lodge 89 E26
Marloes 16 D13
Marlow 22 C44
Marlpit Hill 23 G50
Marlpool 41 A40
Marnhull 9 C33
Marnoch 98 D31
Marple 49 D35
Marr 51 B41
Marrel 103 G26
Marrick 62 G36
Marrister 107 A41
Marros 16 D17
Marsden *T.&W.* 71 G39
Marsden *W.Y.* 50 A36
Marsett 56 A34
Marsh 8 C28
Marshall's Heath 32 G47
Marshalsea 8 D29
Marsham 45 C57
Marshaw 55 D31
Marsh Baldon 21 B41

Marshborough 15 B58
Marshbrook 38 G30
Marsh Chapel 53 C49
Marshfield *Avon* 20 D33
Marshfield *Gwe.* 19 C28
Marshgate 4 A17
Marsh Gibbon 31 F42
Marsh Green *Shr.* 39 D32
Marsh Green *Kent* 23 G50
Marsh Green *Dev.* 7 F26
Marsh Lane 51 E39
Marshside 48 A29
Marsh Street 7 A25
Marshwood 8 E29
Marske 62 F36
Marske-by-the-Sea 63 D41
Marston *H.&W.* 28 C29
Marston *Che.* 49 E32
Marston *War.* 40 F38
Marston *Stf.* 40 D34
Marston *Stf.* 40 C35
Marston *Oxf.* 21 A41
Marston *Wts.* 20 F35
Marston *Lcn.* 42 A44
Marston Green 40 G37
Marston Magna 8 B31
Marston Meysey 20 B37
Marston Montgomery 40 B37
Marston Moretaine 32 D45
Marston on Dove 40 B38
Marston Stannett 28 C31
Marston St Lawrence 31 D41
Marston Trussell 41 G42
Marstow 28 G31
Marsworth 32 G44
Marten 21 E38
Marthall 49 E34
Martham 45 D60
Marthig 100 F10
Martin *Lcn.* 52 F47
Martin *Ham.* 10 C36
Martin Drove End 10 B36
Martinhoe 6 A22
Martin Hussingtree 29 B34
Martinscroft 49 D32
Martinstown 9 F32
Martlesham 35 D58
Martlesham Heath 35 D58
Martletwy 16 C16
Martley 29 B33
Martock 8 C30
Marton *Hum.* 59 F47
Marton *N.Y.* 58 A43
Marton *N.Y.* 57 C40
Marton *War.* 31 B40
Marton *Cle.* 63 E41
Marton *Shr.* 38 E28
Marton *Cum.* 55 B28
Marton *Che.* 49 E34
Marton *Lcn.* 52 D44
Marton Abbey 58 C41
Marton-le-Moor 57 B39
Martyr's Green 22 F46
Martyr Worthy 11 A41
Maruig 100 G7
Marwick 104 D28
Marwood 6 B21
Marybank 96 F20
Maryburgh 96 F21
Maryfield 107 C40
Marygold 77 D33
Maryhill *Grm.* 99 E34
Maryhill *Str.* 74 D21
Marykirk 91 G32
Marylebone *G.M.* 48 B31
Marylebone *G.L.* 23 C48
Maryport *Cum.* 60 C26
Maryport *D.&G.* 64 G17
Marystow 6 G20
Mary Tavy 4 C20
Maryton 83 B32
Marywell *Tay.* 83 C32
Marywell *Grm.* 90 D31
Marywell *Grm.* 91 D35
Masham 57 A38
Mashbury 33 G52
Mastrick 91 C34
Matching 33 G51
Matching Green 33 G51
Matching Tye 33 G51
Matfen 71 F36
Matfield 23 G52
Mathern 19 B31
Mathon 29 D33
Mathry 16 A14
Matlaske 45 B57
Matlock 50 F38
Matlock Bank 50 F38
Matlock Bath 50 G38
Matson 29 G34
Matterdale End 60 D29
Mattersey 51 D42
Mattingley 22 F43
Mattishall 44 D56
Mattishall Burgh 44 D56
Mauchline 67 A20

Maud 99 E35
Maufant 3 G18
Maugersbury 30 F37
Maughold 54 D26
Mauld 88 A19
Maulden 32 E46
Maulds Meaburn 61 E32
Maunby 57 A39
Maund Bryan 28 C31
Maundown 7 C26
Mautby 45 D60
Mavesyn Ridware 40 D36
Mavis Enderby 53 F49
Mawbray 60 B26
Mawdesley 48 A30
Mawdlam 18 C23
Mawgan 2 F12
Maw Green 40 F36
Mawla 2 D12
Mawnan 2 F13
Mawnan Smith 2 F13
Maxey 42 E47
Maxstoke 40 G38
Maxton *Kent* 15 C58
Maxton *Bor.* 70 A31
Maxwellheugh 76 G32
Maxwelltown 65 C25
Maxworthy 4 A18
Maybole 67 C19
Mayen 98 E31
Mayfield *Ltn* 76 D29
Mayfield *Stf.* 40 A37
Mayfield *E.S.* 13 D51
Mayford 22 F45
Mayland 24 A54
Maylandsea 24 A54
Maynard's Green 13 E51
Maypole *Kent* 25 E57
Maypole *I.o.S.* 2 A11
Maypole Green 45 F60
Maywick 107 E39
Meabhag 93 B7
Mead End 10 B36
Meadle 22 A43
Meadowmill 76 C29
Meadowtown 38 E28
Mealabost 100 B9
Mealasta 100 E6
Meal Bank 61 G31
Meals 53 C50
Mealsgate 60 B27
Meanley 56 D33
Mearbeck 56 C34
Meare 19 G30
Mearns 74 E21
Mears Ashby 32 B44
Measham 41 D39
Meathop 55 A30
Meavy 5 D21
Medbourne 42 F43
Meddon 6 D18
Meden Vale 51 F41
Medmenham 22 C44
Medomsley 62 A37
Medstead 11 A42
Meerbrook 49 F35
Meer End 40 A38
Meesden 33 E50
Meeth 6 E21
Meggethead 69 A27
Meidrim 17 B18
Meifod *Clw.* 47 G26
Meifod *Pow.* 38 D27
Meigle 82 C28
Meikle Earnock 74 E22
Meikle Grenach 73 C14
Meikle Kilmory 73 D16
Meikleour 82 D27
Meikle Rahane 74 B18
Meikle Strath 91 F32
Meikle Tarty 91 A35
Meikle Wartle 99 F33
Meinciau 17 C20
Meir 40 A35
Meirheath 40 B35
Melbost 100 D10
Melbourn 33 D49
Melbourne *Hum.* 58 E43
Melbourne *Dby.* 41 C39
Melbury 6 D19
Melbury Abbas 9 C34
Melbury Bubb 8 D31
Melbury Osmond 8 D31
Melbury Sampford 8 D31
Melby 107 B37
Melchbourne 32 B46
Melchet Court 10 B38
Melcombe Bingham 9 D33
Melcombe Regis 9 F32
Meldon *Dev.* 6 F21
Meldon *Nor.* 71 E37
Meldreth 33 D49
Melfort 79 F14
Melgarve 88 E20
Melgum 90 C30
Meliden 47 D26

Melincourt 18 A23
Melincryddan 18 B23
Melin-y-coed 47 F23
Melin-y-ddol 37 E26
Melin-y-grug 37 E26
Melin-y-Wig 37 A26
Melkinthorpe 61 D31
Melkridge 70 G33
Melksham 20 E34
Melksham Forest 20 E35
Melldalloch 73 C15
Melling *Mer.* 48 B29
Melling *Lan.* 55 B31
Melling Mount 48 B30
Mellis 34 A56
Mellon Charles 94 B14
Mellon Udrigle 94 B14
Mellor *G.M.* 49 D35
Mellor *Lan.* 56 F32
Mellor Brook 56 F32
Mells 20 G33
Melmerby *Cum.* 61 C32
Melmerby *N.Y.* 57 B39
Melmerby *N.Y.* 57 A36
Melplash 8 E30
Melrose *Grm.* 99 C33
Melrose *Bor.* 76 G31
Melsetter 105 C28
Melsonby 62 F37
Meltham 50 A37
Melton 35 C58
Meltonby 58 D43
Melton Constable 44 B56
Melton Mowbray 42 D43
Melton Ross 52 B46
Melvaig 94 C13
Melverley 38 D29
Melverley Green 38 D29
Melvich 102 B24
Membury 8 D28
Memsie 99 C35
Memus 83 B30
Menabilly 4 E16
Menai Bridge 46 E21
Mendham 45 G58
Mendlesham 34 B56
Mendlesham Green 34 B56
Menethorpe 58 C43
Menheniot 4 D18
Menie Ho. 91 A35
Mennock 68 C24
Menston 57 E37
Menstrie 75 A24
Mentmore 32 G44
Meoble 86 F13
Meole Brace 38 D30
Meon 11 D41
Meonstoke 11 C42
Meopham 24 E52
Meopham Green 24 E52
Mepal 43 G50
Meppershall 32 E47
Merbach 28 D28
Mercaston 40 A38
Mere *Che.* 49 D33
Mere *Wts.* 9 A34
Mere Brow 48 A30
Mere Green 40 F36
Mereworth 23 F52
Mergie 91 E33
Meriden 40 G38
Merkland 65 C23
Merlin's Bridge 16 C15
Merridge 7 B27
Merrifield 5 F24
Merrington 38 C30
Merrion 16 E15
Merriott 8 C30
Merrivale 5 C21
Merrow 22 F46
Merry Hill 22 B47
Merrymeet 4 D18
Mersham 15 D56
Merstham 23 F48
Merston 12 F44
Merstone 11 F40
Merther 3 D14
Merthyr 17 B19
Merthyr Cynog 27 E25
Merthyr Dyfan 18 D24
Merthyr Mawr 18 D24
Merthyr Tydfil 18 A26
Merthyr Vale 18 B26
Merton *G.L.* 23 E48
Merton *Nfk* 44 F54
Merton *Oxf.* 31 G41
Mertyn 47 E27
Mervinslaw 70 B32
Meshaw 7 D23
Messing 34 G54
Messingham 52 B44
Metfield 45 G58
Metheringham 52 F46
Methil 76 A29
Methlem 36 B17

Methley 57 G39
Methlick 99 F34
Methven 82 E26
Methwold 44 F53
Methwold Hythe 44 F53
Mettingham 45 G59
Metton 45 B57
Mevagissey 4 F16
Mexborough 51 C40
Mey 103 A28
Meysey Hampton 20 B36
Miabhag 100 G6
Miabhig 100 D6
Mial 94 D13
Michaelchurch 28 F31
Michaelchurch Escley 28 E28
Michaelchurch-on-Arrow 28 C28
Michaelston-le-Pit 18 D27
Michaelston-y-Fedw 19 C28
Michaelstow 4 C16
Micheldever 11 A41
Michelmersh 10 B39
Mickfield 35 B57
Mickleby 63 E43
Mickleham 22 F47
Micklehurst 49 B35
Mickleover 40 B38
Micklethwaite 60 A28
Mickleton *Drm* 61 D35
Mickleton *Glo.* 30 D37
Mickletown 57 G39
Mickle Trafford 48 F30
Mickley 57 B38
Mickley Square 71 G36
Mid Ardlaw 99 C35
Midbea 104 B30
Mid Beltie 90 C31
Mid Cairncross 90 F30
Mid Calder 75 D26
Mid Clyth 103 E28
Middle Assendon 22 C43
Middle Aston 31 F40
Middle Barton 31 F40
Middlebie 49 A31
Middle Claydon 31 F43
Middle Drums 83 B31
Middleham 57 A36
Middle Handley 51 E40
Middle Harling 44 G55
Middlehill *Cnw.* 4 D18
Middlehill *Grm.* 99 E34
Middlehope 38 G30
Middle Kames 73 B14
Middle Littleton 30 D36
Middle Maes-coed 28 E29
Middlemarsh 9 D32
Middle Mill 16 B14
Middle Rasen 52 D46
Middle Rigg 82 G26
Middle Salter 56 C32
Middlesbrough 62 D40
Middleshaw 55 A31
Middlesmoor 57 B36
Middlestone Moor 62 C38
Middlestown 50 A38
Middleton *Lan.* 55 D30
Middleton *G.M.* 49 B34
Middleton *Dby.* 50 F38
Middleton *Dby.* 50 G38
Middleton *War.* 40 F37
Middleton *Sfk* 35 B60
Middleton *Shr.* 38 C29
Middleton *Nor.* 77 G36
Middleton *Shr.* 28 A31
Middleton *Esx* 34 E54
Middleton *Cle.* 63 C41
Middleton *Tay.* 82 C27
Middleton *Grm.* 91 B34
Middleton *Tay.* 83 C31
Middleton *Tay.* 82 G27
Middleton *Shr.* 38 F28
Middleton *N.Y.* 58 A43
Middleton *W.Y.* 57 G39
Middleton *Nfk* 44 D52
Middleton *Ltn* 76 E29
Middleton *Nor.* 71 E36
Middleton *Cum.* 56 A32
Middleton *W.G.* 17 F20
Middleton *W.Y.* 57 E37
Middleton *Nmp.* 42 G44
Middleton *Ham.* 21 G40
Middleton Bank Top 71 E36
Middleton Cheney 31 D40
Middleton Green 40 B35
Middleton Hall 70 A35
Middleton-in-Teesdale 61 D34
Middleton of Potterton 91 B35
Middleton One Row 62 E39
Middleton-on-Leven 62 E40
Middleton-on-Sea 12 G45
Middleton on the Hill 28 B31
Middleton-on -the-Wolds 59 D45
Middleton Park 91 B34
Middleton Priors 39 F32
Middleton Quernhow 57 B39

Middleton Scriven 39 G32
Middleton St George 62 E39
Middleton Stoney 31 F41
Middleton Tyas 62 F37
Middle Town 2 A11
Middletown *Pow.* 38 D28
Middletown *Cum.* 60 F25
Middle Tysoe 30 D39
Middle Wallop 10 A38
Middlewich 49 F33
Middle Winterslow 10 A38
Middlewood 49 D35
Middle Woodford 10 A37
Middlewood Green 34 B56
Middleyard 74 G21
Middlezoy 8 A29
Middridge 62 D38
Midfield 102 B21
Midford 20 E33
Midge Hall 55 G31
Midgeholme 61 A32
Midgham 21 E41
Midgley *W.Y.* 57 G36
Midgley *W.Y.* 50 A38
Midhopestones 50 C38
Midhurst 12 D44
Mid Lavant 12 F44
Midlem 70 A31
Mid Letter 80 G16
Mid Lix 81 E21
Mid Mossdale 61 G34
Midpark 73 E15
Mid Sannox 73 F16
Midsomer Norton 19 F32
Midtown *Hgh.* 102 B21
Midtown *Hgh.* 94 C13
Midtown of Barras 91 E34
Midville 53 G49
Mid Yell 106 C40
Migdale 96 B22
Migvie 90 C30
Milarrochy 74 A20
Milber 5 C24
Milbethill 98 D31
Milborne Port 9 C32
Milborne St Andrew 9 E34
Milborne Wick 9 B32
Milbourne 71 F36
Milburn 61 D32
Milbury Heath 19 C32
Milcombe 30 E39
Milden 34 D55
Mildenhall *Sfk* 34 A52
Mildenhall *Wts.* 21 D38
Milebrook 28 A28
Milebush 14 C53
Mile Elm 20 E35
Mile End *Glo.* 28 G31
Mile End *Esx* 34 F55
Mileham 44 D55
Milesmark 75 B26
Milfield 77 G35
Milford *Dev.* 6 C18
Milford *Stf.* 40 C35
Milford *Shr.* 38 C30
Milford *Dby.* 41 A39
Milford *Sry* 22 G45
Milford Haven 16 D15
Milford on Sea 10 E38
Milkwall 19 A31
Milland Marsh 12 D44
Mill Bank 57 G36
Millbank 99 E36
Millbeck 60 D28
Millbounds 104 C31
Millbreck 99 E35
Millbridge 22 G44
Millbrook *Cnw.* 4 E19
Millbrook *Bfd.* 32 E45
Millbrook *Ham.* 10 C39
Millburn *Grm.* 90 A31
Millburn *Grm.* 99 F32
Millcombe 5 F24
Millcorner 14 E54
Millden 91 B35
Milldens 83 B31
Millearn 82 F25
Mill End *Hfs.* 33 E49
Mill End *Bkh.* 22 C43
Mill End Green 33 F52
Millenheath 38 B31
Millerhill 76 D29
Miller's Dale 50 E37
Mill Green *Shr.* 39 C32
Mill Green *Esx* 24 A52
Mill Hill 23 B48
Millholme 61 G31
Millhouse *Cum.* 60 C29
Millhouse *Str.* 73 D15
Millhousebridge 69 E26
Mill Houses 56 C32
Millikenpark 74 D19
Millington 58 D44
Mill Lane 22 F43
Millmeece 40 B34
Millness 88 A19

Mill of Colp 99 E33
Mill of Elrick 99 E35
Mill of Fortune 81 F23
Mill of Kingoodie 91 A34
Mill of Monquich 91 D34
Mill of Uras 91 E34
Millom 54 A27
Millport 73 E17
Mill Street 44 D56
Millthrop 61 G32
Milltimber 91 C34
Millton of Noth 90 A31
Milltown Grm. 90 B30
Milltown Hgh. 97 G25
Milltown D.&G. 69 F29
Milltown Dev. 6 B21
Milltown Dby. 51 F39
Milltown Hgh. 95 F19
Milltown of Aberdalgie 82 E26
Milltown of Auchindoun 98 E29
Milltown of Campfield 91 C32
Milltown of Craigston 99 D33
Milltown of Edinvillie 98 E28
Milltown of Rothiemay 98 E31
Milltown of Towie 90 B30
Milnathort 82 G26
Milngavie 74 C21
Milnrow 49 A35
Milnsbridge 50 A37
Milnthorpe 55 A30
Milovaig 93 F7
Milrig 74 G21
Milson 29 A32
Milstead 14 B54
Milston 20 G37
Milton Oxf. 21 B40
Milton Dyf. 16 D16
Milton Gwe. 19 C29
Milton Cen. 81 G20
Milton Str. 74 C20
Milton Cen. 74 A20
Milton Cen. 81 G21
Milton Tay. 82 C29
Milton Tay. 82 D25
Milton Hgh. 88 A20
Milton Avon 19 E29
Milton Hgh. 96 G21
Milton Hgh. 103 C29
Milton Grm. 98 C31
Milton Hgh. 97 F25
Milton D.&G. 65 C24
Milton Oxf. 31 E40
Milton Not. 51 E42
Milton Stf. 49 G35
Milton Cum. 70 G31
Milton D.&G. 68 E24
Milton Dby. 41 C39
Milton Hgh. 94 G12
Milton Hgh. 90 D23
Milton Abbas 9 D34
Milton Abbot 4 C20
Milton Bridge 76 D28
Milton Bryan 32 E45
Milton Clevedon 9 A32
Milton Coldwells 99 F35
Milton Combe 4 D20
Milton Damerel 6 D19
Miltonduff 97 E27
Milton Ernest 32 C46
Milton Green 48 G30
Milton Hill 21 B40
Miltonhill 97 E26
Milton Inveramsay 91 A33
Miltonise 64 C17
Milton Keynes 32 E44
Milton Keynes Village 32 E44
Milton Lilbourne 20 E37
Milton Lockhart 75 F24
Milton Malsor 31 C43
Milton Morenish 81 D21
Milton of Auchinhove 90 C31
Milton of Balgonie 82 G29
Milton of Cairnborrow 98 E30
Milton of Campsie 74 C22
Milton of Cullerlie 91 C33
Milton of Cushnie 90 B30
Milton of Dalcapon 82 B25
Milton of Tullich 90 D29
Milton on Stour 9 B33
Milton Regis 24 E54
Milton-under-Wychwood
  30 G38
Milverton 7 C27
Milwich 40 B35
Minard 73 A15
Minard Castle 73 A15
Minchington 9 C35
Minchinhampton 20 A34
Mindrum 77 G34
Minehead 7 A25
Minera 48 G28
Minety 20 B36
Minffordd Gwy. 37 D23
Minffordd Gwy. 36 B21
Mingearraidh 84 B3

Miningsby 53 F49
Minions 4 C18
Minishant 67 B19
Minley Manor 22 F43
Minllyn 37 D24
Minnes 91 A35
Minnigaff 64 D19
Minnonie 99 C33
Minskip 57 C39
Minstead 10 C38
Minster Kent 25 E58
Minster Kent 25 D55
Minsterley 38 E29
Minster Lovell 30 G38
Minsterworth 29 G33
Minterne Magna 9 D32
Minting 52 E47
Mintlaw 99 E36
Minto 70 A31
Minton 38 F30
Minwear 16 C16
Minworth 40 F37
Miodar 78 C6
Mirbister 104 D28
Mireland 103 B28
Mirfield 57 G38
Miserden 20 A35
Miskin M.G. 18 C26
Miskin M.G. 18 B26
Misson 51 C42
Misterton Not. 51 C43
Misterton Som. 8 D30
Misterton Lei. 41 G41
Mitcham 23 E48
Mitcheldean 29 G32
Mitchell 3 C14
Mitchelland 60 G30
Mitchel Troy 19 A30
Mitcheltroy Common 19 A30
Mitford 71 E37
Mithian 2 C13
Mitton 40 D34
Mixbury 31 E41
Moar 81 C21
Moat 69 F29
Mobberley 49 E33
Moccas 28 D29
Mochdre Pow. 37 G26
Mochdre Clw. 47 E24
Mochrum 64 F19
Mockbeggar 14 C53
Mockerkin 60 D26
Modbury 5 E22
Moddershall 40 B35
Modsarie 102 B22
Moelfre Gwy. 46 D20
Moelfre Clw. 38 C27
Moffat 69 C26
Mogerhanger 32 D47
Moin'a'choire 72 D9
Moine Ho. 102 B21
Moira 41 D39
Molash 15 B56
Mol-chlach 85 C10
Mold 48 F28
Molehill Green 33 F51
Molescroft 59 E46
Molesworth 32 A46
Mollacott Cross 6 A21
Mollance 65 D23
Molland 7 C24
Mollington Che. 48 F29
Mollington Oxf. 31 D40
Mollinsburn 75 C23
Monachty 26 B20
Monachylemore 81 F20
Moncreiffe 82 F27
Monevechadan 80 G17
Monewden 35 C58
Moneydie 82 E26
Moniaive 68 D23
Monifieth 83 D30
Monikie 83 D30
Monimail 82 F28
Monington 26 D17
Monken Hadley 23 B48
Monk Fryston 58 F41
Monkhill 60 A29
Monkhopton 39 F32
Monkland 28 C30
Monkleigh 6 C20
Monknash 18 D24
Monkokehampton 6 E21
Monkseaton 71 F39
Monks Eleigh 34 D55
Monk's Gate 12 D47
Monks' Heath 49 E34
Monk Sherborne 21 F41
Monkshill 99 E33
Monksilver 7 B26
Monks Kirby 41 G40
Monk Soham 35 B58
Monks Risborough 22 A43
Monkstadt 93 E9
Monk Street 33 F51
Monkswood 19 A29

Monkton T.&W. 71 G39
Monkton Str. 67 A19
Monkton Kent 25 E58
Monkton Dev. 7 E27
Monkton Combe 20 E33
Monkton Deverill 9 A34
Monkton Farleigh 20 E33
Monkton Heathfield 8 B28
Monkton Up Wimborne 10 C36
Monkwearmouth 62 A39
Monkwood 11 A42
Monmore Green 40 F35
Monmouth (Trefynwy) 28 G30
Monnington on Wye 28 D29
Monreith 64 F19
Monsale 25 B55
Montacute 8 C30
Monteach 99 E34
Montford 38 D29
Montford Bridge 38 D30
Montgarrie 90 B31
Montgomery (Trefaldwyn)
  38 F28
Montgreenan 74 F19
Montrave 82 G29
Montrose 83 B33
Monxton 21 G39
Monyash 50 F37
Monymusk 91 B32
Monzie 81 E24
Moodiesburn 74 C22
Moonzie 82 F29
Moor Allerton 57 F39
Moorby 53 F48
Moor Cock 56 C32
Moorcot 28 C29
Moor Crichel 9 D35
Moordown 10 E36
Moore 48 D31
Moor End Hum. 58 F44
Moor End Cum. 55 B31
Moorends 51 A42
Moorgate 55 C31
Moorgreen 41 A40
Moorhall 50 E38
Moorhampton 28 D29
Moorhouse Cum. 60 A29
Moorhouse Not. 51 F43
Moorlinch 8 A29
Moor Monkton 58 D41
Moor Nook 56 F32
Moorsholm 63 E42
Moor Side 53 G48
Moorside 49 B35
Moortown Lcn. 52 C46
Moortown I.o.W. 11 F40
Morangie 96 C23
Morar 86 E12
Morborne 42 F47
Morchard Bishop 7 E23
Morcombelake 8 E30
Morcott 42 E45
Morda 38 C28
Morden Dor. 9 E34
Morden G.L. 23 E48
Mordiford 28 E31
Mordington 77 E35
Mordon 62 D39
More 38 F29
Morebath 7 C25
Morebattle 70 A33
Morecambe 55 C29
Morefield 95 B16
Moreleigh 5 E23
Morenish 81 D21
Moresby 60 D25
Morestead 11 B41
Moreton Esx 23 A51
Moreton Mer. 48 D28
Moreton Oxf. 21 A42
Moreton Dor. 9 F34
Moreton H.&W. 28 B30
Moreton Corbet 38 C31
Moretonhampstead 6 G22
Moreton-in-Marsh 30 E38
Moreton Jeffries 29 D32
Moreton Morrell 30 C38
Moreton on Lugg 28 D31
Moreton Pinkney 31 D41
Moreton Say 39 B32
Moreton Valence 29 G33
Morewellham 4 D20
Morfa Bychan 36 B21
Morfa Glas 18 A24
Morfa Nefyn 36 A18
Morgan's Vale 10 B37
Mork 19 A31
Morland 61 D31
Morley Drm 62 D37
Morley Dby. 41 A39
Morley W.Y. 57 G38
Morley Green 49 D34
Morley St 44 E56
Morningside Ltn 76 C28
Morningside Str. 75 E24
Morningthorpe 45 F58

Morpeth 71 E37
Morphie 91 G33
Morrey 40 D37
Morriston W.G. 17 E22
Morriston Str. 67 C18
Morroch 86 F12
Morston 44 A55
Mortehoe 6 A20
Mortimer 21 E42
Mortimer's Cross 28 B29
Mortimer West End 21 E42
Mortlake 22 D47
Morton Lcn. 42 C47
Morton Shr. 38 C28
Morton Not. 51 G43
Morton Lcn. 51 C43
Morton Dby. 51 G39
Morton Nfk 45 D57
Morton Avon 19 B32
Morton Bagot 30 B37
Morton-on-Swale 62 G39
Morvah 2 E9
Morval 4 E18
Morvich Hgh. 96 A23
Morvich Hgh. 86 B15
Morvil 16 A16
Morville 39 F32
Morwenstow 6 D18
Morwick Hall 71 C38
Mosborough 51 D40
Moscow 74 F20
Mosedale 60 C29
Moselden Height 50 A36
Moseley H.&W. 29 C34
Moseley W.M. 40 G36
Moss S.Y. 51 A41
Moss Clw. 48 G28
Moss Str. 78 C5
Mossat 90 B30
Moss Bank 48 C31
Mossbank 106 E40
Mossblown 67 A19
Mossburnford 70 B32
Mossdale 65 C22
Mossend 75 E23
Mossgiel 67 A20
Mosshead 98 F31
Mosside 83 B30
Mossley 49 B35
Mossley Hill 48 D29
Moss Nook 49 D34
Moss of Barmuckity 98 C28
Mosspaul Hotel 69 D30
Moss-side Hgh. 97 F24
Moss-side Grm. 98 D31
Moss Side 55 F29
Mosstodloch 98 D28
Mosston 83 C31
Mosterton 8 D30
Mostyn 47 D27
Motcombe 9 B34
Motherby 60 D30
Motherwell 75 E23
Mottingham 23 D50
Mottisfont 10 B39
Mottistone 11 F40
Mottram in Longdendale 49 C35
Mottram St Andrew 49 E34
Mouldsworth 48 E30
Moulin 82 B25
Moulsecoomb 13 F49
Moulsford 21 C41
Moulsham 24 A52
Moulsoe 32 D44
Moulton Sfk 33 B52
Moulton Nmp. 31 B43
Moulton Che. 49 F32
Moulton N.Y. 62 F38
Moulton Lcn. 43 C48
Moulton Chapel 43 D48
Moulton Seas End 43 C49
Moulton St Mary 45 E59
Mounie Castle 91 A33
Mount Hgh. 97 G25
Mount Cnw. 2 C13
Mount Cnw. 4 D17
Mountain Ash 18 B26
Mountain Cross 75 F27
Mountain Water 16 B14
Mountbenger 69 A28
Mountblairy 99 D32
Mount Bures 34 E54
Mount Edgcumbe 4 E20
Mountfield 14 E53
Mountgerald 96 E21
Mount Hawke 2 D12
Mountjoy 3 B14
Mount Manisty 48 E29
Mountnessing 23 B51
Mount Oliphant 67 B19
Mounton 19 B30
Mount Pleasant Dby. 41 A39
Mount Pleasant Sfk 35 A60
Mountsorrel 41 D41
Mountstuart 73 E17
Mount Tabor 57 G36

Mousehole 2 F10
Mouswald 69 F26
Mow Cop 49 G34
Mowden 62 E38
Mowhaugh 70 A33
Mowsley 41 G42
Mowtie 91 E34
Moxley 40 F35
Moy Hgh. 87 F17
Moy Hgh. 88 A23
Moy Hgh. 88 F20
Moy House 97 E25
Moyles Court 10 D37
Moylgrove 16 A17
Muasdale 72 F12
Muchalls 91 D34
Much Birch 28 E30
Much Cowarne 29 D32
Much Dewchurch 28 E30
Muchelney 8 B30
Much Hadham 33 G50
Much Hoole 55 G30
Muchlarnick 4 E17
Much Marcle 29 E32
Muchra 69 B28
Muchrachd 87 A18
Much Wenlock 39 F32
Mucking 24 C52
Mucklestone 39 B33
Muckleton 38 C31
Muckletown 90 A31
Muckton 53 D49
Mudale 102 E21
Muddiford 6 B21
Muddles Green 13 E51
Muddleswood 13 E48
Mudeford 10 E37
Mudford 8 C31
Mudgley 19 G30
Mugeary 85 A10
Mugginton 40 A38
Muggleswick 62 A36
Muie 96 A22
Muir 89 F26
Muirden 98 D32
Muirdrum 83 D31
Muirhead Tay. 82 D29
Muirhead Fife 82 G28
Muirhead Grm. 90 B31
Muirhead Grm. 97 E26
Muirhead Str. 74 D22
Muirhouses 75 B25
Muirkirk 68 A22
Muirmill 75 B23
Muir of Fowlis 90 B31
Muir of Lochs 98 C28
Muir of Ord 96 F20
Muirskie 91 D34
Muirtack Grm. 99 E34
Muirtack Grm. 99 F35
Muirton 96 E23
Muirton of Ardblair 82 C27
Muirton of Ballochy 91 G32
Muirtown 82 F25
Muiryfold 99 D33
Muker 61 G34
Mulbarton 45 E57
Mulben 98 D29
Mulhagery 100 G9
Mullach Charlabhaigh 100 C7
Mullion 2 G12
Mumby 53 E51
Munderfield Row 29 C32
Munderfield Stocks 29 C32
Mundesley 45 B59
Mundford 44 F53
Mundham 45 F59
Mundon 24 A54
Mundurno 91 B35
Munerigie 87 D18
Mungasdale 94 B15
Mungoswells 76 C30
Mungrisdale 60 C29
Munlochy 96 F22
Munnoch 74 F18
Munsley 29 D32
Munslow 38 G30
Murchington 6 G22
Murcott 31 G41
Murdostoun 75 E24
Murkle 103 B27
Murlaganmore 81 D21
Murlaggan Hgh. 87 E16
Murlaggan Hgh. 87 F19
Murra 105 A28
Murroes 83 D30
Murrow 32 F44
Mursley 32 F44
Murston 25 E55
Murthill 83 B30
Murthly 82 D26
Murton Drm 62 B39
Murton Nor. 77 F35
Murton Cum. 61 D33
Murton N.Y. 58 D42
Musbury 8 E28

Muscoates 58 A42
Musdale 80 E15
Musselburgh 76 C29
Muston 42 B44
Mustow Green 29 A34
Mutford 45 G60
Muthill 81 F24
Mutterton 7 E26
Mybster 103 C27
Myddfai 27 E23
Myddle 38 C30
Myddlewood 38 C30
Mydroilyn 26 C20
Mylor 3 E14
Mylor Bridge 2 E13
Mynachlog-ddu 16 A17
Myndtown 38 G30
Mynydd-bach 19 B30
Mynytho 36 B18
Myrebird 91 D33
Mytchett 22 F44
Mytholm 56 G35
Mytholmroyd 56 G35
Myton-on-Swale 57 C40

N

Naast 94 C14
Naburn 58 E42
Nackington 15 B57
Nacton 35 D58
Nafferton 59 D46
Nailbridge 29 G32
Nailsea 19 D30
Nailstone 41 E39
Nailsworth 20 B34
Nairn 97 F24
Nancegollan 2 E12
Nancledre 2 E10
Nanhoron 36 B18
Nannau 37 C23
Nannerch 47 F27
Nanpantan 41 D40
Nanpean 3 C15
Nanstallon 4 D16
Nant-ddu 27 G25
Nanternis 26 C19
Nantgaredig 17 B20
Nantgarw 18 C27
Nant-glas 27 B25
Nantglyn 47 F25
Nantlle 46 G20
Nantmawr 38 C28
Nantmel 27 B26
Nantmor 36 A21
Nant Peris 46 G21
Nantwich 49 G32
Nantycaws 17 C20
Nant-y-derry 19 A29
Nant-y-dugoed 37 D24
Nantyffyllon 18 B24
Nantyglo 28 G27
Nant-y-groes 27 B26
Nant-y-moel 18 B25
Nant y Pandy 46 E22
Naphill 22 B44
Nappa 56 D34
Napton on the Hill 31 B40
Narberth 16 C16
Narborough Nfk 44 D53
Narborough Lei. 41 F41
Narrachan 79 F14
Nasareth 46 G20
Naseby 31 A42
Nash Bkh. 31 E43
Nash Shr. 28 A31
Nash Gwe. 19 C29
Nash S.G. 18 D25
Nash H.&W. 28 B29
Nash Lee 22 A44
Nassington 42 F46
Nasty 33 F49
Nateby Cum. 61 F33
Nateby Lan. 55 E30
Nately Scures 21 F42
Natland 55 A31
Naughton 34 D56
Naunton Glo. 30 F36
Naunton H.&W. 29 E34
Naunton Beauchamp 29 C35
Navenby 52 G45
Navestock 23 B51
Navestock Side 23 B51
Navidale 103 G26
Navity 96 E23
Nawton 58 A42
Nayland 34 E55
Nazeing 23 A49
Neacroft 10 E37
Neal's Green 41 G39
Neap 107 B40
Near Cotton 40 A36
Near Sawrey 60 G29
Neasham 62 E39
Neath 18 B23
Neatham 22 G43

Neatishead 45 C59
Nebo Gwy. 47 G24
Nebo Gwy. 46 G20
Nebo Gwy. 46 C20
Nebo Dyf. 26 B21
Necton 44 E54
Nedd 101 E17
Nedderton 71 E38
Nedging Tye 34 D56
Needham 45 G58
Needham Market 34 C56
Needingworth 33 A49
Neen Savage 29 A32
Neen Sollars 29 A32
Neenton 39 G32
Nefyn 36 A18
Neilston 74 E20
Nelson M.G. 18 B26
Nelson Lan. 56 F34
Nelson Village 71 F38
Nemphlar 75 F24
Nempnett Thrubwell 19 E31
Nenthall 61 B33
Nenthead 61 B33
Nenthorn 76 G32
Nercwys 48 F28
Nereabolls 72 E8
Neriby 72 D9
Nerston 74 E22
Nesbit 77 G35
Ness 48 E29
Nesscliffe 38 D29
Ness of Tenston 104 E28
Neston Che. 48 E28
Neston Wts. 20 E34
Nether Alderley 49 E34
Nether Auchendrane 67 B19
Netheravon 20 G37
Nether Barr 64 D20
Nether Blainslie 76 F31
Netherbrae 99 D33
Netherbrough 104 E28
Nether Broughton 41 C42
Netherburn 75 F23
Nether Burrow 56 B32
Netherbury 8 E30
Netherby Cum. 69 F29
Netherby N.Y. 57 E39
Nether Cerne 9 E32
Nether Compton 8 C31
Nethercott 31 F40
Nether Crimond 91 A34
Nether Dalgliesh 69 C28
Nether Dallachy 98 C29
Netherend 19 B31
Nether End 50 E38
Nether Exe 7 F25
Netherfield Str. 75 F23
Netherfield E.S. 14 F53
Netherfield Not. 41 A42
Nether Glasslaw 99 D34
Netherhall 74 D18
Netherhampton 10 A36
Nether Handwick 82 C29
Nether Haugh 51 C40
Nether Headon 51 E43
Nether Hesleden 56 B34
Nether Heyford 31 C42
Nether Kellet 55 C31
Nether Kinmundy 99 E36
Nether Langwith 51 F41
Nether Lenshie 98 E32
Netherley 91 D34
Nethermill 69 E26
Nether Moor 51 F39
Nethermuir 99 E34
Nether Padley 50 E38
Nether Pitforthie 91 F34
Nether Poppleton 58 D41
Netherseal 40 D38
Nethershield 67 A21
Nether Silton 62 G40
Nether Stowey 7 B27
Netherstreet 20 E35
Netherthird D.&G. 65 E23
Netherthird Str. 67 B21
Netherthong 50 B37
Netherthorpe 51 D41
Netherton Dev. 5 C24
Netherton W.M. 40 G35
Netherton W.Y. 50 B37
Netherton H.&W. 29 D35
Netherton Nor. 70 C35
Netherton Tay. 82 B27
Netherton Tay. 83 B31
Netherton Oxf. 21 B40
Netherton Str. 75 E25
Netherton Che. 48 E31
Netherton Mer. 48 B29
Nethertown Hgh. 103 A29
Nethertown Cum. 60 F25
Nether Urquhart 82 G27
Nether Wallop 10 A39
Nether Wasdale 60 F27
Nether Wellwood 68 A22
Nether Whitacre 40 F38

Netherwitton 71 E36
Netherwood D.&G. 65 C25
Netherwood Str. 68 A22
Nether Woodburn 7 C24
Nether Worton 31 E40
Nethy Bridge 89 C26
Netley 11 D40
Netley Marsh 10 C39
Nettlebed 21 C42
Nettlebridge 19 G32
Nettlecombe Dor. 8 E31
Nettlecombe Som. 7 B26
Nettleden 32 G46
Nettleham 52 E46
Nettlestead Sfk 34 D56
Nettlestead Kent 23 F52
Nettlestead Green 23 F52
Nettlestone 11 E42
Nettleton Wts. 20 D33
Nettleton Lcn. 52 B47
Netton Dev. 5 F21
Netton Wts. 10 A37
Neuadd Gwy. 46 C19
Neuadd Dyf. 27 D25
Neuadd Dyf. 26 C20
Nevendon 24 B53
Nevern 16 A16
Nevill Holt 42 F43
New Abbey 65 D25
New Aberdour 99 C34
New Addington 23 E49
New Alresford 11 A41
New Alyth 82 C28
Newark Ork. 104 B33
Newark Cbs. 43 E48
Newark-on-Trent 51 G43
New Arley 40 G38
Newarthill 75 E23
New Ash Green 24 E52
New Barn 24 E52
Newbarn 15 C57
New Barnet 23 B48
Newbarns 55 B28
New Belses 70 A31
New Bewick 71 A36
Newbiggin Nor. 70 G35
Newbiggin Cum. 61 D32
Newbiggin Drm 61 D23
Newbiggin N.Y. 57 A36
Newbiggin Cum. 61 B31
Newbiggin Cum. 60 D30
Newbiggin N.Y. 62 G35
Newbiggin Cum. 55 C28
Newbiggin-by-the-Sea 71 E38
Newbigging Str. 75 F25
Newbigging Tay. 82 C28
Newbigging Grm. 91 D34
Newbigging Grm. 90 E27
Newbigging Tay. 83 D30
Newbigging Tay. 83 D30
Newbiggin-on-Lune 61 F32
Newbold Dby. 51 E39
Newbold Lei. 41 D40
Newbold on Avon 31 A40
Newbold on Stour 30 D38
Newbold Pacey 30 C38
Newbold Verdon 41 E40
New Bolingbroke 53 G49
Newborough Stf. 40 C36
Newborough Cbs. 42 E47
Newborough (Niwbwrch) 46 F19
Newbottle 31 E41
Newbourne 35 D58
New Bradwell 32 D44
Newbridge Cnw. 4 D19
Newbridge Clw. 38 A28
New Bridge 65 C25
Newbridge Ltn 75 C26
Newbridge Oxf. 21 A39
Newbridge Gwe. 19 B28
Newbridge Dyf. 16 A15
Newbridge Cnw. 2 E10
Newbridge I.o.W. 11 F40
Newbridge Ham. 10 C38
Newbridge-on-Usk 19 B29
Newbridge on Wye 27 C25
New Brighton Mer. 48 C29
New Brighton Ham. 11 D43
New Brinsley 41 A40
Newbrough 70 G34
New Broughton 48 G29
New Buckenham 44 F56
Newburgh Lan. 48 A30
Newburgh Grm. 91 A35
Newburgh Grm. 99 C35
Newburgh Fife 82 F82
Newburgh Bor. 69 B29
Newburn 71 G37
Newbury 21 E40
Newby N.Y. 62 E40
Newby Cum. 61 D31
Newby Lan. 56 E34
Newby N.Y. 56 B33
Newby Bridge 55 A29
Newby East 61 A30

New Byth 99 D34
Newby West 60 A29
Newby Wiske 57 A39
Newcastle M.G. 18 D24
Newcastle Shr. 38 G28
Newcastle Gwe. 28 G30
Newcastle Emlyn 26 D18
Newcastleton 69 E30
Newcastle-under-Lyme 40 A34
Newcastle upon Tyne 71 G38
Newcastle (Woolsington) Airport 71 F38
Newchapel Stf. 49 G34
Newchapel Dyf. 16 A17
Newchapel Sry 23 G49
New Cheriton 11 B41
Newchurch I.o.W. 11 F41
Newchurch Gwe. 19 B30
Newchurch Kent 15 D56
Newchurch Lan. 56 G34
Newchurch Lan. 56 F34
Newchurch Dyf. 17 B19
Newchurch Pow. 28 C27
New Clipstone 51 F41
New Costessey 45 D57
Newcott 8 D28
Newcraighall 76 C28
New Cross 27 A22
New Cumnock 68 B22
New Deer 99 E34
Newdigate 22 G47
New Duston 31 B43
New Earswick 58 D42
New Edlington 51 C41
New Elgin 97 E27
New Ellerby 59 F47
Newell Green 22 D44
New Eltham 23 D50
New End 30 C36
Newenden 14 E54
New England 42 E47
Newent 29 F33
Newerne 19 A32
New Farnley 57 F38
New Ferry 48 D29
Newfield Drm 62 C37
Newfield Drm 62 A38
Newfield Hgh. 96 D23
New Fryston 57 G40
Newgale 16 B14
New Galloway 65 C21
Newgate 44 A56
Newgate Street 23 A48
New Gilston 83 G30
Newgord 106 B41
New Grimsby 2 A10
Newhall Dby. 40 C38
Newhall Che. 39 A32
Newham Nor. 71 A37
Newham G.L. 23 C49
Newham Hall 77 G37
New Hartley 71 F38
Newhaven 13 F50
New Haw 22 E46
New Hedges 16 D17
Newhey 49 A35
New Holland 59 G46
Newholm 63 E44
New Horton Grange 71 F37
New Houghton Nfk 44 C53
New Houghton Dby. 51 F41
Newhouse 75 D23
New Houses 56 B34
New Hutton 61 G31
New Hythe 14 B53
Newick 13 D50
Newington Oxf. 21 B42
Newington Kent 24 E54
Newington Kent 15 D57
Newington Bagpath 20 B33
New Inn Gwe. 19 A30
New Inn Dyf. 17 A20
New Inn Gwe. 19 B29
New Inn Fife 82 G28
New Invention W.M. 40 E35
New Invention Shr. 28 A28
New Lanark 75 F24
Newland Glo. 19 A31
Newland N.Y. 58 G42
Newland H.&W. 29 D33
Newlandrig 76 D29
Newlands Nor. 62 A36
Newlands Nor. 70 D31
Newland's Corner 22 G46
Newlands of Geise 103 B26
New Lane 48 A30
New Leake 53 G49
New Leeds 99 D35
New Leslie 90 A31
New Longton 55 G31
New Luce 64 D17
Newlyn 2 F10
Newlyn East 3 C14
Newmachar 91 B34
New Mains 75 G24
Newmains 75 E24

New Mains of Ury 91 E34
New Malden 23 E48
Newmarket W.I. 100 D10
Newmarket Sfk 33 B52
New Marske 63 D42
New Marton 38 B29
New Mill W.Y. 50 B37
New Mill Hfs. 32 G45
Newmill Bor. 69 B30
Newmill Grm. 98 D30
Newmill Grm. 99 E34
Newmill Grm. 91 A33
New Mill Grm. 91 E33
New Mill Cnw. 2 E10
New Mill End 32 G47
Newmill of Inshewan 83 A30
New Mills Pow. 37 E26
New Mills Gwe. 19 A31
New Mills Dby. 50 D36
New Mills Cnw. 3 C15
Newmills 96 E22
Newmiln Tay. 82 D27
Newmiln Tay. 82 E25
Newmilns 74 G21
New Milton 10 E38
New Mistley 35 E57
New Moat 16 B16
Newnham Hfs. 33 E48
Newnham Nmp. 31 C41
Newnham Glo. 29 G32
Newnham H.&W. 29 B32
Newnham Ham. 21 F42
Newnham Kent 14 B55
Newnham Paddox 41 G40
Newnoth 98 F30
New Orleans 66 B13
New Park 4 B17
New Pitsligo 99 D34
New Polzeath 3 B18
Newport Glo. 19 B32
Newport Dyf. 16 A16
Newport Cnw. 6 G19
Newport Nfk 45 D61
Newport Dev. 6 B21
Newport Hum. 58 F44
Newport Hgh. 103 F27
Newport Gwe. 19 C29
Newport Esx 33 E51
Newport Shr. 39 D33
Newport I.o.W. 11 F41
Newport-on-Tay 83 E30
Newport Pagnell 32 D44
Newpound Common 12 D46
New Prestwick 67 A18
New Quay 26 C19
Newquay 2 B13
Newquay (St Mawgan) Airport 3 B14
New Rackheath 45 D58
New Radnor 28 B27
New Rent 61 C30
New Road Side 56 E35
New Romney 15 E56
New Rossington 51 C42
New Row 56 F42
New Sauchie 75 A24
New Sawley 41 B40
New Scone 82 E27
Newseat 98 F32
Newsham N.Y. 62 E37
Newsham N.Y. 57 A39
Newsham Nor. 71 E38
Newsham Lan. 55 F31
Newsholme Hum. 58 G43
Newsholme Lan. 56 D34
New Silksworth 62 A39
Newstead Bor. 76 G31
Newstead Nor. 71 A37
Newstead Not. 51 G40
Newthorpe 57 F40
Newton W.Y. 57 G40
Newton Che. 48 E31
Newton Nfk 44 D54
Newton Tay. 81 D24
Newton Str. 73 A16
Newton Str. 73 E15
Newton Ltn 75 C26
Newton Str. 75 G25
Newton M.G. 18 D24
Newton Dyf. 16 B14
Newton Dyf. 16 D15
Newton W.G. 17 F21
Newton Hgh. 96 G23
Newton Hgh. 103 C28
Newton Hgh. 101 E18
Newton Grm. 99 E36
Newton Grm. 98 D30
Newton Grm. 98 C29
Newton Cum. 55 B28
Newton Lan. 56 B30
Newton G.M. 49 C35
Newton Che. 48 G30
Newton Stf. 40 C36
Newton H.&W. 28 B29
Newton Nor. 71 G36
Newton Sfk 34 D55

Newton *Cbs.* 33 D50
Newton *War.* 31 A41
Newton *Hgh.* 103 D29
Newton *Bor.* 70 A31
Newton *D.&G.* 69 D27
Newton *Bor.* 69 B30
Newton *Lan.* 56 D32
Newton *Nfk* 43 D50
Newton *Nmp.* 42 G44
Newton *Lcn.* 42 B46
Newton *Not.* 41 A42
Newton *Ham.* 10 B38
Newton *W.I.* 92 D4
Newton *Hgh.* 96 E23
Newton *Hgh.* 96 F21
Newton Abbot 5 C24
Newtonairds 68 E24
Newton Arlosh 60 A27
Newton Aycliffe 62 D38
Newton Bewley 62 D40
Newton Blossomville 32 C45
Newton Bromswold 32 B46
Newton Burgoland 41 E39
Newton by Toft 52 D46
Newton Ferrers 5 F21
Newton Flotman 45 F57
Newtongrange 76 D29
Newton Harcourt 41 F42
Newtonhill 91 D34
Newton Kyme 57 E40
Newton-le-Willows 48 C31
Newton-le-Willows 62 G37
Newton Longville 32 E44
Newton Mearns 74 E21
Newtonmill 83 A31
Newtonmore 88 E22
Newton Morrell 62 F38
Newton Mountain 16 D15
Newton Mulgrave 63 E43
Newton of Ardtoe 86 G12
Newton of Balcanquhal 82 F27
Newton of Dalvey 97 F25
Newton of Falkland 82 G28
Newton of Leys 96 G22
Newton-on-Ouse 58 C41
Newton-on-Rawcliffe 63 G43
Newton-on-the-Moor 71 C37
Newton on Trent 51 E43
Newton Poppleford 7 G26
Newton Purcell 31 E42
Newton Regis 40 E38
Newton Reigny 61 C30
Newton Solney 40 C38
Newton Stacey 21 G40
Newton St Cyres 7 F24
Newton Stewart 64 D19
Newton St Faith 45 D58
Newton St Loe 19 E32
Newton St Petrock 6 D20
Newton Tony 21 G38
Newton Tracey 6 C21
Newton under Roseberry
  63 E41
Newton upon Derwent 58 E42
Newton Valence 11 A43
Newtown *Ham.* 11 C41
Newtown *Ham.* 10 C38
Newtown *Wts.* 10 B38
Newtown *Dor.* 10 E36
Newtown *Ham.* 11 C41
Newtown *I.o.W.* 11 E40
Newtown *Brk.* 21 E40
Newtown *Hgh.* 88 D19
Newtown *Wts.* 9 B34
New Town *E.S.* 13 D50
New Town *Ltn* 76 C30
Newtown *Nor.* 71 A36
Newtown *Nor.* 71 C36
Newtown *Grm.* 99 C33
Newtown *I.o.M.* 54 F25
Newtown *Bkh.* 22 A45
New Town *Glo.* 19 D35
Newtown *H.&W.* 29 E32
Newtown *Gwe.* 28 G27
Newtown *H.&W.* 29 D32
Newtown (Y Drenewydd) 38 F27
Newtown *Shr.* 38 B30
Newtown *Stf.* 50 F36
Newtown *Che.* 48 G30
Newtown *Stf.* 49 F35
Newtown *Che.* 40 D35
Newtown *Cum.* 69 G30
Newtown in St Martin 2 F13
Newtown Linford 41 E41
Newtown St Boswells 76 G31
Newtown Unthank 41 E40
New Tredegar 18 A27
Newtyle 82 C28
New Ulva 73 B13
New Walsoken 43 E50
New Waltham 53 B48
New Wimpole 33 D49
New Winton *Ltn* 76 C30
New Yatt 30 G39
New York *Lcn.* 53 G48
New York *T.&W.* 71 F39

Neyland 16 D15
Nibley *Avon* 19 C32
Nibley *Glo.* 19 A32
Nicholashayne 7 D26
Nicholaston 17 F21
Nidd 57 C39
Niddrie 76 C28
Nigg *Grm.* 91 C35
Nigg *Hgh.* 97 D24
Nightcott 7 C24
Nilig 47 G26
Nine Ashes 23 A51
Ninebanks 61 A33
Nine Elms 20 C37
Nine Mile Burn 75 E27
Ninfield 14 F53
Ningwood 11 F40
Nisbet 70 A32
Niton 11 G40
Nitshill 74 D20
Niwbwrch (Newborough)
  46 F19
Nizels 23 F51
Noak Hill 23 B51
Noblehill 65 C25
Nobottle 31 B42
Nocton 52 F46
Noddsdale 74 D18
Noke 31 G41
Nolton 16 C14
No Man's Heath *War.* 40 E38
No Man's Heath *Che.* 38 A31
Nomansland *Dev.* 7 D24
Nomansland *Ham.* 10 C38
Noneley 38 C30
Nonington 15 B58
Nook *Cum.* 55 A31
Nook *Cum.* 69 F30
Noonsbrough 107 B38
Noranside 83 A30
Norbiton 22 E47
Norbreck 55 E28
Norbury *Dby.* 40 A37
Norbury *Che.* 38 A31
Norbury *Shr.* 38 F29
Norbury *Stf.* 39 C33
Norchard 29 B34
Nordelph 43 E51
Norden 9 F35
Nordley 39 F32
Norham 77 F34
Norland Town 57 G36
Norley 48 E31
Norleywood 10 E39
Normanby *N.Y.* 58 A43
Normanby *Cle.* 63 E41
Normanby *Hum.* 52 A44
Normanby by Spital 52 D46
Normanby le Wold 52 C47
Norman Cross 42 F47
Normandy 22 F45
Normann's Ruh 79 C10
Norman's Bay 13 F52
Norman's Green 7 E26
Normanton *Lei.* 42 E45
Normanton *Dby.* 41 B39
Normanton *Lei.* 42 A44
Normanton *Lcn.* 42 A45
Normanton *W.Y.* 57 G39
Normanton *Not.* 51 G48
Normanton le Heath 41 D39
Normanton on Soar 41 C41
Normanton on the Wolds
  41 B42
Normanton on Trent 51 F43
Normoss 55 F29
Norrington Common 20 E34
Norris Hill 41 D39
Northacre 44 F55
Northallerton 62 G39
Northall Green 44 D56
Northam *Dev.* 6 C20
Northam *Ham.* 11 C40
Northampton 31 B43
North Anston 51 D41
North Ascot 22 E44
North Aston 31 F40
Northaw 23 A48
Northay 8 C28
North Baddesley 10 B39
North Ballachulish 80 A16
North Balloch 67 D19
North Barrow 9 B32
North Benfleet 24 C53
North Bersted 12 F45
North Berwick 76 B31
North Boarhunt 11 D41
North Bogbain 98 D29
Northborough 42 E47
Northbourne 15 B58
North Bovey 7 G23
North Bradley 20 F34
North Brentor 6 G20
North Brewham 9 A33
Northbrook 31 F40
North Buckland 6 A20

North Burlingham 45 D59
Northburnhill 99 E33
North Cadbury 9 B32
North Carlton 52 E45
North Cave 58 F44
North Cerney 20 A36
North Chailey 13 D49
Northchapel 12 D45
North Charford 10 B38
North Charlton 71 A37
North Cheriton 9 B32
Northchurch 22 A45
North Cliffe 58 F44
North Clifton 52 E44
North Cockerington 53 C49
North Coker 8 C31
North Cornelly 18 C24
Northcote Manor 6 D22
North Cotes 53 B49
Northcott 6 F19
North Cove 45 G60
North Cowton 62 F38
North Crawley 32 D45
North Cray 23 D50
North Curry 8 B29
North Dallens 80 C15
North Dalton 59 D45
North Dawn 105 A30
North Deighton 57 D39
North Duffield 58 F42
Northdyke 104 D28
North Elkington 53 C48
North Elmham 44 C56
North Elmsall 51 A40
North End *Esx* 33 G52
North End *Bkh.* 32 F44
Northend *War.* 30 C39
Northend *Avon* 20 E33
North End *Avon* 19 E30
North End *Nor.* 71 C37
North End *Nfk* 44 F56
North End *W.S.* 12 E47
Northend *Bkh.* 22 B43
North End *Ham.* 21 E40
North End *Ham.* 11 D42
North Erradale 94 C12
North Essie 99 D36
North Ferriby 59 G45
Northfield *Bor.* 77 D34
Northfield *Grm.* 99 C34
Northfield *Hgh.* 103 D29
Northfield *W.M.* 30 A36
Northfield *Grm.* 91 C34
Northfleet 24 D52
North Frodingham 59 D47
North Gorley 10 C37
North Green 45 G58
North Grimston 58 C44
North Hayling 11 D43
North Hazelrigg 77 G36
North Heasley 7 B23
North Heath 12 D46
North Hill 4 C18
North Hinksey 21 A40
North Holmwood 22 G47
Northhouse 69 C30
North Huish 8 E23
North Hykeham 52 F45
Northiam 14 E54
Northill 32 D47
Northington 11 A41
North Johnston 16 C15
North Kelsey 52 B46
North Kessock 96 G22
North Killingholme 52 A47
North Kilvington 57 A40
North Kilworth 41 G42
North Kyme 52 G47
North Lancing 12 F47
Northlands 53 G49
Northleach 30 G36
North Lee 22 A44
Northleigh *Dev.* 7 F27
Northleigh *Dev.* 6 B22
North Leigh 30 G39
North Leverton with
  Habblesthorpe 51 D43
Northlew 6 F21
North Littleton 30 D36
North Lopham 44 G56
North Luffenham 42 E45
North Marden 12 E44
North Marston 31 F43
North Middleton 76 E29
North Millbrex 99 E34
North Molton 7 C23
Northmoor 21 A40
Northmoor Green or Moorland
  8 A28
North Moreton 21 C41
Northmuir 82 B29
North Mundham 12 F44
North Muskham 51 G43
North Newbald 59 F45
North Newington 30 E39
North Newnton 20 F37

North Newton 8 A28
Northney 11 D43
North Nibley 20 B33
North Oakley 21 F41
North Ockendon 23 C51
Northolt 22 C47
Northop 48 F28
Northop Hall 48 F28
North Ormesby 63 E41
North Ormsby 53 C48
Northorpe *Lcn.* 52 C44
Northorpe *Lcn.* 42 D46
Northorpe *Lcn.* 42 B47
Northover 8 B30
North Owersby 52 C46
Northowram 57 G37
North Perrott 8 D30
North Petherton 8 A28
North Petherwin 4 B18
North Pickenham 44 E54
North Piddle 29 C35
North Poorton 8 E31
North Port 80 E16
Northpunds 107 E40
North Queensferry 75 B27
North Radworthy 7 B23
North Rauceby 42 A46
Northrepps 45 B58
North Reston 53 D49
North Rigton 57 E38
North Rode 49 F34
North Roe 106 D39
North Runcton 44 D52
North Sandwick 106 C41
North Scale 54 C27
North Scarle 52 F44
North Seaton 71 E38
North Shian 79 C14
North Shields 71 G39
North Shoebury 25 C55
North Side 43 F48
North Skelton 63 E42
North Somercotes 53 C50
North Stainley 57 B38
North Stainmore 61 E34
North Stifford 23 C51
North Stoke *W.S.* 12 E46
North Stoke *Avon* 19 E32
North Stoke *Oxf.* 21 C42
North Stoneham 11 C40
North Street *Ham.* 11 A42
North Street *Kent* 15 B56
North Street *Brk.* 21 D42
North Sunderland 77 G37
North Tamerton 4 A18
North Tarbothill 91 B35
North Tawton 6 E22
North Third 75 A23
North Thoresby 53 C48
North Tidworth 21 G38
North Togston 71 C38
North Town *Dev.* 6 E20
Northtown 105 B39
North Town *Ham.* 22 F44
North Tuddenham 44 D56
North Walsham 45 B58
North Waltham 21 G41
North Warnborough 22 F43
North Watten 103 C28
Northway 29 E34
North Weald Bassett 23 A50
North Wheatley 51 D43
North Whilborough 5 D24
Northwich 49 E32
North Wick 19 E31
Northwick 19 C31
North Widcombe 19 F31
North Willingham 52 D47
North Wingfield 51 F39
North Witham 42 C44
Northwold 44 F53
Northwood *Shr.* 38 B30
Northwood *G.L.* 22 B46
Northwood *I.o.W.* 11 E40
Northwood Green 29 G33
North Wootton *Nfk* 44 C52
North Wootton *Som.* 19 G31
North Wootton *Dor.* 9 C32
North Wraxall 20 D34
North Wroughton 20 C37
North Yardhope 70 C34
Norton *I.o.W.* 10 F39
Norton *W.S.* 12 G44
Norton *W.S.* 12 F45
Norton *W.M.* 40 G34
Norton *Wts.* 20 C34
Norton *N.Y.* 58 B43
Norton *Shr.* 38 G30
Norton *Che.* 48 D31
Norton *Cle.* 62 D40
Norton *H.&W.* 30 D36
Norton *Glo.* 29 F34
Norton *Pow.* 28 B28
Norton *H.&W.* 29 C34
Norton *Sfk* 34 B55

Norton *Nmp.* 31 B41
Norton *Hfs.* 33 E48
Norton *Shr.* 39 E33
Norton *Shr.* 38 E31
Norton *Not.* 51 E41
Norton *S.Y.* 51 D39
Norton *S.Y.* 51 A41
Norton Bavant 20 G35
Norton Bridge 40 B34
Norton Canes 40 E36
Norton Canon 28 D29
Norton Disney 52 G44
Norton Ferris 9 A33
Norton Fitzwarren 7 C27
Norton Green 10 F39
Norton Hawkfield 19 E31
Norton Heath 24 A52
Norton in Hales 39 B32
Norton in the Moors 49 G34
Norton-Juxta-Twycross 40 E38
Norton-le-Clay 57 B39
Norton Lindsey 30 B38
Norton Malreward 19 E32
Norton Mandeville 23 A51
Norton St Philip 20 F33
Norton Subcourse 45 F59
Norton sub Hamdon 8 C30
Norton Wood 28 D29
Norwell 51 F43
Norwell Woodhouse 51 F43
Norwich 45 E58
Norwich Airport 45 D58
Norwick 106 A42
Norwood Green 22 D47
Norwood Hill 23 G48
Noseley 42 F43
Noss Mayo 5 F21
Nosterfield 57 A38
Nostie 86 B14
Notgrove 30 F36
Nottage 18 D23
Nottingham *Hgh.* 103 E27
Nottingham *Not.* 41 A41
Notton *Wts.* 20 E34
Notton *W.Y.* 51 A39
Nounsley 24 A53
Noutard's Green 29 B33
Nowton 34 B54
Nox 38 D30
Noyadd Trefawr 26 D18
Nuffield 21 C42
Nunburnholme 58 E44
Nuneaton 41 F39
Nuneham Courtenay 21 B41
Nun Monkton 57 D40
Nunney 20 G33
Nunnington 58 B42
Nunnington Park 7 C26
Nunthorpe 63 E41
Nunton 10 B37
Nunwick *N.Y.* 57 B39
Nunwick *Nor.* 70 F34
Nup End *Glo.* 29 F33
Nup End *Bkh.* 32 G44
Nursling 10 C39
Nursted 11 B43
Nurton 40 F34
Nutbourne *W.S.* 11 D43
Nutbourne *W.S.* 12 E46
Nutfield 23 F48
Nuthall 41 A41
Nuthampstead 33 E49
Nuthurst *War.* 30 A37
Nuthurst *W.S.* 12 D47
Nutley *E.S.* 13 D50
Nutley *Ham.* 21 G42
Nutwell 51 B42
Nyadd 75 A23
Nybster 103 B29
Nyetimber 12 G44
Nyewood 12 D44
Nymet Rowland 6 E22
Nymet Tracey 7 E23
Nympsfield 20 A33
Nynehead 7 C27
Nythe 8 A30
Nyton 12 F45

O

Oadby 41 E42
Oad Street 24 E54
Oakamoor 40 A36
Oakbank *Ltn* 75 D26
Oakbank *Str.* 79 D13
Oak Cross 6 F21
Oakdale 18 B27
Oake 7 C27
Oaken 40 E34
Oakenclough 55 E31
Oakengates 39 D32
Oakenhead 98 C28
Oakenshaw *Drm* 62 C37
Oakenshaw *W.Y.* 57 G37
Oakford *Dev.* 7 C24
Oakford *Dyf.* 26 C20

Oakfordbridge 7 C25
Oakgrove 49 F35
Oakham 42 E44
Oakhanger 11 A43
Oakhill 19 G32
Oakington 33 B49
Oaklands *Hfs.* 33 G48
Oaklands *Clw.* 47 G24
Oakle Street 29 G33
Oakley *Fife* 75 B26
Oakley *Bfd.* 32 C46
Oakley *Sfk* 35 A57
Oakley *Ham.* 21 F41
Oakley Green 22 D45
Oakley Park 37 G25
Oaks 38 E30
Oaksey 20 B35
Oakshaw Ford 70 F31
Oakthorpe 41 D39
Oaktree Hill 62 G39
Oakwoodhill 12 C47
Oakworth 57 F36
Oalinlongart 73 B17
Oare *Wts.* 20 E37
Oare *Som.* 7 A24
Oare *Kent* 25 E55
Oasby 42 B45
Oatfield 66 B12
Oathlaw 83 B30
Oban 79 E14
Obinan 94 B14
Obley 28 A29
Oborne 9 C32
Occlestone Green 49 F32
Occold 35 A57
Occumster 103 E28
Ochiltree 67 A20
Ochr-y-Mynydd 18 A25
Ochtermuthill 81 F24
Ochtertyre *Tay.* 81 E24
Ochtertyre *Cen.* 75 A23
Ockbrook 41 B40
Ockham 22 F46
Ockle 86 G11
Ockley 12 C47
Ocle Pychard 28 D31
Octon 59 C46
Odcombe 8 C30
Odd Down 20 E33
Oddingley 29 C34
Oddington 31 G41
Oddsta 106 C41
Odell 32 C45
Odie 104 D32
Odiham 22 F43
Odstock 10 B37
Odstone 41 E39
Offchurch 30 B39
Offenham 30 D36
Offerton 49 D35
Offham *E.S.* 13 E49
Offham *Kent* 23 F52
Offord Cluny 32 B47
Offord D'Arcy 32 B47
Offton 34 D56
Offwell 7 F27
Ogbourne Maizey 20 D37
Ogbourne St Andrew 20 D37
Ogbourne St George 20 D37
Ogden 57 F36
Ogil 83 A30
Ogle 71 F37
Ogmore 18 D24
Ogmore-by-Sea 18 D24
Ogmore Vale 18 B25
Oil Terminal 105 B29
Okeford Fitzpaine 9 C34
Okehampton 6 F21
Okehampton Camp 6 F21
Okraquoy 107 D40
Old 31 A43
Old Aberdeen 91 C35
Old Alresford 11 A41
Old Arley 40 F38
Old Basford 41 A41
Old Basing 21 F42
Old Belses 70 A31
Oldberrow 30 B36
Old Bewick 71 A36
Old Bolingbroke 53 F49
Oldborough 7 E23
Old Brampton 51 E39
Old Bridge of Urr 65 D23
Old Buckenham 44 F56
Old Burghclere 21 F40
Oldbury *Kent* 23 F51
Oldbury *W.M.* 40 F35
Oldbury *War.* 41 F39
Oldbury *Shr.* 39 F32
Oldbury Naite 19 B32
Oldbury -on-Severn 19 B32
Oldbury on the Hill 20 C33
Old Byland 58 A41
Oldcastle 28 F29

Oldcastle Heath 38 A30
Old Cleeve 7 A26
Old Colwyn 47 E24
Oldcotes 51 D41
Old Craig 91 A34
Old Craighall 76 C29
Old Crombie 98 D31
Old Dailly 67 D18
Old Dalby 41 C42
Old Deer 99 E36
Old Ellerby 59 F47
Old Felixstowe 35 E59
Oldfield *W.Y.* 56 F35
Oldfield *H.&W.* 29 B34
Old Fletton 42 F47
Oldford 20 F33
Old Glossop 50 C36
Old Goginan 37 G22
Old Goole 58 G43
Old Gore 29 F32
Old Grimsby 2 A10
Oldhall *Hgh.* 103 C27
Oldhall *Grm.* 90 D30
Old Hall 53 A48
Oldham 49 B35
Oldhamstocks 77 C33
Old Heath 34 F56
Old Hill 40 G35
Oldhurst 33 A48
Old Hutton 55 A31
Old Kea 3 D14
Old Kilpatrick 74 C20
Old Kinnernie 91 C33
Old Knebworth 33 G48
Oldland 19 D32
Old Leake 43 A49
Old Leslie 90 A31
Old Malton 58 B44
Oldmeldrum 91 A33
Old Micklefield 57 F40
Oldmill 90 C31
Old Milverton 30 B38
Old Netley 11 C40
Old Newton 34 B56
Oldpark 39 E32
Old Philpstoun 75 C26
Old Poltalloch 79 G14
Old Portlethen 91 D35
Old Radnor 28 C28
Old Rattray 99 D36
Old Rayne 91 A32
Oldridge 7 F24
Old Romney 15 E56
Old Scone 82 E26
Old Shields 75 C24
Oldshore Beg 101 C17
Oldshore More 101 C18
Old Sodbury 20 C33
Old Somerby 42 B45
Oldstead 58 A41
Old Stratford 31 D43
Old Sunderlandwick 59 D46
Old Swarland 71 C37
Old Swinford 40 G34
Old Town *Cnw.* 2 A11
Old Town *Cum.* 55 A31
Old Town *Nor.* 70 D34
Oldtown of Aigas 96 G20
Oldtown of Ord 98 D32
Oldwalls 17 E20
Old Warden 32 D47
Oldways End 7 C24
Old Weston 32 A46
Oldwhat 99 D34
Old Windsor 22 D45
Old Wives Lees 15 B56
Old Woking 22 F46
Old Wolverton 32 D44
Old Woods 38 C30
Olgrinmore 103 C26
Oliver 69 A26
Oliver's Battery 11 B40
Ollaberry 106 D39
Ollerton *Shr.* 39 C32
Ollerton *Not.* 51 F42
Ollerton *Che.* 49 E33
Olmstead Green 33 D52
Olney *Bkh.* 32 C44
Olney *Nmp.* 31 D42
Olrig House 103 B27
Olton 40 G37
Olveston 19 C31
Ombersley 29 B34
Ompton 51 F42
Onchan 54 F25
Onecote 50 G36
Ongar Hill 43 C51
Ongar Street 28 B29
Onibury 28 A30
Onich 80 A16
Onllwyn 27 G24
Onneley 39 A33
Onslow Village 22 G45
Opinan 94 D13
Orange Lane 77 F33
Orbliston 98 D28

Orbost 93 G8
Orby 53 F50
Orcadia 73 D17
Orchard 73 D17
Orchard Portman 8 B28
Orchard Wyndham 7 B26
Orcheston 20 G36
Orcop 28 F30
Orcop Hill 28 F30
Ord 86 C12
Ordhead 91 B32
Ordie 90 C30
Ordiequish 98 D29
Ordsall 51 E42
Ore 14 F54
Oreham Common 12 E47
Oreston 5 E21
Oreton 39 G32
Orford *Sfk* 35 D60
Orford *Che.* 49 C32
Orgreave 40 D37
Orleton *H.&W.* 29 B32
Orleton *H.&W.* 28 B30
Orleton Common 28 B30
Orlingbury 32 A44
Ormacleit 84 A3
Ormesby 63 E41
Ormesby St Margaret 45 D60
Ormesby St Michael 45 D60
Ormiscaig 94 B14
Ormiston 76 D29
Ormsaigmore 79 A10
Ormsdale 73 B16
Ormskirk 48 B29
Ormwe 103 B26
Orpington 23 E50
Orrell 48 B31
Orrisdale 54 D25
Orrok Ho. 91 B35
Orroland 65 F23
Orsett 24 C52
Orslow 40 D34
Orston 42 A43
Orton *Nmp.* 31 A44
Orton *Cum.* 61 F32
Orton Longueville 42 F47
Orton-on-the-Hill 40 E38
Orton Waterville 42 F47
Orwell 33 C49
Osbaldeston 56 F32
Osbaldwick 58 D42
Osbaston *Shr.* 38 D31
Osbaston *Lei.* 41 E40
Osborne 11 E40
Osbournby 42 B46
Oscroft 48 F30
Ose 93 G9
Osgathorpe 41 D40
Osgodby *Lcn.* 52 C46
Osgodby *N.Y.* 59 A46
Osgodby *N.Y.* 58 F42
Oskaig 86 A11
Osmaston *Dby.* 40 A37
Osmaston *Dby.* 41 B39
Osmington 9 F33
Osmington Mills 9 F33
Osmotherley 62 G40
Osney 21 A40
Ossett 57 G38
Ossington 51 F43
Ostend 25 B55
Osterley 22 D47
Oswaldkirk 58 B42
Oswaldtwistle 56 G32
Oswestry 38 C28
Otford 23 F51
Otham 14 B53
Othery 8 A29
Otley *Sfk* 35 C58
Otley *W.Y.* 57 E37
Otter 73 C15
Otterbourne 11 B40
Otterburn *N.Y.* 56 D34
Otterburn *Nor.* 70 D34
Otterburn Camp 70 D34
Otterden Place 14 B55
Otter Ferry 73 B15
Otterham 4 A17
Otterhampton 19 G28
Ottershaw 22 E45
Otterswick 106 D41
Otterton 7 G26
Ottery St Mary 7 F27
Ottinge 15 C57
Ottringham 59 G48
Oughterby 60 A28
Oughtershaw 56 A34
Oughtibridge 50 C38
Oulston 58 B41
Oulton *Cum.* 60 A28
Oulton *W.Y.* 57 G39
Oulton *Sfk* 45 F61
Oulton *Nfk* 45 C57
Oulton *Stf.* 40 B34
Oulton Broad 45 F60
Oulton Street 45 C57

Oundle 42 G46
Ousby 61 C32
Ousdale 103 F26
Ousden 34 C53
Ousefleet 58 G44
Ouston *Drm* 62 A38
Ouston *Nor.* 71 F36
Outertown 104 E28
Outgate 60 G29
Outhgill 61 F33
Outlands 39 C33
Outlane 50 A36
Out Newton 59 G49
Out Rawcliffe 55 E30
Outwell 43 E50
Outwood *Sry* 23 G49
Outwood *W.Y.* 57 G39
Oval The 20 E33
Ovenden 57 G36
Over *Avon* 19 C31
Over *Che.* 49 F32
Over *Cbs.* 33 B49
Overbister 104 B32
Overbrae 99 D33
Overbury 29 E35
Overcombe 9 F32
Over Compton 8 C31
Over End 50 E38
Over Haddon 50 F38
Over Kellet 55 B31
Over Kiddington 30 F39
Overleigh 8 A30
Over Norton 30 F39
Over Peover 49 E33
Overpool 48 E29
Over Rankeilour 82 F29
Overscaig Hotel 102 F20
Overseal 40 D38
Over Silton 62 G40
Oversland 15 B56
Oversley Green 30 C36
Overstone 31 B43
Over Stowey 7 B27
Overstrand 45 A58
Over Stratton 8 C30
Over Tabley 49 D33
Overton *Lan.* 55 D30
Overton *Clw.* 38 A29
Overton *Shr.* 28 A30
Overton *Clw.* 38 A29
Overton *Ham.* 21 G41
Overton *Grm.* 91 B34
Overton *N.Y.* 58 D41
Overton *W.G.* 17 F20
Overtown 75 E24
Over Wallop 10 A38
Over Whitacre 40 F38
Over Worton 31 F40
Overy Staithe 44 A54
Oving *Bkh.* 31 F43
Oving *W.S.* 12 F44
Ovingdean 13 F49
Ovingham 71 G36
Ovington *Nor.* 71 G36
Ovington *Nfk* 44 E55
Ovington *Drm* 62 E37
Ovington *Esx* 34 D53
Ovington *Ham.* 11 A41
Ower 10 C39
Owermoigne 9 F33
Owlswick 22 A43
Owmby 52 B46
Owmby by Spital 52 D46
Owslebury 11 B41
Owston 42 E43
Owston Ferry 51 B43
Owstwick 59 F48
Owthorpe 41 B42
Oxborough 44 E53
Oxcombe 53 E49
Oxen End 33 F52
Oxenholme 61 G31
Oxenhope 57 F36
Oxen Park 55 A28
Oxenton 29 E35
Oxenwood 21 F39
Oxford 21 A41
Oxhill 30 D39
Oxley 40 E34
Oxley Green 34 G55
Oxley's Green 13 D52
Oxnam 70 B32
Oxnead 45 C58
Oxnop Ghyll 61 G35
Oxshott 22 E47
Oxspring 50 B38
Oxted 23 F49
Oxton *Not.* 51 G42
Oxton *Mer.* 48 D28
Oxton *Bor.* 76 E30
Oxwich 17 F20
Oxwich Green 17 F21
Oxwick 44 C55
Oykel Bridge 96 A19
Oyne 91 A32

Ozleworth 20 B33

P

Packington 41 D39
Padanaram 82 B29
Padbury 31 E43
Paddington 23 C48
Paddlesworth 15 C57
Paddockhaugh 97 F27
Paddockhole 69 E28
Paddock Wood 23 G52
Paddolgreen 38 B30
Padeswood 48 F28
Padiham 56 F33
Padside 57 D37
Padstow 3 A15
Padworth 21 E42
Pagham 12 G44
Paglesham Churchend 25 B55
Paglesham Eastend 25 B55
Paibeil 92 E3
Paible 92 B6
Paignton 5 D24
Pailton 41 G40
Painscastle 28 D27
Painshawfield 71 G36
Painswick 20 A34
Paisley 74 D20
Pakefield 45 F61
Pakenham 34 B54
Pale 37 B25
Palestine 21 G38
Paley Street 22 D44
Palgowan 67 E19
Palgrave 34 A56
Pallinsburn House 77 G34
Palmerscross 97 E27
Palmerstown 18 E27
Palnackie 65 E24
Palnure 64 D20
Palterton 51 F40
Pamber End 21 F41
Pamber Green 21 F41
Pamber Heath 21 E42
Pamington 29 E35
Pamphill 9 D35
Pampisford 33 D50
Pan 105 B29
Panborough 19 G30
Panbride 83 D31
Pancrasweek 6 E19
Pandy *Clw.* 38 B27
Pandy *Pow.* 37 E25
Pandy *Gwy.* 37 E22
Pandy *Gwe.* 28 F29
Pandy Tudur 47 F24
Panfield 34 F53
Pangbourne 21 D42
Panmure 83 D30
Pannal 57 D38
Panpunton 28 A28
Pant *Shr.* 38 C28
Pant *Clw.* 38 A28
Pantasaph 47 E27
Pantglas 37 F23
Pant-glas 36 A20
Pant Gwyn 37 C24
Pantgwyn 26 D18
Pant-lasau 17 D22
Pant Mawr 37 G24
Panton 52 E47
Pant-pastynog 47 F26
Pantperthog 37 E23
Pant-y-dwr 27 A25
Pantyffordd 48 G28
Pant-y-ffridd 38 E27
Pantyffynnon 17 C22
Panxworth 45 D59
Papcastle 60 C26
Papple 76 C31
Papplewick 51 G41
Papworth Everard 33 B48
Papworth St Agnes 33 B48
Par 4 E16
Parbold 48 A30
Parbrook 8 A31
Parc 37 B24
Parcllyn 26 C18
Parcrhydderch 26 C21
Pardshaw 60 D26
Parham 35 B59
Parish Holm 68 A23
Park 98 D31
Park Corner 21 C42
Parkend *Glo.* 19 A31
Parkend *Cum.* 60 C28
Park End 70 F34
Parkeston 35 E58
Parkford 83 B30
Parkgate *Che.* 48 E28
Parkgate *S.Y.* 51 C40
Parkgate *Sry* 23 G48
Park Gate 11 D41
Parkham 6 C19
Parkham Ash 6 C19
Parkhill *Tay.* 82 C27

Parkhill *Tay.* 83 C32
Parkhouse 19 A30
Parkhurst 11 E40
Park Lane 38 B30
Parkmill 17 F21
Parkmore 98 E29
Parkneuk 91 F33
Parkstone 10 E36
Park Street 22 A47
Parley Cross 10 E36
Parracombe 6 A22
Parrog 16 A16
Parsonby 60 C27
Parson Drove 43 E49
Partick 74 D21
Partington 49 C33
Partney 53 F50
Parton *D.&G.* 65 D22
Parton *Cum.* 60 D25
Partridge Green 12 E47
Parwich 50 G37
Passenham 31 D43
Passfield 12 C44
Passingford Bridge 23 B50
Paston 45 B59
Patcham 13 F49
Patching 12 F46
Patchole 6 A21
Patchway 19 C31
Pateley Bridge 57 C37
Pathe 8 A29
Pathhead *Ltn* 76 D29
Pathhead *Fife* 83 C30
Pathhead *Grm.* 91 G33
Pathhead *Str.* 68 B22
Path of Condie 82 F26
Patmore Heath 33 F50
Patna 67 B19
Patney 20 F36
Patrick 54 E24
Patrick Brompton 62 G38
Patrington 59 G48
Patrishow 28 F28
Patrixbourne 15 B57
Patterdale 60 E29
Pattingham 40 F34
Pattishall 31 C42
Pattiswick 34 F53
Paul 2 F10
Paulerspury 31 D42
Paull 59 G47
Paulton 19 F32
Pauperhaugh 71 D36
Pavenham 32 C45
Pawlett 19 G28
Pawston 77 G34
Paxford 30 E37
Paxhill Park 13 D49
Paxton 77 E35
Payhembury 7 E26
Paynes Hall 33 G49
Paythorne 56 D34
Peacehaven 13 F49
Peacemarsh 9 B33
Peachley 29 C33
Peak Dale 50 E36
Peak Forest 50 E36
Peakirk 42 E47
Pean Hill 25 E56
Pearsie 82 B29
Peasedown St John 20 F33
Peasemore 21 D40
Peasenhall 35 B59
Pease Pottage 13 C48
Peaslake 22 G46
Peasmarsh 14 E54
Peaston 76 D30
Peastonbank 76 D30
Peathill 99 C35
Peat Inn 83 G30
Peatling Magna 41 F41
Peatling Parva 41 G41
Peaton 38 G31
Pebble Coombe 23 F48
Pebmarsh 34 E54
Pebworth 30 D37
Pecket Well 56 G35
Peckforton 48 G31
Peckleton 41 E40
Pedmore 40 G34
Pedwell 8 A30
Peebles 76 F28
Peel 54 E24
Pegswood 71 E38
Peighinn nan Aoireann 84 A2
Peinchorran 85 A10
Peinlich 93 F9
Pelaw 71 G38
Pelcomb Bridge 16 C15
Pelcomb Cross 16 C14
Peldon 34 G55
Pelsall 40 E36
Pelton 62 A38
Pelutho 60 B26
Pelynt 4 E18
Pembrey 17 D20

Pembridge 28 C29
Pembroke 16 D15
Pembroke Dock 16 D15
Pembury 23 G52
Penallt 28 G31
Penally 16 E17
Penalt 28 F31
Penare 3 E15
Penarth 18 D27
Pen-bont Rhydybeddau 37 G22
Penboyr 17 A19
Penbryn 26 C18
Pencader 17 A20
Pencaenewydd 36 A19
Pencaitland 76 D30
Pencarreg 26 D21
Pencelli 27 F26
Pen-clawdd 17 E21
Pencoed 18 C25
Pencombe 28 C31
Pencoyd 28 F31
Pencraig *H.&W.* 28 F31
Pencraig *Pow.* 37 C26
Pendeen 2 E9
Penderyn 18 A25
Pendine 17 D18
Pendlebury 49 B33
Pendleton 56 F33
Pendock 29 E33
Pendoggett 4 C16
Pendomer 8 C31
Pendoylan 18 D26
Penegoes 37 E23
Pen-ffordd 16 B16
Penffordd-Las (Staylittle) 37 F24
Pengam 18 B27
Penge 23 D49
Pengenffordd 28 E27
Pengorffwysfa 46 C20
Pengover Green 4 D18
Pen-groes-oped 19 A28
Pengwern 47 E25
Penhale 2 G12
Penhallow 2 C13
Penhalvean 2 E12
Penhow 19 B30
Penhurst 13 E52
Peniarth 36 E21
Penicuik 76 D28
Penifiler 93 G10
Peninver 66 A13
Penisarcwn 37 D26
Penisar Waun 46 F21
Penistone 50 B38
Penjerrick 2 E13
Penketh 48 D31
Penkill 67 D18
Penkridge 40 D34
Penley 38 A30
Penllech 36 B17
Penllergaer 17 E21
Penllyn 18 D25
Pen-llyn 46 D19
Penmachno 47 G23
Penmaen 17 F21
Penmaenmawr 46 E22
Penmaenpool 37 D22
Penmark 18 E26
Penmon 46 D22
Penmorfa 36 A21
Penmynydd 46 E20
Penn *W.M.* 40 F34
Penn *Bkh.* 22 B45
Pennal 37 E22
Pennan 99 C34
Pennance 2 D13
Pennant *Pow.* 37 F24
Pennant *Dyf.* 26 B21
Pennant Melangell 37 C26
Pennard 17 F21
Pennerley 38 F29
Penninghame 64 D19
Pennington 55 B28
Penn Street 22 B45
Pennsylvania 20 D33
Penny Bridge 55 A28
Pennyfuir 79 D14
Pennyghael 79 E10
Pennyglen 67 B18
Pennygown 79 C11
Pennymoor 7 D24
Penparc 26 D17
Penparcau 36 G21
Penparo 16 A14
Penperlleni 19 A29
Penpillick 4 E16
Penpol 2 E13
Penpoll 4 E17
Penpont *Pow.* 27 F25
Penpont *D.&G.* 68 D24
Penrherber 17 A18
Penrhiwceiber 18 B26
Penrhiwgoch 17 C21
Penrhiw-llan 26 D19
Penrhiw-pal 26 D19
Penrhos *Pow.* 27 G23

Penrhos *Gwy.* 36 B19
Penrhos *Gwy.* 46 D18
Penrhos *Gwe.* 28 G29
Penrhos-garnedd 46 E21
Penrhyn Bay 47 D23
Penrhyn-coch 37 G22
Penrhyndeudraeth 36 B21
Penrhyn-side 47 D23
Penrhys 18 B25
Penrice 17 F20
Penrith 61 C30
Penrose 3 A14
Penruddock 60 D29
Penryn 2 E13
Pensarn *Clw.* 47 E25
Pensarn *Dyf.* 17 C20
Pen-sarn *Gwy.* 36 C21
Pen-sarn *Gwy.* 36 A20
Pensax 29 B33
Pensby 48 D28
Penselwood 9 A33
Pensford 19 E31
Pensham 29 D35
Penshaw 62 A39
Penshurst 23 G51
Pensilva 4 C18
Pensnett 40 G34
Pentewan 4 F16
Pentir 46 F21
Pentire 2 B13
Pentireglaze 3 A15
Pentlepoir 16 D16
Pentlow 34 D53
Pentney 44 D53
Penton Mewsey 21 G39
Pentraeth 46 E21
Pentre *M.G.* 18 B25
Pentre *Pow.* 28 B28
Pentre *Pow.* 38 F28
Pentre *Clw.* 38 A28
Pentre *Pow.* 40 F34
Pentre *Pow.* 37 C26
Pentre *Shr.* 38 D29
Pentre-bach 27 E24
Pentrebach *M.G.* 18 A26
Pentrebach *W.G.* 17 D22
Pentre Berw 46 E20
Pentre-bont 47 G23
Pentre-bwlch 38 A27
Pentrecagal 26 D19
Pentre-celyn 37 E24
Pentre-celyn 47 G27
Pentre-chwyth 17 E22
Pentreclwydau 18 A24
Pentre-cwrt 17 A19
Pentre Dolau 27 D25
Pentredwr 38 A27
Pentre-Dwr 17 E22
Pentrefelin *Dyf.* 17 B21
Pentrefelin *Gwy.* 47 E24
Pentrefelin *Clw.* 38 C27
Pentrefelin *Shr.* 38 C30
Pentrefelin *Gwy.* 36 B21
Pentrefelin *Dyf.* 27 D22
Pentrefoelas 47 G24
Pentre-galar 16 A17
Pentregat 26 C19
Pentre Gwenlais 17 C22
Pentre Gwynfryn 36 C21
Pentre Halkyn 47 E27
Pentreheyling 38 F28
Pentre Isaf 47 F24
Pentre Llanrhaeadr 47 F26
Pentre-llwyn-llwyd 27 C25
Pentre Maelor 38 A29
Pentre-piod 37 B24
Pentre-poeth 19 C28
Pentre'r beirdd 38 D27
Pentre'r-felin 27 E24
Pentre Saron 47 F26
Pentre-tafarn-y-fedw 47 F23
Pentre-ty-gwyn 27 E24
Pentrich 51 G39
Pentridge 10 C36
Pen-twyn 19 A31
Pentwyn 18 C27
Pentyrch 18 C26
Penuwch 26 B21
Penwithick 4 E16
Penwortham 55 G30
Penwyllt 57 A39
Pen-y-banc 17 B21
Pen-y-bont *Dyf.* 27 E23
Penybont 27 B26
Pen-y-bont *Clw.* 38 C27
Pen-y-bont *Pow.* 37 D26
Penybontfawr 37 C26
Pen-y-bryn 37 D22
Penybryn 18 B27
Penycae 38 A28
Pen-y-cae 27 G24
Pen-y-cae -mawr 19 B30
Pen-y-cefn 47 E27
Pen-y-clawdd 19 A30
Pen-y-coedcae 18 C26
Penycwm 16 B14
Pen-y-fai 18 C24

Penyffordd 48 F29
Pen-y-garn 17 A21
Penygarnedd 37 C26
Pen-y-garreg 27 D25
Penygraig 18 B25
Penygroes *Dyf.* 17 C21
Penygroes *Gwy.* 46 G20
Pen-y-Gwryd Hotel 46 G22
Pen-y-Park 28 D28
Pen-yr-hoel 28 G29
Penysarn 46 C20
Pen-y-stryt 47 G27
Penywaun 18 A25
Penzance 2 E10
Penzance Heliport 2 E10
Peopleton 29 C35
Peover Heath 49 E33
Peper Harow 22 G45
Peplow 39 C32
Perceton 74 F19
Percie 90 D31
Perham Down 21 G38
Perivale 22 C47
Perkhill 90 D31
Perkins Beach 38 E29
Perlethorpe 51 E42
Perranarworthal 2 E13
Perranporth 2 C13
Perranuthnoe 2 F11
Perranzabuloe 2 C13
Perry Barr 40 F36
Perry Green 33 G50
Perry Street 24 D52
Persey 82 B27
Pershall 40 C34
Pershore 29 D35
Pert 91 G32
Pertenhall 32 B46
Perth 82 E26
Perthy 38 B29
Perton 40 F34
Peterborough 42 F47
Peterburn 94 C13
Peterchurch 28 E29
Peterculter 91 C34
Peterhead 99 E37
Peterlee 62 B40
Petersfield 11 B43
Peter's Green 32 G47
Peters Marland 6 D20
Peterstone Wentlooge 19 D28
Peterston-super-Ely 18 D26
Peter Tavy 5 C21
Petham 15 B57
Petrockstow 6 E21
Pett 14 F54
Pettaugh 35 C57
Pettinain 75 F25
Pettistree 35 C58
Petton *Shr.* 38 C30
Petton *Dev.* 7 C26
Petty 99 F33
Pettycur 76 B28
Pettymuick 91 A34
Petworth 12 D45
Pevensey 13 F52
Pevensey Bay 13 F52
Pewsey 20 E37
Phesdo 91 F32
Philham 6 C18
Philiphaugh 69 A30
Phillack 2 E11
Philleigh 3 E14
Philpstoun 75 C26
Phoenix Green 22 F43
Phones 88 E22
Phorp 97 F26
Piabil Iarach 101 D11
Piabil Uarach 101 D11
Pibsbury 8 B30
Pica 60 D26
Piccadilly Corner 45 G58
Piccotts End 22 A46
Pickerells 23 A51
Pickering 58 A43
Picket Piece 21 G39
Picket Post 10 D37
Pickford Green 40 G38
Pickhill 58 A43
Picklescott 38 F30
Pickletillem 83 E30
Pickmere 49 E32
Pickstock 39 C33
Pickston 82 E25
Pickwell *Lei.* 42 D43
Pickwell *Dev.* 6 A20
Pickworth *Lei.* 42 D45
Pickworth *Lcn.* 42 B46
Picton *N.Y.* 62 F39
Picton *Che.* 48 E30
Piddinghoe 13 F50
Piddington *Oxf.* 31 G42
Piddington *Nmp.* 31 C43
Piddlehinton 9 E32
Piddletrenthide 9 E32

Pidley 33 A49
Piercebridge 62 E37
Pierowall 104 B30
Pigdon 71 E37
Pikehall 50 G37
Pilgrims Hatch 23 B51
Pilham 52 C44
Pill 19 D31
Pillaton 4 D19
Pillerton Hersey 30 D38
Pillerton Priors 30 D38
Pilleth 28 B28
Pilley *Glo.* 29 G35
Pilley *S.Y.* 51 B39
Pilley *Ham.* 10 E39
Pilling 55 E29
Pilling Lane 55 E29
Pillowell 19 A32
Pilning 19 C31
Pilsbury 50 F37
Pilsdon 8 E30
Pilsgate 42 E46
Pilsley *Dby.* 51 F40
Pilsley *Dby.* 50 E38
Piltdown 13 D50
Pilton *Nmp.* 42 G46
Pilton *Lei.* 42 E45
Pilton *Som.* 19 G31
Pilton *Dev.* 6 B21
Pimperne 9 D34
Pinchbeck 43 C48
Pinchbeck Bars 42 C47
Pinchbeck West 43 C48
Pinchinthorpe 63 E41
Pinfold 48 A29
Pinhay 8 E29
Pinhoe 7 F25
Pinkneys Green 22 C44
Pinley Green 30 B37
Pinminnoch 67 D17
Pinmore 67 D17
Pinn 7 G26
Pinner 22 C47
Pinner Green 22 B47
Pinvin 29 D35
Pinwherry 67 E17
Pinxton 51 G40
Pipe and Lyde 28 D30
Pipe Gate 39 A33
Piperhall 73 E17
Piperhill 97 F24
Pipe Ridware 40 D36
Piper's Pool 4 B18
Pipewell 42 G44
Pippacott 6 B20
Pipton 28 E27
Pirbright 22 F45
Pirnmill 73 F14
Pirton *H.&W.* 29 D34
Pirton *Hfs.* 32 E47
Pisgah 81 G23
Pishill 22 C43
Pistyll 36 A19
Pitagowan 81 A24
Pitblae 99 C35
Pitcairngreen 82 E26
Pitcairns 82 F26
Pitcaple 91 A33
Pitchcombe 20 A34
Pitchcott 31 G43
Pitchford 38 E31
Pitch Green 22 A43
Pitch Place 22 F45
Pitcombe 9 A32
Pitcot 18 D25
Pitcox 76 C32
Pitcur 82 D28
Pitfichie 91 B32
Pitgrudy 96 B23
Pitinnan 99 F33
Pitkennedy 83 B31
Pitkevy 82 G28
Pitlessie 82 G29
Pitlochry 82 B25
Pitmedden 91 A34
Pitminster 7 D27
Pitmuies 83 C31
Pitmunie 91 B32
Pitnacree 82 B25
Pitney 8 B30
Pitroddie 82 E27
Pitscottie 83 F30
Pitsea 24 C53
Pitsford 31 B43
Pitsford Hill 7 B26
Pitstone 32 G45
Pitstone Green 32 G45
Pitt *Dev.* 7 D26
Pitt *Ham.* 11 B40
Pittendreich 97 E27
Pittentrail 96 A23
Pittenweem 83 G31
Pittington 62 B39
Pittodrie Ho. 91 A32
Pitton 10 A37
Pity Me 62 B38

Pityme 3 A15
Pixey Green 35 A58
Place Newton 58 B44
Plaidy 99 D33
Plains 75 D23
Plaish 38 F31
Plaistow 12 C45
Plaitford 10 C38
Plas 17 B20
Plas Gogerddan 37 G22
Plas Gwynant 46 G22
Plasisaf 47 F25
Plas Isaf 37 A26
Plas Llwyd 47 E25
Plas Llwyngwern 37 E23
Plas Llysyn 37 F25
Plas Nantyr 38 B27
Plas-rhiw-Saeson 37 E24
Plastow Green 21 E41
Plas-yn-Cefn 47 E25
Platt 23 F52
Platt Lane 38 B31
Plawsworth 62 B38
Plaxtol 23 F51
Playden 14 E55
Playford 35 D57
Play Hatch 22 D43
Playing Place 3 D14
Plealey 38 E30
Plean 75 B24
Pleasance 82 F28
Pleasington 56 G32
Pleasley 51 F40
Plenmeller 70 G32
Pleshey 33 G52
Plockton 86 A13
Ploughfield 28 D29
Plowden 38 G29
Ploxgreen 38 E29
Pluckley 14 C55
Pluckley Thorne 14 C55
Plumbland 60 C27
Plumley 49 E33
Plumpton Cum. 61 C30
Plumpton E.S. 13 E49
Plumpton End 31 D42
Plumpton Green 13 E49
Plumpton Head 61 C31
Plumstead Nfk 45 B57
Plumstead G.L. 23 D50
Plumtree 41 B41
Plungar 42 B43
Plush 9 D33
Plwmp 26 C19
Plym Bridge 5 E21
Plymouth 5 E21
Plympton 5 E21
Plymstock 5 E21
Plymtree 7 E26
Pockley 58 A42
Pocklington 58 E44
Pocombe Bridge 7 F24
Pode Hole 43 C48
Podimore 8 B31
Podington 32 B45
Podmore 39 B33
Poffley End 30 G39
Pointon 42 B47
Pokesdown 10 E37
Polanach 80 B15
Polapit Tamar 4 B18
Polbae 64 C18
Polbain 101 G15
Polbathic 4 E19
Polbeth 75 D26
Polchar 89 D24
Poldean 69 D26
Polebrook 42 G46
Polegate 13 F51
Pole Moor 50 A36
Poles 96 B23
Polesworth 40 E38
Polglass 95 A16
Polgooth 3 C15
Polgown 68 C22
Poling 12 F46
Poling Corner 12 F46
Polkerris 4 E16
Polla 101 C19
Poll A Charra 84 C3
Polldubh 80 A17
Pollie 102 G23
Pollington 51 A42
Polloch 79 A13
Pollokshaws 74 D21
Polmassick 3 D15
Polmont 75 C25
Polnoon 74 E21
Polperro 4 E18
Polruan 4 E17
Polsham 19 G30
Polstead 34 E55
Poltalloch 73 A13
Poltimore 7 F25
Polton 76 D28
Polwarth 77 E33

Polyphant 4 B18
Polzeath 3 A15
Pondersbridge 43 F48
Ponders End 23 B49
Pond Street 33 E50
Ponsanooth 2 E13
Ponsonby 60 F26
Ponsworthy 5 C23
Pont Aber 27 F23
Pont Aber Glaslyn 36 A21
Pontamman 17 C22
Pontantwn 17 C20
Pontardawe 17 D22
Pontardulais 17 D21
Pontargothi 17 B20
Pontarsais 17 B20
Pontblyddyn 48 F28
Pontbren Llwyd 18 A25
Pont Ceri 26 D18
Pont Crugnant 37 F24
Pont Cyfyng 47 G23
Pont Dolgarrog 47 F23
Pontefract 57 G40
Ponteland 71 F37
Ponterwyd 37 G23
Pontesbury 38 E29
Pontesford 38 E29
Pontfadog 38 B28
Pont-faen 27 E25
Pontfaen 16 A16
Pont-Henri 17 D20
Ponthir 19 B29
Ponthirwaun 26 D18
Pontllanfraith 18 B27
Pontlliw 17 D21
Pontllyfni 46 G20
Pontlottyn 18 A26
Pont Nedd Fechan 18 A24
Pontnewydd 19 B28
Pontnewynydd 19 A28
Pont Pen-y-benglog 46 G22
Pontrhydfendigaid 27 B22
Pont Rhyd-sarn 37 C24
Pont Rhyd-y-cyff 18 C24
Pont-rhyd-y-fen 18 B23
Pont-rhyd-y-groes 27 A23
Pontrhydyrun 19 B28
Pontrilas 28 F29
Pont-rug 46 F22
Ponts Green 13 E52
Pontshaen 26 D20
Pontshill 29 F32
Pontsticill 27 G26
Pont Walby 18 A24
Pontwelly 17 A19
Pontyates 17 D20
Pontyberem 17 C20
Pontybodkin 48 G28
Pontyclun 18 C26
Pontycymer 18 B24
Pont y gwaith 18 B25
Pontymister 19 B28
Pont-y-pant 47 G23
Pontypool 19 A28
Pontypridd 18 B26
Pont yr Alwen 47 G25
Pontywaun 18 B27
Pooksgreen 10 C39
Pool W.Y. 57 E38
Pool Cnw. 2 D12
Pool Bank 55 A30
Poole 9 E35
Poole Keynes 20 B35
Poolewe 94 C14
Pooley Bridge 61 D30
Poolhill 29 F33
Pool of Muckhart 82 G26
Pool Quay 38 D28
Pool Street 34 E53
Pope Hill 16 C15
Popeswood 22 E44
Popham 21 G41
Poplar 23 C49
Porchfield 11 E40
Porin 96 F19
Porkellis 2 E12
Porlock 7 A24
Porlock Weir 7 A24
Portachoillan 73 E13
Port Allen 82 E28
Port Appin 79 C14
Port Askaig 72 D10
Portavadie 73 D15
Port Bannatyne 73 D16
Portbury 19 D30
Port Carlisle 69 G28
Port Charlotte 72 E8
Portchester 11 D41
Port Clarence 62 D40
Port Driseach 73 C15
Port Ellen 72 F9
Port Elphinstone 91 B33
Portencross 73 F17
Port Erin 54 G23
Port Erroll 99 F37

Portesham 9 F32
Portessie 98 C30
Port e Vullen 54 D26
Port Eynon 17 F20
Portfield 79 E13
Portfield Gate 16 C15
Portgate 6 G19
Port Gaverne 4 B16
Port Glasgow 74 C19
Portgordon 98 C29
Portgower 103 G25
Porth M.G. 18 B26
Porth Cnw. 3 B14
Porthallow Cnw. 4 E18
Porthallow Cnw. 2 F13
Porthcawl 18 D23
Porth Colmon 36 B17
Porthcothan 3 A14
Porthcurno 2 F9
Port Henderson 94 D13
Porthgain 16 A13
Porthkerry 18 E26
Porthleven 2 F11
Porthmadog 36 B21
Porth Mellin 2 G12
Porthmeor 2 E9
Porth Navas 2 F13
Portholland 3 D15
Porthoustock 3 F14
Porthpean 4 E16
Porthtowan 2 D12
Porthyrhyd Dyf. 17 C21
Porthyrhyd Dyf. 17 A22
Porth-y-waen 38 C28
Portincaple 73 A17
Portington 58 F43
Portinnisherrich 80 F15
Portinscale 60 D28
Port Isaac 3 A15
Portishead 19 D30
Portknockie 98 C30
Portlethen 91 D35
Portloe 3 E15
Port Logan 64 F16
Portmahomack 97 C24
Portmeirion 36 B21
Port Mor 85 G10
Portmore 10 E39
Port Mulgrave 63 E43
Port na Craig 82 B25
Portnacroish 80 C15
Portnahaven 72 E8
Portnalong 85 A9
Portnaluchaig 86 F12
Portnancon 102 B20
Port Nan Giuran 101 D11
Port Nan Long 92 D4
Port Nis 101 A11
Portobello 76 C28
Port of Menteith 81 G21
Porton 10 A37
Port o' Warren 65 E24
Port Penrhyn 46 E21
Portquin 3 A15
Port Ramsay 79 C14
Portreath 2 D12
Portree 93 G10
Portscatho 3 E14
Portsea 11 D42
Portskerra 102 B24
Portskewett 19 C30
Portslade 13 F48
Portslade-by-Sea 13 F48
Portsmouth 11 E42
Portsoy 98 C31
Port St Mary 54 G24
Port Sunlight 48 D29
Portswood 11 C40
Port Talbot 18 C23
Portuairk 79 A10
Portway War. 30 A36
Portway H.&W. 28 D29
Port Wemyss 72 E8
Port William 64 F19
Portwrinkle 4 E19
Portyerrock 64 G20
Poslingford 34 D53
Postbridge 5 C22
Postcombe 22 B43
Postling 15 D57
Postwick 45 E58
Potarch 90 D31
Potsgrove 32 F45
Potten End 22 A46
Potterhanworth 52 F46
Potterhanworth Booths 52 F46
Potter Heigham 45 C60
Potterne 20 F35
Potterne Wick 20 F35
Potter's Cross 40 G34
Potters Crouch 22 A47
Potterspury 31 D43
Potter Street 23 A50
Potterton 91 B35
Potto 62 F40

Potton 33 D48
Pott Row 44 C53
Pott Shrigley 49 E35
Poughill Cnw. 6 E18
Poughill Dev. 7 E24
Poulner 10 D37
Poulshot 20 E35
Poulton 20 A36
Poulton-le-Fylde 55 F29
Pound Bank 29 A33
Pound Green 13 D50
Pound Green 13 D51
Poundffald 17 E21
Poundgate 13 D50
Poundsgate 5 C23
Poundstock 4 A17
Povey Cross 23 G48
Powburn 71 B36
Powderham 7 G25
Pow Green 29 D32
Powick 29 C34
Powfoot 69 G27
Powerstock 8 E31
Powler's Piece 6 D19
Powmill 75 A26
Poxwell 9 F33
Poyle 22 D46
Poynings 13 E48
Poyntington 9 C32
Poynton Che. 49 D35
Poynton Shr. 38 D31
Poynton Green 38 D31
Poyntzfield 96 E22
Poys Street 35 A59
Poyston Cross 16 C15
Poystreet Green 34 C55
Praa Sands 2 F11
Pratis 82 G29
Pratt's Bottom 23 E50
Praze-an-Beeble 2 E12
Predannack Wollas 2 G11
Prees 38 B31
Preesall 55 E29
Prees Green 38 B31
Preesgweene 38 B28
Prees Higher Heath 38 B31
Prenbrigog 48 F28
Prendergast 16 C15
Prendwick 70 B35
Pren-gwyn 26 D20
Prenteg 36 A21
Prenton 48 D28
Prescot 48 C30
Prescott 38 C30
Presley 97 F25
Pressen 77 G34
Prestatyn 47 D26
Prestbury Che. 49 E35
Prestbury Glo. 29 F35
Presteigne 28 B28
Presthope 38 F31
Prestleigh 19 G32
Prestolee 49 B33
Preston H.&W. 29 E32
Preston Kent 25 E58
Preston Kent 25 E56
Preston T.&W. 71 F39
Preston Sfk 34 C55
Preston Hfs. 32 F47
Preston Bor. 77 E33
Preston Wts. 20 D36
Preston Ltn 76 C31
Preston Nor. 71 A37
Preston Hum. 59 F47
Preston Lan. 55 G31
Preston Glo. 20 A36
Preston Dev. 9 F33
Preston E.S. 13 F49
Preston Dev. 5 C24
Preston Lei. 42 E44
Preston Bagot 30 B37
Preston Bissett 31 F42
Preston Brockhurst 38 C31
Preston Brook 48 D31
Preston Candover 21 G41
Preston Capes 31 C41
Preston Deanery 31 C43
Preston Gubbals 38 D30
Preston on Stour 30 D37
Preston on the Hill 48 D31
Preston on Wye 28 D29
Prestonpans 76 C29
Preston Plucknett 8 C31
Preston-under-Scar 62 G36
Preston upon the Weald Moors 39 D32
Preston Wynne 28 D31
Prestwich 49 B33
Prestwick Str. 67 A19
Prestwick T.&W. 71 F37
Prestwick Airport 67 A19
Prestwold 41 C41
Prestwood 22 A44

Price Town 18 B25
Prickwillow 43 G51
Priddy 19 F31
Priest Hill 55 F31
Priest Hutton 55 B31
Priestland 74 G21
Priestweston 38 F28
Priestwood 7 E24
Primethorpe 41 F40
Primrose Green 44 D56
Princes End 40 F35
Princes Gate 16 C17
Princes Risborough 22 A43
Princethorpe 30 A39
Princetown M.G. 27 G26
Princetown Dev. 5 C21
Prior Muir 83 F32
Prior's Frome 28 E31
Priors Hardwick 31 C40
Priors Marston 31 C40
Priory Wood 28 D28
Priston 19 E32
Prittlewell 24 C54
Privett 11 B42
Prixford 6 B21
Proaig 72 E10
Probus 3 D14
Protsonhill 99 C33
Prudhoe 71 G34
Pubil 81 C20
Publow 19 E32
Puckeridge 33 F49
Puckington 8 C29
Pucklechurch 19 D32
Puddinglake 49 E32
Puddington Dev. 7 D23
Puddington Che. 48 E28
Puddlebrook 29 G32
Puddledock 44 F56
Puddletown 9 E33
Pudleston 28 C31
Pudsey 57 F38
Pulborough 12 E46
Puldagon 103 D28
Puleston 39 C33
Pulford 48 G29
Pulham 9 D32
Pulham Market 45 G57
Pulham St Mary 45 G58
Pulloxhill 32 E46
Pulrossie 96 C23
Pulverbatch 38 E30
Pumpherston 75 D26
Pumsaint 27 D22
Puncheston 16 B15
Puncknowle 8 F31
Punnett's Town 13 D52
Purbrook 11 D42
Purfleet 23 D51
Puriton 19 G29
Purleigh 24 A54
Purley 23 E49
Purley on Thames 21 D42
Purlogue 28 A28
Purls Bridge 43 G50
Purse Caundle 9 C32
Purslow 38 G29
Purston Jaglin 57 G40
Purton Wts. 20 C36
Purton Glo. 19 A32
Purton Stoke 20 B36
Purves Hall 77 F33
Pury End 31 D43
Pusey 21 B39
Putley 29 E32
Putloe 20 A33
Putney 23 D48
Puttenham Sry 22 G45
Puttenham Hfs. 32 G44
Puttock End 34 D53
Putts Corner 7 F27
Puxton 19 E29
Pwll 17 D20
Pwllcrochan 16 D14
Pwlldefaid 36 C17
Pwllgloyw 27 E26
Pwll Trap 17 C18
Pwll-y-glaw 18 B23
Pyecombe 13 E48
Pye Corner Gwe. 19 C29
Pye Corner Hfs. 33 G50
Pye Green 40 D35
Pyle M.G. 18 C24
Pyle I.o.W. 11 G40
Pylle 8 A31
Pymore 43 G50
Pyrford 22 F46
Pyrton 21 B42
Pytchley 32 A44
Pyworthy 6 E19

Q

Quabbs 38 G27
Quadring 43 B48

Quadring Eaudike 43 B48
Quainton 31 G43
Quarley 21 G38
Quarndon 41 A39
Quarr Hill 11 E41
Quarrier's Village 74 D19
Quarrington 42 A46
Quarrington Hill 62 C39
Quarry Bank 40 G35
Quarrybank 48 F31
Quarrywood 97 E27
Quarter 75 E23
Quatford 39 F33
Quatt 39 G33
Quebec 62 B37
Quedgeley 29 G33
Queen Adelaide 43 G51
Queenborough 24 D54
Queen Camel 8 B31
Queen Charlton 19 E32
Queensbury 57 F36
Queensferry 48 F29
Queen's Head 38 C29
Queen Street 23 G52
Queenzieburn 74 C22
Quemerford 20 D35
Quendale 107 E37
Quendon 23 E50
Queniborough 41 D42
Quenington 20 A37
Quernmore 55 C31
Queslett 40 F36
Quethiock 4 D19
Quholm 104 E28
Quidenham 44 G56
Quidhampton Wts. 10 A37
Quidhampton Ham. 21 F40
Quilquox 99 F34
Quina Brook 38 B31
Quindry 105 B30
Quine's Hill 54 F25
Quinhill 73 E13
Quinton Nmp. 31 C43
Quinton W.M. 40 G35
Quintrell Downs 3 C14
Quoditch 6 F19
Quoig 81 E24
Quoigs 81 G24
Quorn 41 D41
Quothquan 75 G25
Quoyloo 104 D28
Quoys 106 A42
Quoys of Reiss 103 C29

R

Raby 48 E29
Rachub 46 F22
Rackenford 7 D24
Rackham 12 E46
Rackheath 45 D58
Racks 69 F26
Rackwick Ork. 105 B28
Rackwick Ork. 104 A30
Radbourne 40 B38
Radcliffe Nor. 71 C38
Radcliffe G.M. 49 B33
Radcliffe on Trent 41 B42
Radclive 31 E42
Radcot 21 B38
Radford Oxf. 31 F40
Radford W.M. 41 G39
Radford Semele 30 B39
Radipole 9 F32
Radlett 22 A47
Radley 21 B41
Radstock 19 F32
Radstone 31 D41
Radway 30 D39
Radway Green 49 G33
Radwell Bfd. 32 C46
Radwell Hfs. 33 E48
Radwinter 33 E51
Radyr 18 C27
Raechester 70 E35
Raemoir Ho. 91 D32
Raffin 101 E16
Rafford 97 F26
Ragdale 41 C42
Raglan 19 A29
Ragnall 51 E43
Rahoy 79 B12
Rainford 48 B30
Rainham Kent 24 E54
Rainham Esx 23 C51
Rainhill 48 C30
Rainhill Stoops 48 C30
Rainow 49 E35
Rainton 57 B39
Rainworth 51 G41
Raisbeck 61 F32
Raise 61 B33
Rait 82 E28
Raithby Lcn. 53 F49
Raithby Lcn. 53 D48
Rake 12 D44

Raleigh's Cross 7 B26
Ram 26 D21
Ramasaig 93 G7
Rame Cnw. 2 E13
Rame Cnw. 4 F20
Ram Lane 14 C55
Rampisham 8 D31
Rampside 55 C28
Rampton Not. 51 E43
Rampton Cbs. 33 B50
Ramsbottom 49 A33
Ramsbury 21 D38
Ramscraigs 103 F27
Ramsdean 11 B43
Ramsdell 21 F41
Ramsden 30 G39
Ramsden Bellhouse 24 B53
Ramsden Heath 24 B52
Ramsey Esx 35 F57
Ramsey I.o.M. 54 D26
Ramsey Cbs. 43 G48
Ramsey Forty Foot 43 G49
Ramsey Heights 43 G48
Ramsey Island 35 A55
Ramsey Mereside 43 G48
Ramsey St Mary's 43 G48
Ramsgate 25 E59
Ramsgate Street 45 B57
Ramsgill 57 B36
Ramsholt 35 D59
Ramshorn 40 A36
Ramsnest Common 12 C45
Ranachan 79 A13
Ranby Lcn. 53 E48
Ranby Not. 51 D42
Rand 52 E47
Randwick 20 A34
Rangemore 40 C37
Rangeworthy 19 C32
Rankinston 67 B20
Rank's Green 34 G53
Rannoch School 81 B21
Ranochan 86 F14
Ranskill 51 D42
Ranton 40 C34
Ranworth 45 D59
Rapness 104 B30
Rascarrel 65 F23
Raskelf 57 B40
Rassau 28 G27
Rastrick 57 G37
Ratby 41 E40
Ratcliffe Culey 41 F39
Ratcliffe on Soar 41 C40
Ratcliffe on the Wreake 41 D42
Ratford Bridge 16 C15
Rathen 99 C35
Rathillet 82 E29
Rathliesbeag 87 F17
Rathmell 56 C33
Ratho 75 C27
Ratho Station 75 C27
Rathven 98 C30
Ratley 30 D39
Ratlinghope 38 F29
Rattar 103 A28
Ratten Row 55 E30
Rattery 5 D23
Rattlesden 34 C55
Rattray 82 C27
Raughton Head 60 B29
Raunds 32 A45
Ravenfield 51 C40
Ravenglass 60 G26
Raveningham 45 F59
Ravenscar 63 F45
Ravensdale 54 D25
Ravensden 32 C46
Ravenshaw 56 E35
Ravenshayes 7 E25
Ravenshead 51 G41
Ravensmoor 49 G32
Ravensthorpe W.Y. 50 A38
Ravensthorpe Nmp. 31 A42
Ravenstone Bkh. 32 C44
Ravenstone Lei. 41 D39
Ravenstonedale 61 F32
Ravenstruther 75 F24
Ravensworth 62 F37
Raw 63 F45
Rawcliffe Hum. 58 G42
Rawcliffe N.Y. 58 D41
Rawcliffe Bridge 58 G42
Rawdon 57 F38
Rawmarsh 51 C40
Rawreth 24 B53
Rawridge 7 E27
Rawtenstall 56 G34
Rawyards 75 D23
Raxton 99 F34
Raydon 34 E56
Raylees 70 D35
Rayleigh 24 B54
Raymond's Hill 8 E29
Rayne 34 F53
Reach 33 B51

Read 56 F33
Reading 21 D42
Reading Street 14 E55
Reagill 61 E31
Rearquhar 96 B23
Rearsby 41 D42
Rease Heath 49 G32
Reaster 103 B28
Reaveley 70 B35
Reawick 107 C39
Reay 103 B25
Reculver 25 E58
Redberth 16 D16
Redbourn 32 G46
Redbourne 52 B45
Redbridge 23 C50
Redbrook 19 A31
Redbrook Street 14 D55
Redburn Hgh. 96 E21
Redburn Hgh. 97 G25
Redcar 63 D42
Redcastle Hgh. 96 G21
Redcastle Tay. 83 C32
Redcliff Bay 19 D30
Redcloak 91 E34
Red Dial 60 B28
Reddish 49 C34
Redditch 30 B36
Rede 34 C53
Redenhall 45 G58
Redesmouth 70 E34
Redford Tay. 83 C31
Redford Grm. 91 G33
Redford W.S. 12 D44
Redgrave 34 A56
Redheugh 83 A30
Redhill Grm. 91 C33
Redhill Grm. 98 E31
Redhill Grm. 98 F32
Redhill Avon 19 E30
Red Hill War. 30 C37
Redhill Shr. 39 D33
Redhill Not. 41 A41
Red Hill Ham. 11 C43
Redhill Sry 23 F48
Redhill Aerodrome & Heliport
 23 G48
Redhouse Grm. 90 A31
Redhouse Str. 73 D14
Redhouses 72 D9
Redisham 45 G60
Redland Avon 19 D31
Redland Ork. 104 D29
Redlingfield 35 A57
Red Lodge 33 A52
Redlynch Som. 9 A32
Redlynch Wts. 10 B38
Redmarley D'Abitot 29 E33
Redmarshall 62 D39
Redmile 42 B43
Redmire 62 G36
Redmoor 4 D16
Rednal W.M. 29 A35
Rednal Shr. 38 C29
Red Oaks Hill 33 D51
Redpath 76 G31
Redpoint 94 E13
Red Post Cnw. 6 E18
Red Post Dev. 5 D24
Red Rock 48 A31
Red Roses 16 C17
Red Row 71 D38
Redruth 2 D13
Redscarhead 76 F28
Redshaw 68 A24
Redstone Bank 16 C16
Red Street 49 G34
Red Wharf Bay 46 D20
Redwick Gwe. 19 C30
Redwick Avon 19 C31
Redworth 62 D38
Reed 33 E49
Reedham 45 E60
Reedness 58 G43
Reepham Nfk 44 C56
Reepham Lcn. 52 E46
Reeth 62 G36
Regaby 54 D26
Regil 19 E31
Regoul 97 F24
Reiff 101 G15
Reigate 23 G48
Reighton 59 B47
Reinigeadal 100 G8
Reisgill 103 E28
Reiss 103 C29
Rejerrah 3 C14
Relubbus 2 E11
Relugas 97 G25
Remenham 22 C43
Remenham Hill 22 C43
Remony 81 C23
Rempstone 41 C41
Rendcomb 29 G35
Rendham 35 B59
Rendlesham 35 C59

Renfrew 74 D20
Renhold 32 C46
Renishaw 51 E40
Rennington 71 B37
Renton 74 C19
Renwick 61 B31
Repps 45 D60
Repton 40 C38
Rescobie 83 B30
Resipole 79 A13
Resolis 96 E22
Resolven 18 A24
Resourie 86 G14
Reston 77 D34
Reswallie 83 B30
Retew 3 C15
Retford (East Retford) 51 D42
Rettendon 24 B53
Rettendon Place 24 B53
Retyn 3 C14
Revesby 53 F49
Rew 5 C23
Rewe 7 F25
Reydon 35 A60
Reymerston 44 E55
Reynalton 16 D16
Reynoldston 17 F20
Rezare 4 C19
Rhandirmwyn 27 D23
Rhaoine 96 A22
Rhayader 27 B25
Rhedyn 36 B18
Rhegreanoch 101 G16
Rheindown 96 G21
Rhelonie 96 B21
Rhemore 79 B11
Rhes-y-cae 47 F27
Rhewl Clw. 47 F27
Rhewl Shr. 38 B29
Rhewl Clw. 38 A27
Rhian 102 G21
Rhicarn 101 F16
Rhiconich 101 C18
Rhicullen 96 D22
Rhidorroch 95 B17
Rhifail 102 D23
Rhigos 18 A25
Rhilochan 96 A23
Rhinduie 96 G21
Rhireavach 95 B16
Rhiroy 95 C17
Rhiw 36 C18
Rhiwargor 37 C25
Rhiwbryfdir 37 A22
Rhiwderin 19 C28
Rhiwlas Gwy. 46 F21
Rhiwlas Clw. 38 B27
Rhiwlas Gwy. 37 B25
Rhodesia 51 E41
Rhodes Minnis 15 C57
Rhodiad 16 B13
Rhodmad 26 A21
Rhonadale 73 G13
Rhonehouse or Kelton Hill
 65 E23
Rhoose 18 E26
Rhos Dyf. 17 A19
Rhos W.G. 18 A23
Rhos-berse 48 G28
Rhoscolyn 46 E18
Rhoscrowther 16 D15
Rhos-ddu 48 G29
Rhosesmor 47 F27
Rhos-fawr 36 B19
Rhosgadfan 46 G20
Rhosgoch Gwy. 46 D20
Rhosgoch Pow. 28 D27
Rhos Hill 26 D17
Rhoshirwaun 36 C17
Rhoslan 36 A20
Rhoslefain 36 E21
Rhosllanerchrugog 38 A28
Rhosmaen 17 B22
Rhosmeirch 46 E20
Rhosneigr 46 E18
Rhosnesni 48 G29
Rhos-on-Sea 47 D24
Rhossili 17 F19
Rhosson 16 B13
Rhostryfan 46 G20
Rhostyllen 38 A29
Rhosybol 46 D20
Rhos-y-brwyner 48 F29
Rhos-y-garth 27 A22
Rhos-y-gwaliau 37 B25
Rhos-y-llan 36 B18
Rhos-y-mawn 47 F24
Rhos-y-Meirch 28 B28
Rhu 74 B18
Rhuallt 47 E26
Rhubodach 73 C15
Rhuddlan 47 E26
Rhue 95 B16
Rhulen 28 C27
Rhumach 86 F12
Rhunahaorine 72 F12

Rhyd Pow. 37 E25
Rhyd Gwy. 37 A22
Rhydargaeau 17 B20
Rhydcymerau 17 A21
Rhydd 29 D34
Rhyd-Ddu 46 G21
Rhydding 18 B23
Rhydlanfair 47 G24
Rhydlewis 26 D19
Rhydlios 36 C17
Rhydlydan Pow. 37 F26
Rhydlydan Clw. 47 G24
Rhydolion 36 C18
Rhydowen 36 D20
Rhyd-rosser 26 B21
Rhydspence 28 D28
Rhydtalog 48 G28
Rhyd-uchaf 37 B24
Rhydwyn 46 D18
Rhyd-y-clafdy 36 B18
Rhydycroesau 38 B28
Rhydyfelin M.G. 18 C26
Rhydyfelin Dyf. 26 A21
Rhyd-y-foel 47 E24
Rhyd-y-fro 17 D22
Rhydmain 37 C23
Rhyd-y-meirch 19 A28
Rhydymwyn 48 F28
Rhyd-yr-onnen 36 E21
Rhydywrach 16 B17
Rhyl 47 D25
Rhymney 18 A26
Rhyn 38 B29
Rhynd 82 E27
Rhynie Grm. 90 A30
Rhynie Hgh. 97 D24
Ribbesford 29 A33
Ribbleton 55 F31
Ribchester 56 F32
Ribigill 102 C21
Riby 52 B47
Riccall 58 F42
Riccarton 74 G19
Richard's Castle 28 B30
Richings Park 22 D46
Richmond 62 F37
Richmond upon Thames 22 D47
Rickarton 91 E33
Rickford 19 F30
Rickinghall 34 A56
Rickling 33 E50
Rickling Green 33 F50
Rickmansworth 22 B46
Riddell 69 A30
Riddlecombe 6 D21
Riddlesden 57 E36
Ridge Wts. 9 A35
Ridge Dor. 9 F35
Ridge Hfs. 23 A48
Ridgebourne 27 C26
Ridge Green 23 G48
Ridge Lane 40 F38
Ridgeway 51 D39
Ridgeway Cross 29 D33
Ridgewell 34 D53
Ridgewood 13 E50
Ridgmont 32 E45
Riding Mill 71 G36
Ridley 24 E52
Ridleywood 48 G29
Ridlington Nfk 45 B59
Ridlington Lei. 42 E44
Ridsdale 70 E34
Riechip 82 C26
Rievaulx 62 G38
Rigg D.&G. 69 G28
Rigg Hgh. 94 F11
Riggend 75 D23
Rigmaden Park 56 A32
Rigsby 53 E50
Rigside 75 G24
Rileyhill 40 D37
Rilla Mill 4 C18
Rillington 58 B44
Rimington 56 E33
Rimpton 8 B31
Rimswell 59 G49
Rinaston 16 B15
Ringford 65 E22
Ringland 45 D57
Ringles Cross 13 D50
Ringmer 13 E50
Ringmore 5 F22
Ringorm 98 E28
Ring's End 43 E50
Ringsfield 45 G59
Ringsfield Corner 45 G60
Ringshall Sfk 34 C56
Ringshall Hfs. 32 G45
Ringshall Stocks 34 C56
Ringstead Nmp. 32 A45
Ringstead Nfk 44 A53
Ringwood 10 D37
Ringwould 15 C59
Rinloan 90 C28

Rinmore 90 B29
Rinnigill 105 B29
Rinsey 2 F11
Ripe 13 F51
Ripley N.Y. 57 C38
Ripley Dby. 51 G39
Ripley Ham. 10 E37
Ripley Sry 22 F46
Riplingham 59 F45
Ripon 57 B38
Rippingale 42 C46
Ripple Kent 15 B59
Ripple H.&W. 29 E34
Ripponden 50 A36
Risabus 72 F9
Risbury 28 C31
Risby 34 B53
Risca 19 B28
Rise 59 E47
Risegate 42 B47
Riseley Brk. 22 E43
Riseley Bfd. 32 B46
Rishangles 35 B57
Rishton 56 F33
Rishworth 50 A36
Risley 41 B40
Risplith 57 C38
Rispond 102 B20
Rivar 21 E39
Rivenhall 34 G54
Rivenhall End 34 G54
River 12 D45
River Bank 33 B51
River Bridge 19 G29
Riverford Bridge 5 D23
Riverhead 23 F51
Rivington 49 A32
Roade 31 C43
Roadhead 69 F30
Roadside Hgh. 103 B27
Roadside Ork. 104 B32
Roadside of Kinneff 91 F34
Roadwater 7 B26
Roag 93 G8
Roa Island 55 C28
Roath 18 D27
Roberton Bor. 69 B30
Roberton Str. 68 A25
Robertsbridge 14 E53
Robertstown 98 E28
Roberttown 57 G37
Robeston Cross 16 D14
Robeston Wathen 16 C16
Robin Hood W.Y. 57 G39
Robin Hood Dby. 50 E38
Robin Hood's Bay 63 F45
Robins 12 D44
Roborough Dev. 6 D21
Roborough Dev. 4 D20
Roby 48 C30
Roby Mill 48 B31
Rocester 40 B36
Roch 16 B14
Rochallie 82 B27
Rochdale 49 A34
Roche 3 B15
Rochester Kent 24 E53
Rochester Nor. 70 D34
Rochford H.&W. 29 B32
Rochford Esx 24 B54
Rock Cnw. 3 A15
Rock H.&W. 29 A33
Rock Gwe. 18 B27
Rock Nor. 71 A37
Rockbeare 7 F26
Rockbourne 10 C36
Rockcliffe Cum. 69 G29
Rockcliffe D.&G. 65 E24
Rock Ferry 48 D29
Rockfield Str. 73 E14
Rockfield Hgh. 97 C25
Rockfield Gwe. 28 G30
Rockhampton 19 B32
Rockhead 4 B16
Rockingham 42 F44
Rockland All Saints 44 F55
Rockland St Mary 45 E59
Rockland St Peter 44 F55
Rockley 20 D37
Rockside 72 D8
Rockwell End 22 C43
Rockwell Green 7 D27
Rodborough 20 A34
Rodbourne 20 C35
Rodbridge Corner 34 D54
Rodd 28 B29
Roddam 71 A36
Rodden 9 F32
Rode 20 F33
Rode Heath 49 G33
Rodeheath 49 F34
Roden 38 D31
Rodhuish 7 B25
Rodington 38 D31
Rodley 29 G33
Rodmarton 20 B35

Rodmell 13 F50
Rodmersham 25 E55
Rodney Stoke 19 F30
Rodsley 40 A37
Rodway 19 G28
Roecliffe 57 C39
Roe Green 33 E48
Roehampton 23 D48
Roesound 107 A39
Roewen 47 E23
Roffey 12 C47
Rogart 96 A23
Rogate 12 D44
Rogerstone 19 C28
Roghadal 92 C6
Rogiet 19 C30
Roker 62 A39
Rollesby 45 D60
Rolleston Stf. 40 C38
Rolleston Not. 51 G43
Rolleston Lei. 42 E43
Rollestone 20 G36
Rolston 59 E48
Rolvenden 14 D54
Rolvenden Layne 14 D54
Romaldkirk 62 D35
Romanby 62 G39
Romannobridge 75 F27
Romansleigh 6 C22
Romford Dor. 10 C36
Romford Esx 23 C51
Romiley 49 C35
Romney Street 23 E51
Romsey 10 B39
Romsley H.&W. 40 G35
Romsley Shr. 39 G33
Ronachan 73 E13
Ronague 54 F24
Ronnachmore 72 E8
Rookhope 61 B35
Rookley 11 F40
Rooks Bridge 19 F29
Rookwith 57 A37
Roos 59 F48
Roosecote 55 C28
Rootpark 75 E25
Ropley 11 A42
Ropley Dean 11 A42
Ropley Soke 11 A42
Ropsley 42 B45
Rora 99 D36
Rorandle 91 B32
Rorrington 38 E29
Rosarie 98 D29
Rose 2 C13
Roseacre 55 F30
Rose Ash 7 C23
Rosebank 75 F24
Rosebrough 71 A37
Rosebush 16 B16
Rosedale Abbey 63 G43
Roseden 71 A36
Rose Green 34 F54
Rosehall 46 A20
Rosehearty 99 C34
Rosehill Grm. 90 D31
Rosehill Shr. 39 B32
Roseisle 97 E27
Rosemarket 16 D15
Rosemarkie 96 F23
Rosemary Lane 7 D27
Rosemount Str. 67 A19
Rosemount Tay. 82 C27
Rosepool 16 C14
Rosewarne 2 E12
Rosewell 76 D28
Roseworthy 2 E11
Rosgill 61 E31
Roshven 86 G12
Roskhill 93 G8
Rosley 60 B29
Roslin 76 D28
Rosliston 40 D38
Rosneath 74 B18
Ross Tay. 81 E23
Ross Nor. 77 G37
Ross D.&G. 65 F22
Rossett 48 G29
Rossie Farm School 83 B32
Rossie Ochill 82 F26
Rossie Priory 82 D28
Rossington 51 C42
Rosskeen 96 D22
Ross-on-Wye 28 F31
Ross Priory 74 B20
Roster 103 E28
Rostherne 49 D33
Rosthwaite Cum. 55 A28
Rosthwaite Cum. 60 E28
Roston 40 A37
Rosyth 75 B26
Rothbury 71 C36
Rotherby 41 D42
Rotherfield 13 D51
Rotherfield Greys 22 C43
Rotherfield Peppard 21 C42

Rotherham 51 C39
Rotherthorpe 31 C42
Rotherwick 21 F42
Rothes 98 E28
Rothesay 73 D16
Rothiebrisbane 99 F33
Rothienorman 98 F32
Rothiesholm 104 D31
Rothley Nor. 71 E36
Rothley Lei. 41 D41
Rothwell Nmp. 42 G43
Rothwell W.Y. 57 G39
Rothwell Lcn. 52 C47
Rotsea 59 D46
Rottal 82 A29
Rottingdean 13 F49
Rottington 60 E25
Roud 11 F41
Roudham 44 G55
Rougham Nfk. 44 C54
Rougham Sfk 34 B55
Rougham Green 34 B54
Roughburn 88 F19
Rough Close 40 B35
Rough Common 15 B56
Roughlee 56 E34
Roughley 40 F37
Roughton Nfk 45 B58
Roughton Shr. 39 F33
Roughton Lcn. 53 F48
Roundhay 57 F39
Roundstreet Common 12 D46
Roundway 20 E36
Rousdon 8 E28
Rousham 31 F40
Rousham Gap 31 F40
Rous Lench 30 C36
Routenburn 74 D18
Routh 59 E46
Rowanburn 69 F29
Rowardennan Lodge 74 A19
Rowberrow 19 F30
Rowchoish 80 G19
Rowde 20 E35
Rowfoot 70 G32
Row Heath 35 G57
Rowhedge 34 F56
Rowhook 12 C46
Rowington 30 B37
Rowington Green 30 A38
Rowland 50 E37
Rowland's Castle 11 C43
Rowlands Gill 62 A37
Rowledge 22 G44
Rowley Drm 62 B36
Rowley Hum. 59 F45
Rowley Dev. 7 D23
Rowley Shr. 38 E29
Rowley Regis 40 G35
Rowlstone 28 F29
Rowly 22 G46
Rowner 11 D41
Rowney Green 30 A36
Rownhams 10 C39
Rowrah 60 E26
Rowsham 32 G44
Rowsley 56 F38
Rowstock 21 C40
Rowston 52 G46
Rowthorne 51 F40
Rowton Che. 48 F30
Rowton Shr. 39 D32
Rowton Shr. 38 D29
Row Town 22 E46
Roxburgh 76 G32
Roxby Cle. 63 E43
Roxby Hum. 52 A45
Roxton 32 C47
Roxwell 24 A52
Royal British Legion Village 14 B53
Royal Leamington Spa 30 B39
Royal Tunbridge Wells 23 G51
Roybridge 87 F18
Roydon Nfk 44 G56
Roydon Nfk 44 C52
Roydon Esx 23 A50
Roydon Hamlet 23 A49
Royston S.Y. 51 A39
Royston Hfs. 33 D49
Royton 49 B35
Ruabon 38 A29
Ruaig 78 C6
Ruanaich 78 E8
Ruan Lanihorne 3 D14
Ruan Major 2 G12
Ruan Minor 2 G13
Ruardean 29 G32
Ruardean Woodside 29 G32
Rubery 29 A35
Ruckcroft 61 B31
Ruckinge 15 D56
Ruckland 53 E49

Ruckley 38 F31
Rudbaxton 16 B15
Rudby 62 F40
Rudchester 71 G37
Ruddington 41 B41
Ruddlemoor 4 E16
Rudford 29 F33
Rudge 20 F34
Rudgeway 19 C32
Rudgwick 12 C46
Rudhall 29 F32
Rudheath 49 E32
Rudley Green 24 A54
Rudry 18 C27
Rudston 59 C46
Rudyard 49 G35
Rufford 48 A30
Rufforth 58 D41
Ruffside 62 A35
Rugby 31 A40
Rugeley 40 D36
Ruilick 96 G20
Ruishton 8 B28
Ruisigearraidh 92 C5
Ruislip 22 C46
Rumbling Bridge 75 A26
Rumburgh 45 G59
Rumford 3 A15
Rumney 19 D28
Rumwell 7 C27
Runacraig 81 F21
Runcorn 48 D30
Runcton 12 F44
Runcton Holme 44 E52
Rundlestone 5 C21
Runfold 22 G44
Runhall 44 E56
Runham 45 D60
Runnington 7 C26
Runsell Green 24 A53
Runswick 63 E43
Runtaleave 82 A28
Runwell 24 B53
Ruscombe 22 D44
Rushall W.M. 40 E36
Rushall Wts. 20 F37
Rushall Nfk 45 G57
Rushall H.&W. 29 E32
Rushbrooke 34 B54
Rushbury 38 F30
Rushden Hfs. 33 E48
Rushden Nmp. 32 B45
Rushford 44 G55
Rush Green 23 C51
Rushlake Green 13 E52
Rushmere 45 G60
Rushmere St Andrew 35 D58
Rushmoor Shr. 39 D32
Rushmoor Sry 22 G44
Rushock 29 A34
Rusholm 49 C34
Rushton Che. 48 F31
Rushton Shr. 39 E32
Rushton Nmp. 42 G44
Rushton Spencer 49 F35
Rushwick 29 C33
Rushyford 62 D38
Ruskie 81 G22
Ruskington 52 G46
Rusko 65 E21
Rusland 55 A29
Rusper 13 C48
Ruspidge 29 G32
Russel 94 G14
Russell's Water 21 C42
Rusthall 23 G51
Rustington 12 F46
Ruston 59 A45
Ruston Parva 59 C46
Ruswarp 63 F44
Rutherend 74 E22
Rutherford 70 A32
Rutherglen 74 D21
Ruthernbridge 3 B15
Ruthin 47 G27
Ruthrieston 91 C35
Ruthven Tay. 82 C28
Ruthven Hgh. 88 E23
Ruthven Grm. 98 E30
Ruthven Hgh. 88 A23
Ruthvoes 3 B15
Ruthwaite 60 C28
Ruthwell 69 G26
Ruyton-XI-Towns 38 C29
Ryal 71 F36
Ryal Fold 56 G32
Ryall 8 E30
Ryarsh 23 F52
Rydal 60 F29
Ryde 11 E42
Rydon 6 E19
Rye 14 E54
Rye Foreign 14 E54
Rye Harbour 14 F55
Rye Park 23 A49
Ryhall 42 D46

Ryhill 51 A39
Ryhope 62 A39
Ryland 52 D46
Rylstone 56 D35
Ryme Intrinseca 8 C31
Ryther 58 F41
Ryton N.Y. 58 B43
Ryton T.&W. 71 G37
Ryton Shr. 39 E33
Ryton Glo. 29 E33
Ryton-on-Dunsmore 30 A39

S

Sabden 56 F33
Sackers Green 34 E55
Sacombe 33 G49
Sacriston 62 B38
Sadberge 62 E39
Saddell 73 G13
Saddington 41 F42
Saddle Bow 43 D51
Sadgill 61 F30
Saffron Walden 33 E50
Sageston 16 D16
Saham Toney 44 E54
Saighdinis 92 E4
Saighton 48 F30
St Abbs 77 D35
St Agnes 2 C12
St Albans 22 A47
St Allen 3 C14
St Andrews 83 F30
St Andrews Major 18 D27
St Anne 3 D17
St Anne's 55 G29
St Ann's 69 D26
St Ann's Chapel 4 C19
St Ann's Chapel 5 F22
St Anthony 2 F13
St Anthony 3 E14
St Arvans 3 B31
St Asaph (Llanelwy) 47 E26
St Athan 18 E25
St Aubin 3 G17
St Audries 7 A26
St Austell 3 C15
St Bees 60 E25
St Blazey 4 E16
St Blazey Gate 4 E16
St Boswells 76 G31
St Brelade 3 G17
St Breock 3 A15
St Breward 4 C17
St Brides 16 C14
St Brides Major 18 D24
St Brides Netherwent 19 C30
St Bride's-super-Ely 18 D26
St Brides Wentlooge 19 C28
St Budeaux 4 E20
Saintbury 30 E36
St Buryan 2 F10
St Catherine 20 D34
St Catherines 80 G16
St Clears 17 C18
St Cleer 4 D18
St Clement 3 D14
St Clether 4 B17
St Columb Major 3 B15
St Columb Minor 3 B14
St Columb Road 3 C15
St Combs 99 C36
St Cross South Elmham 45 G58
St Cyrus 91 G33
St David's 82 E25
St Davids 75 B27
St David's 16 B13
St Day 2 D12
St Decumans 7 A26
St Dennis 3 C15
St Dennis 30 G36
St Dogmaels 26 D17
St Dogwells 16 B15
St Dominick 4 D20
St Donats 18 E24
St Edith's Marsh 20 E35
St Endellion 3 A15
St Enoder 3 C14
St Erme 3 D14
St Erth 2 E11
St Erth Praze 2 E11
St Ervan 3 A14
St Eval 3 B14
St Ewe 3 D15
St Fagans 18 D26
St Fergus 99 D37
St Fillans 81 E22
St Florence 16 D16
St Gennys 4 A17
St George 47 E25
St Georges 19 E29
St George's 18 D26
St Germans 4 E19
St Giles in the Wood 6 D21
St Giles on the Heath 4 A18

St Harmon 27 A25
St Helena 45 D57
St Helen Auckland 62 D37
St Helens *Mer.* 48 C31
St Helen's 14 F54
St Helens *I.o.W.* 11 F42
St Helier 3 G17
St Hilary *S.G.* 18 D25
St Hilary *Cnw.* 2 E11
Saint Hill 13 C49
St Illtyd 19 A28
St Ippollitts 32 F47
St Ishmael 17 D19
St Ishmael's 16 D14
St Issey 3 A15
St Ive 4 D18
St Ives *Cbs.* 33 A48
St Ives *Cnw.* 2 D11
St Ives *Dor.* 10 D36
St James South Elmham
  45 G59
St John *Cnw.* 4 E19
St John *C.I.* 3 F17
St John's *H.&W.* 29 C34
St John's 54 E24
St John's *Drm* 62 C36
St John's *Sry* 22 F45
St John's Chapel 61 C34
St John's Chapel 6 C21
St John's Fen End 43 D51
St John's Highway 43 D51
St John's Kirk 75 G25
St John's Town of Dalry 68 E22
St Judes 54 D25
St Just 2 E9
St Just in Roseland 3 E14
St Katherines 99 F33
St Keverne 2 F13
St Kew 3 A15
St Kew Highway 4 C16
St Keyne 4 D18
St Lawrence *Esx* 25 A55
St Lawrence 3 B15
St Lawrence *I.o.W.* 11 G41
St Leonards *Dor.* 10 D36
St Leonards *E.S.* 14 G53
St Leonards *Bkh.* 22 A44
St Leonards Grange 11 E40
St Leonard's Street 23 F52
St Levan 2 F9
St Lythans 18 D27
St Mabyn 4 C16
St Margarets 28 E29
St Margarets 33 G49
St Margaret's at Cliffe 15 C59
St Margaret's Hope 105 B30
St Margaret South Elmham
  45 G58
St Mark's 54 F25
St Martin *C.I.* 3 G18
St Martin 4 E18
St Martin *Cnw.* 2 F13
St Martin *C.I.* 3 F17
St Martin's 38 B29
St Martins 82 D27
St Mary Bourne 21 F40
St Mary Church 18 D26
St Marychurch 5 D25
St Mary Cray 23 E50
St Mary Hill 18 D25
St Mary in the Marsh 15 E56
St Mary's 105 A30
St Mary's Bay 15 E56
St Mary's Croft 64 D16
St Mary's Grove 19 E30
St Mary's Hoo 24 D53
St Mawes 3 E14
St Mawgan 3 B14
St Mellion 4 D19
St Mellons 19 C28
St Merryn 3 A14
St Mewan 3 C15
St Michael Caerhays 3 D15
St Michael Penkevil 3 D14
St Michaels 28 B31
St Michaels 14 D54
St Michael's on Wyre 55 E30
St Michael South Elmham
  45 G59
St Minver 3 A15
St Monans 83 G31
St Neot 4 D17
St Neots 32 B47
St Nicholas *S.G.* 18 D26
St Nicholas *Dyf.* 16 A14
St Nicholas at Wade 25 E58
St Ninians 75 A23
St Osyth 35 G57
St Ouen 3 F17
St Owen's Cross 28 F31
St Paul's Cray 23 E50
St Paul's Walden 32 F47
St Peter 3 G17
St Peter Port 3 E17
St Peter's 25 E59
St Petrox 16 E15

St Pinnock 4 D18
St Quivox 67 A19
St Sampson 3 E17
St Saviour 3 E16
St Stephen 3 C15
St Stephen's 4 E19
St Stephens *Cnw.* 6 G19
St Stephens *Hfs.* 22 A47
St Teath 4 B16
St Tudy 4 C16
St Twynnells 16 E15
St Veep 4 E17
St Vigeans 83 C32
St Wenn 3 B15
St Weonards 28 F30
Salachail 80 B16
Salcombe 5 G23
Salcombe Regis 7 G27
Salcott 34 G55
Sale 49 C33
Saleby 53 E50
Sale Green 29 C35
Salehurst 14 E53
Salem *Dyf.* 37 G22
Salem *Dyf.* 17 B22
Salem *Gwy.* 46 G21
Salen *Hgh.* 79 A12
Salen *Str.* 79 C11
Salesbury 56 F32
Salford *G.M.* 49 C33
Salford *Bfd.* 32 E45
Salford *Oxf.* 30 F38
Salford Priors 30 C36
Salfords 23 G48
Salhouse 45 D59
Saline 75 A26
Salisbury 10 A37
Salkeld Dykes 61 C31
Sall 45 C57
Sallachan 80 A15
Sallachry 80 F16
Sallachy *Hgh.* 86 A14
Sallachy *Hgh.* 96 A21
Salmonby 53 E49
Salmond's Muir 83 D31
Salperton 30 F36
Salph End 32 C46
Salsburgh 75 D24
Salt 40 C35
Saltash 4 E19
Saltburn 96 E23
Saltburn-by-the-Sea 63 D42
Saltby 42 C44
Saltcoats 74 F18
Saltcotes 55 G29
Saltdean 13 F49
Salterforth 56 E34
Salterhill 97 E27
Salterswall 48 F31
Saltfleet 53 C50
Saltfleetby All Saints 53 C50
Saltfleetby St Clements 53 C50
Saltfleetby St Peter 53 D50
Saltford 19 E32
Salthaugh Grange 59 G48
Salt Hill 22 C45
Salthouse 44 A56
Saltley 40 G36
Saltmarshe 58 G43
Saltney 48 F29
Salton 58 A43
Saltwick 71 E37
Saltwood 15 D57
Salvington 12 F47
Salwarpe 29 B34
Salwayash 8 E30
Sambourne 30 B36
Sambrook 39 C33
Samhla 92 E3
Samlesbury 55 F31
Samlesbury Bottoms 56 G32
Sampford Arundel 7 D26
Sampford Brett 7 A26
Sampford Courtenay 6 E22
Sampford Peverell 7 D26
Sampford Spiney 5 C21
Samuelston 76 C30
Sanaigmore 72 C8
Sancreed 2 F9
Sancton 59 F45
Sand 107 C39
Sandaig *Hgh.* 86 C13
Sandaig *Hgh.* 86 D12
Sanday Airport 104 B32
Sandbach 49 F33
Sandbank 73 B17
Sandbanks 10 F36
Sandend 98 C31
Sanderstead 23 E49
Sandford *I.o.W.* 11 F41
Sandford *Dev.* 7 E23
Sandford *Str.* 75 F23
Sandford *Avon* 19 F29
Sandford *Cum.* 61 E33
Sandford *Dor.* 9 F34
Sandfordhill 99 E36

Sandford-on-Thames 21 A41
Sandford Orcas 9 B32
Sandford St Martin 30 F39
Sandgarth 104 E31
Sandgate 15 D57
Sandgreen 65 E21
Sandhaven 99 C35
Sandhead 64 E16
Sandhills *Dor.* 9 C32
Sandhills *Sry* 12 C45
Sandhoe 70 G35
Sand Hole 58 F44
Sandholme *Hum.* 58 F44
Sandholme *Lcn.* 43 B49
Sandhurst *Kent* 14 E53
Sandhurst *Brk.* 22 E44
Sandhurst *Glo.* 29 F34
Sand Hutton 58 D42
Sandhutton 57 A39
Sandiacre 41 B40
Sandilands 53 D51
Sandiway 49 E32
Sandleheath 10 C36
Sandleigh 21 A40
Sandling 14 B53
Sandness 107 B37
Sandon *Stf.* 40 C35
Sandon *Hfs.* 33 E49
Sandon *Esx* 24 A53
Sandown 11 F42
Sandown Airport 11 F41
Sandplace 4 E18
Sandquoy 104 B33
Sandridge *Wts.* 20 E35
Sandridge *Hfs.* 32 G47
Sandringham 44 C53
Sandrocks 13 D49
Sandsend 63 E44
Sand Side 55 A28
Sandside House 103 B25
Sandsound 107 C39
Sandtoft 51 B43
Sanduck 7 G23
Sandway 14 B54
Sandwich 15 B59
Sandwick *She.* 107 E40
Sandwick *Cum.* 60 E30
Sandwick *W.I.* 100 D10
Sandwith 60 E25
Sandy 32 D47
Sandycroft 48 F29
Sandygate *I.o.M.* 54 D25
Sandygate *Dev.* 5 C24
Sandy Haven 16 D14
Sandylands 55 C29
Sandy Lane *W.Y.* 57 F37
Sandy Lane *Wts.* 20 E35
Sandyway 28 F30
Sangobeg 102 B20
Sanna 79 A10
Sannaig 72 D11
Sanquhar 68 C23
Santon Bridge 60 F27
Santon Downham 44 G54
Sapcote 41 F40
Sapey Common 29 B32
Sapiston 34 A54
Sapperton *Glo.* 20 A35
Sapperton *Lcn.* 42 B46
Saracen's Head 43 C49
Sarclet 103 D29
Sardis 16 D15
Sarisbury 11 D40
Sarn *M.G.* 18 C25
Sarn *Pow.* 38 F27
Sarnau *Pow.* 38 D28
Sarnau *Gwy.* 37 B25
Sarnau *Dyf.* 26 C18
Sarnau *Dyf.* 17 C19
Sarn Bach 36 C18
Sarnesfield 28 C29
Sarn-Meyllteyrn 36 B18
Saron *Dyf.* 17 C22
Saron *Dyf.* 17 A19
Saron *Gwy.* 46 F21
Sarratt 22 B46
Sarre 25 E58
Sarsden 30 F38
Satley 62 B37
Satterleigh 6 C22
Satterthwaite 60 G29
Sauchen 91 B32
Saucher 82 D27
Sauchieburn 91 G32
Sauchrie 67 B18
Saughall 48 E29
Saughall Massie 48 D28
Saughtree 70 D31
Saul 20 A33
Saundby 51 D43
Saundersfoot 16 D17
Saunderton 22 A43
Saunton 6 B20

Sausthorpe 53 F49
Savalbeg 96 A21
Savalmore 96 A21
Sawbridgeworth 33 G50
Sawdon 59 A45
Sawley *N.Y.* 57 C38
Sawley *Lan.* 56 E33
Sawley *Dby.* 41 B40
Sawston 33 D50
Sawtry 42 G47
Saxby *Lei.* 42 D44
Saxby *Lcn.* 52 D45
Saxby All Saints 52 A45
Saxelbye 41 C42
Saxham Street 33 C52
Saxilby 52 E44
Saxlingham 44 B55
Saxlingham Green 45 F58
Saxlingham Nethergate 45 F58
Saxlingham Thorpe 45 F58
Saxmundham 35 B59
Saxondale 41 A42
Saxon Street 33 C52
Saxtead Green 35 B58
Saxtead Little Green 35 B58
Saxthorpe 45 B57
Saxton 57 F40
Sayers Common 13 E48
Scackleton 58 B42
Scadabhagh 93 B7
Scaftworth 51 C42
Scagglethorpe 58 B44
Scalasaig 72 A9
Scalby *Hum.* 58 G44
Scalby *N.Y.* 59 A45
Scaldwell 31 A43
Scaleby 69 G30
Scalebyhill 69 G30
Scale Houses 61 B31
Scales *Cum.* 60 D29
Scales *Cum.* 55 B28
Scalford 42 C43
Scaling 63 E44
Scallasaig 86 C14
Scallastle 79 D12
Scalloway 107 D39
Scamadale 79 E14
Scamblesby 53 E48
Scamodale 86 G14
Scampston 58 B44
Scampton 52 E45
Scaniport 88 A22
Scapa 105 A30
Scar 104 B32
Scarborough 59 A46
Scarcewater 3 C15
Scarcliffe 51 F40
Scarcroft 57 E39
Scardroy 95 F17
Scarff 106 D38
Scarfskerry 103 A28
Scargill 62 E36
Scarinish 78 C6
Scarisbrick 48 A29
Scarning 44 D55
Scarrington 42 A43
Scarth Hill 48 B30
Scartho 53 B48
Scatraig 88 A22
Scaur 65 C24
Scawby 52 B45
Scawton 58 A41
Scayne's Hill 13 D49
Scealascro 100 E7
Scethrog 27 F26
Schaw 67 A20
Scholar Green 49 G34
Scholes *W.Y.* 50 B37
Scholes *W.Y.* 57 F39
Sciberscross 96 A23
Scilly Isles Airport 2 A11
Scleddau 16 A15
Scofton 51 D42
Scole 35 A57
Scolpaig 92 D3
Scolton 16 B15
Sconser 86 A11
Scoor 79 F10
Scopwick 52 G46
Scoraig 94 B15
Scorborough 59 E46
Scorrier 2 D13
Scorriton 5 D23
Scorton *N.Y.* 62 F38
Scorton *Lan.* 55 E30
Sco Ruston 45 C58
Scotby 60 A30
Scotforth 55 D30
Scothern 52 E46
Scotland Gate 71 E38
Scotlandwell 82 G27
Scotnish 73 B13
Scotsburn 96 D22
Scots' Gap 71 E36
Scotston *Tay.* 81 C24
Scotston *Grm.* 91 F33

Scotstown 79 A14
Scotter 52 B44
Scotterthorpe 52 B44
Scottlethorpe 42 C46
Scotton *Lcn.* 52 C44
Scotton *N.Y.* 62 G37
Scotton *N.Y.* 57 D39
Scottow 45 C58
Scoulton 44 E55
Scourie 101 D17
Scourie More 101 D17
Scousburgh 107 D37
Scrabster 103 A26
Scrainwood 70 C35
Scraptoft 41 E42
Scratby 45 D61
Scrayingham 58 C43
Scredington 42 A46
Scremby 53 F50
Scremerston 77 F35
Screveton 42 A43
Scriven 57 D39
Scrooby 51 C42
Scropton 40 B37
Scrub Hill 53 G48
Scruton 62 G38
Scunthorpe 52 A44
Seabank 79 C14
Seaborough 8 D30
Seacombe 48 C28
Seacroft *W.Y.* 57 F39
Seacroft *Lcn.* 53 F51
Seafield *Ltn* 75 D26
Seafield *Str.* 73 B13
Seafield *Str.* 67 A19
Seaford 13 G50
Seaforth 48 C29
Seagrave 41 D41
Seaham 62 A40
Seahouses 77 G37
Seal 23 F51
Sealand 48 F29
Seale 22 G44
Seamer *N.Y.* 62 E40
Seamer *N.Y.* 59 A46
Seamill 73 F17
Sea Palling 45 C60
Searby 52 B46
Seasalter 25 E56
Seascale 60 F26
Seathwaite 60 E28
Seatoller 60 E28
Seaton *Drm* 62 B39
Seaton *Cum.* 60 C25
Seaton *Hum.* 59 E47
Seaton *Nor.* 71 F39
Seaton *Cnw.* 4 E19
Seaton *Dev.* 8 E27
Seaton *Lei.* 42 F44
Seaton Burn 71 F38
Seaton Carew 63 C41
Seaton Delaval 71 F39
Seaton Junction 8 E28
Seaton Ross 58 E43
Seaton Sluice 71 F39
Seatown *Grm.* 99 D37
Seatown *Grm.* 98 C30
Seatown *Grm.* 98 C30
Seatown *Dor.* 8 E30
Seave Green 63 F41
Seaview 11 E42
Seaville 60 A27
Seavington St Mary 8 C29
Seavington St Michael 8 C30
Seawick 35 G57
Sebastopol 19 B28
Sebergham 60 B29
Seckington 40 E38
Second Coast 94 B14
Sedbergh 61 G32
Sedbury 19 B31
Sedbusk 61 G34
Sedgeberrow 29 E35
Sedgebrook 42 B44
Sedgefield 62 D39
Sedgehill 9 B34
Sedgley 40 F34
Sedgwick 55 A31
Sedlescombe 14 F53
Sedlescombe Street 14 F53
Seend 20 E35
Seend Cleeve 20 E35
Seer Green 22 B45
Seething 45 F59
Sefton 48 B29
Seghill 71 F38
Seighford 40 C34
Seilebost 92 B6
Seion 46 F21
Seisdon 40 F34
Seisiadar 101 D11
Selattyn 38 B28
Selborne 11 A43
Selby 58 F42
Selham 12 D45

Selkirk 69 A30
Sellack 28 F31
Sellafield 60 F26
Sellafirth 106 C41
Sellindge 15 D56
Selling 15 B56
Sells Green 20 E35
Selly Oak 40 G36
Selmeston 13 F51
Selsdon 23 E49
Selsey 12 G44
Selsfield Common 13 C49
Selside 56 B33
Selstead 15 C57
Selston 51 G40
Selworthy 7 A25
Semblister 107 B39
Semer 34 D55
Semington 20 E34
Semley 9 B34
Send 22 F46
Send Marsh 22 F46
Senghenydd 18 B26
Sennen 2 F9
Sennybridge 27 F24
Senwick 65 F22
Sequer's Bridge 5 E22
Sessay 57 B40
Setchey 44 D52
Setley 10 D38
Setter *She.* 107 C41
Setter *She.* 107 B39
Settiscarth 104 E29
Settle 56 C34
Settrington 58 B44
Seven Bridges 20 B37
Sevenhampton *Wts.* 20 B37
Sevenhampton *Glo.* 29 F36
Seven Kings 23 C50
Sevenoaks 23 F51
Sevenoaks Weald 23 F51
Seven Sisters 18 A23
Seven Springs 29 G35
Severn Beach 19 C31
Severn Stoke 29 D34
Sevington 15 C56
Sewards End 33 E51
Sewardstone 23 B49
Sewerby 59 C48
Seworgan 2 E13
Sewstern 42 C44
Sexhow 62 F40
Sgarasta Mhor 92 B6
Sgiogarstaigh 101 A11
Sgodachail 96 B20
Shabbington 21 A42
Shackerley 40 E34
Shackerstone 41 E39
Shackleford 22 G45
Shadfen 71 E38
Shadforth 62 B39
Shadingfield 45 G60
Shadoxhurst 14 D55
Shadwell 44 G55
Shaftesbury 9 B34
Shafton 51 A39
Shalbourne 21 E38
Shalcombe 11 F40
Shalden 21 G42
Shaldon 5 C25
Shalfleet 11 F40
Shalford *Sry* 22 G46
Shalford *Esx* 34 F53
Shalford Green 33 F52
Shallowford 7 A23
Shalmsford Street 15 B56
Shalmstry 103 B27
Shalstone 31 E42
Shalunt 73 C16
Shambellie 65 D25
Shamley Green 22 G46
Shandon 74 B18
Shandwick 97 D24
Shangton 41 F42
Shankend 70 C31
Shankhouse 71 F38
Shanklin 11 F41
Shannochie 66 A15
Shantron 74 B19
Shantullich 96 F22
Shanzie 82 B28
Shap 61 E31
Shapwick *Som.* 8 A29
Shapwick *Dor.* 9 D35
Shardlow 41 B40
Shareshill 40 E35
Sharlston 51 A39
Sharnbrook 32 C45
Sharnford 41 F40
Sharoe Green 55 F31
Sharow 57 B39
Sharpenhoe 32 E46
Sharperton 70 C35
Sharpham House 5 E24
Sharpness 19 A32
Sharpthorne 13 C49

Sharrington 44 B56
Shatterford 39 G33
Shaugh Prior 5 D21
Shavington 49 G33
Shaw *G.M.* 49 B35
Shaw *Wts.* 20 E34
Shaw *Wts.* 20 C37
Shaw *Brk.* 21 E40
Shawbury 38 C31
Shawclough 49 A34
Shawell 41 G41
Shawford 11 B40
Shawforth 56 G34
Shawhead 65 C24
Shaw Mills 57 C38
Shawtonhill 74 F22
Sheanachie 66 B13
Sheandow 98 F28
Shear Cross 20 G34
Shearington 69 G26
Shearsby 41 F42
Shebbear 6 E20
Shebdon 39 C33
Shebster 103 B25
Shedfield 11 C41
Sheen 50 F36
Sheepscombe 29 G34
Sheepstor 5 D21
Sheepwash *Nor.* 71 E38
Sheepwash *Dev.* 6 E20
Sheepway 19 D30
Sheepy Magna 41 E39
Sheepy Parva 41 E39
Sheering 33 G50
Sheerness 25 D55
Sheet 11 B43
Sheffield 51 D39
Sheffield Bottom 21 E42
Sheffield Green 13 D50
Shefford 32 E47
Shefford Woodlands 21 D39
Sheigra 101 B17
Sheinton 39 E32
Shelderton 28 A29
Sheldon *Dby.* 50 F37
Sheldon *Dev.* 7 E27
Sheldon *W.M.* 40 G37
Sheldwich 14 B55
Shelf 57 G37
Shelfanger 45 G57
Shelfield 40 E36
Shelford 41 A42
Shellachan *Str.* 80 E16
Shellachan *Str.* 79 F14
Shellbrook Hill 38 B29
Shelley *Sfk* 34 E56
Shelley *W.Y.* 50 A38
Shelley *Esx* 23 A51
Shellingford 21 B39
Shellow Bowells 23 A51
Shelsley Beauchamp 29 B33
Shelsley Walsh 29 B33
Shelton *Bfd.* 32 B46
Shelton *Shr.* 38 D30
Shelton *Nfk* 45 F58
Shelton *Not.* 42 A43
Shelton Green 45 F58
Shelve 38 F29
Shelwick 28 D31
Shenfield 24 B52
Shenington 30 D39
Shenley 22 A47
Shenley Brook End 32 E44
Shenleybury 22 A47
Shenley Church End 32 E44
Shenmore 28 E29
Shennanton 64 D19
Shenstone *Stf.* 40 E37
Shenstone *H.&W.* 29 A34
Shenstone Woodend 40 E36
Shenton 41 E39
Shenval 90 A27
Shepeau Stow 43 D48
Shephall 33 F48
Shepherd's Green 21 C42
Shepherdswell or Sibertswold 15 C58
Shepley 50 B37
Sheppardstown 103 E27
Shepperdine 19 B31
Shepperton 22 E46
Shepreth 33 D49
Shepshed 41 D40
Shepton Beauchamp 8 C30
Shepton Mallet 19 G32
Shepton Montague 9 A32
Shepway 14 B53
Sheraton 62 C40
Sherborne *Glo.* 30 G37
Sherborne *Dor.* 9 C32
Sherborne St John 21 F42
Sherbourne 30 B38
Sherburn *Drm* 62 B39
Sherburn *N.Y.* 59 B45
Sherburn in Elmet 57 F40
Shere 22 G46

Shereford 44 C54
Sherfield English 10 B38
Sherfield on Loddon 21 F42
Sherford 5 F23
Sheriffhales 39 D33
Sheringham 45 A57
Sherington 32 D44
Sherramore 88 E21
Sherrington 9 A35
Sherston 20 C34
Sherwood Green 6 C21
Shettleston 74 D22
Shevington 48 B31
Shevington Moor 48 A31
Sheviock 4 E19
Shiel Bridge 86 C15
Shieldaig *Hgh.* 94 D14
Shieldaig *Hgh.* 94 F13
Shieldhill 75 C24
Shielfoot 79 A12
Shielhill 83 B30
Shiels 91 C32
Shifford 21 A39
Shifnal 39 E33
Shilbottle 71 C37
Shildon 62 D38
Shillingford *Dev.* 7 C25
Shillingford *Oxf.* 21 B41
Shillingford St George 7 G24
Shillingstone 9 C33
Shillington 32 E47
Shillmoor 70 C34
Shilstone 6 E22
Shilton *Oxf.* 21 A38
Shilton *War.* 41 G40
Shimpling *Nfk* 45 G57
Shimpling *Sfk* 34 C54
Shimpling Street 34 C54
Shincliffe 62 B38
Shiney Row 62 A39
Shinfield 22 E43
Shingay 33 D48
Shingle Street 35 D59
Shinner's Bridge 5 D23
Shinness Lodge 102 G21
Shipbourne 23 F51
Shipdham 44 E55
Shipham 19 F30
Shiphay 5 D24
Shiplake 22 D43
Shipley *W.S.* 12 D47
Shipley *W.Y.* 57 F37
Shipley *Nor.* 71 B37
Shipley *Shr.* 39 F33
Shipley Bridge *Dev.* 5 D22
Shipley Bridge *Sry* 23 G49
Shipmeadow 45 F59
Shippon 21 B40
Shipton *N.Y.* 58 D41
Shipton *Shr.* 38 F31
Shipton *Glo.* 30 G36
Shipton Bellinger 21 G38
Shipton Gorge 8 E30
Shipton Green 12 G44
Shipton Moyne 20 C34
Shipton-on-Cherwell 31 G40
Shipton on Stour 30 D38
Shiptonthorpe 58 E44
Shipton-under-Wychwood 30 G38
Shira 80 F17
Shirburn 22 B43
Shirdley Hill 48 A29
Shirebrook 51 F41
Shirehampton 19 D30
Shiremoor 71 F38
Shirenewton 19 B30
Shire Oak 40 E36
Shireoaks 51 D41
Shirland 51 G39
Shirley *G.L.* 23 E49
Shirley *Ham.* 11 C40
Shirley *Ham.* 10 E37
Shirley *Dby.* 40 A38
Shirley *W.M.* 30 A37
Shirl Heath 28 C30
Shirrell Heath 11 C41
Shirwell 6 B22
Shirwell Cross 6 B21
Shiskine 66 A14
Shobdon 28 B29
Shobrooke 7 E24
Shocklach 38 A30
Shoeburyness 25 C55
Sholden 15 B59
Sholing 11 C40
Shooter's Hill 23 D50
Shoot Hill 38 D30
Shop *Cnw.* 6 D18
Shop *Cnw.* 3 A14
Shop Corner 35 C58
Shoreditch 23 C49
Shoreham 23 E51
Shoreham Airport 12 F47
Shoreham-by-Sea 13 F48

Shoremill 96 E23
Shoresdean 77 F35
Shoreswood 77 F35
Shoretown 96 E21
Shorncote 20 B35
Shorne 24 D52
Shorne Ridgeway 24 D52
Shortacombe 6 G21
Short Cross 38 E28
Shortgate 13 E50
Short Green 44 G56
Shortgrove 33 E50
Short Heath *W.M.* 40 F36
Short Heath *Dby.* 40 D38
Shortlanesend 2 D13
Shorwell 11 F40
Shoscombe 20 F33
Shotesham 45 F58
Shotgate 24 B53
Shotley 35 E58
Shotley Bridge 62 A36
Shotleyfield 62 A36
Shotley Gate 35 E58
Shottenden 15 B56
Shottermill 12 C44
Shottery 30 C37
Shottisham 35 D59
Shottle 41 A39
Shottlegate 40 A38
Shotton *Clw.* 48 F28
Shotton *Nor.* 77 G34
Shotton *Drm* 62 C40
Shotton Colliery 62 B39
Shotts 75 D24
Shotwick 48 E29
Shoughlaige-e-Caine 54 E24
Shouldham 44 E52
Shouldham Thorpe 44 E52
Shoulton 29 C33
Shover's Green 13 C52
Shrawardine 38 D29
Shrawley 29 B33
Shrewley 30 B37
Shrewsbury 38 D30
Shrewton 20 G36
Shripney 12 F45
Shrivenham 21 C38
Shropham 44 F55
Shrub End 34 F55
Shucknall 28 D31
Shudy Camps 33 D51
Shurdington 29 G35
Shurlock Row 22 D44
Shurrery 103 C26
Shurrery Lodge 103 C26
Shurton 7 A27
Shustoke 40 F38
Shutford 30 D39
Shute 8 E28
Shut Heath 40 C34
Shuthonger 29 E34
Shutlanger 31 C43
Shuttington 40 E38
Shuttlewood 51 E40
Shuttleworth 49 A34
Siabost 100 C8
Siadar Iarach 100 B9
Siadar Uarach 100 B9
Sibbaldbie 69 E27
Sibbertoft 41 G42
Sibdon Carwood 38 G29
Sibford Ferris 30 E39
Sibford Gower 30 E39
Sible Hedingham 34 E53
Sibsey 53 G49
Sibson *Cbs.* 42 F46
Sibson *Lei.* 41 E39
Sibster 103 C29
Sibthorpe 42 A43
Sibton 35 B59
Sicklesmere 34 C54
Sicklinghall 57 E39
Sidbury *Shr.* 39 G32
Sidbury *Dev.* 7 F27
Sidcot 19 F30
Sidcup 23 D50
Siddington *Glo.* 20 B36
Siddington *Che.* 49 E34
Sidemoor 29 A35
Sidestrand 45 B58
Sidford 7 F27
Sidlesham 12 G44
Sidley 14 G53
Sidlowbridge 23 G48
Sidmouth 7 G27
Siefton 38 G30
Sigford 5 C23
Sigglesthorne 59 E47
Sigingstone 18 D25
Silchester 21 E42
Sileby 41 D41
Silecroft 54 A27
Silfield 45 F57
Silian 26 C21
Silkstone 50 B38

Silkstone Common 50 B38
Silksworth 62 A39
Silk Willoughby 42 A46
Silloth 60 A26
Sills 70 C34
Sillyearn 98 D30
Silpho 63 G45
Silsden 57 E36
Silsoe 32 E46
Silton 9 B33
Silverburn 75 D27
Silvercraigs 73 B14
Silverdale *Lan.* 55 B30
Silverdale *Stf.* 39 A33
Silver End 34 G53
Silver Hill *E.S.* 14 F54
Silver Hill *E.S.* 14 E53
Silverley's Green 35 A58
Silvermoss 99 F33
Silverstone 31 D42
Silverton 7 E25
Silvington 28 A31
Silwick 107 C38
Simonburn 70 F34
Simonsbath 7 B23
Simonstone 56 F33
Simprim 77 F34
Simpson 32 E44
Sinclair's Hill 77 E33
Sinclairston 67 B20
Sinderby 57 A39
Sinderhope 61 A34
Sindlesham 22 E43
Singdean 70 C31
Singleton *W.S.* 12 E44
Singleton *Lan.* 55 F29
Singlewell or Ifield 24 D52
Sinnahard 90 B30
Sinnington 58 A43
Sinton Green 29 B34
Sipson 22 D46
Sirhowy 28 G27
Sisland 45 F59
Sissinghurst 14 D53
Siston 19 D32
Sithney 2 F12
Sittingbourne 25 E55
Siulaisiadar 101 D11
Six Ashes 39 G33
Sixhills 52 D47
Six Mile Bottom 33 C51
Sixmile Cottages 15 C57
Sixpenny Handley 9 C35
Sizewell 35 B60
Skail 102 D23
Skaill *Ork.* 104 E28
Skaill *Ork.* 105 A31
Skares *Grm.* 98 F32
Skares *Str.* 67 B21
Skarpigarth 107 B37
Skateraw 77 C33
Skaw 107 A41
Skeabost 93 G9
Skeabrae 104 D28
Skeeby 62 F37
Skeffington 42 E43
Skeffling 53 A49
Skegby 51 F40
Skegness 53 F51
Skelberry 107 D37
Skelbo 96 B23
Skeldon 67 B19
Skeldyke 43 B49
Skellingthorpe 52 E44
Skellister 107 B40
Skellow 51 A41
Skelmanthorpe 50 A38
Skelmersdale 48 B30
Skelmonae 99 F34
Skelmorlie 73 D17
Skelmuir 99 E35
Skelton *Cum.* 60 C30
Skelton *Cle.* 63 E42
Skelton *N.Y.* 62 F36
Skelton *Hum.* 58 G43
Skelton *N.Y.* 58 D41
Skelton *N.Y.* 57 C39
Skelton Green 63 E42
Skelwick 104 B30
Skendleby 53 F50
Skenfrith 28 E30
Skerne 59 D46
Skeroblingarry 66 A12
Skerray 102 B22
Sketty 17 E22
Skewen 18 B23
Skewsby 58 B43
Skeyton 45 C58
Skidbrooke 53 C50
Skidby 59 F46
Skilgate 7 C25
Skillington 42 C44
Skinburness 60 A26
Skinidin 93 G8
Skinnet 103 B27
Skinningrove 63 D42

Skipness 73 E14
Skipsea 59 D47
Skipton 56 D35
Skipton-on-Swale 57 A39
Skipwith 58 F42
Skirbeck 43 A49
Skirling 75 G26
Skirmett 22 C43
Skirpenbeck 58 D43
Skirwith *Cum.* 61 C31
Skirwith *N.Y.* 56 B33
Skirza 103 B29
Skulamus 86 B12
Skullomie 102 B21
Skye of Curr 89 B25
Slack 98 F31
Slackhall 50 D36
Slackhead 98 C29
Slad 20 A34
Slade 6 A20
Slade Green 23 D51
Slaggyford 61 A32
Slaidburn 56 D33
Slains Park 91 F34
Slaithwaite 50 A36
Slaley 62 A35
Slamannan 75 C24
Slapton *Dev.* 5 F23
Slapton *Bkh.* 32 F45
Slapton *Nmp.* 31 D42
Slate Haugh 98 C30
Slatenber 56 B33
Slattadale 94 D14
Slattocks 49 B34
Slaugham 13 D48
Slaughden 35 C60
Slaughterford 20 D34
Slawston 42 F43
Sleaford *Ham.* 12 C44
Sleaford *Lcn.* 42 A46
Sleagill 61 E31
Sleapford 39 D32
Sledge Green 29 E34
Sledmere 59 C45
Sleights 63 F44
Slepe 9 E35
Slickly 103 B28
Sliddery 66 A15
Sliemore 89 B26
Sligachan 85 B10
Slimbridge 20 A33
Slindon *Stf.* 40 B34
Slindon *W.S.* 12 F45
Slinfold 12 C47
Slingsby 58 B42
Slioch 98 F31
Slip End *Bfd.* 33 E48
Slip End *Bfd.* 32 G46
Slipton 32 A45
Slochd 89 B24
Slockavullin 73 A13
Slogarie 65 D22
Sloley 45 C58
Slongaber 65 C23
Sloothby 53 E50
Slough 22 C45
Sluggan 89 B24
Slyne 55 C30
Smailholm 76 G32
Smallbridge 49 A35
Smallburgh 45 C59
Smallburn *Str.* 68 A22
Smallburn *Grm.* 99 E36
Small Dole 13 E48
Smalley 41 A39
Smallfield 23 G49
Small Hythe 14 D54
Smallridge 8 D28
Smallthorne 49 G34
Smallworth 44 G56
Smannell 21 G39
Smardale 61 F33
Smarden 14 C54
Smaull 72 D8
Smeale 74 C26
Smeatharpe 7 D27
Smeeth 15 D56
Smeeton Westerby 41 F42
Smelthouses 57 C37
Smerral 103 E27
Smethwick 40 G35
Smirisary 86 G12
Smisby 41 D39
Smith End Green 29 C33
Smithfield 69 G30
Smithincott 7 D26
Smith's Green 33 F51
Smithstown 96 G22
Smithy Green 49 E33
Smug Oak 22 A47
Smyrton 66 E16
Smythe's Green 34 G54
Snailbeach 38 E29
Snailwell 33 B52
Snainton 59 A45
Snaith 58 G42

Snape *N.Y.* 57 A38
Snape *Sfk* 35 C59
Snape Green 48 A29
Snarestone 41 E39
Snarford 52 D46
Snargate 14 E55
Snave 15 D56
Sneachill 29 C34
Snead 38 F28
Sneaton 63 F44
Sneatonthorpe 63 F44
Snelland 52 D46
Snellings 60 F25
Snelston 40 A37
Snetterton 44 F55
Snibston 41 D39
Snig's End 29 F33
Snishival 84 A3
Snitter 71 C36
Snitterby 52 C45
Snitterfield 30 C37
Snitton 28 A31
Snodhill 28 D29
Snodland 24 E52
Snowshill 30 E36
Soar *Dyf.* 17 B22
Soar *Dev.* 5 G22
Soberton 11 C42
Soberton Heath 11 C42
Sockburn 62 F39
Sodylt Bank 38 A29
Soham 33 A51
Solas 84 A3
Soldon Cross 6 D19
Soldridge 11 A42
Sole Street *Kent* 15 C56
Sole Street *Kent* 24 E52
Solihull 30 A37
Solihull Lodge 30 A36
Sollers Dilwyn 28 C30
Sollers Hope 29 E32
Sollom 48 A30
Solsgirth 75 A25
Solva 16 B13
Solwaybank 69 F28
Somerby 42 D43
Somercotes 51 G39
Somerford Keynes 20 B36
Somerley 11 E43
Somerleyton 45 F60
Somersal Herbert 40 B37
Somersby 53 E49
Somersham *Sfk* 34 D56
Somersham *Cbs.* 33 A49
Somerton *Oxf.* 31 F40
Somerton *Som.* 8 B30
Somerton *Sfk* 34 C53
Sompting 12 F47
Sonning 22 D43
Sonning Common 22 D43
Sonning Eye 22 D43
Sopley 10 E37
Sopworth 20 C33
Sorbie 64 F20
Sordale 103 B27
Sorisdale 78 A8
Sorn 67 A21
Sornhill 74 G21
Soroba 79 E14
Sortat 103 B28
Sotby 53 E48
Sots Hole 52 F47
Sotterly 45 G60
Soudley 39 C33
Soughton 48 F28
Soulbury 32 F44
Soulby 61 E33
Souldern 31 E41
Souldrop 32 B45
Sound *She.* 107 C40
Sound *Che.* 39 A32
Sound *She.* 107 B39
Soundwell 19 D32
Sourhope 70 A34
Sourin 104 C30
Sourton 6 G21
Soutergate 55 A28
South Acre 44 D53
Southall 22 C47
South Allington 5 G23
South Alloa 75 A24
Southam *War.* 31 B40
Southam *Glo.* 29 F35
South Ambersham 12 E45
Southampton 10 C39
Southampton Airport 11 C40
South Anston 51 D41
South Ascot 22 E45
South Ballachulish 80 B16
South Balloch 67 D18
South Bank 63 D41
Southbar 74 D20
South Barrow 8 B31
South Beddington 23 E48
South Benfleet 24 C53
South Bersted 12 G45

South Blackbog 99 F33
Southborough 23 G51
Southbourne *W.S.* 11 D43
Southbourne *Dor.* 10 E37
South Bowood 8 E30
South Brent 5 D22
South Brentor 6 G20
South Brewham 9 A33
South Broomhill 71 D38
Southburgh 44 E56
South Burlingham 45 E59
Southburn 59 D45
South Cadbury 9 B32
South Carlton 52 E45
South Cave 59 F45
South Cerney 20 B36
South Chard 8 D28
South Charlton 71 A37
South Cheriton 9 B32
Southchurch 24 C54
South Cliffe 58 F44
South Clifton 52 E44
South Cockerington 53 D49
South Common 13 E49
South Cornelly 18 D23
South Corrygills 73 G16
Southcott 6 F21
South Cove 45 G60
South Creagan 80 C15
South Croxton 41 D42
South Dalton 59 E45
South Darenth 23 E51
Southdean 70 C32
South Duffield 58 F42
Southease 13 F50
South Elkington 53 D48
South Elmsall 51 A40
South End *Cum.* 54 C27
South End *Hum.* 52 A47
South End *Bkh.* 32 F44
Southend *Str.* 66 C12
Southend *Grm.* 99 E33
Southend *Brk.* 21 D42
Southend Airport 24 C54
Southend-on-Sea 24 C54
Southerndown 18 D24
Southerness 65 E25
South Erradale 94 D13
Southery 43 F51
South Fambridge 24 B54
South Fawley 21 C39
South Ferriby 59 G45
Southfleet 24 D52
South Flobbets 99 F33
South Garth 106 C41
Southgate *Nfk* 45 C57
Southgate *G.L.* 23 B48
South Gorley 10 C37
South Green *Esx* 24 B52
South Green *Nfk* 44 D56
South Hall 73 C16
South Hanningfield 24 B53
South Harting 11 C43
South Hayling 11 E43
South Hazelrigg 77 G36
South Heath 22 A45
South Heighton 13 F50
South Hetton 62 B39
South Hiendley 51 A39
South Hill 4 C19
South Hole 6 D18
South Holmwood 22 G47
South Hornchurch 23 C51
South Hourat 74 E18
South Huish 5 F22
South Hykeham 52 F45
South Hylton 62 A39
Southill 32 D47
Southington 21 G40
South Kelsey 52 C46
South Kessock 96 G22
South Killingholme 52 A47
South Kilvington 57 A40
South Kilworth 41 G41
South Kirkby 51 B40
South Kirkton 91 C33
South Kyme 52 G47
South Lancing 12 F47
South Ledaig 80 D15
Southleigh 8 E28
South Leigh 21 A39
South Leverton 51 D43
South Littleton 30 D36
South Lopham 44 G56
South Luffenham 42 E45
South Malling 13 E50
South Marston 20 C37
South Milford 58 F41
South Milton 5 F23
South Mimms 23 A48
Southminster 25 B55
South Molton 7 C23
South Moor 62 A37
South Moreton 21 C41
Southmuir 82 B29

South Mundham 12 G44
South Muskham 51 G43
South Newbald 59 F45
South Newington 31 E40
South Newton 10 A36
South Normanton 51 G40
South Norwood 23 E49
South Nutfield 23 G48
South Ockendon 23 C51
Southoe 32 B47
Southolt 35 B57
South Ormsby 53 E49
Southorpe 42 E46
South Otterington 57 A39
Southowram 57 G36
South Oxhey 22 B46
South Park 23 G48
South Perrott 8 D30
South Petherton 8 C30
South Petherwin 6 G19
South Pickenham 44 E54
South Pool 5 F23
South Queensferry 75 C27
South Radworthy 7 B23
South Rauceby 42 A46
South Raynham 44 C54
South Redbriggs 99 E33
Southrepps 45 B58
South Reston 53 D50
Southrey 52 F47
Southrop 20 A37
Southrope 21 G42
South Runcton 44 E52
South Scarle 52 F44
Southsea *Clw.* 48 G28
Southsea *Ham.* 11 E42
South Shian 80 C15
South Shields 73 G39
South Skirlaugh 59 F47
South Somercotes 53 C50
South Stainley 57 C39
Southstoke 20 E33
South Stoke *Oxf.* 21 C42
South Stoke *W.S.* 12 F46
South Street *E.S.* 13 E49
South Street *Kent* 24 E52
South Tawton 6 F22
South Thoresby 53 E50
South Tidworth 21 G38
South Town 11 A42
Southtown *Ork.* 105 B30
Southtown *Nfk* 45 E61
South Upper Barrack 99 E35
South View 107 C39
Southwaite *Cum.* 60 B30
Southwaite *Cum.* 61 F33
South Walsham 45 D59
Southwark 23 D49
South Warnborough 22 G43
Southwater 12 D47
Southway 19 G30
South Weald 23 B51
Southwell *Dor.* 9 G32
Southwell *Not.* 51 G42
South Weston 21 B42
South Wheatley *Not.* 51 D43
South Wheatley *Cnw.* 4 A18
Southwick *Ham.* 11 D42
Southwick *Wts.* 20 F34
Southwick *T.&W.* 62 A39
Southwick *W.S.* 13 F48
Southwick *Nmp.* 42 E45
South Widcombe 19 F31
South Wigston 41 F41
South Willesborough 14 C55
South Willingham 52 D47
South Wingate 62 C40
South Wingfield 51 G39
South Witham 42 D44
Southwold 35 A61
South Wonston 11 A40
Southwood *Som.* 8 A31
Southwood *Nfk* 45 E59
South Woodham Ferrers 24 B54
South Wootton 44 C52
South Wraxall 20 E34
South Yardley 40 G37
South Zeal 6 F22
Sowerby *W.Y.* 57 G36
Sowerby *N.Y.* 57 A40
Sowerby Bridge 57 G36
Sowerby Row 60 B29
Sowton 7 F25
Soyal 96 B21
Spa Common 45 B58
Spadeadam 70 F31
Spalding 43 C48
Spaldington 58 F43
Spaldwick 32 A46
Spalefield 83 G31
Spalford 52 F44
Spanby 42 B46
Sparham 44 C56
Spark Bridge 55 A29
Sparkford 8 B31

Sparkwell 5 E21
Sparrowpit 50 D36
Sparrow's Green 13 C52
Sparsholt *Ham.* 11 A40
Sparsholt *Oxf.* 21 C39
Spartylea 61 B34
Spaunton 63 G43
Spaxton 8 A28
Spean Bridge 87 F18
Speddoch 68 E24
Speen *Bkh.* 22 A44
Speen *Brk.* 21 E40
Speeton 59 B47
Speke 48 D30
Speldhurst 23 G51
Spellbrook 33 G50
Spelsbury 30 F39
Spencers Wood 22 E43
Spen Green 49 F34
Spennithorne 57 A37
Spennymoor 62 C38
Spetchley 29 C34
Spetisbury 9 D34
Spexhall 45 G59
Spey Bay 98 C29
Speybridge 89 B26
Speyview 98 E28
Spilsby 53 F50
Spindlestone 77 G37
Spinkhill 51 E40
Spinningdale 96 B22
Spirthill 20 D35
Spital *Hgh.* 103 C27
Spital *Brk.* 22 D45
Spitalbrook 23 A49
Spital in the Street 52 C45
Spithurst 13 E50
Spittal *D.&G.* 64 E19
Spittal *D.&G.* 64 D20
Spittal *Dyf.* 16 B15
Spittal *Nor.* 77 E36
Spittal *Ltn* 76 C30
Spittalfield 82 C26
Spittal of Glenmuick 90 E29
Spittal of Glenshee 89 G26
Spixworth 45 D58
Spofforth 57 D39
Spondon 41 B39
Spooner Row 44 F56
Spoonley 39 B32
Sporle 44 D54
Sportsman's Arms 47 F25
Spott 76 C32
Spratton 31 B43
Spreakley 22 G44
Spreyton 6 F22
Spridlington 52 D46
Springburn 73 C16
Springfield *Str.* 73 C16
Springfield *Tay.* 82 D27
Springfield *Fife* 82 F29
Springfield *Grm.* 97 E26
Springfield *D.&G.* 69 G28
Springfield *W.M.* 40 G36
Springholm 65 D23
Springkell 69 F28
Springleys 99 F33
Springside 74 G19
Springthorpe 52 D44
Springwell 62 A38
Sproatley 59 F48
Sproston Green 49 F33
Sprotbrough 51 B41
Sproughton 35 D57
Sprouston 77 G33
Sprowston 45 D58
Sproxton *N.Y.* 58 A42
Sproxton *Lei.* 42 C44
Spurstow 48 G31
Square Point 65 C23
Squires Gate 55 F28
Sron Doire 73 C14
Sronphadruig Lodge 88 G22
Stableford 39 B33
Stackhouse 56 C33
Stackpole 16 E15
Stacksteads 56 G34
Staddiscombe 5 E21
Staddlethorpe 58 G44
Stadhampton 21 B42
Stadhlaigearraidh 84 A3
Staffield 61 B31
Staffin 93 E10
Stafford 40 C35
Stagden Cross 33 G52
Stagsden 73 D45
Stagshaw Bank 70 G35
Stain 103 B29
Stainburn 57 E38
Stainby 42 C44
Staincross 51 B39
Staindrop 62 D37
Staines 22 D46
Stainfield *Lcn.* 42 C46
Stainfield *Lcn.* 52 E46
Stainforth *N.Y.* 56 C34

Stainforth *S.Y.* 51 A42
Staining 55 F29
Stainland 50 A36
Stainsacre 63 F44
Stainton *N.Y.* 62 G36
Stainton *Cle.* 62 E40
Stainton *Drm* 62 E36
Stainton *Cum.* 61 D30
Stainton *Cum.* 55 A31
Stainton *S.Y.* 51 C41
Stainton by Langworth 52 E46
Staintondale 63 G45
Stainton le Vale 52 C47
Stainton with Adgarley 55 B28
Stair *Str.* 67 A20
Stair *Cum.* 60 D28
Staithes 63 E43
Stakeford 71 E38
Stake Pool 55 B30
Stalbridge 9 C33
Stalbridge Weston 9 C33
Stalham 45 C59
Stalham Green 45 C59
Stalisfield Green 14 B55
Stallingborough 53 A48
Stalling Busk 56 A35
Stalmine 55 E29
Stalybridge 49 C35
Stambourne 33 E52
Stamford *Nor.* 71 B38
Stamford *Lcn.* 42 E45
Stamford Bridge 58 D43
Stamfordham 71 F36
Stanborough 32 G47
Stanbridge *Bfd.* 32 F45
Stanbridge *Dor.* 9 D35
Stanbridge Earls 10 B39
Stanbury 56 F35
Stand 75 D23
Standburn 75 C25
Standeford 40 E34
Standen 14 C54
Standford 12 C44
Standish 48 A31
Standlake 21 A39
Standon *Stf.* 39 B33
Standon *Hfs.* 33 F49
Standon *Ham.* 11 B40
Stane 75 E24
Stanfield 44 C55
Stanford *Kent* 15 D57
Stanford *Bfd.* 32 D47
Stanford Bishop 29 C32
Stanford Bridge 29 B33
Stanford Dingley 21 D41
Stanford in the Vale 20 A38
Stanford-le-Hope 24 C52
Stanford on Avon 31 A41
Stanford on Soar 41 C41
Stanford on Teme 29 B32
Stanford Rivers 23 A51
Stanghow 63 E42
Stanground 42 F47
Stanhope *Drm* 62 C35
Stanhope *Bor.* 69 A27
Stanion 42 G45
Stanley *Dby.* 41 A40
Stanley *Stf.* 49 G35
Stanley *Tay.* 82 D26
Stanley *Wts.* 20 D35
Stanley *Drm* 62 A37
Stanley *W.Y.* 57 G39
Stanley Common 41 A40
Stanmer 13 F49
Stanmore *G.L.* 22 B47
Stanmore *Brk.* 21 D40
Stannersburn 70 E32
Stanningfield 34 C54
Stannington *S.Y.* 50 D38
Stannington *Nor.* 71 F37
Stansbatch 28 B29
Stansfield 34 C53
Stanstead 34 D54
Stanstead Abbots 33 G49
Stansted 23 E51
Stansted Airport 33 F51
Stansted Mountfitchet 33 F50
Stanton *Stf.* 40 A37
Stanton *Nor.* 71 D37
Stanton *Sfk* 34 A55
Stanton *Glo.* 30 E36
Stanton *Dby.* 40 D38
Stanton by Bridge 41 C39
Stanton by Dale 41 B40
Stanton Drew 19 E31
Stanton Fitzwarren 20 B37
Stanton Harcourt 21 A39
Stanton Hill 51 F40
Stanton in Peak 50 F38
Stanton Lacy 28 A30
Stanton Long 38 F31
Stanton on the Wolds 41 C42
Stanton Prior 19 E32
Stanton St Bernard 20 E36
Stanton St John 21 A41
Stanton St Quintin 20 C34

Stanton Street 34 B55
Stanton under Bardon 41 D40
Stanton upon Hine Heath
38 C31
Stanton Wick 19 E31
Stanwardine in the Fields
38 C29
Stanway *Esx* 34 F55
Stanway *Glo.* 30 E36
Stanwell 22 D46
Stanwell Moor 22 D46
Stanwick 32 A45
Stanwix 60 A29
Stanydale 107 B38
Stape 63 G43
Stapehill 10 D36
Stapeley 39 A32
Staple 15 B58
Staple Cross 14 E53
Staplefield 13 D48
Staple Fitzpaine 8 C28
Stapleford *Lcn.* 52 G44
Stapleford *Hfs.* 33 C45
Stapleford *Cbs.* 33 C50
Stapleford *Lei.* 42 D44
Stapleford *Not.* 41 B40
Stapleford *Wts.* 10 A36
Stapleford Abbotts 23 B50
Stapleford Tawney 23 B50
Staplegrove 7 C27
Staplehurst 14 C53
Staplers 11 F41
Stapleton *Lei.* 41 F40
Stapleton *H.&W.* 28 B29
Stapleton *Shr.* 38 E30
Stapleton *Cum.* 69 F31
Stapleton *N.Y.* 62 E38
Stapleton *Som.* 8 B30
Stapleton *Avon* 19 D31
Stapley 7 D27
Staploe 33 B47
Staplow 29 D32
Star *Avon* 19 F30
Star *Dyf.* 17 A18
Star *Fife* 82 G29
Starbotton 56 B35
Starcross 5 G25
Starkigarth 107 E40
Starling's Green 33 E50
Starr 67 D20
Starston 45 G58
Startforth 62 E36
Startley 20 C35
Statham 49 D32
Stathe 8 B29
Stathern 42 B43
Station Town 62 C40
Staughton Green 32 B47
Staughton Highway 32 B47
Staunton *Glo.* 29 F33
Staunton *Glo.* 28 G31
Staunton Harold Hall 41 C39
Staunton on Arrow 28 C29
Staunton on Wye 28 D29
Staveley *Cum.* 61 G30
Staveley *N.Y.* 57 C39
Staveley *Dby.* 51 E40
Staveley-in-Cartmel 55 A29
Staverton *Nmp.* 31 B41
Staverton *Dev.* 5 D23
Staverton *Glo.* 29 F34
Staverton *Wts.* 20 E34
Staverton Bridge 29 F34
Stawell 8 A29
Stawley 7 C26
Staxigoe 103 C29
Staynall 55 E29
Staythorpe 51 G43
Stean 57 B36
Steane 31 E41
Stearsby 58 B41
Steart 19 G28
Stebbing 33 F52
Stebbing Green 33 F52
Stedham 12 D44
Steel Cross 13 C51
Steele Road 70 D31
Steel Works 19 C29
Steen's Bridge 28 C31
Steep 11 B43
Steeple *Dor.* 9 F35
Steeple *Esx* 25 A55
Steeple Ashton 20 F35
Steeple Aston 31 F40
Steeple Barton 31 F40
Steeple Bumpstead 33 D52
Steeple Claydon 31 F42
Steeple Gidding 42 G47
Steeple Langford 10 A36
Steeple Morden 33 D48
Steeton 57 E36
Stein 93 F8
Steinmanhill 99 E33
Stella 71 G37

Stelling Minnis 15 C57
Stemster *Hgh.* 103 B27
Stemster *Hgh.* 103 D27
Stemster House 103 B27
Stenalees 4 E16
Stenhousemuir 75 B24
Stenigot 53 D48
Stenness 106 E37
Stenscholl 93 E10
Stenton *Ltn* 76 C32
Stenton *Tay.* 82 C26
Stepaside 16 D17
Stepney 23 C49
Steppingley 32 E45
Stepps 74 D22
Sternfield 35 B59
Sterridge 6 A21
Stert 20 F36
Stetchworth 33 C52
Stevenage 33 F48
Stevenston 74 F18
Steventon *Oxf.* 21 B40
Steventon *Ham.* 21 G41
Stevington 32 D46
Stewartby 32 D46
Stewarton *D.&G.* 64 F20
Stewarton *Str.* 74 F20
Stewkley 32 F44
Stewton 53 D49
Steyning 12 E47
Steynton 16 D15
Stibb 6 D18
Stibbard 44 C55
Stibb Cross 6 D20
Stibb Green 21 E38
Stibbington 42 F46
Stichill 76 G32
Sticker 3 C15
Stickford 53 F49
Sticklepath 6 F21
Stickney 53 G49
Stiffkey 44 A55
Stifford's Bridge 29 D33
Stillingfleet 58 E41
Stillington *N.Y.* 58 C41
Stillington *Cle.* 62 D39
Stilton 42 G47
Stinchcombe 20 B33
Stinsford 9 E33
Stirchley *Shr.* 39 E32
Stirchley *W.M.* 40 G36
Stirkoke House 103 C28
Stirling *Grm.* 99 E37
Stirling *Cen.* 75 A23
Stisted 34 F53
Stithians 2 E12
Stittenham 96 D22
Stivichall 30 A39
Stix 81 C23
Stixwould 52 F47
Stoak 48 E30
Stobo 75 G27
Stoborough 9 F34
Stoborough Green 9 F35
Stobwood 75 E25
Stock 24 B52
Stockbridge *Cen.* 81 G23
Stockbridge *Ham.* 10 A39
Stockbury 24 E54
Stockcross 21 E40
Stockdalewath 60 B29
Stockerston 42 F44
Stock Green 29 B35
Stockingford 41 F39
Stocking Pelham 33 F50
Stockland 8 D28
Stockland Bristol 19 G28
Stock Lane 21 D38
Stockleigh English 7 E24
Stockleigh Pomeroy 7 E24
Stockley 20 E35
Stocklinch 8 C29
Stockport 49 D34
Stocksbridge 50 C38
Stocksfield 71 G36
Stockton *Wts.* 9 A35
Stockton *Nfk* 45 F59
Stockton *Shr.* 39 F33
Stockton *War.* 31 B40
Stockton *H.&W.* 28 B31
Stockton Heath 49 D32
Stockton-on-Tees 62 D39
Stockton on Teme 29 B33
Stockton on the Forest 58 D42
Stock Wood 29 C35
Stockwood 8 D31
Stodday 55 D30
Stodmarsh 25 E57
Stody 44 B56
Stoer 101 F16
Stoford *Som.* 8 C31
Stoford *Wts.* 10 A36
Stogumber 7 B26
Stogursey 7 A27
Stoke *W.M.* 30 A39
Stoke *Kent* 24 D54

Stoke *Dev.* 6 C18
Stoke *Ham.* 11 D43
Stoke *Ham.* 21 F39
Stoke Abbott 8 D30
Stoke Albany 42 G44
Stoke Ash 35 A57
Stoke Bardolph 41 A42
Stoke Bliss 29 B32
Stoke Bruerne 31 C43
Stoke by Clare 34 D53
Stoke-by-Nayland 34 E55
Stoke Canon 7 F25
Stoke Charity 11 A40
Stoke Climsland 4 C19
Stoke D'Abernon 22 F47
Stoke Doyle 42 G46
Stoke Dry 42 F44
Stoke Ferry 44 F52
Stoke Fleming 5 F24
Stokeford 9 F34
Stoke Gabriel 5 E24
Stoke Gifford 19 D32
Stoke Golding 41 F39
Stoke Goldington 32 D44
Stokeham 51 E43
Stoke Hammond 32 F44
Stoke Heath 29 C32
Stoke Holy Cross 45 E58
Stokeinteignhead 5 C25
Stoke Lacy 28 D31
Stoke Lyne 31 F41
Stoke Mandeville 22 A44
Stokenchurch 22 B43
Stoke Newington 23 C49
Stokenham 5 F23
Stoke on Tern 39 C32
Stoke-on-Trent 40 A34
Stoke Orchard 29 F35
Stoke Poges 22 C45
Stoke Prior *H.&W.* 28 C31
Stoke Prior *H.&W.* 29 B35
Stoke Rivers 6 B22
Stoke Rochford 42 C44
Stoke Row 21 C42
Stokesay 38 G29
Stokesby 45 D60
Stokesley 63 F41
Stoke St Gregory 8 B29
Stoke St Mary 8 B28
Stoke St Michael 19 G32
Stoke St Milborough 38 G31
Stoke sub Hamdon 8 C30
Stoke Talmage 21 B42
Stoke Trister 9 B33
Stoke Wake 9 D33
Stolford 19 G28
Stonar Cut 25 E59
Stondon Massey 23 A51
Stone *Kent* 23 D51
Stone *Kent* 14 E55
Stone *H.&W.* 29 A34
Stone *Bkh.* 31 G43
Stone *Stf.* 40 B35
Stone *Glo.* 19 B32
Stone Allerton 19 F29
Ston Easton 19 F32
Stonebridge *E.S.* 13 D51
Stonebridge *War.* 40 G38
Stonebroom 51 G39
Stone Cross *E.S.* 13 F52
Stone Cross *Kent* 13 C51
Stone Cross *Kent* 15 D56
Stoneferry 59 B35
Stonefield *Str.* 74 E22
Stonefield *Str.* 73 C14
Stonegate 13 D52
Stonegrave 58 B42
Stonehaugh 70 F33
Stonehaven 91 E34
Stonehouse *Nor.* 61 A32
Stone House 56 A33
Stonehouse *Str.* 75 F23
Stonehouse *Glo.* 20 A33
Stonehouse *Dev.* 4 E20
Stonehouse *D.&G.* 65 D24
Stoneleigh 30 A39
Stonely 32 B46
Stoner Hill 11 B43
Stonesby 42 C44
Stonesfield 30 G39
Stones Green 35 F57
Stone Street *Sfk* 45 G59
Stone Street *Kent* 23 F51
Stonestreet Green 15 D56
Stonethwaite 60 E28
Stoneyburn 75 D25
Stoney Cross 10 C38
Stoneygate 41 E41
Stoneyhills 25 B55
Stoney Houghton 51 F40
Stoneykirk 64 E16
Stoney Stanton 41 F40
Stoney Stoke 9 A33
Stoney Stratton 9 A32
Stoney Stretton 38 E29
Stoneywood 91 B34

Stonganess 106 B41
Stonham Aspal 35 C57
Stonnall 40 E36
Stonor 22 C43
Stonton Wyville 42 F43
Stonybreck 106 A37
Stonyhurst College 56 F32
Stony Stratford 31 D43
Stoodleigh 7 D24
Stopham 12 E46
Stopsley 32 F46
Stoptide 3 A15
Storeton 48 D28
Stornoway 100 D9
Stornoway Airport 100 D10
Storridge 29 D33
Storrington 12 E46
Storth 55 A30
Storwood 58 E42
Stotfield 98 B28
Stotfold 32 E47
Stottesdon 39 G32
Stoughton *Lei.* 41 E42
Stoughton *Sry* 22 F45
Stoughton *W.S.* 11 C43
Stoul 86 E13
Stoulton 29 C34
Stourbridge 40 G34
Stourpaine 9 D34
Stourport-on-Severn 29 A33
Stour Provost 9 B33
Stour Row 9 B34
Stourton *Wts.* 9 A33
Stourton *War.* 30 E38
Stourton *Stf.* 40 G34
Stourton Caundle 9 C33
Stove 104 C32
Stoven 45 G60
Stow *Bor.* 76 F30
Stow *Lcn.* 52 D44
Stow Bardolph 44 E52
Stow Bedon 44 F55
Stowbridge 43 E51
Stow cum Quy 33 B50
Stowe *Shr.* 28 A28
Stowe *Stf.* 40 C35
Stowe *Glo.* 19 A31
Stowell *Glo.* 30 G36
Stowell *Som.* 9 B32
Stowey 19 F31
Stowford 6 G20
Stowlangtoft 34 B54
Stow Longa 32 A47
Stow Maries 24 B54
Stowmarket 34 C56
Stow-on-the-Wold 30 F37
Stowting 15 C56
Stowupland 34 B56
Stracathro 91 G32
Strachan 91 D32
Strachur 80 G16
Stradbroke 35 A58
Stradishall 34 C53
Stradsett 44 E52
Stragglethorpe 52 G44
Straiton *Str.* 67 C19
Straiton *Ltn.* 76 D28
Straloch *Tay.* 82 A26
Straloch *Grm.* 91 A34
Stramshall 40 B36
Strang 54 F25
Strannda 92 C6
Stranraer 64 D16
Strata Florida 27 B23
Stratfield Mortimer 21 E42
Stratfield Saye 21 F42
Stratfield Turgis 21 F42
Stratford 29 E34
Stratford St Andrew 35 B59
Stratford St Mary 34 E56
Stratford sub Castle 10 A37
Stratford Tony 10 B36
Stratford-upon-Avon 30 C37
Strath 103 C28
Strathan *Hgh.* 86 E15
Strathan *Hgh.* 101 F16
Strathaven 74 F22
Strathblane 74 C21
Strathdon 90 B29
Strathgirnock 90 D29
Strathkanaird 95 A17
Strathkinness 83 F30
Strathmiglo 82 G27
Strathpeffer 96 F20
Strathrannoch 96 D19
Strathwhillan 73 G16
Strathy 102 B24
Strathyre 81 F21
Stratton 20 A35
Stratton *Dor.* 9 E32
Stratton *Cnw.* 6 E18
Stratton *Gratton* 31 F42
Stratton-on-the-Fosse 19 F32
Stratton St Margaret 20 C37
Stratton St Michael 45 F58
Stratton Strawless 45 C58

Stravanan 73 E16
Stravithie 83 F31
Streat 13 E49
Streatham 23 D48
Streatley Brk. 21 C41
Streatley Bfd. 32 F46
Street Som. 8 A30
Street N.Y. 63 F43
Street Lan. 55 D31
Street Dinas 38 B29
Street End Kent 15 B57
Street End W.S. 12 G44
Streethay 40 D37
Streetlam 62 G39
Streetly 40 F36
Street on the Fosse 8 A31
Strefford 38 G30
Strensall 58 C42
Strensham 29 D34
Stretcholt 19 G28
Strete 5 F24
Stretford 49 C33
Stretford Court 28 C30
Strethall 33 E50
Stretham 33 A50
Strettington 12 F44
Stretton Dby. 51 F39
Stretton Che. 30 D32
Stretton Che. 48 G30
Stretton Stf. 40 C38
Stretton Lei. 42 D45
Stretton Stf. 40 D34
Stretton en le Field 41 D39
Stretton Grandison 29 D32
Stretton Heath 38 D29
Stretton-on-Dunsmore 31 A40
Stretton-on-Fosse 30 E37
Stretton Sugwas 28 D30
Stretton under Fosse 41 G40
Stretton Westwood 38 F31
Stribers 55 A29
Strichen 99 D35
Stringston 7 A27
Strixton 32 B44
Stroat 19 B31
Stromeferry 86 A14
Stromemore 86 A14
Stromness 105 A28
Stronachlachar 80 G19
Strone Hgh. 87 F17
Strone Hgh. 88 B21
Strone Str. 73 B17
Strone Cen. 81 F20
Stronechrubie 101 G18
Stronenaba 87 F17
Stronlonag 73 B16
Stronmilchan 80 E17
Stronsay Airport 104 D32
Strontian 79 A14
Strontoiller 79 E14
Stronvar 81 F21
Strood 24 E53
Strood Green 12 D46
Stroquhan 68 E24
Stroud Glo. 20 A34
Stroud Ham. 11 B43
Stroud Common 22 G46
Stroud Green 20 A34
Stroul 74 B18
Stroxton 42 B44
Struan Hgh. 85 A9
Struan Tay. 81 A23
Strubby 53 D50
Strumpshaw 45 E59
Struthers 82 G29
Struy 96 G19
Stryt-issa 38 A28
Stryt-yr-hwch 38 A29
Stuartfield 99 E35
Stubbington 11 D41
Stubbins 49 A33
Stubhampton 9 C34
Stubley 51 E39
Stub Place 60 G26
Stubton 42 A44
Stuck Str. 73 D16
Stuck Str. 73 A17
Stuckbeg 74 A18
Stuckgowan 80 G18
Stuckindroin 80 F18
Stuckreoch 73 A16
Stuckton 10 C37
Studdon 61 A34
Studfold 56 B34
Stud Green 22 D44
Studham 32 G46
Studholme 60 A28
Studland 10 F36
Studley Wts. 20 D35
Studley War. 30 B36
Studley Common 30 B36
Studley Roger 57 B38
Stuggadhoo 54 F24
Stump Cross 33 D50
Stuntney 33 A51
Stunts Green 13 E52

Sturbridge 40 B34
Sturmer 33 D52
Sturminster Common 9 C33
Sturminster Marshall 9 D35
Sturminster Newton 9 C33
Sturry 25 E57
Sturton by Stow 52 D44
Sturton le Steeple 51 D43
Stuston 35 A57
Stutton Sfk 35 E57
Stutton N.Y. 57 E40
Styal 49 D34
Styrrup 51 C41
Suainebost 101 A11
Suardail 100 D10
Succoth Str. 80 G18
Succoth Grm. 98 F30
Succothmore 80 G17
Suckley 29 C33
Sudborough 42 G45
Sudbourne 35 C60
Sudbrook Gwe. 19 C30
Sudbrook Lcn. 42 A45
Sudbrooke 52 E46
Sudbury Dby. 40 B37
Sudbury Sfk 34 D54
Sudbury G.L. 22 C47
Sudgrove 20 A35
Suffield Nfk 45 B58
Suffield N.Y. 63 G45
Sugarloaf 14 D55
Sugnall 39 B33
Suie Lodge Hotel 81 E20
Sulby 54 D25
Sulgrave 31 D41
Sulham 21 D42
Sulhamstead 21 E42
Sullington 12 E46
Sullom 106 E39
Sullom Voe Oil Terminal
    106 E39
Sully 18 E27
Sumburgh 107 E37
Summer Bridge 57 C38
Summercourt 3 C14
Summerhill 48 G28
Summer-house 62 E37
Summerleaze 19 C29
Summerseat 49 A33
Summertown 21 A40
Summit 49 A35
Sunadale 73 F13
Sunbury 22 E46
Sundaywell 68 E23
Sunderland T.&W. 62 A39
Sunderland Cum. 60 C27
Sunderland Bridge 62 C38
Sundhope 69 A29
Sundon Park 32 F46
Sundridge 23 F50
Sundrum 67 A20
Sunhill 20 A36
Sunipol 78 B9
Sunk Island 53 A48
Sunningdale 22 E45
Sunninghill 22 E45
Sunningwell 21 B40
Sunniside Drm. 62 C38
Sunniside T.&W. 62 A38
Sunny Bank 60 G28
Sunnylaw 75 A23
Sunnymead 21 A40
Sunnyside Nor. 70 G35
Sunnyside Grm. 91 D34
Sunnyside W.S. 13 C49
Sunwick 77 E34
Surbiton 22 E47
Surfleet 43 C48
Surfleet Seas End 43 C48
Surlingham 45 E59
Sustead 45 B57
Susworth 52 B44
Sutcombe 6 D19
Suton 44 F56
Sutors of Cromarty 96 E23
Sutterton 43 B48
Sutton Cbs. 42 F46
Sutton Not. 42 B43
Sutton W.S. 12 E45
Sutton G.L. 23 E48
Sutton Sry 22 G47
Sutton Lcn. 52 G44
Sutton Not. 51 D42
Sutton S.Y. 51 A41
Sutton Shr. 39 G33
Sutton Stf. 39 C33
Sutton Sfk 35 D59
Sutton Shr. 38 E30
Sutton Shr. 39 B32
Sutton Bfd. 33 D48
Sutton Cbs. 33 A50
Sutton Nfk 45 C59
Sutton Oxf. 21 A40
Sutton Kent 15 C59
Sutton Dyf. 16 C15
Sutton at Hone 23 E51

Sutton Bassett 42 G43
Sutton Benger 20 D35
Sutton Bonington 41 C41
Sutton Bridge 43 C50
Sutton Cheney 41 E40
Sutton Coldfield 40 F37
Sutton Courtenay 21 B40
Sutton Crosses 43 C50
Sutton Grange 57 B38
Sutton Green 22 F46
Sutton Holms 10 C36
Sutton Howgrave 57 B38
Sutton in Ashfield 51 G41
Sutton-in-Craven 56 E35
Sutton in the Elms 41 F41
Sutton Lane Ends 49 E35
Sutton Leach 48 C31
Sutton le Marsh 53 D51
Sutton Maddock 39 E33
Sutton Mallet 8 A29
Sutton Mandeville 9 B35
Sutton Montis 9 B32
Sutton-on-Hull 59 F47
Sutton on Sea 53 D51
Sutton-on-the-Forest 58 C41
Sutton on the Hill 40 B38
Sutton on Trent 51 F43
Sutton Poyntz 9 F32
Sutton Scotney 11 A40
Sutton St Edmund 43 D49
Sutton St James 43 D50
Sutton St Nicholas 28 D31
Sutton-under-Brailes 30 E39
Sutton-under-Whitestonecliffe
    57 A40
Sutton upon Derwent 58 E43
Sutton Valence 14 C54
Sutton Veny 20 G34
Sutton Waldron 9 C34
Sutton Weaver 48 E31
Sutton Wick 21 B40
Swaby 53 E49
Swadlincote 40 C38
Swaffham 44 E54
Swaffham Bulbeck 33 B51
Swaffham Prior 33 B51
Swafield 45 B58
Swainby 57 F40
Swainshill 28 D30
Swainsthorpe 45 E58
Swainswick 20 E33
Swalcliffe 30 E39
Swalecliffe 25 E57
Swallow 52 B47
Swallow Beck 52 F45
Swallowcliffe 9 B35
Swallowfield 22 E43
Swalwell 71 G37
Swampton 21 F40
Swanage 9 G35
Swanbach 39 A32
Swanbourne 31 F43
Swanbridge 18 E27
Swancote 39 F33
Swanlaws 70 B33
Swanley 23 E51
Swanmore 11 C41
Swannington Lei. 41 D39
Swannington Nfk 45 D57
Swanscombe 23 D51
Swansea 17 E22
Swansea Airport 17 E21
Swan Street 34 F54
Swanton Abbot 45 C58
Swanton Morley 44 D56
Swanton Novers 44 B56
Swanwick Dby. 51 G39
Swanwick Ham. 11 D41
Swarby 42 A46
Swardeston 45 E57
Swarkestone 41 C39
Swarland 71 C37
Swaton 42 B47
Swavesey 33 B49
Sway 10 E38
Swayfield 42 C45
Swaythling 11 C40
Swaythorpe 59 C46
Sweetshouse 4 D16
Sweffling 35 B59
Swell 8 B29
Swepstone 41 D39
Swerford 30 E39
Swettenham 49 F33
Swffryd 19 B28
Swiftsden 14 E53
Swilland 33 C57
Swillbrook 55 F30
Swillington 57 F39
Swimbridge 6 B22
Swimbridge Newland 6 B22
Swinbrook 30 G38
Swincliffe 57 D38
Swinderby 52 F44
Swindon Glo. 29 F35
Swindon Wts. 20 C37

Swindon Stf. 40 F34
Swine 59 F47
Swinefleet 58 G43
Swineshead Bfd. 32 B46
Swineshead Lcn. 43 A48
Swineshead Bridge 43 A48
Swiney 103 E28
Swinford Oxf. 21 A40
Swinford Lei. 31 A41
Swingfield Minnis 15 C58
Swinhoe 71 A37
Swinhope 52 C47
Swining 107 A40
Swinithwaite 57 A36
Swinscoe 40 A37
Swinside Hall 70 B33
Swinstead 42 C46
Swinton S.Y. 51 C40
Swinton G.M. 49 B33
Swinton Bor. 77 F34
Swinton N.Y. 58 B43
Swinton N.Y. 57 B38
Swintonmill 77 F33
Swithland 41 D41
Swordale 96 E21
Swordland 86 E13
Swordle 79 A11
Swordly 102 B23
Sworton Heath 49 D32
Swyddffynnon 27 B22
Swyncombe 21 B42
Swynnerton 40 B34
Swyre 8 F31
Syde 29 G35
Sydenham Oxf. 22 A43
Sydenham G.L. 23 D49
Sydenham Damerel 4 C20
Sydling St Nicholas 9 E32
Sydmonton 21 F40
Syerston 42 A43
Syke 49 A34
Sykehouse 51 A42
Sykes 56 D32
Sylen 17 D21
Symbister 107 A41
Symington Str. 75 G25
Symington Str. 74 G19
Symondsbury 8 E29
Symonds Yat 28 G31
Synod Inn 26 C19
Syre 102 D22
Syreford 30 F36
Syresham 31 D42
Syston Lcn. 42 A45
Syston Lei. 41 D42
Sytchampton 29 B34
Sywell 32 B44

T

Taagan 95 E16
Tabost W.I. 101 A11
Tabost W.I. 100 F9
Tacher 103 D27
Tackley 31 G40
Tacleit 100 D7
Tacolneston 45 F57
Tadcaster 57 E40
Tadden 9 D35
Taddington 50 E37
Taddiport 6 D20
Tadley 21 E42
Tadlow 33 D48
Tadmarton 30 E39
Tadworth 23 F48
Tafarnaubach 27 G26
Tafarn-y-bwlch 16 A16
Tafarn-y-Gelyn 47 F27
Taffs Well 18 C26
Tafolwern 37 E24
Tai-bach 38 C27
Taibach 18 C23
Tain Hgh. 103 B28
Tain Hgh. 96 C23
Tai'n Lon 46 G20
Tairbeart (Tarbert) 100 G7
Tai'r Bull 27 F25
Tairlaw 67 C20
Takeley 33 F51
Takeley Street 33 F51
Talachddu 27 E26
Talacre 47 D27
Talardd 37 C24
Talaton 7 F26
Talbenny 16 C14
Talbot Green 18 C26
Talerddig 37 E25
Talgarreg 26 C20
Talgarth 28 E27
Taliesin 37 F22
Talisker 85 B9
Talke 49 G34
Talkin 61 A31
Talla Bheith 81 B21
Talladale 94 D14
Talla Linnfoots 69 A27

Tallarn Green 38 A30
Tallentire 60 C26
Talley 17 A22
Tallington 42 E46
Talmine 102 B21
Talog 17 B19
Tal-sarn 26 C21
Talsarnau 36 B21
Talskiddy 3 B14
Talwrn Clw. 38 A28
Talwrn Gwy. 46 E20
Tal-y-bont Gwy. 47 F23
Tal-y-bont Gwy. 46 E21
Talybont 37 G22
Tal-y-bont Gwy. 36 C21
Talybont-on-Usk 27 F26
Tal-y-Cae 46 F21
Tal-y-cafn 47 E23
Talyllyn 27 F26
Tal-y-llyn 37 E22
Talysarn 46 G20
Tal-y-wern 37 E24
Tamavoid 74 A21
Tamerton Foliot 4 D20
Tamworth 40 E37
Tandridge 23 F49
Tanerdy 17 B20
Tanfield 62 A37
Tangiers 16 C15
Tanglandford 99 F34
Tangley 21 F39
Tangmere 12 F44
Tangwick 106 E38
Tangy 66 A12
Tankerness 105 A30
Tankersley 51 C39
Tan-lan 37 A22
Tannach 103 D29
Tannachie 91 E33
Tannachy 96 A23
Tannadice 83 B30
Tannington 35 B58
Tannochside 75 D23
Tansley 51 G39
Tansor 42 F46
Tantobie 62 A37
Tanton 63 E41
Tanworth in Arden 30 A37
Tan-y-fron 47 F25
Tan-y-graig 36 B18
Tanygrisiau 37 A22
Tan-y-groes 26 D18
Tan-y-pistyll 37 C23
Taobh A Deas Loch Baghasdail
    84 C3
Taobh Tuath 92 C5
Taoth Siar 100 G7
Tapeley 6 C20
Taplow 22 C44
Taravocan 80 C15
Tarbat Ho. 96 D23
Tarbert (Tairbeart) 100 G7
Tarbert Hgh. 79 A12
Tarbert Str. 73 D14
Tarbert Str. 72 E12
Tarbert Str. 72 B12
Tarbet Str. 80 G19
Tarbet Hgh. 101 D17
Tarbet Hgh. 86 E13
Tarbolton 67 A19
Tarbrax 75 E26
Tardebigge 29 B35
Tardy Gate 55 G31
Tarfside 90 E30
Tarland 90 C30
Tarleton 55 G30
Tarlscough 48 A30
Tarlton 20 B35
Tarnbrook 55 D31
Tarnock 19 F29
Tarporley 48 F31
Tarr 7 B26
Tarrant Crawford 9 D35
Tarrant Gunville 9 C35
Tarrant Hinton 9 C35
Tarrant Keyneston 9 D35
Tarrant Launceston 9 D35
Tarrant Monkton 9 D35
Tarrant Rawston 9 D35
Tarrant Rushton 9 D35
Tarrel 97 C24
Tarring Neville 13 F50
Tarrington 28 D31
Tarrnacraig 73 G15
Tarsappie 82 E27
Tarskavaig 86 D11
Tarves 99 F34
Tarvie Tay. 82 A26
Tarvie Hgh. 96 F20
Tarvin 48 F30
Tarvin Sands 48 F30
Tasburgh 45 F58
Tasley 39 F32
Taston 30 F39
Tatenhill 40 C37
Tatham 55 C31

Tathwell 53 D49
Tatsfield 23 F50
Tattenhall 48 G30
Tatterford 44 C54
Tattershall 53 G48
Tattershall Bridge 52 G47
Tattershall Thorpe 53 G48
Tattingstone 35 E57
Tatworth 8 D29
Tauchers 98 E29
Taunton 8 B28
Tavelty 91 B33
Taverham 45 D57
Tavernspite 16 C17
Tavistock 4 C20
Taw Bridge 6 E22
Taw Green 6 F22
Tawstock 6 B21
Taxal 49 E35
Tayburn 74 F21
Tayinloan 72 F12
Taylors Cross 6 D18
Taynafead 80 F16
Taynish 73 B13
Taynton Oxf. 30 G38
Taynton Glo. 29 F33
Taynuilt 80 D15
Tayock 83 B32
Tayovullin 72 C8
Tayport 83 E30
Tayvallich 73 B13
Tealby 52 C47
Team Valley 71 G38
Teanamachar 92 E3
Teasses 82 G29
Tebay 61 F32
Tebworth 32 F45
Tedburn St Mary 7 F24
Teddington Glo. 29 E35
Teddington G.L. 22 D47
Tedstone Delamere 29 C32
Tedstone Wafre 29 C32
Tees-side Airport 62 E39
Teeton 31 A42
Teffont Evias 9 A35
Teffont Magna 9 A35
Tegryn 17 A18
Teigh 42 D44
Teigngrace 5 C24
Teignmouth 5 C25
Telford 39 E32
Telham 14 F53
Tellisford 20 F33
Telscombe 13 F50
Telscombe Cliffs 13 F49
Tempar 81 B22
Templand 69 E26
Temple Cnw. 4 C17
Temple Ltn 76 E29
Temple Bar 26 C21
Temple Cloud 19 F32
Templecombe 9 B32
Temple Ewell 15 C58
Temple Grafton 30 C36
Temple Guiting 30 F36
Temple Hirst 58 G42
Temple Normanton 51 F40
Temple Sowerby 61 D31
Templeton Dyf. 16 C16
Templeton Dev. 7 D24
Templeton Bridge 7 D24
Templewood 83 A31
Tempsford 32 C47
Tenbury Wells 28 B31
Tenby 16 D17
Tendring 35 F57
Tenga 79 C11
Ten Mile Bank 43 F51
Tenterden 14 D54
Tepersie Castle 90 A31
Terally 64 F17
Terling 34 G53
Ternhill 39 B32
Terregles 65 C25
Terrington 58 B42
Terrington St Clement 43 C51
Terrington St John 43 D51
Tervieside 98 F28
Teston 14 B53
Testwood 10 C39
Tetbury 20 B34
Tetbury Upton 20 B34
Tetchill 38 B29
Tetcott 6 F19
Tetford 53 E49
Tetney 53 B49
Tetney Lock 53 B49
Tetsworth 21 A42
Tettenhall 40 E34
Tettenhall Wood 40 F34
Tetworth 33 C48
Teuchan 99 F36
Teversal 51 F40
Teversham 33 C50
Teviothead 69 C29

Tewel 91 E34
Tewin 33 G48
Tewkesbury 29 E34
Teynham 25 E55
Thainston 91 F32
Thainstone 91 B33
Thakeham 12 E47
Thame 21 A42
Thames Ditton 22 E47
Thames Haven 24 C53
Thamesmead 23 C50
Thanington 15 B57
Thankerton 75 G25
Tharston 45 F57
Thatcham 21 E41
Thatto Heath 48 C30
Thaxted 33 E51
Theakston 57 A38
Thealby 52 A45
Theale Som. 19 G30
Theale Brk. 21 D42
Thearne 59 F46
The Bage 28 D28
The Banking 99 F33
The Bar 12 D47
Theberton 35 B60
The Birks 91 C33
The Bog 38 F29
The Bourne 22 G44
The Bratch 40 F34
The Bryn 19 A29
The Burf 29 B34
The Burn 90 F31
The Camp 20 A35
The Chequer 38 A30
The City 22 B43
The Common 10 A38
The Craigs 96 B20
The Cronk 54 D25
Thedden Grange 11 A42
Theddingworth 41 G42
Theddlethorpe All Saints 53 D50
Theddlethorpe St Helen 53 D50
The Den 74 E19
The Dicker 13 F51
The Drums 82 A29
The Eaves 19 A31
The Flatt 70 F31
The Folly 32 G47
The Grange Shr. 38 B29
The Grange Sry 23 G49
The Green Str. 78 C5
The Green Wts. 9 A34
The Haven 12 C46
The Hermitage 23 F48
The Howe 54 G24
The Isle 38 D30
The Knowle 23 G52
The Laurels 45 F59
Thelbridge Barton 7 D23
The Leacon 14 D55
The Lee 22 A44
The Lhen 54 C25
Thelnetham 34 A56
The Lodge 73 A17
Thelveton 45 G57
Thelwall 49 D32
The Marsh 38 F28
Themelthorpe 44 C56
The Moor 14 E53
The Mumbles 17 F22
The Mythe 29 E34
The Neuk 91 D33
Thenford 31 D41
The Node 32 G47
Therfield 33 E49
The Rhos 16 C15
The Rowe 40 B34
The Sands 22 G44
The Shoe 20 D34
The Smithies 39 F32
The Stocks 14 E55
Thetford 44 G54
The Vauld 28 D31
The Wrythe 23 E48
The Wyke 39 E33
Theydon Bois 23 B50
Thickwood 20 D34
Thimbleby N.Y. 62 G40
Thimbleby Lcn. 53 E48
Thirkleby 57 B40
Thirlby 57 A40
Thirlestane 76 F31
Thirn 57 A38
Thirsk 57 A40
Thistleton Lei. 42 D44
Thistleton Lan. 55 F30
Thistley Green 33 A52
Thixendale 58 C44
Thockrington 70 F35
Tholomas Drove 43 E50
Tholthorpe 57 C40
Thomas Chapel 16 D16
Thomastown 98 F31
Thompson 44 F54
Thomshill 97 F27

Thong 24 D52
Thoralby 56 A35
Thoresby 51 E42
Thoresway 52 C47
Thorganby Lcn. 52 C47
Thorganby N.Y. 58 E42
Thorgill 63 G42
Thorington 35 A60
Thorington Street 34 E56
Thorlby 56 D35
Thorley 33 G50
Thorley Street Hfs. 33 G50
Thorley Street Ham. 10 F39
Thormanby 57 B40
Thornage 44 B56
Thornborough N.Y. 57 B38
Thornborough Bkh. 31 E43
Thornbury H.&W. 29 C32
Thornbury Dev. 6 E19
Thornbury Avon 19 B32
Thornby 31 A42
Thorncliff 49 G35
Thorncombe 8 D29
Thorncombe Street 22 G46
Thorncote Green 32 D47
Thorndon 35 B57
Thorne 51 A42
Thorner 57 E39
Thornes 40 E36
Thorne St Margaret 7 C26
Thorney Not. 52 E44
Thorney Som. 8 B30
Thorney Cbs. 43 E48
Thorney Bkh. 22 D46
Thorney Hill 10 D38
Thorn Falcon 8 B28
Thornford 8 C31
Thorngrove 8 A29
Thorngumbald 59 G48
Thornham 44 A53
Thornham Magna 34 A56
Thornham Parva 35 A57
Thornhaugh 42 E46
Thornhill Ham. 11 C40
Thornhill Dby. 50 D37
Thornhill W.Y. 50 A38
Thornhill D.&G. 68 D24
Thornhill M.G. 18 C27
Thornhill Cen. 81 G22
Thornholme 59 C47
Thornicombe 9 D34
Thornley Drm 62 B39
Thornley Drm. 62 C37
Thornliebank 74 E21
Thorns 34 C53
Thornsett 49 D35
Thornthwaite Cum. 60 D27
Thornthwaite N.Y. 57 D37
Thornton Lan. 55 E29
Thornton Lei. 41 E40
Thornton Hum. 58 E43
Thornton W.Y. 57 F36
Thornton Mer. 48 B29
Thornton Nor. 77 F35
Thornton Fife 76 A28
Thornton Dyf. 16 D15
Thornton Tay. 82 C26
Thornton Tay. 82 C29
Thornton Cle. 62 E40
Thornton Lcn. 53 F48
Thornton Bkh. 31 E43
Thornton Cross 6 F21
Thornton Curtis 52 A46
Thornton Dale 58 A44
Thorntonhall 74 E21
Thornton Hough 48 D29
Thornton-in-Craven 56 E35
Thornton-le-Beans 62 G40
Thornton-le-Clay 58 C42
Thornton-le-Moor 57 A39
Thornton le Moor 52 C46
Thornton-le-Moors 48 E30
Thornton-le -Street 57 A39
Thorntonloch 77 C33
Thornton Park 77 F35
Thornton Rust 56 A35
Thornton Steward 57 A37
Thornton Watlass 57 A38
Thornwood Common 23 A50
Thornyhill 91 F32
Thornylee 76 G29
Thoroton 42 A43
Thorp Arch 57 E40
Thorpe Hum. 59 E46
Thorpe N.Y. 57 C36
Thorpe Nfk 45 F60
Thorpe Dby. 50 D37
Thorpe Lcn. 53 D50
Thorpe Sry 22 E46
Thorpe Abbotts 45 G57
Thorpe Acre 41 D40
Thorpe Arnold 42 C43
Thorpe Audlin 51 A40
Thorpe Bassett 58 B44

Thorpe Bay 25 C55
Thorpe by Water 42 F44
Thorpe Constantine 40 E38
Thorpe Culvert 53 F60
Thorpe End Garden Village 45 D58
Thorpe Green 34 C55
Thorpe Hall 58 B41
Thorpe Hesley 51 C39
Thorpe in Balne 51 A41
Thorpe in the Fallows 52 D45
Thorpe Langton 42 F43
Thorpe Larches 62 D39
Thorpe-le-Soken 35 F57
Thorpe le Street 58 E44
Thorpe Malsor 32 A44
Thorpe Mandeville 31 D40
Thorpe Market 45 B58
Thorpe Morieux 34 C55
Thorpeness 35 C60
Thorpe on the Hill Lcn. 52 F44
Thorpe on the Hill W.Y. 57 G38
Thorpe Salvin 51 D41
Thorpe Satchville 42 D43
Thorpe St Andrew 45 E58
Thorpe St Peter 53 F50
Thorpe Thewles 62 D39
Thorpe Tilney Dales 52 G47
Thorpe Underwood 57 D40
Thorpe Waterville 42 G46
Thorpe Willoughby 58 F41
Thorpland 43 E51
Thorrington 34 G56
Thorverton 7 E24
Thrandeston 34 A56
Thrapston 32 A45
Threapland 56 C35
Threapwood 38 A30
Three Bridges 13 C48
Three Burrows 2 D13
Three Chimneys 14 D54
Three Cocks 28 E27
Three Crosses 17 E21
Three Cups Corner 13 D52
Three Holes 43 E51
Threekingham 42 B46
Three Leg Cross 13 C52
Three Legged Cross 10 D36
Three Mile Cross 22 E43
Threemilestone 2 D13
Threlkeld 60 D28
Threshers Bush 23 A50
Threshfield 56 C35
Threxton Hill 44 E54
Thriepley 82 D28
Thrigby 45 D60
Thringarth 61 D35
Thringstone 41 D40
Thrintoft 62 G39
Thriplow 33 D50
Throcking 33 E49
Throckley 71 G37
Throckmorton 29 C35
Throphill 71 E37
Thropton 71 C36
Throwleigh 6 F22
Throwley 14 B55
Throws 33 F52
Thrumpton 41 B40
Thrumster 103 D29
Thrunton 71 B36
Thrupp Glo. 20 A34
Thrupp Oxf. 31 G40
Thrushelton 6 G20
Thrussington 41 D42
Thruxton H.&W. 28 E30
Thruxton Ham. 21 G38
Thrybergh 51 C40
Thulston 41 B39
Thundergay 73 F14
Thundersley 24 C53
Thunderton 99 E36
Thundridge 33 G49
Thurcaston 41 D41
Thurcroft 51 D40
Thurdistoft 103 B27
Thurgarton Nfk 45 B57
Thurgarton Not. 41 A42
Thurgoland 50 B38
Thurlaston War. 31 A40
Thurlaston Lei. 41 F40
Thurlbear 8 B28
Thurlby Lcn. 52 F44
Thurlby Lcn. 42 D47
Thurleigh 32 C46
Thurlestone 5 F22
Thurloxton 8 A28
Thurlstone 50 B38
Thurlton 45 F60
Thurmaston 41 E41
Thurnby 41 E42
Thurne 45 D59
Thurnham 14 B54
Thurning Nmp. 42 G46
Thurning Nfk 44 C56
Thurnscoe 51 B40

Thursby 60 A29
Thursford 44 B55
Thursley 12 C44
Thurso 103 B26
Thurstaston 48 D28
Thurston 34 B55
Thurstonfield 60 A28
Thurstonland 50 B37
Thurton 45 E59
Thurvaston 40 M38
Thuster 103 C28
Thuxton 44 E56
Thwaite N.Y. 61 G34
Thwaite Sfk 34 B56
Thwaite Head 55 A29
Thwaite St Mary 45 F59
Thwing 59 C46
Tibbermore 82 E26
Tibberton Shr. 39 C32
Tibberton Glo. 29 F33
Tibberton H.&W. 29 C35
Tibbie Shiels Inn 69 A28
Tibenham 45 F57
Tibertich 79 G14
Tibshelf 51 F40
Tibthorpe 59 D45
Ticehurst 13 C52
Tichborne 11 A41
Tickencote 42 E45
Tickenham 19 D30
Tickhill 51 C41
Ticklerton 38 F30
Ticknall 41 C39
Tickton 59 E46
Tidcombe 21 F38
Tiddington Oxf. 21 A42
Tiddington War. 30 C37
Tidebrook 13 D52
Tideford 4 E19
Tidenham 19 B31
Tidenham Chase 19 B31
Tideswell 50 E37
Tidmarsh 21 D42
Tidmington 30 E38
Tidpit 10 C36
Tiers Cross 16 C15
Tiffield 31 C42
Tifty 99 E33
Tigerton 83 A31
Tighachnoic 79 C12
Tigh A Ghearraidh 92 D2
Tighnablair 81 F23
Tighnabruaich 73 C15
Tighnacomaire 80 A15
Tigley 5 D23
Tilbrook 32 B46
Tilbury 24 D52
Tile Cross 40 G37
Tile Hill 30 A38
Tilehurst 21 D42
Tilford 22 G44
Tillathrowie 98 F30
Tillers' Green 29 E32
Tillery 91 A35
Tilley 38 C30
Tillicoultry 75 A24
Tillingham 25 A55
Tillington H.&W. 28 D30
Tillington W.S. 12 D45
Tillington Common 28 D30
Tillyarblet 83 A30
Tillybirloch 91 C32
Tillycairn Castle 91 B32
Tillycorthie 91 A34
Tillydrine 90 D31
Tillyfar 99 E34
Tillyfour 90 B31
Tillyfourie 91 B32
Tillygreig 91 A34
Tillypronie 90 C30
Tilmanstone 15 B58
Tilney All Saints 43 D51
Tilney High End 43 D51
Tilney St Lawrence 43 D51
Tilshead 20 G36
Tilstock 38 B31
Tilston 48 G30
Tilstone Fearnall 48 F31
Tilsworth 32 F45
Tilton on the Hill 42 E43
Tiltups End 20 B34
Timberland 52 G47
Timberland Dales 52 F47
Timbersbrook 49 F34
Timberscombe 7 A25
Timble 57 D37
Timperley 49 D33
Timsbury Avon 19 F32
Timsbury Ham. 10 B39
Timsgearraidh 100 D6
Timworth Green 34 B54
Tincleton 9 E33
Tindale 61 A32
Tingewick 31 E42
Tingley 57 G38
Tingrith 32 E45

Tingwall 104 D29
Tinhay 6 G20
Tinney 4 A18
Tinshill 57 E38
Tinsley 51 C39
Tinsley Green 13 C48
Tintagel 4 B16
Tintern Parva 19 A31
Tintinhull 8 C30
Tintwistle 50 C36
Tinwald 68 E25
Tinwell 42 E45
Tipperty *Grm.* 91 E33
Tipperty *Grm.* 91 A35
Tiptoe 10 E38
Tipton 40 F35
Tipton St John 7 F26
Tiptree 34 G54
Tiptree Heath 34 G54
Tirabad 27 D24
Tirdeunaw 17 E22
Tiree Airport 78 C5
Tirindrish 87 F18
Tirley 29 F34
Tirphil 18 A27
Tirril 61 D30
Tir-y-dail 17 C22
Tisbury 9 B35
Tissington 50 G37
Tister 103 B27
Titchberry 6 C18
Titchfield 11 D41
Titchmarsh 32 A46
Titchwell 44 A53
Tithby 41 B42
Titley 28 B29
Titsey 23 F50
Titson 6 E18
Tittensor 40 B34
Tittleshall 44 C54
Tiverton *Dev.* 7 D25
Tiverton *Che.* 48 F31
Tivetshall St Margaret 45 G57
Tivetshall St Mary 45 G57
Tixall 40 C35
Tixover 42 E45
Toab *She.* 107 E37
Toab *Ork.* 105 A31
Tobermory 79 B10
Toberonochy 79 G13
Tobha Mor 84 A3
Tobson 100 D7
Tocher 98 F32
Tockenham 20 D36
Tockenham Wick 20 C36
Tockholes 56 G32
Tockington 19 C31
Tockwith 57 D40
Todber 9 C33
Toddington *Bfd.* 32 F45
Toddington *Glo.* 30 E36
Toddington *W.S.* 12 F46
Todenham 30 E38
Todhills *Cum.* 69 G29
Todhills *Tay.* 83 D30
Todlachie 91 B32
Todmorden 56 G35
Todwick 51 D40
Toft *She.* 106 E40
Toft *Cbs.* 33 C49
Toft *Lcn.* 42 D46
Toftcarl 103 D29
Toft Hill 62 D37
Toft Monks 45 F60
Toft next Newton 52 D46
Toftrees 44 C54
Tofts 103 B29
Toftwood 44 D55
Togston 71 C38
Tokavaig 86 C12
Tokers Green 22 D43
Tolastadh 101 C11
Tolastadh a Chaolais 100 D7
Tolastadh Ur 101 C11
Tolland 7 B26
Tollard Royal 9 C35
Tollcross 74 D22
Toller Down Gate 8 D31
Toller Fratrum 8 E31
Toller Porcorum 8 E31
Tollerton *Not.* 41 B41
Tollerton *N.Y.* 57 C40
Toller Whelme 8 D31
Tollesbury 25 A55
Tollesby 62 E40
Tolleshunt D'Arcy 34 G55
Tolleshunt Knights 34 G55
Tolleshunt Major 34 G54
Toll of Birness 99 F35
Tolpuddle 9 E33
Tolvah 89 E24
Tolworth 22 E47
Tom an Fhuadain 100 F9
Tomatin 88 B23
Tombreck 88 A22
Tomchrasky 87 C18

Tomdoun 87 D17
Tomdow 97 G25
Tomich *Hgh.* 87 B19
Tomich *Hgh.* 96 A22
Tomich *Hgh.* 96 D22
Tomintoul 90 B27
Tomnacross 96 G20
Tomnamoon 97 F26
Tomnaven 98 F29
Tomnavoulin 90 A27
Tomvaich 89 A26
Tonbridge 23 G51
Tondu 18 C24
Tonfanau 36 E21
Tong 39 E33
Tonge 41 C40
Tongham 22 G44
Tongland 65 E22
Tong Norton 39 E33
Tong Street 57 F37
Tongue 102 C21
Tongue Ho. 102 C21
Tongwynlais 18 C27
Tonna 18 B23
Ton-Pentre 18 B25
Ton-teg 18 C26
Tonwell 33 G49
Tonypandy 18 B25
Tonyrefail 18 C25
Toot Baldon 21 A41
Toot Hill 23 A50
Toothill 10 C39
Topcliffe 57 B39
Topcroft 45 F58
Topcroft Street 45 F58
Top End 32 B46
Toppesfield 34 E53
Toppings 49 A33
Topsham 7 G25
Topsham Bridge 5 E23
Torastan 78 A8
Torbain 90 B27
Torbeg *Grm.* 90 D29
Torbeg *Str.* 66 A14
Torbryan 5 D24
Torcastle 87 G17
Torcross 5 F24
Tordarroch 88 A22
Tore 96 F21
Toreduff 97 E26
Toremore 103 E27
Torgyle 87 C18
Torksey 52 E44
Torlum 92 F3
Torlundy 87 G17
Tormarton 20 D33
Tormisdale 72 E8
Tormore 73 G14
Tormsdale 103 C27
Tornagrain 96 G23
Tornahaish 90 C28
Tornaveen 90 C31
Torness 88 B21
Torpenhow 60 C27
Torphichen 75 C25
Torphins 90 C31
Torpoint 4 E20
Torquay 5 D25
Torquhan 76 F30
Torr 5 E21
Torran *Hgh.* 94 G11
Torran *Hgh.* 96 D22
Torran *Str.* 79 G14
Torrance *Str.* 74 E22
Torrance *Str.* 74 C22
Torrancroy 90 B29
Torrich 97 F24
Torridon 94 F15
Torrin 86 B11
Torrisdale *Hgh.* 102 B22
Torrisdale *Str.* 73 G13
Torrish 103 G25
Torrisholme 55 C30
Torroble 96 A21
Torry *Grm.* 91 C35
Torry *Grm.* 98 E30
Torryburn 75 B26
Torsonce 76 F30
Torterston 99 E36
Torthorwald 69 F26
Tortington 12 F45
Tortworth 19 B32
Torvaig 93 G10
Torver 60 G28
Torwood 75 B24
Torworth 51 D42
Tosberry 6 C18
Toscaig 86 A12
Toseland 33 B48
Tosside 56 D33
Tostarie 78 C9
Tostock 34 B55
Totaig 93 F8
Tote 93 G10
Totegan 102 B24

Totford 11 A41
Tothill 53 D50
Totland 10 F39
Totley 51 D39
Totnes 5 D23
Toton 41 B40
Totronald 78 B7
Tottenham 23 B49
Tottenhill 44 D52
Totteridge 23 B48
Totternhoe 32 F45
Tottington *G.M.* 49 A33
Tottington *Nfk* 44 F54
Totton 10 C39
Touchen-End 22 D44
Toulton 7 B27
Toux 99 D35
Tovil 14 B53
Toward 73 D17
Towcester 31 D42
Towednack 2 E10
Towersey 22 A43
Towie *Grm.* 99 C34
Towie *Grm.* 90 A31
Towie *Grm.* 90 B30
Towiemore 98 E29
Tow Law 62 C37
Town End *Cbs.* 43 F49
Townend 74 C20
Town End *Cum.* 55 A30
Town Green 48 B30
Townhead 65 F22
Townhead of Greenlaw 65 D23
Townhill 75 B26
Town Row 13 C51
Townshend 2 E11
Town Street 44 G53
Town Yetholm 70 A33
Towthorpe *N.Y.* 58 D42
Towthorpe *Hum.* 58 C44
Towton 57 F40
Towyn 47 E25
Toynton All Saints 53 F49
Toynton Fen Side 53 F49
Toynton St Peter 53 F50
Toy's Hill 23 F50
Trabboch 67 A20
Traboe 2 F13
Tradespark *Hgh.* 97 F24
Tradespark *Ork.* 105 A30
Trafford Park 49 C33
Trallong 27 F25
Tranch 19 A28
Tranent 76 C29
Trantlebeg 102 C24
Trantlemore 102 C24
Tranwell 71 E37
Trapp 17 C22
Traprain 76 C31
Traquair 76 G29
Trawden 56 F35
Trawsfynydd 37 B22
Trealaw 18 B25
Treales 55 F30
Trearddur 46 E18
Treaslane 93 F9
Trebanog 18 C26
Trebanos 17 D22
Trebarrow 4 A18
Trebartha 4 C18
Trebarwith 4 B16
Trebetherick 3 A15
Treborough 7 B25
Trebudannon 3 B15
Trebullett 4 C18
Treburley 4 C19
Trebyan 4 D16
Trecastle 27 F24
Trecwn 16 A15
Trecynon 18 A25
Tredavoe 2 F10
Tre-ddiog 16 B14
Tredegar 18 A27
Tredington *War.* 30 D38
Tredington *Glo.* 29 F34
Tredinnick *Cnw.* 4 E18
Tredinnick *Cnw.* 3 A15
Tredissi 16 A16
Tredomen 27 E26
Tredunnock 19 B29
Treen 2 F9
Treeton 51 D40
Trefaldwyn (Montgomery) 38 F28
Trefasser 16 A14
Trefdraeth 46 E19
Trefecca 28 E27
Trefeglwys 37 F25
Trefenter 26 B21
Treffgarne 16 B15
Treffynnon 16 B14
Trefgarn Owen 16 B14
Trefil 28 G27
Trefilan 26 C21
Treflach 38 C28

Trefnanney 38 D27
Trefnant 47 E26
Trefonen 38 C28
Trefor *Gwy.* 36 A19
Trefor *Gwy.* 46 D19
Treforest 18 C26
Treforest Ind. Est. 18 C26
Trefriw 47 F23
Trefynwy (Monmouth) 28 G30
Tregadillett 4 B18
Tregaian 46 E20
Tregare 28 G30
Tregaron 27 C22
Tregarth 46 F21
Tregavethan 2 D13
Tregear 3 C14
Tregeare 4 B18
Tregeiriog 38 B27
Tregele 46 C19
Tregidden 2 F13
Treglemais 16 B13
Tregolds 3 A14
Tregole 4 A17
Tregonetha 3 B15
Tregony 3 D15
Tregoyd 28 E27
Tre-groes *Dyf.* 26 D20
Tre-groes *M.G.* 18 C25
Treguff 18 D26
Tregurrian 3 B14
Tregynon 37 F26
Trehafod 18 B26
Treharris 18 B26
Treherbert 18 B25
Trekenner 4 C19
Trelash 4 A17
Trelassick 3 C14
Trelawnyd 47 E26
Trelech 17 A18
Trelech a'r Betws 17 B18
Trelewis 18 B26
Trelights 3 A15
Trelill 4 C16
Trelissick 3 E14
Trelleck 19 A30
Trelleck Grange 19 A30
Trelogan 47 D27
Trelystan 38 E28
Tremadog 36 A21
Tremail 4 B17
Tremain 26 D18
Tremaine 4 B18
Tremar 4 D18
Trematon 4 E19
Tremeirchion 47 E26
Tremethick Cross 2 E9
Trenance 3 B14
Trenarren 4 F16
Trench *Shr.* 39 D32
Trench *Clw.* 38 B29
Treneglos 4 B18
Trenewan 4 E17
Trent 8 C31
Trentham 40 A34
Trentishoe 6 A22
Treoes 18 D25
Treorchy 18 B25
Tre'r-ddol 37 F22
Tre-Rhys 26 D17
Trerule Foot 4 E19
Tresaith 26 C18
Trescott 40 F34
Trescowe 2 E11
Tresham 20 B33
Treshnish 78 C9
Tresillian 3 D14
Tresinney 4 B17
Tresinwen 16 A14
Treskinnick Cross 4 A18
Tresmeer 4 B18
Tresparrett 4 A17
Tresparrett Posts 4 A16
Tressait 81 A24
Tresta *She.* 107 B39
Tresta *She.* 106 C42
Treswell 51 E43
Trethurgy 4 E16
Tretio 16 B13
Tretire 28 F31
Tretower 28 F27
Treuddyn 48 G28
Trevalga 4 A16
Trevalyn 48 G29
Trevanson 3 A15
Trevarren 3 B15
Trevarrick 3 D15
Tre-vaughan 17 B19
Trevaughan 16 C17
Trevellas 2 C13
Trevelmond 4 D18
Treverva 2 E13
Trevescan 2 F9
Trevethin 19 A28
Trevigro 4 D19
Trevine *Dyf.* 16 A14
Trevine *Str.* 80 E16

Treviscoe 3 C15
Trevone 3 A14
Trevor 38 A28
Trewalder 4 B16
Trewarmett 4 B16
Trewarthenick 3 D14
Trewassa 4 B17
Trewellard 2 E9
Trewen 4 B18
Trewern 38 D28
Trewidland 4 E18
Trewilym 26 D17
Trewint 4 A17
Trewithian 3 E14
Trewoon 3 C15
Trewornan 3 A15
Treyarnon 3 A14
Treyford 12 E44
Triangle 57 G36
Trickett's Cross 10 D36
Trimdon 62 C39
Trimdon Colliery 62 C39
Trimdon Grange 62 C39
Trimingham 45 B58
Trimley St Martin 35 E58
Trimley St Mary 35 E58
Trimpley 29 A33
Trimsaran 17 D20
Trimstone 6 A21
Trinafour 81 A23
Trinant 18 B27
Tring 32 G45
Trinity 83 A31
Trislaig 87 G16
Trispen 3 C14
Tritlington 71 D37
Trochry 82 C25
Troedyraur 26 D19
Troedyrhiw 18 A26
Trondavoe 106 E39
Troon *Str.* 74 G19
Troon *Cnw.* 2 E12
Trosaraidh 84 C3
Troston 34 A54
Troswell 4 A18
Trottiscliffe 24 E52
Trotton 12 D44
Troughend 70 D34
Troustan 73 C16
Troutbeck 60 F29
Troutbeck Bridge 60 F29
Trowbridge 20 F34
Trow Green 19 A31
Trowle Common 20 F34
Trowley Bottom 32 G46
Trows 76 G32
Trowse Newton 45 E58
Trudernish 72 E10
Trudoxhill 20 G33
Trull 8 B28
Trumaisge Arraidh 92 D4
Trumpan 93 E8
Trumpet 29 E32
Trumpington 33 C50
Trunch 45 B58
Trunnah 55 E29
Truro 3 D14
Trusham 7 G24
Trusley 40 B38
Trusthorpe 53 D51
Truthan 3 C14
Trysull 40 F34
Tubney 21 B40
Tuckenhay 5 E23
Tuckingmill 2 D12
Tuddenham *Sfk* 34 A53
Tuddenham *Sfk* 35 D57
Tudeley 23 G52
Tudhoe 62 C38
Tudweiliog 36 B18
Tuffley 29 G34
Tufton *Dyf.* 16 B16
Tufton *Ham.* 21 G40
Tugby 42 E43
Tugford 38 G31
Tughall 71 A37
Tuirnaig 94 C14
Tulchan 82 E26
Tullibody 75 A24
Tullich *Str.* 80 F16
Tullich *Cen.* 81 D21
Tullich *Hgh.* 88 B22
Tullich *Grm.* 98 E29
Tullich *Str.* 79 F14
Tullich *Hgh.* 97 D24
Tullich Muir 96 D23
Tulliemet 82 B25
Tulloch *Hgh.* 96 B22
Tulloch *Grm.* 97 F26
Tulloch *Grm.* 99 F34
Tullochgorm 73 A15
Tullochgribban High 89 B25
Tullochvenus 90 C31
Tulloes 83 C30
Tullybannocher 81 E23
Tullybelton 82 D26

Tullyfergus 82 C27
Tullymurdoch 82 B27
Tullynessle 90 B31
Tumble 17 C21
Tumby 53 G48
Tumby Woodside 53 G48
Tummel Bridge 81 B23
Tundergarth Mains 69 E27
Tunga 100 D10
Tunstall *N.Y.* 62 G37
Tunstall *Nfk* 45 E60
Tunstall *Hum.* 59 F49
Tunstall *Lan.* 55 B31
Tunstall *Stf.* 49 G34
Tunstall *Sfk* 35 C59
Tunstall *Kent* 24 E54
Tunstead 45 C58
Tunworth 21 G42
Tupsley 28 E31
Turbiskill 73 B13
Turclossie 99 D34
Turgis Green 21 F42
Turin 83 B31
Turkdean 30 G36
Tur Langton 42 F43
Turnastone 28 E29
Turnberry 67 C17
Turnchapel 4 E20
Turnditch 40 A38
Turner's Green 30 A37
Turners Hill 13 C49
Turners Puddle 9 E34
Turnford 23 A49
Turnworth 9 D33
Turret Bridge 88 E19
Turriff 99 D33
Turton Bottoms 49 A33
Turvey 32 C45
Turville 22 B43
Turville Heath 22 B43
Turweston 31 E41
Tutbury 40 C37
Tutnall 29 A35
Tutshill 19 B31
Tuttington 45 C58
Tuxford 51 E43
Twatt *She.* 107 B39
Twatt *Ork.* 104 D28
Twechar 74 C22
Tweedmouth 77 E35
Tweedsmuir 69 A26
Twelveheads 2 D13
Twenty 42 C47
Twerton 19 E32
Twickenham 22 D47
Twigworth 29 F34
Twineham 13 D48
Twinhoe 20 F33
Twinstead 34 E54
Twiss Green 49 C32
Twitchen *Dev.* 7 B23
Twitchen *Shr.* 28 A29
Twizell House 71 A37
Two Bridges 5 C22
Two Dales 50 F38
Two Gates 40 E38
Twycross 41 E39
Twyford *Dby.* 41 C39
Twyford *Brk.* 22 D43
Twyford *Ham.* 11 B40
Twyford *Bkh.* 31 F42
Twyford *Nfk* 44 C56
Twyford *Dor.* 9 C34
Twyford *Lei.* 42 D43
Twyford Common 28 E31
Twynholm 65 E22
Twyning 29 E34
Twyning Green 29 E34
Twynllanan 27 F23
Twyn-yr-odyn 18 D26
Twyn-y-Sheriff 19 A29
Twywell 32 A45
Tyberton 28 D29
Tyburn 40 F37
Tycroes 17 C21
Tycrwyn 37 D26
Tydd Gote 43 D50
Tydd St Giles 43 D49
Tydd St Mary 43 D50
Tye Common 24 B52
Tye Green 34 F53
Ty-hen 36 B17
Tyldesley 49 B32
Tyle-garw 18 C26
Tyler Hill 25 E57
Tylers Green *Esx* 23 A51
Tylers Green *Bkh.* 22 B44
Tylorstown 18 B25
Tylwch 27 A25
Ty-mawr *Clw.* 38 A27
Ty-mawr *Clw.* 37 A25
Ty-nant *Gwy.* 37 C25
Ty-nant *Clw.* 37 A25
Tyndrum 80 D19
Tyneham 9 F34
Tynehead 76 E29

Tynemouth 71 F39
Tynewydd 18 B24
Tyninghame 76 C31
Tynribbie 80 C15
Tynron 68 D23
Tyn-y-cefn 37 A26
Tyn-y-Cwm 37 G24
Tyn-y-ffridd 37 B26
Tyn-y-graig 27 D25
Tynygraig 27 B22
Tyringham 32 D44
Tythegston 18 D24
Tytherington *Som.* 20 G33
Tytherington *Avon* 19 C32
Tytherington *Wts.* 20 G34
Tytherington *Che.* 49 E34
Tytherleigh 8 D28
Ty-uchaf 37 C25
Tywardreath 4 E16
Tywardreath Highway 4 E16
Tywyn *Gwy.* 36 E21
Tywyn *Gwy.* 47 E23

U

Uachdar 92 F3
Uags 86 A13
Ubbeston Green 35 A59
Ubley 19 F31
Uckerby 62 F38
Uckfield 13 D50
Uckinghall 29 E34
Uckington 29 F34
Uddingston 74 D22
Uddington 75 G24
Udimore 14 F54
Udny Green 91 A34
Udny Station 91 A34
Udstonhead 75 F23
Uffcott 20 D37
Uffculme 7 D26
Uffington *Shr.* 38 D31
Uffington *Lcn.* 42 E46
Uffington *Oxf.* 21 C39
Ufford *Cbs.* 42 E46
Ufford *Sfk* 35 C58
Ufton 30 B39
Ufton Nervet 21 E42
Ugborough 5 E22
Uggeshall 35 A60
Ugglebarnby 63 F44
Ugley 33 F51
Ugley Green 33 F50
Ugthorpe 63 E43
Uig *Hgh.* 93 E9
Uig *Hgh.* 93 F7
Uig *Str.* 78 B7
Uig *Str.* 73 B17
Uigen 100 D6
Uiginish 93 G8
Uigshader 93 G10
Uisgebhagh 92 G4
Uisken 78 F9
Ulbster 103 D29
Ulcat row 60 D29
Ulceby *Lcn.* 53 E50
Ulceby *Hum.* 52 A47
Ulceby Cross 53 E50
Ulcombe 14 C54
Uldale 60 C28
Uldale House 61 G33
Uley 20 B33
Ulgham 71 D38
Ullapool 95 B17
Ullenhall 30 B37
Ullenwood 29 G35
Ulleskelf 58 E41
Ullesthorpe 41 G40
Ulley 51 D40
Ullingswick 28 D31
Ullinish 85 A9
Ullock 60 D26
Ulpha 60 G27
Ulrome 59 D47
Ulsta 106 D40
Ulting 24 A53
Uluvalt 79 E11
Ulverston 55 B28
Ulwell 10 F36
Ulzieside 68 C23
Umberleigh 6 C22
Unapool 101 E18
Underbarrow 60 G30
Underhoull 106 B41
Underriver 23 F51
Underwood *Not.* 51 G40
Underwood *Gwe.* 19 C29
Undy 19 C30
Unifirth 107 B38
Union Croft 91 D34
Union Mills 54 F25
Unstone 51 E39
Unthank 60 C30
Upavon 20 F37
Up Cerne 9 D32

Upchurch 24 E54
Upcott *H.&W.* 28 C29
Upcott *Dev.* 6 F20
Upend 33 C52
Up Exe 7 E25
Uphall *Dor.* 8 D31
Uphall *Ltn* 75 C26
Uphall Station 75 C26
Upham *Dev.* 7 E24
Upham *Ham.* 11 B41
Uphampton 29 B34
Up Hatherley 29 F34
Uphill 19 F29
Up Holland 48 B31
Upleadon 29 F33
Upleatham 63 D42
Uplees 25 E55
Uploders 8 E31
Uplowman 7 D25
Uplyme 8 E29
Up Marden 11 C43
Upminster 23 C51
Up Nately 21 F42
Upottery 7 E27
Upper Affcot 38 G30
Upper Ardroscadale 73 D16
Upper Arley 39 G33
Upper Arncott 31 G42
Upper Aston 40 F34
Upper Astrop 31 E41
Upper Basildon 21 D41
Upper Beeding 12 E47
Upper Benefield 42 G45
Upper Bighouse 102 C24
Upper Boat 18 C26
Upper Boddington 31 C40
Upper Borth 36 G21
Upper Boyndlie 99 C35
Upper Brailes 30 D38
Upper Breakish 86 B12
Upper Breinton 28 D30
Upper Broughton 41 C42
Upper Bucklebury 21 E41
Upper Burgate 10 C37
Upper Burnhaugh 91 D34
Upper Caldecote 32 D47
Upper Camster 103 D28
Upper Catshill 29 A35
Upper Chapel 27 D26
Upper Chute 21 F38
Upper Clatford 21 G38
Upper Coberley 29 G35
Upper Cound 38 E31
Upper Cwmbran 19 B28
Upper Dallachy 98 C29
Upper Dean 32 B46
Upper Denby 50 B38
Upper Derraid 89 A26
Upper Diabaig 94 E14
Upper Dicker 13 E51
Upper Dovercourt 35 F58
Upper Dunsforth 57 C40
Upper Eastern Green 40 G38
Upper Eathie 96 E23
Upper Elkstone 50 G36
Upper End 50 E36
Upper Farringdon 11 A43
Upper Framilode 29 G33
Upper Froyle 22 G43
Upper Gills 103 A29
Upper Glendessarry 86 E15
Upper Godney 19 G30
Upper Gornal 40 F35
Upper Gravenhurst 32 E47
Upper Green *Esx* 33 E50
Upper Green *Gwe.* 28 G29
Upper Green *Brk.* 21 E39
Upper Gylen 79 E14
Upper Hackney 50 F38
Upper Halliford 22 E46
Upper Halling 24 E52
Upper Hambleton 42 E45
Upper Hardres Court 15 B57
Upper Hartfield 13 C50
Upper Hawkhillock 99 F36
Upper Hayton 38 G31
Upper Heath 38 G31
Upper Helmsley 58 D42
Upper Hergest 28 C28
Upper Heyford 31 F40
Upper Hill 28 C30
Upper Hopton 50 A37
Upper Horsebridge 13 E51
Upper Hulme 49 F35
Upper Inglesham 20 B37
Upper Kilchattan 72 A9
Upper Killay 17 E21
Upper Knockando 97 G27
Upper Lambourn 21 C38
Upper Langwith 51 E41
Upper Largo 83 G30
Upper Lochton 91 D33
Upper Longdon 40 D36
Upper Ludstone 40 F34
Upper Lybster 103 E28
Upper Lydbrook 29 G32

Upper Maes-coed 28 E29
Upper Midhope 50 C37
Uppermill 49 B35
Upper Minety 20 B36
Upper Mitton 29 A33
Upper North Dean 22 B44
Upper Norwood 23 D49
Upper Obney 82 B30
Upper Oddington 30 F37
Upper Ollach 85 A10
Upper Poppleton 58 D41
Upper Quinton 30 D37
Upper Ridinghill 99 D36
Upper Rochford 29 B32
Upper Sanday 105 A31
Upper Sapey 29 B32
Upper Seagry 20 C35
Upper Shelton 32 D45
Upper Sheringham 45 A57
Upper Skelmorlie 74 D18
Upper Slaughter 30 F37
Upper Sonachan 80 E16
Upper Soudley 29 G32
Upper Stoke 41 G39
Upper Stondon 32 E47
Upper Stowe 31 C42
Upper Street *Sfk* 35 E57
Upper Street *Nfk* 45 D59
Upper Street *Ham.* 10 C37
Upper Sundon 32 F46
Upper Swell 30 F37
Upper Tean 40 B35
Upperthong 50 B36
Upper Thurnham 55 D30
Upper Tillyrie 82 G26
Upperton 12 D45
Upper Tooting 23 D48
Uppertown 103 A29
Upper Town 19 E30
Upper Tysoe 30 D39
Upper Upham 21 D38
Upper Upnor 24 D53
Upper Victoria 83 D31
Upper Wardington 31 D40
Upper Weald 31 E43
Upper Weedon 31 C42
Upper Welson 28 C28
Upper Wield 11 A42
Upper Winchendon 31 G43
Upper Woodford 10 A37
Upper Wootton 21 F41
Upper Wraxall 20 D33
Upper Wyche 29 D33
Uppingham 42 F44
Uppington *Dor.* 10 D36
Uppington *Shr.* 38 E31
Upsall 57 A40
Upsettlington 77 F34
Upshire 23 A49
Up Somborne 11 A40
Upstreet 25 E57
Up Sydling 9 D32
Upton *Nfk* 45 D59
Upton *Som.* 7 C25
Upton *Dor.* 9 E35
Upton *Cnw.* 4 C18
Upton *Nmp.* 31 B43
Upton *Bkh.* 31 G43
Upton *Cbs.* 32 A47
Upton *Lcn.* 52 D44
Upton *Mer.* 48 D28
Upton *Dev.* 5 F23
Upton *Che.* 48 F30
Upton *W.Y.* 51 A40
Upton *Not.* 51 E43
Upton *Not.* 51 G43
Upton *Dev.* 7 E26
Upton *Ham.* 10 C39
Upton *Brk.* 22 D45
Upton *Ham.* 21 F39
Upton *Oxf.* 21 C40
Upton *Cbs.* 42 E47
Upton Bishop 29 F32
Upton Cheyney 19 D32
Upton Cressett 39 F32
Upton Cross 4 C18
Upton End 32 E47
Upton Green 45 D59
Upton Grey 22 G43
Upton Hellions 7 E24
Upton Lovell 10 G35
Upton Magna 38 D31
Upton Noble 9 A33
Upton Pyne 7 F25
Upton Scudamore 20 G34
Upton Snodsbury 29 C35
Upton St Leonards 29 G34
Upton upon Severn 29 D34
Upton Warren 29 B35
Upwaltham 12 E45
Upware 33 B51
Upwell 43 E51
Upwey 9 F32
Upwood 43 G48
Uradale 107 D39
Urafirth 106 E38

Urchany 97 G24
Urchfont 20 F36
Urdimarsh 28 D31
Ure 106 E38
Urgha 93 B7
Urlay Nook 62 E39
Urmston 49 C33
Urquhart *Grm.* 98 C28
Urquhart *Hgh.* 96 F21
Urra 93 F41
Urray 96 F20
Ushaw Moor 62 B38
Usk 19 A29
Usselby 52 C46
Uton 7 F24
Utterby 53 C48
Uttoxeter 40 B36
Uwchmynydd 36 C17
Uxbridge 22 C46
Uyeasound 106 B41
Uzmaston 16 C15

V

Valley 46 E18
Valleyfield *Fife* 75 B25
Valleyfield *D.&G.* 65 E22
Valley Trudde 4 B17
Valsgarth 106 A42
Vange 24 C53
Vardre 17 D22
Varteg 19 A28
Vatten 93 G8
Vaul 78 C6
Vaynor 27 G26
Vaynor Park 38 E27
Veaullt 28 C27
Veensgarth 107 C39
Velindre *Dyf.* 16 A16
Velindre *Pow.* 28 E27
Vellow 7 B26
Veness 104 D31
Venn 5 F23
Vennington 38 E29
Venn Ottery 7 F26
Ventnor 11 G41
Vernham Dean 21 F39
Vernham Street 21 F39
Vernolds Common 38 G30
Verwig 26 D17
Verwood 10 D36
Veryan 3 E15
Vicarage 8 F28
Vickerstown 54 C27
Victoria 3 B15
Vidlin 107 A40
Viewfield 103 B26
Viewpark 75 D23
Vigo 40 E36
Vigo Village 24 E52
Villavin 6 D21
Vinehall Street 14 E53
Vine's Cross 13 E51
Viney Hill 19 A32
Virginia Water 22 D45
Virginstow 6 F19
Virley 34 G55
Vobster 19 G32
Voe *She.* 106 D39
Voe *She.* 107 A40
Vowchurch 28 E29
Voy 104 E28

W

Wackerfield 62 D37
Wacton 45 F57
Wadborough 29 D34
Waddesdon 31 G43
Waddingham 52 C45
Waddington *Lcn.* 52 F45
Waddington *Lan.* 56 E33
Waddingworth 52 E47
Wadebridge 3 A15
Wadeford 8 C28
Wadenhoe 42 G45
Wadesmill 33 G49
Wadhurst 13 C52
Wadshelf 50 E38
Wadsley Bridge 51 C39
Wadworth 51 C41
Wadworth Hill 59 G48
Waen 47 F26
Waen-fach 38 D28
Waen-wen 46 F21
Wag 103 F26
Wainfleet All Saints 53 G51
Wainfleet Bank 53 G50
Wainhouse Corner 4 A17
Wainscott 24 D53
Wainstalls 57 G36
Waitby 61 F33
Wakefield 57 G39
Wakerley 42 F45
Wakes Colne 34 F54

Walberswick 35 A60
Walberton 12 F45
Walcot Lcn. 42 B46
Walcot Shr. 38 G29
Walcot Lcn. 52 G47
Walcot Hum. 58 G44
Walcot Shr. 38 D31
Walcot Dales 52 G47
Walcote War. 30 C37
Walcote Lei. 41 G41
Walcot Green 45 G57
Walcott 45 B59
Walden 57 A36
Walden Head 56 A35
Walden Stubbs 51 A41
Walderslade 24 E53
Walderton 11 C43
Walditch 8 E30
Waldley 40 B37
Waldridge 62 A38
Waldringfield 35 D58
Waldron 13 E51
Wales 51 D40
Walesby Lcn. 52 C47
Walesby Not. 51 E42
Walford Shr. 38 C30
Walford H.&W. 28 F31
Walford H.&W. 28 A29
Walgherton 39 A32
Walgrave 31 A43
Walhampton 10 E39
Walkden 49 B33
Walker 71 G38
Walkerburn 76 G29
Walker Fold 56 E32
Walkeringham 51 C43
Walkerith 51 C43
Walkern 33 F48
Walker's Green 28 D30
Walkerton 82 G28
Walkhampton 5 D21
Walk Mill 56 F34
Walkwood 30 B36
Wall Nor. 70 G35
Wall Stf. 40 E36
Wallacehall 69 F28
Wallacetown 67 C18
Wallasey 48 C28
Wall Bank 38 F30
Wallbottle 71 G37
Wallend 24 D54
Waller's Green 29 E32
Wall Heath 40 G34
Wallingford 21 C41
Wallington G.L. 23 E48
Wallington Ham. 11 D41
Wallington Hfs. 33 E48
Wallis 16 B16
Wallisdown 10 E36
Walliswood 12 C47
Walls 107 C38
Wallsend 71 G38
Wall under Heywood 38 F31
Wallyford 76 C29
Walmer 15 B59
Walmer Bridge 55 G30
Walmersley 49 A33
Walmley 40 F37
Walpole 35 A59
Walpole Cross Keys 43 C51
Walpole Highway 43 D51
Walpole St Andrew 43 D51
Walpole St Peter 43 D51
Walsall 40 F35
Walsall Wood 40 E36
Walsden 56 G35
Walsgrave on Sowe 41 G39
Walsham le Willows 34 A55
Walsoken 43 D50
Walston 75 F26
Walsworth 32 E47
Walterstone 28 F29
Waltham Kent 15 C56
Waltham Hum. 53 B48
Waltham Abbey 23 B49
Waltham Chase 11 C41
Waltham Forest 23 B49
Waltham on the Wolds 42 C44
Waltham St Lawrence 22 D44
Walthamstow 23 C49
Walton Cbs. 42 E47
Walton Lei. 41 G41
Walton Stf. 40 B34
Walton Cum. 70 G31
Walton N.Y. 57 E40
Walton Pow. 28 C28
Walton Bkh. 32 G44
Walton War. 30 C38
Walton Bkh. 32 E44
Walton Shr. 38 D31
Walton Sfk 35 E58
Walton Dby. 51 F39
Walton W.Y. 51 A39
Walton Mer. 48 C29
Walton Som. 8 A30
Walton Cardiff 29 E34

Walton East 16 B15
Walton-in-Gordano 19 D30
Walton-le-Dale 55 G31
Walton-on-Thames 22 E47
Walton on the Hill 23 F48
Walton-on-the-Hill 40 C35
Walton on the Naze 35 F58
Walton on the Wolds 41 D41
Walton-on-Trent 40 D38
Walton Park 65 C23
Walton West 16 C14
Walwen Clw. 47 E27
Walwen Clw. 48 E28
Walwick 70 F34
Walworth 62 E38
Walwyns Castle 16 C14
Wambrook 8 D28
Wanborough Sry 22 G45
Wanborough Wts. 20 C37
Wandel 68 A25
Wandon 71 A36
Wandsworth 23 D48
Wandylaw 71 A37
Wangford Sfk 44 G53
Wangford Sfk 35 A60
Wanlip 41 D41
Wanlockhead 68 B24
Wannock 13 F51
Wansford Nmp. 42 F46
Wansford Hum. 59 D46
Wanstead 23 C49
Wanstrow 19 G32
Wanswell 19 A32
Wantage 21 C39
Wapley 19 D32
Wappenbury 30 A39
Wappenham 31 D41
Warblebank 60 B28
Warbleton 13 E52
Warborough 21 B41
Warboys 33 A48
Warbstow 4 A18
Warburton 49 D33
Warcop 61 E33
Warden Kent 25 D56
Warden Nor. 70 G34
Ward End 40 G37
Wardgate 40 A38
Ward Green 34 B56
Wardhouse 98 F31
Wardington 31 D40
Wardle G.M. 49 A34
Wardle Che. 48 G31
Wardley 42 E44
Wardlow 50 E37
Wardy Hill 43 G50
Ware Hfs. 33 G49
Ware Kent 25 E58
Wareham 9 F35
Warehorne 14 D55
Warenford 71 A37
Waren Mill 77 G37
Warenton 77 G36
Wareside 33 G49
Waresley 33 C48
Warfield 22 D44
Warham 44 A55
Wark Nor. 77 G34
Wark Nor. 70 F34
Warkleigh 6 C22
Warkton 32 A44
Warkworth Nmp. 31 D40
Warkworth Nor. 71 C38
Warlaby 62 G39
Warland 56 G35
Warleggan 4 D17
Warley 40 G35
Warley Town 57 G36
Warlingham 23 F49
Warmfield 57 G39
Warmingham 49 F32
Warminghurst 12 E47
Warmington Nmp. 42 F46
Warmington War. 30 D39
Warminster 20 G34
Warmlake 14 C54
Warmley 19 D32
Warmsworth 51 B41
Warmwell 9 F33
Warndon 29 C34
Warnford 11 B42
Warnham 12 C47
Warningcamp 12 F46
Warninglid 13 D48
Warren Dyf. 16 E15
Warren Che. 49 E34
Warrenby 63 D41
Warren House 6 G22
Warren Row 22 C44
Warren Street 14 B55
Warrington Che. 49 D32
Warrington Bkh. 32 C44
Warroch 82 G26
Warsash 11 D40
Warslow 50 G36

Warsop 51 F41
Warter 58 D44
Warthill 58 D42
Wartle 90 C31
Wartling 13 F52
Wartnaby 41 C42
Warton War. 40 E38
Warton Lan. 55 G30
Warton Lan. 55 B30
Warton Nor. 71 C36
Warwick War. 30 B38
Warwick Cum. 60 A30
Warwick Bridge 61 A30
Wasbister 104 C29
Washaway 4 C16
Washbourne 5 E24
Wash Common 21 E40
Washfield 7 D25
Washfold 62 F36
Washford 7 A26
Washford Pyne 7 D24
Washingborough 52 E46
Washington T.&W. 62 A38
Washington W.S. 12 E47
Washmere Green 34 D55
Wasing 21 E41
Waskerley 62 B36
Wasperton 30 C38
Wass 58 B41
Watchet 7 A26
Watchfield Som. 19 G29
Watchfield Oxf. 21 B38
Watchgate 61 G31
Watendlath 60 E28
Water 56 G34
Waterbeach 33 B50
Waterbeck 69 F28
Water Eaton 31 G41
Water End Hfs. 32 G46
Water End Hfs. 23 A48
Waterfall 50 G36
Waterfoot Lan. 56 G34
Waterfoot Str. 74 E21
Waterford 33 G48
Waterhead D.&G. 68 E23
Waterhead Cum. 60 F29
Waterhill of Bruxie 99 E35
Waterhouses Drm 62 B37
Waterhouses Stf. 50 G36
Wateringbury 23 F52
Waterloo Grm. 99 F36
Waterloo Mer. 48 C28
Waterloo Nfk 45 D58
Waterloo Str. 75 E24
Waterloo Dyf. 16 D15
Waterloo Dor. 9 E35
Waterloo Tay. 82 D26
Waterloo Cross 7 D26
Waterloo Port 46 F20
Waterlooville 11 C42
Watermeetings 68 B25
Watermillock 60 D30
Water Newton 42 F47
Water Orton 40 F37
Waterperry 21 A42
Waterrow 7 C26
Watersfield 12 E46
Waterside Str. 74 F20
Waterside Str. 74 C22
Waterside Bkh. 22 A45
Waterside Grm. 90 B29
Waterside Grm. 91 A36
Waterside Str. 67 C20
Waterstock 21 A42
Waterston 16 D15
Water Stratford 31 E42
Waters Upton 39 D32
Water Yeat 55 A28
Watford Nmp. 31 B41
Watford Hfs. 22 B47
Wath N.Y. 57 C37
Wath N.Y. 57 B39
Wath Brow 60 E26
Wath upon Dearne 51 B40
Watlington Nfk 44 D52
Watlington Oxf. 21 B42
Watnall 41 A40
Watten 103 C28
Wattisfield 34 A56
Wattisham 34 C55
Watton Nfk 44 E54
Watton Hum. 59 E46
Watton at Stone 33 G49
Watton Green 44 E55
Wattston 75 D23
Wattstown 18 B25
Wattsville 18 B27
Waunarlwydd 17 E21
Waunclynda 17 A22
Waunfawr 46 G21
Waun Fawr 37 G22
Waun y Clyn 17 D20
Wavendon 32 E44
Waverbridge 60 B27
Waverton Cum. 60 B27
Waverton Che. 48 F30

Wawne 59 F46
Waxham 45 C60
Waxholme 59 G49
Wayford 8 D29
Way Gill 56 C35
Waytown 8 E30
Way Village 7 D24
Wayshyburn 98 D32
Weald 21 A38
Wealdstone 22 C47
Weare 19 F29
Weare Giffard 6 C20
Wearhead 61 B34
Wearne 8 B30
Weasenham All Saints 44 C54
Weasenham St Peter 44 C53
Weathercote 56 B33
Weaverham 49 E32
Weaverthorpe 59 B45
Webheath 29 B35
Webton 28 E29
Wedderlairs 99 F34
Weddington 41 F39
Wedhampton 20 F36
Wedmore 19 G30
Wednesbury 40 F35
Wednesfield 40 E35
Weedon 32 G44
Weedon Bec 31 C42
Weedon Lois 31 D42
Weeford 40 E37
Week 7 D23
Weekley 42 G44
Week Orchard 6 E18
Week St Mary 4 A18
Weeley 35 F57
Weeley Heath 35 F57
Weem 81 B24
Weeping Cross 40 C35
Weethley 30 C36
Weeting 44 G53
Weeton Hum. 59 G49
Weeton W.Y. 57 E38
Weeton Lan. 55 F29
Weir Lan. 56 G34
Weir Esx 24 C54
Weirbrook 38 C29
Welbeck Abbey 51 E41
Welborne 44 E56
Welbourn 52 G45
Welburn 58 C43
Welbury 62 F39
Welby 42 B45
Welches Dam 43 G50
Welcombe 6 D18
Weldon 42 G45
Welford Nmp. 41 G42
Welford Brk. 21 D40
Welford-on-Avon 30 C37
Welham Not. 51 D43
Welham Lei. 42 F43
Welham Green 23 A48
Well Ham. 22 G43
Well Lcn. 53 E48
Well N.Y. 57 A38
Welland 29 D33
Wellbank 83 D30
Well End 22 C44
Wellesbourne 30 C38
Well Hill 23 E50
Welling 23 D50
Wellingborough 32 B44
Wellingham 44 C54
Wellingore 52 G45
Wellington Shr. 39 D32
Wellington H.&W. 28 D30
Wellington Cum. 60 F26
Wellington Som. 7 C27
Wellington Heath 29 D32
Wellington Marsh 28 D30
Wellow Avon 20 F33
Wellow Not. 51 F42
Wellow I.o.W. 10 F39
Wells 19 G31
Wellsborough 41 E39
Wells-Next-The-Sea 44 A55
Well Town 7 E25
Wellwood 75 B26
Welney 43 F51
Welshampton 38 B30
Welsh Bicknor 28 G31
Welsh End 38 B30
Welsh Frankton 38 B29
Welsh Hook 16 B14
Welsh Newton 28 G30
Welshpool (Y Trallwng) 38 E27
Welsh St Donats 18 D26
Welton Avon 19 F32
Welton Cum. 60 B29
Welton Nmp. 31 B41
Welton Lcn. 52 D46
Welton Hum. 59 G45
Welton le Marsh 53 F50
Welton le Wold 53 D48
Welwick 59 G49

Welwyn 33 G48
Welwyn Garden City 33 G48
Wem 38 C31
Wembdon 8 A28
Wembley 22 C47
Wembury 4 F20
Wembworthy 6 E22
Wemyss Bay 74 D18
Wenallt Gwy. 37 C24
Wenallt Gwy. 37 A25
Wendens Ambo 33 E50
Wendlebury 31 G41
Wendling 44 D55
Wendover 22 A44
Wendron 2 E12
Wendy 33 D49
Wenhaston 35 A60
Wenlli 47 F24
Wennington Lan. 56 B32
Wennington Cbs. 33 A48
Wennington Esx 23 C51
Wensley Dby. 50 F38
Wensley N.Y. 62 G36
Wentbridge 51 A40
Went Hill 13 G51
Wentnor 38 F29
Wentworth S.Y. 51 C39
Wentworth Cbs. 33 A50
Wentworth Castle 51 B39
Wenvoe 18 D27
Weobley 28 C29
Weobley Marsh 28 C30
Wepham 12 F46
Wepre 48 F28
Wereham 44 E52
Wergs 40 E34
Wernyrheolydd 28 G29
Werrington Dev. 6 G19
Werrington Nmp. 42 E47
Werrington Stf. 40 A35
Wervil Brook 26 C19
Wervin 48 E30
Wesham 55 F30
Wessington 51 G39
West Aberthaw 18 E26
West Acre 44 D53
West Allerdean 77 F35
West Alvington 5 F23
West Amesbury 20 G37
West Anstey 7 C24
West Ashby 53 E48
West Ashling 12 F44
West Ashton 20 F34
West Auckland 62 D37
West Ayton 59 A45
West Bagborough 7 B27
West Barkwith 52 D47
West Barnby 63 E44
West Barns 76 C32
West Bay 8 E30
West Beckham 45 B57
West Benhar 75 D24
Westbere 25 E57
West Bergholt 34 F55
West Bexington 8 F30
West Bilney 44 D53
West Blatchington 13 F48
West Boldon 71 G39
Westborough 42 A44
Westbourne W.S. 11 D43
Westbourne Dor. 10 E36
West Bradenham 44 E54
West Bradford 56 E33
West Bradley 8 A31
West Bretton 50 A38
West Bridgford 41 B41
West Bromwich 40 F35
Westbrook 21 D40
West Buckland Som. 7 C27
West Buckland Dev. 6 B22
West Burrafirth 107 B38
West Burton N.Y. 57 A36
West Burton W.S. 12 E45
Westbury Wts. 20 F34
Westbury Shr. 38 E29
Westbury Bkh. 31 E41
Westbury Leigh 20 G34
Westbury-on-Severn 29 G33
Westbury on Trym 19 D31
Westbury-sub-Mendip 19 G30
West Butterwick 52 B44
Westby 55 F29
West Byfleet 22 F46
West Cairncake 99 D34
West Caister 45 D60
West Calder 75 D25
West Camel 8 B31
West Charleton 5 F23
West Chelborough 8 D31
West Chevington 71 D38
West Chiltington 12 E46
West Chinnock 8 C30
West Chisenbury 20 F37
West Clandon 22 F46

West Cliffe 15 C59
Westcliff-on-Sea 24 C54
West Clyne 97 A24
Westcombe 9 A32
West Coker 8 C31
West Compton *Dor.* 8 E31
West Compton *Som.* 19 G31
Westcote 30 F37
Westcott *Bkh.* 31 G42
Westcott *Dev.* 7 E26
Westcott *Sry* 22 G47
Westcott Barton 30 F39
West Cross 17 F22
West Curry 4 A18
West Curthwaite 60 B29
West Dean *Wts.* 10 B38
Westdean 13 G51
West Dean *W.S.* 12 E44
West Deeping 42 E47
West Derby 48 C30
West Dereham 44 E52
West Ditchburn 71 A37
West Down 6 A21
Westdowns 4 B16
West Drayton *G.L.* 22 D46
West Drayton *Not.* 51 E42
West Dullater 81 G21
West Dunnet 103 A27
West Edington 71 E37
West Ella 59 G46
West End *Hum.* 59 C46
West End *N.Y.* 57 D37
West End *Sfk* 45 G60
West End *Nfk* 45 D60
West End *Str.* 75 F25
West End *Oxf.* 21 A40
West End *Avon* 19 D30
West End *Lan.* 55 C30
West End *Lcn.* 53 C49
West End *Kent* 25 E57
West End *Bfd.* 32 C45
West End *Sry* 22 E45
West End *Sry* 22 E46
West End *Ham.* 11 C40
West End Green 21 E42
Wester Aberchalder 88 B21
Wester Badentyre 99 D33
Wester Culbeuchly 98 C32
Westerdale *N.Y.* 63 F42
Westerdale *Hgh.* 103 C26
Wester Dechmont 75 C26
Westerfield *She.* 107 B39
Westerfield *Sfk* 35 D57
Wester Fintray 91 B34
Westergate 12 F45
Wester Gruinards 96 B20
Westerham 23 F50
Wester Lealty 96 D21
Westerleigh 19 D32
Wester Lonvine 96 D22
Wester Newburn 83 G30
Wester Ord 91 C34
Wester Parkgate 69 E26
Wester Quarff 107 D40
Wester Skeld 107 C38
Westerton *Tay.* 83 B32
Westerton *Grm.* 91 D33
Westerton *Drm* 62 C38
Westerton *Tay.* 81 F24
Westerwick 107 C38
West Farleigh 14 B53
West Farndon 31 C41
West Felton 38 C29
Westfield *Nfk* 44 E55
Westfield *Cum.* 60 D25
Westfield *Ltn* 75 C25
Westfield *E.S.* 14 F53
Westfield *Hgh.* 103 B26
Westfield Moor 14 F54
West Firle 13 F50
West Fleetham 71 A37
West Garforth 57 F39
Westgate *Drm* 61 C34
Westgate *Nfk* 44 A55
Westgate *Nor.* 71 F37
Westgate *Hum.* 51 B43
Westgate Hill 57 G38
Westgate on Sea 25 D58
West Ginge 21 C40
West Glen 73 C16
West Grafton 21 E38
West Green 22 F43
West Grimstead 10 B38
West Grinstead 12 D47
West Haddlesey 58 G41
West Haddon 31 A42
West Hagbourne 21 C41
West Hagley 40 G34
West Hall 70 G31
Westhall *Sfk* 45 G59
Westhall *Grm.* 91 A32
West Hallam 41 A40
West Halton 59 G45
Westham *Som.* 19 G29
Westham *Dor.* 9 G32
Westham *E.S.* 13 F52

West Ham 23 C50
Westhampnett 12 F44
West Handley 51 E39
West Hanney 21 B39
West Hanningfield 24 B53
West Hardwick 51 A40
West Harptree 19 F31
West Harting 11 B43
West Hatch 8 B28
Westhay 19 G30
Westhead 48 B30
West Heath *W.M.* 30 A36
West Heath *Ham.* 22 F44
West Helmsdale 103 G25
West Hendred 21 C40
West Heslerton 59 B45
Westhide 28 D31
Westhill *Grm.* 91 C34
West Hill *Avon* 19 E30
West Hill *Dev.* 7 F26
Westhill *Hgh.* 96 G23
West Hoathly 13 C49
West Holme 9 F34
Westhope *H.&W.* 28 C30
Westhope *Shr.* 38 G30
West Horndon 24 C52
Westhorpe *Sfk* 34 B56
Westhorpe *Lcn.* 42 B47
West Horrington 19 G31
West Horsley 22 F46
West Horton 77 G36
West Hougham 15 C58
Westhoughton 49 B32
Westhouse 56 B32
Westhouses 51 G39
West Humble 22 F47
West Hyde 22 B46
West Hythe 15 D57
West Ilsley 21 C40
Westing 106 B41
West Itchenor 12 F44
West Keal 53 F49
West Kennett 20 E37
West Kilbride 74 F18
West Kingsdown 23 E51
West Kington 20 D34
West Kirby 47 D27
West Knapton 58 B44
West Knighton 9 F33
West Knoyle 9 A34
West Kyloe 77 F36
Westlake 5 E21
West Lambrook 8 C30
West Langdon 15 C59
West Langwell 96 C34
West Lavington *Wts.* 20 F36
West Lavington *Wts.* 12 D44
West Layton 62 E37
West Leake 41 C41
Westleigh *G.M.* 49 B32
Westleigh *Dev.* 6 C20
Westleigh *Dev.* 7 D26
Westleton 35 B60
West Lexham 44 D54
Westley *Shr.* 38 E29
Westley *Sfk* 34 B54
Westley Heights 24 C52
Westley Waterless 33 C51
West Lilling 58 C42
West Lingo 83 G30
Westlington 22 A43
West Linton 75 E27
Westlinton 69 G29
West Littleton 20 D33
Westloch 76 E28
West Lockinge 21 C40
West Looe 4 E18
West Lulworth 9 F33
West Lutton 59 C45
West Lydford 8 A31
West Lyng 1 B29
West Lynn 44 D52
West Mains 77 F36
West Malling 23 F52
West Malvern 29 D33
West Marden 11 C43
West Markham 51 E43
West Marsh 53 A48
Westmarsh 25 E58
West Marton 56 D34
West Melton 51 B40
West Meon 11 B42
West Meon Hut 11 B42
West Mersea 34 G56
Westmeston 13 E49
Westmill 33 F49
West Milton 8 E30
West Minster 25 D55
West Molesey 22 F47
West Monkton 8 B28
West Moors 10 D36
West Mostard 61 G32
Westmuir 82 B29
West Muir 83 A31
West Ness 58 B42

Westness 104 D29
Westnewton *Cum.* 60 B27
West Newton *Hum.* 59 F48
West Newton *Nfk* 44 C53
Westnewton *Nor.* 77 G33
West Norwood 23 D49
West Ogwell 5 D24
Weston *Dor.* 9 G32
Weston *Hfs.* 33 E48
Weston *Brk.* 21 D40
Weston *Avon* 20 E33
Weston *N.Y.* 57 E37
Weston *Dev.* 7 G27
Weston *Nmp.* 31 D41
Weston *Shr.* 38 F31
Weston *Shr.* 38 C31
Weston *Che.* 49 G33
Weston *Che.* 48 D30
Weston *Grm.* 98 C30
Weston *Not.* 51 F43
Weston *Ham.* 11 B43
Weston *Lcn.* 43 C48
Weston *Stf.* 40 C35
Weston Beggard 28 D31
Westonbirt 20 C34
Weston by Welland 42 F43
Weston Colville 33 C51
Weston Corbett 21 G42
Weston Coyney 40 A35
Weston Favell 31 B43
Weston Green *Cbs.* 33 C52
Weston Green *Nfk* 45 D57
Weston Green *Sry* 22 E47
Weston Heath 39 D33
Weston Hills 43 C48
Westoning 32 E46
Weston-in-Gordano 19 D30
Weston Jones 39 C33
Weston Longville 45 D57
Weston Lullingfields 38 C30
Weston-on-the-Green 31 G41
Weston-on-Trent 41 C39
Weston Patrick 21 G42
Weston Point 48 D30
Weston Rhyn 38 B28
Weston Subedge 30 D36
Weston-super-Mare 19 E28
Weston Turville 22 A43
Weston-under-Lizard 40 D34
Weston under Penyard 29 F32
Weston under Wetherley
 30 A39
Weston Underwood *Bkh.* 32 C44
Weston Underwood *Dby.* 40 A38
Westonzoyland 8 A29
West Orchard 9 C34
West Overton 20 E37
Westow 58 C43
West Park *Grm.* 91 D33
West Park *Mer.* 48 C30
West Parley 10 E36
West Peckham 23 F52
West Pennard 8 A31
West Pentire 2 B13
West Perry 32 B47
West Porlock 7 A24
Westport *Som.* 8 C29
Westport *Str.* 66 A12
West Putford 6 D19
West Quantoxhead 7 A27
West Rainton 62 B39
West Rasen 52 C46
Westray Airport 104 A30
West Raynham 44 C54
Westrigg 75 D25
West Rounton 62 F39
West Row 33 A52
West Rudham 44 C54
West Runton 45 A57
Westruther 76 F32
Westry 43 F49
West Saltoun 76 D30
West Sandwick 106 D40
West Scrafton 57 A36
Westside 91 D34
West Somerton 45 D60
West Stafford 9 F33
West Stockwith 51 C43
West Stoke 12 F44
West Stonesdale 61 F34
West Stoughton 19 G29
West Stour 9 B33
West Stourmouth 25 E58
West Stow 34 A54
West Stowell 20 E37
West Stratton 21 G41
West Street 8 B55
West Tanfield 57 B38
West Taphouse 4 D17
West Tarbert 73 D14
West Tarring 12 F47
West Thorney 11 D43
West Thurrock 23 D51
West Tilbury 24 D52
West Tisted 11 B42
West Tofts *Nfk* 44 F54

West Tofts *Tay.* 82 D26
West Torrington 52 D47
West Town *Avon* 19 E30
West Town *Ham.* 11 E43
West Tytherley 10 A38
West Tytherton 20 D35
West Walton 43 D50
West Walton Highway 43 D50
Westward 60 B28
Westward Ho! 6 C19
Westwell *Oxf.* 30 G38
Westwell *Kent* 14 C55
Westwell Leacon 14 C55
West Wellow 10 B38
West Wemyss 76 A29
West Wick 19 E29
Westwick *Nfk* 45 C58
Westwick *Drm* 62 E36
Westwick *Cbs.* 33 B50
West Wickham *Cbs.* 33 D51
West Wickham *G.L.* 23 E49
West Williamston 16 D16
West Winch 44 D52
West Winterslow 10 A38
West Wittering 11 E43
West Witton 57 A36
Westwood *Wts.* 20 F34
Westwood *Dev.* 7 F26
West Woodburn 70 E34
West Woodhay 21 E39
Westwood Heath 30 A38
West Woodlands 20 G33
Westwoodside 51 C43
West Worldham 11 A43
West Worlington 7 D23
West Worthing 12 F47
West Wratting 33 C51
West Wycombe 22 B44
West Yell 106 D40
Wetheral 60 A30
Wetherby 57 E40
Wether Cote Fm 63 G42
Wetherden 34 B56
Wetheringsett 35 B57
Wethersfield 33 E52
Wethersta 107 A39
Wetherup Street 35 B57
Wetley Rocks 40 A35
Wettenhall 48 F31
Wettenhall Green 49 G32
Wetton 50 G36
Wetwang 59 D45
Wetwood 39 B33
Wexcombe 21 F38
Weybourne 45 A57
Weybread 45 G58
Weybridge 22 E46
Weycroft 8 D29
Weydale 103 B27
Weyhill 21 G39
Weymouth 9 G32
Whaddon *Cbs.* 33 D49
Whaddon *Bkh.* 31 E44
Whaddon *Glo.* 29 G34
Whaddon *Wts.* 10 B37
Whaddon Gap 33 D49
Whale 61 D31
Whaley 51 E40
Whaley Bridge 50 D36
Whaligoe 103 D29
Whalley 56 F33
Whalton 71 E37
Wham 56 C33
Whaplode 43 C49
Whaplode Drove 43 D49
Whaplode St Catherine 43 D49
Wharfe 55 C33
Wharles 55 F30
Wharncliffe Side 50 C38
Wharram le Street 58 C44
Wharram Percy 58 C44
Wharton *Che.* 49 F32
Wharton *H.&W.* 28 C30
Whashton 62 F37
Whatcote 30 D38
Whatfield 34 D56
Whatley 20 G33
Whatlington 14 F53
Whatstandwell 50 G38
Whatton 42 B43
Whauphill 64 F19
Whaw 62 F35
Wheatacre 45 F60
Wheatenhurst 20 A33
Wheathampstead 32 G47
Wheathill 39 G32
Wheatley *Ham.* 22 G43
Wheatley *Oxf.* 21 A41
Wheatley Hill 62 C39
Wheatley Lane 56 F34
Wheaton Aston 40 D34
Wheddon Cross 7 B25
Wheedlemont 90 A30
Wheelerstreet 22 G45
Wheelock 49 G33
Wheelton 56 G32

Wheen 90 F29
Wheldrake 58 E42
Whelford 20 B37
Whelpley Hill 22 A46
Whelpo 60 B28
Whenby 58 C42
Whepstead 34 C54
Wherstead 35 D57
Wherwell 21 G39
Wheston 50 E37
Whetley Cross 8 D30
Whetsted 23 G52
Whetstone 41 F41
Whicham 54 A27
Whichford 30 E38
Whickham 71 G37
Whiddon Down 6 F22
Whifflet 75 D23
Whiggstreet 83 C30
Whilton 31 B42
Whim 76 E28
Whimple 7 F26
Whimpwell Green 45 C59
Whinburgh 44 E56
Whin Lane End 55 E29
Whinnyfold 99 F36
Whippingham 11 E40
Whipsnade 32 G45
Whipton 7 F25
Whisby 52 F44
Whissendine 42 D43
Whissonsett 44 C54
Whistley Green 22 D43
Whiston *S.Y.* 51 C40
Whiston *Mer.* 48 C30
Whiston *Nmp.* 32 B44
Whiston *Stf.* 40 D34
Whiston *Stf.* 40 A36
Whitbeck 54 A27
Whitbourne 29 C32
Whitburn *Ltn* 75 D25
Whitburn *T.&W.* 71 G39
Whitby *Che.* 48 E29
Whitby *N.Y.* 63 E44
Whitchurch *Oxf.* 21 D42
Whitchurch *Shr.* 38 A31
Whitchurch *Dev.* 4 C20
Whitchurch *Bkh.* 31 F43
Whitchurch *Avon* 19 E31
Whitchurch *Dyf.* 16 B14
Whitchurch *Ham.* 21 G40
Whitchurch *S.G.* 18 D27
Whitchurch Canonicorum 8 E29
Whitchurch Hill 21 D42
Whitcombe 9 F32
Whitcott Keysett 38 G28
Whiteacen 98 E28
Whitebog 99 D35
Whitebridge *Hgh.* 103 A28
Whitebridge *Hgh.* 88 C20
Whitebrook 19 A31
Whiteburn 76 F31
Whitecairn 64 E17
Whitecairns 91 B34
Whitecastle 75 F25
White Chapel 55 E31
Whitechurch 16 A17
White Colne 34 F54
White Coppice 49 A32
Whitecraig 76 C29
Whitecroft 19 A32
Whitecrook 64 E17
White Cross *Dev.* 7 F26
White Cross *Cnw.* 3 B14
White Cross *H.&W.* 28 D30
Whitecross 2 E11
White End 29 F33
Whiteface 96 C22
Whitefield *Tay.* 82 D27
Whitefield *Grm.* 91 A33
Whitefield *Hgh.* 88 B21
Whitefield *Hgh.* 103 C28
Whitefield *G.M.* 49 B33
Whiteford 91 A32
Whitegate 49 F32
Whitehall 104 D32
Whitehaven 60 E25
Whitehill *Str.* 74 E18
Whitehill *Kent* 14 B55
Whitehill *Ham.* 11 A43
Whitehills 98 C32
Whitehouse *Str.* 73 D14
Whitehouse *Grm.* 91 B32
Whitekirk 76 B31
White Lackington 9 E33
Whitelackington 8 C29
White Ladies Aston 29 C35
Whitelaw 77 E34
Whiteleen 103 D29
Whitelees 74 G19
Whiteley 11 D41
Whiteley Bank 11 F41
Whiteleys 64 E16
Whiteley Village 22 E46
Whitemans Green 13 D49

28 D28

White Mill 17 B20
Whitemire 97 F25
White Moor 41 A39
White Notley 34 G53
Whiteparish 10 B38
White Pit 53 E49
Whiterashes 91 A34
White Roding 33 G51
Whiterow 103 D29
Whiteshill 20 A34
Whiteside *Ltn* 75 D25
Whiteside *Nor.* 70 G33
Whitesmith 13 E50
Whitestaunton 8 C28
Whitestone *Dev.* 7 F24
Whitestone *Str.* 73 G13
Whitestone *Grm.* 91 D32
Whitestripe 99 D35
White Waltham 22 D44
Whiteway 29 G34
Whitewell *Lan.* 56 E32
Whitewell *Grm.* 99 C35
Whiteworks 5 C22
Whitewreath 98 D28
Whitfield *Kent* 15 C58
Whitfield *Nor.* 61 A33
Whitfield *Avon* 19 B32
Whitfield *Nmp.* 31 E41
Whitfield *H.&W.* 28 E30
Whitford *Dev.* 8 E28
Whitford *Clw.* 47 E27
Whitgift 58 G44
Whitgreave 40 C34
Whithorn 64 F20
Whiting Bay 66 A16
Whitkirk 57 F39
Whitlam 91 A34
Whitland 16 C17
Whitland Abbey 16 C17
Whitletts 67 A19
Whitley *N.Y.* 58 G41
Whitley *Brk.* 21 E42
Whitley Bay 71 F39
Whitley Chapel 61 A35
Whitley Lower 50 A38
Whitley Row 23 F50
Whitlock's End 30 A36
Whitminster 20 A33
Whitmore *Stf.* 39 A33
Whitmore *Dor.* 10 D36
Whitnage 7 D26
Whitnash 30 B39
Whitney 28 D28
Whitrigg *Cum.* 60 C28
Whitrigg *Cum.* 60 A28
Whitsbury 10 C37
Whitsome 77 E34
Whitson 19 C29
Whitstable 25 E56
Whitstone 4 A18
Whittingham 71 B36
Whittingslow 38 G29
Whittington *Shr.* 38 B29
Whittington *Dby.* 51 E39
Whittington *Glo.* 29 F36
Whittington *Nfk* 44 F52
Whittington *H.&W.* 29 C34
Whittington *Stf.* 40 G34
Whittington *Stf.* 40 E37
Whittington *Lan.* 55 B31
Whittlebury 31 D42
Whittle-le-Woods 55 G31
Whittlesey 43 F48
Whittlesford 33 D50
Whitton *Cle.* 62 D39
Whitton *Hum.* 59 G45
Whitton *Nor.* 71 C36
Whitton *Pow.* 28 B28
Whitton *Shr.* 28 A31
Whitton *Sfk* 35 D57
Whittonditch 21 D38
Whittonstall 62 A36
Whitway 21 F40
Whitwell *I.o.W.* 11 G41
Whitwell *Lei.* 42 E45
Whitwell *Nfk* 45 C57
Whitwell *N.Y.* 62 G38
Whitwell *Dby.* 51 E41
Whitwell *Hfs.* 32 F47
Whitwell-on-the-Hill 58 C42
Whitwick 41 D40
Whitwood 57 G39
Whitworth 49 A34
Whixall 38 B30
Whixley 57 D40
Whorlton *N.Y.* 62 F40
Whorlton *Drm* 62 E37
Whygate 70 F33
Whyle 28 B31
Whyteleafe 23 F49
Wibdon 19 B31
Wibsey 57 F37
Wibtoft 41 G40
Wichenford 29 B33
Wichling 14 B55
Wick *W.S.* 12 F46

Wick *Dor.* 10 E37
Wick *Wts.* 10 B37
Wick *H.&W.* 29 D35
Wick *Avon* 19 D32
Wick *M.G.* 18 D25
Wick *Hgh.* 103 C29
Wicken *Cbs.* 33 A51
Wicken *Nmp.* 31 E43
Wicken Bonhunt 33 E50
Wickenby 52 D46
Wickerslack 61 E31
Wickersley 51 C40
Wickford 24 B53
Wickham *Brk.* 21 D39
Wickham *Ham.* 11 C41
Wickham Bishops 34 G54
Wickhambreaux 15 B57
Wickhambrook 34 C53
Wickhamford 20 D36
Wickham Heath 21 E39
Wickham Market 35 C58
Wickhampton 45 E60
Wickham Skeith 34 B56
Wickham St Paul 34 E54
Wickham Street *Sfk* 34 C53
Wickham Street *Sfk* 34 A56
Wick Hill *Brk.* 22 E44
Wick Hill *Kent* 14 C54
Wicklewood 44 E56
Wickmere 45 B57
Wick St Lawrence 19 E29
Wickwar 20 C33
Widdington 33 E51
Widdop 56 F35
Widdrington 71 D38
Widecombe in the Moor 5 C22
Widegates 4 E18
Widemouth Bay 6 E18
Wide Open 71 F38
Widewall 105 B30
Widford *Hfs.* 33 G50
Widford *Esx* 24 A52
Widmerpool 41 C42
Widnes 48 D31
Widworthy 7 F27
Wigan 48 B31
Wiggaton 7 F27
Wiggenhall St Germans 44 D52
Wiggenhall St Mary Magdalen
   43 D51
Wiggenhall St Mary the Virgin
   43 D51
Wiggenhall St Peter 44 D52
Wiggington 58 D41
Wigginton *Hfs.* 32 G45
Wigginton *Oxf.* 30 E39
Wigginton *Stf.* 40 E37
Wigglesworth 56 D34
Wiggonby 60 A28
Wiggonholt 12 E46
Wighill 57 E40
Wighton 44 B55
Wightwizzle 50 C38
Wigmore *H.&W.* 28 B29
Wigmore *Kent* 24 E54
Wigsley 52 E44
Wigsthorpe 42 G46
Wigston 41 F41
Wigston Parva 41 F40
Wigthorpe 51 D41
Wigtoft 43 B48
Wigton 60 B28
Wigtown 64 E20
Wilbarston 42 G43
Wilberfoss 58 D43
Wilburton 33 A50
Wilby *Nmp.* 32 B44
Wilby *Nfk* 44 F56
Wilby *Sfk* 35 A58
Wilcot 20 E37
Wilcott 38 D29
Wilcrick 19 C29
Wildboarclough 49 F35
Wilden *H.&W.* 29 A34
Wilden *Bfd.* 32 C46
Wildhern 21 F39
Wildhill 23 A48
Wildsworth 51 C43
Wilford 41 B41
Wilkesley 38 A31
Wilkhaven 97 C25
Wilkieston 75 D26
Willand 7 D26
Willaston *Che.* 49 G32
Willaston *Che.* 48 E29
Willen 32 D44
Willenhall *W.M.* 30 A39
Willenhall *W.M.* 40 F35
Willerby 59 G46
Willersey 30 D36
Willersley
Willesborough 14 C55
Willesborough Lees 14 C55
Willesden 23 C48
Willesley 20 C34
Willett 7 B26

Willey *War.* 41 G40
Willey *Shr.* 39 F32
Williamscot 31 D40
Williamthorpe 51 F39
Willian 33 E48
Willimontswick 70 G33
Willingale 23 A51
Willingdon 13 F51
Willingham *Cbs.* 33 A49
Willingham *Lcn.* 52 D44
Willington *War.* 30 E38
Willington *T.&W.* 71 G38
Willington *Drm* 62 C37
Willington *Bfd.* 32 D46
Willington *Dby.* 40 C38
Willington Corner 48 F31
Willisham 34 C56
Willitoft 58 F43
Williton 7 A26
Willoughby *Lcn.* 53 E50
Willoughby *War.* 31 B40
Willoughby on the Wolds
   41 C42
Willoughby Waterleys 41 F41
Willoughton 52 C45
Willows Green 34 G53
Willsworthy 6 G21
Wilmcote 30 C37
Wilmington *Dev.* 8 D28
Wilmington *W.S.* 13 F51
Wilmington *Kent* 23 D51
Wilmslow 49 D34
Wilnecote 40 E37
Wilpshire 56 F32
Wilsden 57 F36
Wilsford *Wts.* 20 G37
Wilsford *Wts.* 20 F36
Wilsford *Lcn.* 42 A45
Wilsill 57 C37
Wilsley Green 14 D53
Wilson 41 C39
Wilstead 30 C46
Wilsthorpe 42 D46
Wilstone 32 G44
Wilton *Bor.* 69 B30
Wilton *Som.* 8 B28
Wilton *Cum.* 60 E26
Wilton *N.Y.* 58 A44
Wilton *Cle.* 63 D41
Wilton *Wts.* 21 E38
Wilton *Wts.* 10 A36
Wimbish 33 E51
Wimbish Green 33 E52
Wimblebury 40 D35
Wimbledon 23 D48
Wimblington 43 F49
Wimborne Minster 9 E35
Wimborne St Giles 10 C36
Wimbotsham 44 E52
Wimpstone 30 D37
Wincanton 9 B32
Wincham 49 E32
Winchburgh 75 C26
Winchcombe 29 F35
Winchelsea 14 F55
Winchelsea Beach 14 F55
Winchester 10 B39
Winchet Hill 14 C53
Winchfield 22 F43
Winchmore Hill *G.L.* 23 B48
Winchmore Hill *Bkh.* 22 B45
Wincle 49 F35
Wincobank 51 C39
Windermere 60 G30
Winderton 30 D39
Windhill 96 G21
Windlesham 22 E45
Windley 40 A38
Windley Meadows 41 A39
Windmill Hill *Som.* 8 C29
Windmill Hill *E.S.* 13 E52
Windrush 30 G37
Windsor 22 D45
Windygates 82 G29
Windy Yet 74 E20
Wineham 13 D48
Winestead 59 G49
Winewall 56 F35
Winfarthing 44 G56
Winford 19 E31
Winforton 28 D28
Winfrith Newburgh 9 F33
Wing *Bkh.* 32 F44
Wing *Lei.* 42 E44
Wingate 62 C39
Wingates *Nor.* 71 D36
Wingates *G.M.* 49 B32
Wingerworth 51 F39
Wingfield *Sfk* 35 A58
Wingfield *Bfd.* 32 F45
Wingfield *Wts.* 20 F34
Wingham 15 B58
Wingmore 15 C57
Wingrave 32 G44
Winkburn 51 G42
Winkfield 22 D44

Winkfield Row 22 D44
Winkhill 50 G36
Winksley 57 B38
Winksley Banks 57 B38
Winkton 10 E37
Winlaton 71 G37
Winlaton Mill 71 G37
Winless 103 C28
Winmarleigh 55 E30
Winnards Perch 3 B15
Winnersh 22 D43
Winscombe 19 F29
Winsford *Som.* 7 B24
Winsford *Che.* 49 F32
Winsham 8 D29
Winshill 40 C38
Winskill 61 C31
Winslade 21 G42
Winsley 20 E33
Winslow 31 F43
Winson 20 A36
Winsor 10 C39
Winster *Cum.* 60 G30
Winster *Dby.* 50 F38
Winston *Sfk* 35 B57
Winston *Drm* 62 E37
Winstone 20 A35
Winswell 6 D20
Winterborne Came 9 F32
Winterborne Clenston 9 D34
Winterborne Houghton 9 D34
Winterborne Kingston 9 E34
Winterborne Monkton 9 F32
Winterborne Stickland 9 D34
Winterborne Whitechurch
   9 E34
Winterborne Zelston 9 E35
Winterbourne *Avon* 19 C32
Winterbourne *Brk.* 21 D40
Winterbourne Abbas 9 E32
Winterbourne Bassett 20 D36
Winterbourne Dauntsey
   10 A37
Winterbourne Earls 10 A37
Winterbourne Gunner 10 A37
Winterbourne Monkton 20 D37
Winterbourne Steepleton 9 F32
Winterbourne Stoke 20 G36
Winterburn 56 D35
Wintercleugh 68 B25
Winteringham 59 G45
Winterley 49 G33
Wintersett 51 A39
Wintershill 11 C40
Winterslow 10 A38
Winterton 52 A45
Winterton-on-Sea 45 D60
Winthorpe *Lcn.* 53 F51
Winthorpe *Not.* 52 G44
Winton *Cum.* 61 E33
Winton *Dor.* 10 E36
Wintringham 58 B44
Winwick *Che.* 49 C32
Winwick *Nmp.* 31 A42
Winwick *Cbs.* 42 G46
Wirksworth 50 G38
Wirswall 38 A31
Wisbech 43 E50
Wisbech St Mary 43 E50
Wisborough Green 12 D46
Wiseton 51 D42
Wishaw *Str.* 75 E23
Wishaw *War.* 40 F37
Wisley 22 F46
Wispington 52 E47
Wissett 35 A59
Wissington 34 E55
Wistanstow 38 G30
Wistanswick 39 C32
Wistaston 49 G32
Wiston *Str.* 75 G25
Wiston *Dyf.* 16 C16
Wiston *W.S.* 12 E47
Wistow *N.Y.* 58 F41
Wistow *Cbs.* 43 G48
Wiswell 56 F33
Witcham 33 A50
Witchampton 9 D35
Witchburn 66 B12
Witchford 33 A50
Witcombe 8 B30
Witham 34 G53
Witham Friary 20 G33
Witham on the Hill 42 D46
Withcote 42 E43
Witherenden Hill 13 D52
Witherhurst 13 D52
Witheridge 7 D24
Witherley 41 F39
Withern 53 D50
Withernsea 59 G49
Withernwick 59 F46
Withersdale Street 45 G58
Withersfield 33 D52
Witherslack 55 A30

Witherslack Hall 55 A30
Withiel 3 B15
Withiel Florey 7 B25
Withington *G.M.* 49 C34
Withington *Shr.* 38 D31
Withington *H.&W.* 28 D31
Withington *Glo.* 30 G36
Withington *Stf.* 40 B36
Withington Green 49 E34
Withleigh 7 D24
Withnell 56 G32
Withybrook 41 G40
Withycombe 7 A25
Withycombe Raleigh 7 G26
Withyham 13 C50
Withypool 7 B24
Witley 12 C45
Witnesham 35 C57
Witney 90 F31
Wittering 42 E46
Wittersham 14 E54
Witton 90 F31
Witton Bridge 45 B59
Witton Gilbert 62 B38
Witton-le-Wear 62 C37
Witton Park 62 C37
Wiveliscombe 7 C26
Wivelsfield 13 D49
Wivelsfield Green 13 E49
Wivenhoe 34 F56
Wiveton 44 A56
Wix 35 F57
Wixford 30 C36
Wixoe 33 D52
Woburn 32 E45
Woburn Sands 32 E45
Wokefield Park 21 E42
Woking 22 F46
Wokingham 22 E44
Wolborough 5 D24
Woldingham 23 F49
Wold Newton 53 C48
Wolfelee 70 C31
Wolferlow 29 B32
Wolferton 44 C52
Wolfhampcote 31 B40
Wolfhill 82 D27
Wolfpits 28 C27
Wolf's Castle 16 B15
Wolfsdale 16 B15
Woll 69 A30
Wollaston *Nmp.* 32 B44
Wollaston *Shr.* 38 D29
Wollaston *Stf.* 40 G34
Wollerton 38 C31
Wolsingham 62 C36
Wolstenholme 49 A34
Wolston 30 A39
Wolvercote 21 A40
Wolverhampton 40 F34
Wolverley *Shr.* 38 B30
Wolverley *H.&W.* 29 A34
Wolverton *Bkh.* 31 D44
Wolverton *War.* 30 B38
Wolverton *Ham.* 21 F41
Wolvesnewton 19 B30
Wolvey 41 G40
Wolviston 62 D40
Wombleton 58 A42
Wombourne 40 F34
Wombwell 51 B40
Womenswold 15 B57
Womersley 51 A41
Wonastow 28 D30
Wonersh 22 G46
Wonson 6 G22
Wonston 11 A40
Wooburn 22 C44
Wooburn Green 22 C45
Woodale 57 B36
Woodbastwick 45 D59
Woodbeck 51 E43
Woodbine 16 C15
Woodborough *Wts.* 20 E36
Woodborough *Not.* 41 A42
Woodbridge 35 D58
Wood Burcote 31 D42
Woodbury 7 G26
Woodbury Salterton 7 G26
Woodchester 20 A34
Woodchurch *Mer.* 48 D28
Woodchurch *Kent* 14 D55
Woodcote *Oxf.* 21 C42
Woodcote *Shr.* 39 D33
Woodcott 21 F40
Woodcroft 19 B31
Woodcutts 9 C35
Wood Dalling 44 C56
Woodditton 33 C52
Woodeaton 31 G41
Wood End *Hfs.* 33 F49
Wood End *War.* 30 A36
Woodend *Nmp.* 31 D41
Wood End *Bfd.* 32 D45
Woodend *Hgh.* 88 B23
Woodend *Grm.* 91 B32

Woodend *Tay.* 81 C23	Woodyates 9 C35	Wormit 82 E29	Wyboston 32 C47	Y Bryn 37 C24
Woodend *W.S.* 12 F44	Woofferton 28 B30	Wormleighton 31 C40	Wybunbury 39 A32	Y Drenewydd (Newtown) 38 F27
Woodend *Cum.* 60 G27	Wookey 19 G30	Wormley *Hfs.* 23 A49	Wychbold 29 B35	Yeading 22 C46
Wood End *War.* 40 F38	Wookey Hole 19 G31	Wormley *Sry* 12 C45	Wych Cross 13 C50	Yeadon 57 E37
Woodend *Hgh.* 79 A13	Wool 9 F34	Wormshill 14 B54	Wyck 11 A43	Yealand Conyers 55 B30
Wood Enderby 53 F48	Woolacombe 6 A20	Wormsley 28 D30	Wyck Rissington 30 F37	Yealand Redmayne 55 B30
Woodfalls 10 B37	Woolaston 19 B31	Worplesdon 22 F45	Wycliffe 62 E36	Yealmpton 5 E21
Woodford *G.L.* 23 B49	Woolavington 19 G29	Worrall 50 C38	Wycoller 56 F35	Yearby 63 D41
Woodford *Glo.* 19 B32	Woolbeding 12 D44	Worsbrough 51 B39	Wycomb 42 C43	Yearsley 58 B41
Woodford *Nmp.* 32 A45	Wooler 70 A35	Worsley 49 B33	Wycombe Marsh 22 B44	Yeaton 38 D30
Woodford *G.M.* 40 D34	Woolfardisworthy *Dev.* 7 E23	Worstead 45 C59	Wyddial 33 E49	Yeaveley 40 A37
Woodford *Cnw.* 6 D18	Woolfardisworthy *Dev.* 6 C18	Worsted Lodge 33 C51	Wye 15 C56	Yedingham 58 B44
Woodford Bridge 23 B50	Woolfords Cottages 75 E25	Worsthorne 56 F34	Wyke *W.Y.* 57 G37	Yelford 21 A39
Woodford Green 23 B49	Woolhampton 21 E41	Worston 56 E33	Wyke *Dor.* 9 B33	Yelland *Dev.* 6 B20
Woodford Halse 31 C41	Woolhope 28 E31	Worswell 5 F21	Wyke *Shr.* 39 E32	Yelland *Dev.* 6 F21
Woodgate *H.&W.* 29 B35	Woollage Green 15 C58	Worth *Kent* 15 B59	Wyke Regis 9 G32	Yelling 33 B48
Woodgate *Nfk* 44 D56	Woolland 9 D33	Worth *W.S.* 13 C48	Wykey 38 C29	Yelvertoft 31 A41
Woodgate *W.M.* 40 G35	Woollard 19 E32	Wortham 34 A56	Wylam 71 G36	Yelverton *Nfk* 45 E58
Woodgate *W.S.* 12 F45	Woollaton 6 D20	Worthen 38 E29	Wylde Green 40 F37	Yelverton *Dev.* 5 D21
Wood Green 23 B48	Woolley *Cbs.* 32 A47	Worthenbury 38 A29	Wyllie 18 B27	Yenston 9 B32
Woodgreen 10 C37	Woolley *Avon* 20 E33	Worthing *Nfk* 44 D56	Wylye 9 A35	Yeoford 7 F23
Woodhall 62 G35	Woolley *W.Y.* 51 A39	Worthing *W.S.* 12 F47	Wymering 11 D42	Yeolmbridge 4 B18
Woodhall Spa 52 F47	Woolmere Green 29 B35	Worthington 41 C39	Wymeswold 41 C41	Yeomadon 6 E18
Woodham *Sry* 22 E46	Woolmer Green 33 G48	Worth Matravers 9 G35	Wymington 32 B45	Yeo Vale 6 C20
Woodham *Drm* 62 D38	Woolmersdon 8 A28	Wortley *Glo.* 20 B33	Wymondham *Nfk* 45 E57	Yeovil 8 C31
Woodham Ferrers 24 B53	Woolpit 34 B55	Wortley *S.Y.* 50 C38	Wymondham *Lei.* 42 D44	Yeovil Marsh 8 C31
Woodham Mortimer 24 A54	Woolscott 31 B40	Worton 20 F35	Wyndham 18 B25	Yeovilton 8 B31
Woodham Walter 24 A53	Woolstaston 38 F30	Wortwell 45 G58	Wynford Eagle 8 E31	Yerbeston 16 D16
Woodhaven 82 E29	Woolsthorpe *Lcn.* 42 C44	Wotherton 38 E28	Wynnstay 38 A29	Yesnaby 104 E28
Wood Hayes 40 E35	Woolsthorpe *Lcn.* 42 B44	Wotton 22 G47	Wyre Piddle 29 D35	Yetlington 70 C35
Woodhead 99 F33	Woolston *Ham.* 11 C40	Wotton-under-Edge 20 B33	Wyresdale Tower 56 D32	Yetminster 8 C31
Woodhill 39 G33	Woolston *Shr.* 38 G30	Wotton Underwood 31 G42	Wysall 41 C41	Yettington 7 G26
Woodhorn 71 E38	Woolston *Shr.* 38 C29	Woughton on the Green 32 E44	Wyson 28 B30	Yetts o'Muckhart 82 G25
Woodhouse *Lei.* 41 D41	Woolston *Che.* 49 D32	Wouldham 24 E53	Wythall 30 A36	Y Fan 37 G25
Woodhouse *Cum.* 55 A31	Woolstone 21 C38	Wrabness 35 E57	Wytham 21 A40	Y Felinheli 46 F20
Woodhouse *S.Y.* 51 D39	Woolston Green 5 D23	Wrae 99 D33	Wythburn 60 E29	Y Ffor 36 B19
Woodhouse Eaves 41 D41	Woolton 48 D30	Wrafton 6 B20	Wyton 33 A48	Yielden 32 B46
Woodhouses 40 D37	Woolton Hill 21 E40	Wragby 52 E47	Wyverstone 34 B56	Yiewsley 22 D46
Woodhuish 5 E25	Woolverstone 35 E57	Wragholme 53 C49	Wyverstone Street 34 B56	Ynysboeth 18 B26
Woodhurst 33 A48	Woolverton 20 F33	Wramplingham 45 E57	Wyville 42 C44	Ynysddu 18 B27
Woodingdean 13 F49	Woolwich 23 D50	Wrangham 98 F32	Wyvis Lodge 96 D20	Ynyshir 18 B26
Woodland *Dev.* 5 D23	Woonton 28 C29	Wrangle 53 G50		Ynyslas 36 F21
Woodland *Drm* 62 D36	Wooperton 71 A36	Wrangle Lowgate 53 G50	**Y**	Ynysmendwy 18 A23
Woodlands *Shr.* 39 G32	Woore 39 A33	Wrangway 7 D27		Ynystawe 17 D22
Woodlands *Ham.* 10 C38	Wootton *Bfd.* 32 D45	Wrantage 8 B28	Yaddlethorpe 52 B44	Ynysybwl 18 B26
Woodlands *Dor.* 10 D36	Wootton *Nmp.* 31 C43	Wrawby 52 B46	Yafford 11 F40	Yockenthwaite 56 B34
Woodlands Park 22 D44	Wootton *Oxf.* 31 G40	Wraxall *Avon* 19 D30	Yafforth 62 G39	Yockleton 38 D18
Woodleigh 5 F23	Wootton *Oxf.* 21 A40	Wraxall *Som.* 8 A31	Yalding 14 C53	Yokefleet 58 G43
Woodlesford 57 G39	Wootton *Kent* 15 C57	Wray 55 C31	Yanworth 30 G36	Yoker 74 D20
Woodley 22 D43	Wootton *Stf.* 40 A37	Wray Castle 60 F29	Yapham 58 D43	Yonder Bognie 98 E31
Woodmancote *W.S.* 13 E48	Wootton *Shr.* 28 A30	Wraysbury 22 D46	Yapton 12 F45	York 58 D41
Woodmancote *W.S.* 11 D43	Wootton *Ham.* 10 E38	Wrea Green 55 F29	Yarburgh 53 C49	Yorkletts 25 E56
Wood-mancote 20 A35	Wootton *Stf.* 40 C34	Wreay *Cum.* 60 B30	Yarcombe 8 D28	Yorkley 19 A32
Woodmancote *Glo.* 29 F35	Wootton *Hum.* 52 A46	Wreay *Cum.* 60 D30	Yardley 40 G37	Yorton 38 C30
Woodmancott 21 G41	Wootton Bassett 20 C36	Wrecclesham 22 G43	Yardley Gobion 31 D43	Youldon 6 E18
Woodmansey 59 F46	Wootton Bridge 11 E41	Wrekenton 62 A38	Yardley Hastings 32 C44	Youldonmoor Cross 6 E19
Woodmansterne 23 F48	Wootton Common 11 E41	Wrelton 58 A43	Yardro 28 C28	Youlgreave 50 F37
Woodminton 10 B36	Wootton Courtenay 7 A25	Wrenbury 38 A31	Yarkhill 28 D31	Youlstone 6 D18
Woodmoor 38 E28	Wootton Fitzpaine 8 E29	Wreningham 45 F57	Yarlet 40 C34	Youlthorpe 58 D43
Woodnesborough 15 B58	Wootton Green 32 D45	Wrentham 45 G60	Yarley 19 G30	Youlton 57 C40
Woodnewton 42 F46	Wootton Rivers 20 E37	Wrenthorpe 57 G39	Yarlington 9 B32	Young's End 34 G53
Wood Norton 44 C56	Wootton St Lawrence 21 F41	Wrentnall 38 E29	Yarm 52 F45	Yoxall 40 D37
Woodplumpton 55 F30	Wootton Wawen 30 B37	Wressle 58 F43	Yarmouth 10 F39	Yoxford 35 B59
Woodrising 44 E55	Worcester 29 C34	Wrestlingworth 33 D48	Yarnacott 6 B22	Ysbyty Cynfyn 27 A23
Woodseaves *Stf.* 39 C33	Worcester Park 23 E48	Wretham 44 G54	Yarnbrook 20 F34	Ysbyty Ifan 37 A24
Woodseaves *Shr.* 39 B32	Wordsley 40 G34	Wretton 44 F52	Yarnfield 40 B34	Ysbyty Ystwyth 27 A23
Woodsend 21 D38	Wordwell 34 A54	Wrexham 38 A29	Yarnscombe 6 C21	Ysceifiog 47 E27
Woodsetts 51 D41	Worfield 39 F33	Wribbenhall 29 A33	Yarnton 31 G40	Ysgubor-y-coed 37 F22
Woodsford 9 E33	Work 104 E30	Wrightington Bar 48 A31	Yarpole 28 B30	Ystalyfera 18 A23
Woodside *Fife* 82 G28	Workington 60 D25	Wrightpark 74 A22	Yarrow 46 A29	Ystrad 18 B25
Woodside *Grm.* 91 C35	Worksop 51 E41	Wrinehill 39 A33	Yarrow Feus 69 A29	Ystrad Aeron 26 C20
Woodside *Tay.* 82 D27	Worlaby 52 A46	Wrington 19 E30	Yarrowford 69 A29	Ystradfellte 27 G25
Woodside *Str.* 74 E19	Worlds End 11 C42	Writhlington 19 F32	Yarsop 28 D29	Ystradffin 27 D23
Woodside *Shr.* 38 G29	World's End 21 D40	Writtle 24 A52	Yarwell 42 F46	Ystradgynlais 27 G23
Woodside *D.&G.* 69 F26	Worle 19 E29	Wrockwardine 38 D31	Yate 19 C32	Ystrad Meurig 27 B22
Woodside *W.M.* 40 G34	Worleston 49 C33	Wroot 51 B43	Yateley 22 E43	Ystrad Mynach 18 B27
Woodside *Hfs.* 23 A48	Worlingham 45 F60	Wrotham 23 F51	Yatesbury 20 D36	Ystradowen *S.G.* 18 D26
Woodside *Brk.* 22 D45	Worlington 33 A52	Wrotham Heath 23 F52	Yattendon 21 D41	Ystradowen *Dyf.* 27 G23
Woodstock 31 G40	Worlingworth 35 B58	Wrotham Hill 24 E52	Yatton *Avon* 19 E30	Ythanwells 98 F32
Woodstock Slop 16 B16	Wormbridge 28 E29	Wrotham Park 23 B48	Yatton *H.&W.* 28 B30	Ythsie 99 F34
Woodston 42 F47	Wormegay 44 D52	Wroughton 20 C37	Yatton Keynell 20 D34	Y Trallwng (Welshpool) 38 E27
Wood Street 22 F45	Wormelow Tump 28 E30	Wroxall 11 G41	Yaverland 11 F42	
Woodthorpe *Lei.* 41 D41	Wormhill 50 E37	Wroxeter 38 E31	Yaxham 44 D56	**Z**
Woodthorpe *Dby.* 51 E40	Wormiehills 83 D31	Wroxhall 30 A38	Yaxley *Sfk* 35 A57	
Woodton 45 F58	Wormingford 34 A54	Wroxham 45 D58	Yaxley *Cbs.* 42 F47	Zeal Monachurum 6 E22
Woodtown *Grm.* 90 F31	Worminghall 21 A42	Wroxton 30 D39	Yazor 28 D29	Zeals 9 A33
Woodtown *Dev.* 6 C20	Wormington 30 E36	Wstrws 26 D19		Zelah 3 C14
Woodville 40 D38	Worminster 19 G31	Wyaston 40 A37		Zennor 2 E10
Woodwalton 42 G47	Wormistone 83 G31	Wyberton 43 A49		

DISTANCE IN KILOMETRES

Places (along the diagonal):

ABERYSTWYTH, AYR, ABERDEEN, BIRMINGHAM, BRADFORD, BRISTOL, CAMBRIDGE, CARDIFF, CARLISLE, COVENTRY, DERBY, DONCASTER, DOVER, EDINBURGH, EXETER, FISHGUARD, FORT WILLIAM, GLASGOW, GLOUCESTER, HARWICH, HOLYHEAD, HULL, INVERNESS, KENDAL, LEEDS, LEICESTER, LINCOLN, LIVERPOOL, MANCHESTER, NEWCASTLE UPON TYNE, NORWICH, NOTTINGHAM, OXFORD, PENZANCE, PERTH, PLYMOUTH, PORTSMOUTH, SALISBURY, SHEFFIELD, SHREWSBURY, SOUTHAMPTON, SOUTHEND-ON-SEA, STOKE-ON-TRENT, STRANRAER, THURSO, WORCESTER, YORK, LONDON

DISTANCE IN MILES

ROAD SIGNS

THE SIGNING SYSTEM

The shapes give

 orders

warnings

information

EXCEPTIONS ARE FOR EMPHASIS

The colours give

a positive instruction

a negative instruction

general information

directions on primary routes

SIGNS GIVING ORDERS — mostly circular

 Stop and Give Way

 Give way to traffic on major road

No vehicles

No entry for vehicles

 No right turn

 No left turn

 No U turns

No overtaking

 Give priority to vehicles from opposite direction

STOP POLICE

 School Crossing Patrol

 Maximum speed

 National speed limit applies

 No horse-drawn vehicles

 No vehicles carrying explosives

 Overall length of vehicle or combination of vehicles limit

 Total weight limit

 Axle weight limit

Width limit

Height limit

 Manually operated temporary Stop sign

At any time — Continuous prohibition on waiting, except for loading/unloading

No loading at any time — No loading/unloading

 Times of (upper) no waiting, (lower) no loading/unloading

 Parking reserved for permit holders

No stopping ('Clearway')

 URBAN CLEARWAY Monday to Friday — No stopping during times indicated except for up to 2 minutes to set down or pick up passengers

Lane ahead for buses and pedal cycles only

Bus lane – buses and pedal cycles only

No vehicles with over 12 seats except regular scheduled school and work buses

 No pedestrians

 No cycling

No goods vehicles over specified unladen weight

End of restriction on prohibition of goods vehicles

 No motor vehicles

No motor vehicles except motor cycles without side-cars

Plates below some signs qualify their message

End — End of restriction

Except buses and coaches — Exception for vehicles with over 12 seats

Except for loading — Exception for loading/unloading goods and access to off-street garaging

 Ahead only

One-way traffic

 Turn left (right if symbol reversed)

 Turn left ahead (right if symbol reversed)

Keep left (right if symbol reversed)

 Vehicles may pass either side to reach same destination

Mini-roundabout

 Route to be used by pedal cyclists only

Minimum speed

 End of minimum speed

WARNING SIGNS — mostly triangular

Cross roads

Side road

Staggered junction

T Junction

Priority through junction indicated by thickened line

Traffic merging with equal priority from right

Traffic merging with equal priority from left

Bend to right (left if symbol reversed)

Double bend first to left

Double bend first to right

 Sharp deviation of route to left / Sharp deviation of route to right

Road narrows on both sides

Road narrows on right (left if symbol reversed)

Dual carriageway ends

Roundabout

Two-way traffic straight ahead

Two-way traffic crosses one-way road ahead

Right-hand lane of a three lane carriageway closed to traffic ahead

Change to opposite carriageway (may be reversed)

 Steep hill upwards (gradient shown as ratio 1:6=16%)

 Steep hill downwards (gradient shown as percentage 10%=1:10)

 AUTOMATIC BARRIERS STOP when lights show — Level crossing with automatic barrier and flashing lights

Level crossing with other barrier or gate ahead

Level crossing without barrier or gate ahead

Location of level crossing without barrier or gate

'Count-down' markers approaching concealed level crossing

Height limit (eg. low bridge) with available width of headroom indicated

Hump bridge

Overhead electric cable

Low flying aircraft or sudden aircraft noise

 Roadworks

Traffic signals ahead

Pedestrian crossing ahead

Ford — Worded warning sign

Opening or swing bridge

Quayside or river bank

Slippery road

Uneven road

Risk of fallen or falling rocks

Loose chippings

Cattle

Wild animals

 Accompanied horses or ponies crossing the road ahead

 School — Children going to or from school

 Accident — Other danger (plate indicates nature)

 STOP 100 yds — Distance to STOP sign ahead

 GIVE WAY 50 yds — Distance to GIVE WAY sign ahead

Hazard markers

1 mile — Distance to hazard

For 2 miles — Distance over which hazard extends